A History of
Western Education

Second Edition

H. G. Good

The Ohio State University

New York **THE MACMILLAN COMPANY**

PREFACE

THE FIRST EDITION OF THIS BOOK WAS PUBLISHED IN 1947 WHEN
the world, after many years of small and large wars, was
trying to regain its sanity. Great social changes were taking place. Not
colonies merely but colonialism was being abolished in large areas. New
nations and new social systems were developing in Japan, China, India,
and Africa. Russia, controlling the "heartland" of Eurasia, had firmly established its form of state socialism and was a great world power. Nazism and
Fascism had been defeated on the battlefields but not destroyed. In such
a time it needed no prophetic inspiration to declare in the preface of the
first edition that the period was more critical than most, in a world in
which all periods are critical, and in which change is more evident than
permanence. Change would clearly overtake the school systems as well as
other institutions of society.

Educational change had already begun. Before the book appeared, England had undertaken to put into effect a new comprehensive school law
that was to broaden her educational services and, in particular, to provide
secondary schooling for all children to the age fifteen or even sixteen years.
France was once again struggling with her need to close the gap between
her primary and secondary school systems and to develop her facilities for
vocational education. West Germany was removing the Nazi taint from
her schools and returning to the democratic proposals of the Weimar Republic. Even greater changes were taking place in Russian education; and
the new weight of that country in the world's councils and her position
and power in relation to the United States make it necessary to consider
her school system in this book. This does not alter the general plan of
the book, but the changes in Western Europe and the necessity for the
inclusion of Russia are the main reasons that a revision of the text has
been deemed advisable. Many pages in the latter half of the book have

[v]

been brought up to date; the chapter references have been revised, and new titles have been added; and two new chapters have been written to describe more fully the new developments mentioned earlier in this paragraph.

The book has been kindly received in Europe and the Far East, but it was originally prepared for the American public and teachers and has been used mainly by them. For this reason more attention has been given to education in the United States than to that of other countries. The second purpose was to provide a broad base for the understanding of Western education by tracing its origins in the ancient world, its growth in its progress westward, and its fuller development in those large countries of Western Europe which are most closely related, politically and intellectually, to the United States. This feature is in harmony with the great and growing interest in comparative education of the present time.

To include several smaller countries, especially Switzerland, Holland, Scotland, and one of the Scandinavian countries would seem desirable from some standpoints. In fact a chapter along these lines was written for the original manuscript; but the space in a textbook is limited, and beginning students in the history of education need to concentrate their attention rather than to spread it over a wide and diverse field. There was also the problem of selection. If Norway were to be treated, why not Chile or Uruguay? These and similar reasons persuaded the writer to omit even Switzerland which has exercised so many beneficent influences upon education in the United States.

Western education in its development has followed a democratic trend. It has grown through free discussion in a free press, a free radio, and other free means of communication, freedom of assembly, and the use of a secret ballot in elections that offer genuine choices. The existence of private schools is another test of democracy in education; so is equality of educational opportunity; and still another is the reasonable distribution of control over schools between the local constituency and parents and the central government. A little consideration may suggest other tests to the student. There is not enough space here to expand upon this theme, but among all the questions of this book, this one should be kept in mind: How fares democracy in the various educational systems considered in courses on the history of Western education?

The author is grateful for help given him on the first edition by James D. Teller, Forest L. Shoemaker, Roscoe H. Eckelberry, and Dan H. Eikenberry, all sometime on the staff of The Ohio State University. For aid on this edition his cordial thanks are offered to Professor W. W. Brickman of New York University and to the editorial staff of The Macmillan Company. Several of the illustrations are based upon photographs taken by the late Professor F. C. Wooton of the University of California at Los Angeles. In the permission to use these heretofore unpublished pictures the author acknowledges a last kindness from his friend.

H. G. Good

CONTENTS

PART I

1. PERSPECTIVE AND PROSPECT   3
2. EDUCATION IN ANCIENT GREECE   18
3. ROMAN EDUCATION   42
4. EDUCATION IN THE EARLIER MIDDLE AGES   58
5. FROM MONASTIC SCHOOLS TO UNIVERSITIES   80
6. THE RENAISSANCE IN ITALY   111
7. THE REFORMATION ERA   139

PART II

8. FROM HUMANISM TO REALISM   170
9. NEW VIEWS OF NATURE AND HUMAN NATURE   201
10. NEW SCHOOLS FOR OLD   225
11. NEW SYSTEM-BUILDERS: HERBART   250
12. NEW SYSTEM-BUILDERS: FROEBEL   268
13. NATIONAL EDUCATION IN FRANCE   292
14. NATIONAL TRENDS IN GERMAN EDUCATION   318
15. EDUCATION IN ENGLAND   344

PART III

16. AMERICAN BEGINNINGS   367
17. UNDER THE NEW CONSTITUTION   398
18. THE AMERICAN SYSTEM   434
19. TRANSFORMING THE ELEMENTARY SCHOOL   461
20. CREATING THE HIGH SCHOOL   496
21. WAR AND PEACE   533
22. SOVIET AND AMERICAN EDUCATION   570
    INDEX   607

A History of
Western Education

1 PERSPECTIVE AND PROSPECT

THE HISTORY OF EDUCATION IS THE HISTORY OF MAN BECOM-
ing civilized and enlightened and of the institutions he
has created and propagated to preserve and to advance those features of
civilized life which he has learned to prize. To those who have the wit to
understand and the imagination to realize the contrast between the naked,
ignorant, and terrified savage and the humane, cultivated citizen of the
twentieth century, and who can bring home to themselves also the realities
of the hard but successful ascent toward civilization, this must be the
story of an exciting adventure.

Education is sometimes thought to be a dull affair, but that is a radical
error. It is ignorance and the lack of education, when for long stretches
of time nothing happens within the mind of child or race, that occasion
the tedium and boredom of our human existence. Education as a process
of active inquiry and the pursuit of knowledge and of ideas, especially
when the inquiry is rewarded by even slight discoveries, is never dull.

We should also notice at the outset that the word education or learning is used in two senses. Both are implied in the preceding words and
both are essential meanings in life and school. The first sense is involved
in the request: "Tell me, or show me, for I wish to learn." Here learning
depends upon preservation and transmission. And the second meaning is
implied in the contrary demand: "Do not tell me, because I want to learn
for myself." Here learning results from discovery. Both are essential processes in education, but it is the second, self-education, that is the more
inspiring. The education of mankind has proceeded through the discovery
and the transmission of the elements of civilization.

1. EARLY LIFE AND EDUCATION OF MAN

Man has lived on the earth for a period so long, reaching back into the
illimitable past so far, that it has to be computed not in decades or even

3

centuries but in thousands of years. Of man's early progress we know only what we may surmise from the condition of present-day savages and what a few skeletons, cave drawings, and artifacts such as stone fist hatchets, scrapers, and knives may reveal. Of course there are no records and no deliberate monuments from those early times of our race. Long ago, we do not know how early in his career, man also developed language and learned to speak. Both tools and language had to be invented, and these useful skills had to be transmitted from the older generation to the young. Along with speech and perhaps even before tools man also developed ideas. He began to present in his imagination what was not present to his sight and touch, and perhaps to forecast what was to come—after the hunt, a feast. Ideas were also transmitted to companions and to the young, ideas of physical comfort, of the seasons, and of nature in calm or fearsome mood, of human association, and of life and death. Civilization and education are based upon three characteristics which distinguish man from the other animals, the powers of articulate speech, of connected thought, and of inventing and making tools, weapons, clothing, and shelters.

Man is the builder of civilization; and he builds it by pyramiding, generation after generation, the experiences and discoveries of the present upon those of the past. Stone tools were displaced by copper, those by bronze, and these again by iron in a progression of cultures which occupied thousands of years. All these years man was learning. At all times and in every generation the old culture and the new had to be learned by the children. Civilization is never inherited. To speak of social inheritance is to employ a violent figure of speech. Every item of civilization, if it is not to be lost, must be learned by some individual; and this succession of discovery and transmissions was the earliest education. The young of the distant past learned as we still do by experiment, by actively taking part in life, by imitation, and, speaking loosely, by an apprenticeship to life, without schools.

It would be a great mistake to suppose that the early process of civilization building was always an upward and forward-going process that was carried on without error. Errors were then, as they still are, far more numerous than ten-strikes. Man, for example, acquired a vast array of magical beliefs and superstitions which he long prized and many of which still survive. Magic is an attempt to control the forces of nature or the gods, to gain food, assure victory, or satisfy other needs or desires, by irrational means. Primitive man did not distinguish magic from science; and both science and religion were filled with such supposed short-cuts to power. An American historian, Lynn Thorndike, has traced the history of science as the gradual process of replacing magical with rational processes in dealing with nature. One of the early arts of man in the Stone Age, the drawing

nd painting of animals and hunters on the walls of caves, is supposed to
ave had a magical purpose. In the form of magic there employed, called
ympathetic magic, a desired result is supposed to be brought about by

FIGURE 1.

FROM V. GORDON
CHILDE, "MAN MAKES
HIMSELF." LONDON,
WATTS AND CO., 1936

mimicking that result. A drawing of a deer, especially if it is pierced by an
arrow, will bring game within reach of the hunter's weapon. The illustration shows such a supposedly magical drawing.

These ancient cave drawings and paintings, of which many have been
found, are among the most remarkable of man's early achievements. The
subject is altogether too large for treatment here and it is also too remote
from our purpose; but if, as archaeologists believe, such works of art had
a magical purpose they serve to illustrate the thought of this paragraph,
that man in his ascent toward civilization followed many blind trails from
which he had again to rescue himself.

Social inventions such as the family, the clan, and the tribe, with their
forms of government and fixed customs, paralleled the accumulation of
natural knowledge and the invention of new and better tools and weapons.
Bands of hunters with the bow and arrow and half-tamed wolflike animals,
the ancestors of the dog, roamed the forests. Fishermen with spears and
nets and rude boats followed the streams and paddled on the inlets of
the seas. When man began to domesticate animals for their flesh, skins,

and milk, the tribes of herdsmen had to find pasture for their flocks by following the rains from north to south and back again through the seasons of the year. When he began to cultivate the wild grasses from which wheat and barley were evolved he had to settle in one place, usually a river valley with fertile soil, for the cultivable land and the growing crop could not be moved. Even in the last Stone Age, villages of wooden houses with wooden furniture, pottery molded by hand without the wheel, and fields of barley and wheat existed on the shores of Swiss lakes. These lands were not owned by individual farmers but were the property of the whole community which controlled them by custom and law and worked them in common. With the rise of individual ownership and personal liberty one of the greatest of human problems arose. It is the problem of the proper relation of the individual to the group, the problem of individual rights and social duties.

The age of specialization was then beginning. The earliest specialization was the division of labor between men and women. Men provided the materials for food and clothing and the women prepared them for use. Men, perhaps, raised the flax and invented and built the loom and women spun the thread and wove the cloth. A second form of specialization was the setting apart of chieftains and medicine men for special duties. But the phrase, the age of specialization, implies much more. It means that some men developed special manual skills while the rest continued to follow the common relatively unskilled occupations. Men began to practice trades, woodworking and building, pottery, mining. The introduction of metals and of the potter's wheel were great technological advances and had the most far-reaching influences upon the development of a higher civilization. We shall not be able to follow the course of man's civilization building in detail but it is important to understand that long periods of time were involved. The age of man on earth reaches back perhaps three hundred thousand years; that of high civilization only five or ten thousand.

2. HIGH CIVILIZATION OF THE TWIN RIVERS

It was in the valley of the Nile and in the valleys of the Tigris and Euphrates that a technological civilization based upon science, government, and religion developed more than six thousand years ago. For a fuller account of these topics the student should turn to the excellent work on *Ancient Times* by James Henry Breasted and to the works which he cites.

We have noticed the rise of the age of specialization. This was closely followed by another epoch-making advance, the invention of writing which marks the dawn of history, with names, inscribed monuments, and dated events. The oldest dated event, according to Breasted, is the establishment in Egypt about 4200 B.C. of a civil calendar with three hundred and sixty-five days to a year; but this date is not accepted by all students. Obviously events could not be accurately dated before a calendar was established and records were kept. The year having been determined, each passing year could then be marked by a great event such as a flood or a war or they could be numbered in a series of years. Nature herself has, of course, kept a sort of record in the fossils and artifacts deposited in the successive strata of the sedimentary rocks, but these ages can only be estimated and with a large allowance for possible error. Through human records, events can be dated precisely; and records also furnish the thoughts and opinions of the recorder. But here allowance must be made for the frailty and the perversity of the human agent. The period before records is known as prehistory. History is based upon records and began in the Near East where high civilization began. The origins of writing and records are traced in many books including the one which has just been m ntioned. A word should also be said about the mistaken notion that Chinese civiliza-tion is older than that of the Near East. Metals were not used and no records were kept in China before about 1200 B.C., and this is several thousand years later than the rise of government, writing, and great buildings and monuments in Egypt and Mesopotamia.

Both specialization in work and the art of writing had evident implications for education. The former led directly to education through apprenticeship and the latter to the invention and establishment of the school. In the early days of our race, work was work and education as a separate activity hardly existed; and yet education had to be carried on, consciously or unconsciously, if discoveries and inventions were to be retained. Long before schools were established, children were taught in the family, the daughters by the mother and the sons by the father. The customary tools, weapons, and materials were at first fashioned by those who intended to use them. When occupations became specialized, careful and long-continued training became necessary and apprenticeship arose. The Code of Hammurabi, which will be presently noticed again, indicates that apprenticeship even then, four thousand years ago, was in an advanced stage both as a customary practice and as a legal institution. It was common in ancient times not only in Babylonia but also in China, India, and Egypt. Apprenticeship must be the earliest form of organized education and the parent of many later forms. Its great virtues are that it is real, real work and not make-believe work, work and not play; that success and failure are concrete and demonstrable; that the apprentice's work, if well done, is socially valuable and will be rewarded; and that the process is one which fosters, rather than retards, maturity.

Before we can consider the origin of the school in western Asia we must trace the history of Babylonia, as the region of the Tigris and Euphrates rivers is called. Babylon was not the first center of culture in this section. The oldest high civilization between the Twin Rivers, as on the Nile, was developed in the lower valleys with their rich and easily watered soils. A people called Sumerians lived on these fertile bottomlands perhaps before 4000 B.C. They learned the art of irrigation and became wealthy in the pursuits of agriculture and animal husbandry. The city-kingdoms of Sumer carried on an extensive commerce, developed a system of numerals with sixty as the base, standard weights and measures, and a serviceable calendar. Before 3000 B.C. they employed a form of picture writing from which the cuneiform or wedge-shaped writing of later Babylonia was developed. Great quantities of business records such as bills, receipts, and notes have been found on the sites of Sumerian towns. The center of a Sumerian town was the temple with its priests, assisted by scribes. The chief priest was the ruler of the town and was in charge of defense, irrigation, and taxation, as well as religion.

When Sumer had become luxurious, foreign invaders came down the Tigris from Akkad, a Semitic country toward the north. The army of vigorous tribesmen was led by a great chief, Sargon, who conquered Sumer about 2500 B.C. and then, with it as a base, established a great kingdom that reached to the Mediterranean. In time the nomad herdsmen and warriors settled down in Sumer and adopted the Sumerian civilization. They learned to write the Sumerian script and to use the weights and measures, the arts and culture of the country which they had overrun. This is an early example of a process that has been repeated many times in history. As conquered Sumer "took captive its rude conqueror" and civilized him so the Aegeans civilized the invading Hellenes, so the Greeks in turn softened the asperities and refined the taste of the Romans, and so the Romans and the Roman Church taught the Germans, Goths, and Vandals the arts of peace and civilized life.

After the tribesmen of Akkad and the city dwellers of Sumer had lived together for several centuries and after the Sargon dynasty declined, some of the cities again regained control. One of the best known of these was the city of Ur, whence according to the Bible came the Hebrew patriarch Abraham. Silver and gold came to be used as the mediums of exchange. A pound of silver was called a mina, and one sixtieth of a pound was a shekel. "Sixty shekels make a mina," the schoolboys were taught to say, for now there were schools, books, and exercise tablets by which numbers, money, weights, business forms, writing, and literature were taught. Before 2000 B.C. there were grammars and dictionaries in the schools of Ur. By that time the old Sumerian speech had gone out of common use and had come to be regarded as more sacred than the Semitic tongue which had displaced it. But the Sumerian language continued in religious use after it was no longer commonly spoken, another early example of a frequent historical process. The tongue of ancient Sumer became a sacred language as Greek, Latin, Hebrew, and Arabic are today in different parts of the world.

The city which was to give its name to this whole region, Babylon, had remained an insignificant town on the Euphrates until about 2000 B.C., when it became the cultural and political capital of the country of the Twin Rivers. A century later (1948–1904 B.C.) Hammurabi, an enlightened ruler and the greatest king since Sargon, came to the throne and gave laws to the region, the famous Code of Hammurabi which has already been mentioned. This Code consisted of old Sumerian laws collected and new laws added, all systematically arranged, and carved on a splendid stone shaft which was set up in the temple of the great god Marduk. This is the oldest surviving code of laws. It regulated the administration of justice, business, apprenticeship, marriage, and other social relations.

The old Sumerian gods were still worshiped in Babylon, but the name of the Semitic god, Marduk, was now inserted in the religious stories where that of Enlil, the great god of Sumer, had been previously read; and that of Ishtar, the goddess of love who became the Venus of Rome, was added. To train priests and clerks for the temple and for business, schools were established in connection with the temple. There even were women scribes. The ruins of a schoolhouse with the exercise tablets of the children of four thousand years ago has been found in Babylon. One of these tablets has a proverb that was set as a writing and memory copy. Like the old Spencerian copybook maxims of modern America, it was intended to encourage the pupils in well-doing. It read: "He who shall excel in tablet-writing shall shine as the sun." On the following page we give from Breasted a plan of this ancient schoolhouse.

After the Babylonians, another semibarbarous and conquering race, the Assyrians, subdued the country of the Twin Rivers. The ages of copper (c. 4000–2000 B.C.) and of bronze (2000–1000 B.C.) had passed, and the Assyrians came armed with iron weapons. They built the great city of Nineveh and under a succession of warrior-emperors ruled the entire region. They built great palaces and temples with tall square towers, and aqueducts and the roads upon which the royal messengers traveled to every part of the empire. They were the Romans of ancient western Asia. As they became civilized they pursued aesthetic and intellectual interests. They developed or inherited a musical notation with a scale of five tones and played on a harp of twenty-two strings, an instrument that was widely used later. Their animal sculpture was vigorous and lifelike. They erected great libraries into which they gathered the religious, scientific, and literary works of their own and past times. These collections reached their height

FIGURE 2.

A SCHOOLHOUSE OF THE TIME OF HAMMURABI

The drawing at the top shows the entrance, and the walls of sun-dried brick, of a schoolhouse that was built more than four thousand years ago. The lower figure shows the plan of the building. The court marked "C" was probably open to the sky. The building was uncovered in 1894 by French archaeologists. A supply of clay for writing tablets was found in it.

Drawing after Schiel. Redrawn from James H. Breasted's *Ancient Times* (1935), by permission of the publishers, Ginn and Company.

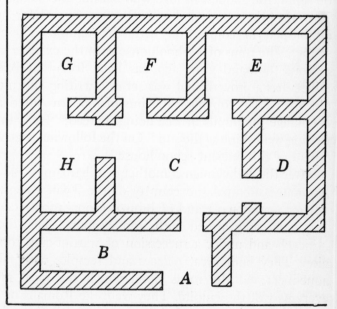

under Ashurbanipal (r. 668–626 B.C.) who was known to the Greeks as Sardanapalus. Ashurbanipal has left us a boastful eulogy of his own accomplishments in learning, the only such account of an Assyrian youth and one of the earliest of autobiographies. Although it is only a fragment, it shows what skills and knowledge were valued by the cultured men of his time; and it indicates the degree in which they and other ancient peoples attributed their learning to the gods.

As presented by A. H. Sayce and A. N. J. Whymant (*Encyclopedia Britannica*, 14th edition, 2,851) the eulogy reads as follows: "I, Ashurbanipal, understood the wisdom of Nabu; all the art of tablet writing of every kind of clerk, I acquired their understanding. I learned to shoot the bow, to ride horses, and chariots, and to hold the reins." Nabu, who is again mentioned below, was one of their gods and since he is also called "the scribe," the art of writing may have been attributed to him as the Egyptians ascribed the same art to their god Thoth or Theuth of whom we read in Plato's *Phaedrus*. Ashurbanipal also wrote: "Marduk, the wise one of the gods, presented me with information and understanding as a gift. Nabu, the scribe, granted me all the understanding of his wisdom as a present. Enurta and Nergal made me virile and strong, of incomparable force. I understood the craft of the wise Adapa, the hidden secrets of all the scribal art; in heavenly and earthly buildings I read and pondered, in the meetings of clerks I was present, I watched the omens, I explained the heavens with the learned priests, recited the complicated multiplications and divisions which are not immediately apparent. The beautiful writings in Sumerian that are obscure, in Akkadian that are difficult to bear in mind, it was my joy to repeat." He goes on to describe his skill in horsemanship and the arts of war and concludes with a flourish, thus: "At the same time I learnt what is proper for lordship, I went my royal ways." How all these matters were learned and taught, who were the teachers, and how widespread such learning and pride in learning were, we do not know. Ashurbanipal was king of Assyria from 668 to 626 B.C., two centuries before the flowering time of Athens in Greece. To the Greeks in their rough western mountains he seemed a luxurious and rather effeminate prince.

3. HEBREW RELIGION AND EDUCATION

This brief sketch of the country of the Twin Rivers must suffice on the early high civilizations which arose between the Nile and the Tigris. Elam which lay beyond the Tigris, east and south, where the great oil fields now are, had a civilization as early as Sumer. For the story of the Hittites, the Phoenicians, and the great Persian Empire the student must go to a general history of the ancient world. Even Egypt, which antedated and paralleled the achievements of Babylonia and surpassed her in technology, in the great pyramids, temples, and tombs with their superlative art, will be omitted for lack of space and because it would add no essentially new educational features to this rapid survey. History tells much of the life of these countries and peoples over great stretches of time beginning five or six thousand years ago. Of their schools we know very little. The Hebrews, a small people who have had a great and continuing influence upon the West, we cannot altogether omit.

When the Hebrews first appear in history they were nomadic herdsmen from the Arabian desert who were moving into Palestine about 1200 B.C. Some of them had been enslaved in Egypt, and these were led out by Moses who became one of their great heroes. Palestine, where they eventually settled, was inhabited by the Philistines, from whom the name Palestine was derived, and by the Canaanites. These peoples were further advanced in the arts of civilization than the Hebrews. They lived in cities and carried on agriculture and trade which the Hebrews learned from them. About the year 1000 B.C. the Hebrews formed a national government under a succession of warrior kings, Saul, David, and Solomon, and established their capital at Jerusalem. They gradually developed a monotheistic religion, a system of ethics, and an important body of literature, much of which is included in the Bible; and through these they radically influenced the West. The religion of the early Hebrews was practically synonymous with patriotism, but eventually they accepted the idea that their god, Yahweh, was the God of all the earth. They taught that they, the Hebrews, were God's Chosen People, that man was made in His likeness, and that personal holiness before God was the end of man's existence. Character, not knowledge, or skill, or wealth, was the purpose of life. They had a high regard for womanhood and taught their children to honor father and mother and stressed a pure family life. The father was the ruler, priest, and teacher of the family, and the teaching of the children remained in his hands for many centuries. The Temple in Jerusalem with its sacred objects was the center of their religious life and had a great nationalizing influence among them.

The tribes that invaded Canaan, later called Palestine, were entirely illiterate and remained so until the eighth century. They acquired writing from the Philistines who had obtained their alphabet from Egypt. As the Hebrews developed town life and commerce, they became wealthy and luxurious and began to take on the manners, the religious ideas, and the forms of worship of their neighbors. Those who remained faithful to the Hebrew God called this idolatry. Under these conditions a new class of religious teachers, called prophets, arose. It was the prophets who began to teach that their God, Yahweh, was different from other gods in His moral character and that He dealt righteously, ethically, with His People. They taught that the reverses of the Chosen People were His punishments and were visited upon them for their idolatry and sin. The early prophets delivered their messages orally, but about 750 B.C. the first literate prophets, Amos, Hosea, and those who followed, wrote down their teachings for posterity. Amos was a "herdsman of Tekoa"; and that he and others who came from the common people were able to write shows that book learning had by the eighth and seventh centuries spread to some among the masses of the people.

Although common people, like Amos, learned to read and write, we hear nothing of schools in this early period. The religious teachings which were called "the Law" and the art of writing were inculcated in the family. The prophets held that the object of education was to teach children to know the Law and to follow it; and the responsibility for this teaching was laid upon the father. In Deuteronomy, the sixth chapter, we read: "Thou shalt teach the Laws diligently unto thy children, and shalt talk of them when thou sittest in thine house and when thou walkest by the way."

Palestine is not a rich country. The southern part, especially, is chiefly dry desert and grazing country, but in the north there are fertile valleys. Although not desired for its fertility by its powerful neighbors on the north, east, and southwest, it had great importance for these strong states because it lay on the direct route between them. Every peaceful or hostile mission, every caravan and army between the Nile and the Twin Rivers had to pass through Palestine to avoid the Arabian desert. In the northern part of Palestine lay the battlefield of Armageddon, modern Megiddo, where the fate of more than one great army was sealed. Thus the Hebrews were frequently the victims of their neighbors' quarrels. Nor could they agree among themselves. The nation which had been united under Saul and David broke up into two, Judah in the south and Israel in the north. Early in the sixth century a catastrophe overtook the southern kingdom. The people of Judah were carried into captivity by Nebuchadrezzar of Babylon, and held for more than fifty years before they were again released. Their return was marked by the growth of a world religion, the rebuilding of the Temple, strict observance of the Law, and strong national feeling. The prophecy of Isaiah beginning with chapter forty gives noble expression to this new sense that the God of the Hebrews is the God of the whole earth.

Meanwhile a language change had occurred. The Hebrews no longer spoke their ancient tongue but had come to speak a derivative speech, the Aramaic language. The Hebrew was still used for the Law and the religious worship and thus came to be a sacred language; and a learned, literary class became necessary to keep and transcribe the text of the Law and to interpret it to the people. These were the Scribes. And a teaching institution, the synagogue, was set up in the towns and villages in order that the Law might be read and explained to the people. The new era needed education more than ever, and later Judaism was intensely concerned with the teaching of the young as well as adults. Josephus (c. A.D. 37–95) wrote in *Contra Apion*: "We take most pains of all with the instruction of the children and esteem the observance of the laws and the piety corresponding with them the most important matter of our whole life." By about 100 B.C. schools for children were attached to the synagogues, and in A.D. 64 the High Priest, Joshua ben Gamala, ordered the opening of an elementary school in every village where attendance was to be compulsory for boys from the age of six. This is the earliest attempt at compulsory school attendance. The instruction was apparently dogmatic and memoriter but there were also "disputations" in which there was opportunity for difference of opinion and argument. The girls were taught at home.

We have now sketched, very briefly indeed, but with all the fullness that our space will allow, the rise of civilization and the origin of schools. Schools in the pre-Greek world seem everywhere to have been connected with the temples and the worship of the gods. As the art of writing developed, as religious doctrines and forms of worship came to be written down, schools became necessary to teach priests and people to read the sacred literature. They became still more essential as the language changed and the older language of the cult, which had become standardized and invariable, ceased to be intelligible without special study. This, as we have just noted, occurred among the Hebrews, but it had also taken place in Babylonia. Ashurbanipal, we recall, was proud that he had learned to read "the beautiful writings in Sumerian that are obscure" and "in Akkadian that are difficult to bear in mind."

But writing and reading had not merely a religious but also a business and political use. Commercial and administrative records had to be kept, and for this it was necessary that "the hidden secrets of the scribal art" should be known to the large body of clerks that served in the temples, counting-houses, and chanceries of the great cities. A similar atmosphere of secrecy enveloped the skills of the trades. Those who had learned an art or craft, whether the tanning of leather, or the smelting of metals, or the ceramic crafts, were interested to conceal the "mystery" which they had acquired from those who had not undergone a similar apprenticeship. Their purpose was to preserve to the initiated the rewards of their privileged position.

The notion that learning should be spread as far as possible and should be freely open to all is a recent idea. Such thoughts were foreign to the pre-Greek world and did not become widespread until modern times. In the next chapter when we come to study the schools of ancient Athens we shall see that the Greeks introduced the idea that literary education, at least, was not to be a cult or trade secret but that it should be spread abroad and that its purpose should be the development of personality and preparation for citizenship. But even there these generous aims were applied only to the sons of citizens. Even the most liberal of the Athenians did not propose to educate slaves or girls whether slave or free. And with all her achievements in the arts and sciences, Greece enabled only a few of her talented sons to go beyond the elements of learning. It was, in the Greek social and political scheme, inevitable that this should be so.

This chapter summarizes the history of civilization to the point at which schools and other formal means of education were employed to maintain and raise the level of culture. We deal only with the high civilization which influenced the Greeks and Hebrews who, in their turn, became our intellectual and spiritual ancestors. The opening sentence of the chapter announces the theme of the book. The theme is that education is the process by which man, through the discovery and preservation of all that he considers valuable, becomes civilized and enlightened. This has been a slow, though cumulative process. Man has often suffered from the defects of his own perverse nature; and apparently valuable discoveries have many times turned out to be fool's gold.

In the fertile valleys of the Nile and the Tigris and Euphrates rivers, agriculture and commerce flourished; populous cities and powerful empires arose. Economic and political power was in the hands of the priests; and the temples were administrative as well as religious institutions. In early times teaching and learning were carried on by participation in the common activities of life, and by family and priestly teaching. Apprenticeship arose with the rise of specialized occupations. Four thousand years ago, it was already an old and widespread institution. Schools arose to promote religion and to teach writing and calculation. Learning was restricted to selected groups. Both literary and manual skills were confined to the initiated.

The Hebrews who lived in Palestine, on the high road between Egypt and Babylonia, developed an ethical monotheistic religion and literature which have had an important influence in Western education.

The Greeks, who will be treated in the next chapter, borrowed from the neighboring empires and the Aegean region. Being a creative people, they refined the arts, increased knowledge, and, through a free, inquiring spirit, released education from some of the mystery in which it had been confined.

QUESTIONS

1. What other essential characteristics of man, besides speech, thought and the invention and construction of tools, can be named? Would the possession of conscience be one? What is the bearing upon education of each of the characteristics you name?

2.   What is "social inheritance"? Give examples. How are teaching and learning related to the "social inheritance" of a particular people?

3.   The text mentions some of the advantages of apprenticeship as a method of learning. What are its disadvantages?

4.   What, from the standpoint of your own ideals, were the defects of the education of Ashurbanipal?

5.   Compare the educational ideals of the Hebrews and other ancient peoples, using the information of this chapter.

6.   Why was education in early times confined to a small class and, only long after, more widely extended?

FOR FURTHER READING AND STUDY

The bibliography in Breasted's *Ancient Times* will make it unnecessary to name many titles. The ones listed below are general and elementary and do not, therefore, presuppose any technical knowledge of anthropology or archaeology. Special mention should be made of an article on "Jewish Education" in the *Cyclopedia of Education*, edited by Paul Monroe (New York, Macmillan Co., 1911–1913, 5 vols.), Vol. III, pp. 542–553. In addition to the books dealing with the topics of the present chapter we give below also the titles of several of the standard history of education texts. These can be consulted on the topics of this and the following chapters.

Boyle, Mary E., *Man Before History*, Boston, Little, Brown and Co., 1926, 135 pp. A useful primer on prehistory.

Breasted, James Henry, *Ancient Times. A History of the Early World*, Boston, Ginn and Co., 1935, 823 pp. It is important to use this second and revised edition. The "Library Edition" of the same book was issued under the title *The Conquest of Civilization* and is a new work edited by Edith Williams Ware in 1938 (New York, the Literary Guild of America, Inc., 669 pp.).

Childe, V. Gordon, *Man Makes Himself*, London, Watts and Co., 1939, 275 pp.

Kramer, S. N., *From the Tablets of Sumer*, Indian Hills, Colorado, The Falcon's Wing Press [1956], 293 pp.

Peake, Harold J., *Early Steps in Human Progress*, Philadelphia, J. B. Lippincott Co., 1933, 256 pp.

Sayce, R. U., *Primitive Arts and Crafts. An Introduction to the Study of Material Culture*, Cambridge University Press, 1933, 291 pp.

Swift, Fletcher H., *Education in Ancient Israel, from Earliest Times to 70 A.D.*, Chicago, The Open Court Publishing Co., 1919, 134 pp.

Some Standard American Texts of the History of Education:

Brubacher, John S., *A History of the Problems of Education*, New York, McGraw-Hill Book Co., 1947, 688 pp.

Butts, R. Freeman, *A Cultural History of Western Education*, Second Edition, New York, McGraw-Hill Book Co., 1955, 645 pp.

Cubberley, Ellwood P., The History of Education, Boston, Houghton Mifflin Co., 1920, 849 pp.; Readings in the History of Education, Boston, Houghton Mifflin Co., 1920, 684 pp.; Public Education in the United States, Boston, Houghton Mifflin Co., 1934, 782 pp.

Duggan, Stephen, A Student's Textbook in the History of Education, New York, D. Appleton-Century Co., 1936, 486 pp.

Eby, Frederick, and C. F. Arrowood, The Development of Modern Education, New York, Prentice-Hall, 1934, 922 pp.; The History and Philosophy of Education, Ancient and Medieval, New York, Prentice-Hall, 1940, 966 pp.

Edwards, Newton, and H. G. Richey, The School in the American Social Order, Boston, Houghton Mifflin Co., 1947, 880 pp.

Graves, Frank P., A Student's History of Education, New York, The Macmillan Company, 1936, 567 pp.

Kane, W., An Essay Toward a History of Education, Chicago, Loyola Press, 1935, 637 pp.

Monroe, Paul, A Text-Book in the History of Education, New York, The Macmillan Company, 1905, 772 pp.

Mulhern, James, A History of Education, New York, The Ronald Press, 1946, 647 pp.

Parker, Samuel C., A Textbook in the History of Modern Elementary Education, Boston, Ginn and Co., 1912, 505 pp.

Reisner, Edward H., Historical Foundations of a Modern Education, New York, The Mamillan Company, 1927, 513 pp.

Wilds, Elmer H., The Foundations of Modern Education, New York, Farrar and Rinehart, 1936, 634 pp.

2 EDUCATION IN ANCIENT GREECE

MORE THAN TWO THOUSAND YEARS AGO THE GREEKS DEveloped the basic forms of the arts and sciences, of literature, and of philosophy. They were the first to study systematically the closely related subjects of ethics, politics, and education; and their schools, although they were not public institutions, aimed at public and civic purposes. The Greeks were the first to use the school as a means of preparing citizens for citizenship.

None of the older civilizations has so directly and fruitfully influenced the West. Therefore, we share with the Greeks a close intellectual and political kinship, while the Babylonian and Egyptian civilizations developed on lines that seem to us foreign. In race and language also, the Greeks were our near relatives. The dominant Greek stock was Indo-European. They were the cousins of the Aryans of India, of the ancient Persians, and of most of the races of Europe. The term Indo-European is, however, properly applied to languages, not races; and calling the Greeks Indo-Europeans really means that their language belongs to the same family as the Latin, the English, and the other major European languages.

The ancient Greek people called their land Hellas and themselves Hellenes after a mythical ancestor, Hellen, from whom they claimed to be descended. Our modern accounts are different. They were the issue of a mingling of several groups of people. About 1500 B.C. some tribes of warriors with long iron swords came from the north into the Greek peninsula and the islands of the Aegean Sea, and conquered the highly civilized people who were living in those territories. Conquered and conquerors amalgamated to form the people whom we know as the Greeks of ancient history. Their descendants gradually became farmers, skilled artisans, traders, and colonizers; and eventually they spread over much of the Mediterranean world. None of the Greek cities was far from the sea. Wherever they settled, on the mainland, on the islands of the Aegean, in Asia Minor, in Italy and Sicily, on the coasts of modern France and Spain, or far eastward on the shores of the Black Sea, the Greeks were a commercial and seafaring people. Association with foreign races helped to make them observant, inquiring, and thoughtful.

The unit of political life was the city and the surrounding territory which was often enclosed by ranges of mountains or the arms of the sea. On the mainland and the islands there were many of these small, independent, and sovereign city-states such as Sparta, Athens, Achaea, Thebes, and Argos. On the average, each had a total population of between one hundred thousand and three hundred thousand. The forms of government included monarchy, oligarchy, democracy, and tyranny. The earliest examples of democracy developed among the Greek people; and their experience and their political theory were carefully studied by Hamilton, Madison, Jefferson, and other founders of our republic. They did not succeed in forming a unified nation-state, they did not invent representative democracy, and the unions they formed were only temporary leagues, yet their experiments in government were valuable to later ages.

The evil of slavery formed one of the darkest blots upon ancient civilization; and it was found everywhere in the ancient world, including Greece. In Sparta and Athens, the only Greek states with which we shall deal, the slaves were far more numerous than the citizens. Some of them were owned by the state; and their lot, under this public exploitation, was much worse than that of the privately owned and, especially, the domestic slaves. None of them had any political rights; and they usually received no education, although, because they could be used as writers and as merchants, there were exceptions to this rule. But they were after all slaves, and slavery corrupts both the master and the slave.

Sparta and Athens developed the two best known types of ancient Greek education, but the difference between them is often made to appear more radical than it was. Their practices and philosophies were, indeed, somewhat different, but their basic purposes were similar. Both took for their chief aims the training and education of strong and courageous soldiers and loyal citizens thoroughly imbued with the conventional morality. Neither intended to give much freedom to the individual, although Athens gave far more attention to intellectual and aesthetic elements and allowed more individual liberty than Sparta.

1. SPARTA

There were three classes of people in Sparta: the Spartiates, or Spartans proper, who were descendants of the Dorian conquerors and were the citizens; the *Perioeci* who tilled the land in a sort of feudal economy, and who were free but had no political rights; and the Helots who were public slaves owned by the state. The two servile classes outnumbered the Spartiates many times and were the descendants of the ancient inhabitants of the land. Their agricultural products and other goods were heavily taxed for the support of the army and the families of their conquerors and oppressors. Thus the Spartiates were freed from all manual and menial labor to devote themselves to military and civil activities. The country was divided into about nine thousand plots of land, each of which was made to furnish the support of one able-bodied soldier and his family and dependents. These citizen-soldiers lived in barracks in companies and took their meals together. The scheme was entirely static and unprogressive. The economic system was a form of state communism.

The characteristic fact about Spartan education is that it was carried out on military lines, because it was organized and controlled by a state that was founded upon conquest and which always remained an armed camp. The utmost emphasis was, therefore, placed upon physical and military training, and upon moral and civil training. The aim was to develop courage, military skill, obedience to law and to custom, and reverence for the elders. The ideal was a man who was determined, courageous, of moderate desires, who did not give way to his feelings, and who was no babbler. They shared the Greek religion and the Greek language and its great literary monuments, the Homeric poems, with all the Hellenes; but they placed little emphasis upon intellectual education.

Only healthy children could be used by such a state, and all others were by legal command exposed to die or were adopted by the Helots or *Perioeci*. Every vigorous little boy who was approved by the elders was brought up at home by his mother until the age of seven, when he was transferred to barracks for public training in a company of about sixty cadets of his own age. These were organized in military fashion. At the head of each company there was an *Eiren*, a young man of twenty or more who had completed his training and had taken his oath of citizenship and loyalty to the state. A general superintendent, the *paidonomos*, ruled very strictly over the whole system.

The physical education was intended not only to develop endurance and to harden the muscles, but also to toughen the mental and moral fiber and stamina. The cadets slept without cover on beds of straw or of rushes which, as they grew older, they had to pull for themselves from the banks of the small Spartan river, the Eurotas. They were purposely limited in garments also and they went shoeless in winter as in summer. Their food was curtailed to encourage foraging which would tend to develop craftiness, since severe punishment followed upon detection. And the lash was applied, not only for punishment, but also to develop hardihood and endurance; before the altar of Artemis Orthia, in the final test for citizenship, boys were scourged so severely that death sometimes resulted. Gymnastic exercises and sports were among the chief means of education; and these included the pentathlon: running, jumping, throwing the discus and the javelin, and wrestling. Ball games were also played. The pancratium was a combination of wrestling, boxing, and fighting and was not governed by any rule or restraint. Older boys were trained in the use of arms.

Mental and moral training was involved in the dances and in the musical education which was provided. Boys and young men were taught to play the lyre and to sing, both solo and in chorus. Doric chant and dance helped to develop and to express patriotic and religious feeling; and to a great degree these two came to the same thing, for Greek religion was largely a racial and civic religion. Their gods were the gods of the Greek people and the religious rites were enjoined by the state. Doric music was intended to make men brave, reverent, and proud of their fatherland. The marching songs of Tyrtaeus were highly prized.

Reading and writing were not included in the public education. These were sometimes taught privately; and then Homer, and Pindar who was the poet of athletes and the athletic games, were read and memorized. But science and intellectual learning received small attention. Poetry, except as it taught patriotism and morality, and oratory were not as highly regarded as practical sense and laconic speech. Short and witty apothegms, such as the Spartan mother's farewell word to her son leaving for a campaign, were highly praised. She said: "Return with your shield or on it." The trainers often asked the boys to sing a song or to give a short and pithy answer to such a question as "who is the best man in Sparta?" At the public tables the youth listened to the discussion of public questions by older men; and this was regarded as a means of political education. An iron discipline gripped the boy and held him from his seventh to his thirtieth year when full citizenship was granted. All adult men had the right and the duty to take part in the education of youth and were empowered to punish faults and bad conduct. At thirty, when full adulthood was finally attained, came the liberty and obligation to establish a home and raise a family. From thirty until forty-five they were enlisted in the national army and until sixty in the home guards.

Girls were given a similar public athletic training. Women's highest duty was the bearing of healthy children for the state, that is, for the army. This sounds very much like some modern German or Italian propaganda. Like the boys they were organized by ages into troops and exercised in jumping, running, wrestling, and throwing the discus. Dancing and choral singing, marching, and participation in religious rites were carried out. But they lived at home, not in a public institution. Young Spartan maidens were not so expert in spinning and weaving as their

Athenian cousins, but they were excellent housekeepers and managers and also took their share in the discussion of public questions. The Spartan matron, like the Roman, had more influence in family and state than the more oriental Athenian *hausfrau*. This Spartan regard for the opinion of women was so unusual that it seemed odd to most of the Greeks.

Spartan life and education was thus directed almost exclusively toward military success at home and abroad, and the individual's personal desires were given little consideration. Herodotus (VII, 104) makes the exile say to Xerxes: "The Spartans are the best of all men when fighting in a body; for, though free, yet they are not free in all things, since over them there is set law as a master, which they fear much more than your subjects do you." Sparta was long a firmly established but never a progressive or developing state and it produced no great poets, painters, sculptors, or philosophers but only soldiers and politicians. Even the exact site of the ancient town is in doubt because she had no monuments and no great buildings. Her men were courageous and her women virtuous, but they lacked most of the finer intellectual interests and moral traits which civilization should develop. According to Aristotle, government should aim to develop character in the citizens, making them good and capable of fine actions. In the *Politics* (VII, 14) he declares that legislators are less likely to frame governments, make laws, and set up educational plans with a view to cultivating the virtues than to tend, "in a vulgar spirit," to stress those matters which promise to be useful and profitable. Many modern writers, he continues, have taken a similar view: they commend the Lacedaemonian constitution, and praise the legislator for making conquest and war his sole aim, a doctrine which "may be refuted by argument and has long since been refuted by facts." Sparta in continuing its military system according to old custom, having lost her independence, was, he said, also losing the chance to become civilized.

Spartan education is historically important not only for its example but also because it influenced the thought of the great Greek philosopher, Plato, and through him the thought of the world. Plato's *Republic* and *Laws* borrow a great deal from the Spartan experience. The hardening system of training which is intended to toughen body and spirit and to build up resistances and immunities had an early historical expression in Spartan practice whence it passed over into the works of Montaigne, Locke, and Rousseau, and many modern masters. And there is a related and still more important point. The modern cult of physical education is not altogether Spartan, but in its militaristic form in some states like Nazi Germany, with its youth movement, and Fascist Italy, with its Balilla, it came close to the Spartan philosophy that the end of life is power. Thus this very early topic of our survey is not only ancient history but modern politics as well.

2. ATHENS

The peninsula of Greece, projecting into the eastern Mediterranean like an open hand, has for its thumb the little country of Attica pointing eastward toward Asia Minor and the colonies where the Seven Wise Men lived and the higher Greek culture first developed. The city-state of Attica, for which the name Athens, its capitol, is almost universally substituted, was somewhat smaller than Rhode Island and in its prosperous days had a population of about two hundred thousand. The state enjoyed an income from the rich silver mines of Laurium, which were worked by slave labor. The soil was not particularly fertile, but the olive and the vine flourished and various manufactures, especially that of pottery, were carried on. Many Athenians engaged in the extensive commercial undertakings and the large carrying-trade for which their state was admirably situated. These overseas connections led to the importation from the East and Egypt not only of commercial goods but also of ideas. Of both classes of imports the gifted Athenian people made full use, and by the end of the Persian Wars, about 480 B.C., Athens had become a wealthy and highly cultured city, and the leader of the Greek city-states.

Although the Greeks were unable to achieve political unity, Greece, or Hellas, was not merely a geographical term. There was a strong cultural unity based upon language, religion, similar customs, and the consciousness of a common origin and history, together with the great games which drew their contestants, spectators, and audiences from all the regions in which the Greek people had settled. Athens was the great center of this cultural development, which reached its most creative period in the fifth and fourth centuries before Christ. The spirit of the Athens of that epoch is portrayed in a famous "speech" of Pericles (c. 495–429 B.C.), as reported or composed by the historian Thucydides.

Thucydides (c. 464–410 B.C.) makes Pericles, in the "Funeral Oration," praise the people and the polity of his city as follows:

Our form of government does not enter into rivalry with the institutions of others. We do not copy our neighbors, but are an example to them. It is true that we are called a democracy, for the administration is in the hands of the many and not of the few. But while the law secures equal justice to all alike in their private disputes, the claim of excellence is also recognized; and when a citizen is in any way distinguished, he is preferred to the public service, not as a matter of privilege, but as the reward of merit. Neither is poverty a bar, but a man may benefit his country whatever the obscurity of his condition.

And we have not forgotten to provide for our weary spirits many relaxations from toil; we have regular games and sacrifices throughout the year; at home the style of our life is refined; and the delight which we daily feel in all these things helps to banish melancholy. Because of the greatness of our city the fruits of the whole earth flow in upon us, so that we may enjoy the goods of other countries as freely as our own.

Then, again, our military training is in many respects superior to that of our adversaries [the Spartans]. . . . And in the matter of education, whereas they from early youth are always undergoing laborious exercises which are to make them brave, we live at ease, and yet are ready to face the perils which they face.

If, then, we prefer to meet danger with a light heart, but without laborious training are we not greatly the gainers? . . . An Athenian citizen does not neglect the state because he takes care of his own household; and even those of us who are engaged in business have a very fair idea of politics. . . .

To sum up, I say that Athens is the school of Hellas, and that the individual Athenian in his own person seems to have the power of adapting himself to the most varied forms of action with the utmost versatility and grace. This is no passing and idle word, but truth and fact; and the assertion is verified by the position to which these qualities have raised the state. For in the hour of trial Athens alone among her contemporaries is superior to the report of her. No enemy who comes against her is indignant at the reverses which he sustains at the hands of such a city; no subject complains that his masters are unworthy of him. And we shall assuredly not be without witnesses; there are mighty monuments of our power which will make us the wonder of this and of succeeding ages: we shall not need the praises of Homer or of any other panegyrist, whose poetry may please for the moment, although his representation of the facts will not bear the light of day. For we have compelled every land, every sea, to open a path for our valour, and have everywhere planted eternal memorials of our friendship and of our enmity.

This supposed speech is, however, the statement of a great ideal rather than a dispassionate account of the actual conditions. To prove this we need only recall that citizenship was the privilege of only one-fourth of the population; and that those who actually controlled the Athenian city-state were only a small part of its citizenry. But the ideal is a noble one and could have been formed only in a great and noble state.

3. THE ATHENIAN SCHOOLS

In wealthy families, nurses who were usually slaves cared for the children in their infant years; and for this purpose Spartans were often preferred because they were considered especially capable. That the Athenian parents loved and indulged their children is shown in literature and many inscriptions. There were cradle songs, children's stories, and many toys, and games. The manufacture of dolls was an Athenian industry. The games were such universal favorites as marbles, leapfrog, hoops, ball games, and knuckle-bones. Children's games are among the most conservative and persistent of customs.

Formal education began at the age of seven. Each family had a pedagogue, a *paidagogos* or man-servant, whose duty it was to escort the boys to school where he waited until their lessons were done when he conducted them home again. The pedagogue was to permit no loitering and gadding about, for modesty was one of the ideals of conduct for boys. He had the direction of the morals of his charges and was allowed to use the whip, but he was not always highly esteemed or willingly obeyed by the boys. Only the boys were sent to school. The girls were given domestic education by the mother in the home.

There were three separate elementary schools for boys in Athens: the letters school for reading, writing, and the elements of arithmetic, the music school which taught lyric poetry and the mastery of the seven-stringed lyre, and the gymnastic school or palaestra. All of these were private schools and the parents paid the fees by the month. Both the qualifications and the social standing of the teachers were low. The boys commonly attended the letters school or the music school in the morning and the palaestra in the afternoon; but the schools were quite independent of each other and almost entirely unregulated by law. There was an Athenian law which restricted schools to daylight hours; and another which said that only fathers who sent their boys to school could expect aid in old age from their sons. The former law indicates the fact that the Athenian school day was a long one. The latter suggests, what is also a fact, that all the sons of Athenian citizens were given the chance to learn to read. Athenian schooling for boys extended from the age of seven until they went to work in early adolescence; but rich lads attended school longer. In the later period of Greek history, after about 340 B.C., the young men of the upper classes were enrolled in the ephebic corps and served as frontier patrols for two years between the ages of eighteen and twenty.

Before we consider the school exercises, we must notice that among the Greeks the word music had a wider application than it has with us. In Athenian education, literature, including reading and writing, together with music in our sense, were the concern of the Muses; and, indeed, all intellectual studies were considered forms of music. The aim of both the music and the gymnastics, or, in other words, of mental and physical education, was moral excellence.

The letters school taught first the alphabet, then syllables, then words, and reading, and writing. The master was called a *grammatist* from *grammata*, meaning letters, and from this our word grammar is derived. The teaching methods were mechanical and the motive was often supplied by the rod. The teacher pronounced the name of the letter or the word; the pupil pronounced after him. The school had little equipment. Potsherds from the large potteries west of the city were used for practice writing. Wax tablets consisting of thin wax-covered boards hinged together were also used for the same purpose. Books were costly and were in the form of a roll, a form which is very inconvenient for reference and school use, although quite handy for continuous reading. Besides Homer the children were taught Aesop, Hesiod, and later the lyric poets. Partly because books were scarce, the children were required to memorize long passages from Homer and other poets. In later times when grammar, in the modern sense, became a subject of study and when literature became more common, the courses of study grew longer and secondary education, chiefly literary

FIGURE 3.

ATHENIAN SCHOOL SCENE FROM A
VASE PAINTING

in content, was developed. This is the reason for the term grammar school as applied to secondary or intermediate education. But it was the Romans, not the Greeks, who first fully organized the secondary school and made it a school of literature.

Writing was taught from a copy set by the master on a wax tablet with the stylus. This copy the boy traced, following the groove; and the master also guided the boy's hand at the beginning until he was able to imitate the copy. When sufficient skill had been attained the master dictated a text which the pupil wrote down and memorized. With the scarcity of books dictation was an unavoidable exercise and among the Romans *dictata* came to mean schoolbooks; and later a derived form, *dictamen*, meant the writing of legal papers and forms and the study of law. Arithmetic was little taught in schools, partly because of its connection with the menial occupations of commerce—from Plato's *Laws* one would gather that educated men were often wholly ignorant of arithmetic—but partly also because the Greeks had a poor and difficult method of writing numbers. Although they counted by tens, they used twenty-seven or more characters in their arithmetical notation. With all its acuteness the ancient world did not succeed in inventing an appropriate symbolism for calculation. The schools therefore taught little arithmetic beyond counting and the addition and subtraction of whole numbers. In the business world finger reckoning with an elaborate system of signs and gestures prevailed. This could be carried on between persons who were wholly illiterate. Business, and perhaps the school also, used the abacus or counting-board in calculation.

FIGURE 4.

FROM THE REVERSE OF THE SAME VASE

Instruction in music, in our sense of the word, usually began after some progress had been made in reading, and both were taught by the same teacher in early times; but later a separate school and teacher, the *citharist*, arose. Singing and the playing of the lyre were taught. These were practiced at the same time, for the boy was taught to play an accompaniment to his own voice rendering the words of the lyric poets. This ability was a social requirement, lack of which marked one as uneducated. The lyre was in a way the national instrument which, it was believed, Apollo himself had used. Another Greek instrument was the Asiatic pipe, commonly called the flute, although it was not the modern instrument. This was not favored in the school because it was used in Bacchic festivals and was supposed to be sensual in its effects.

Among the Greeks music was an essential element of education. It was not a mere recreation but was regarded as a means of forming the character and disposition and of ethical-religious education. It was never in old days considered apart from poetry. The words were an essential part, and the later appearance of purely instrumental music was lamented as a symbol of decadence. Music was also directly connected with physical education through the dance and the procession, with their religious and military significance. Dancing was an important element in religious and civic festivals and in the theater.

Gymnastics, as a form of education, was older and just as important as music. The pentathlon provided the basic exercises. Greek vases and sculptures show the various forms of activity and the equipment used in them. Among the latter were the boxing thongs instead of gloves, the jumping weights, the punching bag which was not inflated but filled with seeds, the jumping pit and the pickax for loosening the ground, the spear, the discus, and the strigil for cleaning the body after exercise. The Greeks aimed at health, strength, and endurance, and also at skill, grace, and beauty of figure; and the Greek sculptures show how well they succeeded. Gymnastics further had a moral aim, to develop courage, so that, as Plato says, the young man need not "play the coward in war or on any other occasion." Hunting, swimming, riding, the use of arms, and other exercises were sometimes practiced. Physical education was taught in a special school, the *palaestra*, under a special teacher and continued in adolescence and throughout life in the public gymnasiums of which almost every Greek city had one or more. In the latter half of the fourth century the ephebic institution was introduced. Then, between the ages of eighteen and twenty, the boy as an *ephebos* received military training and patrolled the frontiers of Attica. At twenty years of age, having received a set of weapons and having sworn the famous ephebic oath, he became a full Athenian citizen.

Girls did not attend the schools and, as we have said, they received their education, mostly moral and domestic training, from their mothers in the home. Marriage and the family were closely regulated by law and custom. The women and girls lived in separate apartments, had no share as hostesses or guests at men's social gatherings in the homes, and were kept in almost oriental seclusion. Matrons seldom appeared in public except at religious ceremonies. It was their task to order the household and direct the work of the domestic slaves. Spinning and weaving were typical occupations. Romantic love between the sexes did not commonly exist and was hardly an ideal; but it was the Athenian wife's primary function to bear strong, healthy children. If the marriage proved to be childless the husband could return the wife to her parents together with her dowry. In no sense was she the mental, spiritual, or social companion of her lord. Athens was "a man's town," and except for female participation in religion, Athenian culture was a male culture. Pericles in the famous funeral oration, which has been quoted in part, put the spirit of this phase of it into a sentence: "And if I am to speak of womanly virtues to those of you who will henceforth be widows, let me sum them up in one short admonition: To a woman not to show more weakness than is natural to her sex is a great glory, and not to be talked about for good or evil among men."

Although the schools of ancient Athens were not secular they did not teach religion as a separate subject because religion was not separate from the domestic, economic, and political life. Greek religion was largely a matter of ritual and ceremony and was to be scrupulously carried out by the individual or the official priest at sacred shrines and on sacred days. The state watched carefully over the public worship of the gods because their aid was believed necessary to the public welfare. There was no church because the Greeks were unable to conceive of a separation between civil and ecclesiastical powers. There was no church because there was no secular state. The state itself performed the functions of a church and the gods of nature were also the gods of the family and the state. Apollo, the god of the sun, was also the god of healing and the fine arts. Poseidon, or Neptune, the monarch of the ocean, took a lively interest in the affairs of men. The sailor who upon rounding a headland saw Athene's golden spearhead shining above the Acropolis saw more than a symbol of his city and homeland. Pallas Athene, the goddess of wisdom, who sprang from the head of Jove, was the spiritual element as well as the protectress of the city of beauty, wisdom, and knowledge.

As Athene presided over Athens, so every schoolroom was presided over by the Muses, and for the schoolboy to play truant or to slight his lessons was to flout the Muses. Religion was taught in Greek schools by means of Homer and the poets and in Greek life by participation in the great public festivals and the smaller religious acts and by the presence of the great temples and statues dedicated to the deities.

As the Greek conception of man's relations to the divine became more spiritualized, the advanced thinkers became dissatisfied with the old conceptions of the gods and their very imperfect morality. Thus Plato would amend Homer to make him teach that the gods (or God) never do evil or cause evil to be done, never mislead anyone, and never change. But the religion of the ordinary citizen included a great deal of crude superstition. For him religion was a means of foretelling the future, of placating jealous gods, of averting misfortune, and of increasing his health or prosperity. The Greek religion contained a minimum of doctrine and a great deal of art, ceremony, and ritual; and rather than a belief it was a spiritual atmosphere in which the whole of Greek life, private and public, was lived. Because it contained so little of dogma and belief and positive intellectual claim it did not tend to hamper investigation as much as later Christian churches sometimes did. Yet we must remember that in 399 B.C. Socrates was executed by Athens, the most enlightened Greek state, for "introducing new gods and corrupting the youth."

4. THE PERICLEAN AGE AND AFTER

The Athens of Pericles jealously guarded its constitutional democracy; but in spite of the political equality there was a small class of so-called best families which really controlled public affairs. With the perhaps unique exception of Socrates only the wealthy and well-born were admitted to this upper caste; nor would Socrates have been admitted if he had accepted fees for teaching. In that case he would have been classed with the Sophists, whom one paid well and treated with outward deference but really despised because they were professionals and no better than trades-men. Praxiteles, the painter, and Phidias, the sculptor, were only workmen, artisans, in the eyes of the aristocratic class; and the great vase painters who placed the figures of beautiful aristocratic youths upon their creations could gaze upon their models only by stealth and from a distance. And yet the common people of Athens were proud of the social aristocracy. When Alcibiades sent a number of chariots to the Olympic Games and won a race with the speediest of them, the whole populace gloried in the honor which they felt that they shared. This does not really differ from the condition today when a whole city rises to its feet, so to speak, for the local football hero whom most of them never see.

With all their snobbery and more serious misconduct the aristocracy had their value. It was they who erected the structure of higher education and created its materials. The Sophists, most of them foreigners in Athens, were those who undertook to prepare young men for active life and public service. The word was originally taken to mean wise and educated persons; but it came to have a derogatory meaning as in the modern word sophistry, from the polemic which Plato directed against this class of teachers. None of the well-known Sophists except Socrates were Athenians, and this stirred up the opposition which criticism of foreigners usually arouses. As a group they charged fees, sometimes very high fees, and some made excessive claims for their teaching and argumentative powers. A few seem to have had less interest in imparting the truth than in showing how, by rhetorical and logical devices, one might win a case or an argument despite the weight of the evidence on the opposite side. Thus all were smudged with the terms, sophistry and sophistical, which many of them did not deserve.

The Sophists may be given chief credit for the invention and develop-ment of the formal subjects of grammar, rhetoric, dialectic or logic, and mathematics. The last of these came to its flowering-point at a later time than the others and will be treated in a later section. The first three, gram-mar, rhetoric, and logic, became the elementary curriculum of the Middle Ages. Their origins will be treated here.

Literary and grammatical instruction was greatly broadened in the age of Pericles, and from being a subject for schoolboys it now became a study for men. During this period, about 450 B.C., the Sophists Protagoras and Hippias of Elis, who were relatively as learned in their time as Aristotle in the following century, founded the study of grammar as a science. They investigated the speech sounds, distinguished the genders, and the several tenses and moods. As a result of their investigation and influence formal grammar became a subject of study and instruction in higher schools.

It is significant that prose was then studied and cultivated as well as poetry. This led to the development of rhetoric or the art of public speaking. Gorgias, commonly called the father of rhetoric, and after whom Plato named one of his dialogues, came to Athens in the year of Plato's birth (427 B.C.). Gorgias was known for his ornate style, the use of poetical words, symmetrical clauses, a strongly marked rhythm, and parallelism of structure. He had a great influence upon the most famous Greek teacher of rhetoric, Isocrates. Oratory had a remarkable development. It became a science and a profession, useful in the courts and in the popular assemblies, and a deliberately cultivated fine art as well. At the great games the Sophists delivered carefully wrought speeches which were intended to serve as models for their students.

Young men who wished to enter public life needed to acquire facility in reasoning. The Sophists attempted to develop this facility by means of conversation, that is, the dialogue; and from this came the name dialectic for the art of logic. Zeno, of Elea in southern Italy, may be regarded as the founder of logic. He flourished about 460 B.C. Two of his arguments became especially famous. These, which are known, respectively, as the flying arrow and as Achilles and the tortoise, still serve to puzzle students. The Sophists developed logic; and its comprehensive exposition was given by Aristotle. Logic was the instrument of knowledge, and Aristotle was called the "master of those who know."

All three, grammar, rhetoric, and logic, developed as formal disciplines, useful not so much for their own content but as instruments for handling the content of other sciences. Those sciences and subjects which are packed with information, such subjects as history, geography, chemistry, and agriculture, are called realistic, that is, objective and informational subjects treating of "real" things. The formal subjects are implements that aid us in handling the realistic ones.

The realistic subjects were also cultivated in this great period. History flowered in the storytelling of Herodotus and the critical history of Thucydides. Historical and political studies were introduced into the ephebic college, and the orator Demosthenes is said to have copied the history of Thucydides many times as a means of becoming thoroughly familiar with its contents. Hippocrates of Cos by his personality and achievements earned the title of Father of Medicine and the honorary citizenship of the city of his adoption. Astronomy and geography were cultivated. For Homer the solid earth had been shaped like a shield surrounded along the edges by "the ever-flowing river of Ocean"; but by the end of the Periclean age the most advanced of the Greeks considered the earth as a sphere. The Sophists also taught law and constitutional theory and practice. Even city planning did not escape the writers of this period.

The higher education of ancient Athens, like the primary, was wholly private. There were no state examinations and no state curricula, indeed no set curricula of any kind. Nor did the state provide any support. In spite of the political democracy, the tone of the intellectual life was set by a social aristocracy, as we have already seen. Plato (427–347 B.C.), the greatest of the Greek philosophers and one of the world's greatest thinkers, first organized the higher instruction in Athens at a fixed place and in a regular institution, the Academy. He founded the Academy (c. 387 B.C.) in his own grounds, a grove dedicated to the minor deity Academus. Because he was a wealthy aristocrat he did not, like the Sophists, accept fees. The institution seems to have had a continuous history of more than nine hundred years. It was closed by Justinian in A.D. 529. The scholars of the Academy formed a closed brotherhood and the care which they bestowed upon Plato's writings is doubtless the cause for the excellent state in which these have been preserved. The succeeding heads of the Academy, called scholarchs, took over the grounds which formed the home of the school, but the vicissitudes of time compelled the Academy to move on several occasions. It was a research as well as a teaching institution and devoted itself to mathematics, politics, ethics, and other subjects, not omitting botany and zoology. Like the teachers of rhetoric, the philosophers also prepared men for public and private life; and, while rhetoric was supposed to be more practical and especially to serve as an introduction to statesmanship, philosophy came to be regarded as the highest and final discipline of the Athenian educated classes. The theater and practical politics might be considered incidental but effective forms of adult education during this great creative age, which for intellectual and artistic productiveness was not equaled until the thirteenth or perhaps the nineteenth century of our era.

5. GREEK EDUCATIONAL THEORY

Everyone has heard of the teaching of Socrates (469–399 B.C.), who is considered the founder of ethics. He turned aside from speculations about the nature of the physical world to consider the nature of virtue or good conduct. He felt that to "know oneself" would be the most important knowledge of all. He did not conduct a school but went about in the city talking with the youth and trying to develop clear ideas about such virtues as courage, temperance, and justice. He demanded not examples but a definition. Engaging a young man in conversation and pretending that others were wiser than he, Socrates by clever questioning led his respondent to admit that his ideas were confused and his statements self-contradictory, and that he really did not know the essential meaning of the term he had used. This step was called the Socratic Irony, a necessary stage in becoming wise, for no one can learn until he becomes humble and admits his present lack of wisdom.

The next step was Definition. By interrogating men of all classes, shoemakers, merchants, soldiers, or wealthy young aristocrats, and by abstracting what was common to all the plausible definitions and descriptions of such a term as courage, Socrates attempted to arrive at its essential meaning.

The third step, called the Maieutic, was taken in order to draw out the implications of the ideas which had already been defined. An example of the maieutic process is shown in Plato's dialogue, the Meno, in which a slaveboy who has never studied geometry draws true conclusions as soon as the figure and definitions of the terms are set before him.

This means that by nature everyone possesses the power to think; and that learning is a process not of gathering information but of seeing meanings. But it should be noted that this conclusion was drawn from a mathematical exercise, not from the study of history. In human affairs, the drawing of necessary conclusions and the making of precise predictions are not generally possible. Even ethics, the special field which Socrates cultivated, is not yet a science. Socrates was not justified in using mathematics as the typical example of the truth-finding process. This criticism should not divert us from the main point, namely, that Socrates, by his Irony, Definition, and Maieutic, began the development of rational methods of teaching. He was the founder, not only of ethics, but also of educational method.

Socrates turned from the study of nature to that of ethics because a generation of orators and teachers had called in question the old Athenian customs and morals and raised doubts about all principles of morality. These teachers were the Sophists. He was also moved to study ethics and politics because Athens was passing through a revolutionary period when the very foundations of government were quaking. He came to the conclusion that "virtue is knowledge" and that a state or an individual life can be good only when it is based upon wisdom. He believed that wisdom could be attained by men, and, although he insisted that he was not wise, he meant to keep on seeking. But in 399 B.C. he was accused of corrupting the youth by false teaching, was condemned, and was executed by the city which h(. had tried to instruct. His greatest pupil, Plato, who had been with him for eight years, continued his work.

Plato erected an imposing edifice of educational theory. His teachings are found in his famous dialogues, especially the *Laws*, *Protagoras*, *Symposium*, and *Phaedrus*, and in the *Republic*, from every standpoint his most important work. He was one of the most original and comprehensive thinkers of all time. His views on education were influenced by Socrates, by the Sophists, by Spartan practice, and by current political conditions in Athens.

We shall offer only a brief, simplified account of Plato's theory of education as found in the *Republic*. In that work Plato accepted some of the main outlines of the education and practice of Athens but offered criticism also. The poets, he said, had misrepresented the gods as quarreling among themselves, as changing their minds, and as often doing evil deeds. God must be represented, said Plato, as perfect, unchanging, and never doing evil. The heroes must be depicted as truly heroic and, therefore, as proper models for the youth. Homer must be expurgated before being used in the schools. Music and gymnastic, likewise, were to be simplified and purified in order that they might be fitted to lead the boy to become temperate, courageous, healthy, and devoted to the state.

Plato proposed to extend the educational system to include a series of mathematical studies, arithmetic, geometry, astronomy, and music, and finally logic, or the science of thinking and of final truth. He recognized the practical values of such studies but his main purpose was to teach the meaning and the method of attaining truth as distinct from mere opinion.

In addition to its educational function the school had also a selective function. Pupils were to be sent to school only as long as they received real benefit from the instruction and Plato thought many pupils would be dismissed early in the course because they lacked capacity for advanced study. He considered that only a few were able to profit from the study of logic or advanced mathematics. His scheme of selection was fairly complex and was applied in a series of stages which were intended to select gradually but more and more closely the most able from the less gifted. His criteria were such as the following: love of knowledge, ability to learn, strength and skill, self-control, devotion to the public good, aptness to resist evil and deceit, and capacity for abstract thinking. Those who passed the successive tests and reached the highest levels of wisdom and devotion to the state were to rule the state. The government was, therefore, to be based upon knowledge of principles and truth. Not power or propaganda, but science and philosophy were to control. The philosopher was to be king.

The same scheme which selected the rulers also separated out, first, the working classes and, secondly, the soldiers or defenders of the state. Thus there were to be three classes of citizens. The lowest were the producers of food, clothing, and shelter, the merchants, the bankers, all those who provided the economic resources of the state. These, he thought, were moved mainly by desires and appetites and they were to be controlled by those wiser than themselves. The middle class was composed of soldiers who were to be men of honor and courage. The thinkers or philosophers formed the highest and ruling class. This social scheme was paired with a psychological scheme to which it was parallel and upon which it depends. Each person, said Plato, is composed of three kinds of elements, appetite, spirit, and reason, and these seek, in the same order, wealth, honor, and wisdom. That one is a just or righteous person in whom reason rules the body and the appetites; and that is a just state in which the most completely rational, the wise, rule, the soldiers fight, and the workers labor. The state is an individual "writ large." The problem of the *Republic* is the problem of justice or righteousness. Plato's justice, therefore, is a harmony in which all qualities and all individuals are in their proper places performing their proper functions; and, to repeat it in more general form, that is a just state or society in which each individual is in the place for which his nature and capacity fit him, and is doing those things and only those which he can do best.

For Plato the state was "the Great Society," the highest ethical community, which alone made the good life of the individual possible. To the state, therefore, the individual owed a natural loyalty and obedience. Plato's educational scheme was throughout a social, not an individualistic scheme, and this is also true of Greek educational theory as a whole. His ideal state was to have power over the political, economic, domestic, and cultural life of its citizens; and he concerned himself a great deal with the upper classes in all those relations and not with the lower classes. The laboring and industrial groups were considered mainly as means.

Plato feared change because it seemed, and in his day tended to be, destructive, not constructively progressive. He feared ambition, individualism, and egoism, because they destroyed the needed unity of society. The state was to control and regulate property, children, and the family. All selfishness which might stem from family interests or the pursuit of wealth and power were to be suppressed by a firmly established communism. Loyalty to the state was to be the highest loyalty and education the state's highest function.

The educational system of the *Republic* is an intellectualist scheme based upon knowledge and understanding. Virtue is the result of intelligence. This leaves little room for poetry and art and in his more ascetic moods Plato would have suppressed both. The *Republic* is itself, however, a great work of art as well as of thought; and it has influenced most of the world's philosophers, political thinkers, and educators.

Aristotle's scheme is found in his *Politics*. Either this work was left incomplete or its later books have been lost. As far as we have it, its argument follows Plato closely. Both regard education as a branch of politics, and Aristotle teaches that each form of state, the aristocratic, democratic, or monarchical, has a particular form of education which is most appropriate to it. Education is to be administered by the state. He turns aside from his positive theory to criticize Spartan education, which he considered narrow and brutal. Both Plato and Aristotle began with infancy and the care and hygiene of the young child. Education, Aristotle said, depends upon nature, habit, and reason, and the end is understanding, or contemplation. The elementary subjects, about which "there is a dispute," should be reading and writing, gymnastics, music, and drawing. These are useful in practical life, but the final end is not utilitarian but the development of an actively good man. Human goodness is of two kinds: goodness of character which is produced by habituation, and goodness of conduct and intellect which is produced by teaching. As has already been suggested by his reference to Sparta, Aristotle was opposed to hard and strenuous physical training for boys. Before adolescence only the lighter exercises were to be used. He has an extended discussion of music in education which was to offer pleasure, train character, and provide an outlet for overwrought feelings. We know nothing of Aristotle's views on the intellectual education of the older adolescent and young adult.

6. THE HELLENISTIC AGE (300 B.C. AND AFTER)

The creative powers of the Greek mind were almost exhausted by the time of Alexander. A great deal of useful intellectual work was still being done, but it was less original. It was the work of Euclid, Claudius Ptolemy, Erasistratus, and of the Alexandrian grammarians, men who were not primarily original thinkers but rather specialists, scholars, and interpreters; but their work greatly increased knowledge and it was important. The chief characteristics of the period were that learning now became specialized and thought became cosmopolitan. Greece had lost her independence. Philosophy had been the universal science including all other sciences; philosophy now became differentiated into special subjects such as astronomy, geography, mathematics.

Greek learning and views, overflowing their former national and racial boundaries, were spread by Alexander (356–323 B.C.) among the civilized people of the Mediterranean regions and as far as India. His successors followed the same policy of conquest; and Greek and Oriental learning and religions were combined into a new but vague and homeless culture. The Greek language became the common language of learning in the East and Greek science, art, and coinage, the common possessions of the Eastern peoples.

Athens long continued to hold her historical supremacy in letters and learning. So in the time of Cicero, Athens was still an intellectual center. But other cities, favored by situation or by the support of their rulers, could also boast of their schools. A professional class of teachers, the successors to the old Sophists, arose and devoted themselves to research and to instruction. The scholar's beard and gown became familiar in Pergamum, Rhodes, Antioch in Syria, but especially in Alexandria which first rivaled and then surpassed Athens as a center of learning. Alexandria was founded by the great conqueror whose name it bears in 332 B.C. Under the rule of the Ptolemies, the Museum, or home of the Muses, and great libraries and schools flourished. The city became a meeting place of Greek, Hebrew, and Egyptian learning, and was famed for philology, science, and mathematics.

Little creative literature, either in poetry or prose, was produced in this period. The great works of the fifth and fourth centuries were now considered as classics, that is, as models. From these examples, rules were drawn as guides to practice. For philology it was, first of all, necessary to have correct, authentic texts of the classics, especially of Homer. The explanation of difficult passages, the solution of grammatical, historical, and literary problems occupied the philologists of the time. Grammars, commentaries, and dictionaries were prepared and became the tools of the scholar and the schoolmaster. Famous teachers laid the foundations of Roman and modern language study.

Science received a strong impulse from Aristotle, who was a student of zoology not only in books but by observation. Charles Darwin in his later years expressed regret that he had not earlier read Aristotle's *History of Animals*. Aristotle's pupil, Theophrastus, was the founder of scientific botany and mineralogy. Dissection was carried on by Alexandrian physicians and prepared the way for the development of anatomy and surgery. Euclid worked in Alexandria about 290 B.C. His system of geometry became a schoolbook and remained for twenty centuries the standard work on that subject; and it is still the chief source of high school geometry. Archimedes also lived in Alexandria for a time; and there Hero (c. 100 B.C.) showed that a reflected ray of light follows the shortest possible path, invented the first steam engine which however remained a toy until recent times, and laid the foundations of geodesy. Hero and Archimedes were physicists as well as mathematicians. Aristarchus of Samos (280 B.C.) developed a system of astronomy in which the earth was supposed to move while sun and stars were fixed. Eratosthenes was a physical geographer, and Claudius Ptolemy put much of the Greek knowledge of astronomy and geography into scientific form. Like other sciences, geography is based upon two kinds of mental operations, the bit-by-bit observation of earth and heavens by scientists and practical men like sailors and traders and the classification and argumentation which unites the facts into a consistent whole. By such work the Greek world produced maps and charts, another set of tools for use in education.

These advances in science and language gave to education an intellectual character which tended to decrease the importance of music, of gymnastics, and of the moral content of the older schools. Less attention was paid to the all-round education of the classical days and more to a purely intellectual culture. There was a second result. The ideal of an encyclopedic knowledge led, in the Alexandrian period, to a multiplication of subjects and to the growth of specialism. In the schools a fixed group of subjects formed itself into an *encyclopaedia*, which means a circle of the arts and sciences appropriate for the education of boys. Thence came our word encyclopedia for a work of all-inclusive knowledge. This was, in part, the result of the internationalizing of Greek culture. The older Athens had a well-rounded scheme of education for her boys. Sparta had a military one. Each was intended to form the citizens of its states. Even in Plato we already see an effort to unite these two; but no Greek of classical days ever dreamed that other peoples, "the barbarians," could desire a similar schooling. Under the Alexandrian influence the distinction between Greek and foreigner tended to fade and that between the learned and the unlearned was raised to a high power. The subjects which were gradually included in the encyclopedia were grammar, rhetoric, and dialectic, the language studies; and arithmetic, geometry, astronomy, music as a science, and other scientific studies. The last four had, indeed, been named in this order by Plato. The whole group, called the Seven Liberal Arts, although the number and content became fixed only in the early Middle Ages, passed on to Rome and came to form the regular, unvarying curriculum of schools. The first three of these were in all times much more widely studied than the last four. Everywhere terminology became standardized, textbooks were prepared, and the school acquired the materials and methods which were to remain with little change for more than a thousand years. Intellectualism, specialism, fixity, and sterility, tended to characterize the secondary education of the later Greek, and of the Roman and the Middle Ages. And these are evils which the school has always had to fight against.

The final stages in the education of a learned man of Hellenistic times were devoted to rhetoric which prepared for public speaking, law, and statesmanship; and to philosophy which was directed toward religion and morals. Great schools of philosophy were founded: the Academy of Plato, the Lyceum of Aristotle, the Stoic school of the Porch of Zeno, and the Garden of Epicurus. Individual philosophers or Sophists, lecturing for fees which they collected from their hearers and employing "barkers" to bring in new students, featured the so-called Greek universities. These "institutions," however, had no formal unity, no organization, equipment, or requirements. They were merely the customary congregations of students and teachers of the higher disciplines. For centuries the Hellenistic centers were frequented not only by local students but by some who came from a great distance; so, Cicero studied for a time at Athens, Rhodes, and elsewhere, and later also sent his son, the young Marcus, to Athens. This young scion of a great family, provided by an indulgent father with too much money and a fine house, did not become "a second Cicero." There were many such dilettantes, and we may now add another characteristic to the list given above. Education in Hellenistic and in later Roman times tended to become decorative, a means to amusement and idle distinction for young men without serious purposes. In the Byzantine empire and throughout the East a fading Greek civilization lived on, but Rome had already become the ruler and civilizer of the West.

The primary purpose of Greek education was the preparation of citizens. This emphasis upon public ends represents a radical change from earlier practice. Among older peoples, education had been restricted to special classes such as priests, officials, and skilled craftsmen. It had often been controlled by the priests and was regarded as a "mystery," to be concealed from the uninitiated. The Greeks recognized no such mystery and accepted no such restriction.

This statement must not, however, be interpreted too broadly. In Greece there was neither concealment nor control by a priestly caste; and the opportunity for education was open to all the sons of citizens. But the opportunity was also confined to them. Girls were not admitted to the schools of Athens and received only limited training in Sparta. And everywhere both boys and girls of the lowest and more numerous classes were generally barred, and slaves, the most numerous class of all, were altogether excluded. As a result, only about one in eight or ten of the whole population could attend school in Athens or receive training in the Spartan system. The Greeks did not conceive of universal education.

The Athenians developed the materials of secondary and higher education. They created the literary and art forms, several of the sciences, and the tools of learning, such as grammar, rhetoric, logic, and mathematics. The Spartan state communism was entirely unprogressive; but the Athenians and other Greeks, through trade and travel, came into contact with many cultures. Being a creative and inquiring people, they learned from the past and the present and they transformed all that they borrowed. They were observant, critical, and sensitive to beauty. They developed those ideals of art and of political freedom, of free investigation, and of rational interpretation which the modern world still pursues.

The schools had a simple, well-rounded, and active curriculum. They attempted to meet the needs of the spirit, intellect, and physical nature. It has been said that two-thirds of the school program consisted of activities in music and games that most boys must have regarded as play. They kept before the child the idea of public activity in peace and war; and, in the ephebic oath, the young men vowed to try to hand over their city to their successors, "not less than but more noble" than it was when they received it from their elders.

With their independence, they lost also their national spirit. Education became cosmopolitan, technical, specialized, and diffuse. It no longer had a central purpose. Before this occurred, the Greek language had become the universal language of learning throughout the eastern Mediterranean world.

QUESTIONS

1. Consider the following statement: We must necessarily fail in any attempt to explain Greek achievement on the basis of race, geography, or the influence of previous civilizations. True, partly true, or wholly false? Why do we consider the factors named and similar ones?
2. Do Spartan conditions help to explain Spartan education?
3. The ancient Spartan ideals and practices affected later education. Is the modern Spartanism in certain countries likely to affect education in other countries?
4. Distinguish between "formal education" in the sense in which this phrase is used on page 15, formalized education, and formative education.
5. Compare ancient Greek education with the educational provision of an American city or school district, considering the pupils and classes of people, the curriculum, the methods, the equipment, the purposes, and any other features.
6. Why did the Sophists lay great stress upon argumentation and oratory?
7. Why did the Athenian schools give little attention to informational subjects?
8. Why is the Socratic method inappropriate in the teaching of botany?
9. Write a commentary on the passage quoted from Plato's *Protagoras*.
10. Compare and distinguish between the politics and education of Plato's *Republic* and those of modern totalitarian states.

FOR FURTHER READING AND STUDY

The Homeric poems, in a good translation such as that of Lang, Leaf, and Myers, are the best sources for early Greek life and education. Paul Monroe's *Source-Book in the History of Education for the Greek and Roman Period* (New York: Macmillan Co., 1901, 515 pp.) has selections from later sources. The *Review of Educational Research* (Washington, D. C.) for October, 1939, has a longer reading list on Greek and Roman education than we can provide here. The student should have at hand a good history of ancient Greece such as that by G. W. Botsford, or J. B. Bury.

Burnet, John, *Aristotle on Education*, fifth edition, Cambridge, Mass., Harvard University Press, 1928, 141 pp.

Dobson, John F., *Ancient Education and Its Meaning to Us*, New York, Longmans, Green and Co., 1932, 205 pp.

Drever, James, *Greek Education: Its Principles and Practice*, Cambridge, Mass., Harvard University Press, 1912, 107 pp.

Forbes, Clarence A., *Greek Physical Education*, New York, Century Company, 1929, 300 pp.

Freeman, Kenneth J., *Schools of Hellas* . . . third edition, London, Macmillan Co., Ltd., 1932.

Gardiner, E. Norman, *Athletics of the Ancient World*, London, Oxford University Press, 1930, 246 pp. A detailed treatment by the author of *Greek Athletic Sports and Festivals* (1910).

Hatch, Edwin, *The Influence of Greek Ideas and Usages Upon the Christian Church*, London, William and Norgate, 1914, 359 pp.

Jaeger, Werner, *Paideia, the Ideals of Greek Culture*, New York, Oxford University Press, 1939–1944, 3 vols.

Kenyon, Frederic G., *Books and Readers in Ancient Greece and Rome*, New York, Oxford University Press, 1932, 136 pp. "Two Greek School Tablets," *Journal of Hellenic Studies*, 29:29–40 (1909).

Klein, Anita E., *Child Life in Greek Art*, New York, Columbia University Press, 1932, 62 pp.

Marrou, H. I., *A History of Education in Antiquity*, New York, Sheed and Ward, 1956, 466 pp.

Moore, Ernest C., *The Story of Instruction: the Beginnings*, New York, The Macmillan Company, 1936, 380 pp.

Nettleship, Richard L., *Lectures on the Republic of Plato*, London, Macmillan Co., Ltd., 1936, 364 pp. A useful interpretation of Plato's Republic. Also useful but less important is the same author's *The Theory of Education in Plato's Republic*, New York, Oxford University Press, 1935, 155 pp.

Sidgwick, Henry, "The Sophists," *Journal of Philosophy*, Cambridge, England, 4 (1872–73): 288–307.

Ulich, Robert, *History of Educational Thought*, New York, American Book Company, 1945, 412 pp.

Van Hook, LaRue, *Greek Life and Thought*, New York, Columbia University Press, 1923, 329 pp.

Walden, John W. H., *The Universities of Ancient Greece*, New York, Charles Scribner's Sons, 1909, 367 pp.

Woody, Thomas, *Philostratus: Concerning Gymnastics*, Ann Arbor, Michigan, American Physical Education Association, 1936, 30 pp. The text of a Greek sophist's literary essay on athletic training and competition.

3 ROMAN EDUCATION

G REEK ACHIEVEMENT IN THE REALMS OF THE INTELLECT and the imagination was an important factor in the making of the modern mind and society. No one would doubt this. Another ancient civilization which made a great contribution to Western culture was the Roman. Not only were the qualities of these two peoples and of their civilizations strikingly different, but they were supplementary to each other, so that at several important points the strength of one covered the weakness of the other. Rome was strongest in law and administration, in practical work such as architecture and engineering, and in the art of spreading a civilization over wide areas and among many peoples.

The art of spreading a civilization is a form of education, in a broad sense of the word. The Romans civilized western Europe, from which our own civilization was to come. The foundations of this extension of civilization were their native legal and administrative institutions, their technology, and their language and literature. In these fields, although they borrowed much from the Greeks, they were creative. Through the Latin language, the Roman schools, and those powerful institutions, the Roman empire and the Roman Catholic Church, Roman achievements and many of the Greek contributions were preserved and transmitted to the future. The Romans were great educators.

When the curtain of history rises on the Italian peninsula we find its southern parts and a large portion of Sicily settled by the Greeks. They were by far the most civilized of Italy's early inhabitants. The Italic tribes, of whom the Latins were one, occupied the middle of the peninsula, while at the north the fierce, barbarous Gauls had come across the Alps into the valley of the Po and had pushed back the Etruscans. These latter were an important people living in strongly fortified cities and carrying on both agriculture and commerce. The Etruscans were builders of massive walls of hewn stone, of roads, and of imposing tombs. And they were able to write;

but, unfortunately, the little Etruscan writing that remains has not been deciphered.

The Latins lived on the left bank of the Tiber just across from the Etruscans. They were a race of farmers and shepherds. This rural background had great and continuing influence upon Roman life and literature, as may be seen, for example, in Vergil's *Bucolics* and *Georgics* and in the works of many other writers. The ancient Latins lived in straw-thatched huts grouped around hills which they had fortified. Some of these hill towns grew into cities and were united into a league for defense and offence. This people had a common worship and an annual festival which they celebrated on the Alban Mount. By 510 B.C. the Latins had secured for themselves both banks of the Tiber and held a protectorate over a long strip of the coast stretching south from Tiber-mouth and far inland. Two and a half centuries later (250 B.C.) they held all of southern Italy including the Greek cities on the mainland. In the next fifty years they added Sicily, Sardinia, and Spain. Carthage fell to Roman arms in 146 B.C.

We need not follow the expansion of the Roman dominions step by step. When her conquests were completed, Rome controlled all the old countries that bordered upon the Mediterranean Sea: Carthage, Egypt, Palestine, Syria, and Mesopotamia, and most important of all for our interests Athens, Alexandria, Syracuse, and the whole Greek world. In the old days of the later republic and the empire, "all roads led to Rome" and from the center they radiated to all the provinces. Through the mediation of Roman institutions, the contributions of any section of a great empire became the property of all. And yet this gift of disseminating culture was less than it might have been if the Roman nature had been more flexible and receptive.

The Romans had not the restless, sensitive nature nor the inquiring mind of the Greeks; and consequently they did not show so keen an interest in art and pure science. In these fields they were pupils and not always very attentive ones. Scientific investigation did not flourish in Rome; but this we shall consider more fully below. In oratory and still more in philosophy the dependence of the Romans upon their predecessors is very evident. Cicero spent several of the later years of his life in translating the thought of Plato and the Greek moralists into Latin. To do this he had to coin and borrow the words and almost literally to fashion a new philosophical language. Ethics, because it deals with conduct, was the branch of speculation which was most congenial to the Roman mind; and in the works of Seneca and of the emperor-philosopher, Marcus Aurelius, the Stoic ethics is given admirable though hardly original statement. Metaphysics and logic interested them little.

In poetry and history they consciously followed Hellenic models; but they were not mere imitators. Vergil took his idea of the pastoral from Theocritus and of the epic from Homer. But he did not copy Theocritus and Homer. Being a great artist, "majestic in his sadness at the doubtful doom of human kind," he wrote a great poem of his own, not an artless, elemental epic but a great national and self-conscious epic phrased like the *Iliad* in the "stateliest measure ever moulded by the lips of man." The *Aeneid* immediately became a schoolbook and has never ceased being a schoolbook since Tucca and Varius published the poem over two thousand years ago. The Latin literature is, however, less original than the Greek, and the Romans were even less creative in sculpture and painting, in dancing and athletics, and in philosophy and science. Their genius was that of adapting means to ends for the accomplishment of objective results. The Romans excelled as doers rather than as thinkers or artistic creators.

1. BEGINNINGS OF ROMAN EDUCATION

Education in ancient Rome was likewise practical; and, as elsewhere among the early culture-peoples, it was carried on in the family. The people, or some of them, must have been able to read in the time of Appius Claudius (450 B.C.) because at that time the Laws of the Twelve Tables were set up in the Forum for their instruction. Boys were required to memorize the text of the laws. This does not prove that there were schools. It is a great mistake to suppose that all people must be illiterate where there are no schools although doubtless many will be illiterate or only slightly literate under such conditions. And it would be a greater mistake to suppose that literacy was the only or the main objective of early education at Rome or elsewhere. Obedience to law and custom, the maintenance of religion and morals were the main objectives of early education. But when schools were established, and sometimes before, attention was directed to the teaching of reading and writing and of arithmetic, all of which were usually taught for practical use.

Whether education was conducted in the family as in very early times, or in the family and the school as in later times, what the Romans most cared about was that the children should acquire and embody the moral and social virtues. Such virtues were piety, which meant love of country, and justice, truthfulness, and *gravitas*. The family in Rome had a much larger place in life, greater unity and purity, and greater influence than in Greece and the East. The mother, although she had no part in public affairs, was held in esteem, contributed to the family councils, and deeply affected the tone of society. Rome produced such high-minded women as Cornelia, the mother of the Gracchi, the great leaders and martyrs of the struggle for social justice. Some upper class matrons were educated women who aided in the intellectual as well as the moral development of their sons. Quintilian takes occasion to name a number of these. He makes no reference whatever to girls as pupils in schools, but he was dealing with the highest or rhetoric schools which girls did not attend. Only the elementary school, and perhaps the second stage, the grammar school, were open to them. Roman education like the Greek was chiefly boys' education. In any case only elementary schools existed in the early times. Even these were lightly regarded. At least this has been inferred from the fact that the word *ludus* for the most elementary school means play. The extensive development of grammar schools and especially of rhetoric schools came in the second century before Christ and continued during the empire until such schools had been established in all the important towns, even in the provinces.

Practical education was taken up by the father where the mother left off. The boy was present while his father conducted the religious rites about the sacred fire which was kept burning upon the family altar. He went with his father into the fields and acquired skill with mattock and reaping hook and in the common operations of agriculture. He accompanied his father on social occasions. An upper class boy saw his father deal out justice among his clients and order his business. In the forum he obtained insight into the domestic and foreign affairs of his nation. The public debates were a school of politics and at the same time of public speaking. The tradition of learning by participation and observation was deeply rooted and continued long. Cicero and Tacitus both insist that citizenship and public speaking can be learned only by active participation. "The school is life," was first spoken by Roman lips. Its modern currency does not make it a modern coinage. The fact is, rather, that as schools became more active and practical among the common people of western Europe and America, the old phrase returned. Learning by doing is especially emphasized where doing is considered more important than thinking and feeling. Ancient Rome and modern America are notable for their practical activity and economic interests; and this is the source of their emphasis upon an active school which more intellectual, contemplative, and aristocratic peoples are less concerned to foster.

On the completion of his sixteenth year the young Roman solemnly exchanged his boyhood toga, with its purple stripe, for the plain white *toga virilis*, the dress of a man. With this, if not before, his school days came to an end. In later periods, those who belonged to the aristocratic and official classes or who meant to become orators continued their studies into their adult years.

2. GREEK INFLUENCE

All the peninsular part of Italy was under the control of Rome by 280 B.C. except the Greek cities in the south; and Tarentum, the last of these to hold out, was reduced eight years later. These Greek cities on the coast had grown into wealthy commercial centers. They were also centers of art and letters and a rich spoil for the conquerors. It was from this region that Livius Andronicus (c. 284–204 B.C.) was brought as a slave to Rome where, having been given his freedom, he became a teacher of the Greek and Latin languages. He is sometimes called the first Roman poet because he translated the *Odyssey* into Latin. This became a schoolbook. Other translations were made; and the beginnings of a native Latin literature were further indications of the development of culture and the improvement of education.

In Plutarch and Suetonius we have some mention of the introduction of Greek teachers at Rome. Plutarch names Spurius Carvilius who opened a grammar school about 260 B.C. Ennius was like Andronicus a Greek translator as well as a teacher. He was also the author of a historical poem called *Annals*, which later authors came to use as a quarry out of which they dug old words to salt their sentences. Quintilian, using a different figure, says of him: "Ennius we may venerate, as we venerate groves sacred from their antiquity; groves in which gigantic and aged oaks affect us not so much by their beauty, as by the religious awe with which they inspire us." Suetonius names Crates of Mallos as the first teacher of Greek in Rome; but as he arrived in 157 B.C. this is clearly an error. Crates was however a man of importance and may have given a considerable impulse to Greek studies. The fact that he was allowed to teach at all is significant because, only four years before his arrival, the Senate had decreed that no Greek philosophers or rhetoricians were to be permitted to teach at Rome. Suetonius is on firm ground when he speaks of the gradual growth of Greek studies. He says: "The science of grammar was in ancient times far from being in vogue in Rome; indeed it was of little use in a rude state of society, when the people were engaged in constant war and had not much time to bestow upon the cultivation of the liberal arts. At the outset its pretensions were very slender, for the earliest men of learning, who were both poets and orators, may be considered as half Greek."

The victory over Pyrrhus and the fall of Tarentum had made Rome supreme over southern Italy and its Greek population. A century later (168 B.C.) Macedonia and the mainland of Greece fell to the Roman army. By reason of these conquests and the mingling to which they led, the soldiers, administrative officers, and Roman traders came into close contact with Greek civilization. L. Aemilius Paullus was the commander who conquered Greece. Although too old to acquire the full flavor of her culture, he was not insensible to her charm for he filled his Roman villas with Greek marbles, manuscripts, and slaves; and, most significant, he gave his sons a thorough Greek education. In increasing numbers now, Greek slaves were taken to Italy as teachers, musicians, artists, and personal servants. The upper classes became rapidly Hellenized by employing Greek tutors in the family so that the Greek language might be acquired by natural methods almost as readily and at almost as early an age as the Latin. Greek scholars, finding themselves able to earn a living by giving instruction in rhetoric and philosophy, flocked to the capital. But there was also another side. The lightest, showiest, and the most frivolous products of the Greek mind were also imported. It was noted that new slang, although it appeared first in the coast towns, was almost immediately carried on to Rome. Cicero's father expressed the mind of many, no doubt, when he declared that his fellow-countrymen were like the slaves on his estate in that "the more Greek they know the less they are worth." Cato the Elder (234–149 B.C.) had attempted to stem this tide; but the decrees against Greek philosophers and rhetoricians, which the Senate passed at his instigation, were ineffectual. And it is sufficiently curious that in his old age Cato himself undertook to learn the Greek language. There also developed a fashionable circle who learned Greek as an accomplishment somewhat as a similar class of German aristocrats, in the eighteenth century, learned French. The high born and the wealthy in this way prepared for a social career.

3. SCHOOL EXERCISES (100 B.C. TO A.D. 100)

Schools were private institutions in this period and did not all follow the same curriculum. Yet the Roman genius for organization produced a degree of uniformity which permits us to call this the first organized system of schools with three clearly marked out levels, the elementary, secondary, and higher. In Greece, the organization of secondary education was vague and indefinite; and the university was a chance and customary grouping of students and professors. At Rome the institutions were more clearly outlined. Elementary education began about the age of seven under the *ludi magister*, the master of the play school, who taught boys reading, writing, moral maxims, good conduct, and the Laws of the Twelve Tables. First came the letters, then syllables and spelling, then words and reading. Moral maxims were used as writing copies. The Greek boy learned a poem, Homer, but the Roman boy was taught the laws of his country. Counting and calculating were also taught in the *ludus*. The Romans, like the Greeks, had an inconvenient way of writing numbers, the still well-known Roman numerals. How inconvenient they were the reader can test by setting himself a sum in division, or even in addition, using these numerals. Calculation was carried out on the counting board, on the fingers, or by purely mental processes. The solution being found, it could then be written down in the Roman numerals.

The second stage in Roman education was that of the grammar school, which received pupils at the age of about ten years and taught both Latin and Greek. Most Romans did not, as Quintilian advised, teach Greek first to their children and Latin afterwards. The grammar school taught chiefly literature; hence the name grammar, from *grammata*, or letters, was translated by the word *literatura*. Grammar, in the sense of syntax, was of course taught as a necessary instrument in the study of literature.

Even as early as the time of Cicero (106–43 B.C.), Roman boys learned Greek not only that they might have a command of that language but also in order that they might be able to profit from the instruction of Greek teachers and the use of Greek textbooks. Greek scholars neglected the Latin as an uncultivated tongue and they even felt some measure of contempt for the Roman culture.

The rhetoric school, likewise, was based upon both Greek and Latin learning; and teachers of rhetoric sometimes taught public speaking in either tongue. But the rhetoric school included much besides public speaking: rhetoric, mathematics, music, astronomy, history, law, and other subjects. Students were given training in three or more types of speeches: the deliberative, dealing with policy; the judicial, dealing with the application of law to cases; and the eulogistic, in praise of some person or deed. The school aimed to prepare for an effective public life in the practice of law, public service, and statesmanship. Although the teachers of rhetoric dealt with much which had no immediate application, their aim was a practical one and included the development of good character both for its own sake and as a requirement in the public service. Many writers have described the rhetoric school. Tacitus, Cicero in *De Oratore*, and Quintilian in the *Institutes of Oratory* are among these; and the last-named book became, at the time of the Renaissance, the most generally accepted work on education. It was widely read and frequently quoted. It influenced the modern secondary school which long regarded training in eloquence as one of its important aims and devoted much of its time to the study of oratorical literature, especially the orations of Cicero and Demosthenes. Thus secondary schools in the Renaissance and later reflected the practice of Rome and the doctrine of Quintilian.

The chief exercises of the ancient rhetoric school were carried out somewhat as follows. The master announced a topic, usually historical and political or legal in character, and involving a statement of facts and principles or laws. He discussed with the school the proper treatment of this question and perhaps assigned parts pro and con. Then each of the pupils wrote his draft of a speech which was corrected by the master and re-written until it won his approval. The speeches having been learned, they were delivered in an appropriate order and this performance was subjected to the master's criticism. Then each oration was repeated to show whether the boy had benefited by the criticism. Finally the master took the theme and treated it as only a master could. In later decadent days the master often invited the public to hear him and made of the occasion a public event which sometimes became the talk of the aristocratic set of the capital city. In republican times the schools had been less sensational. The master in those days was content to prepare good and loyal citizens and to train public servants instead of catering to the perverted tastes of an amusement-loving populace.

4. THE ROMAN SYSTEM AFTER A.D. 100

The Roman schools had reached their highest point of development by A.D. 100. Then came gradual decline, although this did not become pro-nounced for another century. As a result of their natural genius for sys-tem and order, the Roman people were able to organize their schools more definitely than the Greeks. Let us look at this again. There were three levels with distinct aims and subjects. The ludus took the child at seven and taught him reading, writing, arithmetic, and good manners and morals. The grammar school received the boy after he had spent from three to five years in the ludus. It taught him language and literature, often two languages and two literatures, and also astronomy and geometry, together with the ethics and other knowledge which could be learned from these materials. Even the elements of rhetoric were often taught by the gram-maticus or teacher of the grammar school; but to this the rhetor tended to object. "Let each stick to his last," was his injunction. The schools of rhetoric were founded on Greek lines and were often at first conducted by Greek teachers. Quintilian included good character as essential to the orator; and so did Cicero. An orator, according to their definition, is a good man skilled in speaking.

Although there were these three levels, the highest can hardly be said to have furnished a higher education, certainly not in the modern sense and not even in the sense of the Greek university. The Roman rhetorical edu-cation was usually completed before the youth had become fully mature. The whole of that training was of a nature which would today be called secondary. The lack of the spirit of investigation and absence of student freedom point to the same conclusion. It is true that philosophy was taught both in the schools and by private teachers, but a university can hardly be claimed for Rome. It early became the custom for young Romans to complete their education in the East, in rhetoric usually at Rhodes and in philosophy at Athens. As familiar examples, we name Cicero, Brutus, Horace, and Titus Pomponius Atticus, who was Cicero's banker, publisher, and friend. Roman education became richer, it was both more literary and more philosophical, than it would have been without the Greek influence. This also made it bilingual, the first bilingual education in history.

5. ROMAN SCIENCE

The Romans' lack of interest in pure science and mathematics had unfortunate effects in education and upon the world at large. If they had been able to acquire and to transmit the Greek wonder in the presence of natural phenomena, the history of the whole medieval period might have been different. The more observant among them admitted and deplored their deficiency. Cicero stated the case exactly when he remarked that "the Greek mathematicians lead the field in pure geometry while we confine ourselves to the practice of measuring." The Romans built great engineering works with rule-of-thumb mathematics; they developed a practical hygiene and sanitation without a Roman science of medicine; and they traveled to and fro over the wide world without any interest in scientific geography. The Roman farmer or country gentleman was a practical and not infrequently a sympathetic or poetic observer of nature, but not an inquiring one; and Vergil was quite in the Roman tradition as a "landscape lover" who sang in tenderest accents of

wheat and woodland,
tilth and vineyard, hive and horse and herd.

A similar mood is shown in Roman art which reproduces faithfully and lovingly the graceful symmetry of vines, flowers, and bees. The Roman saw nature as a farmer and a poet but not as a natural scientist. Theory, experiment, and reasoned conclusion he did not systematically employ.

It might be difficult to find a sufficient explanation for this aversion from the investigation of natural phenomena. The Romans were busy with practical matters, but there was no lack of leisure for study. The peaceful centuries ushered in by Augustus should have been fruitful for science, but they produced no great scientists. The English and Americans are practical peoples as were the ancient Babylonians, and all these have been noted for their scientific work. It has been claimed that at Rome the vogue for magic and superstition even among upper classes was a retarding factor;

and, no doubt, the influence of the rhetoric schools was another. The prevailing Stoic philosophy, while it demanded "conformity to nature," held that nature was made for man. The Stoics studied nature in order to derive rules for conduct, as expressed for example in the sentiment: "Geometry teaches me the art of measuring acres; teach me to measure my appetites, and to know when I have enough." The Stoic attitude of resignation is not favorable to science. For whatever reasons, science at Rome was not creative; and when the springs of research cease to flow the rivers of knowledge soon dry up.

Rome produced no great scientists, but there were a number of writers on scientific and technical subjects. Most of these dealt with practical interests like agriculture, medicine, architecture, the water supply; or they were encyclopedists who presented collections of information. Lucretius, the philosophic poet, was a writer of a wholly different class. Although his great poem, De Rerum Natura, contains no new observations or independent theory, its philosophy deeply affected the thought of the Renaissance.

Of the Roman encyclopedists, Varro (116–27 B.C.) was one of the earliest. He was extremely industrious and economical in the use of his almost ninety years; and he has been called the most learned of Roman scholars and most voluminous of Roman writers. He wrote many books, including: On the Latin Language; Res Rusticae, on agriculture, which was used as a textbook, is still reprinted, and is very pleasant reading for boys who grew up on a farm; and, most important for our purposes, Of School Studies in nine books. This became one of the models for the numerous medieval works on the liberal arts. Varro distinguished nine arts by including medicine and architecture along with the seven which later became traditional.

A similar encyclopedist was Pliny the Elder (A.D. 23–79) whose Natural History was intended to cover the whole field of the physical sciences. Pliny regards all nature as made for man. Each plant and herb has its medical use and every phenomenon suggests a moral principle. Gibbon described the Natural History as "that immense register where Pliny has deposited the discoveries, the arts and the errors of mankind." It is a formless, uncritical work culled from an incredible number of earlier writers including Aristotle. Seneca (4 B.C.–A.D. 65) wrote a work entitled Natural Questions. He dealt with astronomy, physical geography, and other large-scale phenomena, which he treated in a philosophical manner. As a writer on nature he is remarkable because he held in common with modern science the hope that our knowledge of nature can be indefinitely extended. "How many discoveries are reserved for the ages to come," he wrote, "when our memory shall be no more, for this world of ours contains matter for the investigation of all generations." As a moralist the Middle Ages regarded him as almost or altogether a Christian, which, although an error, was a plausible one.

When we come to the applications of science the story of the Romans takes on an abrupt change. They made no advances in medical science and they produced no eminent physician, but they excelled in developing medical education and medical practice. Under the empire, medical societies were formed and a school of medicine was established. The government built halls for medical teaching. The aim seems to have been to provide physicians and surgeons for the army. The same object was aided by the development of a system of military hospitals. The remains of such institutions have been found in old Roman camps on the Rhine and the Danube as well as in the city of Rome where the first one had been established.

Travelers, merchants, and commanders were interested in itineraries. The Romans provided road maps and route books giving distances and other practical information. They made no contribution to scientific geography. Under Julius Caesar, with the aid of Sosigenes, a Greek mathematician from Alexandria, the calendar was reformed. Their use of the arch in buildings and aqueducts as well as their great roads testify to Roman engineering skill. But all this fine achievement stops as we approach the line that divides practice from free investigation in the search for pure knowledge. The narrowly practical nature of the Roman intelligence was one of the causes of Roman decline and of the unprogressiveness of the early Middle Ages; it was, as we shall see, not the only one.

6. DECADENCE UNDER THE EMPIRE

Augustus became emperor in 27 B.C. in a period which overlaps the late Hellenistic centuries. This period, like the Alexandrian age, was characterized by a cosmopolitan spirit and a mingling of ideas, languages, and races. Individualism, with its search for personal culture, with its aestheticism, and with its emphasis on utility and vocation, on the striving for personal success and the struggle to achieve virtuosity, now tended to displace the old national and moral virtues. Language also reflected the change by becoming colloquial and corrupted with foreign words, often the names of imported luxuries and vices. Literature and rhetoric tended to become artificial and bombastic. And there was a decadence also in the field of morality. How shall we interpret the care exercised by Horace's father, a "witness incorruptible" at all his son's lessons? Was he concerned over the possible careless morality of the teachers? Clearly moralists under the empire placed more and more weight upon the selection of teachers, with especial emphasis upon their moral character. Quintilian, a century after Horace, prefers school education to a family education because of the immoralities of the home. Tacitus speaks of the education of his day as a rhetorical circus. The comparative decadence of both school and home seems certain, although one must not accept too literally the statements of the satirists.

Citizenship was an honor no longer sought as eagerly as it had been because the empire was becoming a centralized despotism. The free citizens were required to bear an almost intolerable burden of taxation while an extravagant aristocracy found ways of evading its due contribution. In the general loss of the old Roman freedom, the loss of freedom of speech was involved. The loss of free speech affected the rhetoric schools where the most unreal situations were now taken as topics. When the schools had been in a healthy state the rhetors assigned topics based upon actual cases in which the facts and law were real and of public significance. In the decadence of the later empire both the facts and the law used in school exercises were often imaginary and even fanciful.

The speeches that were most popular in the schools of the later empire were not deliberative and judicial but eulogistic speeches. These permitted the piling up of adjectives which made of the resulting oration a gaudy patchwork of rhetoric in the bad sense of that ambiguous word. Actual questions of public policy could no longer be publicly discussed under the autocratic rule of the late Caesars. The proper response to this condition would have been to close the rhetorical schools. They no longer performed a proper function. But schools in all ages have tended to invent an artificial purpose when it was no longer possible to follow the real one. So it was in ancient Rome. The less the rhetoricians dared to deliberate and pronounce judgment upon living issues the more the schools cultivated the art of talking brilliantly about unreal and unimportant subjects. Even from Quintilian, who wrote in the first century of the empire, we catch glimpses of this showy and hollow rhetoric.

It was in this decadence, when Romans had come to think of what the state would do for them rather than of their duty to their country, that schools and libraries were first aided with public funds. The poor had by that time come to expect bread and circuses; the great demanded power; and the scholars, privilege. Julius Caesar, in the desire to secure the favor of all classes, granted the franchise to the Greek philosophers. That was the first governmental grant of privilege to teachers. Caesar had also contemplated the building of a great national library for which the scholar Varro was to help select the books. The dictator's death prevented this achievement. Vespasian, who ruled from A.D. 70 to 79, began the practice of paying the salaries of teachers of grammar and rhetoric out of the treasury. This was a new idea; and Quintilian was the first to be appointed to an imperial chair. Later emperors expanded this policy. Chairs in provincial cities were established; and many cities not thus favored established their own municipal professorships. With the development of this system came public competitions which served as qualifying examinations for the prospective professors.

The fifth century saw the final phase of Roman education. Rome fell to Alaric in 410. The Vandals conquered North Africa, and the Visigoths held Gaul and Spain. The population was declining; the central government had grown weak and corrupt; brigandage was making the roads unsafe; and commerce was decaying. In the large cities the schools continued for another century, but their teaching had grown formal. Greek was disappearing from the West. And it was an ominous fact that astrology had become one of the most popular of the school subjects. Education had come to be a veneer and an amusement for those who could still afford it. The Christian church was emphasizing faith and conduct, not learning. The old system was dying. The emperor, Theodosius, attempted to reinvigorate it in the East by founding the University of Constantinople. He was partly successful and Greek learning survived in the Byzantine empire. But Western civilization had reached a turning point, the Dark Ages of the medieval period.

7. ROMAN EDUCATIONAL WRITERS

The Roman writers on education did not compose stimulating and speculative philosophies like that of Plato; but, instead, they discussed practical problems in a matter-of-fact way. The two greatest were Cicero and Quintilian. Cicero's *Brutus* and *De Oratore* provide a very complete description of the education and the profession of the orator in his day. Quintilian wrote the *Institutes of Oratory* which has been the source of many of the ideas of later writers. It is in twelve books and was written a little before A.D. 100. He dealt with early education as well as with the more advanced stages. He advised that the early lessons should be playful, that study and recreation should be duly proportioned, and proposed the use of educational toys. He opposed corporal punishment and urged that children should be won for learning rather than driven to it. He placed great emphasis upon morals and declared that an orator, however skillful he may be, cannot be called great unless he is also good. Most of his work deals with matters of speech, language, rhetoric, and literature. He illustrates the fact, which has been stated earlier in this chapter, that Roman education was much more bookish and less well rounded than Greek education. His overemphasis upon words and style and his treatment of philosophy betray the further fact that Roman education was becoming artificial. Quintilian was partly aware of this; but his fulsome eulogy of the emperor Domitian suggests that he may not have realized how greatly the independence and virility of the Romans had declined. In the Italian city-states of the Renaissance, Quintilian was read more than any other ancient educational writer. And his book helped to foster the cult of eloquence and the imitation of Cicero, which debased the Italian humanism as it had debased the humanism of Rome.

In considering Roman education, one is almost involuntarily drawn to contrast it with the Greek. The Greeks were speculative, aesthetic, warm, and pliable; but each one was closely attached to his own small city-state. The Roman genius was practical and administrative, the Roman mood austere and puritanical, and the Roman outlook as wide as the known world.

The characteristics of the Roman people shaped Roman education. In early times it was what the education of rude peoples has generally been, namely, a static education gained by observation, participation, and custom. While the young Greek learned a poem, the young Roman learned the Laws of the Twelve Tables. The learning of the schools, when schools developed, was book learning, lacking the music and gymnastics which had given the Athenian curriculum a well-rounded character. As in Greece, the schools were private, but the Romans made one improvement. They organized them into a chain of articulated schools; the ludus prepared for the grammar school, and this for the rhetoric school. This was the result of the Roman demand for an orderly system.

Roman education borrowed its higher values and its theory, methods, and advanced curriculum from the Greeks. Roman rhetoric and philosophy were imported from the same sources. And the aristocratic Romans, for the first time in recorded history, studied a foreign tongue, the Greek language. The Hellenization of Roman education was only an interlude between the later republic and the later empire and affected only the upper classes. The originality of the Romans was not expressed in education but in war, law, administration, and architecture, and most of all in their conceptions of the Roman peace and universal empire. For this, a heavy price of conquest and exploitation was exacted. But it made the Latin language the universal language of learning in the West, as Greek was in the East.

In the decadence which accompanied and resulted from absolutism in government, learning became decorative and showy. The cultivation of eloquence, always too prominent in Roman education, became its chief end. Virtuosity in public speech engrossed abilities that should have been devoted to investigation and the attainment of broader and deeper knowledge. Instead of encouraging original investigation, the Romans made second-hand collections of information from earlier and more original writers; and thereby they set the pattern for the Middle Ages. The empire and Roman law set the pattern for the organization of the medieval church. After the medieval period the Roman literary and educational classics played a great part in the education of the Renaissance and later ages.

QUESTIONS

1. What kinds of education did the Romans mean to include when they used the saying, "The school is life?"
2. In what ways and by what means were Roman culture and education influenced by the Greeks?
3. Is it more surprising that the Romans studied the Greek language than that the Greeks excluded all foreign language study from their schools?
4. How did Roman education differ in spirit, content, and organization from Greek education?
5. Explain the function and character of rhetorical instruction as preparation for public life in Rome. In addition to the text, Cicero's De Oratore may be used.
6. In what ways and why did Roman education decline under the empire?
7. Analyze the early chapters of Quintilian's *Institutes of Oratory*. Indicate your agreements and disagreements with your reasons for the position you take.
8. Using the edition of W. J. Chase, describe and trace the history of the short grammar (*Ars Minor*) of Donatus.
9. Compare the *iuvenes*, as described by S. L. Mohler, with the ephebes of Athens.
10. Compare with the present chapter the account of Roman education in H. W. Johnston's *The Private Life of the Romans*.

FOR FURTHER READING AND STUDY

The *Source Book* by Paul Monroe which is given in the list for the preceding chapter has several selections from Roman sources. There is a good translation of Quintilian's *Institutes of Oratory* by J. B. Watson in the Bohn classical series; and another which also contains the Latin text in the Loeb series (New York, G. P. Putnam's Sons). The texts and translations of Virgil, Cicero, and other works which have been schoolbooks for two thousand years are also included in the latter series. A few special studies are included in the present list, but all have a direct connection with Roman education.

Abbott, Frank Frost, *Society and Politics in Ancient Rome*, New York, Charles Scribner's Sons, 1909, 267 pp.; *The Common People of Ancient Rome*, New York, Charles Scribner's Sons, 1917, 290 pp. The latter book has material on the influence of the Latin language, and also Diocletian's edict fixing "ceiling prices" of goods and services including teachers' fees.
Becker, W. A., *Gallus, or Roman Scenes of the Time of Augustus*. Translated by F. Metcalfe, London, Longmans, Green and Company, 1876, 535 pp.
Boissier, Gaston, *Tacitus and Other Roman Studies*. Translated by W. G. Hutchison, London, Constable and Company, Ltd., 1906, 277 pp. Has a chapter upon "Schools of Declamation at Rome."

Carrington, Roger C., *Pompeii*, London, Oxford University Press, 1936, 179 pp.

Chase, W. J., translator and editor, *The Distichs of Cato*, University of Wisconsin Studies in the Social Sciences and History, No. 7, 1922, 43 pp.; *The Ars Minor of Donatus*, same series, No. 11, 1926, 55 pp. Each is a translation and history of the use in schools of the work treated.

Clark, Donald, *Rhetoric in Greco-Roman Education*, New York, Columbia University Press, 1957, 285 pp.

Fowler, W. Warde, *Social Life at Rome in the Age of Cicero*, New York, The Macmillan Company, 1926, 362 pp.

Friedländer, Ludwig, *Roman Life and Manners under the Early Empire*, London, George Routledge & Sons, Ltd., 1908–1913, 4 vols.

Gwynn, Aubrey Osborn, *Roman Education from Cicero to Quintilian*, London, Oxford University Press, 1926, 260 pp.

Johnston, Harold Whetstone, *The Private Life of the Romans*. Revised by Mary Johnston, Chicago, Scott, Foresman and Company, 1932, 430 pp.

Jullien, Emile, *Les professeurs de littérature dans l'ancienne Rome, et leur enseignement depuis l'origine justqu'a la mort d'Auguste*, Paris, Ernest Lerous, 1885, 379 pp.

Mohler, S. L., "The Iuvenes and Roman Education," *Transactions of the American Philological Association*, 68:442–479 (1937).

Odgers, Merle M., "Quintilian's Rhetorical Predecessors," *Transactions of the American Philological Association*, 65:25–36 (1935); "Quintilian's Use of Earlier Literature," *Classical Philology*, 28:182–188 (July, 1933).

Petersson, Torsten, *Cicero, a Biography*, Berkeley, University of California Press, 1920, 699 pp. There are many accounts of Cicero but this is a very full one.

Pharr, Clyde, "Roman Legal Education," *Classical Journal*, 34:257–70 (February, 1939).

Thompson, James Westfall, *Ancient Libraries*, Berkeley, California, University of California Press, 1940, 120 pp.

Ulich, Robert, *History of Educational Thought*, New York, American Book Company, 1945, 412 pp.

Wilkins, A. S., *Roman Education*, New York, The Macmillan Company, 1905, 100 pp.

4 EDUCATION IN THE EARLIER MIDDLE AGES

THE MIDDLE AGES MAY BE TAKEN TO SPAN THE THOUSAND years from about A.D. 500 to 1500; but this is only a rough approximation. Roman civilization had been declining during two or three centuries before 500, and for several centuries before 1500 a remarkable revival of culture and learning was in progress. We shall, therefore, divide the Middle Ages into two unequal parts: the Dark Ages, as the fifth and sixth centuries are called, an earlier period of barbarian invasion, civil disorder, and cultural decline; and, beginning about 1100, a later period of progress in commerce, urban development, and education. We shall deal with the former period (500–1100) in this chapter and with the latter in the following chapter.

The Roman Catholic Church was the dominant institution in the Middle Ages. By the sixth century, the old Roman schools, after a long decadence, were closed. The church, through its monastic, cathedral, parish, and chantry schools, became the educator of western Europe. Although the Latin language was the language of the church and the schools, the learning of the schools was not merely Roman learning but included much of Greek and Hebrew culture. Indeed, the major characteristic of medieval education is just this combination of Greek, Roman, and Hebraic-Christian ideas and ideals. We have called the third group of ideas Hebraic-Christian because the church presented the Old Testament through a Christian interpretation. The elements which were combined can be clearly seen by examining the curriculum of the medieval schools. The curriculum was composed of the Seven Liberal Arts and these were divided into two parts, the trivium and the quadrivium. The trivium comprehended grammar, rhetoric, and dialectic, or logic; and the quadrivium included arithmetic, geometry, astronomy, and music. The less advanced schools taught only a part of this curriculum, only the trivium perhaps, and these were called trivial schools. This term indicated the subjects taught and not the quality of the work. After the Seven Liberal Arts had been completed, the most advanced schools added courses in philosophy and theology. As we have shown, these subjects except theology were developed by the Greeks; and theology was also much indebted to Greek thinkers. But the subjects came into the medieval schools not directly from Greece but by way of Rome. They had been given Roman form and much of the content and the speculative spirit of Greek learning had been lost. Many of the Latin Church Fathers, including Tertullian, Jerome, and Augustine, had been educated in Roman schools. In their writing and teaching, the ancient learning still lived but their message was the Christian message. This was derived from the Hebrew and Christian Scriptures. It is, therefore, clear that the school learning of the Middle Ages was a combination of the learning of the Greeks, the Hebrews, and the Romans. It was one important task of the period to make this synthesis.

1. THE CHURCH IN THE WEST

At the beginning of the Middle Ages, the church had been in existence for five centuries. Christianity began with the work of Jesus. He taught that God is our Father; that we, His children, are brothers and should live brotherly lives; and that through His grace we may do so. He taught the infinite worth of the individual. He was gentle, and looked upon children and people of all ages with kindly sympathy and a deep compassion, and upon nature with the eyes of a poet. He did not use the language of philosophy and did not attempt to prove his intuition by argument. His life was a living example of his teaching. The church and the churches tried, almost from the first, and largely in vain, to embody the example and the teaching in rigid doctrinal statements, the Creeds.

Christianity spread quickly to the large cities of the Roman empire. By the middle of the first century (A.D. 50) there was a Christian group in Rome to whom St. Paul addressed his *Letter to the Romans*. Antioch, Corinth, and Alexandria were other early centers of the movement. For three centuries the Christians were often assailed by mobs and persecuted by the government. They refused to worship at Roman shrines, and this was construed as treason. Early in the fourth century Christianity was first recognized as a legal religion, and was accepted by Constantine in 325 as the official religion of the empire.

The Catholic church received her school curriculum through Rome and she also copied the imperial pattern of organization. At the beginning of the Middle Ages the governmental unit of the church was the city with its congregations. This was called a diocese. The bishop was the ruler of the diocese and the head of its clergy. The church of the bishop was called a cathedral; and a school was often attached to it. The dioceses usually included a varying area about the city, small in the east and in Italy where the cities were numerous and the population dense, and very large in the western provinces and in North Africa where the opposite conditions prevailed. The dioceses or bishoprics were grouped into sees or metropolitanates, under head bishops called metropolitans or, when they were of the highest rank, patriarchs. In all the east there were four patriarchates: Alexandria, Jerusalem, Antioch, and Constantinople, the last being the highest or ecumenical patriarchate. In the West there was only one comparable center, Rome, which became the seat of the papacy and the capital of the whole of western Christendom. The forms of the civil government became the models for the church government.

The church was the main institution for the preservation and transmission of the learning of the ancient world during the Middle Ages. It was the main institution because it was able to keep its organization intact through the successive invasions, the decay of civilization, and the gradual breakup of the civil government. The empire fell; but the church stood. It not only stood but it spread and increased in power. In 476, when the last Roman emperor was deposed, the Bishop of Rome remained, unchecked by any strong secular power, the sole patriarch of Italy, North Africa, France, and Spain. Ireland, where St. Patrick ended his labors about 416, was the last province before the fall of Rome to come under the sway of the church. The first to be added after that event were Scotland and the country of the Salic Franks. In 496, Clovis, the Frankish chieftain, and three thousand of his warriors were baptized. Columba was the great missionary to Scotland. From Ireland and Scotland, Christianity was carried to England, where the monastery of Lindisfarne was founded in 634. Pope Gregory had, meanwhile, sent a party of missionaries into southern England. They established themselves at Canterbury and completed the religious conquest of all that region within a half-century. Next came Germany. Neither the legions of Rome nor the missionaries of the church had been able to secure a permanent foothold on the right bank of the Rhine until the time of Boniface (c. 680–754). He firmly established the church in Hesse, Bavaria, and Thuringia, and founded the monastery of Fulda in 744. This monastery was destined to become a center of learning for all central Germany. Wherever the church was established, its monasteries, cathedrals, and schools were agencies for the preservation and later for the advancement of learning.

2. CHRISTIANITY AND THE ANCIENT LEARNING

To understand medieval education we must study the complex relations which developed between Christianity and the ancient learning. From the beginning Christianity was in contact with Hebrew, Greek, and Roman ideas. The Hebrew and Roman influences are obvious; and the Greek influence is apparent in the New Testament, especially in the fourth gospel and the writings of St. Paul. But Greek thought also affected Christianity directly through the Greeks and Hellenized Jews who became members of Christian congregations.

The Hellenizing of many of the Jews had taken place several centuries before Christ. One evidence of this was the Greek version of the Hebrew Scriptures called the Septuagint. This translation was made in Alexandria and it shows that there was a large and influential section of the dispersed Jewish people who preferred a Greek to the original Hebrew text. When the New Testament writers quoted from the Old Testament they used the Septuagint version. The union of Hebrew and Greek thought is also indicated by the work of Philo (c. 20 B.C.–A.D. 53) who taught at Alexandria. Philo was a faithful Jew; but in his philosophy he was a Neo-Platonist. He was convinced that the Greek thinkers had drawn all that was truest and best in their thought from the Hebrew Scriptures; and he attempted to show that there was no essential conflict between the two. Christianity also was deeply affected by Neo-Platonist thought. Neo-Platonism taught the real unity of man and God; but man was bound in the toils of matter and the evils of the flesh and he could win his way back to his real home by overcoming the material phase of his being and participating fully in the spiritual Reason or *Logos*. Western Christianity was influenced by the Roman tradition also. St. Paul's *Letter to the Romans*, written about A.D. 53, shows that the Roman Christians of that early time were already more institutionally minded and more inclined to follow authority and law, that is, more Roman, than a religious mystic and individualist such as Paul was could approve.

In two centuries after the Christian religion and Greek philosophy met face to face, the religion had itself become a philosophy for many. "We teach the same as the Greeks," said Justin Martyr (c. 100–165), "although we only are hated for our teachings." "Our books show," said Tertullian, addressing the emperor, "that our doctrines are not new"; and even our opponents admit that Christianity is a philosophy, teaching the approved virtues of chastity, justice, and temperance. "Therefore," he added, "you should not persecute us."

Other opposing tendencies within Christianity struggled for mastery from early times. One was the ascetic attitude which led men to renounce the world. Opposed to this was the missionary spirit which led men to attack the evils of the world. And the great body of Christians were neither monks nor evangelists but laymen who followed ordinary vocations without accepting the world's beliefs or indulging in its immoralities. Some

Christians rigorously excluded all pagan literature from their lives. One of these was Tatian, born about A.D. 110 and liberally educated in Greek learning. He had a speculative mind and was won for Christianity by its monotheism or, as he said, "by the assertion of the government of all by one Being," a doctrine which, at one stroke, liberated him from "the tyranny of a thousand demons." In his *Address to the Greeks* he launched a violent attack upon pagan thought. Another, already mentioned, was Tertullian, born in Carthage about the year 160, deeply schooled in philosophy and rhetoric and intended for the law. As a Christian he became an austere puritan who, in hostility to pagan learning, outdid Tatian. Christianity was to him a mighty supernatural reality which had no concern with the pallid theories of the philosophers. In Greek philosophy, it seemed to him, lurked the sources of all future heresies, a view widely held in later times. But even Tertullian was unable to do without the secular learning he so vigorously assailed. This is a symbol of what happened in the church at large. Pagan learning could not be either accepted or rejected; a middle ground had to be found.

With a little historical imagination we can bring home to ourselves some of the difficulties of the Christians in those times. Daily life presented many scenes, in the circus, the theater, the games, and even in the school celebrations, that to Christians were repulsive and scandalous. All the literary schools were pagan, and ceremonies and festivals dedicated to the gods were a part of the ordinary school program. Some of the books studied were the very same which Plato had condemned for their low morality and false religion. Quintilian too had said: "The Greeks are licentious in many of their writings and I should be loath to interpret Horace in certain passages." Why should we be surprised that Christians condemned schoolbooks which had offended the moral sense of Plato and Quintilian? The old system of thought and ritual continued to have a strong appeal as the effort of Julian (r. 361–363), unsuccessful though it was, proves. The ideas of Christian home and pagan school not only were different, but violently contradicted each other. Was it wise to expose a boy to such cross-currents; and what could be done to avoid it without denying him the opportunity for a liberal education? Tertullian, in a passage on "the difficulties of schoolmasters," attempted to deal with the problem; but there was really no answer that was satisfactory to the Christians until the schools themselves became Christian.

Attempts to set up Christian schools were made in the second century. These were the catechumenal and the catechetical schools. Although their history is obscure, it appears that catechumenal schools were organized by individual churches to induct catechumens, that is, new believers, into the doctrines, discipline, and morals of the church and thus to prepare them for membership. They taught the Scriptures and the hymns of the church and performed the functions of a modern Sunday School or communicants' class. Perhaps they met for only one or two hours a week. The instruction cannot be compared to that of the regular schools of literature and rhetoric.

The catechetical school was more ambitious. It was one of the main agencies through which the synthesis of philosophy and church doctrine was achieved, and it was of the same type as the schools of the philosophers. Each catechetical school was a private lectureship or chair occupied by an outstanding teacher. One would expect Alexandria to have provided the conditions for such a school. About 125 Basilides opened a school at Alexandria for the philosophical teaching of Christian doctrine. This may have been the first. His disciple Valentinus established a similar school at Rome. Another Alexandrian cathechetical school whose history is more fully known was founded in 179. Two of its famous teachers were Clement (c. 150–c. 220), and Origen (c. 185–c. 254). Origen established another one at Caesarea; and others existed at Antioch, Edessa, Nisibis, Carthage, and other places.

The catechetical schools seem to have taught chiefly theology, but also the philosophy and science which were necessary to the consideration of theological questions. Their purpose was to defend Christianity against attacks from the outside. In this, Origen was the master mind of his age. His educational practice is described for us by Eusebius, the first great church historian, who wrote in the fourth century. It was an individual method of personal consultation and argument, but he also directed the reading of his students and delivered lectures. The catechetical schools gave advanced instruction to mature men and their purpose was apologetic, the defense of the church doctrines against the attacks of pagan philosophy. Neither the catechumenal nor the cathechetical school could take the place of the ordinary elementary and secondary schools. For general education, children had to be sent to Greek or Latin schools although some of these were from an early period conducted by Christian teachers.

That there were Christian teachers in some of the regular schools in the early centuries is shown by Tertullian's writings and also by Julian's decree in the middle of the fourth century against Christian teaching in the literary schools. Meanwhile the homes gave moral and religious instruction to counteract the pagan influence of the schools. The problem was not solved at any given time, but the desired result was achieved gradually in the course of centuries. The edict of Justinian (529) closing the pagan schools was hardly needed because most of these institutions had already disappeared.

3. THE PRESERVATION OF LEARNING

In the difficult transition from the empire to the church, much knowledge and many books were lost. Much was also saved by the copyists, the schools, the great churchmen, and the less great but useful writers of textbooks. Among the great churchmen was Jerome (340–420), one of the most learned men of the early Roman church. He devoted most of his life to literary work, and at the request of Pope Damasus he prepared the Latin version of the Bible which is known as the Vulgate. This was his greatest work, but he wrote much, including many letters. The admiration Erasmus felt for him is not surprising, for the two had much in common. Among other similarities, each had a sharp tongue. Augustine (354–430) was a colorful, many-sided individual, a great philosopher, and a great writer. His glowing *Confessions*, which portray his education and the growth of his mind, and the *City of God*, which contains his philosophy of history, are important sources on the educational conditions of his time. In a book on doctrine, he recommended the study of classical literature as a preparation for theology.

The *Consolations of Philosophy* by Boethius (480–524) was loved and read for many centuries. Boethius also wrote textbooks on arithmetic, geometry, and music. He had planned a Latin version of the works of Plato and Aristotle but completed only a small part of this large project. It has been said that if he had succeeded in providing a translation of Aristotle's *History of Animals*, or any good book on an observational science, "the whole mental history of the race might have been different." He completed a small part of the logic of Aristotle; and this had an important influence upon medieval thought.

The Seven Liberal Arts were treated in *The Marriage of Philology and Mercury* by Martianus Capella, a fifth-century writer. This title may be paraphrased as the union of learning and practical affairs. The book was an arid and fantastic allegory, but it was extensively used as a schoolbook, in the cathedral and the monastic schools, after the first difficulties of grammar and rhetoric had been mastered.

For aid in mastering those earliest difficulties, the pupil was directed to Donatus, who wrote a short grammar, the *Ars Minor*, and also a longer textbook in the same subject. The *Ars Minor* was in such universal use all through the Middle Ages that in Chaucer and other writers "donatus," or "donat," is the name for any grammar textbook. A more extended grammar was written by Priscian, who flourished about 500.

Cassiodorus, who served King Theodoric the Great (c. 454–526) and his successors as secretary and minister, founded (c. 540) the monastery of

Vivarium, or Viviers, in the extreme south of Italy. This afforded him a learned retirement near the sea after his public life was ended. His books of "instructions in sacred and secular letters," written for his monks, dealt with the Seven Liberal Arts. He wrote a *History of the Goths,* in twelve books; and he published the public documents and letters which he had written in the name of his royal masters. He devoted his wealth to the collection and copying of manuscripts and thus saved many works from destruction. One of these was an ancient, illustrated herbal which, as he said, "describes and figures the herbs of the field with wonderful faithfulness." The practice of dating events from the Christian era is said to have originated in his monastery; and there also the number of the liberal arts, which had varied somewhat among the Romans, was settled. Until then architecture, medicine, and other subjects had sometimes been included; but, thereafter, the seven we have named became canonical.

The *Etymologies* of Isidore of Seville purported to be a compend of all knowledge. But Isidore had neither the philosophic interests of Boethius nor the learning and genial outlook of Cassiodorus. The *Etymologies* was a compilation, in twenty "books" or chapters, dealing with forty or more subjects extending from agriculture to medicine and public games. The contents of some books are extremely diverse. For example, Book IX deals with languages, races, kingdoms, the army, citizens, and kinship. Much of the material was taken at second hand. Such encyclopedias, sometimes even drier and less nourishing than the *Etymologies,* became common in the Middle Ages. Isidore's work was so popular that it was included in most medieval libraries.

The decline in learning had begun in Roman times; and this tendency was accelerated in the dark sixth and seventh centuries through the invasions, the decrease of wealth and population, and the growing distaste of churchmen for secular learning. The investigative spirit was never as strong in Rome as it had been in Greece, and it was further weakened in the Middle Ages; the lack of investigation was accompanied by the relative absence of both the critical sense and the historical sense. The habit of taking a knowledge of words for the understanding of things, the practice of summarizing large fields of learning in meager outlines and of compiling from previous compilations became almost general. We have called this section, "The Preservation of Learning." Many books were preserved that, for a long period, were not much used; but it is important to understand that the best way to preserve learning is to use it and to attempt to advance it. The early Middle Ages tended to forget this, because the churchmen studied secular learning merely as a preparation for sacred learning; but, as we said in the first chapter, for fruitful learning, intrinsic interest is necessary. This was lacking in the period we are considering.

4. THE MONASTERIES AND LEARNING

Asceticism was implied in many of the philosophies and religions of the ancient world; and monastic practices and institutions were widespread in India and China, as in some religions with which early Christianity came into contact. Chastity was an obligation of the vestal priesthood in Rome. The priests of Isis were forbidden the use of woolen clothing, of wine, and of many articles of food, and monasticism was definitely recognized. Cloistered ascetics under strict rules were a part of the temple service of Serapis, and in the worship of Mithra monks and virgins of several grades were employed. Monasticism was, therefore, not peculiar to Christianity; indeed for two centuries after the Founder it was hardly to be found in Christianity. Nor, if we except two relatively unimportant sects, were monastic life and ascetic practice found among the Hebrews.

The word monasticism comes from the Greek word "monos" meaning alone. Monks ought, according to this derivation, to live as hermits; but the purely solitary condition of life proved too drastic for most people. It was also too individualistic and socially useless to secure permanent approval, at least among an active people. Men are by nature social, as Aristotle pointed out, and any institution for average humanity has to recognize this fact. In the monastery, as it developed in Europe, the monk's individual cell gave sufficient opportunity for solitary retirement and meditation while the common services and the cooperative work of the institution provided the humanly necessary social life. The vows of poverty, chastity, and obedience, the daily work and the services of worship, the meditation and silence, provided quite enough self-denial. It should be understood that the vow of poverty applied to the monk as an individual only. The monastery as an institution could hold property and often became wealthy. Wealth and resulting luxury, indeed, often led to a decline in monastic fervor and gave occasion, over the centuries, for numerous reforms of the monastic life.

In the fourth century, monasticism was introduced into Europe. The disorders of the invasions and the disturbed conditions of the time drove many into the monastic fold. Among the early leaders were St. Martin of Tours (371) and John Cassian (415). But the great organizer of monasticism in the West was Benedict of Nursia. At a time traditionally given as 529, he established a monastery at Monte Cassino in Italy and formulated the most influential of monastic Rules. By Rule we are to understand a system of life and government for the monks, who are hence called regular clergy, from the Latin word "regula," meaning rule or constitution. Priests and other clergy who did not retire into a monastery to live in accordance with a Rule but remained active in the "world" were, by contrast, known as secular clergy. There were other monastic rules in the West, but as the Benedictine was the only one that was widely applied, the earlier half of the Middle Ages is often called the Benedictine period. The order spread gradually from Italy, and in about two and a half centuries its houses were established even in the British Isles and in Germany.

The Rule of St. Benedict shows that its author had considerable understanding of human nature and a gift for organization. The discipline was strict but not too severe for zealous men. At the head of each monastery there was an abbot who, although empowered to command obedience, was required to consult all the brothers down to the humblest before major decisions were made. Novices had to undergo a period of probation. When this was safely passed the irrevocable vows of chastity, poverty, and obedience were administered. Stress was placed upon worship and work, especially worship; and the whole day was to be occupied, for Benedict called idleness "the enemy of the soul." To prevent idleness, the Rule divided the day into seven periods of which four were spent in worship and the rest in manual labor, chiefly in the fields and shops, and in reading. The Benedictine Rule and the practice of the monks helped to dignify labor. Under monasticism, work became the normal occupation, not of slaves as in Greece and Rome but of freemen and brothers. Each monastery became a hive of industry. Much of the agricultural development and restoration of Europe was due to the monks who drained the swamps, cleared the land, and transformed deserts into gardens. Since renunciation of the world and retirement from it were at the very foundation of monasticism, the houses were often located in secluded and even desolate places which gave opportunity for improvement.

A worthy form of labor was that of copying manuscripts. A specified period of each day, varying with the season, was given over to reading. Books were given out for this purpose and supervision was often provided to ensure that they were read. One brother was appointed to read to the monks during meals. This implied the existence of a library, and an old saying had it that "a monastery without a library is like a castle without an armory." Books had to be manufactured on the spot, for the most part; the parchment was prepared, the desired manuscript was copied, often with beautiful illumination, and the work was finally bound, frequently in rich, decorative covers. Such books were so costly that only the wealthy, or societies like the monasteries, could own them. The wide dissemination of learning had to wait upon cheaper books. Those who had a taste for reading and literature had almost no refuge in the early Middle Ages except the monasteries.

Monasteries were not always small institutions. They varied greatly in size, but some comprised numerous buildings such as hospitals, quarters for travelers and for the poor, kitchens and refectories and dormitories for several hundred monks, farm buildings and shops, residence halls with separate cells for individual monks, and always a church. Upon the monastery church a great deal of the love and wealth of the society was lavished. The main monastic buildings were often grouped around a green quadrangle called the garth. Surrounding the garth there was an open arcade or colonnade called the cloister. This word and its adjective, cloistral, are often applied to the monastery or the monastic life in general. Hence also comes the term cloistral schools.

As monasteries were often large so, in the prosperous days of the system, they were also numerous. New ones were continually founded and the old ones remained. At the Reformation, England counted more than six hundred monasteries, with more than one hundred hospitals and about an equal number of important monastery schools. In France at the Revolution, two hundred and fifty years later, there were one thousand abbeys of which about one-fourth were for women. Spain had a similar number. They were most numerous in Italy which in the nineteenth century suppressed more than two thousand monasteries.

We have already named a few of the monasteries which were famous for their educational endeavors. Cassiodorus of Vivarium, by example and writing, had a great influence upon monastic education. St. Patrick, who lived for a considerable time at Lerins in southern France, spread Christianity in Ireland in the fifth century. Under his direct successors a group of institutions famous for their learning were founded in Ireland. The Irish monastic schools were at their high point in the sixth and seventh centuries when learning was in danger of extinction on the continent. The Irish monks became missionaries of both religion and learning. We have noted their influence in Scotland and England. Wearmouth-Jarrow in England was in the eighth century the home of the Venerable Bede (673–735), the author of the *Ecclesiastical History of the English Nation* and also of several important schoolbooks. The Irish helped to re-Christianize Europe after the Dark Ages. Columbanus set out from the Irish monastery of Bangor and planted a similar institution in Burgundy at Luxeuil. His disciple Gallus gave his name to the Swiss foundation of St. Gall, while Columbanus went on to found Bobbio in Italy. Neighbor to St. Gall was the famous monastery of Reichenau. Fulda in Germany we have already named. Intermittently, Monte Cassino, the mother monastery of the whole Benedictine order, was educationally important. Many others had a notable share in the preservation and progress of learning in a time when learning was in need of friends.

5. THE MONASTIC SCHOOLS

Schools were a practical necessity in monasteries because boys were often dedicated to the religious life at seven or earlier. These children, as well as illiterate elders, were to be taught to read and sometimes to write. Not all monks in all periods were able to read, but we have no figures. Again the monastery frequently accepted pupils who were not to be dedicated at all. In this respect, also, practice varied, and, indeed, few statements about monasticism are true for all times and places. St. Benedict admitted the children of some of the rich Roman families into his school. In the Dark Ages, the monastery or convent in many places offered the only opportunity for schooling. Those children who were intended for the monastic life were called oblati, and the others externi. At times and in some monasteries there were two schools, inner schools for the oblati and outer schools for the externi. The outer school was placed outside the walls as a separate boarding school, but such a plan could be carried out only in larger institutions. Poor boys might secure their maintenance without loss of self-respect by begging or might earn support by working. The schools did not charge fees but were glad to accept donations from wealthy patrons.

Books for use in the schools, and service books and Bibles for use in the church, were produced in the scriptorium or writing room. Chronicles and lives of the saints were written. Bede composed his *Ecclesiastical History* in a monastery.

Early in the period, some of the monasteries began to collect books for the use of their members. The monastic Rules, beginning even with that of Pachomius, contain directions for the care of these collections and for loaning books to the monks. The supply of a particular monastery could be increased in various ways: by gift or purchase; by making duplicates of books already in the collection or borrowed for this purpose; and finally by the writing of new works by monastic chroniclers or other original authors. The collections, small in the early centuries of the Middle Ages, gradually grew until in late medieval times the more intellectual centers had acquired considerable libraries. Alcuin in the eighth century listed about forty authors who were represented in the library at York. There were included in that library numerous Church Fathers, several of the Latin classics, some grammarians, and some late Christian writers. This collection is often cited as an example of the scholarly opportunities of Alcuin. It must be judged from the standpoint of its time when few other institutions were equally well stocked with books. The arts, politics, law, medicine, mathematics, the sciences, and many other large departments were hardly represented.

Libraries increased rapidly in succeeding centuries. In a fire which destroyed the monastery at Croyland about 1100, a library of seven hundred books was lost. Two or three centuries later a monastery of similar standing might have had one or even two thousand volumes. In the late fifteenth century, the German monastery of Sponheim, under a learned and vigorous abbot, had two thousand books. A number of monasteries manufactured books for sale or exchange and, when printing was invented, some of the early presses were set up in monasteries. The first English printer, John Caxton, set up a press in the abbey of Westminster, whose abbot was one of his most munificent patrons.

Such facts must not lead one to overestimate the intellectual activities of the monks; and it will be a wholesome safeguard against such overestimate to remember that the monasteries were always primarily religious, not intellectual, institutions, and were always based upon the principle of renunciation. Libraries and schools were ancillary and not primary features of monasticism.

The monk who was set to direct the school or schools was called the principal or head master, if we take a literal translation of the words used. Most of the schools were very small, but when they became large, assistants were provided. The schools of Corvei, founded in 817, sometimes required the services of twenty or more of the brethren. To prepare monks to take part in the services of the church, instruction in song and chant was given by a cantor who sometimes also had charge of the library and scriptorium. That the young might be guarded against violation of the rules and against frivolity, idleness, and sin, a watcher or "custos" was named. If the pupils were few they were all taught together; otherwise they were divided into separate groups and classes; but, in any case, much of the instruction was oral and memoriter.

Monastic school discipline in the West was usually strict and somber. The boys, one may be sure, did not always benefit from a relaxation of the Rule intended for their elders. The oblati were given little opportunity for play; and when monastic reformers were in control, the rule of silence was enforced upon small boys, even in the pauses between lessons. The rod, or more frequently a bundle of switches, compulsory fasting, and confinement were the usual punishments. The way and spirit in which they were used must have varied widely. Long school vacations seem not to have been common; but there was a multitude of feasts and holy days, somewhat irregularly distributed through the year, in addition to the Sundays. The most joyful and even boisterous day of the school year was Childermas or Holy Innocents' Day, the twenty-eighth of December. On this festival the children were the masters and were allowed to put their usual enemies, the teachers, into their proper place.

The general course of study was everywhere the same. It comprised the elements of Latin, followed by the Seven Liberal Arts. Pupils in the school, like the monks in the cloister and in the church, had to speak in Latin. One of the first tasks of the school was, therefore, to teach this language, which to most of western Europe was not the common tongue. The ordinary words and phrases were taught at first through the boys' own vernacular, but this was discontinued as soon as possible. Of the formal subjects, the first was grammar. When the boy had mastered the rudiments he was set to read the fables of Aesop in the collection of Avianus (c. 400) and the moral sentences known as the *Distichs of Cato*. This little book in couplets was not written by Cato but it was in existence in the fourth century and was used as a beginning reading book for a very long time. One of the main problems was that of building up a vocabulary. Verse helped in locating the "longs" and "shorts" in Latin words. Music was taught to the small boys along with the grammar and reading since it was important for participation in the church services.

For further reading matter the master might turn to Vergil or to some of the Christian poets like Prudentius (c. 400), and to the psalms. One of the great difficulties was the costliness of books and hence their scarcity. A monastery might have a considerable library without being able to supply individual schoolbooks to its pupils. Not more than three boys to a book was the aim of one cloister. There was no paper or other cheap writing material and hence no easy way to provide for written exercises or notebooks.

Rhetoric followed grammar. But it was no longer the rhetoric of the ancient world. Oratory was of no use to those who had retired from active life. Even preaching did not, according to Isidore, require "the rhetor's wordy display." The rhetoric of the Middle Ages, therefore, dealt with composition, letter writing, the keeping of chronicles and monastic records, and with legal papers. Indeed the very word clerk, in both French and English, meant clergyman; and "benefit of clergy" was conferred upon those who were able to read and write. The elements of law and the drawing up of legal papers, sometimes called "dictamen," became a branch of rhetoric. *Ars Dictamen* is the title of many medieval schoolbooks. Dialectic or logic was the third subject and was based upon some slight remains of Aristotle until the later twelfth and thirteenth centuries, when the complete logical works of Aristotle were recovered.

The group of four subjects which followed the trivium, arithmetic, geometry, astronomy, and music, was called the quadrivium. Only a few of the pupils who completed the trivium also undertook the mathematical and scientific studies of the quadrivium. Several of these latter subjects were of importance in the calculation of the movable festivals of the church, such as Easter. This art was called the *computus* and special books were devoted to it. Arithmetic still followed the Greek and Roman tradition and used their clumsy notations. The astronomy of the monastic schools followed Ptolemy, of course, but it was only a meager treatment. Even so, it contained encyclopedic materials from meteorology and geography. Geography was also mixed with the subject of geometry. The usual text in geometry was not Euclid, whose work had been practically lost, or even the text of Boethius, but the sixth book of Martianus Capella. He dealt chiefly with geography but at the end he stated a few of Euclid's propositions. The common remark is probably correct that in the earlier Middle Ages few were able to pass over the "pons asinorum" or "bridge of asses," as the fifth proposition of Euclid was called from the resemblance of its figure to the truss of a bridge. Geometry, really geography, included a good deal of an uncritical and credulous natural history borrowed by the medieval textbook writers from Pliny and by him from all the libraries of Rome. These writers were not interested in cause and effect or in practical use but rather in remarkable occurrences, strange races, animal monsters, and, in general, the unusual. This was the state of school learning. There were some scientific observers of nature in the Middle Ages, but their work did not influence the schools. Music, as a subject of the quadrivium, was a theoretical study based upon Greek sources and taught from the work of Boethius.

These were the school studies which everyone pursued who proposed to become a scholar. These were the basic studies in the schools of Europe for about a thousand years. They were pursued, not for themselves, but as a preparation for the highest study of all, theology, "the queen of the sciences." Obviously education in the monasteries did not exist for its own sake. It had a religious purpose. The school existed for the monastery, and the monastery was for the deepening of the spiritual life and the salvation of souls. Training and practice in the Rule and instruction in religion began immediately when novices were admitted and accompanied all the work in the subjects we have described. That was the important matter required of all. The intellectual training was less important.

We may here consider some of the religious teachings and practices. Benedict's description of a well-qualified master of novices is that he should be "a person fitted for winning souls." Immediately upon admission to the cloister the novice began his year of probation which was to end either in his formal acceptance as a brother of the house and order, or in his rejection. His instruction began with matters of form and custom: how to wear his habit and cowl, how to walk and bow on various occasions, a somewhat complicated matter, and in general how to deport himself with monastic decorum. Control of the eyes, showing respect for brothers and uperiors, the rule of silence, all demanded study and practice. The Rule, prayers, psalms, and hymns were committed to memory. He learned to ing and chant. He was to become familiar with the Holy Scriptures and re received the instruction which prepared him for confession. Such was he elementary religious instruction that accompanied his literary studies.

The deepest trough of the depression in education is to be placed in he sixth century. But conditions varied in different regions, and this was a century of great activity in Ireland. A further revival is linked with the Carolingian line of sovereigns in Frankland. The revival began under Charlemagne's predecessors but was carried to its high point in his own reign and under his own leadership. To this movement we must now turn.

6. REVIVAL UNDER CHARLEMAGNE—CATHEDRAL AND PARISH SCHOOLS

Charlemagne, or Charles the Great (742–814), was one of the great men of history and his period is one of the great moments in the development of Europe. In 732 his grandfather turned back the Mohammedans at the decisive battle of Tours. About the same time the eastern emperor relinquished his ambition to control the West. These events made it certain hat civilization in Europe would be Christian and not Moslem, Occidental not Byzantine. When Charles came to the throne in 768 the current of progress was, therefore, already in motion, but he gave it new impetus and helped to construct the channels in which it was to run. If it were not or the tradition of the historians, the time of Charlemagne would make a reasonable beginning of modern history.

Charles was not only a great man but a very attractive figure. His biographer speaks of his merry eyes; he was tall, robust, and well proportioned. Whether in action or repose he impressed everyone with a ense of dignity and authority. He was great as a commander, as a ruler, as a builder; and to the church he was a faithful son, although his personal ife did not always embody the church's ideals. As a statesman he realized he power of opinion and morale and, therefore, of education and religion, but he was also interested in ideas for himself and for themselves. Although he never learned to write, he was an eager student of ideas and a liberal patron of the arts.

To his court at Aachen he invited every kind of talent. His educational counselors included three from Italy, still the most cultivated portion of his empire and most closely connected with the Roman see. These were Peter of Pisa, Paulinus of Aquileia, and Paul the Deacon, who wrote a History of the Lombards which won the praise of Gibbon. Another, Theodulf, came from southern France or Spain. Charles, who appointed his own bishops, made Theodulf bishop of Orleans, and this scholar became one of the emperor's staunchest supporters. He was also a poet and author of the hymn "All glory, laud and honor." Best known of Charlemagne's educational advisers was Alcuin (735–804) from the cathedral school of York where he had been educated in the Roman church tradition—a requirement to Charles who, as early as 769, had declared his whole-hearted "allegiance to the apostolic see in all things." Alcuin had qualities adapted to the life of the court. He was big and burly, fond of jokes and riddles and of the pleasures of the table. Most of his poetry is light and when it is serious it is dull. He was loved as a teacher, influential as an adviser in educational policy, but not a great scholar or a great intellect. It was in 781 that he met Charles at Parma and was invited to become head of the palace school; and he remained in this position until 796 when, upon his own request, he was allowed to retire to a monastery, St. Martin's of Tours, as abbot.

In the first years of his reign Charles followed in the steps of Pepin and Charles Martel, his father and his grandfather. He supported the successors of Boniface in their efforts to Christianize the people and to extend the sway of the Roman church. He introduced the Benedictine Rule into the monasteries, and the semimonastic collegiate system of Chrodegang of Metz into the cathedrals. The bishops, who were made the main supports of his government, were given a certain control over the monasteries. Beginning in 773, Charles made some military expeditions into Italy and visited Rome. He was astonished at the remains of Roman buildings and art which spoke to him of the glory of the ancient city and awakened in him the desire to emulate the ancient civilization. His returning armies brought back across the Alps columns, mosaics, and other works of art. He built Frankish churches in imitation of those he had seen at Rome and at Ravenna, and he engaged Italian scholars to act as teachers of the Frankish clergy.

Charles turned his palace into a school, with the English Alcuin as its head. The princes and princesses of his own family and the sons of the nobility were given instruction in the liberal arts, and the king, in the intervals of his campaigns, attempted to set them a studious example. Grammar and rhetoric were studied, and efforts were made to cultivate a classical style. Charles was especially interested in astronomy, and in Greek, on account of its diplomatic importance in the relations of the western with the eastern empire. Alcuin could teach him such knowledge of astronomy as the times afforded but he knew no Greek; and Paul the Deacon who had studied Greek was not able to teach him very much of that language. It was not possible for the busy ruler of a realm which covered what is now included in France, Germany, Switzerland, Belgium,

Holland, most of Italy, and parts of Czecho-Slovakia, to spend much time in study.

Soon after Alcuin came to the court the king took occasion to instruct the clergy on matters of education. The scholar was probably responsible for the form and not the matter of the famous capitulary of 786, "On the cultivation of letters." The royal author said: Churchmen write incorrectly. What if their understanding of the Bible is equally defective? Therefore, let them study literature, including rhetoric, for the Bible contains many figures of speech. Let men willing and able to teach be selected to set up schools. This is the task of all bishops and abbots and is laid upon their consciences as a solemn duty to God and His church.

Also, soon after Alcuin came to the court, the king had him make correct copies of all the books of the Old and New Testaments and then gave command that all copies of the Bible should be corrected to correspond to Alcuin's model. Many missals and service books were so corrupt that they could not be properly emended. This gave Charles the opportunity to change to the Roman liturgy, which he doubtless intended to do in any case, and he supplied all cathedrals and abbeys with the new service books and ordered that correct copies should be made for them.

As soon as Charlemagne was assured that the higher clergy favored his efforts to improve education he made more stringent regulations. He directed the Council of Aachen (789) to include education within the scope of its deliberations; and the Council passed the decree that every convent and cathedral must establish schools in which boys were to be taught the Psalter, singing, the *computus*, and grammar. Priests had to pass a literary examination and those who could not meet the standard were deposed. All who were preparing for the clerical calling were instructed upon a regular plan. The newly erected Saxon bishoprics were assigned chiefly to men who had been pupils of Alcuin. Charlemagne through his scouts or *missi* gave attention to the schools and had only gifted teachers appointed. The Abbey of St. Martin's of Tours, under Alcuin after 796, became a school for the preparation of teachers and higher churchmen. The cathedral school of Metz was another of the great schools of the kingdom. Charlemagne supplied it with teachers from Rome, who were masters of all the liberal arts and who were especially noted for their skill in the teaching of music.

Even the children of the common people came within the scope of Charlemagne's endeavor. In spite of some opposition the monastery gates were opened to admit into the convent schools many children who were not intended for the monastic life. The same result was proposed in some rescripts of Charlemagne issued about 801. Finally, the great emperor caught a fleeting vision of universal education and compulsory attendance

at schools. It was only a glimpse and came about in this way. Charles discovered and revived the old decree of the synod of Vaison held (529) almost three centuries earlier. This decree ordered that all pastors, "as is the
very salutary custom all over Italy," should receive young persons into
their parish houses to teach them singing and reading and the commands
of God. Charles ordered that all priests were, without charge, to maintain
schools in villages and parish houses and were not to refuse any who came
to them for instruction in letters. It was further ordered that "no one
should henceforth dare to administer baptism to anyone who was unable
to repeat the Creed and Lord's Prayer"; and severe penalties were prescribed for those who would not learn these formularies in the Latin tongue.
It soon became evident that such laws were unenforceable in that age;
but the strict duty was still imposed upon parents that they were to "send
their sons to school whether to the cloister or to the parish priest so that
they should rightly learn the Catholic faith and the Lord's prayer and
should also be able to teach them to others at home."

The new system of education, wherein the church performed pre-
eminent service, was to some extent the achievement of Charlemagne and
Alcuin. Charles, as we know, ruled by his personal influence, and after his
death the empire rapidly disintegrated; but his influence upon education
never wholly disappeared. In the next century the English king, Alfred the
Great (849–901), displayed an interest very similar to that of Charlemagne
in the better education of the clergy. He even encouraged the cultivation
of the vernacular language and caused translations to be made of Pope
Gregory's *Pastoral Care* and Boethius' *Consolations of Philosophy*. Beginning in the eighth century the Northmen devastated and recolonized
large parts of Britain and France; but by the end of the tenth century
they had became civilized and the "intellectual depression" which followed the fall of Rome had been overcome.

By conquering and colonizing, Alexander the Great had spread the language
and learning of Greece so widely in the Eastern world that he has been called
the Apostle of the Greeks. Alexandria became a second Athens. In the early
Christian centuries, Greek philosophy deeply influenced Christian thought. The
catechumenal and catechetical schools were established to teach Christian doctrine and to erect a defense against philosophical attack. In defending itself,
Christian theology absorbed much of Neo-Platonic thought.

A similar union was formed in the school curriculum of the West. This curriculum was composed of the remains of Greek, Hebrew, and Roman ideas and
learning. It was the first task of the Middle Ages to make this synthesis; and this
was accomplished under the auspices of the church and her schools. In the
period of political decline, barbarian invasion, and civil disorder, the church preserved what it could use. Much of ancient culture had already disappeared from

the West; and of what remained, much was neglected. The spirit of investigation and criticism, the sense of history, and the hope of progress were almost entirely absent. Learning, embodied in outlines, summaries, and selections, was merely preserved.

The monastic and cathedral schools taught the Seven Liberal Arts, philosophy, and theology. In the scriptoria, books were copied and new ones written. Libraries, though never large, gradually increased in size. Charlemagne drew to his court learned men from several parts of his empire and attempted to stimulate the clergy to increased scholastic activity. He even hoped to spread some slight degree of learning among the laity. This example of state interest in education was not to be followed until much later. In the next century the great English king, Alfred, exhibited a similar concern for education, although on a smaller stage. But the period of educational quiescence was now over, and in the next period the Middle Ages became much more active and progressive.

QUESTIONS

1. Was the medieval period, in its educational development, a coherent historical unit or did it include divergent trends?
2. Show that the Middle Ages attempted a synthesis of Greek, Roman, and Judean-Christian knowledge and ideas. Was this union inevitable or might it have been avoided; and if so, with what results?
3. Why did the Christian teachers in spite of their opposition to pagan literature after all use it in their schools? And how did they justify its use?
4. How did the Roman civil organization affect the organization of the Christian church? How did this affect the schools?
5. Why did the schoolbooks of the Middle Ages tend to become formal and abstract summaries?
6. Why did Western monasticism develop only after the great persecutions came to an end?
7. Why did the monasteries carry on a great variety of economic activities; and why did they also foster reading, schools, the manufacture of books, singing, and other arts?
8. Outline the virtues and the defects of the monastic schools. Were the reasons for their defects at all comparable to those which characterized early modern common schools in rural sections?
9. Why were books expensive in the Middle Ages?
10. From the account of Eginhard or Einhard (see bibliography), write a paper on the character and personality of Charlemagne.
11. Why did Charlemagne draw his educational advisers from Italy and England rather than from his own Frankland?
12. In what respects do Charlemagne's efforts mark an advance upon the education of preceding centuries? How did his efforts differ from those of the Roman emperors? Was this an example of genuine state activity in education?
13. From J. M. Clark's history of The Abbey of St. Gall write an account of the intellectual and musical activities of that monastery. Were all or most monasteries as enlightened as St. Gall?

FOR FURTHER READING AND STUDY

Education in the Middle Ages was closely connected with the medieval church, and a background of church history is desirable. Although we have no space to list the major works, a course of reading in that field is to be recommended to those who have access to a good library. Equally, or more, important is reading in the general history of the Middle Ages. Two one-volume books that may be recommended are Carl Stephenson's *Medieval History, Europe from the Fourth to the Sixteenth Century* (New York, Harper and Brothers, 1935, 797 pp.) : and Francis J. Tschan, Grimm, and Squires on *Western Civilization. The Decline of Rome to 1660* (Philadelphia, J. B. Lippincott Company, 1942, 783 and xciii pp.). Many of the books in the following list will be useful for the next chapter also.

Abelson, Paul, *The Seven Liberal Arts*, New York, Teachers College, Columbia University, 1906, 150 pp.

Adams, George Burton, *Civilization during the Middle Ages*, New York, Charles Scribner's Sons, 1913, 463 pp. First published in 1894, but still useful.

Clark, James Midgeley, *The Abbey of St. Gall as a Center of Literature and Art*, Cambridge, University Press, 1926, 322 pp.

Church, R. W., *Saint Anselm*, London, Macmillan & Company, Ltd., 1884, 303 pp.

Deansley, Margaret, *A History of the Medieval Church*, 590–1500, London, Methuen & Co., Ltd., 1938, second edition, 284 pp.

Eginhard (Einhard), *Life of Charlemagne*. Translated from the text of Monumenta Germaniae by Samuel Epes Turner, Cincinnati, American Book Company, 1883, 83 pp.

Gasquet, F. A., Cardinal, *English Monastic Life*, London, Methuen & Co., Ltd., 1919, fifth edition, 326 pp. Excellent on the life and material arrangements of monasteries.

Glover, Terrot R., *Life and Letters in the Fourth Century*, New York, G. E. Stechert & Company, 1924, 398 pp. First published in 1901.

Halliday, William Reginald, *Greek and Roman Folklore*, New York, Longmans, Green and Company, 1927, 154 pp. (Our Debt to Greece and Rome Series.) Useful on medieval traditions derived from the ancients.

Hannah, Ian C., *Christian Monasticism, A Great Force in History*, New York, The Macmillan Company, 1925, 270 pp.

Labriolle, Pierre de, *History and Literature of Latin Christianity from Tertullian to Boethius*. Translated by Herbert Wilson, London, Kegal Paul, Trench, Trübner & Co., 1929, 555 pp.

Laistner, M. L. W., *Thought and Letters in Western Europe A.D. 500 to 900*, London, Methuen & Co., 1931, 354 pp.

Mullinger, J. Bass, *The Schools of Charles the Great and the Restoration of Education in the Ninth Century*, London, Longmans, Green and Company, 1877, 193 pp.

O'Connor, The Very Rev. J. B., *Monasticism and Civilization*, New York, P. J. Kennedy and Sons, 1921, 253 pp. Deals with monastic libraries.

Pope, R. Martin, *An Introduction to Early Church History*, London, Macmillan & Company, Ltd., 1918, 163 pp.

Rand, Edward K., *Founders of the Middle Ages*, Cambridge, Harvard University Press, 1928, 365 pp.

Sanford, Eva M., Translator, *On the Government of God, by Salvian*, New York, Columbia University Press, 1930, 241 pp. Fifth century document giving views of taxation, games, manners, and morals, of Romans and barbarians.

Singer, Charles, *From Magic to Science. Essays on the Scientific Twilight*, New York, Boni and Liveright, 1928, 253 pp.

Specht, Franz Anton, *Geschichte des Unterrichtswesens in Deutschland . . . bis zur Mitte des dreizehnten Jahrhunderts*, Stuttgart, J. B. Cotta, 1885, 441 pp.

Taylor, Henry Osborn, *The Medieval Mind: A History of Thought and Emotion in the Middle Ages*, New York, The Macmillan Company, 1927, 2 vols.

Wishart, Alfred Wesley, *A Short History of Monks and Monasteries*, Trenton, N. J., Albert Brandt, 1902, 462 pp. Anti-Catholic bias.

Workman, Herbert B., *The Evolution of the Monastic Ideal*, London, Charles H. Kelly, 1913, 368 pp.

5 FROM MONASTIC SCHOOLS TO UNIVERSITIES

T HE ELEVENTH CENTURY MARKS THE TURNING POINT IN medieval history. The previous losses, the long-accumulated deficits on the balance sheet of knowledge, culture, and welfare were overcome between the eleventh century and the end of the Middle Ages and there were positive gains sufficient to make the period from 1100 to 1500 one of Europe's great periods of progress. To be sure the people of that age were not able to realize all their ideals, and some of their greatest accomplishments led to new problems of health and morals, religion and politics, problems which had not troubled their ancestors. Economic dislocation, corruption in the church, a depressed and poverty-stricken working class, new diseases and devastating plagues were some of these ills. The educational advances included an increase in the number of schools and the wider extension of learning, especially in the cities; new and better books and methods; the beginning of instruction in the vernacular languages, which led, in modern times, to the common school; and most striking, perhaps most important, the creation of the medieval universities.

The most important factors in this progress were the growth of commerce and the rise of cities; new improvements in the crafts, including the art of building the great cathedrals; the establishment of stronger governments; the crusades and the rise of chivalry; the extraordinary effects of the recovery of the ancient learning from the Mohammedans; the development of scholastic logic, philosophy, and theology; and in the fourteenth century the renaissance of secular art, literature, and learning. We shall devote the present chapter and the following one to these subjects; but we must begin with a period of destruction.

1. DECLINE AFTER CHARLEMAGNE

The great achievements that distinguished the later centuries of the Middle Ages did not grow directly out of the Carolingian period. At

least two centuries of feudalism, invasions, civil disorder, and religious decline followed the close of Charlemagne's reign. His successors were not
exceptionally weak but they were not able to lead and dominate as Charlemagne had done. Many monasteries were pillaged by the Vikings, as the
Scandinavian invaders were called, and cities and towns were laid waste.
There were armed clashes on three frontiers, north, south, and east, and a
revolt in Italy. In two decades the Vikings plundered the valleys of the
Rhine, the Seine, and the Loire and raided the Mediterranean coasts. In
many places they remained as permanent settlers, and thence came the
Norman kingdoms of Sicily and of Normandy in France. The extent to
which they penetrated into the country and the importance of the cities
they destroyed show how weak the central government had become. Since
each locality had to provide for its own defense, local interests and local
chieftains became stronger, on their own ground at least, than the king.
In other words, the feudal system which the great Carolingian rulers had
held in check came to prevail. And yet the Normans, like the modern
Scandinavians, were easily assimilated by the people whom they had conquered. They accepted the Christian religion, developed the Norman-
French speech, and became leaders in their new home.

 Meanwhile the Moslems held control of Spain and of the whole western
Mediterranean sea, including the islands of Sicily, Corsica, and Sardinia.
They raided the coasts of Italy and France. Their pirates plundered the
shipping of the Italian cities and controlled the leading ports. They burned
the church of St. Peter at Rome and they sacked the mother monastery of
the Benedictines at Monte Cassino. It was not until 1095 that Genoa and
Pisa, combining their fleets, recovered control of their sea routes, which
had the most direct influence upon the prosperity of those cities and
upon the support they were able to give to the crusades.

Other enemies attacked the tottering empire of Charlemagne by land.
In the ninth century the Magyars, driven up the Danube by the pressure
of Asiatic tribes, united with the Avars, who had settled in those regions
long before. Moving west, they broke through the defenses of the empire
and invaded the plains of northern Italy and southern Germany. They
even reached into Saxony and into eastern France. By attacks from all
directions from without, and the spread of feudal conditions within, the
empire of Charlemagne was destroyed, and the ground was thereby prepared for the rise of modern nation-states. East of the Rhine the first step
was taken in 918 when Henry, the Saxon, was elected king; and in France
a similar occasion presented itself when Hugh Capet attained the throne
in 987. The rise of nation-states is significant in the history of education,
for ultimately, but not yet for many centuries, they were to become the
chief educators of their citizens.

2. MOSLEM LEARNING

Signs of the coming renewal of Western learning can be seen in numerous places from the eighth century onward. Even without stimulation from abroad, Europe would have developed a civilization not wholly different from the one which actually came to be. It would have taken much longer, discovery and creation would not have followed the paths which we find in the historical record, and some features, the crusades, for example, would have been missing altogether. This internal development was, however, stimulated by contributions from ancient Greece, from eastern Christianity, and from the Arabs.

As mediators and carriers of borrowed culture the Arabs were more effective than any other people with whom medieval Europe came into contact; but they were also more than carriers and mediators. Although they were not freely creative on the grand scale of ancient Greece, they yet made many contributions in agriculture, the arts and sciences, medicine, and philosophy. The Mohammedan religion, which developed in Arabia in the seventh century, set these people upon a career of conquest. Arabia was quickly unified, Syria fell after a single battle, Persia offered only weak resistance; and when the East had submitted the armies turned westward.

Their amazing conquest laid at the feet of the caliphs a vast domain stretching from eastern Persia across the Fertile Crescent and equally fertile Nile to the Pyrenees in the west. In all these conquests, however, they never met a first-class power. The world which the Arabs conquered was a decrepit world, divided against itself, and everywhere ready to break into pieces and to accept new alignments. Nor were they able to build a lasting and unified empire. Their political unity began to dissolve the moment their soldiers stopped marching.

Not political but religious unity and the wide extension of the Arabic tongue were the permanent results of these conquests. Although, as in Christianity, there are many sects in Islam, its pretensions have been well sustained. Spain is the only large country from which a firmly planted Islam has ever been uprooted. The real supremacy of the Arabs in the Middle Ages was religious, scientific, and commercial, and their great educational service was the transmission of learning from the slumbering East to the awakening West. Arabic became the universal language of learning and culture in large areas of three continents. The science and the philosophy of Greece and the East were taken up into this new cultural speech, carried to the West, translated into Latin, and placed before the scholars of Christian Europe. How this came about and what its effects were is the subject of our present inquiry.

3. SOURCES OF MOSLEM LEARNING

The main body of the knowledge which the Arabs were to carry to Europe was ancient Greek knowledge, preserved in the Greek language; but the early Arab conquerors were semibarbarian Bedouins. From the time when they came into the light of history down to Mohammed (c. 570–632) the peoples of the interior of Arabia were wild and predatory tribesmen. They were of Semitic stock, belonging to the same division of the human family as the Hebrews. They lived in tents and moved from pasture to pasture with their herds of camels.

Nature in the Arabian deserts has been so sparing of her gifts to man that the Arabs were usually hungry and ready to prey upon caravans or upon their neighbors, especially those in the fixed settlements. These desert warriors would not stoop to work in regular occupations such as agriculture or industry, for work was considered fit only for slaves. They practiced only one fine art, that of poetry. In the southwestern part of Arabia, near the Gulf of Aden, there were settlements; farther north there were cities of which Mecca and Medina were the chief; and frankincense and spices from Arabia itself, pearls from the Persian Gulf, and rich luxurious products from India were carried along the coast of the Red Sea to Egypt, Palestine, and even to distant Rome. The young Mohammed engaged successfully in this caravan trade. But of learning and letters the desert Arabs had none and the trading Arabs very little. Those were the days which the Moslems themselves consider the times of ignorance, although they refer mainly to their ignorance of the faith, before Mohammed. It is thought that the Prophet was unable to read or write.

When the Arabs came into the outside world all this was changed. They quickly became literate and many of them became learned. Aroused to a burning zeal for their new spiritual values, driven also by the pangs of physical hunger, and, when the campaigns succeeded, led by ambition and the well-established Arabian desire for loot, they conquered the whole extent of the Fertile Crescent, invested Alexandria in 642, swept across the ancient Roman province of Africa to the Atlantic, and in 711 crossed the thirteen-mile-wide straits of Gibraltar into Spain, which became one of their fairest provinces. They marched as conquerors but they were in turn taken captive by the civilizations which they found. No other people which began at so low a level of civilization was raised so quickly to such a high plane of culture as these Semitic tribesmen. They accomplished as much in two centuries as the Germanic barbarians in six and the ancient invaders of Greece in eight or ten. The chief instruments were Indo-Persian, Syrian, and Hellenic books, teachers, and schools at such centers as Antioch, Edessa, Harran, Jundi-Shapur, and the Islamic capitals, Damascus and Bagdad.

The history of Moslem scholarship as far as it concerned the medieval West comprises two main parts. The first task of the Arabs was to acquire the ancient learning of the Hindus, Persians, and Greeks. To this learning they gradually added their own achievements. The second act of the drama was played in the twelfth century in Moslem Spain and consisted again of translation, this time from Arabic into Latin. Much of this knowledge had once been available in the West, but some was lost in Roman times and still more during the Dark Ages. The return of this forgotten knowledge through translations from the Arabic into Latin had the most stimulating effect upon the mind of the West and was one of the main influences in the rise of the medieval universities.

4. BYZANTIUM AND PERSIA

The books and learning which made the translations possible were preserved in the Byzantine empire, which has been called the rearguard of European civilization. The capital city of Constantinople, founded by Constantine the Great in A.D. 330, was the center of the empire, some of whose outposts of learning have already been mentioned. Constantine set up new schools and endowed old ones. Theodosius also provided for the higher learning in literature and philosophy, both Greek and Latin. Libanius, the great sophist of the fourth century, taught at Antioch. Gaza on the southeastern edge of the great sea was long famous for its schools of rhetoric; and Alexandria and Athens continued to produce valuable work in geometry in the fourth and fifth centuries of our era. The law schools of the Byzantine empire were famous, especially those of Berytus, so that, when Justinian in the sixth century desired to make a definite code of the Roman law, there was no want of competent legal scholars to carry out the imperial project.

Alexandria had once been the rival of Athens as a center of learning. The great library, variously estimated from four to seven hundred thousand rolls, was founded early in the third century before Christ; and it was supplemented by a smaller one of perhaps two hundred thousand rolls in the Serapeum. There was also the great Museum with its provision for the work and residence of a body of scholars who received public support. There is a mistaken tradition that all this was destroyed by the Moslems. The fact is that both of the libraries had been destroyed long before Mohammed, the greater and older of the two when Alexandria was besieged by Caesar in 48 B.C. and the smaller one about A.D. 450. Orosius, the historian, mourned over the ruins a generation after the latter date.

The Greek learning of Byzantium was frequently translated not directly into Arabic but in a roundabout way through Syriac, Hebrew, Persian, and finally into Arabic. Many of the scholars who made the translations were Christians with heretical tendencies, who were driven toward the East by persecution. The two most important groups were the Nestorians and the Monophysites, each dividing from the orthodox faith and from each other on the question of the nature of Christ. Both the Nestorians and the Monophysites originated in the fifth century and spread far and wide in the East before the Moslem conquests in the eighth century. Persia had an important scientific center in the medical school of Jundi-Shapur, near the Persian Gulf. The name, Jundi-Shapur, is variously spelled and means "Conquered by Shapur," one of a dynasty of kings. It was also noted for the study of astronomy, or astrology, which was connected with medicine through the belief that the stars influenced human health and destiny. The school reached its highest point in the sixth century. Damascus, where al-Khwarizmi worked, and other cities of western Asia were equally famous for their schools.

5. TRANSLATION INTO ARABIC

One of the greatest translators into Arabic was Hunayn-ibn-Ishaq (809–873), a physician and noted investigator. Hunayn, known in Latin as Joannitius, was a Nestorian who worked at Jundi-Shapur and later served as physician to the caliph at Bagdad. He was an admirable character as well as a scholar. One story tells that when Hunayn refused to poison a political enemy of the ruler he was threatened with death. Commanded to reveal the reason for his refusal, he replied: "Two things: my religion and my profession. My religion decrees that we should do good even to our enemies; and my profession is instituted for the benefit of humanity. Besides," he added, referring to the oath of Hippocrates, "every physician is under oath never to give anyone a deadly potion." He was released and continued to hold the favor of the caliph.

Hunayn's position as medical librarian at Bagdad led to his work as a translator. He was careful not only to give a true rendering but also to secure the most accurate manuscripts. Some of the treatises of Hippocrates and nearly all those of Galen, some dialogues of Plato, and several works of Aristotle were translated into Arabic under Hunayn. The Greek text of Galen's seven books on anatomy has been lost, but the contents have been preserved in Hunayn's Arabic version.

Other schools of translators at Bagdad and elsewhere flourished from the eighth to the twelfth centuries. Most of the Greek works on geography, astronomy, mathematics, and medicine were translated into the Arabic tongue; and many new works were written. Among the leaders were al-Khwarizmi, a mathematician, al-Razes and ibn-Sina, commonly known as Avicenna, medical writers, Omar Khayyám, a poet and mathematician, and the philosopher ibn-Rushd, known to us as Averroes.

6. FROM ARABIC INTO LATIN

Spain was quickly conquered by the Moslems, but they found the country hard to pacify and to govern. But during periods of vigorous government, Moslem Spain was prosperous and her cities rivaled in wealth, luxury, and pleasure the cities of the East. Cordova, the capital, competed with Bagdad and Constantinople in the arts of civilized life and far excelled Paris and every other city north of the Pyrenees. In the ninth and tenth centuries, Cordova had a half-million inhabitants for whom it provided well-lighted, paved streets, public baths, and a bridge across the Guadalquiver to connect the city with its southern suburbs. The royal palace was built of Numidian marble, and the grand mosque attracted pilgrims from the whole of Moslem Spain. Seville, Valencia, and Granada were other famous cities, but the greatest center of scholarship was Toledo, famed also for its manufacture of "Toledo blades," which vied for pre-eminence with the swords of Damascus. Intellectual activity and particularly the work of translation continued at Toledo even after the city was retaken by the Christians in 1085. Archbishop Raymond was, in the twelfth century, the founder and patron of a vigorous school of translators which flourished for a long time. Arabic continued in Toledo to be the official language in law and business for two hundred years after the Christian conquest. Many Christians whose faith and practice were assimilated to those of Islam lived in a separate quarter of the city, regularly spoke two languages, Arabic and a form of Low Latin which was on the way to become Spanish, and were known as Mozarabs. The Latin language was written with Arabic letters, Spanish kings used Arabic characters on their coins, and even the ritual of the Catholic church showed Mozarabic influences. Similar assimilation in the direction of Islam was shown by the Jews of Spain, of whom many adopted the language, dress, and manners, and a very few the faith, of the Arabs. Cordova, the capital of Moslem Spain, was also the seat of a flourishing Talmudic school and a center of Jewish culture.

The recovery of ancient science and philosophy in the twelfth and thirteenth centuries was an important cause of the medical renaissance. The Moslems were not interested in Homer, Herodotus, and the Greek dramatists. Their religion did not permit the development of painting and sculpture. Like the Romans, they were not able to acquire the whole range of Hellenic culture. If they had been, the renaissance of classical literature in Italy might have occurred in the thirteenth century along with the revival of logic and the development of scholasticism. The medieval renaissance revived instead ancient logic, philosophy, and science, not pure literature, and this revival stemmed from the translation into Latin of the numerous Arabic texts of Greek and Hindu authors that had been written in the East during the three or four preceding centuries. This era of transla-tion divides the educational history of the Middle Ages into two clearly marked periods. The earlier one we have already described. In that, to quote Renan's *Averroes*, the human mind had to satisfy its curiosity with the meager fragments of Roman school education which such writers as Martianus Capella, Bede, and Isidore had preserved in their dry outlines. But in the later period, after 1100, the West learned far more of Greek science than Rome had been willing or able to acquire. The whole body of Greek and Arabic medicine, Greek and Arabic mathematics, astronomy, and alchemy, all of Aristotle, and numerous works from India, Syria, and Persia were by 1300 available to Latin Europe in its own language. The recovery of this learning promoted the educational renaissance of the Middle Ages.

Sicily was, next to Spain, the most important gateway through which the ancient learning was brought back to Europe. Sicily was of particular im-portance because it was ruled by the Arabs for two centuries before the Normans conquered it and continued to hold a large Moslem population afterwards.

But more important than location and sources is the eagerness of Euro-pean scholars for learning. It was not the Arabs who translated their works into Latin; it was the Latins of Christian Europe who translated from the Arabic into the language of the West. Europe was awakening, and Euro-pean scholars such as Adelhard of Bath went in search of the manuscripts, acquired the necessary knowledge of languages and subject matter, and carried through the translations. Before the twelfth century monastic and cathedral libraries had only the usual Latin books. By 1300 the translators had done their work and much of the ancient knowledge was again avail-able.

With the dozen or more first-line European translators we can deal only briefly. Adelhard of Bath translated Euclid's *Elements* and the astronomical tables of al-Khwarizmi and wrote original works on "natural questions," a science miscellany that was popular in the Middle Ages, and on astronomy and the use of the astrolabe. Another mathematical translator was the Italian, Plato of Tivoli, who lived in Barcelona for a dozen years after 1134. Leonardo Fibonacci was not a translator but an original writer on mathematics and the first to explain the Hindu numerals to Christian Europe. This he did in 1202 in his *Liber Abaci*, the book on the abacus.

He was the author of other, more advanced, mathematical works. Robert of Chester translated the algebra of al-Khwarizmi and revised Adelhard's version of the astronomical tables of the same author. Robert, in 1143, completed the Latin version of the Koran requested by Peter the Venerable.

How the scientific and mathematical minds of the later twelfth century were affected by the discovery of Arabic science is seen in the *Philosophia* of Daniel of Morley. He found the scholastics of Paris filled with "a pretentious ignorance" and hastened to Toledo "to hear the world's great masters." There he became a pupil of Gerard of Cremona, one of the most prolific and learned translators of that time. Gerard had received a thorough Latin education in Italy, studied Arabic in Spain where he found and translated Ptolemy's *Almagest*. Meanwhile, in Sicily and northern Italy, scholars had begun again to translate directly from Greek into Latin. By the close of the thirteenth century, Greek science and the Aristotelian philosophy were available in their entirety in the Christian schools and universities of Europe.

7. THE RECOVERY OF ARISTOTLE

Aristotle was to scholasticism, to theology, and to advanced studies in the liberal arts what Galen was to medicine and the Code of Justinian to law. When we take into account the wide range of the subjects that Aristotle treated and the persistence of his influence down to our own day we see that he was the most important single author in the medieval renaissance. The material for that revival was at hand, when Aristotle's works became available and not before.

The introduction of Aristotle into Western education occurred between 1100 and 1300. Abelard knew only parts of two of his works on logic. About 1128, James of Venice translated from Greek into Latin four other logical works by Aristotle, the *Topics*, the *Prior* and *Posterior Analytics*, and another dealing with logical fallacies. The whole group came to be called the "New Logic," new in the sense of having been previously unknown to Latin readers. Nearly at the same time the old version of Boethius again came into circulation. At least two new translations from the Arabic were also made. All of these versions of the logical works came into use in the twelfth century.

The other writings of Aristotle appeared in the West a little later. Several of the shorter works dealing with natural history were introduced before 1200. Most of these, like his works on logic, came by one of two independent routes, direct from the Greek or by way of the Arabic. The works dealing with social and ethical questions, the *Politics*, the *Ethics*, the *Eco-*

nomics, and the *Rhetoric,* were translated in the thirteenth century. By 1275 the whole of Aristotle was again available, and most of his works became required reading in the universities, but before that came about, the scholarship of the West had passed through an acute crisis.

The crisis which Aristotle precipitated in the schools arose because of the necessity for an accommodation between his teaching and that of the Christian church. The same difficulty arose in Islam and in Judaism, because all three religions taught that the world, including the matter of which it is composed, was created by God, while Aristotle taught the eternity of matter. There were other points of disagreement, but this was the central one. The men who dealt most incisively with this contradiction were ibn-Rushd (Averroes) in Islam, Moses Maimon in Judaism, and Thomas Aquinas in Christendom. Ibn-Rushd wrote his commentaries on what later educators have called the spiral plan. There were three turns in his spiral. The first was an elementary summary for beginners and that was followed by an intermediate and this, finally, by a full text and definitive interpretation. These three commentaries corresponded to three levels of education just as, to compare great things with small, a primary, intermediate, and advanced school geography series does today. We shall see that Comenius came back to this idea but it was already old when ibn-Rushd used it, for it was a common plan in the higher schools of Islam.

Aristotle's own doctrines were considered dangerous, but when they appeared in the dress of a Moslem philosopher, Averroes, they were alarming. The church tried to suppress both at once. In 1210 the teaching of Aristotle was forbidden at Paris by the provincial council on threat of excommunication. In 1215 the study of the logic was permitted but that of the *Metaphysics* was again forbidden together with everything that smacked of Averroes and Averroism. At this point the great scholastic doctors undertook the task of harmonizing the teachings of the Greek philosopher and the church. Albert the Great and, especially, Thomas Aquinas were so successful in reconciling reason with revelation that Aristotle was considered a safe author. By 1275 the whole of Aristotle, interpreted in a Christian sense, was admitted to the university course.

8. THE CRUSADES

The first crusade was preached by a monk of Cluny who had become Pope Urban II. The church had long wished to check the constant civil warfare which feudal conditions had brought about in Europe. The monks of Cluny, with the support of powerful laymen, had moved for the restoration of law and order, the Peace of God as it was called. All who committed outrages, attacked noncombatants, or violated sacred places were solemnly excommunicated. The Peace of God was supplemented by the Truce of God which banned all fighting from Wednesday evening to the following Monday morning. Four days of peace each week had a salutary effect upon practical affairs. Pope Urban was in Clermont in the heart of his native France seeking a renewal of the Truce of God when, in November 1095, by an eloquent and moving address, he launched the first crusade. "Dieu le veut"—God Wills It! shouted the people in unison. So says the legend. The ensuing crusade was altogether real.

The crusades were made possible by the new unity of Christendom under the leadership of the papacy, and since they were in one sense military pilgrimages to the holiest of Christian shrines, they were an expression of the rising spirit of asceticism. All through the Middle Ages, pilgrimages were a favored form of penance, and in preaching the first crusade Pope Urban felt himself justified in promising immediate entrance into paradise to any crusader who died repenting of his sins.

The time was favorable for such campaigns. The West enjoyed comparative peace. The invasions by Northmen and Hungarians were over. National and commercial interests and activities were still in their early beginnings. The spirit of adventure and knight errantry was strong. There were few competing claims upon the rising power of the great barons and kings. The religious attitude of the time, we have noted, was ascetic. The papacy was powerful. Numerous smaller crusades had already been undertaken with the blessing of the church in Spain, in northern Africa, and in aid of the Eastern emperor. Under all these conditions, the enthusiasm for the great adventure of 1096 can be readily understood.

This first crusade was followed by others. There were eight major and numerous smaller ones during the next two centuries. We shall deal only with the influence of these military pilgrimages upon civilization and education. They were not wholly or mainly "holy wars" nor were the crusaders wholly disinterested and chivalrous men risking their lives in a noble cause. The purposes and the results were certainly in part economic. In the second place, the crusaders were less civilized than those whom they sought to conquer. The capture of Jerusalem in 1099 led immediately to a wholesale massacre of Moslem and Jewish inhabitants. In Europe the crusades were the occasions for widespread outbreaks of anti-Jewish persecutions and pogroms. The crusaders suffered greatly because they knew nothing or almost nothing of hygiene, and they seem to have been responsible for the increase of leprosy in Europe. On the other hand the crusades had a direct influence in the improvement of surgery and the increase of hospitals.

Many of the lords who went on crusade never returned to claim their fiefs. Meanwhile the serfs escaped to neighboring towns, and they and their descendants helped to swell the numbers of the growing middle class of free workmen and artisans. The removal of the barons enabled the kings to strengthen their power. The crusaders who came back returned with a wider knowledge of the world and its civilizations. They had learned of new and desirable commodities in the luxurious East and of the trade routes. Commerce was stimulated. More and more the later crusaders traveled by sea from Italy over the Mediterranean. They depended upon the Italian cities to furnish transport, supplies, ships, and sailors. Italy became the purveyor to the crusading armies, and a great impulse to her developing commerce ensued. The crusades were an important factor in preparation for the Italian Renaissance. Chivalry developed from the crusading movement; and in chivalry there arose an aristocratic educational system which was to have far-reaching influences.

9. CHIVALRIC EDUCATION

The institution of chivalry, based on a feudal society, received its greatest impetus during the period of the crusades. It continued in full vigor for centuries, however, and exercised an influence upon education which lasted into modern times. The word itself is derived from the French *cheval*, a horse, whence *chevalier*, which as a military term meant cavalryman or knight. For the origin of much of the elaborate etiquette and many of the terms of chivalry one must also go to the French. But the institution was by no means purely French. Some of its basic customs originated among the early Germans. Many of its moral ideas such as loyalty, truthfulness, respect for womanhood, and knightly honor were developed under the influence of Christianity. But, although chivalry may have moderated the customs and manners of a rude age, it can hardly be held that the institution was ever truly Christian. It was too aristocratic and recognized no obligations to the common man. It set a moral and social gulf between the noblemen who lived in the castle and those who labored on the manor, the artisans in the city, and even the priest who ministered in the church. Chivalry was based upon a caste system.

In the early feudal age the young nobleman was not expected to have a literary education. His profession was that of a mounted warrior. At seven the boy became a page and learned to serve at table, to carve the roast or fowl, and to hunt. Heraldry and chess were not omitted. At fourteen he became a squire and had to serve as valet to his knight, to help him dress, to put on his armor, and to groom his horse. Fourteen years of service as page and squire prepared the young man of twenty-one for knighthood. After a night of vigil in the church, communion was administered. The candidate was invested with his arms and armor, he knelt at the altar, the sword was laid across his shoulder in the *adoubement*, and he rose a full-fledged knight.

Chivalric education was not a uniform and static system but one which exhibited considerable adaptability and the power to survive under different conditions. In later times it included many refinements which would have been scorned in ruder days, music both vocal and instrumental, dancing, the art of love as well as of war, and even some of the sciences, especially the mathematical and military ones. Chaucer's squire is an illustration. He could ride the war horse but he was equally adept at singing and composing songs, playing on the flute, and dancing. In Chaucer's description his skill in drawing gets as much emphasis as his ability to unhorse an antagonist. Chivalric tendencies did not die out with chivalry. Schemes for the education of the prince and later of the gentleman and the lady showed traces of chivalric influence. Writers like Castiglione and Sir Thomas Elyot were deeply affected by chivalric ideals. The French academies, the knightly academies of Germany, the writings of Montaigne, Locke, and many others down to the eighteenth century were influenced by the practices of the medieval knight. Basedow's scheme (1774) of physical education was one result of his experience as a teacher in a knightly academy. As feudalism was at war with commerce, the knight with the burgher, so the chivalric education was opposed to the practical and democratic education of modern life.

10. MEDIEVAL TOWNS AND TOWN LIFE

All through Western history educational progress has been dependent upon industry, commerce, and urban prosperity. There are many more illustrations of this rule than exceptions to it. Today in the United States the great cities are also great educational centers. In Europe, likewise, the great capitals have long been famous for their universities and schools. So it was in the ancient world whose great schools and famous teachers were to be found in Athens, Antioch, and Alexandria, rather than in the provinces. The history of the Middle Ages proves the same truth. With the decline of urban life in the West, education also declined; and when cities rose again on the old sites or in new locations, schools became larger, more numerous, and better. The fact does not need any elaborate explanation. Schools must have students, funds, and cooperation, and all of these are more readily found in urban than in rural regions.

The growth of cathedral towns had an important influence upon education. The decline of commerce and of a commercial population increased the relative importance of the bishops. The clerical population of a cathedral town included not only the cathedral clergy with numerous secretaries and legal advisers but also priests, teachers, and students in the schools as well as the monks of any local monasteries. Most towns had markets on one or more days a week; many had an annual fair for the sale of cloth, armor, weapons, and other products. Of such a town and the surrounding communities which formed his diocese, the bishop was both the religious and the civil head. He administered the law, repaired the streets and the walls, and organized the defense in case of attack.

Other towns in the ninth and tenth centuries grew up around fortified places. This is the meaning of the word borough or burg. The borough did not at first have any commercial importance, but eventually commercial quarters developed under the walls of many boroughs. These quarters frequently had to be walled in for security, and in such a community we have the beginning of a modern city. Often neither the episcopal town nor the fortified borough was a genuine city, for they frequently had no middle class population, no corporate privileges, and no commercial or industrial importance.

Industry and commerce have been the usual bases of urban development, and these are intimately related to each other. Industry requires supplies of raw materials, industrial skill, and markets, while commerce finds the markets, brings the raw materials, disposes of the manufactured goods, and supplies the needs of the workers. Both industry and commerce are aided by compact populations, political stability, just laws, good roads, or by adequate shipping and an open sea. Money and credit, weights and measures, ready methods of calculation, and adequate business records are other essentials. These at once suggest the importance of education, and it is fair to say that education, in a broad sense, is fundamental to the whole economic structure.

The Italian cities were ready to take advantage of the new knowledge and new markets that developed from the crusades. As a direct result, Venice and Pisa developed their shipping and employed their sailors to transport goods across the great sea. Venice became the most important link between the East and the West. She kept up her connection with Constantinople and prospered from the business of provisioning that great city.

From Venice the produce of the Levant and Egypt were carried northward by several routes. An eastern route reached Ratisbon and used the Danube to Vienna; a western crossed Switzerland to the Rhine and then followed the Seine to Paris; but the Brenner Pass gave the most convenient access to the north. This last track led to Innsbruck whence the goods were carried in many directions, to the Flemish coast, to Scandinavia, and to all parts of Germany. Trade routes were determined by natural conditions, mountain passes and river valleys. At strategic points, cities arose.

Venice catered especially to the German trade in later centuries and as early as 1228 a German chamber of commerce was to be found on the Rialto. Young German businessmen were sent to Italy to study business methods; and they always learned a great deal besides. Italian exchanges and business and banking houses were likewise established in the northern towns when these towns developed. But the cities of the north remained culturally undeveloped for a considerable time. Their trade was in raw materials and their people were engaged in harder labor and exposed to greater risks. On the other hand, southern German towns like Nuremberg and Augsburg were more easily affected by Italian art and ideas.

Pisa first became prominent through an immigration of Sardinians who fled from the Moslems in the eighth century. Genoa was its commercial rival, but the two towns adjusted their differences for a combined and successful attack upon Mohammedan sea power. Both towns also took large part in the crusades. In the course of the thirteenth century Pisa succumbed to Genoan competition and arms and eventually it became merely the port for the trade of Florence.

Florence, which was to become the capital of the Italian Renaissance, became wealthy through its manufactures of wool and silk and the work of its artists and artisans, especially the goldsmiths. The power of the Florentine state was in the hands of a succession of noble families although in form its government was democratic. Its powerful gilds gave political training to the "free" Florentines. Before and during the Renaissance it was the most turbulent but also the wealthiest city of Tuscany and the industrial center of all Italy.

Commerce not only followed the natural trade routes but it demanded their improvement. Roads were repaired, and bridges replaced fords. Boats and barges were provided for river transport. To protect their packs and cargoes, merchants traveled in armed bands. Church and state each tried to do its share in making the roads and the seas safer. The church excommunicated pirates and highwaymen and invoked its Truce of God especially for the protection of travelers, pilgrims, and merchants. Treaties between nations began to include safe-conduct clauses for traders. England's Magna Charta guaranteed legal protection to them; and many cities, eager for the success of their annual fairs or their regular trade, granted them privileges and legal safeguards. Commercial needs led to the establishment of a postal service between important Italian towns in the twelfth century. Ancient Rome had established a postal service, but it was used for official business only. The twelfth-century commercial post transmitted private letters as well. By its means a letter could be carried at the rate of fifty miles or more a day. In the north postal service did not develop until the thirteenth century. Public transport service for heavy merchandise was provided. The coinage of gold, which had to be abandoned in Carolingian times because there was no gold in Gaul nor any use for gold coins in a feudal society, was now resumed. The gold florin, so called because coined in Florence, marks the high noon of the commercial renaissance. With the increasing complexity of commercial relations, more elaborate records became necessary, and so it came about that the Italians invented double-entry bookkeeping sometime in the twelfth century. As late as the eighteenth century American schoolmasters advertised in the newspapers lessons in bookkeeping "after the Italian method of double-entry." About the same time (1202), also, the Hindu-Arabic numerals were imported into Latin Europe, more precisely into Italy whence they followed the trade routes northward and, although it took four centuries, were adopted by the whole commercial world.

In northern Europe the Netherlands began as early as the time of Charlemagne to engage in maritime commerce. This was due not only to the great rivers, such as the Rhine and the Scheldt, but also to the closing of the Mediterranean by the Moslems. But these early commercial beginnings were destroyed by the Northmen, whose invasion of the country was made easier by the same wide and deep estuaries which had favored foreign trade. By the tenth century the Northmen had become settlers, themselves engaged in peaceful pursuits instead of destruction. They now became the link to join the economic resources of the Arab and the Byzantine empires with those of the north. It was the Scandinavian shipping that aroused the Flanders coast to economic activity. The existence, since Roman times, of an extensive woolen industry increased the commercial importance of the region. Its cloths and Frisian cloaks were famous throughout the Middle Ages. Bruges was the Venice of the north, the first city in the Netherlands to develop an overseas commerce. The same forces that raised Bruges to commercial importance developed Ghent, Ypres, and other cities of that region. The trade routes which converged upon the Low Countries came down the Rhine and followed the south shores of the Baltic. Through Lübeck passed the Russian trade which brought to the west the "wealth of Ormus and of Ind," and that city was the pivot of the Baltic Hanseatic or merchant league. By the tenth and eleventh centuries the commercial area of the Roman empire had been greatly extended, for not only the Mediterranean but also the Baltic and the North Seas were now commercial highways connecting the busy and populous towns that enlivened their shores. Back of this trading and transportation activity were the great wholesale merchants who handled wool and woolen cloths, silks, furs, spices, and other products. As the transactions increased some of the great merchants also became bankers supplying capital and credit to the smaller houses and the retail trade.

11. THE GILDS

The merchants and craftsmen of the towns were usually organized into gilds or associations with statutes, officers, and economic, and often also political, rights. They were established for the mutual protection of the members and the advancement of their interests. Some gilds were of the nature of labor unions and cooperative societies combined, while the greater gilds more nearly resembled manufacturers' associations and chambers of commerce. The gilds are of importance in social and educational history because they carried on the medieval system of vocational education and gave the middle class an opportunity for education in liberty and democratic processes.

Gilds varied in scope. They might be simple, comprising only those engaged in a single trade or craft; or complex, including several occupations. They varied in organization, some being democratic, others oligarchic or capitalistic in structure. Furthermore, democratic gilds not infrequently passed into the control of a special class which exploited the less privileged members. Gilds which treated their employees as little better than serfs were not infrequent. Evidently the word gild stands for diverse social phenomena. Most students hear only of the small-industry gilds, the friendly personal relations between apprentice and teacher-employer, and the room at the top for every apprentice to become a master workman. The facts were often otherwise.

Craftsmen under the gild system passed through three stages. Just as in chivalry one became first a page, then a squire, and finally a knight, so under the gilds the young worker became an apprentice, a journeyman, and, finally, a master workman. But the sequence was not inevitable. The gilds were or tended to become monopolies in their special crafts and often controlled the number of workers in each class. The number of apprentices which any master might take was limited by the gild. The usual number was two or three, but sons of the master were not counted and new apprentices might be taken on before the term of those about to finish was quite completed. This was to prevent the difficulty that a master might be left at any one time with only inexperienced helpers. Some apprentices were never allowed to become master workmen, while the son of a master workman might be promoted to his father's rank without passing through the usual course of training.

Children were apprenticed at an early age. The period of apprenticeship was from two to ten years long, but seven years was perhaps the most frequent term. Both the age at entrance and the length of the training varied from trade to trade and in relation to other circumstances. Only master workmen of good character were allowed to take apprentices. At the beginning there was usually a short period of probation for the young worker. This was followed by a contract, called an indenture, between the master and the father of the boy. The master agreed to teach his trade, to supply food, clothes, and lodging, and to stand *in loco parentis* to the apprentice. In the usual small crafts the boy became a member of the master's household and ate at the family table. The apprentice in his turn covenanted to be obedient and dutiful, not to marry during the term of his training, to keep the secrets of the craft, and to work faithfully and conduct himself honorably. The indenture was executed before witnesses by a notary and sealed with the proper oaths. Abuses such as running away from the master or excessive cruelty to the boy were to be laid before the gild officers. When the apprenticeship was completed the master was required to give the young man a certificate of the fact. He could then continue to work for his old master for wages or go to seek other employment, whence he was then called a journeyman.

The gilds were the channels of vocational education; and apprenticeship was the means for providing an adequate succession of skilled workers. The workshop was the technical school of the Middle Ages. At a time when all the common articles of daily use were made by hand, skill in a craft gave the journeyman the means to earn an adequate living, establish a family, perform his civic duties, and attain a satisfying life among his equals. Literary education was not included in apprenticeship; but late medieval and modern indentures provided that the boy must be given the opportunity to learn the rudiments of reading, writing, and arithmetic. These were acquired in evening sessions in private or town schools.

Gilds also established schools. These were of two kinds, literary, that is, Latin secondary schools, and vocational or apprenticeship schools. The former of these are commonly known as the medieval gild schools. They were numerous. Of thirty-three English gilds which A. F. Leach studied, twenty-eight at some time maintained gild schools. Such schools belonged to the prevailing type of Latin grammar schools. The primary purpose in establishing them was philanthropic. It must be repeated, for students constantly misunderstand the facts, that these did not teach trades but gave a literary education to boys who later might go to a university and prepare for a profession. So a gild of Worcester, England, "time out of mind," maintained a school which at the Reformation had "above the number of a hundred scholars." Famous London gild schools were the Stationers School, the Mercers School, and, one of the most distinguished of all, the Merchant Taylors School.

Gilds also, especially in Germany, established continuation apprenticeship schools. Apprenticeship in the workshop was replaced by regular trade teaching in schools of different types. In the city of Munich the associations of artisans maintained numerous technical schools until about 1900 when Kerschensteiner incorporated them into the public school system. So in Berlin the merchants' association maintained six continuation schools for the commercial education of apprentices, and the tailors' association had a school taught by master tailors, cutters, and designers from the large tailoring establishments.

One other highly important but incidental educational function of the gilds resulted from the opportunities they gave for the political education of their members. Especially in the free towns or communes the gilds joined forces with all the discontented classes against the rich and powerful. Each gild formed a corporation whose members, as in a little republic, deliberated and voted and received a practical civic education. There were struggles between groups within a gild, between two or more gilds, and between the gilds and the city itself. The medieval gilds frequently were units for the holding of elections, for the supply of soldiers, and for taxation purposes. A major question always concerned the apportionment of the privileges and responsibilities of these separate republics. Under such conditions oratorical ability, political skill, and leadership were developed.

Unfortunately in the large commercial cities the greater gilds developed into oligarchies. In the small crafts the social distances between master, journeyman, and apprentice were not great. But in the great commercial and industrial associations the inequalities became staggering. The masters, bound together to support their interests, were rich and powerful capitalists separated from their workers by an impassable gulf. The labor difficulties of modern automobile or mining industries merely repeat, hardly in a more intense degree, the struggles that developed in the woolen industry in the Middle Ages. Florence, where the Arte di Calimala controlled the woolen industry, furnishes a striking example of such struggles between the haves and the have-nots. The Arte di Calimala had twenty or thirty thousand "members," but of these the great mass had no powers whatever. Even the gilds of the Middle Ages had learned the device of farming out their work to unorganized and unorganizable domestic laborers, compelled by circumstances to work for mere subsistence under sweatshop conditions. With the profits from such industry the monopolistic gilds then endowed schools and hospitals for those who belonged to or would graduate into the upper classes.

The gilds were established for the benefit of their members but they also rendered many public services. Some of these were educational, some economic, and others benevolent. With the rise of powerful national states the gilds came under state regulation, and with the increasing specialization and mechanization of industry apprenticeship declined in importance.

(2

12. NEW SCHOOLS IN THE CITIES

The urban schools which arose in the later Middle Ages were of greater importance than the people could realize at that time. They were of two types, both closely connected with the secular life of the city and less closely with the church than the cathedral and monastic school. There we find the first slight beginnings of a secularism which was to supplant the church as the chief educational agency. This change required hundreds of years, but from 1300 if not before it was under way.

One type of new school was the city or gild Latin school; and the second was the city or private writing and reckoning school. The city Latin school was controlled, not by churchmen but by the civil authorities, usually the town council, and its students were the sons of merchants and other well-to-do burghers. No extended description of the city Latin school is needed because, except in personnel and administration, it differed little from the Latin schools of the church.

Documents from Cologne show the existence of city Latin schools in 1234. Breslau in 1267 asked leave to build a city school so placed that the children would not need to cross unsafe bridges. Hamburg by appeal to the Pope against the local clergy secured permission to establish a city school, a proposal which the cathedral authorities had fought for eight years.

The struggle at Hamburg was not unusual. Local church authorities opposed the city schools as an invasion of their privileges. The cathedral might be willing to have city schools teach the elements of Latin and some writing and arithmetic but would reserve to itself the right to teach the more advanced subjects such as rhetoric. Although there was no question of faith or morals involved in this warfare, the church used its usual weapon, excommunication; the towns retaliated with court actions; and when a conflict was finally adjusted the city had often won at least a part of its contention. Such cases were sometimes important enough to be carried to the head of the church. In such instances, the Pope was likely to decide in favor of the town and its schools and against the interests of the local clergy. When the patricians or the town council established Latin schools they also usually conferred upon the teachers a monopoly of secondary education. The fight here was chiefly against private elementary schools whose teachers taught Latin to the disadvantage of the recognized teachers.

The writing school was even freer from church control. It taught reading, writing, business arithmetic, and bookkeeping to the sons of artisans and businessmen and sometimes to their daughters. Private, secular schools of the *ars dictaminis*, the art of writing legal papers, existed in the large towns of Italy as early as the tenth century. In the early centuries of our period, business letters and records were still in Latin, but in the thirteenth century, with the development of the vernacular languages, these commercial schools turned to the common language as their medium. The three chief adjectives which are to be applied to the city schools of the later Middle Ages are, therefore, public, middle class, and practical; but we must add that they only gradually tended to acquire these qualities. In the thirteenth century beginnings were made, but only beginnings.

Many of the private schools were commercial and vernacular schools of handwriting and arithmetic. Others were still more elementary and taught only the alphabet, spelling, and reading. It is to these types that we must look for the beginnings of the elementary or common schools. The church was but little interested in them because they seemed to be vocational and related to business rather than to religion. Their early history is obscure and must always remain so because they seemed too insignificant for careful record.

The vernacular schools, although they multiplied rapidly, were often humble enough. They were often called "reading and writing" or "writing and reckoning" schools. That many of them existed in England, Scotland, Germany, and elsewhere long before the Reformation is clear. They grew rapidly about 1350 or 1400, which is about a century later than the beginnings of the city Latin schools. They became almost general by 1500; a Mainz leaflet of 1498 asserted that "everybody now wants to read and write." It has been estimated that the city of Nuremberg in the sixteenth century had about fifty reckoning, that is, arithmetic, masters; and they formed a gild. This is an early example of a teachers' association.

Most of our information about these early vernacular schools comes from records of disputes and lawsuits. Lübeck had several German schools about 1400, and in 1418 a formal agreement was drawn up between the city and the scholasticus. The latter consented to the maintenance of four German writing schools on condition that one-third of the fees received should be turned over to the cathedral. A similar solution was reached at Brunswick (1420). It was agreed that the writing masters should confine themselves to the common language, teaching no Latin at all. That the contract had to be reaffirmed later in the century is evidence that it was not always observed.

On the other hand, Latin schools often gave elementary instruction. This was true of the burg schools of Scotland which go back to the thirteenth or even the twelfth century, as in Stirling and Perth. In Amsterdam the city Latin schools had to fight against encroachment by the writing masters. Hamburg, about 1400, limited the number and attendance of common schools to protect the interests of the Latin schools. But all this legislation was the effort to sweep out the ocean with a broom. At the end of another century (1500) the Hamburg scholasticus complained that "new schools are almost daily opened by old women and other persons." This was changing the words but not the spirit of the Mainz leaflet quoted above; and it shows again that many unauthorized schools were being opened everywhere, in homes, tailors' shops, and other rooms where indoor occupations could be combined with elementary teaching. The poor were seeking education for their children. The closing Middle Ages saw vigorous competition in school-founding.

The writing and reckoning schools taught arithmetic and bookkeeping and were the chief agencies to introduce the Hindu-Arabic numerals and the new methods of computation into the West. The rise of commerce and cities both changed and increased the educational demands of the times. Bookkeeping, commercial arithmetic, the need for commercial and manorial records, the recording of city and gild minutes and accounts all gave employment to a growing class of men who made their living as writers, accountants, and secretaries. Private correspondence also increased, and men made a business of writing letters for those who could not write their own. Setting up their desks in the open at a busy corner, they plied their trade. These were often teachers, who earned an extra penny in this way. A vernacular literature was growing up rapidly and with it grew the general desire to learn to read. The wealthy and influential people of the towns desired a regular education in Latin and the Seven Liberal Arts for their sons. The common people demanded vernacular schooling and a ready acquaintance with figures and the pen. With the growth of the cities, both classes of schools multiplied. Meanwhile knowledge also advanced rapidly. In the last three centuries of the Middle Ages the population of Europe may have doubled but the available knowledge multiplied many times— knowledge of the sciences and medicine, of law, philosophy, and theology. It was this great increase in knowledge which led to the foundation of the universities. The schools, which had served the West as the main carriers of its rather meager learning, now became inadequate.

13. THE RISE OF UNIVERSITIES

The universities arose in cities. For purely physical as well as intellectual reasons an institution which enrolled hundreds or thousands of students could exist in the larger centers only. They arose when the spirit of inquiry, the need for a trained professional class, and a great accumulation of ancient knowledge developed. The earliest arose in Bologna, where legal studies had been carried on for several hundred years, and in Paris, where theological questions had begun to occupy some of the best minds. In Bologna, at the crossroads of northern Italy, Irnerius and other famed teachers of the Roman law had been interpreting the civil rights of the Italian cities. These claims for freedom from domination by the empire were based upon ancient Roman charters. In Paris the cathedral school of Notre Dame had become a leading center of higher education through the teaching and controversies of William of Champeaux (1070–1121), Abelard (1079–1142), and other theological scholars. Abelard's *Sic et Non* was a new form of textbook. It dealt with a large number of theological questions. After each one, he presented arguments on both sides, drawn from the Bible and the Church Fathers, without stating any conclusions. He declared that it was his aim to stimulate thinking, "for through doubt we are led to inquire, and through inquiry we discover truth." Other writers soon prepared other textbooks which employed this disputational method. The pursuit of learning directly implied freedom to think and to report the results obtained by thinking; and the struggle for this academic freedom from external control—which still continues and will continue—was another of the main causes of the rise of organized bodies of independent scholars, that is, of universities.

The universities of the Middle Ages, like those of the present, were incorporated schools and what distinguished them from other lower or advanced schools was the fact of legal incorporation. They were corporate bodies of teachers and students, equipped with a charter, seal, bylaws, and officers. Other schools were directly controlled by church, city, gild, or private founder but the universities were themselves legal persons, free from external control. Being in the same world, they were, naturally, not free from external influences, and both the church and the empire as well as kings, bishops, and the Dominican and Franciscan Orders found ways of shaping their policies and of using them for other purposes than the pursuit and promulgation of knowledge and truth.

The earliest universities developed in the twelfth century. The Universities of Bologna, Paris, and Oxford are examples. These all grew out of previously existing schools, Paris from the cathedral school of Notre Dame, Oxford from a similar institution, and Bologna from law schools which, as noted, had existed many years before the university was chartered. These, the oldest universities, have had a fairly continuous history of more than seven centuries. Salerno, a city below Naples that was noted for its medicinal waters, attracted students and teachers of medicine early, but as these were never incorporated, Salerno cannot be counted as a university. Later it became the seat of the medical faculty of the University of Naples. The other three are often called the mother universities because they provided the models for later incorporations. Bologna, which was controlled mainly by the students, was imitated in the southern countries. The charter of Paris, which placed the governing power in the faculties, was most influential in the north. The earliest universities were shaped by circumstances and evolved gradually; but most of the later ones were founded outright and equipped with a charter from the beginning.

About eighty universities were open by 1500. The movement spread outward by a process of diffusion and imitation from the original centers. Only Bologna, Paris, and Oxford can be definitely assigned to the twelfth century, but Montpellier in France and Cambridge in England belong to the early thirteenth if not to the twelfth. Besides these two, the thirteenth century saw the establishment of one or several in Italy, in Spain, and in southern France. The movement, therefore, spread first in the Mediterranean area. In the fourteenth century it advanced to new locations in these countries and also into Germany, where the first university was established at Prague in 1347. This was a partly Czech foundation; but as the Czechs did not get along well with the Germans they later separated. The university of Vienna was opened in 1365, the Polish university of Cracow in 1364, and the one at Buda in Hungary in 1389. Altogether about twenty new universities were opened in the fourteenth century, the largest numbers in Italy and France. By 1400, Italy was fairly well supplied with universities, but in France four or five new ones were added in the fifteenth century. In that century, also, the movement advanced into Scotland. And so it continued until, if we include the new foundations of the twentieth century, it had extended around the world. Thus the Middle Ages created an educational institution which, though greatly modified and even transformed, is considered more useful and necessary today than ever before.

The university charters gave grants of privileges or rights to the institutions and their students. The most important of the rights granted to the universities was the right of self-government. This permitted them to control their own organization and their members. Thereby students came to be subject to the law of the university instead of the law of the land. The universities had the right to arrest offenders, to try them in the university court, and to discipline them by fine or imprisonment; and the city authorities were required to hand students over to the university for these purposes. The students were eager to claim this right because they were frequently foreigners in the university city, and expected more considerate treatment from their own group than from municipal courts. In the heated state of public opinion, which resulted from the "town and gown" riots of a turbulent age, this was a matter of importance.

Universities also had the right to suspend lectures and to go on strike against the city when the rents or prices of food were raised or when students were assaulted or even, as sometimes happened, killed by citizens. Since a university was a valuable financial asset to a city a strike, called *cessatio*, often secured redress of grievances; but if it did not, the university as a whole or in part might move to another city. Many of the newer universities were founded as a result of such a migration. Since the early universities owned no real estate, being conducted in rented buildings, and had no university library or laboratories, it was easy for them to move. They often resorted to the stoppage of the lectures and the threat to migrate for apparently trivial reasons.

In the third place, the universities had the right to examine and to license their own professors and to control their own degrees. This implied the right to determine the studies and exercises which should qualify students for degrees, one of the most essential functions of these institutions.

The faculties of Arts, Law, Medicine, and Theology formed the full complement of the usual medieval university. Some universities lacked one or more of these and some had two law faculties, one for canon and another for civil law. After the Reformation some also had two theological faculties, one Protestant and the other Catholic. The universities were, therefore, professional schools although the Arts faculty in earlier centuries gave preparatory work, mainly in logic but also in others of the Seven Liberal Arts. The dean was the head of each faculty and the rector was the head of the university. The rector's term of office was usually for one year only, and he had no such extensive powers as we associate with the office of university president in the United States. In some universities his main duty was to deliver an inaugural address, in others, to preside at convocations or meetings of a university senate, and in still others he exercised some administrative functions. The students were organized into "nations" according to the regions from which they had come. At the head of each nation stood an elected councillor who represented the interests of this body and its members.

All instruction, all exercises, and all books were in Latin. The main exercises were of three kinds: the lecture, the repetition, and the disputation. Lectures themselves were of two kinds: formal and cursory. In the earlier period of university development the university hall was unheated and had practically no furniture, although the professor perhaps always had a dais and reading desk or lectern, for lecture meant reading. The students sat on bundles of straw and, in writing with their quill pens, they supported their parchments on their knees.

In the formal lecture, the professor read the text slowly and the students took it down word for word. In southern universities the lecturer was fined for reading too fast or too slow or for skipping passages. After a passage had been completed the professor added his comments and interpretation. When books became accessible students could buy the basic texts or rent them from university stationers. Thereafter, the formal lecture was outlawed, and the cursory lecture was substituted. This consisted of a free rendering and interpretation of the text. But throughout the medieval period, university instruction was based upon authors such as Galen in medicine or the *Institutes of Justinian* in civil law. The systematic presentation of a subject or field of study developed only in modern times.

The repetition consisted of a rehearsal and discussion of the matter of a lecture and was usually led by advanced students, to each of whom was assigned a small group of students each equipped with lecture notes. The disputation was a debate between two or more students pitted against each other and presided over by a professor. They argued a stated thesis or point of doctrine; and the disputation was used both as a practice and teaching exercise and as an examination for the coveted degree.

There were three stages in the progress toward a degree. The student was at first a freshman, although this is a modern term, or *bejaunus*, meaning yellow-beak, then he became a *baccalaureus*, and finally a master or doctor. The last two terms were equivalent, and each means qualified to teach. The English universities later took over the term master while the continental universities appropriated the term doctor. To this was added the name of the faculty in which the degree was taken as in the phrase Doctor of Medicine, or of Law. The arts faculty was eventually placed upon an equality with the others and in Germany and elsewhere the name was changed to philosophy, whence the degree of Doctor of Philosophy. Still later the term philosophy in this connection came to include all the non-professional subjects so that now we have Doctors of Philosophy who have specialized in various fields such as mathematics, history, or languages. In the medieval universities, most of the students did not remain to complete the six to nine years of study which were required before the doctor's or master's degree could be attained.

The students at first lived in rented rooms and later in halls, often under university supervision. When instructors were assigned to such a student-hall, when an organization was effected, and when some of the elementary instruction was also given in the hall, this constituent part of a university was called a college. The English universities of Oxford and Cambridge have retained this collegiate form and exhibit most fully the medieval arrangement. These English colleges bear something of the same relation to their controlling university as the states of the Union bear to the government of the United States. They have their own personnel, organization, and internal regulations and are constituent parts of their university.

The medieval students were young, often arriving at the age of twelve or thirteen; hence the need for regulation and supervision. They were foreigners in a strange land. Their rooms were without warmth, the streets were unlighted, and the police were not numerous. There were no or few legitimate means of amusement. From the records one gathers that life in the medieval university was often irregular and sometimes incredibly violent.

The university was the outcome of a genuinely popular movement. The institutions arose and grew because they met a popular demand. They were fostered by pope, emperor, and kings partly because these powers expected to benefit from their work; but they prospered because the people felt the need for them and because they offered opportunities that had not been available before. The numbers of their students were not as large as the medieval chroniclers report. Perhaps no medieval university, not even Paris or Bologna, ever had more than six thousand students at any time, and the smaller institutions counted their numbers in hundreds rather than thousands.

The instruction was bookish and authoritarian. We can no longer fully realize or understand the subservience of the human mind which was shown in the Middle Ages to the authority of Aristotle, or Galen, or the theological textbooks of the university. Lectures were not contributions to knowledge or systematic treatments of a field, but rather commentaries upon a book and explanations of its statements, or efforts to harmonize conflicting views. In the disputation such opposing positions were set over against each other and some originality was demanded; but even in this exercise there was often an accepted conclusion which, it was assumed, would emerge triumphantly from the debate. But although orthodoxy in medicine, law, and theology was favored, heresy gradually increased as the arguments were sharpened and new knowledge accumulated until in the sixteenth century Peter Ramus at the University of Paris argued that all that Aristotle had taught is false.

The universities prepared learned men for the professions, stimulated writing in the great fields of human interest and need, developed a growing band of scholars, and aided in the appeal from force to reason. They prepared many of the early leaders of the Renaissance. The Studium or university took its place beside those other great medieval institutions, the Imperium or empire and the Sacerdotium or church, and helped to bring into being the modern world.

After Charlemagne, the Viking invasions disturbed the civilization of Europe, piracy interfered with seaborne commerce, and the feudal system reached its height. The Moslems developed an advanced civilization in Spain and Sicily.

They brought Greek, Hindu, and Persian learning to the West, and much of this was translated and incorporated into the Latin culture. Scientific, medical, and mathematical knowledge and the works of Aristotle became available and were given an important place in university instruction. The logical and scientific writings of Aristotle profoundly influenced Christian thought after 1300. The effect of Aristotle upon theology in the later Middle Ages formed an interesting parallel with the influence of the Neo-Platonists upon Christian thought in the third and fourth centuries.

The crusades served to unite the West, increased its knowledge of the world, developed means of transport, and made Europe aware of a civilization that was more advanced than its own. When barons were long absent or failed to return, their serfs and villeins often escaped to the cities and joined the growing class of urban freemen. Each of these changes tended to stimulate commerce. Commerce promoted the growth of cities, capital, markets, and travel. A money economy displaced the old system of barter. Schools increased in numbers and became more diversified in nature. Bookkeeping became a new and important subject of study; and its pursuit implied skill in commercial arithmetic and handwriting. In the later centuries of the Middle Ages many schools taught the vernacular languages.

Chivalric education developed ideals of knightly honor, service, skill, and courtesy; and out of this grew the education of the prince, diplomat, and gentleman. Upper class education was long influenced by its aims and practice.

The gilds controlled apprenticeship, set standards of workmanship, conducted vocational education, and aided their members in sickness and old age. They also established many Latin schools. Before the end of the Middle Ages, capitalism and the new system of domestic manufacture had begun to break the gild monopoly of skilled industry.

Universities began to form themselves in the twelfth century. They were independent corporations of students and professors devoted to higher learning. Their most important privileges were the right of self-government, and of granting their degrees and selecting their teachers without outside interference. They educated new classes of professional servants of state and church, increased learning, multiplied books, and served as arbiters in disputed matters of government and religion. Their inability to free themselves from dependence upon authors, who were regarded as authorities, was their chief intellectual defect. Before the end of the Middle Ages, other authors, the literary masters of Greece and Rome, were again recovered in the Italian Renaissance. Gradually the full complement of ancient culture was restored; but, as we shall see in the next chapter, this was not only an age of restoration but also a creative period.

QUESTIONS

1. Show how this period illustrates the dependence of education upon civil order and stability.
2. On a map of the Eastern hemisphere trace the present extent of Moslem civilization.
3. Compare the influence of Greek culture upon ancient Rome with that influence as it was spread by the Moslems in the Middle Ages. Consider extent, methods, and subject matter.

4. Why did the intellectual activity of the Moslems when they came face to face with ancient Greek culture take a turn so different from that of the Romans when they came into contact with the same materials?

5. The Moslem civilization of Spain reached its height in the ninth and tenth centuries but the Latin borrowing came later. Why?

6. Did any of the learning transmitted by the Moslems directly affect the lives of the common people? Consider also the broader topic, namely, the degree to which the learning of the Greeks, the Romans, the medieval schools affected the common people. Why?

7. How was the recovery of Aristotle's works on logic related to the systems of thought among the Moslems and the Christians?

8. How were the intellectual, religious, and administrative reforms of Cluny related to each other?

9. How did the crusades affect the intellectual and political condition of Europe?

10. How did chivalric education differ from that of the schools of the same period? Consider the aims of the people concerned, the means used, and other factors. Consider the statement that it was a form of "activity education."

11. Show that the growth of commerce developed a European in place of a Mediterranean civilization; and compare the influences upon education of the ancient cities and late medieval cities.

12. Compare apprenticeship with chivalric and school education. What was the nature of the gild schools?

13. Why were the local clergy less favorable than the Papacy to the extension of education in the cities?

14. Do you agree with the judgment that the university was the greatest educational achievement of the Middle Ages? Why, or why not?

FOR FURTHER READING AND STUDY

The monastic and cathedral schools remained and became more important in the later Middle Ages and to these the universities were added. The rise of universities in the twelfth century was made possible by the recovery of ancient learning and by the increase of commerce, cities, gilds, and wealth. The crusades were followed by the development of chivalry, which had a profound influence upon later education. Many of the following books will aid the student to understand the "renaissance of the twelfth century" and the following centuries which led to the Italian "revival of learning."

Ashley, William J., *Introduction to English Economic History and Theory*, New York, G. P. Putnam's Sons, 1894, 2 vols.

Baldwin, Charles S., *Medieval Rhetoric and Poetic*, New York, The Macmillan Company, 1928, 321 pp.

Bland, C. C. Swinton, *The Autobiography of Guibert, Abbot of Nogent-sous-Coucy*, New York, E. P. Dutton & Company, 1925, 224 pp. Guibert de Nogent lived 1053–1124.

Compayre, Gabriel, *Abelard and the Origin and Early History of Universities*, New York, Charles Scribner's Sons, 1893, 315 pp.

Cornish, F. W., *Chivalry*, New York, The Macmillan Company, 1901, 369 pp.

Davis, William Stearns, *God Wills It. A Tale of the First Crusade*, New York, The Macmillan Company, 1901. A novel. *Life on a Medieval Barony . . . in the Thirteenth Century*, New York, Harper & Brothers, 1923, 414 pp.

Gautier, Leon, *Chivalry*, London, George Routledge & Sons, Ltd., 1891, 499 pp.

Gibbins, H. deB., *The History of Commerce in Europe*, London, Macmillan & Company, Ltd., 1909, 233 pp.

Giry, A., and A. Reville, *Emancipation of Medieval Towns*, New York, Henry Holt and Company, 1907, 69 pp. A translation of a chapter from the general history of Lavisse and Rambaud.

Haskins, Charles Homer, *The Normans in European History*, Boston, Houghton Mifflin Company, 1915, 258 pp.; *Studies in Medieval Culture*, New York, Oxford, Clarendon Press, 1929, 295 pp.; *The Renaissance of the Twelfth Century*, Cambridge, Harvard University Press, 1933, 437 pp.; *The Rise of Universities*, New York, Henry Holt and Company, 1923, 134 pp. The last of these contains some interesting student letters.

Hitti, Philip K., *History of the Arabs*, London, Macmillan & Company, Ltd., 1937, 767 pp. A careful history of the Arabs from pre-Islamic times giving attention to language, literature, the sciences and arts, architecture, and medicine.

Irsay, Stephen d', *Histoire des universités françaises et étrangères*, Paris, A. Picard, 1933, 1935, 2 vols.

Krey, August A., *The First Crusade, the Accounts of Eye-Witnesses and Participants*, Princeton, N. J., Princeton University Press, 1921, 299 pp.

Leach, Arthur Francis, *Educational Charters and Documents*, 598–1909, Cambridge, University Press, 1911, 582 pp.; *The Schools of Medieval England*, New York, The Macmillan Company, 1915, 349 pp.

Liebeschütz, Hans, *Medieval Humanism in the Life and Writings of John of Salisbury*, London, The Warburg Institute, University of London, 1950, 126 pp.

Luchaire, Achille, *Social France in the Time of Philip Augustus*. Translated by E. B. Krehbiel, New York, Peter Smith, 1929, 441 pp. Intimate social history including school and university life.

MacCabe, Joseph, *Peter Abelard*, New York, G. P. Putnam's Sons, 1901, 402 pp.

Madan, Falconer, *Books in Manuscript*, New York, Empire State Book Co., 1927, 203 pp. First published in 1893.

Norton, Arthur O., *Readings in the History of Education. Medieval Universities*, Cambridge, Harvard University Press, 1909, 155 pp.

Painter, Sidney, *French Chivalry; Chivalric Ideas and Practices in Medieval France*, Baltimore, The Johns Hopkins Press, 1940, 179 pp.

Paulsen, Friedrich, *Geschichte des gelehrten Unterrichts*, Leipzig, Veit and Company, 1919–1921, 2 vols.

Pirenne, Henri, *Medieval Cities; Their Origins and the Revival of Trade*. Translated by Frank D. Halsey, Princeton, N. J., Princeton University Press, 1925, 249 pp.; *A History of Europe from the Invasions to the XVI Century*. Translated by Bernard Miall, New York, W. W. Norton & Company, Inc., 1939, 624 pp.

Rait, Robert S., *Life in the Medieval University*, Cambridge, University Press, 1912, 164 pp.

Rashdall, Hastings, *The Universities of Europe in the Middle Ages*. Revised by F. M. Powicke and A. B. Embden, New York, Oxford, Clarenden Press, 1936, 3 vols. The best authority in English on its subject.

Renard, Georges, *Guilds in the Middle Ages*. Translated by Dorothy Terry, with introduction by G. D. H. Cole, London, George Bell & Sons, Ltd., 1919, 139 pp.

Sandys, John Edwin, *A History of Classical Scholarship*, Cambridge, University Press, 1903–1908, 3 vols. Covers ancient, medieval, and modern times.

Sarton, George, *Introduction to the History of Science*, Baltimore, The Williams & Wilkins Company, 1927, 1931, 3 vols., Carnegie Institution of Washington, Publication No. 376. Covers ancient and medieval periods, with emphasis upon Arabic science. A reference work.

Thomas, Bertram, *The Arabs. The Life Story of a People*, New York, Doubleday, Doran & Company, Inc., 1937, 364 pp. A readable, popular work.

Thorndike, Lynn, *A History of Magic and Experimental Science During the First Thirteen Centuries of our Era*, New York, The Macmillan Company, 1923–1941, 6 vols.; *History of Medieval Europe*, Boston, Houghton Mifflin Company, 1928, 682 pp.

Watson, Foster, *English Grammar Schools to 1660*, Cambridge, University Press, 1908, 548 pp.

Westlake, Herbert F., *The Parish Gilds of Medieval England*, London, Society for Promoting Christian Knowledge, 1919, 242 pp.

6 THE RENAISSANCE IN ITALY

W E SHALL BEGIN WITH THE MEANING OF THE WORD RENAIS-
sance. Every age which, through the revival of an earlier
culture, develops new life and creative activity forms a renaissance. The
medical and physical sciences are today the centers of a great scientific
renaissance; the whole western world after the French Revolution experienced a renaissance of liberalism, humanitarianism, and democracy; but,
with those who wish to emphasize the continuity of human evolution, the
word is out of favor. These students point out that the Middle Ages were
not as dark, the transitions of history not as abrupt, and "the Renaissance"
not as glorious as they have been painted; but yet the word has its uses
and is not to be too lightly given up. And the desired continuity of history
may be secured by recognizing the large number of renaissance periods,
noting their interconnections, and tracing their causes. We shall, therefore, with C. H. Haskins, speak of the rapid progress after 1100 as "the
twelfth-century renaissance," which continued through the thirteenth century; and shall consider the development of northern Europe after 1500
as the northern renaissance. Between these two occurred the Italian Renaissance of the fourteenth and fifteenth centuries with its recovery of classical
humanism, which is our present topic.

The Italian Renaissance was more than the revival of ancient learning
and the recovery of the ideal of liberal education. Intimately related to
the revival of learning was the artistic revival and a great development
of civil and political life. Indeed it was more than a revival for, like every
true renaissance, it was a creative period. The artistic achievements between
Giotto and Tintoretto were accomplished by many painters, sculptors, and
architects, each great enough to mark an epoch. Their age was dominated
by the ideals of the fine arts quite as much as our time is controlled by
scientific concepts. Furniture and costume, war and religion, morality, and
politics were all judged by artistic standards. Symonds said: "From the
Pope upon St. Peter's chair to the clerks in the Florentine counting-house,

every Italian was a judge of art, and estimated all things in terms of their artistic qualities." But the wonder of their age is not their ability to judge and criticize but to produce. They solved difficult technical problems of perspective, coloring, and composition; but more than that, they had something of importance to say together with the genius to create an art-language capable of saying it effectively.

We owe to Italy also the fuller recovery of the two ancient literatures of Greece and Rome which is called the revival of learning; and that service to civilization was rendered in the fourteenth century, at the last possible moment because Constantinople, which had preserved the most important Greek manuscripts, was captured by the Turks in 1453. The Moslems of the Middle Ages had paid little attention to the literary and artistic work of Greece; and now, in the fourteenth century, the Italians were the only people immediately capable of understanding Greek poetry and philosophy. It was Italy in turn which roused the sleeping North. With the recovery of the classics we shall have to deal at some length, but we shall see that the recovery itself was a creative act. It was no mere physical discovery of dead books but a taking to heart and into the understanding of the thought and feelings of the ancients.

The period was marked not only by the recovery of old literatures but also the rise of a new one, the modern Italian. The first great modern classic was the epic of Dante. The prose and verse of Petrarch and Boccaccio as well as the development of the sonnet as a literary art form were further Italian contributions to the earliest great literature in a modern tongue.

The development of Italian literature was closely related to the growth of Italian political institutions. The unit was the city-state, recalling the similar organizations of ancient Greece. Each of these political entities was composed of several classes, the nobility, merchants, mercenary soldiers, and workingmen organized into powerful gilds. The population was torn with the strife and dissension of the classes; and between the several cities there existed competition and even hatred rather than cooperation. Each of these states, with their concentration of wealth, extensive public works, and oligarchical or democratic government, was able to reward its abler citizens with positions of honor, power, or wealth; and the intense civic development of the times is merely the other side of an equally intense individualism. The Italian city-state was a cause of the decline of those medieval institutions, the universal church, the empire, and feudalism; and a money economy was becoming general. One evidence of this latter change was the coinage of the states, the gold florin of the great financial center, Florence, being a prime example. Meanwhile the use of gunpowder, the mariner's compass, paper and printing, the march of geographical discovery were other features of the Italian Renaissance. If the age must have a set beginning and ending we may take the birth of Petrarch in 1304 and the sack of Rome in 1527 as these dates. At the birth of Petrarch, Dante still had seventeen years to live; and in any case most of the period falls within the conventional period of the Middle Ages. When Charles V secured control of the peninsula (1527), the Renaissance in Italy was over, the Reformation in Germany was in full career, and Catholicism was preparing the Counter-Reformation.

1. CLASSICAL HUMANISM

The recovery of classical literature and the humanistic movement which together make up the "revival of learning" are, for the student of education, the most important phases of the Renaissance. Humanism combined the aims of self-realization and self-expression with the older ideal of a liberal education. Aristotle's concept of a liberal education as the culture of citizens, free men in a free state, again acquired the secular connotation that it had in Greek times; but also it was often given an individualistic, even an egoistic turn. As a reaction against medieval feeling, humanism stressed the interests of a worldly, civilized life in an earthly city in contrast with preparation for a world to come. On the other hand, humanism generally accepted Greek and even Christian ethics and was therefore opposed to all radical naturalism. But actually the philosophies of the Italian humanists were so divergent that no simple classification would do justice to all their views.

In education, humanism was the study of great human achievements and thoughts as these are preserved in the greatest writers. Such study is necessarily historical, for we can no longer interview Pericles or Plato and we can speak of them with assurance only if we know them as characters in their times. The works of man are of the most various kinds, but most of them are anonymous and can be studied only as they have affected the material world, tradition, or the written record. The humanists studied the record chiefly, although the beginnings of classical archaeology fall within the Italian Renaissance. Books, however, contain more than information; they offer inspiration and guidance also. As DeQuincey taught, there is a literature of knowledge but there is also the literature of power. It was the latter, the drama, epic, oratory, philosophy, in general the great authors who are notable for form and expression as well as content which formed the humanistic curriculum. The matters treated by these writers are chiefly human life and values; hence the term humanism is appropriate to such studies.

The values which were stressed most in the Italian Renaissance were aesthetic, ethical, and political: the interest in beauty and the aesthetic experience; and the interest in conduct and political life. In both respects the Italians of the fourteenth century believed that they could learn from the ancients, and there were at that time no other literatures so rich in beauty, so freighted with meaning, and so competent to give guidance as the Greek and Roman. In addition, the Roman literature was the product of their own ancestors on their own soil, and it therefore appealed powerfully to their patriotic feeling. They gradually discovered, also, that the Roman writers had been inspired and taught by the Greeks and that they could be fully understood only by those who were acquainted with the Greek models.

Those studies are humanistic which present, analyze, and criticize human thought and conduct. History, literature, philosophy, and social anthropology are leading humanistic studies. The writings of the Greeks and Romans in these and cognate fields are sometimes called the ancient or classical humanities; and comparable writings, in modern tongues, may be called modern humanities. Whether ancient or modern, humanism emphasizes man, not God or nature but man, as a politically, ethically, and aesthetically free being. Human freedom is one of the postulates of humanism; and the Renaissance demand for individual freedom is of the essence of the new education. The humanist education of that age was not professional like that of the medieval universities. The humanists contrasted their own general, liberal, and preprofessional culture with all that was technical, narrowly practical, and vocational. This contrast is still accepted by many, who urge that a balanced education must give due attention both to the purposes of life and the means of living, both to the humanistic and the technical needs of the student.

2. THE LATIN LANGUAGE

At the Renaissance the Latin was still a living language, in constant use by the church, in the professions, and in the schools. Just because it had been in continuous use for many centuries it was no longer the Latin of the Romans. Quintilian, who lived until about A.D. 100, is sometimes called the last of the classical writers. In this long stretch of time the Christian church had introduced new ideas and a new vocabulary, and great changes had taken place even in the structure and the idioms of the language. Medieval Latin in itself may have been no worse than classical Latin but it was different. In one respect, the history of medieval Latin had been unfortunate; it frequently had to grow in a foreign soil. It developed largely among a non-Latin and a barbarous people who spoke Teutonic or Slavic dialects and who learned Latin only at school. Because they frequently did not really know what the accepted Latin forms were the language was corrupted through the ignorance of its users.

The Italian humanists, having fallen in love with the works of the great Roman authors, especially Cicero, readily discovered the difference between contemporary and classical Latin. They hastily jumped to the conclusion that Ciceronian speech should be made the standard for their own day, and like schoolboys went about trying to find mistakes in the letters and books of the dignitaries of their time; and they found them. "Ignoramus! blockhead!" they shouted, just as though Europe had not changed since the time of Cicero. They set up an inappropriate language standard for literature and the schools; and it was, in part, their pedantic imitation that killed the Latin language. But its demise was hastened by the growth of the modern tongues which had been reduced to writing and gradually displaced the ancient even in books for scholars. Yet the Latin lived on for a long time. Secondary schools and universities were conducted in classical Latin, and Latin textbooks were used until about 1700, or even later; and the Catholic church, for some purposes, uses it today. Schools and universities, of course, still teach Latin and Greek, but they no longer generally use either as the language of instruction.

3. WHY THE RENAISSANCE BEGAN IN ITALY

The earlier view that the Italian Renaissance was a sudden upheaval and revolt against the Middle Ages is now discredited. It occurred in the later Middle Ages because the earlier had prepared the way for it. The Renaissance is a good example of historical continuity, although the people who lived at that time thought they were creating a fundamental break with tradition. Even in the Middle Ages, the idea of a revival or renaissance was common; but what men looked for was a religious revival. The monastic reformers, especially Francis of Assisi, are examples. With the religious hopes arose also visions of the rise of Italy and the reestablishment of the Roman empire. Dante, in his de Monarchia, following the argument of Thomas Aquinas, proposed a world empire. In 1347, Rienzi (1313-1354), the orator and tribune, believed himself to have reopened a new and glorious period of Roman supremacy. The papacy had deserted Rome for Avignon on the banks of the Rhone. Rienzi restored the republic, revived the self-government of the city, and invited all Italy to aid in establishing a united nation. This political scheme was based upon archaeology and the traditions and laws of antiquity. Rienzi failed tragically, but his ideas lived on and were adopted by Petrarch, the greatest writer then living. Ideas of a revival and rebirth were therefore not new; and certain features of the Renaissance can certainly be traced from the twelfth century onward. Italy was the focal point. Because of her location, Italy had long been the bridge between the East and the West over which trade and travel passed in either direction. It was her location which had enabled Italy to control the whole Mediterranean area during imperial times. Because of this, and because Italy had been the seat of the Roman empire, it was practically inevitable that the revival of the ancient civilization should first take place there. There were the ancient sites and monuments, the names, the traditions of past grandeur, there the Italian language furnished access by easy stages to the Latin from which it was derived, there the Roman law was still a living institution. The humanists were the first classical archaeologists. The popes and princes of Italy were the first collectors of ancient sculptures. And the artists studied the antique for inspiration for their own creations. Insofar as the Renaissance was a Latin revival, it was clearly inevitable that it should begin in Italy. And until 1396 the revival was almost wholly Latin. Neither Petrarch nor Boccaccio knew much Greek, and Petrarch at least, just because he was one of the most highly cultivated men of his time, felt this as a serious defect. Again the revival took place in Italy because of her centers of wealth and taste and her active public and patriotic spirit. The private and public means for gratifying taste in art and learning were at hand. Wealthy individuals, cities, despots, and the church established libraries, galleries, and schools and maintained collectors, copyists, scholars, and teachers.

4. THE SPIRIT OF THE RENAISSANCE

The first modern man, a new psychological phenomenon, is often said to have appeared in the Renaissance. Instead of the humble and penitent member of a class or an order, we see a self-conscious and self-sufficient individual seeking power and fame through art, learning, war, and even crime. George Eliot in *Romola* depicts such a one in the head of the Bardi family, who demands an eternity of fame as a scholar and collector of books.

The humanists frequently lived by the patronage of the great, and they often reflected the egotism and arrogance which they caught from their sponsors. From their pedestals they looked down upon the vulgar, who knew not Cicero and who spoke only the lowly vernacular. Thus Petrarch said: "Who indeed could excite envy in me, who do not envy even Vergil?" and as for Dante, "our poet," who wrote in the common tongue of tavern keepers, weavers, and butchers, we must realize "how little the plaudits of the unschooled multitude weigh with scholars." It is for us today to realize how far such men were from any concept of popular education.

The man of the Renaissance was the all-sided man, *l'uomo universale*, showing often the most extraordinary versatility. Dante was a publicist, theologian, philosopher, and poet. Leonardo da Vinci and Raphael had the widest interests and were skilled in the most various arts. Or consider Leon Battista Alberti (c. 1404–1472). He was the author of a famous work on education, *The Care of the Family*, was a noted gymnast, a scholar, author, musician, and an important art critic, but his *forte* was architecture in which he achieved real greatness. Only a little less variously gifted was Cellini (1500–1571), the author of a well-known autobiography which presents a picture, not only of himself, but of his times.

These, and the other great men of the time, were strongly individualistic; but this applied only to the great and those of the upper classes. The peasants and the workingmen were not yet free. The lower gilds were held in subjection. It was the rulers, courtiers, condottiere, and the scholars and artists who freed themselves from tradition and exhibited *virtu*, that is, self assertion and personal independence. Good examples of this radical individualism are found in Machiavelli, the author of the *Prince*, in Cellini, who was so extreme that he was not typical, and, at the other end of the scale, the sensitive and refined Botticelli. As another caution against broad generalization on the men of the Renaissance, we may recall that the Middle Ages also were not without their individuals, for they produced Abelard. Yet we do not mean to withdraw the statement that individualism is a basic characteristic of the greater men of the fourteenth century. Further evidence is contributed by literature with its abundance of personal writing, autobiographies, memoirs, and letters.

The men of the Renaissance were notable letter writers. This was a type of literature little cultivated in the Middle Ages. Petrarch and Erasmus are among the great letter writers of all time, and that is the reason why we know their characters so well. One has to keep in mind that many letters were written for publication; but, carefully handled, the personal correspondence of the period is a good measure of the new individualism. In letters and autobiographies the souls of these men are opened to the gaze of all who read.

Almost from the first of the revival of learning, men feared the return of paganism, a renewal of the old struggle between the ancient gods and Christianity. These fears were in some measure realized. Increasing attention was paid to Stoicism and especially to Seneca's *Morals*; but under cover of Stoicism, practice was often Epicurean. Bembo, who was an officer of the papal household, advised Sadoleto to omit from his studies the letters of St. Paul lest the barbarous Latin of the Vulgate should spoil his style. Even for the titles of the officers of the church, the classical style was employed: Thus the pope was designated *Pontifex Maximus* and the college of cardinals *Senatus Sacer*. These were not the diversions of outsiders; churchmen themselves became humanists. One of the great events which assured the success of the new learning was the election (1447) of Pope Nicholas V (1397–1455). "On that day the new learning took possession of the Holy See, and Rome began to be considered the capital of the Renaissance." The most skeptical humanists and artists did not launch an open attack against a church which gave them employment or which might turn upon them and chain them to the stake; but veiled sarcasm and oblique attacks on the Christian faith and institutions were common. Poggio, Filelfo, and Valla used such tactics. Though indifferent or hostile to religion and the church, in all ceremonial matters they conformed. Macaulay has brilliantly vindicated Machiavelli's cynical and amoral political theory on the ground that in the *Prince* the virtues of a great mind shine through the corruptions of a degenerate age. This is to say that the virtues are those of the author and the vices those of his time! This picture again is not true of all humanists and not of many of the teachers. Vittorino was much concerned for the moral and religious education of his pupils as were Vergerius, Sadoleto, and others.

5. FRANCESCO PETRARCH

Petrarch was one of the first and greatest of the humanists. In his life and work he exemplified the eager search for manuscripts, the early interest in Greek, the passionate love of Cicero, and that literary temperament which led him and his contemporaries to lay too much emphasis upon words and mere eloquence. This is a matter of importance for education. The exaggerated attention to style and the constant effort to imitate the sounding periods of Cicero were defects, not only of Petrarch, but of the whole revival and its education. The schools came to put eloquence upon a par with intellect and good character and, in fact, it was too often accepted as a substitute for them.

Petrarch, a Florentine by nationality, was born at Arezzo in 1304 where his parents, "poor but honorable folk," were living in exile. His childhood was spent near Florence, at Pisa, and, from his ninth year, at Avignon where the pope had "long held the Church of Christ in shameful exile." In these words Petrarch revealed his loyalty to Rome. He regarded the Romans as his ancestors and the ancient empire as his country. In his brief autobiography, he told the story of his life to the age of forty-seven. He studied law at Montpellier and Bologna. What impressed him most in this study was the frequent reference to Roman antiquity. He described the transfer of his allegiance from the law to the classics. He returned home at the age of twenty-two, not as a lawyer but as a humanist. The Colonna family became his patrons and bestowed benefices upon him. He traveled in the north to collect manuscripts. On a journey to Paris and the Netherlands, he discovered some lost orations of Cicero. In Italy, he found the manuscript of some of Cicero's letters to Atticus, to his brother Quintus, and to Brutus. "Whenever I took a journey," he said, "I always turned aside to any old monasteries that I chanced to see in the distance, saying to myself, 'who knows whether some scrap of the writings that I covet may not lie there?' " He recovered some of these writings, but he was more successful in stimulating others than in making great finds himself.

Upon his return from his northern journey, Petrarch settled near Avignon in a beautiful, secluded spot called Vaucluse. There he lived the life which he praised in his *De Vita Solitaria*, or "on the secluded life." Many of the books which were to make him famous were written at Vaucluse, where he lived a retired but epicurean life. There he received, on the same day, letters from the Senate at Rome and from the University of Paris offering him the crown of laurel for his poetry. The coincidence does not seem so remarkable to us, for we know it was contrived by Petrarch himself. Most of his books are conscious or unconscious autobiography, and the *De Vita Solitaria* belongs to this class. It is dedicated to a clerical friend. The title itself should call to mind the fact that monasticism was still a very active force in the world. Petrarch's only brother was a monk, and Petrarch admits that the brother had made the better choice. Nor was this merely a formal concession. Petrarch himself wished to be a sincere follower of the faith as well as a humanist, and there was a lifelong conflict in his soul.

Three historical trends met in him to be resolved as they might be. From ancient times came the ideal of a liberal education, literally an education appropriate for freemen, not for slaves or the working class. This was the view expressed by Plato in the *Theatetus*, that only the man of leisure has opportunity to pursue truth for its own sake. All other men are driven by circumstances to sacrifice truth to expediency. The lawyer must serve his client; the merchant, the politician, and every practical man must seek a practical and never the ideal result. From the Middle Ages, in the second place, the monastic and in general the religious life called to Petrarch and his contemporaries to renounce the world and to accept truth from the hand of revelation. And recently, men had come to see again the greatness of ancient Rome and Roman literature. The way to truth and beauty seemed to Petrarch to lie in the study of the thoughts of the ancients, Cicero, Vergil, and Seneca. Each of these three traditions had a part in forming the mind of Petrarch.

In form, the *De Vita Solitaria* is an extended letter. The friend to whom it was addressed was never long absent from his thought as he penned its three hundred pages. And friendly converse was to be one of the chief pleasures of this epicurean hermitage, for "no solitude is so profound, no house so small, no door so narrow, but it may open to a friend." In substance, he is writing about himself as one does in a letter, he is writing a vindication, an *apologia pro vita sua*. The book was written, as we have seen, at beautiful Vaucluse to extol the simple life. Occasionally we almost seem to catch the accents of Rousseau praising the life according to nature and leading an attack upon that sink of wickedness which is the city; but not for long. Almost immediately Petrarch turns upon himself to say that only a learned solitude is tolerable, one well stocked with books and applied to study and writing, in words like these "to read what our forerunners have written and to write what later generations may wish to read, to pay to posterity the debt which we cannot pay to the dead for the gift of their writings, and yet not remain altogether ungrateful to the dead, but to make their names more popular if they are unknown, to restore them if they have been forgotten, to dig them out if they have been buried in the ruins of time and to hand them down to our grandchildren as objects of veneration, to carry them in the heart, and by cherishing, remembering, and celebrating their fame in every way, to pay them a homage that is due to their genius even though it is not commensurate with their genius"—this is his ideal of the solitary life.

To what books did this fourteenth-century man of letters have access? His library of about two hundred volumes contained the great Roman historians, with the exception of Tacitus, and the great Roman poets, with the exception of Lucretius. He had the greater part of Quintilian and often quoted him. His Seneca and Cicero were not complete, but he had most of them; and he had several of the great Latin Fathers, Ambrose, Jerome, and Augustine, and used them. Petrarch was not able to read Greek but he had Latin translations of the *Timaeus* of Plato, the *Ethics* and *Politics* of Aristotle, and a crude version of Homer which Leontius Pilatus made for him and Boccaccio.

Some remarkable Latin finds were not made until after Petrarch's time. Niccolo Niccoli discovered a complete copy of Cicero's *De Oratore* which contains the orator's theory of education and his criticism of ancient educational practice. Poggio, in 1416, found at St. Gall a complete copy of Quintilian, a discovery which created remarkable enthusiasm among scholars. He also discovered a number of other rare works in the same monastery, including six of Cicero's orations.

6. THE RECOVERY OF GREEK AUTHORS

Most Greek literary manuscripts which remained had been transcribed within the bounds of the Byzantine empire. Even before the dispersion of the manuscripts, which followed the fall of the capital to the Turks in 1453, Greeks had found their way to Italy and had taught their language there. The first of importance was Manuel Chrysoloras (c. 1350–1415) who came as an ambassador from the emperor and was persuaded by the city of Florence to stay to teach the Greek language. This engagement, said Symonds, assured the future of Greek in Europe. Beginning in 1396 he taught for three years at Florence and had among his pupils Guarino, Fifelfo, Poggio, Leonardo Bruni, and Traversari. Chrysoloras seems to have left Florence for Pavia to escape the jealousy and spite of Niccolo Niccoli, Lorenzo de Medici's literary adviser. Chrysoloras taught in Pavia until about 1400. His work was of the utmost importance to the study of Greek, and therefore to the proper understanding of the Latin authors and to the whole development of learning in the West.

Other Greeks came early in the fifteenth century. G. G. Plethon (c. 1355–1450), who was born at Constantinople, lectured in Florence and inspired the founding there of a Platonic academy, which affected the thought not alone of Italy but also of Germany. Bessarion (1403–1472), who had been a pupil of Plethon, attended the Council of Florence in 1439, joined the Church of Rome, became a cardinal, and in 1471 was almost elected pope. His large collection of Greek manuscripts became the nucleus of the famous library of St. Mark's in Venice. Theodore Gaza (c. 1400–1475), another Greek, came to Italy in 1438. He became a teacher of Greek and, at the same time, a pupil in Latin in the school of Vittorino. Cardinal Bessarion became his patron and Pope Nicholas V invited him to Rome, in 1451, to aid in an ambitious program for the translation of the Greek classics into Latin. The death of the pope interfered with these plans, but Bessarion translated parts of Theophrastus and Aristotle into Latin and Cicero On Old Age and On Friendship, into Greek. He prepared the first fairly complete Greek grammar to be written in Italy. It was used long and widely as a textbook. Before this, Greek could be learned only by word of mouth, and competent teachers were scarce in the West before the time of Erasmus. Once the knowledge of the language had been recovered, and especially after Gaza and others had prepared grammars, classical Greek manuscripts became more important than Greek scholars. If, to the three whom we have already named, we add three more, George of Trebizond, called Trapezuntius (1424–1500), J. Argyropoulos (1416–1486), and Demetrius Chalcondylas (1424–1511), we shall have exhausted the list of the greatest of those who arrived in Italy before the fall of Constantinople. Trapezuntius, like Gaza, taught Greek and learned Latin under Vittorino and, like him also, prepared useful elementary grammars of the Greek language. These men were scholars as well as teachers, but they were primarily teachers.

Not only did Greek teachers come to Italy in the first half of the fifteenth century, but a movement in the opposite direction also took place. Italian scholars went to Constantinople, and resided there for long periods to learn the language and to gather manuscripts. Among these was Guarino da Verona (c. 1370–1460). For five years he lived at Constantinople, in the family of Chrysoloras, whose daughter he married. Returning to Italy he taught in Venice, where Vittorino was his pupil, later at Florence and Verona, and finally he became head of the famous Italian court-school at Ferrara. Guarino was active as an editor and commentator and served as translator to the Council of Ferrara (1438). He had a son, Battista, who succeeded him in the court-school of Ferrara. Battista wrote an account of his father's methods of teaching. It shows that a knowledge of Greek was by that time considered essential to the understanding of the Latin language and literature. The recovery of Greek had changed the Renaissance perspective of the history of culture and civilization.

Fifteen years later than Guarino, Aurispa (c. 1370–1459), a scholar from Sicily, visited Constantinople and returned in 1423 with more than two hundred manuscripts. Filelfo (1398–1481) served in a diplomatic post in the city on the Bosphorus and worked for seven years in its great libraries, returning with another large collection of Greek authors. Later he became a wandering scholar and lectured on the classics in the leading Italian cities. This illustrates the fact that there were few permanent positions for humanists in the Italian universities until the middle of the fifteenth century. The universities expended their energies upon the professional studies of law, medicine, and theology, and made no provision for liberal studies. Only very gradually did they establish chairs of rhetoric and poetry. The humanists, meanwhile, served as free-lance lecturers, took private pupils, found positions as secretaries or librarians, or enlisted under the banner of a wealthy patron.

7. DIFFUSION OF THE SOURCES

The next step to be taken, when many of the famous authors had been recovered, was the multiplication of copies in manuscript and printed form and the founding of libraries. The fifteenth century saw the formation of many remarkable collections; and their story was told by the shrewd but gossipy bookseller Vespasiano da Bisticci in his *Memoirs* of the illustrious men of his time. Libraries were built up by rulers like the Medici of Florence and the Sforza of Milan, by the higher clergy including the popes who developed the Vatican Library, by wealthy merchants and bankers, and by scholars. Vespasiano, who had every reason to be interested in the movement because he was the agent for many buyers, described the assembling of almost a score of great libraries. Books were obtained by purchase when possible, but more frequently by having skillful writers make manuscript copies.

Classical libraries flourished for a half-century before the development of printing. A new class of professional writers distinguished both for their learning and their beautiful handwriting produced the finest manuscripts. Those who had mastered Greek received the honorable title of *scrittori* and were well paid, because they were few. The less highly educated and less skillful writers had to work for a moderate wage. Frequently scholars made their own copies, either because they were poor or because *scrittori* were not to be had. Petrarch thus copied with his own hand a work of Cicero, because he would not put up with the "vile sloth" of the available copyists. Not only the *scrittori* but some of the great scholars wrote the beautiful Italian hand which had come into use in the fourteenth century. Parchment was always used for the books that were intended for the great collections. The writing in these manuscripts is artistic and regular yet individual; and they are so appropriately ornamented with scrolls, miniatures, and borders that they are a delight to the eye. Every such book had a character of its own and was usually decked out with a sumptuous binding, often of velvet with silver clasps.

To provide some illustrative details we now turn to Vespasiano da Bisticci's *Lives of Illustrious Men of the Fifteenth Century*, usually called the Vespasiano Memoirs. The author lived from 1421 to 1498 and, through his business, came into intimate contact with many of the leading humanists, princes, and popes of that century. But he was more than a mere trader in manuscripts. He read widely and was a keen observer and a good judge of what would prove interesting about the life and character of the famous men whom he met. He was not a stylist; but his greatest weakness as a writer is due to his amiability; he presents his characters in a favorable light only.

From Vespasiano we learn that Nicholas V, before he became pope, wished for money to do two things: to build great edifices and to buy books. He did the latter even in his days of poverty, and during his pontificate he did both. His personal library included the complete works of St. Augustine in twelve fine volumes. He annotated the works of the ancients with his own hand. He was himself one of the finest of calligraphers. He was familiar with the whole of Latin and Greek literature; and he was more skilled in classifying books than anyone of his time. Hence, when Cosimo de Medici was furnishing a great library, he sent to Nicholas V for directions to guide him in organizing the collection. The pope gave similar aid to other library founders. All men of letters, said Vespasiano, owed much of the high regard in which their craft was held to the good offices of Pope Nicholas. It was the purpose of this first humanist pope to found a great library at St. Peter's for the general use of the Roman court, and Vespasiano gave a list of the works which Pope Nicholas collected and the writers whom he employed.

Vespasiano presented even more elaborate accounts of the libraries of Federigo, Duke of Urbino, and of Cosimo de Medici. Duke Federigo's collection cost thirty thousand ducats, about seventy thousand dollars, worth three or four times that sum today. He spared neither cost nor labor and when he heard of a fine book, whether in Italy or elsewhere, he sent for it. After gathering all the notable titles in Latin, Greek, Hebrew, and Italian, he determined to dress every author worthily by binding him in scarlet and silver. "In this library," this dealer in fine manuscripts tells us, "all the books are superlatively good, and written with the pen, and had there been one printed volume it would have been ashamed in such company." From the account we learn that Vespasiano had before him complete catalogues of all the principal Italian libraries and even one of the library of Oxford University. We likewise have descriptions of the libraries established by Cosimo de Medici in Florence. When he did not have books enough to furnish the library of St. Mark's as it deserved, the executors of Niccolo Niccoli agreed to transfer all the books left by that scholar to St. Mark's, "letting the books be at the general service of all those who might like to use them." This contains the germ of the public library idea. In each book, there was a note indicating that it had belonged to the collection of Niccoli. When Cosimo wished to furnish the library of San Lorenzo he applied to Vespasiano, who told him that such a collection could not be purchased but that the books would have to be transcribed. And Vespasiano was commissioned to have the books copied. "He was anxious that I should use all possible despatch, and, after the library was begun, as there was no lack of money, I engaged forty-five scribes and completed two hundred volumes in twenty-two months, taking as a model the library of Pope Nicholas and following directions written by his own hand, which Pope Nicholas had given to Cosimo." According to this, it took one scribe about five months to complete a volume. The libraries of Bessarion, Alessandro Sforza, and others are also described by the genial bookseller of Florence. When the life of Vespasiano closed, in 1498, the day of the printed book was already far advanced. And, although the printing press was necessary for the wide dispersion of learning, the beginnings of humanism were made with manuscript sources. Petrarch and all the early scholars knew no other.

The use of movable type for printing on paper first came in about 1438. It had a very great influence in the spread of the classical authors and in providing books for schools. Now for the first time books became cheap and uniform. Copies of the same edition were as like as two peas, paging and all. This was a great convenience for pupils and teachers. Grammars, dictionaries, phrase and conversation books, and other aids to learning came from the press. By and by even scholars and the wealthy purchased printed books; and printing in its turn became a fine art. Among the Renaissance printers who took a scholarly and an artistic interest in their products were Aldus of Venice, Froben of Basle, and the Estiennes of Paris and Geneva. The Aldine classics, in handy pocket form, were and are famous. Although the editions were small according to modern standards, running about three hundred copies each on the average, the printing press made possible a far wider distribution of good literature than the world had ever known.

The discovery and distribution of classical books led to critical work. Two forms of criticism are the textual and the historical. The autographs of the classics had all long since disappeared, and by repeated copyings the text had become corrupt, but the printers desired to issue the most accurate or authentic text that scholarship could produce. The textual critic, by collating the available manuscripts, attempted to settle from the various readings what the true or original reading was. Historical criticism aimed to determine the authorship, time of writing, the purpose of the author, and similar matters that were in doubt. Laurentius Valla worked along such lines in proving that the so-called *Donation of Constantine* was a forgery, produced not in the fourth century, as had been claimed, but in the seventh or some later time.

8. AN EARLY HUMANIST WRITER ON EDUCATION

The first great writer on education to recommend the new learning and to propose a liberal education as his aim was Pier Paolo Vergerio, or Vergerius. Vergerius was born in 1349 and became a professor at Padua and Florence. He lived too early to find a place in Vespasiano's gallery of famous humanists. When Chrysoloras came to Florence to introduce the study of Greek, Vergerius was already forty-seven years old, but so great was his enthusiasm for the new study that he took his place at school among the boys who were learning their declensions. His treatise, "On Character and Liberal Studies," was written eight years later (1404); and it is such a book as ought to be expected of a man of noble character who has devoted his days and nights to liberal studies. It is wise in its practical demands, elevated in tone, and charmingly written. For two centuries the little book was used as a guide by humanist educators; and today it provides an excellent introduction to the greatest of those teachers, Vittorino da Feltre. Before we take up Vittorino's school and the other humanist schools we shall review the writings which served as guidebooks to the teachers of that time.

Vergerius wrote his little book for a particular boy of his acquaintance, one of the noble Carrara family. "Your distinguished ancestor," he said to the lad, "used to say that a parent owes his child three advantages: a good name, a country to be proud of, and a sound education. The last of these is the most important and failure in it is beyond remedy. You bear an honored name, you are of a house long eminent in 'our ancient and most learned city of Padua.' The most important aim, now, is that you should secure a good education."

Until boys come to the age of understanding, rivalry is a necessary spur to learning. Talents differ, and those with only modest capacities have the most need of education that their defects may be made good. Evil conduct and sin must be rigorously repressed. Language must be carefully guarded. An unsocial temper must be mellowed and friendliness developed. Idleness, and intemperance in food and drink, are to be shunned. Children must not be too much indulged and therefore family education should be avoided.

Vergerius, like Vittorino, aimed to combine Christian faith and conduct with ancient learning. His definition of a liberal education has become classic and we quote it. "We call those studies liberal," he wrote, "which are worthy of a free man; those studies by which we attain and practice virtue and wisdom; that education which calls forth, trains, and develops those highest gifts of body and mind which ennoble men and which are rightly judged to rank next in dignity to virtue only, for to a vulgar temper gain and pleasure are the one aim of existence, to a lofty nature, moral worth and fame." Such an education must be begun early for we shall not attain wisdom in our later years unless in our earliest we enter sincerely on its search. To be able to speak and write with elegance is of the utmost advantage for both public and private life. And a knowledge of literature enables us to use our leisure pleasantly and profitably. Think, by contrast, of Domitian, who, although he was the son of an emperor, could find nothing more amusing for his leisure hours than killing flies. Literature we must remember consists not of facts alone but of thoughts and style also. I do not think that thoughts without style and certainly not facts alone will be likely to attract much notice or secure a sure survival. What greater charm can life offer than this power of making the past, the present, and even the future, our own by means of literature. We may say, with Cicero, How bright a household is the family of books.

Thus Vergerius had already begun to debate that common Renaissance topic, namely, what subjects of study are to be considered essential in a liberal education. The first and foremost is literature. An important part of literature is history, which is both attractive and useful. Moral philosophy and eloquence follow close after. By philosophy we learn what is true; eloquence teaches us to say it convincingly; and history carries the light of experience. Poetry, music, logic, arithmetic, and geometry should be added and, if necessary, a professional study such as medicine or law.

How shall we teach and how learn? Vergerius warns against attempting too much at once or passing too rapidly from one subject to another. Only if we are systematic and put our heart into one subject at a time can we hope to succeed. Again, we must remember that mental endowments differ. Tasks and guidance must be adapted to the child's powers. Given good ability, three methods will be found useful: a systematic review every evening of what was done during the day; the practice of discussing each lesson with another student or with several; and the teaching to a younger student of what we have recently learned. Perseverance is essential. To give a set period to study every day, to work vigorously and to permit no interruption, is a practice which may be strongly recommended.

Education is to call forth and develop the highest gifts of body and mind. We have been speaking of the mind but you, he said to the boy, have wisely chosen to excel in both. And for physical and military fitness, courage and endurance are required. Here the Spartans and the Romans have set us the prime examples. "The Lacedaemonian discipline was indeed severe. The boys were so trained that in their contests they could not yield nor confess themselves vanquished; the severest tests produced no cry of pain, though blood might flow and consciousness itself give way. The result was that all antiquity rehearses the deathless courage of the Spartans in the field; their arms were to them part of their very selves, to be cast away, or laid down, only with their lives."

Training in arms should begin early, as soon as the boy is able to use his limbs. Those exercises should be chosen which will strengthen the body and maintain its health. Physical education, like mental, must be adapted to the child's nature and capacities. The Greek pentathlon, swimming, horsemanship, use of shield, spear, sword, and club all are necessary in the training of the soldier. The chariot of the Homeric Greeks and the legion of the Romans have both disappeared. We must adapt our training to our own day in which cavalry is the chief arm; and it is desirable to include the wider aspects of the art of war, such as strategy and tactics, discipline, supplies, and the management of encampments and winter quarters. Both war and peace will demand recreation, such as ball games, hunting, hawking and fishing, and, indoors, games of skill, not chance, music and song, and especially good books. Lastly we must not be neglectful of our personal habits. Our dress should be suitable to time, place, and circumstance, we should learn to be gracious in manner and of a cheerful spirit.

9. OTHER HUMANIST WRITERS

Some of the humanists favored the education of upper class girls in the new learning. Vittorino and his contemporaries acted on this principle, admitting girls to their classes. Within a year after Vergerius issued his treatise on the education of boys, Leonardo Bruni addressed an educational tract to Baptista Malatesta, daughter of the famous ducal house of Urbino. The tract covers only a few pages, and he used this space chiefly to select the subjects Baptista is to study. He recommended a full course of literature, history, and poetry. Like most humanists he condemned astrology; and for girls, mathematics was considered unsuitable. Rhetoric and oratory lie outside a woman's sphere of activity. Religion and ethics are, however, very important. Morals have been treated by the noblest minds of Greece and Rome. The Greek, Roman, and Christian ethical writers demand the serious study of a cultivated Christian lady. This, and all other studies, depend upon a sound foundation without which nothing can be accomplished; and that foundation consists in a thorough knowledge of the Latin language.

More elaborate was the treatise written for young King Ladislas of Bohemia by Aeneas Sylvius Piccolomini who afterwards became Pope Pius II. His contemporary, the famous architect L. B. Alberti, wrote a work on the management of a family which contains important sections on educational aims and the curriculum. One of the most systematic treatises of the whole Renaissance, arranged in six books, is by Maffeo Vegio. And Battista, the son and successor of Guarino da Verona, wrote an interesting and discriminating account of his father's views and practice.

Altogether we owe to the Italian humanists of the fourteenth and fifteenth centuries many works which deal wholly or in part with education. There was among these writers a singular unanimity in philosophy, curriculum, and method. This agreement was due to their limited materials, to the similarity of the conditions, and in particular to their dependence upon the same authorities, namely, Plato, Aristotle, Cicero, and especially Quintilian, whose *Institutes of Oratory* formed the great guidebook of the educators of the Renaissance.

The tract "Upon the Method of Teaching and of Reading the Classical Authors" by Battista Guarino (1459) is the first to give a prominent place to Greek studies. It, therefore, shows that the fifteenth century began a new phase in humanistic education. This is also shown by its narrower scope and its greater emphasis upon scholarship.

The sections upon methods of private study contain much good advice, some of which had already been given by Vergerius. Let the young student think of himself as preparing to teach what he is studying, advice which Quintilian gave us long ago. Let him read not only the text but every commentary. The precise meaning and force of every word is to be determined. He must write out his notes as if for publication. The practice of making extracts is to be commended, as is that of providing parallel passages from several authors. Like the Pythagoreans, he must review each evening what he learned by day, each month the whole reading of the preceding four weeks. Translation and the comparison of translations by others are useful exercises. Reading aloud is valuable to mind and body. Definite hours must be devoted to study, and the plan decided upon must be followed without interruption. We must recognize the crucial importance of a regular system in study; it is as important as "harmony of time and note" in a chorus. In conclusion, Battista Guarino quotes Cicero on literature as the inspiration of youth, the joy of old age, the ornament of success, and the solace of adversity. Books do not offend or rebuke, call up no empty hopes or fears. Through books alone will our converse be with the best and greatest minds among all the mighty men of the past. No leisure could be more nobly occupied than one spent among books.

Such were the views on education of writers in the Italian revival during the fourteenth and fifteenth centuries. Education had come to mean the cultivation of mind and body, the coordination of Greek and Christian morals, and the development of man as a citizen. Letters were not to be an excuse for withdrawal from active life. Aesthetic cultivation, good conduct, polite manners, and patriotism were all supposed to grow out of the liberal education which all the humanists sought and praised. Letters and philosophy were regarded as the ideal preparation for professional study. Ancient writers were studied for aid in war, politics, agriculture, and other practical concerns. Yet some even then began to sense a danger in the compromises which were involved in the union of the new learning and the old, compromises between Greek and Christian ethics, between the new thirst for fame and the old humility, between the pagan classics and the Christian gospel. Individualism was becoming rampant and in extreme spirits overstepped all bounds in the later Renaissance. The old struggle between antiquity and Christian faith and morals was again breaking out. Among teachers who were able to effect a working compromise were Guarino da Verona and Vittorino da Feltre.

10. TWO GREAT TEACHERS

Guarino we have already noticed as a scholar in Greek and a collector of Greek manuscripts. His school at Ferrara attained a European reputation, and pupils came from distant countries, from Germany, France, and even England. He made available in a Latin translation the educational essay which was attributed to Plutarch and which came to stand beside Quintilian on the humanist teacher's shelf of professional books. His moral character and his influence upon his students were greatly praised, and he read the Christian scriptures and the Church Fathers with his pupils. He was a thoroughgoing humanist scholar and a particular admirer of Cicero and Vergil. In a letter to a pupil he outlined a method of study which he ascribed to his father-in-law Chrysoloras. This concerns reading and interpretation. By reading aloud comprehension is aided. This is to be followed by grammatical analysis and a careful study of the exact sense, by repetition, and by a careful summary. Translation is not to be slavish but faithful. Beautiful passages are to be copied into a book of selections and to be memorized. The books that are read are to be discussed with other students and with friends. The educational doctrines given to the world by his son Battista, which have already been mentioned, were confessedly those of the father also.

Vittorino was more exclusively a teacher than Guarino. He wrote nothing, collected no manuscripts, took no part in public affairs, yet his fame was equally widespread and has proved just as lasting. Vittorino Rambaldoni of Feltre was born in a mountain village of the eastern Alps in 1378. The father, though poor, had some education and the town, though remote and lacking in cultural resources, yet gave Vittorino the opportunity to acquire the rudiments of Latin. At the age of eighteen he entered the university of Padua, with which Petrarch had been associated. He even studied under one of Petrarch's disciples; and he may have met Vergerius who was a Paduan professor. Being very poor, he earned his way by tutoring pupils in Latin. He studied mathematics, which was still a rare accomplishment, for Euclid was just being revived. For a while he lived in the house of Gasparino Barzizza, who was regarded as the greatest Latin scholar of that time. Among his companions were men soon to become famous such as Filelfo, and George of Trebizond. He studied Greek with Guarino, who upon his return from Constantinople set up a school in Venice.

He was a spare, active man, simple in his habits, dress, and tastes, and beloved in the best social circles of the city and the university. For twenty years he had been a student and a private and public teacher at Padua and at Venice. His schools had drawn to him the sons of the great families of the two cities. But he taught not only the rich. Remembering his own youthful struggles, he received some poor boys free while the rich paid the usual fees. In 1423, the Marquis of Mantua, Gianfrancesco Gonzaga, invited him to become head of the Mantuan court school. He had to be persuaded; concessions were offered. Vittorino might fix his own salary, have complete control of school and pupils, continue his custom of giving free education to some talented poor boys; and it was urged as a great opportunity for a great teacher to have the chance to educate the future Marquis of Mantua. Although somewhat unwillingly, Vittorino consented and spent the remaining twenty-three years of his life as head of the court-school of Mantua.

The children of the prince formed the nucleus of the school. There were three boys and a girl when the master arrived. Another daughter, Cecilia, and a son were born later. The sons of the nobility and of rich merchants, together with poor boys of ability and many foreigners, swelled the numbers until there was a large boarding school. Learned Greeks from the East came to study Latin with Vittorino. The ages of the pupils varied. Some were as young as six or eight years and several stayed on until they were in the middle twenties and beyond. Valla, who was one of Vittorino's most famous pupils, remained until he was twenty-three but apparently served as an assistant. Sassuolo was twenty-one when he entered but he had charge of the music instruction and was, therefore, a teacher as well as a pupil. Other famous pupils were John Andrea, later a bishop, Corraro, Perotti, who became a professor of rhetoric and an official in the Roman Curia, and Ognibene, who was to be Vittorino's successor as head of the school.

The school was housed in a large casino or clubhouse, which had been called the House of Pleasure but which Vittorino renamed the Pleasant House and redecorated with murals of children at play. Surrounding this schoolhouse, which was flanked by other buildings used for sleeping and dining quarters, were large grounds with trees and gardens. Through the plain below, the Mincio River flowed. The great teacher was the father and companion of his school family. He took care of their health, took part in their games, and accompanied them to the foothills or the lakeshore in the hot summer. No luxuries were allowed even to princes. Strict discipline of the body by games and exercises, good manners and good conduct, and serious study were demanded of all. But the dominating influence in the school was the Christian spirit and the personality of Vittorino.

The youngest pupils began with letter games, spelling, and reading. Speaking and reading aloud with careful attention to articulation, tone, accent, and every quality of good speech were practiced daily. Declamation was taught as a means of eloquence. Composition and rhetoric were subjects of the greatest value to the future leader in public affairs or in the church. The Latin language was the language of instruction and the main subject of study. Greek was taught but not Italian, and this is what would be expected of a humanist. Few doubted and everyone hoped that classical Latin was henceforth to be the universal language of scholars and leaders.

The common people might have to be content with the common tongue. Vittorino laid great emphasis upon the parallel study of Greek and Latin, each reinforcing the other; the study of the languages implied the deep and broad study of their literatures. The school gave a complete education in both ancient languages, in literature, poetry, rhetoric, history, and mathematics. This was also one of the first Renaissance schools to include games and physical activities. The historians came in for particular attention, especially Livy. It was no accident that a pupil of Vittorino prepared the first printed edition of Livy. Arithmetic was taught for practical use and for training in accuracy. In its early stages it was taught in games as Plato had advised. Geometry was one of the studies which Vittorino loved and in which he had acquired fame as a teacher. Astronomy and the elements of physics or natural philosophy were also included. Among the school activities there were choral singing, instrumental music, and dancing.

Famous schools in the Renaissance were numerous, but none embodied more fully its educational ideals, the complete training of man for leisure and action, and especially for service to state and church, by means of the ancient literatures. The later humanists lost the fine early enthusiasm. Schools became harsh and the teaching more and more grammatical. Cicero became the sole model of style and was slavishly imitated. In the later schools, also, only short selections of the main authors were read, the scientific subjects were dropped out, mathematics was curtailed, and the time saved was devoted to the formal aspects of language, to prose style, and to the making of verses, against which Milton was to utter his maledictions. The freedom and spontaneity which had produced a Vittorino were lost from both the language and the schools of the humanists.

11. INFLUENCE OF THE REVIVAL ON EDUCATION

The most obvious educational influence from the Revival, if not the most important, came in the transformation and expansion of the curriculum. The classical Roman authors and some Greek writers, together with the necessary language studies, displaced the medieval trivium of grammar, rhetoric, and dialectic. Many more authors and greater ones were read in the humanist than in the medieval schools and the curriculum was thereby greatly enriched. The new aims were the understanding of literature and of life through literature, rather than skill in logic and the scholastic philosophy or the professional study of law or medicine. The humanists intended to offer a liberal, not a professional, education.

Of the authors, Cicero held the largest place. Not only his orations but also his letters, his De Oratore and Brutus, and his essays on friendship and old age were read. In this connection, the imitation of Cicero's prose became far too much an aim of the schools. This degenerate stylism was known as Ciceronianism, a word which designates the formalism of the late Renaissance education. This was one of the decadent tendencies against which Erasmus broke a lance. As education became more formal, grammatical, and stylistic, the great literary works received less attention.

Besides Cicero, other prose writers, Quintilian, and the historians, Sallust, Curtius, Caesar, and Livy were read. Virgil was the great poet of the schools, but others were introduced, especially Horace, Ovid, and Lucan. In the Greek, Homer, the dramatists, the historians and biographers Xenophon, Herodotus, Plutarch, and the orators Demosthenes and Isocrates were studied. Greek always received less emphasis than Latin. When the pupil could read and speak Latin he began rhetoric, composition, and oratory. Oratory again became one of the fine arts and held a much larger place in the Renaissance schools than it had in the Middle Ages. Latin composition and Latin verse-making were taught and usually Greek prose also. History as a science, the effort to learn what actually happened, was hardly understood in the Renaissance. On the contrary, it was more nearly a branch of ethics. Both history and ethics were studied for the same purpose, to improve public and private conduct.

Among the nonliterary studies, although the Revival and its schools were primarily literary, there were music and physical education including skill in the use of weapons. The new emphasis upon the body in the Renaissance was one of the most striking contrasts with the Middle Ages. This remarkable change of interest and values is exhibited even more clearly in painting and sculpture, but it is also evident in education. The medieval schools did not engage in sports and games and the use of arms. Then the body was to be mortified, but now it was to be developed, admired, and used for civic and personal success and glory. Music also came into the schools. Vittorino had a special teacher of music, Sassuolo. Alberti was one of the noted organists of the time and included music in his proposed curriculum. For their theory of education in music both Vittorino and Alberti went back to Aristotle, who held that music had several functions: it is good for diversion, recreation, moral and civic education, and purification or catharsis. Castiglione assigned an important place to music in the education of the courtier and the high-born lady. Many of the Renaissance writers distinguished between elevating and debasing music and insisted upon careful selection of the compositions which were to be used. Some were also critical of the general run of music masters, who seem to have had a bad name. Dancing was not generally approved by the Renaissance educators, although Vittorino taught it. Drawing was not usually included because it was regarded as a practical study, too closely connected with geometry, surveying, and engineering to be considered among the liberal studies. The natural sciences aroused little interest before the seventeenth century.

One of the greatest defects of the Renaissance curriculum was the complete omission of the vernacular; and this suggests the even more basic fact that the humanists had no conception of universal education and no message for the common people. The new studies appealed, however, to groups of people who might not have attended the medieval schools, such as the nobles, ruling classes, merchants, and bankers. When the poor were admitted into the new schools, they were drawn into the upper social strata. But the humanists, with few exceptions, did nothing to provide an appropriate education for the poor. The education of girls made some progress among the upper classes.

Important improvements were made in the equipment of the schools. The printing press provided uniform texts which made class discussion and the interpretation of the text feasible. It was no longer necessary to dictate the texts or to correct the numerous errors of manuscript copies. Aids to language study, grammars, lexicons, phrase books, and colloquies became numerous. Vastly more reading material became available. Themes, notebooks, and many new kinds of exercises were made possible through the use of paper.

New schools were founded, court-schools in Italy, collèges and lycées in France, the gymnasium in Germany, and the reformed grammar school in England. Schools were a little less likely to be controlled by the church. Their physical equipment was improved, playing fields were sometimes added, and there was a new attention to the health of the pupils. Friendlier relations were developed between teachers and pupils in the early Renaissance. Some of these gains were lost as the schools again became formal and standardized in the sixteenth century. And then a new, a realist revival occurred.

12. THE CLASSICS CROSSING THE ALPS

The great Latin classics were not widely studied in the north until about a century after their revival in Italy; and then, as in Italy, the Greek revival followed the Latin at a distance of about fifty years.

One of the earliest humanist circles in the north formed itself around Duke Humphrey of England about 1425. He was the first English patron of humanists, collector of classical manuscripts, and contributor to the classical collections of his own university, Oxford, where he had been a student of Balliol College. Among the Italian translators whom he employed was Antonio Beccaria who had been a pupil of Vittorino. Not long after, young Englishmen began to go to Italy to study the classics just as, during the Middle Ages, they had gone to study law.

Holland and the Rhine country were not earlier in the field but were more important than England as centers of the rising northern humanism. In Holland the voluntary religious society called the Brethren of the Common Life was founded in the fourteenth century. The members, mostly ordinary middle class people, devoted themselves to pious works, the physical and spiritual care of students, copying manuscripts, teaching, and the establishment of schools. They were a loosely knit body, the members took no formal vows, and it is often difficult to distinguish the brothers from others who were only associated with them. Their early schools were not humanistic, but by 1500 a change in this respect was noticeable. Hegius, rector of the Brethren's school at Deventer, for example, placed that institution in the front rank of their schools; and, at his death in 1498, it was fairly classical in the content and spirit of its teaching.

Humanism developed slowly in France, where the University of Paris long opposed its introduction. The support of classical studies, in that country as in Italy, came more from the court and the princes than from the universities. When Francis I became king in 1515, the humanists rejoiced in the prospect of support for their studies and they were not disappointed. William Budé, a distinguished scholar, was made royal librarian; the Collège de France, a humanist institution, was founded; and a royal printing press was established, with Robert Estienne as printer. The city of Bordeaux in 1534 founded the Collège de Guyenne, where Élie Vinet and Mathurin Cordier later became teachers.

In Germany John Sturm organized the classical gymnasium of Strassburg about 1538. Rudolph Agricola was, however, the greatest of the early German classicists. But since the Reformation was, at first, a German revolution, we shall deal with the German humanists in the next chapter.

The transition from medieval to modern times is called the Renaissance. Many phases of life were affected, including the fine arts, politics, exploration, and scholarship. The scholarly phase, or Revival of Learning, was a return to ancient literature. Roman law, never wholly lost, was revived in the Middle Ages. Science, medicine, mathematics, and the works of Aristotle were brought by the Moslems. The humane letters of Greece and Rome had not yet been revived. The appreciative and critical study of these classical authors formed the Revival of Learning. This study implied the use of classical instead of medieval Latin.

The Renaissance was hardly less creative in education than it was in the fine arts. The Greek ideal of liberal education was revived and it marks a radical change from medieval humility and submission. The Renaissance man tended to be proud, aggressive, and self-sufficient. These new attitudes influenced education in the direction of freedom for the individual; but the great teachers occupied an intermediate position on the question of freedom versus authority. The humanist schools thus repeated history by again attempting to combine classical and Christian ideals. They aimed to cultivate both mind and body; they tried to prepare their pupils for active work in the world; and they developed intelligent methods of study and teaching and introduced a new curriculum. The curriculum still was, as in the Middle Ages, a collection of authors; but these were the great writers of Greece and Rome, not mere summarizers; they were read in their own language; and they were read critically and with historical perspective, not as final authorities. The humanists favored the education of girls of the upper classes. They wrote industriously, but with limited originality, on educational theory. They created a new type of secondary school which still retains its prestige in large parts of the world, although it has everywhere come under heavy attack.

Humanism early developed a decadent tendency. It lost contact with science and with national and economic development; and the humanists were not interested in the education of the common people, nor in the common life, language, or literature. Humanist education acquired the faults of the ancient Roman schools. It became formal, stylistic, and declamatory; and it came to be, itself, in need of reform. Education was in transition but it did not in the Renaissance become fully modern.

QUESTIONS

1. How did the Italian Renaissance differ from the "Renaissance of the Twelfth Century"?
2. Consider chivalric education as a form of humanism.
3. If mathematics were to be regarded as a humanistic study, how should it be taught?
4. Were the great Greek and Roman writers humanists? Could humanism in the fourteenth century have developed without the ancient classics?
5. Did the Italian scholars become humanists because they studied the classics or did they study the classics because they were humanists?
6. What were the main characteristics of the Renaissance scholars? Which of these characteristics were exhibited in the life of Petrarch? Was Petrarch a wholly modern man?
7. Criticize, pro and con, the educational theory of Vergerius.
8. Discuss the judgment that the chief educational contribution of the Italian Renaissance was its emphasis upon individual liberty of thought and expression.
9. Does Vittorino deserve his fame as a great teacher? Why, or why not?
10. Compare the curricula of the Renaissance schools and the medieval schools.
11. What improvements in the equipment and the methods of the schools occurred during the Renaissance?

12.   Compare the spread of the new learning to the north with the spread of commerce to the north.
13.   To what new classes of the population, not reached by the medieval schools, did the humanist learning appeal?

FOR FURTHER READING AND STUDY

While there are many English books on the Italian Renaissance, to make a first-hand study of the period one would need a knowledge of other languages, especially Italian and Latin. Some of the sources are given in Woodward's *Vittorino da Feltre*, which is listed below. Attention should again be called to *A History of Classical Scholarship* by J. E. Sandys which is listed in Chapter V. Volume II of Sandys deals with classical scholarship in Italy in the fourteenth and fifteenth centuries. Burckhardt and Symonds, in the present bibliography, are of prime importance.

Burckhardt, Jakob, *The Civilization of the Renaissance in Italy*. Translated by S. G. C. Middlemore, New York, Harper & Brothers, 1929, 526 pp.
Ferguson, Wallace K., *The Renaissance*, New York, Henry Holt and Company, Inc., 1940, 148 pp.
Field, Lilian F., *An Introduction to the Study of the Renaissance*, London, Smith, Elder and Company, 1898, 304 pp.
Funck-Brentano, Frantz, *The Renaissance*, London, Geoffrey Bles, Ltd., 1936, 320 pp.
Gee, John A., *The Life and Works of Thomas Lupset* . . . , New Haven, Yale University Press, 1928, 357 pp.
George, William, and Emily Waters, Translators, *The Vespasiano Memoirs, Lives of Illustrious Men of the XV Century*, New York, Lincoln Mac-Veagh, Dial Press, Inc., 1926, 475 pp.
Hudson, William H., *The Story of the Renaissance*, London, Cassell & Co., Ltd., 1912, 268 pp.
Hulme, Edward M., *The Renaissance, the Protestant Revolution, and the Catholic Reformation*, New York, Century Company, 1914, 589 pp.
Lanciani, Rodolfo A., *The Golden Days of the Renaissance in Rome*, Boston, Houghton Mifflin Company, 1906, 340 pp.
Laurie, Samuel S., *Studies in the History of Educational Opinion from the Renaissance*, Cambridge, University Press, 1903, 261 pp.
Lucas, Henry Stephen, *The Renaissance and the Reformation*, New York, Harper & Brothers, 1934, 767 pp.
Mitchell, R. J., *John Tiptoft, 1427–1470*, New York, Longmans, Green and Company, 1938, 263 pp.
Nelson, Brother Joel Stanislaus, *Æneae Silvii De Liberorum Educatione, a Translation with an Introduction*, Washington, D. C., The Catholic University of America Press, 1940, 241 pp.
Robinson, James Harvey, and H. W. Rolfe, *Petrarch, the First Modern Scholar and Man of Letters*, New York, G. P. Putnam's Sons, 1914, 477 pp.
Sandys, John Edwin, *Harvard Lectures on the Revival of Learning*, Cambridge, University Press, 1905, 212 pp.

Santillana, Giorgio de, *The Age of Adventure, the Renaissance Philosophers*, Boston, Houghton Mifflin Company, 1957, 283 pp.

Sichel, Edith Helen, *The Renaissance*, New York, Henry Holt and Company, Inc., 1914, 256 pp.

Symonds, John Addington, *Renaissance in Italy*, New York, Charles Scribner's Sons, 1914–1915, 7 volumes. Of this there is also a two-volume "Modern Library" edition, New York, 1935. Volume two of the complete edition is entitled *The Revival of Learning*. Symonds has written and translated many works dealing with the Renaissance.

Watson, Foster, *Vives on Education; A translation of the De tradendis disciplinis*, Cambridge, University Press, 1913, 328 pp.

Woodward, William Harrison, *Vittorino da Feltre and Other Humanist Educators*, Cambridge, University Press, 1912, 261 pp.

Zeitlin, Jacob, *The Life of Solitude by Francis Petrarch*, Urbana, Ill., University of Illinois Press, 1924, 316 pp. A translation with introduction and notes. This work by Petrarch shows that he was not wholly "modern."

7 THE REFORMATION ERA

THE PROTESTANT REFORMATION AND THE DEVELOPMENT OF humanism north of the Alps were so closely interlinked that they may be treated together. Erasmus, who "laid the egg which Luther hatched," became prominent and his ideas influential between 1500 and 1520; and his lifetime of seventy years spans almost the whole period of humanistic development in the north. When Erasmus was born, sometime before 1470, the earliest northern humanists were still young. The Brethren of the Common Life, a famous Netherlands teaching society, did not become genuinely humanistic until the latter part of the fifteenth century. Greek was not much studied in the north before 1500. Most of the famous classical schools, including those established or reformed by Colet in London, Sturm in Strassburg, and Élie Vinet and his predecessors in Bordeaux, were products of the sixteenth century. The great system of the Jesuit classical schools hardly began before 1550.

All this shows the error of treating the northern revival of learning as if it had run its course before the Reformation. And the two movements were not merely contemporary but they were causally interrelated. They developed together and each modified the other. The individualist and critical attitudes of the Revival of Learning, its study of ancient authors, its tendency to regard original sources as authoritative, and its effort to recapture the glories of a great past could all be turned to the study of the Bible and to the establishment of a pure Bible text and to an attempt to recover the virtues of the primitive church. They not only could be but they were turned in these directions. On the other hand, by this preoccupation with the Bible and by the addition of Hebrew studies, northern humanism became differentiated from the Italian.

Although contemporary and causally interrelated, the two movements were not of equal scope. The Reformation was much broader than humanism and broader than all purely intellectual and aesthetic interests together. It developed into a social revolution, accented by the demand of the common man for recognition. It also was, what it has been traditionally considered to be, a religious movement, but not so purely religious as the church historians would have it. To regard it as the Renaissance of the north is suggestive, a renaissance less individualistic, less pagan, less aesthetic, more economic, and more popular and democratic than the Italian.

The Reformation and humanism even came into direct conflict at times, so that Erasmus was led to say that "where Lutherism rules, letters die." There was much truth and some half-truth in this declaration of the great humanist. The truth was that the Reformation produced new orthodoxies, creeds, persecutions; a religion, dogmatic, harsh, narrow, leaving little freedom for humanistic studies; and the half-truth, the implication that these evils were of the essence of the Reformation and could not be overcome. Erasmus would not have denied that he had done much to release the revolutionary forces. He was the most effective critic of the evils of the time; and his edition of the Greek New Testament was the basis of vernacular translations into many languages, including the English.

1. BEFORE LUTHER

Other causes of the Reformation were political and economic. One of these was the rise of nations, whose interests conflicted with those of the international Roman church. Competition and rivalry between nations led to wars, such as the Hundred Years' War (1337–1453) between England and France, and wars have always been costly. At the same time an economic revolution was substituting a money economy and taxation for the old feudal services. But the vast lands and other properties of the church were not subject to taxation, and besides the pope secured much of his very large income through tithes, special taxes like the annates, the sale of indulgences, and other means. All this was drawn from the very same people whom the kings wanted to tax for the expenses of government. Whatever moneys the pope drew out of a kingdom, whatever lands and wealth were privileged and untaxable because they belonged to the church, were so much wealth withdrawn from civil and national uses, and the kings did not like the system. Here was the basis for a fundamental conflict between state and church.

The theory of papal supremacy over the civil power was reasserted by Pope Boniface VIII about 1300 in two famous bulls named, as is usually done, from their opening words, "Unam Sanctum" and "Clericis Laicos." In the latter document he forbade all civil authorities to collect, from the clergy, any taxes which he had not approved. The gage thus thrown down was taken up by Philip, king of France. In 1302 he called the first parliament, the Estates General of France, and secured from them a denial of the right of the pope to interfere in the internal affairs of the nation and especially in taxation and fiscal matters. Although public opinion did not altogether favor the king, the majority supported him, thereby showing that in the fourteenth century the strongest nations were already capable of challenging the power of the papacy in matters of domestic policy. In England the issues were somewhat different, but the outcome was similar and resulted in limiting papal interference. Spain, beginning in 1381, set limits to the amount of papal taxes that could be imposed and insisted that only Spaniards might hold the episcopal office. That was the century of Dante who in his de Monarchia asserted the principle that the civil power should be separated from the ecclesiastical and that only the latter should be vested in the papacy. Nationalism was one of the modern forces which were to limit the power of the church; and we have pointed especially to the fiscal issue. The Protestant Reformation was to carry the matter much further until instead of one church a number of independent national churches were set up.

Meanwhile one nation, France, secured a preponderant influence over the papacy by removing its seat from Rome to Avignon, a city in the Rhone valley on the borders of France, where it was to remain for seventy years (1305–1377). This removal of the capital of Christendom and the resulting interference by the French kings in papal policy is called the "Babylonian Captivity" of the church. Following the death of Boniface VIII, the king of France secured the election of a French prelate to the papal chair. By removing to Avignon, the new pope, Clement V, and the church lost all that the Eternal City signified, and suffered incalculably in prestige and influence. The college of cardinals was packed with French ecclesiastics, and the Avignon popes, seven in number during these seventy years, were pro-French in policy. England, which during this long period was at war with France, came to regard the pope as the ally of her enemy. Even in German states a similar feeling developed. The German Diet of Frankfort (1338) solemnly declared that the king derived his right to rule from God directly and not through the pope. This version of the doctrine of the divine right of kings was thus a weapon to be used against the papacy and in the interest of national independence.

The Great Schism still further undermined the prestige and unity of the church. In 1377, Pope Gregory XI returned to Rome to recover his power over the papal states in Italy. When Gregory died, a disputed papal election led to the choice first of Urban VI, an Italian, and then of Clement VII, a Frenchman. France and her allies, including Scotland and Naples, supported Clement, while England led the party which favored

Urban. For forty years this division of the church continued, with two popes, hostile to each other, and each supported by an international party. This was the Great Schism. Many plans to heal the wounds of the church were proposed: arbitration, voluntary or forced resignations, the withdrawal of obedience from both incumbents, and the calling of a General Council. This last plan was the one finally adopted but not carried through until 1414.

The effects of the division were felt not only in religion but also in education. University students and professors were divided into hostile parties; and how, asked one great Paris master, can knowledge be acquired except in peace; but now, he added, scholars avoid the university altogether on account of this cursed division in the church. Heretics multiplied in number and boldness, and indeed a man might be a heretic under one pope and a true believer under the other.

Except for the Great Schism, Wycliffe might have remained a quiet theologian at Oxford. From the outbreak of the schism he began to move away from his earlier views until he had become a vigorous critic of the church. In his later years he did not scruple to call the pope Antichrist and to declare that no such office as the papacy is recognized in the Bible. Even the Apostles, he said, considered themselves only brethren. Wycliffe fought the church in England with "two swords," one his wandering, wayside preachers called Lollards, one of whom is described in Chaucer's *Prologue*, and the other his English version of the Bible for the common people. He anticipated later Protestants in his belief that all religious problems should be solved by direct reference to the Bible; and this helps to justify his historic title, "The Morning-Star of the Reformation." Wycliffe was protected by the powerful noble, John of Gaunt. But when Henry IV became king, with a somewhat doubtful title, he sought to gain the support of Rome by crushing all dissent in his kingdom. John of Gaunt and Wycliffe had already passed from the stage, but Wycliffe's wayside preachers were hunted down until by 1430 Lollardry had become practically extinct. Wycliffe's ideas, however, were carried to far-off Bohemia where they fell upon fertile soil among the Czechs.

The marriage of King Richard II to Anne of Bohemia and the presence of a great many Germans at their own University of Prague led many Bohemian students to migrate to Oxford. Many of these, when they returned home, brought back Wycliffe's ideas and his books. The age-old hostility of the Czechs toward the Germans, coupled with the fact that the church and the government of Bohemia were in German hands, made them the more hospitable to Wycliffe's anti-Roman Catholic principles. But even earlier, evangelical influences had been introduced among the Czechs from the Waldenses, a widely scattered body of heretics who originated in the Rhone valley and in Switzerland. The Waldenses were simple peasants who took the Bible as their rule of life. In this respect they were similar to Wycliffe's preachers, and they spread their doctrines far and wide, a fact embodied in the poet Whittier's "The Vaudois Teacher." The persecution which they suffered during long periods led John Milton to write one of his most stirring sonnets, "Avenge, O Lord, Thy Slaughtered Saints." In Bohemia, they provided one of the influences which led to the reform activities of John Huss and Jerome of Prague. There were many of these evangelical groups, in many countries, in the later Middle Ages. Another heretical sect, which diverged much farther from orthodox Christianity, was the Albigenses who were ruthlessly exterminated by the Inquisition. The existence of all these dissenters, whether they were more or less radical, shows the widespread dissatisfaction that existed before the Reformation and the potential following that awaited any powerful leader who should appear. Huss was such a leader.

John Huss was a popular preacher interested in practical religion and critical of conditions in the church. Already somewhat acquainted with Wycliffe's writings, he was completely converted to Wycliffe's views by Jerome of Prague who returned from Oxford in 1401 with some Wycliffe's later books. His Czech countrymen supported him the more heartily, because he was opposed by the Germans. The common people especially rallied around him while the higher clergy attacked his theological and social views. Meanwhile, the Council of Pisa had been called and had chosen another pope, John XXIII, thus adding a third contender to the claimants of the papal office. Conditions in Bohemia were one of the concerns of the Council of Pisa; and the new pope, in an effort to curb the growing heresy, granted special indulgences to those who would help to put down the Hussite movement. Jerome of Prague, in reply, led a mob in burning the papal bull in the public square of Prague. National aspirations, racial hatreds, the demand for purer living by the clergy, free thought stimulated by Bible reading, the financial exactions of the Roman church, and the scandal of the schism had reinforced each other to produce the Bohemian rebellion and a century later, were to cooperate to produce the great revolution which is called the Reformation.

In the efforts to heal the Great Schism two parties developed. The conciliar party held that the authority of a general council is superior to that of a pope. The opposing party held that the pope was supreme and that only the pope could call a council to deal with the ills of the church. The conciliar party, supported by the most noted theologians of the University of Paris and aided by the failure of all other efforts to heal the schism, won a temporary victory in the Council of Pisa; and won a further victory in persuading Pope John XXIII to call the Council of Constance.

John thought he could dominate that Council, but he was mistaken. On assembling at Constance in the autumn of 1414, the new Council adopted rules of procedure which assured that the prelates who favored extensive reforms would have control and that the influence of the Italian clergy would be curbed. Pope John was displeased with this action because he had expected to have his own election confirmed and the other contenders, Gregory XII and Benedict XIII, deposed. Instead he was now to be treated as one of three rivals. John left the Council and denounced its proceedings, but the leaders were not to be intimidated and eventually they deposed all three of the contenders.

One of the main problems to come before the Council of Constance was the Hussite rebellion. Huss had been summoned before the Council and came with an assurance of safe conduct from the Emperor, Sigismund. In May 1415, the previous condemnation of Wycliffe was reaffirmed and his writings were committed to the flames. Next Huss was brought up for trial, was condemned, and went to the stake bravely refusing to recant unless his errors could be demonstrated from the Scriptures. The emperor protested these measures but eventually agreed to violate his pledged word because he was assured that promises to a heretic have no binding force. After this the Council reached a stalemate. Controversy over the reform of the episcopal system and the papal administration and even over the question of future regular meetings of church councils so divided the prelates that little further was accomplished. The conciliar party had a plan to moderate the absolutism of the pope but failed to get it adopted. The most that was accomplished was to provide for the calling of future councils at intervals of five, seven, and ten years. By 1417 the Council of Constance was so divided that they were just barely able to agree on a procedure to elect a new pope. The choice fell upon an Italian cardinal, who took the name of Martin V, and who became the head of a reunited church. The Great Schism was over, and in April 1418 the new pope dissolved the Council. It is doubtful whether it could have accomplished anything more by continuing its meetings.

It was during the Council of Constance that Poggio Braccolini, who attended as a secretary, visited the monastic library of St. Gall and discovered there a complete copy of Quintilian, a find which aroused the greatest enthusiasm among the Italian humanists. Unfortunately, the prelates attending the Council also borrowed from the library, for use at the meetings, large numbers of the most valuable books, such as copies of the Church Fathers and books on canon law, and these were never returned. The manuscript library of one of the most famous monasteries of Europe was, therefore, definitely poorer because the Council had met in its neighborhood.

2. INVENTION OF PRINTING

Meanwhile printing had come into use throughout western Europe, and its influence in informing the people and creating a large and active public in favor of reform is one of the most weighty factors in the success of the German revolt under Luther. It was also highly important in education, in both the humanistic and the popular schools. Indeed, the influence of printing upon popular education and the spread of knowledge which it facilitated would be hard to overestimate; and it is hard even to realize it without a good deal of thought and study. Not only were books made accessible at lower cost and in uniform editions, but in printed books spelling began to be standardized, a great improvement over the chaotic spellings of the Middle Ages; reference books such as dictionaries and books of selections appeared; and beyond the school itself printing aided the development of a popular literature which all the people were eager to read.

The free use of paper further aided in transforming school exercises. The writing of themes and letters, the collection of favorite passages and of word lists, the taking of reading and lecture notes were made possible. Arithmetic, which had been taught with counters and the abacus, could now be carried on "with the pen."

Paper had been introduced into Europe, and paper mills had gradually increased in number in the later medieval centuries. Movable type was invented in Holland or Germany, perhaps about 1425, probably by more than one inventor, and the Gutenberg Bible was printed in 1456 at Mainz. From Holland and Germany, printing spread to other countries. The first press in Italy was set up near the Benedictine monastery of Monte Cassino in 1465. Caxton, the first English printer, set up his press in a monastery in 1477. He was not only the first printer in England but also the first to print in the English language. The famous Aldine press was established at Venice in 1490 and at once became famous for its handy-volume editions of the classics. Froben of Basel conducted a press notable for its editions of the great Church Fathers. Erasmus worked for both the Aldine and the Froben presses. The press of the Estiennes was first set up in Paris but, when this family joined the Protestant cause, they removed it to Geneva where they long continued to serve the cause of learning and the reformed religion.

Printing was well developed and widely spread before the Lutheran revolt began and became a powerful agency for the dissemination not only of humanist learning but also of Lutheran doctrine. It became also a similarly important influence in developing literacy. Luther's tracts, sermons, and addresses were bought in great numbers, showing that many people could read. His address *To the Christian Nobility of the German Nation* sold five thousand copies within a very short time. In the quarter-century between 1500 and 1525, the annual number of books published in German rose from forty to five hundred. Many of these books dealt with the questions which were raised by the reform tendencies of the Reformation, and a large number were written by Luther himself. Many tracts, pamphlets, and sermons were published and widely circulated— "winged words," they were called. It has been said that Luther created the book trade in Germany, but this is an exaggeration. He greatly stimulated the circulation of books, but there were already a growing literature and many vernacular readers before he was born.

3. VERNACULAR BIBLES

The Bible was the favorite book among the common people. We have seen that it was circulated in manuscript copies by the Lollards in England; and on the continent there were many other translations of the Bible before the Reformation. They must have had a great influence in furthering the movement. One evidence is the fact that many of the clergy opposed its circulation and regarded its promiscuous reading as a cause of heresy. Over and over the medieval church, or at least some of the churchmen, forbade the reading of the Scriptures by laymen; but again, in other cases, they tolerated the reading of it by pious people when there was no danger of controversy. The bishops disagreed among themselves. When Tyndale's translation of the New Testament was smuggled into England, the archbishop of Canterbury burned every copy he could find, while the bishop of Norwich highly commended the work. Humanists, though devout Catholics, were generally favorable; but these were merely personal and unofficial opinions. Sir Thomas More is an example. He wrote: "I myself have seen and can show you Bibles fair and old, written in English, which have been known and seen by the bishop of the diocese, and left in the hand of laymen and women, whom he knew to be good Catholic people who used the books with devotion and soberness." More estimated that sixty per cent of the English people in the sixteenth century could read their own language, a valuable bit of testimony, although too generous perhaps, on the extent of literacy at that time. Erasmus also expressed the liberal Catholic position. He wrote with his usual eloquence: "I wish that even the weakest woman might read the Gospels and the Epistles of St. Paul. I wish they were translated into all the languages so as to be read and understood not only by Scots and Irishmen but even by Saracens and Turks. But the first step to their being read is to make them intelligible to the reader. I long for the day when the ploughman would sing a text of the Scripture at his ploughbeam; and that the weaver at his loom with this would drive away the tediousness of time, and the way-faring man with this pastime would overcome the weariness of his journey. And to be short, I would that all the conversation of the Christian should be of the Scripture, for in a manner such are we ourselves as our daily tales are." This was the attitude of a liberal who favored a liberal but Catholic Christianity. The day of liberal Christianity had already dawned when Erasmus wrote, but in a large part of Europe it was no longer to be Catholic. Of the old church, it is perhaps fair to say that it tolerated rather than approved, when it did not condemn the reading of the Bible in the common tongue.

Especially in Germany, the land of many early printing presses, there had been many vernacular translations. This was partly due to the variety of languages and dialects spoken in the German lands, a region which extended from the Netherlands in the west to the lower Danube valley on the east. The early German presses produced devotional books and Bibles in much larger numbers than classical works. Conrad Celtes, the humanist and university teacher, warned the priests that soon every village ale-house, if not every family, would have a Bible. Twenty-two editions of the Psalms, twenty-five of the New Testament or large portions of it, and fourteen or more of the whole Bible were printed on German presses before the Lutheran Reformation began. All of these were translated from the Latin Vulgate; they have no connection with the still earlier translations by Wycliffe, the Waldenses, and the Hussites. Their existence shows the strong religious interests of the German people; and those who read them had their minds prepared for the teachings of the reformers. Their wide circulation shows the growth of a laymen's evangelical religion of personal devotion.

This personal religion of Holland and Germany was not wholly un-organized even before the Reformation. As early as the beginning of the fourteenth century, mystics like Eckhart, Tauler, and the author of the *Imitatio Christi* gathered their followers into devotional groups. One of the largest and most influential of these societies was the one founded by Gerhard Groot in the Netherlands and called the Brethren of the Common Life, also called Hieronymians, a word derived from Jerome.

The Hieronymians were especially important for their schools. By 1384 they had more than forty centers where they taught children and copied manuscripts; and they set up Latin schools as well. At first they taught the subjects of the Trivium, and Erasmus was one of their pupils. When the revival of learning developed in the north, their schools, as we have seen, became classical and they enlisted a long line of famous humanist teachers. Alexander Hegius was headmaster at Deventer of a school which at one time enrolled two thousand pupils. Meanwhile they continued their popular teaching, gathering children and adults into schoolrooms and reading and expounding the New Testament and other religious books in the vernacular. They raised questions and led in discussions to solve the religious difficulties of their audiences. Spreading over western Germany, they did much to arouse and foster the religious life. There is evidence of their connection with the Hussites and the Waldenses in the fact that all of these used the same catechism for the instruction of children. It was printed in the German, French, Italian, Czech, and perhaps other languages. Such religious conditions are as important for the history of vernacular education as they are for the history of the Reformation.

4. TOWNS AND SCHOOLS

Town life developed rapidly in Germany in the last two centuries of the Middle Ages, and a great desire for education spread in all these growing centers. Prague secured a university in 1348, the first such foundation in Germany. It became the center of the Bohemian heresy, as we have seen. Between 1348 and 1500, thirteen other German universities were established, including the famous ones of Heidelberg, Leipzig, and Tübingen. Wittenberg, where Luther taught, was founded in 1502. Numerous schools also sprang into life, founded by wealthy citizens or by the municipalities themselves. Students came long distances, often from foreign countries, to attend school or university. This was also the era of the wandering scholars who secured food by begging and often by stealing. The autobiography of Thomas Platter, a Swiss lad who spent several years with a band of students or *vagantes* traveling from school to school, convinces the reader that many of these institutions were of little value. Breslau was famous for a whole system of cathedral, gild, and vernacular schools. Thomas Platter, who attended one of its Latin schools, has left a graphic description of its arrangements and exercises. "In the school of St. Elizabeth," he wrote, "nine bachelors of arts read lectures at the same hour in the same room. Greek had not yet penetrated into that part of the world. No one had any printed books except the preceptor, who had a Terence. What was read had first to be dictated, then punctuated, then construed, and at last explained." This was in the sixteenth century. No wonder he soon moved on in search of better instruction! He finally found it and became a learned man and a famous teacher. Indeed, there were many good schools. Luther himself had been a begging student who sang for his bread in the streets of "the dear town of Eisenach" until kind Frau Cotta gave him a home. In after years he denounced the begging system as a waste of valuable time and a temptation to vagrancy and worse. Germany had no lack of schools by 1450 or 1500, but the curriculum in most was still medieval, giving training in logical forms but little usable knowledge.

5. INTRODUCTION OF HUMANISM IN THE NORTH

The founders of the new order of humanistic education obtained their inspiration in Italy. One of the first was Nicholas of Cusa (1401–1464), who became a cardinal and a philosopher. As a student of astronomy, he came close to anticipating Copernicus. Thoroughly trained in the scholastic learning, he learned to love the classics which he studied in Italy. A less reputable and indeed notorious figure among the early German humanists was Peter Luder (1415–1474). He also began as a churchman, but he acquired in Italy not only the classics but also a total contempt for religion and even ordinary morals. He taught classical learning at Heidelberg but met great opposition, partly because of disreputable conduct, and he ended as a teacher of medicine at Vienna. John Wessel of Groningen (1420–1489) studied with the Brethren of the Common Life at their large school at Zwolle where he made contact with Thomas à Kempis, who influenced him profoundly. When he reached the highest class he also did some teaching in the lower classes, for that was the practice in the school. He had been a poor boy, a baker's son, but his ability won him generous patrons, including Pope Sixtus IV. When he had finished his studies in Italy and was ready to return home, the Pope said to the young scholar, "Ask what you please as a parting gift." "Give me," was the request, "books from your library, Greek and Hebrew." One of the books given him was a copy of the Gospels in Greek which is thought to have reached the hand of Erasmus when he was working on the second edition of his New Testament. Wessel taught at Heidelberg and also worked as a reformer of schools. In his views on indulgences he seems to have held a position similar to Luther's.

Rudolph Agricola (1444–1485), like Erasmus, was the son of a priest. From childhood he was passionately fond of music, learned to play the organ, and built a small one for himself. It is said that he added the vox humana stop to the instrument. Like other humanists, he studied in numerous places, the elements at Erfurt, at Cologne, and at Louvain, where he attained the master's degree, law and rhetoric at Pavia, and the classics at Ferrara, where, he said "literae humaniores seem to be in the very air." He was a pupil of the younger Guarino and of Theodore Gaza. Unlike most of the humanists, he paid considerable attention to the modern languages, learning German, French, and Italian. He wrote a few books and taught for a short time at Heidelberg but he died early. Like Erasmus, he taught that the true end of liberal education is moral conduct. He had a great reputation among his contemporaries, and his stimulating example was his chief contribution to German humanism.

The greatest of the northern humanists, perhaps the greatest of all humanists, was Erasmus. He treasured not only the classical heritage but that of the gospels as well. Between the two he saw no deep gulf but believed that they could be joined together and that their union would produce the fruits of sound learning, peace, moral conduct, and the good life. His influence extended throughout civilized Europe, among Catholics and Protestants, and has continued through succeeding centuries.

His first schoolbook came into the world almost by accident. This was the *Adages or Familiar Quotations from the Classics*. It is a collection of brief passages from the great writers. Each of these is used as a text for his own commentary; and the commentary is often studded with further apt quotations from ancients and moderns. It began as a small manuscript but with every successive edition it became larger. Although it was intended for schoolboys, it was read and quoted by everyone who read Latin literature and later was also translated into all the modern tongues. Very similar was the growth and history of his *Colloquies* which was intended to aid the acquisition of an easy Latin style while also imparting information and stimulating the thought of students. Schoolbooks in the form of colloquies or conversations were provided by many authors in the Renaissance. Next to that of Erasmus in popularity was one written by Corderius, the great Genevan teacher. Erasmus wrote an *Enchiridion*, which may mean either handbook or dagger, for the Christian soldier. He wrote a great satire, the *Praise of Folly*, and an argument against war, the *Complaint of Peace*. Dealing with education in the professional sense were his *On the Right Method of Teaching*, and *Training Young Children in Virtue and Sound Learning*. He collaborated with William Lyly in preparing a Latin grammar for St. Paul's school in London. He prepared a new edition of an elementary Latin reading book, the *Distichs of Cato*. For advanced classes he prepared editions of the Greek and Roman classics; and he also wrote on the pronunciation of the ancient languages.

Of all the books prepared by Erasmus, his edition of the New Testament in the original Greek had the widest influence and revealed best his central purpose, namely, to make the "philosophy of Christ" prevail. The revival of learning had brought the classics back to life and into current use; but in the north, attention was soon focused upon the classics of the church, the Old and New Testaments, and the writings of the Fathers. Valla, in his critical works, had already shown the method by which these were to be studied to bring out their true historical sense. Erasmus had, in 1504, found a copy of Valla's *Notes on the New Testament*. Even earlier, perhaps, Colet's lectures had convinced him of the need for a critical edition of that central Christian book. Many other scholars also were beginning to feel the same need if they were to deal historically and critically with the sources. Spanish scholars, under the lead of Cardinal Ximenes, were producing a careful edition of the whole Bible from several ancient editions and versions, the Complutensian Polyglot. The earliest volume of this extensive work contained the New Testament in Greek and was printed in 1514 but was not published until 1520. Meanwhile Erasmus issued his Greek New Testament in 1516. He continued to work on the text, collating new manuscripts, and prepared a second edition in 1519 and a third in 1522. New vernacular translations from Erasmus's text were made almost immediately. Luther made his German translation at the Wartburg in 1519; Lefévre, a French version in 1520; and Tyndale, in 1525, the first English New Testament to be translated out of the Greek. A Spanish translation from the Erasmian text came out in 1543. The reformed churches introduced these new translations into their church services and the common people read them in their homes.

The new textual scholarship was greatly indebted to the printing press. Before books were printed no scholar could be sure that his text would remain in the form which he had given it. No one could be certain that later manuscript copies would agree in all respects with the originals. Copyists carelessly or ignorantly introduced many errors. Thus two students working on different copies of the same work could never be sure that they had the same text before them. They had to expect omissions, interpolations, crude errors such as misplaced lines, and other forms of inaccuracy. Uniform texts hardly existed. And a text once rectified would not stay corrected in later copies but would again become corrupt. Under such conditions, to correct a manuscript would hardly seem worth the pains. But when printing came in, all this was changed. Erasmus's *New Testament*, when struck off by Froben's press, was the same in its hundredth copy as in its first. This made the gradual improvement of a text possible as new and better manuscript authorities were discovered.

This is what was actually done with the *New Testament* and all the ancient books. Textual criticism became a progressive and is by now almost an exact science. This was a gain, not only for the textual critic and the scholar, but also for the humblest teacher who could now be assured that his own copy of Terence, for example, and those of his schoolboys were identical, an obvious advantage in school exercises. And there was another and greater advantage. The text was brought into closer agreement with the original.

6. THE STUDY OF HEBREW

Before the Reformation, another literary controversy introduced a third language, the Hebrew, into the repertoire of northern scholars. Ranged against the New Learning was the whole weight of scholasticism and the power of the Dominican Order, then in a dominant position in the most powerful universities. The central figure in the controversy over the study of Hebrew was John Reuchlin; and it finally ended in the publication in 1516 of one of the most famous satires of that time, the *Epistolae Obscurorum Virorum*, or the *Letters of Obscure Men*. The anonymous authors, self-styled obscure, directed their shafts against ignorance but also against the sloth and immorality of the monks and those in high places in the church. And theirs was not the first such attack upon vice and obscurantism among the shepherds of the flock. Three centuries earlier a German minnesinger, Walther von der Vogelweide, had put into verse the northern resentment against papal exactions. He wrote:

> All their goods will be mine,
>   Their silver is flowing into my far-away chest;
> Their priests are feeding on poultry and wine,
>   And leaving the foolish fellows to fast.

Chaucer had slyly pictured the monk, dressed in fur, with a "love-knot" on the gold pin in his cravat and riding a fine horse among the footsore pilgrims to a holy shrine. Sebastian Brandt's *Ship of Fools* and Erasmus's *Praise of Folly* were more recent attacks upon hypocrisy and other evils among the privileged classes. The *Letters of Obscure Men* was only the most sarcastic attack and the last before Luther. It was occasioned by the controversy over Reuchlin's Hebrew studies.

The scholar and Hebraist, John Reuchlin, was born in 1455 in a little town in the Black Forest, the son of a burgher family. Entering the university at fifteen, he quickly mastered the Latin tongue. At Paris and Basel he studied Greek and at Orleans and Poitiers he became a doctor of laws. He continued his Greek studies in Italy and made such progress that it was said in eulogy, "Greece has flown over the Alps." At that time he was only twenty-six. Returning home he was employed in judicial and diplomatic work but continued his studies; and in 1492 he again visited Italy where he came under the spell of Pico della Mirandola who taught him to believe that in the mysteries of the Jewish *Cabbala* there lay the key to unlock the common Truth, which Plato in his philosophy and Christianity in its doctrine had separately expressed. But to use the *Cabbala*, he needed a knowledge of the Hebrew language. This he at once proceeded to acquire from learned Italian Jews. As the Jews had never at any period ceased to read their ancient works in the original, there was no question of a recovery; but Reuchlin was one of the first Gentile humanists to become skilled in the Hebrew language. Within a few years he published an enthusiastic eulogy of that tongue, the holy language, in which "God speaks with men." Upon returning to Heidelberg he was welcomed by the learned but was soon employed by the Elector Philip on a diplomatic mission to Italy where he renewed the opportunity to study the language. In 1506 he published an elementary Hebrew grammar and dictionary which introduced many to Semitic studies. A few years later (1509) an unexpected controversy arose over his work. It was started by John Pfefferkorn, a Jew recently converted to Christianity. With the zeal of a new convert and the support of the Dominicans of Cologne he conceived the plan of compelling all Jews to become Christians by confiscating all their ancient books, the Old Testament alone excepted. He secured the qualified support of Emperor Maximilian. Reuchlin refused to lend his aid to the scheme; but the universities and scholars generally divided into hostile camps over the issue, with the humanists and liberals supporting Reuchlin. The dispute led to much virulent writing and was finally carried up to the Papal Court for decision. The humanist Pope, Leo X, was not much interested in the quarrel but with the aid of Dominican funds the case dragged on for years. Those to whom the matter was referred voted in favor of Reuchlin but the decision was not published until 1520. By that time the Reformation had broken out, and the former decision was reversed and sentence was given against Reuchlin. Reuchlin died soon after without having been further molested.

7. THE LUTHERAN MOVEMENT

The attack of Luther upon the papacy, like most great historical movements, grew out of an incident, a campaign for the sale of indulgences in the neighborhood of Wittenberg. The idea of indulgences and reconciliation for sinners was very old. In early days of Christianity the congregations themselves expelled flagrant offenders against the Christian code and readmitted them upon confession and penitence. In time this right of the congregations and their control over the penalties imposed for sin were taken over by the priests, then by the bishops, and at last by the pope. In the thirteenth century the doctrine of a treasury of good works was developed. Under this conception the sinner was to benefit from the good deeds of the pious and the virtues of the saints. All these merits could be dispensed by the church to erring brethren as indulgences to release their souls from the penalties imposed by the church. Some of the indulgence-sellers, however, claimed much more for their wares and great abuses arose from the fact that the indulgences came to be sold for cash. Thus a money payment was added to or even substituted for penance. As early as the first crusade, Pope Urban II (1095) promised the crusaders a complete remission of all penances for taking part in the movement. The privilege of selling indulgences was also granted to cathedrals and to religious orders as a means of raising money. In the sixteenth century, the rebuilding of St. Peter's at Rome was under way and money for the work was raised by the sale of indulgence-tickets. Tetzel, the papal agent who had charge of the sale near Wittenberg, seems to have used reprehensible methods to increase his sales. This aroused Luther, who on All-Saints Day of 1517 posted his Ninety-five Theses against indulgences and other prac-tices of which he did not approve. He attacked claims that indulgences could remove guilt and remit punishment for sin, and declared that the true treasury of merits is the Gospel. The Theses had an unprecedented circulation and were translated out of the original Latin into German and within two weeks were read all over Germany.

Luther had intended to hold an ordinary university disputation with his colleagues; instead, he found himself the leader in a national movement which led step by step to a complete break with the Roman church. The sale of indulgences fell off rapidly, but the matter did not end there. At-tacks upon the Theses were answered by Luther in words that were read even more widely than the original document. His colleagues at Witten-berg supported him, and the students burned the countertheses of Tetzel and other opponents. Luther was summoned to Rome but he did not go. He appealed to his prince, the Elector Frederick, who took a deep interest in the quarrel and who was too powerful to be overawed. It was the disputation at Leipzig in 1519 which really opened Luther's eyes and the eyes of all Germany to the meaning of the revolution which was in progress. They now saw that the result would be separation from the church of Rome and the substitution of the Bible for the medieval ecclesiastical system as the rule of life. The young German humanists, the burghers in the cities, the common people who desired a free national church, and the princes who wanted to avoid the drain of money from their states generally supported the reforming party. Luther's pen was never at rest. He issued sermons, pamphlets, and books which were read everywhere. The printing press of Froben was very active in spreading his writings. All this is further evidence that many thousands in Germany could read and that there must have been many schools which have left no trace in the record, schools in homes and in the shops of tailors, saddlers, and other indoor workers. Many also may have learned to read without actually going to school.

Three of Luther's early books may be named: *The Liberty of a Christian Man; To the Christian Nobility of the German Nation*, which called for extensive educational reforms; and *On the Babylonian Captivity of the Church*. These "three great Reformation treatises" were written in 1520. In that year also the pope issued his excommunication of Luther, but he found the greatest difficulty in having it even published in Germany. The Electoral Council of Saxony, universities, and even bishops pretended to believe that it was not genuine. On December 10, in the presence of students, professors, and citizens, Luther solemnly burned the papal bull of excommunication outside the Elster Gate of Wittenberg. The separation from Rome was a fact.

When ecclesiastical measures failed to crush Luther, the church turned to the empire; when he could not be reached as a heretic, they attempted to have him declared an outlaw. Charles V became emperor in 1520 and held his first German Diet early in the next year. Luther was summoned to appear under a safe-conduct and did so in April 1521. In the august assembly, addressing the emperor and the princes, Luther not only refused to recant but reaffirmed his teaching in a quiet but determined speech which received the enthusiastic approval of the German princes and people and was roundly condemned by the emperor and his party. A month later Luther was placed under the imperial ban; but the ban could not be executed. For his own safety, Luther was concealed in the Wartburg by his friends. Political conditions made impossible the execution of the ban, for Charles was never free to exert the whole weight of the empire against the Germans. The imperial rule was threatened on the east by the invading Turks, who had come up the Danube valley until they were at the gates of Vienna, and on the west by the kingdom of France. Before the emperor was free from these threats to his power, the Reformation had proceeded to a point where it was impossible to crush it even by the united power of pope and emperor. Before Luther's death, in 1546, much the larger portion of the German empire had become Protestant. That area stretched along the Baltic from Holland to East Prussia and south in lines meeting in Switzerland. In this general region Protestant churches and schools had been established. Some regions within this triangle, however, remained Catholic, and large sections outside it became Protestant.

Since the Protestant churches regarded teaching as one of their main functions, they were even more interested in schools than the Catholic church had been; and we have seen that the Catholic church was the one great teaching institution for many centuries. Protestantism, however, held that everyone should be taught the Scriptures as the basis of his faith and life, of his private devotions and his participation in public worship, and of his duties as a member or vestryman, elder, or other official of the church. The new churches were as much concerned for the education of leaders and more than the old church had been for the education of members, men and women, boys and girls. This last point is significant, for the Reformation gave the first widely applicable reason for the education of girls. Only a few nuns and a few wealthy or noble women were educated in earlier periods. Though Luther was not a humanist, he favored the education both of the common people and of future leaders in church and state. He did not create vernacular education, which had been growing for several centuries, but he did what he could to further it. And in the vernacular schools, which developed after the Reformation, the children of the common people, boys and girls, received an elementary education.

The educational needs of the new period were greater and the resources were less than they had been. The Reformation, like all revolutions, was the cause of disorder and destruction which tended to make the improvement and even the maintenance of schools more difficult. The monasteries and their schools and scriptoria were closed; foundations, scholarships, and endowments were embezzled by princes and nobles; many positions which had been filled by learned men were abolished; and much civil disorder and religious warfare resulted from the Reformation.

The large number of positions which were abolished may be seen from the fact that a city of fifty thousand people sometimes had as many as eight hundred priests, or one for every sixty-five of the population. To this we must add the persons connected with monasteries, chantries, and other institutions if we would get a full measure of the vast number of clergy in the medieval church. And, Luther said, because selfish parents see that they can no longer place their children on the bounty of monasteries and cathedrals, they refuse to educate them. "Why," they say, "should we educate our children if they are not to become priests, monks, and nuns, and thus earn a support?" The hollow piety and selfish aims of such persons, he adds, are sufficiently evident from their confession.

School and university attendance declined rapidly in the period. The universities of Erfurt and Rostock never recovered from the losses sustained; but the numbers at Cologne, Vienna, Leipzig, and Basel also were greatly reduced. Professorships were abandoned because there were no students to be taught. Only little Wittenberg, founded in 1502, said Luther, is doing its best; but even Wittenberg lost three-fourths of its enrollment in the disastrous 1520's.

Luther attempted to stem the tide by his *Address to the Christian Nobility of Germany* (1520); by a *Letter to the Mayors and Aldermen in Behalf of Christian Schools* (1524); and by a *Sermon on the Duty of Sending Children to School* (1530). We should notice that these writings are addressed to rulers, civil officers, and parents, not to the clergy or the churches. One reason for this was that he realized the need of the state for educated public servants; and another that he needed the aid of the state to preserve the Reformation and to carry out his program for church and school. He was the first modern writer to urge compulsory attendance and proposed that the state should pass such legislation and enforce it. It was not until long after his death that any state followed his suggestion. Many of the larger nations did not enact compulsory attendance laws until the latter part of the nineteenth century, but the little state of Weimar, in 1619, demanded the compulsory education of all children in the vernacular. In all states, large and small, enforcement of such laws lagged considerably behind enactment.

Luther favored a broader curriculum for the vernacular school. Such schools at that time usually taught merely reading or reading with writing and arithmetic. There were also special schools of writing, arithmetic, and bookkeeping. He proposed to have music, poetry, and history, and "the whole course of mathematics" introduced. Luther was himself musical and would have both singing and instrumental music taught. He placed a high estimate upon the work of the teacher and declared that his vocation was, next to that of the ministry, "the highest and best." Schools were to be cheerful and pleasant so that children might take delight in acquiring knowledge. In language typically vigorous and violent, he described the old school of the Middle Ages as "a hell or purgatory in which children were tortured and in which with much flogging and wretchedness they learned nothing." Unfortunately school discipline was not so easily reformed but remained harsh even until recent times. To show how easily an education might be acquired, he declared that he would be satisfied with a school which should be in session only two hours a day. With good methods and stimulating, friendly teachers that would be enough. The rest of the child's day could be devoted to play and to the learning of a trade. Luther did not propose any innovation in industrial education, as is sometimes claimed. Apprenticeship was common and effective and he was satisfied with its results. On secondary education, in which he was greatly interested, he had fewer suggestions to make. Along with all the other reformers, he supported the current classical program and emphasized the study of "the holy languages," Latin, Greek, and Hebrew. They were considered "holy" as well as "learned" because they were considered essential in the study of the Scriptures. Every "promising lad" was to be enabled and encouraged to attend a secondary school and, after that, the university.

In northern Germany, John Bugenhagen reorganized the churches, the Latin schools, and the parish schools in which German reading and writing were taught. Bugenhagen also worked in Denmark, and schools were developed for the common people in all the Scandinavian countries. Ability to read was made a requirement for confirmation and this, in turn, a prerequisite to marriage. Thus an indirect form of compulsory schooling was developed. Melanchthon reformed the schools of Saxony, providing for elementary schools and especially Latin schools, in which he was most interested. John Sturm organized his Protestant humanistic gymnasium at Strassburg in 1538. This school, with its nine-year course, was the first example of a type which became the dominant secondary school of Germany for centuries and which remains to the present. One important fact about these and other German schools of the Reformation era is that state and church cooperated in their establishment and maintenance. The Reformation marks an important period in the transfer of the educational functions from the church to the state. From this time on, for several centuries, we see the increasing activity of the state in education until, in the eighteenth and early nineteenth centuries and after the democratic revolutions, the state took over these functions almost completely. As a result of this movement, elementary and secondary schools have become secular and civil rather than religious institutions.

8. SPREAD OF THE REFORMATION

The movement inaugurated by Luther spread far beyond Germany. The leader in Switzerland was a young humanist who was so fond of music that he had contemplated entering a monastery to secure the leisure for developing his musical talents. His family did not wish him to become a monk and he became an eloquent and popular preacher instead. His name was Ulrich Zwingli. Coming to Zürich in 1519, he became the admired leader of a circle of young liberals. The reform movement began there almost immediately. Zwingli read one of the books of John Huss and was led to the conclusion that church tithes were or should be only voluntary offerings. From this he went on until Zürich, Basel, and Berne became fully Protestant. The mass was abolished by the citizens and council of Berne in 1528. The Swiss, in 1529, separated themselves from the Lutheran movement and developed an independent church, the German Reformed. The American branch of this Zwinglian church is now called the Reformed Church of the United States.

Geneva, in western Switzerland, became the capital of Calvinism. In the same year (1536), the city became politically independent and Protestant. Calvin's doctrinal position was accepted by the Huguenots of France, the Dutch Reformed communion of Holland, the Presbyterians of Scotland, and the Puritans of England and America.

John Calvin (1509–1564) grew up in Picardy, among a people known for their sympathy with Wycliffe and Huss. He was a brilliant student and was thoroughly educated in the classics, the law, and theology. Mathurin Cordier, already mentioned in connection with the Collège de Guyenne, was one of his teachers. At the University of Paris, Calvin belonged to the Collège de Montaigu, Erasmus's old school. About the same time another student, who was to become a world-famous leader, entered the same college. His name was Ignatius Loyola. Whether the future reformer and the founder of the Society of Jesus ever met is not known. Calvin was a Protestant as early as 1532, but he was not compelled to flee from France until three years later. After short periods at Strassburg and Basel he came to Geneva.

Calvin is often blamed for the harsh laws and cruel criminal code of Geneva. These accusations are not altogether justified. The city of Geneva was a free republic. Although Calvin was extremely influential in the government, the city was ruled by the Council. The citizens and the Council must share the blame for its "blue laws" and criminal code. Calvin did not create them; but he acquiesced in them, and he did not attempt to change them. The "blue laws," or sumptuary laws, of Geneva were similar to those of Nuremberg and other cities at that time. Restrictions which we would regard as gross tyranny were common. In Geneva, the dress of the different classes of citizens, the number of guests at weddings, and similar matters were prescribed by law. So with the burning of Michael Servetus (1509–1553) the scientist. Servetus was condemned as a criminal in a regular trial and punished according to law by the Council of Geneva. Servetus was a unitarian; this was his heresy; and heresy was then considered as treason. Servetus was executed by the barbarous method which was then used in such cases. He was burned at the stake. The Protestants of France and Switzerland, in 1903, erected an "expiatory monument" to him. In the inscription they acknowledge their debt to the great reformer, Calvin, but condemn his error, which they say "was the error of his time."

The secondary school of Geneva had seven classes. It was a humanistic school with a thorough course in Latin, Greek, and rhetoric. Calvin drew several famous teachers to Geneva, including Cordier, Theodore Beza (1519–1605), who prepared a French translation of the New Testament, and Castellion (1515–1563), the author of a book of *Colloquies*. The Academy of Geneva (1559) was the nucleus of a university; but, at first, it gave instruction only in advanced humanistic studies and theology. Medicine and theology were added later. The schools of the city attracted many foreign students who in their turn spread the educational influence of Geneva. And, in fact, Calvinism had an international aspect. Its interest in universal education, in the separation of church and state, and in a church government in which laymen participated influenced many countries. Two of these countries, Holland and Scotland, were particularly influential in promoting these principles in America.

10. THE REFORMATION IN ENGLAND

The Reformation in England was a political change rather than a religious movement among the people. Parliament in 1534 passed the Act of Supremacy, which separated England from Rome. The English Bible became common in the homes and the English language was used in the services of the church. An English catechism and the *Book of Common Prayer* were provided.

In England as in Germany the Reformation was educationally destructive. The monasteries and chantries were closed and their funds for the most part appropriated to political ends. Along with the monasteries, the monastic grammar schools were abolished and England was left poorer in educational opportunities than it had been before the Reformation. Although some schools were refounded, and some new schools were opened, the losses of the Reformation were not made good for a long time. Nothing was done by the government and little by the Anglican church for elementary education. Private schools of the most diverse qualities grew up in villages and towns. Many of these were mere dame schools. Thus England developed a *laissez faire* attitude in education which was to delay the development of an educational system and of universal opportunity for schooling until the latter nineteenth century, and of secondary education until the twentieth century. English individualism tended to restrict the functions and powers of government within narrow limits, and these limits did not permit the government to deal with schools. English religious toleration and the consequent growth of many dissenting sects, coupled with the desire to inculcate some form of religious belief in each school, further limited the educational activity of government. Churches and private individuals or groups, however, established schools. The dissenting academies of the seventeenth century were one such response.

A difficult social problem and a great deal of hardship to the poor were occasioned by the decline of the gilds, the destruction of the monasteries, and the Enclosure Acts, all at the same period. The Reformation dried up many of the old streams of charitable aid, and the enclosing of the common lands for use as "sheep walks" or ranches deprived the poor of means of subsistence and firewood which they had from the commons. Thomas More, in his *Utopia*, refers to England as a country in which "sheep eat men." A series of laws were passed to restrict begging, to require the parishes to support their poor, and to provide for the teaching of trades by means of a system of publicly supported apprenticeship. The intention was to prevent the growth of a pauper class by aid to vocational education. Near the close of the reign of Elizabeth, the previous fragmentary legislation was codified in the English Poor and Apprenticeship Law of 1601 which, among other obligations, enjoined the overseers of the poor in each locality to furnish materials, to build workhouses or to bind out children, and to make systematic arrangements to teach useful trades to the young poor. Similar laws were passed but not well enforced in the colonies which were soon to be founded in America. The Massachusetts education law of 1642 and a Virginia statute of nearly the same time exhibit the influence of English experience with apprenticeship laws during the preceding century.

11. THE JESUITS

The Society of Jesus, commonly known as the Jesuits, was founded in 1534, through the efforts of Ignatius Loyola (1491–1556), and was recognized by the Roman church six years later. They immediately became active as preachers, missionaries, teachers, and school founders. They became a kind of flying squadron to recover for the Roman church the territories lost through the Protestant revolution and to spread her influence to new countries. Active almost everywhere in Europe, the Jesuits soon came to America with the purpose of converting the Indians. As a result, they also became explorers in Canada and in the Mississippi and Ohio valleys. They went to Africa, to China, to India as missionaries. All those who were sent out to distant lands as well as those who worked in Europe were given a thorough education in the schools they established.

Ignatius Loyola was chosen General of his order and received the vows of his companions in 1541. The new Society became famous almost immediately, and numbers sought to join. A strict military discipline was decided upon from the first. There were four classes of associates: the novices, who were all carefully selected for zeal, devotion, and ability; the scholastics, who had been novices for at least two years and who had to spend at least five years in study and five more as teachers in junior classes; the coadjutors, who were preachers and teachers and from whom the heads of schools and houses were chosen; and the professed, who alone could share in the government of the Society. This long winnowing process assured that every Jesuit was a picked and a marked man. The Constitution gave the General almost absolute power over the lives, the consciences, and the activities of the members; yet it also provided for a system of surveillance and an elaborate use of the confessional intended to keep everybody, even the General, in the line of duty and to prevent all illicit changes in the Constitution. The government of the Society is autocratic and absolute and the General is a veritable Czar. Historians, for example Ranke in his *History of the Papacy*, have not been slow to point out that, along with much that is good, this Society has done a great deal of evil through its secret and ruthless political machinations, its casuistry, and its blind obedience to the Catholic church.

The Society became powerful almost at once in Italy and Portugal. Progress was slower in Spain where the hostile Dominican Order was in power. Schools and colleges were developed early in these countries. In France, also, there was much opposition, but colleges were founded at St. Omer, Douai, and Rheims. From the beginning, Ignatius saw a promising field in Germany and, while the Society was not able to destroy the work of the Reformation, they effectively prevented its spread to regions which were in imminent danger of becoming Protestant. This statement applies particularly to Austria where the colleges, which were founded at Vienna and Ingolstadt, became centers of Jesuit propaganda and education. In a century, the Society had six hundred schools; and in two centuries, eight or nine hundred. Some of their schools were large, the largest ones enrolling as many as a thousand or even two thousand pupils. Many of the most famous schools were in France.

At the height of their power, the Jesuits were the most successful educators in Europe. Their schools were permanent, well supported, and well organized, their teachers were selected and thoroughly educated in what they taught and in the methods of discipline and teaching. Everything was prescribed, not only the subjects and methods, but also the interpretations. The teachers had no freedom, and no innovations or experiments were allowed. They had a limited and attainable aim and used every available means to reach it. The fourth part of the Jesuit *Constitution* is the plan of studies, called the *Ratio Studiorum*. The *Ratio* was fully worked out and several times revised in the light of experience in teaching between the years 1584 and 1599, when it was adopted and issued to the schools. This work is a set of directions to teachers and school officers and it prescribes a system which leaves little to their judgment. It is an ironclad scheme. Once adopted, it became the law of Jesuit education until the suppression of the Society by the pope in 1773. After the Society was reestablished in 1814, the *Ratio* was revised again (1832) and some emphasis was placed upon the vernacular language.

The Jesuit schools are almost exclusively secondary and higher institutions. At first, Loyola had devoted a portion of his efforts to social reform. He set up two orphanages in Rome, one for boys and one for girls. In these two hundred children were fed, clothed, and taught. The teaching included some handwork and vocational work. But this was soon given up, and thereafter the Society, except as an occasional work of charity, devoted all its educational efforts to the classical and theological education of boys and young men. There were no Jesuit schools for girls. The colleges were divided into junior and senior divisions. The former had a six-year course devoted to Latin grammar, literature, and rhetoric, and the latter a four-year course in literature, rhetoric, and logic. After completing the junior division, the future member of the Society was occupied for two years in the religious activities of his novitiate; and the senior division was followed by a period of several years in cadet or practice teaching under supervision. The whole program occupied the Jesuit up to the age of thirty or longer, when he became a full member of the Society and a professor. In the higher colleges, mathematics, logic, philosophy, and theology were taught in a course of from four to six years. The Greek and Hebrew languages were included but the emphasis throughout was upon the Latin. It was the language of instruction and conversation, in and out of school, although even in the *Ratio* of 1599 the vernacular was permitted as an aid in teaching beginning pupils. Extraordinary emphasis was placed upon skill in speaking and writing idiomatic Latin fluently. Equal emphasis was placed upon skill in argument, upon a knowledge of philosophy and theology, and upon the development of character and complete devotion to the Society and the Roman church. It may be as well to say that these ends do not seem to have been always compatible, each with the others.

The colleges were supported by endowments and donations; instruction was free. Externs, that is those who had not the intention of becoming Jesuits, were admitted, and contributions were often obtained from their parents. The Society became rich and has always catered to the wealthy, the aristocratic, and the powerful classes. But the success of the schools was due neither to money, which gave the means, nor to the curriculum, which was simply the formalized humanism of the sixteenth century. Their success was due to their organization, methods, and men. The conduct of the pupils at their lessons and at play, and the methods of the teachers, were closely supervised. Supervision was exercised by the rector of each school and by his prefect of studies and prefect of discipline. The teachers were as carefully supervised as the pupils. A system of spying, or "manifestation" as it is called by Jesuits, was used in the schools and in the Society. Once a year each school was inspected by the provincial who had charge of the schools over a large area. The discipline, while firm, was mild and gentle, especially as compared with the brutality which ruled in the schools of the sixteenth century. Much use was made of rivalry and competition. Each boy had his opponent, each group of ten was pitted against another group of ten, and classes vied with classes.

One of the striking elements of Jesuit method was the assignment or prelection. We give a greatly shortened example from the *Ratio*. It says: Let the teacher read the whole passage through. Let him explain the topic and its connection with what went before. After reading a single Latin sentence, let him explain the difficult words and phrases, not merely substituting one hard word for another. The vernacular may be used if necessary. Let him explain the allusions and make observations suitable to each class. Such was the prelection.

Another element in Jesuit method was the repetition. "At the end of the lectures some students, about ten at a time, will repeat during half an hour what they have heard, one of their fellow students of the Society, if possible, being put in charge of each group of ten." This passage illustrates another practice of the Jesuit schools, the use of monitors in teaching. Systematic daily, weekly, monthly, and yearly reviews were also carried out. Carefully organized written examinations were given. Add to this that the teachers were men selected for their ability and zeal; that they were prepared for their work by study and by teaching under the guidance of skillful teachers; and that they prepared to devote their lives to this profession, and we shall understand why Francis Bacon, who was not a Jesuit, could say that the Jesuit schools were the best in Europe. He should have said, best for the purpose which the Society followed.

12. OTHER CATHOLIC SOCIETIES

Other teaching societies, besides the Jesuits, developed Catholic schools. The Oratory of Divine Love grew up in Rome as a voluntary association, originally of fifty or more laymen and clergy, who were interested in church reform and devoted to humanism, a pure life, and the theology of St. Augustine. Scattered by the sack of Rome in 1527, some of them found new homes in Venice, Genoa, and other cities where they formed groups of "Christian academies." Influenced by this Italian Oratory, the French Cardinal de Berulle in 1611 established the Oratory of France. De Berulle and his followers were devout Catholics who wished to improve the discipline and education of priests. The Oratory grew rapidly and established some famous schools such as the one at Juilly. They were influenced by the writings of Descartes; and the philosopher Malebranche was a member of the order. They aimed to cultivate close personal relations between teachers and pupils. Their schools were conducted in French and taught mathematics, physics, and the natural sciences. Polite accomplishments such as dancing and various games were taught. The Oratorians paid special attention to music and were known as "les pères au beau chant." Palestrina had been an adherent of St. Philip Neri, one of the founders of the Italian Oratory, and had composed music for the congregation. The learned languages were not neglected, but their schools were realistic, a type which will be treated in the next chapter. The word oratorio seems to be derived from the name of these societies.

The Port Royalists, or Jansenists, which were founded by St. Cyran and Cornelius Jansen, established schools that resembled those of the Oratory. The theology of both groups was derived from St. Augustine; and their ascetic outlook led the Port Royalists to supervise their pupils very closely. For this reason, the schools and classes were kept small and the teachers lived with their pupils. The curriculum was, in general, similar to that of the Oratorians, although dancing was omitted. The Port Royalists, however, made an advance over the Oratorians by their excellent teaching of the French language and of logic. In logic, they used the inductive method. Their teachers wrote textbooks in grammar and logic that were widely used. The "Little Schools of Port Royal" lasted only from about 1646 to 1661 when, through the opposition of the Jesuits, the society was dispersed. Their influence was far greater than their small numbers and short period of activity would suggest. Blaise Pascal was their greatest defender.

Catholic charity schools for the poor were established by several societies. One of these was the Brothers of the Christian Schools, founded by Jean Baptiste de la Salle in 1684. They were required to dedicate their lives to teaching and agreed not to become priests. They taught the vernacular language and religion. La Salle wrote a book of directions on organizing schools and teaching. It is called *The Conduct of Schools* and in general purpose, not in content, might be compared with the *Ratio Studiorum* of the Jesuits. The Christian Brothers developed a class system of teaching as compared with individual instruction. They classified their students into proficiency groups, used monitors to teach the younger pupils, and established a normal school for the preparation of teachers. Their schools increased rapidly in France and spread to foreign countries.

The Order of Ursulines was a society of nuns, devoted to the education of girls. France, in the seventeenth century, showed a strong interest in the best types of education for girls. The Abbé Fénelon wrote a widely influential book, *On the Education of Girls*. Fénelon believed that girls should be educated for homemaking and the care of a household as a career. This involved some training in law and business affairs and economic principles. An example of Fénelon's influence is seen in the fact that when the Philadelphia physician, Benjamin Rush, wrote on the education of American girls he followed the French abbé's outline. Fénelon had the direction of the education of some pupils of the royal family of France and prepared some historical and ethical books for them. These were read not only by schoolboys but by almost all readers of French literature. The most famous was *Télémaque*, a story which teaches that rulers should be the servants of their peoples.

The Reformation period greatly extended the educational opportunities of the common people, Catholic and Protestant, boys and girls. In secondary education, it continued the humanistic tradition and used the old humanities for the service of the church. At the same time, it tended to overemphasize grammar and style and thus narrowed the meaning of humanism until it became largely linguistic. The Reformation also gave an opening for the civil governments to participate more actively in education; and this trend toward state education continued to grow in the following centuries.

The Reformation was a social evolution growing out of political, economic, moral, intellectual, and religious changes. Intellectually, the Reformation was connected with the humanist movement. Both appealed to individual judgment, original sources, and the inspiration which was to be derived from a revered past. The Reformation directed its intellectual activity not so much toward aesthetic and political ends as to Bible study by means of the original tongues. Old Testament scholarship demanded a knowledge of Hebrew; and New Testament studies were aided by the revival of Greek and the more authentic Greek texts of Erasmus and others. The Reformation was, therefore, related to the Revival of Learning, but it was a broader movement.

The Reformation was a popular, not an aristocratic movement. Salvation by faith was an individualist principle. It applied to everyone of both sexes. It implied individual understanding. The Protestant religion became the religion of a book, the Bible; and personal faith presupposed knowledge and understanding of the Bible. On this path the reformers were led to support universal education. The Reformation was also a nationalist movement and resulted in the creation of national churches which used the national language in their services and their parish schools. The Reformation promoted, and was promoted by, the increasing use of the printing press. The vernacular school was adopted by the new churches with the favor and sometimes with the financial support of the government. This was the opening stage of the long progress toward national education, a result which the reformers neither foresaw nor desired.

Catholic education, which did not follow this trend, was led by the late humanistic secondary schools of the Jesuits and the schools of the Christian Brothers which provided elementary, vernacular education for poor children. The schools of the Christian Brothers taught reading, writing, arithmetic, morals, religion, and sometimes spinning or some other manual work. The curriculum of the elementary schools, both Protestant and Catholic, rarely extended beyond these subjects. These were class schools and only much later were they superseded by the common, civil schools.

QUESTIONS

1. In what respects may the Renaissance in the north and the Reformation be linked as parts of a single movement? In what respects may they be distinguished from each other?

2. Which of the causes of the Reformation affected education and in what ways?

3. Was the extraordinary emotion generated by the Reformation due solely to piety and interest in religion? Explain.

4. Consider the invention of printing as a means in the democratization of knowledge. In what sense do you use the word "democratization"?

5. Consider the influence of the invention of printing upon the Reformation movement.

6. Find some good books on the subject and trace the early history of the English Bible.

7. How did humanism in the north differ from humanism in Italy? How was it related to the Reformation?

8. Why did the Protestant churches regard teaching as one of their chief functions? The Roman Catholic Church had conducted schools for a long time. Was the Protestant attitude on education different from the Catholic?

9. What were the names of the secondary schools of the Renaissance-Reformation period in the several countries? How similar or different were they?

10. In what way is the political doctrine of Calvin of importance in education?

11. Why was Holland a center of great educational activity in the Reformation period?

12. Trace the different uses of the word "public" as it has been, in different places and periods, applied to schools and education.

13. How did the Reformation affect education in the American colonies?

14. Why were the Jesuit schools highly praised in the sixteenth and seventeenth centuries?

FOR FURTHER READING AND STUDY

The Reformation and the Society of Jesus are both highly controversial sub-jects, and although we have space for only a few titles, an attempt has been made to give representation to several interpretations. A few biographies of Erasmus and of Luther out of many are given.

Allen, Percy S., *The Age of Erasmus*, New York, Oxford, Clarendon Press, 1934, 303 pp.; *Erasmus: Lectures and Wayfaring Sketches*, Oxford, Clarendon Press, 1934, 216 pp. Mr. Allen edited *Sir Thomas More: Selections from his English Works and from the Lives of Erasmus and Roper*, Oxford, Clarendon Press, 1924, 191 pp.; and an edition of Erasmus's *Letters*, in Latin, 10 vols.

Bailey, Nathan, Translator, and E. Johnson, Editor,*The Colloquies of Erasmus*, London, Reeves and Turner, 1878, 2 vols.

Bainton, Roland H., *Here I Stand; A Life of Martin Luther*, New York, Abingdon-Cokesbury Press, 1950, 422 pp.; *Hunted Heretic; the Life and Death of Michael Servetus, 1511–1553*, Boston, Beacon Press, 1953, 270 pp.

Barrett, Edward J. B., *The Jesuit Enigma*, New York, Boni and Liveright, 1927, 351 pp. An unfriendly and personal account by one who was dismissed from the Society.

Beard, Charles, *The Reformation of the Sixteenth Century in its Relation to Modern Thought and Knowledge*, London, Williams & Norgate, Ltd., 1907, 451 pp.

Born, Lester K., Editor, *The Education of a Christian Prince, by Desiderius Erasmus*, New York, Columbia University Press, 1936, 277 pp.

Eby, Frederick, *Early Protestant Educators*, New York, McGraw-Hill Book Company, Inc., 1931, 312 pp.

Farrell, Allan P., *The Jesuit Code of Liberal Education; Development and Scope of the Ratio Studiorum*, Milwaukee, The Bruce Publishing Company, 1938, 478 pp.

Fitzpatrick, Edward A., *St. Ignatius and the Ratio Studiorum*, New York, McGraw-Hill Book Company, Inc., 1933, 275 pp.

Froude, James A., *Life and Letters of Erasmus*, New York, Charles Scribner's Sons, 1894, 433 pp.

Grisar, Hartmann, *Martin Luther, His Life and Work*. Adapted from the second German edition by Frank J. Eble, St. Louis, B. Herder Book Company, 1935, 609 pp. This is an impartial biography by a Catholic author. Has a bibliography.

Harney, Martin Patrick, *The Jesuits in History, the Society of Jesus through Four Centuries*, New York, The American Press, 1941, 513 pp.

Lindsay, Thomas M., *A History of the Reformation*, New York, Charles Scribner's Sons, 1906, 1907, 2 vols.

McCabe, Joseph, *A Candid History of the Jesuits*, New York, G. P. Putnam's Sons, 1913, 451 pp.

McGucken, William Joseph, *The Jesuits and Education; the Society's Principles and Practice, especially in Secondary Education in the United States*, Milwaukee, The Bruce Publishing Company, 1932, 352 pp.

Mangan, John J., *Life, Character, and Influence of Desiderius Erasmus*, New York, The Macmillan Company, 1927, 2 vols.

Monroe, Paul, *Thomas Platter and the Educational Renaissance of the Sixteenth Century*, New York, D. Appleton and Company, 1904, 227 pp.

Murray, Robert Henry, *Erasmus and Luther: Their Attitude Toward Toleration*, London, Society for Promoting Christian Knowledge, 1920, 503 pp.

Nichols, Francis M., *The Epistles of Erasmus*, New York, Longmans, Green and Company, 1901–1918, 3 vols. The selected letters, extending down to 1520, are in English and fully annotated.

Painter, F. V. N., *Luther on Education*, Philadelphia, Lutheran Publication Society, 1889, 282 pp. Luther's *Letter* (1524) and *Sermon* (1530) on education in English. The long introduction provided by the editor is uncritical.

Schwickerath, Robert, *Jesuit Education; Its History and Principles*, St. Louis, B. Herder Book Company, 1904, 687 pp.

Smith, Preserved, *Erasmus; a Study of His Life, Ideals, and Place in History*, New York, Harper & Brothers, 1923, 479 pp.; *The Age of the Reformation*, New York, Henry Holt and Company, Inc., 1920, 861 pp.

Stokes, Francis Griffin, *Epistolae Obscurorum Virorum*, London, Chatto & Windus, 1925, 560 pp. The Latin text with an English translation and notes.

Woodward, William Harrison, *Desiderius Erasmus concerning the Aim and Method of Education*, Cambridge, University Press, 1904, 244 pp.; *Studies in Education during the Age of Renaissance*, Cambridge, University Press, 1924, 336 pp. The latter title contains material on the northern humanists.

8 FROM HUMANISM
TO REALISM

NOT ONLY THE MEANING BUT ALSO THE PRACTICAL VALUE OF science was becoming clear in the seventeenth century as its application to military affairs and to surgery and medicine came to be recognized. New schools, called academies, began to provide a more practical education, including some of the sciences and mathematics. The French and German academies were intended for the noble and fashionable classes but in England the academy was patronized by the mercantile and manufacturing classes, who were beginning to share in the leadership of society. The advances in natural science and education were paralleled by new doctrines of religious and political liberty, by the rise of international law, and by the foundation of modern philosophy. Both the national and cosmopolitan trends of the century helped to place the modern languages in a more favored position than they had ever occupied. The great writers of the time, Bacon, Locke, Descartes, began to make more use of the mother tongue, and the realist schools gave a place to modern foreign languages in their schedules.

Educational writers, such as Comenius and Locke, gave further emphasis to the need for modern curricula and improved methods, while Comenius and Mulcaster favored universal education. A deep and widespread optimism characterized the century, and utopists like Campanella and Andreae attempted to bring education into closer connection with society itself. One of the ways in which they attempted to do this was by supporting industrial and vocational education in schools. This was a new demand. Schools had always dealt with words and ideas but now they were asked to introduce materials and tools and to teach trades. Much progress was made in the century but more would have been possible had it not been for the religious wars that followed the Reformation: the Huguenot wars in France, the Puritan struggle in England, and the terrible and devastating Thirty Years War in Germany. The utilitarian and realist tendencies in education were also held back by the continued success of the Jesuit schools in Catholic countries. In the seventeenth century the Jesuits were still the greatest educators in Europe, and realism could make little progress wherever their formal classicism was dominant. In spite of these deterrent influences, the seventeenth and eighteenth centuries, not the Renaissance, mark the real beginning of modern education.

1. THE MEANING OF REALISM

Realism in education may be compared with realism in philosophy, or art, or literary criticism. It connotes concrete knowledge, practical and vocational skills, the learning of languages for commercial or diplomatic rather than for literary use, and the study of history, politics, law, and the sciences. It is, negatively, a reaction against the literary and artistic purposes of the Renaissance and against the classics. Among the realists, the fine arts, music, dancing, and even literature, were given very little place or none at all. Greek had always been a poor second to Latin in the schools of western Europe and the realists wished to dispense with it altogether. In the seventeenth century, they still demanded instruction in Latin, not for the humanistic reason that it is the key to a great literature, but because it continued to be widely used as the medium of communication in public affairs, in the sciences, by the universities, in international correspondence, and by the Catholic church.

One of the catchwords of realism was "things before words," and this was sometimes taken to mean "things and not words." But words themselves are "things" and will repay careful study. On the other hand, many real things can hardly be studied at all except by the extensive and careful use of words. Such "things" are the French Revolution, courage, loyalty, devotion to duty and country, and the doctrine of evolution. No one recommends mere verbalism, but neither should we attempt to teach a science, a craft, or even swimming, without the use of words. And yet the realists emphasized an important element in all education, namely, the value of direct experience as a basis for teaching and learning.

A broad curriculum was one of the features of realism. It is not unusual to find seventeenth-century realists proposing the study of twenty-five or thirty subjects, including two or three languages such as Latin, French, and the vernacular, two or three branches of mathematics, several social studies, a number of sciences, philosophical, military, and vocational branches, and a variety of polite accomplishments. The number, variety, and necessarily superficial treatment of the many studies was a general characteristic of realist education.

New methods came in with the new subjects. Languages were to be taught by direct methods, by conversation and by composition. Travel, observation, demonstration, and the early beginnings of the laboratory facilitated new methods. Botanical gardens, cabinets of minerals, pictures, drawings, maps, globes, and instruments were introduced. Because better methods were used and the children actively engaged in doing things in school, the discipline became milder.

Realism was partly but not wholly an upper class movement. The English academy was a middle class school, Comenius and Mulcaster were concerned with the vernacular education of the common people, and the vocational education of mechanics was proposed by several realists. The Reformation and Counter-Reformation had laid emphasis upon the vernacular languages for the common people; and this emphasis was greatly increased by realism. Thus the realist movement of the seventeenth century gradually affected almost every phase of education, but the classical schools and the universities were still the dominant institutions. These long resisted the new influences.

2. A HUMANIST WITH REALIST LEANINGS

Early in the sixteenth century the Spanish scholar Juan Luis Vives (1492–1540) urged the study of nature, and accepted the principles of utility and practical application as criteria for judging education and life. To modern languages, he assigned a place in the curriculum along with the ancient. He proposed two devices, the use of notebooks for lists of words, idioms, and eloquent passages, and, secondly, the method of double translation from the foreign tongue into the native speech and back again. The Englishman Roger Ascham, who recommended the same two devices, may have obtained these ideas from Vives.

Vives was one of the few great humanists who was also versed in modern tongues. He knew Spanish and French and was acquainted with Flemish and English; and in this interest in the vernaculars he was not alone, for the famous Spaniard Antony de Lebrija had prepared the first Spanish grammar and dictionary in 1492, the year of Vives' birth. When children go to school, Vives declared, they are to speak in their own tongue, not in Latin. It is the duty of mother and teacher to preserve a pure native language.

History and geography were to be taught as means of developing practical understanding and knowledge of public affairs. The school histories, Vives held, should not emphasize war but rather the arts and achievements of civilization. Modern history should be emphasized, not only the history of the great states but also that of the smaller progressive nations. Like Erasmus, he was interested in the problem of international peace.

In his psychology, Vives struck out along new lines. The senses are our first teachers and sight is the chief of the senses. Children vary widely in capacity, in ability to observe and distinguish, in intelligence and judgment, but also in persistence and power to pay attention, and in mental vigor and energy. Some children are notable for skill with the hands as in painting or weaving. Some of these ideas he may have read in his favorite Quintilian and he certainly found there the thought that we can best discover the nature of children by watching them at play. The psychological principle for which Vives is best known is the Greek doctrine of association. He said: If two ideas occur together then at a later time the less important one will tend to call up the more important. He dealt also with forgetting and ascribed it to physical conditions, to imperfect understanding, and other features. The teacher should help the pupil recall what has been learned, by teaching the connections between ideas, by the use of surprise and wonder, by means of rhymes, and by serial arrangements. In Vives, we have some of the elements of an educational psychology, and he also anticipated Bacon and the inductive method of science. His ideal school or academy was to be a public institution, and education was to be extended to boys and girls. He prepared a highly successful book of school dialogues or colloquies somewhat like those of Erasmus, Cordier, and Castellion. In this little schoolbook, he incidentally threw much light upon the educational conditions of his time.

3. REALIST UTOPIAS

The Utopia of Thomas More had little to say about education but it contemplated having all men learn both a trade and the art of agriculture; and it declared that the Utopians "have all their learning in their own tongue." Industrial education and the use of the vernacular by scholars were proposals characteristic of realism. Other realist utopias of the early modern period were the *Christianopolis* by John Valentine Andreae (1586–1654), the *Nova Solyma* of Samuel Gott, the *Commonwealth of Oceana* (1650) of James Harrington, and the *City of the Sun* of Thomas Campanella (1568–1639). Campanella was an Italian Dominican who got into difficulties with the Spanish government and the Inquisition and wrote his book in prison. The political features of the *City of the Sun* are drawn from Plato, but in his educational views Campanella was a realist and an encyclopedist. His city was to be equipped with gardens and collections of all kinds. The walls and public buildings were to be covered with pictures, maps, diagrams and illustrations of the mechanical arts and various instruments, with portraits of their inventors and of other historical figures. He anticipated the idea of the planetarium. Such devices, together with specimens of all created things and all human constructions, were to be used in the education of the young. Education started at birth, but children began to study the sciences at the age of six and this was followed with instruction in the practical arts. The city was opposed to narrow specialization and favored instead an encyclopedic and more general knowledge and training. In regard to languages, however, the reverse of this policy was in force. The citizens held that, although languages must be studied, they need not be studied by all; they may be assigned to a sufficient but small number of specialists. In this utopia, each citizen worked four hours a day, and the rest of the time was to be spent in "learning joyously" and in other recreations. Special attention was given to industrial education, and even the officials and rulers had to be skilled in the physical sciences and practical arts.

England in the seventeenth century had a number of minor writers, such as Samuel Hartlib, John Dury, and William Petty, who gave expression to new ideas on vocational education. Hartlib was not English. He was a Polish merchant living in London and was bent upon the establishment in his adopted city of an institute for physical investigation. This project made him the center of the group which invited Comenius to England. It is important to notice that this was just before the Royal Society was started. Hartlib's *Description of Macaria* was a utopia in which all children, both boys and girls, were taught industrial occupations and agriculture. He proposed a national bureau of vocational guidance and employment, an idea much discussed in his day and again in ours. John Dury, inspired by Hartlib, wished to have trades taught to the common people and science to the future scholars, while William Petty of the same circle proposed a college for the highly skilled occupations. He named a dozen of these skilled trades including the manufacture of scientific instruments. Petty also had advanced notions on vocational guidance. All of these writers exhibited other realist tendencies as well. Dury, in the *Reformed School*, declared for object teaching, for the use of the mother tongue, and for an encyclopedic curriculum. Proposals for industrial education also cropped up in Germany and some actual schools were opened in the following century.

4. JOHN MILTON ON EDUCATION

The little book, *Of Education*, by John Milton (1608–1674), which was written at the request of Samuel Hartlib, is as famous for its prose as for its proposals. It is usually criticized on the ground that it makes extravagant demands upon the pupils, and Milton admits that his program is not "a bow for every man to shoot with that calls himself a teacher." And yet the English academies carried out nearly all that Milton recommended although much of it was done superficially. Milton's own education at St. Paul's, at Cambridge, and in private study at home was rounded out, as the custom was, with a period of travel. There is no sufficient reason to raise a doubt about his statement that he met Galileo in Italy. Upon his return, Milton taught a school which is described in Edward Phillips' life of the poet. It was during that period that he wrote *Of Education*.

In this little tract, Milton insisted that good teaching must begin with sensory ideas; and that the sole function of language is to convey ideas. "Though a linguist," he wrote, "should pride himself to have all the tongues that Babel cleft the world into," it is only through the information and wisdom which these languages transmit that he becomes learned and wise. Languages should be learned through oral instruction in an easy book and by extensive reading. What languages? He named Latin, Greek, Hebrew, Chaldee, Syriac, and Italian. He did not mention French and he noticed English only incidentally. He proposed to have the beginning student of Latin read the opening chapters of Quintilian, and thereby learn about education and the Latin language at the same time.

Milton's realism is further shown by the extensive and varied course of study, from arithmetic and geometry learned as games, "the easy grounds of religion," and Bible stories to navigation, architecture, and fortification. Writing in the midst of the civil wars, he had the education of soldiers in view and proposed daily exercises in the use of weapons and instruction in tactics. Like Vives, he was a humanist as well as a realist and did not neglect social and aesthetic studies. Poetry and the drama, history and political oratory were to be studied. Again like Vives, he proposed a special institution which he called an academy and which was to be both school and university, educating boys to the age of twenty-one.

5. THE ENGLISH ACADEMIES

At the Restoration (1660), when their clergy were driven from their positions and their youth excluded from the universities, the Puritans established their own schools for secondary and theological education and these they called academies. The first was established at Sheriffhales (1663) in a spacious manor house with close-clipped lawns and ancient trees. Not many of the academies could afford such beautiful homes, but otherwise the first was typical of the seventy or eighty such schools which were established later. They were generally small, enrolling from twenty to fifty students. Without endowment, they depended upon fees for their support.

Sheriffhales may be taken as an example. The founder, John Woodhouse, had studied at Cambridge and was a family chaplain when the Act of Uniformity silenced him in 1662. He conducted the academy for thirty-four years until 1697 when it was closed because of his advanced age. Like others of these private schools, its success depended mainly upon the principal. The course of study occupied four years and included three ancient languages, English, and a wide range of subjects to be followed by some professional work in law, anatomy, and theology. While much use was made of textbooks and lectures, there were practical exercises in surveying, dissecting, constructions, debating, and other activities. There was a close connection between the academies and the Scottish universities. The Scotch and the Puritans were dissenters and realists. Excluded from Oxford and Cambridge, many academy students attended northern universities, where after a residence of a year or longer they obtained a degree. In their preference for the English language as the means of instruction instead of Latin, the academies and the Scottish universities further resembled each other. Charles Morton, who later came to America and was vice-president of Harvard College, made this change by using English in his teaching at his academy at Newington Green in 1680. This was several years before the German University of Jena took a similar step. Philip Doddridge at Northampton Academy and the noted ethical teacher Frances Hutcheson, at the University of Glasgow, changed to English in 1729. This phase of the realist movement, the driving out of Latin by the vernacular as the language of schools and universities, was, of course, a very important change.

Newington Green under Morton was progressive in other ways. His academy had a form of self-government where the pupils in a school republic legislated for themselves. Others of the academies also became centers of democratic politics where future Whigs received their early training in public affairs. Many of the dissenters sympathized with the American Revolution and later with the French Revolution. Among these was Joseph Priestley, who like Charles Morton came to America. Many manufacturers and businessmen of the north of England sent their sons to the academies, so that sometimes half the students were preparing for a business career. But the Puritans could not adequately support the schools. Some were closed, others became secondary schools, and a few were transformed into higher institutions. Manchester Academy became Manchester College of Oxford University. By 1820, when the somewhat similar institutions in the United States were in their prime, the great era of the English dissenting academy was over.

In Germany, a religious movement known as Pietism paralleled the English Puritanism and had a somewhat similar influence upon education. August Hermann Francke (1663–1727) became the leading Pietist school founder. Near the end of the seventeenth century, he established at Halle a group of institutions known as the Halle Foundation. It included a vernacular school for poor children, a Latin school for the middle class, and a science school for nobles. To these, a school for teachers was later added. At the time of Francke's death, his schools had more than two thousand pupils. The distinguishing feature of all the schools was their realist curriculum. They provided cabinets of minerals and of natural history, a chemistry laboratory, and a workshop for wood and glass. One of Francke's teachers was Christopher Semler (1669–1740) who planned a realist secondary school; and, in a pamphlet of 1739, he described his proposed school, calling it a *Realschule* or Realist School. A few years later, in 1747, a clergyman, Julius Hecker (1707–1768), who had been a pupil in Francke's schools, established such a school in Berlin. In this six-year school, instruction was given in three languages, German, French, and Latin, and in mathematics, drawing, history, geography, human anatomy, mechanics, and architecture. There were also some vocational classes. Schools of this type were gradually opened in other cities. They prospered and in the nineteenth century the courses were extended to nine years; and these new *Oberrealschulen*, or Higher Realist Schools, were accepted as one of the major types of the official secondary school system of Germany.

6. MODERN SCIENCE AND PHILOSOPHIES

Twenty-five years (1518–1543) will cover Magellan's circumnavigation of the globe, the new astronomy of Copernicus, and the new anatomy of Vesalius. Such achievements might lead one to assign the rise of modern science to the early decades of the Reformation period, but the real power of science was not understood until the following century.

In the seventeenth century, science came to be recognized as an international and cooperative enterprise. The first great scientific societies were founded in that century in Italy, England, France, and other countries. The Accademia dei Lincei (that is, of the Lynxes) was founded in 1603 at Rome by G. della Porto (1541–1615), a prolific but not very original writer on physical science. Of this body, Galileo was a member; and some pupils of Galileo founded the Accademia del Cimento (experiment) at Florence in 1657. The Royal Society of London began somewhat casually but by 1660 it had developed into a well-organized association of scientists and it was chartered in 1662. Similar was the early history of the French Academy of Sciences, founded in 1666. Under the leadership of Leibnitz, a royal academy was founded in Berlin in 1700. In informing scientists of work already done or in progress and in calling attention to new problems, the publications of these associations were invaluable.

A deliberate effort to define scientific method developed. Two of the pioneers in this field were Francis Bacon and René Descartes. In his definition of the inductive method, Bacon insisted upon observation, experiment, and the industrious collecting of facts, but he did not sufficiently emphasize the importance of ideas, insights, and happy guesses as guides to investigation and to generalization. Mere labor alone, however unsparing, will not produce science. Genius is demanded and those investigators are most successful who are most adept in raising significant, answerable questions. Although Bacon did not see this clearly yet by his literary power he did much to stimulate interest in discovery and in calling attention to the practical value of scientific knowledge.

While Bacon demanded experiment and new discoveries, Descartes called for incontrovertible proofs which he sought by rational and mathematical methods. Descartes' *Discourse on Method* (1637), his *Rules for the Direction of the Mind,* and his *Search after Truth by the Light of Nature* are examples of a whole class of psychological and educational books. Locke wrote one which he called the *Conduct of the Understanding* (1706), and recent examples of the same class are sometimes entitled "How to use your mind" and "How we think." Descartes reduced his method to four "rules" somewhat as follows:

1. Accept as true nothing that it is possible to doubt.
2. Analyze every statement into its simplest elementary propositions.
3. Review each of these elementary propositions one by one.
4. Make your final enumeration so complete that nothing shall be omitted.

Descartes was impressed by the success of mathematics in finding indisputable proofs of its propositions and took the mathematical methods as his ideals in scientific investigation. But, although he was keenly aware that the senses may lead us into error, he did not neglect inductive and experimental work. He carried out dissections and was deeply interested in the work of Harvey and of Gilbert.

Scientific method is a compound of induction and deduction. Induction begins with some question and proceeds by observation and experiment. Deduction begins with an assumed or a demonstrated truth and draws its necessary implications. The proofs of elementary geometry are the handiest examples of deduction. Both induction and deduction are likely to involve unrecognized assumptions which may introduce errors into the conclusions. Every natural science seems to depend for its new matter upon observation and induction, while necessary inference and deduction supply proofs of its general principles.

An example of scientific method which involved both the Baconian and the Cartesian elements together with a description of the progress of his thought had already been furnished by Copernicus who published his *De Revolutionibus Orbium Coelestium* in 1543. In the dedication of that work he explained how he had obtained his results. He said that (1) he became dissatisfied with the growing intricacy of the Ptolemaic theory; (2) he studied all previous views; (3) he proposed to himself a new and simpler theory; and (4) by observation and calculation he proved that his theory accounted for all known facts. A simplified account of his method might read about as follows: "When I had thought long on the traditional views concerning the paths of the heavenly bodies, it seemed to me lamentable that no better explanation had yet been proposed. Then I read the writings of the ancients and found that some of the Greeks had held that the earth moves about the sun and turns upon its axis. Gathering confidence from these suggestions, I conceived that I as well as they should have liberty to propose a more satisfactory theory of the motions in question. I then assumed the motions which I describe in the present work, and after careful investigation extending through years, I found that if the movements of the other planets were referred to the motion of the earth in its orbit about the sun all their observed phenomena can be satisfactorily explained and that a simple and harmonious system is the result. In accordance with this theory I have drawn up the plan of my work." He had kept the manuscript of his book not for nine years as Horace recommends but for thirty-six years before he decided to publish it.

The invention of new instruments to aid observation, manipulation, and measurement was a third development in seventeenth-century science. Lenses were known to Archimedes, but spectacles seem to have been made in Italy about 1289 and the telescope was developed in the Netherlands about 1600. Leeuwenhoek with a simple microscope discovered bacteria. Galileo who made good use of the telescope is said to have occasioned the invention of the compound microscope. Huyghens (1629–1695) invented an improved eyepiece. He also invented the pendulum clock although Galileo in 1582 had used the pendulum, kept swinging by hand, to measure small intervals. The barometer, air pump, and thermometer are other instruments of the same period. Mathematical inventions of the same time were decimal fractions, logarithms, better symbols and notations, the analytic geometry of Descartes, and the calculus of Leibnitz and Newton. All these had much to do with the rapid development of science and its proper applications.

For the history of science one must go to special books, and there are now many good ones; but a few names will provide a little orientation. We have already mentioned William Harvey who discovered the circulation of the blood in 1616 but did not publish his complete results until 1628. Two famous microscopists, Malpighi and Leeuwenhoek, demonstrated the capillaries which Harvey had been unable to see; and Leeuwenhoek, with his keen sight and manipulative skill, figured the blood corpuscles and many forms of bacteria and protozoa. Harvey, with a simple lens, made contributions to embryology and developed the doctrine that each individual begins as a fertilized egg. Thomas Sydenham who followed the principles of Hippocrates in tracing the natural history of diseases had John Locke for an assistant and pupil. Sydenham is sometimes regarded as the founder of modern clinical medicine.

The contributions to physics and mechanics were equally notable. William Gilbert in his De Magnete (1600) founded the new science of electricity. The genius of Galileo was shown, as Lagrange pointed out, not so much by his work in astronomy which needed only a telescope and industry but by his discoveries in mechanics. Near the end of his life, he published at Leyden a book, Two New Sciences, in which he announced the laws of falling bodies and the pendulum, determined the component motions of a projectile and its parabolic path, and described other experimental discoveries in dynamics, statics, and hydrostatics. The foundations of modern chemistry were laid by Robert Boyle who defined "element" as an irreducible substance, thus distinguishing between elements and compounds. Boyle also experimented on electricity and on the physiology of respiration. He is best known for his law that gas pressure and volume vary inversely. In the seventeenth century, the new mathematics which was needed as a scientific tool was supplied by Napier who developed logarithms, by Descartes, Leibnitz, and Newton whom we have already named, and by many lesser men. The work of Newton on light and gravitation was the crowning achievement of science in this period.

Although we shall be anticipating the developments of several centuries, it will be useful to indicate here some of the influences which the sciences gradually exerted upon education. The first was that the sciences themselves were included in the curricula of schools. Many sciences were introduced into the realist schools of the seventeenth century, although unfortunately they were usually taught from books. Secondly, the methods were gradually improved. Collections of minerals and of instruments such as the air pump, barometer, or prism were shown and demonstrated. Later on, laboratory demonstrations were given by the teacher, and still later the students were asked to carry on experiments. Observation and field excursions were used early, but the student laboratory was not common until the nineteenth century. The scientific method of discovery, somewhat after the manner described by Copernicus, was recommended by Rousseau as a method of teaching and was so employed by Pestalozzi and later teachers. Problems and projects were introduced not only in science but in other fields also. In the third place, science aided the improvement of the physical plant and the equipment of schools and provided the basis for the study and practice of hygiene, home economics, agriculture, and other practical arts and vocations. Fourthly, beginning with the inductive psychology of Vives and Locke, natural science furnished the model and some of the tools for a science of education, which began to develop in the present century. Finally, the greatest effect of science upon education came from its influences upon the spirit of the school. It made education more inductive and investigative and less authoritarian and memoriter. These changes, however, came slowly, and are not yet by any means complete or universal. We shall come across them again.

7. EDUCATION FOR STATESMEN AND MEN OF AFFAIRS

One result of the advancement of science was that a strong current of optimism was generated. This is felt in the views of the scientists and philosophers as well as in those of the educators whose task demands an optimism which, however, it does not always help to generate. Descartes and Bacon, Locke, Comenius, and the utopists were all optimists and prepared the way for the "theory of progress" in the following century. The sciences, said Descartes, should not be acquired singly like a skill or an art. All the sciences are merely applications of human wisdom or brains to the facts of nature; and they are so interconnected and so based upon a common foundation that they may all be acquired together instead of attacking them one at a time. Reason, it seemed to Descartes, is evenly distributed among men and by his method, which we noticed above, anyone should be able to arrive at the scientific truths of nature. Bacon also thought that a good method would enable anyone to become a scientist and even a discoverer. Most of the great educators show the influence of the same current of optimism. This applied especially to Comenius but also to the most influential of all English writers on education, John Locke.

John Locke (1632–1704) was a man of the council table rather than the study, prudent and skillful rather than scintillating. Known for his genial friendliness, he was equally noted for self-restraint and ability to hold his tongue. In that period of violent party strife, Locke was the confidential agent of Lord Shaftesbury. The same Dr. Fell of Oxford, whose unpopularity is still an unsolved mystery, celebrated in the stanza,

> I do not like you, Dr. Fell,
> The reason why I cannot tell;
> But this I know and know full well,
> I do not like you, Dr. Fell,

was commissioned to spy upon him and set traps for him; but he was completely baffled by Locke's reserve and caution. In his *Some Thoughts Concerning Education*, Locke urged that children should early be taught to guard their speech.

Although Locke was not a man of the study, he wrote many books, and this in spite of the fact that he devoted much of his time for twenty years to a single one, the *Essay Concerning Human Understanding*. It is little of an exaggeration to say that Locke applied only his spare time to composition and that most of his works are occasional writings, called out by the practical demands of the hour. Even the titles, the *Essay*, noted above, the *Letters on Toleration, Some Observations on Printed Money*, or *Some Thoughts Concerning Education* show that many of his works were tracts for the times.

Born near Bristol, Locke was the son of a country lawyer who was a Puritan, who sent him to Westminster School and to Oxford. He became a lecturer in his college and his connection with the university lasted for thirty years, although much of this time he was not in residence. Like Milton, he had a highly unfavorable opinion of current education. What he thought of the English Public Schools is clear from his *Thoughts*. The scholastic course was still in vogue, and he sometimes wished that he had never gone to the university; but in that case we might never have heard of him. Oxford, with all its defects, was the making of him.

The bent of his mind is clearly shown by his early studies. In a fragment on the art of medicine, he wrote down this principle: "True knowledge grew first in the world by experience and rational observation; but proud man, not content with the knowledge that he was capable of, and which was useful to him, would needs penetrate into the hidden cause of things," and even presumed to lay down his own laws which nature is to follow. In his Oxford period, Locke joined a chemistry club for which Boyle secured a lecturer from Germany. Anthony à Wood, another member and later a political opponent, reported that Locke would not take notes quietly like the rest but was "always prating and troublesome." This may simply mean that Locke's practical mind was "content with the knowledge that he was capable of" instead of attempting to "penetrate into the hidden causes of things" as the alchemists tried to do. Locke was graduated a bachelor of medicine and sometimes prescribed for patients but, owing to difficulties with the university authorities, he never secured his final medical degree.

Returning from a diplomatic mission to Brandenburg in May 1666, Locke resumed his work in Oxford. That summer, through some medical services, Locke made the acquaintanceship of the Earl of Shaftesbury. He was to serve for many years as secretary and as adviser in the education of the children and later the grandchildren of this patron. He was elected a Fellow of the Royal Society, which brought him into the circle of "the incomparable Mr. Newton." A mutual friend was Robert Boyle, who chose Locke as his literary executor. A question raised in a social group about this time started Locke on the composition of his *Essay Concerning the Human Understanding*. The question was, what is the mind capable of knowing; and in developing his answer he came to consider psychological and logical questions and earned the reputation of being one of the founders of modern psychology as well as of a new species of philosophy, the critical philosophy which was carried forward by Berkeley, Hume, Kant, and later thinkers. The *Essay* occupied him intermittently for twenty years and appeared in the bookshops early in 1690. For the manuscript, upon which he had worked so long, he received thirty pounds.

Two periods of foreign residence, first in France where he had charge of a pupil about 1675 and later in Holland, broadened Locke's experience of life. In France, he translated but did not publish the moral essays of the Jansenist, Pierre Nicole. This must have brought him close to the sphere of activity of the Abbé Fleury. Lord Shaftesbury wrote to Locke to inquire what books were used in the education of the dauphin, one of whose tutors Fleury was. We must mention this educator more particularly because of the likeness between his views and those of Locke. Claude Fleury (1640–1723) wrote a *Treatise on the Choice and Method of Studies* which includes an early, perhaps the first, account of the history of education. It was, however, written to outline and defend a utilitarian course of study. Although it was finished in 1675, it was not immediately published. Locke was in France, during these years, but there is no evidence that the two authors met. Perhaps the explanation of the close similarity of their views is that both were influenced by Descartes, by Port Royal, and by the contemporary conditions in England and France. Be that as it may, Fleury's *Treatise* came out in 1686, shortly before Locke's *Thoughts Concerning Education*. Five editions of the *Thoughts* appeared in Locke's lifetime and a great many afterward. The first French translation (1695), by Pierre Coste, reached at least five editions. Besides the Dutch version (1698) mentioned by Locke in a preface, the book was also translated into Swedish, German, and Italian, and no doubt other languages.

Nor did the author dismiss the subject after the book had appeared but, as new editions came out, he added here a paragraph and there a page to the earlier text. This manner of composition explains the repetitions, digressions, and badly constructed sentences that one occasionally finds. There are also some deviations from Locke's usual good sense. But its merits were so great that we should not dwell on its imperfections. And it was influential. Much of the philanthropinist movement of the eighteenth century was in harmony with Locke's views, and he was read in the nineteenth century as well.

The educational optimism of the century was shown by Locke in the first paragraph of the *Thoughts*. He declared that men are, at least nine parts out of ten, formed by education rather than by heredity. This might mean that the school can make of a man what it will just as a river at the source could easily be turned in a direction other than the one which it has taken. As we have already noted, this view of Locke and others that the nature of men can be changed by education gave rise to an optimism in regard to society which was to lead in the succeeding age to a well-defined theory of progress.

Four principles form the foundation of Locke's educational doctrine. These may be named the principles of utility, of rationality, of practice or conditioning, and of direct experience; they will be discussed in this order. Early in life, Locke prepared a short guide to conduct which would have delighted Benjamin Franklin. A man's proper business, he wrote, is to seek happiness and avoid misery. The most lasting pleasures come through health, reputation, knowledge, doing good, and the hope of eternal happiness. "In life," he added, "I must carefully look that it cross not any of those great and constant pleasures above mentioned." In again considering the aims of life and education in the *Thoughts*, he included health, virtue, practical prudence, courtesy, industry, and knowledge. Virtue is here the greatest and controlling aim and in defining it Locke announces his principle of rationality. He wrote: "As the strength of the body lies chiefly in being able to endure hardship, so also does that of the mind. And the great principle and foundation of all virtue is placed in this, that a man is able to deny himself his own desires, cross his inclinations, and purely follow what reason directs as best, though appetite lean the other way." This is the cornerstone of Locke's theory. He believed, with Descartes, that a man's reason can control his desires and stormy emotions and bring to a peaceful and rational end the conflict which otherwise rages between the good and evil forces of his inner life.

The ability to reason originates early in life and should be cultivated from the first, according to Locke; but, although it begins early, it develops slowly and therefore children must for a considerable time be directed by adults. Before the child can be permitted to make his own choices, at least in difficult cases and on weighty occasions, he must be conditioned, as the psychologists say, to make the right choices. And the right choices are those approved by reason. Conditioning or training in good habits is Locke's third principle. As Locke in one place put it, children are not in the right way until they take delight in laudable things. Claude Fleury, who held the same view, declared that he who can make pleasant what it is desired that children shall do will have discovered the great secret of education.

By example, by repetition and constant practice, through praise and blame, rewards and punishments, said Locke, good habits are to be formed and the moral law made clear, easy, and palatable. It is, therefore, necessary that children shall be brought up in a good society. This is the basis of Locke's attack upon schools with their "herds of unruly boys"; and of his fear of the evil influence of vicious servants. "Children," he wrote, "are not to be taught by rules which will be always slipping out of their memories. What you think necessary for them to do, settle in them by an indispensable practice as often as the occasion returns," and even make occasions. Until children can reason and will follow reason, even though desire lean the other way, they must be habituated, trained, and conditioned to good and right conduct.

Both wisdom in practical affairs and good manners are best learned by experience. This is Locke's fourth principle, and he applied it chiefly in moral education. The world is full of cheats, follies, and faults, and to be forewarned is to be forearmed. This experience of the world must be carefully guarded so that the child may learn the true state of an evil world and may become a good judge of men without becoming corrupted. Knowledge of the world of men is to be given through this guarded experience; but Locke proposed to give knowledge of the physical world also through sensory experience, knowledge of countries and customs through travel, and skill in fencing and dancing and in the use of tools through practice and participation. This is an important principle, but Locke did not make as much use of it as some other realists. In geography and science he did not propose, as on his principles he should have done, to take children into the field.

Health is treated first in the *Thoughts*. His advice was mainly hygienic and was directed to the development of a strong constitution. He gave attention to diet, exercise, clothing, sleep, and good health habits. His main idea is the Spartan one of hardening and inuring the body to overcome any tendency to weakness and effeminacy. To the attainment of health and the moral and practical qualities, Locke devotes two-thirds of his book. In one of the most important sections, the ninety-fourth, he said: "The great work of a governor is to fashion the carriage and form the mind; to settle in his pupil good habits and the principles of virtue and wisdom; to give him little by little a view of mankind, and work him into a love of imitation of what is excellent and praiseworthy; and in the prose· cution of it, to give him vigor, activity, and industry. The studies which he sets him upon are but as it were the exercises of his faculties, and employment of his time, to keep him from sauntering and idleness, to teach him application, and accustom him to take pains, and give him some little taste of what his own industry must perfect." Information can be obtained as needed. "But of good breeding, knowledge of the world, virtue, industry, and love of reputation, he cannot have too much; and if he have these he will not long want information." And yet he devoted one-third of his space to school subjects.

In the selection of these studies, he followed his utilitarian principle, keeping his eye upon his main object, the education of a gentleman. The attaining of knowledge depends for a motive upon curiosity which is an "appetite" for knowledge and which is to be carefully fostered in children for it is "the great instrument of nature for overcoming the ignorance they were born with." We must encourage their questions and answer them truly and seriously. Children are travelers just landed in a new country and we who are old residents should be helpful to them.

When a child is able to talk it is time to teach him to read, and this may be done playfully with ivory letters and some easy, pleasant book. Writing should follow reading and should be begun soon afterward. He thought shorthand might be worth learning by young gentlemen. After English, French and then Latin were to be taken up. Languages should be learned by a conversational and nongrammatical method. Grammar should be taught only after a great deal of progress had been made in the languages; and Latin themes, verses, and the memorizing of long passages were to be omitted.

Arithmetic is recommended for early study because it offers the "easiest sort of abstract reasoning" but also because it is useful. Geography and astronomy are to be presented as mathematical subjects. The Copernican system is favored as the simplest and also the likeliest to be true. Geometry should follow, and the first six books of Euclid are enough for a gentleman. In every subject we should begin with what is simplest and plainest and should consider carefully what the child is capable of understanding. Many subjects were included in the scheme, history, rhetoric, logic, ethics, civil law, and biblical history. Greek he thought unnecessary for a gentleman. Music he condemned because it wastes so much of a young man's time. Dancing, fencing, and a trade were to be taught. He named several suitable trades, but he favored gardening and carpenter work. From such occupations were to be derived exercise, recreation, and a practical understanding of working conditions, and also knowledge and experience which would be useful when the boy himself became an employer. The last period, when the boy was fairly mature, was to be spent in foreign travel with a tutor. Locke himself had served as the traveling tutor of a boy whom he directed through France.

Finally, he advised parents to consult their own reason in planning the education of their children rather than to follow old custom merely. In the *Thoughts* he did not deal with the education of the working class, but we know from other documents that he would have offered them only meager schooling. He dealt with a somewhat special subject, the education of an English gentleman, and he dealt with that subject, not exhaustively but comprehensively. The distinctive quality of Locke's educational doctrine is not only its common sense and cool realism; it is that he saw men as the sculptor sees them, "in the round," as physical, intellectual, social, practical, moral, political, and religious beings. Education was to enable men to live well in all these dimensions.

8. THE LANGUAGE QUESTION

Educators in the seventeenth century were more conscious of language than ever before or since. The ancient Greeks studied only one language, their own; the Romans in the classical period added Greek to Latin, but by the fourth century Greek was again disappearing from the schools of the West; and the schools of the earlier Middle Ages were conducted in Latin and taught no other language. With the Renaissance, we came into a new era. The classical Latin took the place of the medieval Latin and fifty years later Greek was reintroduced. With the development of biblical investigation, Hebrew also was added, and trilingual colleges flourished at Salamanca, Paris, and Louvain. Meanwhile, the vernaculars were taught in the new elementary schools, and modern foreign tongues began to knock at the doors of academies and municipal schools. Obviously there was a language question. The languages tended to monopolize a curriculum which was at the same time hard pressed to admit more mathematics, history, science, and other subjects including several practical arts. The realists offered various suggestions including the following: limiting the time for languages and devoting the rest of the school time to other subjects; teaching fewer languages, omitting Greek, and of course Hebrew, which was never widely taught; concentrating on languages as tools and omitting literature; using supposedly more effective methods of language teaching such as conversation, extensive, easy reading, careful selection of the vocabulary, and various crutches like interlinear translations or having the teacher translate instead of the pupils. The writers who dealt with the subject did not confine themselves to it, and to the greatest of them, Comenius, the language question is only a detail in a complete system of educational philosophy.

Vernacular schools had become far more numerous since their first appearance in the Middle Ages; and the church used the vernacular to teach the catechism and Bible, but usually only to the poor and to those who would receive no further schooling. In the seventeenth century the civil and practical advantages of vernacular education came to fuller recognition. Educators such as Ratke and Comenius, Peter Ramus of France who wrote a grammar of the French language, a few Spaniards already mentioned, and several prominent English educators argued vigorously in favor of the vernacular.

Among the English reformers of language instruction was Richard Mulcaster (1530–1611), who was headmaster of Merchant Taylors' School for twenty-five and of St. Paul's for twelve years and to whom we are indebted for a prophetic work on the teaching of English, *The First Part of the Elementarie which entreateth Chieflie of the right writing of the English Tung* (London, 1582). He demanded that all children should be taught reading, writing, drawing, singing, and playing an instrument. With such a foundation, he declared that he could teach the boys in the grammar school more Latin in four years, between twelve and sixteen, than they could have learned without it in ten years. One of Mulcaster's chief interests was the improvement of the English language. He urged the preparation of an English dictionary and prepared a word list to aid in stabilizing English spelling. This was his list of the eight thousand most frequently used English words. He also proposed to reform the English universities and to establish in each a college of education.

Other English masters of the period who had the same concern were Brinsley and Hoole. John Brinsley (c. 1570–c. 1630) in his *Ludus Literarius or the Grammar Schoole* (London, 1612) expressed his conviction that boys should learn good English before undertaking Latin; and he insisted that the Latin school must take care to preserve and extend skill in the mother tongue. Too often, he declared, Latin was allowed to crowd out the English so that boys came up to the university unable to read and write their own language. And Charles Hoole (1610–1667), "Master of Arts and teacher of a private grammar school in Lothbury Garden, London," devoted a whole section of his *New Discovery of the Old Art of Teaching School* (London, 1660) to the teaching of English.

The most distinguished of the immediate predecessors of Comenius was Wolfgang Ratke (1571–1635) who was educated in the Johanneum in Hamburg, the school that Basedow later attended. Ratke's grandiose plans won the support of Prince Ludwig of Anhalt-Köthen who had founded the "Fruit-Bearing Society" for the purpose of improving the German language. Ratke favored the High German of Luther's Bible as the national speech and insisted that it must be taught first, before Latin. His plan for teaching the elements of Latin did not succeed, and Prince Ludwig withdrew his aid from the school. Ratke read the plays of Terence over and over with his class, both in Latin and in translation, but they still could not read Latin because they had been merely passive listeners. He proposed to develop a science of education which he intended to base upon psychology and upon an analysis of the subjects that were to be taught. He argued that the government should support the schools because of their great social and political importance. Of Ratke's influence we shall speak later. Comenius, who is one of the world's great educators, also dealt with the language question, but only as one element of his broad and profound conception of education.

9. THE MASTER KEY TO UNIVERSAL EDUCATION

John Amos Comenius (1592–1670), a Czech and a Moravian, was one of the great system builders in education. He came from the lower middle class—his father was a miller—and did not attend secondary school until he was sixteen. This late beginning is supposed to have forcibly directed his attention to the methods employed in teaching languages, about which he had a good deal to say. One of his teachers in the university at Herborn was the celebrated J. H. Alsted (1588–1638), from whom he acquired ideas on the scope and organization of the sciences. After a year at the university of Heidelberg, he became first a teacher, then pastor, and later bishop of the Moravian churches. The Thirty Years War began just when he became pastor at Fulneck which was in the path of the invading armies. The little city was sacked, its people massacred, his wife killed, his library and manuscripts destroyed, and Comenius was driven into exile in Poland. There he taught in the gymnasium at Lissa. By that time his writings had already brought him a European reputation; and he was invited (1641) to come to England to serve as the head of a projected college of research. This scheme miscarried, and Comenius accepted from the Chancellor of Sweden a commission to prepare textbooks for the Latin schools of that country. During those years he lived in Elbing and also taught in the gymnasium of that town. About 1650 he was called back to central Europe to reform the schools of Sáros-Patak, but after several years, when warfare again broke out in that region, he retired to Amsterdam where he continued to write to the end of his life.

Comenius produced about a hundred and seventy works, large and small, some in Czech and others in Latin. In the field of education, he wrote schoolbooks and works on theory. His most important theoretical work was *The Great Didactic* (1628) or "the art of teaching all things to all men," that is, the master key with which to unlock all educational doors. Three years later he published the first of his language books, the Latin textbook, *Janua Linguarum Reserata* (1631), the open door to the languages. We shall consider the language texts first. The idea for the

Janua came from Elias Boodin. A book of the same kind prepared by William Bateus, a Spanish Jesuit, was in wide use; but when Comenius issued his *Janua* it swept all similar books off the boards. It was used in the schools of Europe for three centuries.

This famous textbook was based upon eight thousand common Latin words arranged in sentences. The sentences are simple in the beginning and become progressively more difficult as we proceed through the book. Each page in a parallel column gave also the vernacular translation of the Latin. Connectives and other structural words were repeated, but each basic word was used only once. Verbal illustrations of the grammatical constructions were given. The book had a hundred chapters and told the story of the earth, man, and the divine government of the universe. The topics included the creation of the world, the heavens, the elements, the earth and its minerals, its plants, and its animals, man his body and his mind, the mechanic arts, social institutions, the various branches of knowledge, and the providence of God. The book, as we have said, became extremely popular but it had two serious defects. It was as dry as a dictionary and like a dictionary it used each word only once. To acquire the complete vocabulary, it would have been necessary to commit it to memory.

The rest of Comenius's textbooks were built upon the same plan as the *Janua*. The *Vestibulum* was to precede the *Janua*, which had proved too difficult for beginners; and the *Atrium* and *Palatium* were to follow the *Janua*. The *Thesaurus* was a reading book made by culling extracts from the great Latin writers and was the most advanced book in this series. Lexicons were to be provided. The books were to be read and read again, the *Vestibulum* ten times over, until they were practically memorized.

The *Janua* and his other schoolbooks reveal another element in Comenius's educational philosophy. He believed that the correct way to build a curriculum was to follow the spiral plan as it was later called. By this plan even the small child was to receive instruction about nature, man, and God, and all the topics named from the *Janua*. As the child grew and entered upon a more advanced stage the same round of topics was treated again but more fully and more penetratingly—and so on stage after stage. This plan of providing instruction in every department of knowledge at each period of growth was known as pan-sophism or encyclopedism.

On his visit to Sweden, Comenius had agreed to prepare the textbooks demanded by the chancellor for the schoolboys of that country. It was in November 1642 that he settled down in Elbing for that purpose, but he found it difficult to devote his whole time to the work. He had a patron, de Geer, who provided assistants, and Elbing was a quiet town by the sea. But the difficulties of his exiled brethren and his propaganda for church union, the union of all Protestants, constantly diverted his thoughts from the schoolbooks. The town council of Elbing persuaded him to teach in their Latin school four times a week. Although they paid him, that did not reduce the extent of the interruption. In 1645 he had to attend a religious conference called by the King of Poland. It was not until 1647 that the schoolbooks were about completed, together with the *Methodus Linguarum Novissima*, the newest language method. The best way to keep a language pure, he declared, is to found societies for this purpose such as the Fruit-Bearing Society (Fruchtbringende Gesellschaft) at Weimar. He did some practical work in this field by bringing out a German dictionary.

The Hungarian Count Rakoczky invited him to organize a school at Sáros-Patak where he arrived in May 1650. The count agreed to build a schoolhouse with classrooms and boarding facilities and to furnish a printing press together with equipment and the staff to operate it. To arouse popular interest in the plan, Comenius delivered some public lectures on educational topics, and published his *Sketch of the Pan-Sophic School.* Owing to the death of his patron in 1652 the plan, which included a seven-year course, was not put into full operation, yet he carried on the school and the printing establishment, and got out new editions of his schoolbooks. And, most important, he prepared for the beginners at Sáros-Patak the most celebrated of all his works, the *Orbis Sensualium Pictus* (1657), the world of the senses in pictures. There were one hundred and fifty lessons on all subjects in the pan-sophic manner. Each lesson was illustrated. The text below the picture was in parallel columns, Latin in one and a translation in the other. Reference numbers helped the child to link the word with the pictured object.

The *Orbis Pictus* was immediately successful. The English version, for example, was made by a famous teacher, Charles Hoole, whose preface is dated, "From my school in Lothbury, London, January 25, 1658," less than a year after the first issue. The *Orbis Pictus* was neither altogether original with Comenius nor was it the first illustrated schoolbook; and its pictures were rather rough wood-cuts. But it had so many good qualities that it was introduced into schools in most of Europe and remained in use for a long time. One hundred years after its first introduction Goethe, telling the story of his childhood, wrote: "No libraries for children had at that time been established. The old people themselves still had childish notions, and found it convenient to impart their own education to their successors. Except the *Orbis Pictus* of Amos Comenius, no book of the sort fell into our hands; but the large folio Bible, with copper plates by Merian, was diligently gone over leaf by leaf."

The *Schola Ludus* was also written at Sáros-Patak. And while the *Orbis Pictus* may be called a much simplified and an illustrated *Janua*, this new work, the *Schola Ludus*, was the *Janua* dramatized. Unfortunately, Comenius was not a dramatic genius and the book had no success; but it merits brief description for it shows one of the ways in which he tried to put a leading idea to work. This Latin "play school" book had eight dramatic pieces presenting the whole pan-sophia, the physical world, man, work and workers, the family, state, church, and other institutions, thus forming, according to the subtitle, a living encyclopedia. The parts which were to be taken by schoolboys symbolized elements of the physical world, social world, mankind, and so on, and the purpose of the plays, as of the *Janua*, was to teach at one and the same time the Latin tongue and the whole round of knowledge. But Comenius saw other values also. On the school stage the pupils were to learn manners, carriage, and self-assurance in facing the public, all of which he considered of great use in preparing them for life. And, further, these plays were intended to attract parents to the school. The successes of their children would please them, he thought, and would dispose them to pay school fees more willingly. In a preface Comenius traced the history of the book and offered his dedication to the school board of Sáros-Patak. Though the ideas had merit, the work was dramatically lifeless and had no success. But the other schoolbooks of Comenius formed one of the chief means by which he influenced education.

The other means by which Comenius exerted influence was through *The Great Didactic* and other works on educational theory. To give a full account of the philosophy of Comenius would require many pages, but we must constantly remember that he was a Christian minister and a Neo-Platonist and that, although no scientist, he was much influenced by the scientific activities of his time. He compares our whole life to a school; the world was created to serve as the training ground of the human race. Through man's failures, darkness and confusion have entered this school, but harmony and order may be restored through the cultivation of the understanding and the application of true knowledge. Mankind, he said, anticipating later theories of progress, has already passed through six stages and we are now entering upon a seventh, that of pan-harmony in which the whole world will be enlightened. To accomplish this, there would be needed universal books, universal schools, a universal language, and an academy of science drawing its members from all the world. Education for Comenius was not a matter of learning this or that; it was the means to redeem mankind from the evils which made life worthless and unbearable.

There have been few works of educational theory as systematic and comprehensive as *The Great Didactic*, or that have claimed as much. Here is set forth "the whole art of teaching all things to all men," making them learned, virtuous, and pious. This claimed to be the master key to universal education. And this is not to introduce anything new into human nature.

The "seeds" of learning, virtue, and piety are implanted in all men by nature. Let us first take learning or knowledge. Man is *naturally* capable of acquiring a knowledge of all things. His senses and his reason are given him for this purpose. Comenius stands in awe of "the marvelous wisdom of God" who was able to contrive the brain of man which is able to receive and retain the impressions and images of a lifetime. Similarly, the seeds of virtue and piety are equally a part of the original nature of man.

A skeptic might be inclined to ask why, if it is "natural" for man to grow learned, virtuous, and pious, the world so often goes begging for those qualities. The answer of Comenius would not be different from the one which Rousseau actually gave, that conditions, society, and the schools have been so bad that the "seeds" have had no chance to sprout and grow. Some of the defects of schools in the past have been that they have excluded the common people, have used poor methods, have taught words merely and not real knowledge, and have been cruel institutions for stuffing and flogging children rather than teaching them. We must build up good schools, "true forging-places of men." He gave no bad definition who called man the teachable animal, but a man must be actually taught and taught well if he is to develop true manhood. All men need education, the clever and the stupid, the rich and the poor, that they may become men. There is in the doctrines of Comenius no ground for class education; to him education is an elemental human need, not a privilege. Schools must be universal and open to all. Girls as well as boys are to have a thorough education and one that shall be suitable to their duties in life.

Man can be most easily formed in youth while he is plastic and before the labor of adult life begins. Indeed, God has given man a long period of immaturity for this purpose. It is the long period of plasticity and growth that enables the child to become a man. This doctrine of Comenius is a surprising anticipation of a corollary to the doctrine of evolution which John Fiske developed under the term "the meaning of infancy."

All studies are to be taught to all children, for Comenius is an encyclopedist, but not all can be fully mastered. Much can be done by applying to teaching the principles of which we find constant examples in nature. By applying these principles, Comenius believed that sure, easy, quick, and permanent learning may be attained. The principles were such as the following: Nature observes a suitable time; Nature prepares the material before she gives it form; in all operations of Nature, development is from within; Nature proceeds step by step without a break. These are four of the nine principles which deal with the certainty of learning; and there are similar groups dealing with ease or facility, permanence, and rapidity of learning. Altogether he considers thirty-seven principles of nature which are to guide our teaching. From them we are advised as follows: to teach what will be useful in life; to appeal to the senses and understanding rather than to the authority of books; that studies must not only be understood but must also be impressed upon the memory; that studies must be carefully graded and organized; that it is useful to have pupils teach other pupils for we learn nothing so well as what we teach to others.

Lest the student should think that these pages of *The Great Didactic* are devoted wholly to abstract discussion, we quote one of the finest passages, one that might have been written by Vittorino or Vives. Comenius wrote: "The school itself should be a pleasant place, and attractive to the eye both within and without. Within, the room should be bright and clean, its walls ornamented with pictures, portraits of celebrated men, geographical maps, historical plans, or other ornaments. Without, there should be an open place to walk and play in, for this is absolutely necessary for children, as we shall show later, and there should also be a garden attached, into which the scholars may be allowed to go from time to time, and where they may feast their eyes on trees, flowers, and plants. If this be done, boys will, in all probability, go to school with as much pleasure as to fairs, where they always hope to see and hear something new."

A golden rule for teachers is that everything should be presented to the senses, and to several of the senses, whenever possible. Sensation is the foundation of knowledge and there is nothing in the understanding that was not originally derived from the senses. The senses also are the most trusty servants of the memory and we always remember what we have first tasted, heard, or seen. The anatomy of the human body can be remembered better from a single dissection than from reading exhaustive volumes. If objects are not at hand, pictures or models may be used. The arts should be taught by practice. We learn to carve by carving, to dance by dancing, to write, talk, reason, by carrying on these activities. In this way schools will become workshops, humming with activity. Rules and theory are essential, but they should follow and not precede observation and practice.

Languages are tools and only those languages which are necessary tools should be learned. But languages may be tools for different purposes because they may be used to arouse emotion, to stimulate speculation, to convey fact and information, or to lead us in the conduct of life itself. And yet Comenius, in agreement with all the realists, does not value language largely for its beauty of phrase or as a vehicle of noble emotion but chiefly as the carrier of information. For this function the mother tongue is most important, then the languages of neighboring nations, and then Latin. Only specialists will need other languages. Languages and concrete knowledge of fact should always be learned together. Some languages we must learn to speak, but of others a reading knowledge is sufficient.

And we must not let the languages crowd more necessary subjects out of the course of study.

Knowledge, virtue, and piety are the three great ends of education. Virtue and piety should be taught by the practice of virtuous and religious acts but also through example and through reason. The Bible should rank above all other books in Christian schools; and Erasmus has shown, said Comenius, that it is suitable for children of all ages.

The plan of school organization which Comenius advised is one of the most striking features of his program, for he proposed to develop a one-class society or rather he assumed that such a society already existed. He planned a complete system of education for all children of every rank and class. There were to be four periods of six years in this system and a school corresponding to each period; the school of infancy for the first six years, the vernacular school from six to twelve, the Latin school from twelve to eighteen, and the college of research from eighteen to twenty-four. Instead of this democratic plan, Erasmus accepted the dual system, with one school for the lower classes and another secondary-university sequence for the directing classes. Two hundred years after Comenius wrote his *Great Didactic*, the American democracy undertook to develop a single-track scheme in which all schools were to be open to "all the children of all the people."

A chapter in the *Great Didactic* is given to the school of infancy or, as the Germans translated the idea, the mother-school. About the same time Comenius wrote a separate book which he called *The School for Little Children* (1633). This anticipated Pestalozzi's manual for mothers and also foreshadowed the kindergarten of Froebel. Everywhere, but here especially, Comenius revealed his kindly nature and his sympathetic observation of little children. He gives sensible advice on the care of their health and their safety. A healthy child is God's most precious gift to the home. Childhood should be joyous, and whatever promotes innocent joy should be given to children. Fables, stories, and songs are highly desirable; and children must play with other children. Natural objects, toys, tools, and a garden should be provided. Lessons and all learning must be made pleasant and the parents should prepare the child for school by showing him that school is a happy place. The encyclopedic curriculum appears in the plan of the school of infancy as well as in that of the more advanced schools.

10. INFLUENCE OF RATKE AND COMENIUS

Recently the democracy of Comenius has been out of fashion in several countries especially in Germany where race, and autocracy were in the saddle and rode mankind; but forty or fifty years ago the name of Comenius was honored the wide world over and especially in Germany where, in 1891, a Comenius-Gesellschaft was founded to study his work and to spread his views on popular education. Even in the seventeenth century both Comenius and Ratke had considerable influence in several German states. Ratke's influence was most evident in the Weimar ordinance of 1619; and that of Comenius in the school programs of Saxe-Gotha, Brunswick, Hesse, and other German states and cities.

Ratke's patroness was the Duchess Dorothea Maria of Weimar who provided for the introduction of his principles. The school instructions which were drawn up in 1619 instituted compulsory attendance the year around, except for four weeks in harvest, between the ages of six and twelve. This seems to be the earliest example of a compulsory attendance requirement by the civil authority. The school day was kept short, only four hours, and a long recess was allowed between classes. Corporal punishment was forbidden. Each pupil was to have his own book and each teacher his own classroom. The German language was to be thoroughly taught before the Latin was taken up. These were Ratkean ideas.

Duke Ernest, called "the Pious," of Saxe-Gotha (1601–1675) took another step toward a common school, in which the influence of both Ratke and Comenius may be seen. Duke Ernest was the son of Dorothea Maria of Weimar, and as advisers in the reform of the schools of his duchy he called first Sigismund Evenius, a moderate Ratkean, and then Andreas Reyher, a friend of Evenius and a disciple of Comenius. Others of his advisers show the same influence. Reyher was made rector of the gymnasium at Gotha. His instructions of 1641 began the reform and were in part copied in the ordinance of 1642, known as the Saxe-Gotha School Method.

Pietism was strong in Gotha, religious teaching was emphasized, and the clergy were appointed school visitors. Nor was this a mere form, for the local pastor was to visit the schools several times a week and to keep a list of all children between the compulsory attendance ages of five and twelve. In the year when Gotha adopted these requirements (1642), Massachusetts passed a law which was intended to achieve similar ends. By the age of twelve, the children in Gotha were expected to read German, repeat the catechism and Bible verses, report the main heads of a sermon, write legibly, calculate accurately, and sing, at least in chorus. A public examination of all children who were about to complete the course was held to determine whether they might be excused from further attendance. Two points are noteworthy: this was an example not of civil control but of state and church cooperation; and the objectives of the school were stated in terms of achievement and not formally in terms of years.

Reyher also prepared a *Brief Text Book* (1657) which followed Comenian lines. This dealt with four main topics, natural objects, useful knowledge, political and social duties, and domestic affairs. The code of 1642 was amended to include these realist topics in the course of study. The first part deals with the heavens, the earth, minerals, plants, and other subtopics. In the third part, we have the introduction into school-education of home geography, a German curriculum idea which was later taken up by Rousseau and given an observational and inductive turn. A new edition of this code, the Saxe-Gotha Method (1672), emphasizes observation of actual things, school experiences, and visits to farms and to the local court sessions. Duke Ernest also established continuation classes and improved the school equipment. His peasants, it was said, were better educated than the princes of other lands.

Next to Saxe-Gotha the old city and territories of Magdeburg show most clearly the direct influence of Comenius. Its school code of 1658 established a four-level school system, each level comprising six years. The Comenian textbooks were used and Comenian aims were professed. Other states also introduced Comenian ideas, but almost everywhere the traditional humanism was still too strong for the new realism. Yet the doctrines of Comenius were here and there kept alive and his textbooks remained in use until Basedow and Salzmann developed a new realism in the following century.

The definition of realism, as of other historical movements, depends upon the standpoint occupied by the one who defines it. It may be regarded either as a broader humanism or as a reaction against humanism. Prominent realists occupied each of these positions. It was the result of the early efforts to introduce science and practical arts into education, to rationalize methods of teaching, and to base education upon direct experience. Realist education appealed especially to skilled workmen and to those who employed skilled workmen, the landlords and manufacturers. But there was also a fringe of aristocratic realists who outlined the education of gentlemen, men of affairs, military leaders, and even princes. At the other extreme, were realists like Mulcaster and Comenius who urged universal vernacular schools. The realists, therefore, proposed the transformation of the schools of all levels and for all classes.

Realist education was generally characterized by a broad curriculum, involving twenty or thirty subjects, including history and geography, the sciences, the modern languages and sometimes Latin, several polite accomplishments such as dancing or fencing, a trade, and a period of travel. Those with less money would have to omit some of these features. The realists developed new methods. They taught languages through translations, or other semidirect methods such as Ratke's. They introduced illustrative materials and tried to base their teaching upon actual experience. Where possible they attempted to follow the method of science in the process of discovering new scientific laws. The Copernican method of discovery and the Cartesian method of proof began to influence instruction. In England the various inductive processes came to be known as the Baconian method.

Locke and Comenius were doubtless the most influential realists. Locke employed the principles of utility, rationality, conditioning, and direct experience; and his aims were health, virtue, practical sense, courtesy, industry, and "learning," that is, knowledge. Of these he considered learning both last and least; but he devoted more than half of his *Thoughts* to learning.

The master mind of Comenius attempted to fashion the master key of universal education, or to create the art of teaching all things to all men. Like all the realists he was an optimist, and his *Great Didactic* was an unconscious utopia, although an inspiring one. The noblest of his many noble conceptions was that of a one-class society and a ladder system of universal schools. The world of his day was not worthy of him; and, indeed, we still have to look forward to glimpse the Comenian goal.

QUESTIONS

1. Why did realism appeal to pupils who were not reached by humanism?
2. Illustrate the statement in the text that "words are things," and will repay careful study. Using the *Oxford English Dictionary*, trace the history of the word "academy."
3. What relations can be made out between the new psychology and philosophy and the new methods of teaching?
4. Why were the seventeenth-century leaders optimists and authors of utopias?
5. Why did both Puritans and Pietists lean toward realism?
6. Why has modern science been more successful than Greek science? Name several ways in which the two movements and the conditions surrounding them differ.
7. What is meant by saying that Locke proposed an all-round education? How, in this respect, does Locke's scheme differ from medieval education? Compare it with the ancient Athenian plan.
8. Why, if the realists had the whole truth, do the problems of language teaching, language learning, and the use of language occupy so large a place in educational discussion in all ages?
9. Compare the spiral plan of Comenius with the similar scheme of the Moslem schools. Can you find any similar plans today?
10. How can we, as Comenius proposed, "follow nature" in education? This topic is of special importance for we shall meet it again in connection with Rousseau and other educators.
11. How influential was Comenius and in what ways?

FOR FURTHER READING AND STUDY

Many new and original educational plans, both utopian and practical, mark the transition from humanism to realism, and several of these are included in the present list. Some of the writings of the period, for example, those of Hartlib, Petty, Dury, and Ratke, have been left out because no convenient editions are available; but selections from these and others may be found in Henry Barnard's *American Journal of Education* (Hartford, Connecticut, 1855–1881). Barnard's *Journal* is indexed. Nearly all of Milton's *Tractate* and passages from Montaigne and Fénelon are included in Painter's *Great Pedagogical Essays* which is entered below.

Adamson, John William, *The Educational Writings of John Locke*, New York, Longmans, Green and Company, 1912, 272 pp. Contains the *Conduct of the Understanding* and the larger portion of the *Some Thoughts*. Adamson also wrote *Pioneers of Modern Education, 1600–1700*, Cambridge, University Press, 1921, 285 pp.

Barnard, H. C., *The Little Schools of Port Royal*, London, Cambridge University Press, 1913, 263 pp. *The Port Royalists on Education*, London, Cambridge University Press, 1918, 276 pp.; *The French Tradition in Education*, London, Cambridge University Press, 1922, 319 pp. The second of these has extracts from the Port Royalist writings and the third work begins with Ramus and comes down to the eighteenth century.

Campagnac, E. T., Editor, *A New Discovery of the Old Art of Teaching Schoole* by Charles Hoole, Liverpool, The University Press, 1913, 357 pp.; *Ludus Literarius; or the Grammar Schoole*, by John Brinsley, London, Constable & Company, Ltd., 1917, 363 pp.; *Mulcaster's Elementarie*, London, Clarendon Press, 1925, 292 pp.

Comenius, John Amos, *The Orbis Pictus*, Syracuse, N. Y., C. W. Bardeen, 1887. English and Latin in parallel columns. The English is that of Charles Hoole from the English edition of 1727. This reprint resembles the original but is not a facsimile.

Fleury, Claude, *Traité du Choix et de la Méthode des Études*, Paris, Louis Janet, 1822, 466 pp. This work, several times printed, which contains a short history of education, the first ever composed it is said, was written in 1675 but not published until 1686. There is an English edition, issued in London in 1695, with the title *The History, Choice, and Method of Studies by Monsieur Fleury*.

Fox Bourne, H. R., *The Life of John Locke*, New York, Harper & Brothers, 1876, 2 volumes.

Graves, Frank Pierrepont, *Great Educators of Three Centuries*, New York, The Macmillan Company, 1912, 289 pp.; *Peter Ramus and the Educational Reformation of the Sixteenth Century*, New York, The Macmillan Company, 1912, 226 pp.

Held, Felix Emil, *Christianopolis . . . by John Valentin Andreae*, New York, Oxford University Press, 1916, 287 pp.

Keatinge, M. W., *The Great Didactic by John Amos Comenius*, London, A. & C. Black, Ltd., 1910, 2 volumes. First edition, 1896.

McLachlan, H., *English Education under the Test Acts, being the History of the Non-Conformist Academies, 1662–1820*, Manchester, Manchester University Press, 1931, 341 pp.

Monroe, Will S., *Comenius' School of Infancy*, Boston, D. C. Heath and Company, 1893, 99 pp.; *Comenius and the Beginnings of Educational Reform*, New York, Charles Scribner's Sons, 1900, 184 pp.

Morley, Henry, Editor, *Ideal Commonwealths*, London, George Routledge & Sons, Ltd., 1893, 284 pp.

Oliphant, James, *The Educational Writings of Richard Mulcaster*, Glasgow, J. Maclehose and Sons, 1903, 245 pp.

Painter, F. V. N., *Great Pedagogical Essays. Plato to Spencer*, New York, American Book Company, 1905, 426 pp.

Quick, Robert Hebert, Editor, *Mulcaster's Positions*, New York, Longmans, Green and Company, 1888, 309 pp.; *Some Thoughts Concerning Education by John Locke*, Cambridge, University Press, 1895, 240 pp.; *Essays on Educational Reformers*, New York, D. Appleton & Company, 1907, 568 pp. The *Essays* went through several editions. Chapters V to XIII deal with sixteenth and seventeenth century subjects.

Spinka, Matthew, *John Amos Comenius; that Incomparable Moravian*, Chicago, University of Chicago Press, 1943, 117 pp.

Turnbull, George Henry, *Samuel Hartlib; a Sketch of his Life and his Relation to J. A. Comenius*, London, Oxford University Press, 1920, 79 pp.

Young, Robert Fitzgibbon, *Comenius in England*, London, Oxford University Press, 1932, 99 pp.

9 NEW VIEWS OF NATURE AND HUMAN NATURE

THE EIGHTEENTH CENTURY IS CALLED THE AGE OF REASON, but it was also an age of benevolence, toleration, and political democracy, partly because these attitudes were considered reasonable but also in response to humane feeling. It was a humanitarian age which attempted to abolish slavery, to reform the prisons and the criminal law, to alleviate the miseries of the peasants, to educate the blind and the deaf, and to deal with children both kindly and intelligently. In the political sphere, events led to democratic revolutions in America and France. In literature, the century turned from classicism to romanticism and produced the novels of Richardson and the New Héloise of Rousseau; and in religion, the spread of pietism and the rise of Methodism belong to the history of this hundred years as truly as Voltaire, Frederick the Great, and the French Encyclopedists. It was an age of faith and hope as well as reason. Even the skeptical rationalists had a faith, a new confidence in the power of reason to solve all problems and to bring in the millennium, faith in progress and the perfectibility of man and society.

Rationalism held that the world is entirely subject to natural law and ruled out everything supernatural and all revealed religion as contrary to the uniformity of nature and to natural law. The only kind of religion that was acceptable to the rationalists was some form of deism or natural religion which made no use of any special revelation. In politics, rationalism opposed autocracy and the divine right of kings and supported what were considered the natural rights of the individual, such as the rights to life, liberty, and the pursuit of happiness, as Jefferson stated them in the Declaration of Independence. The comparable catch words of the French Revolution were liberty, equality, and fraternity. The common term here is liberty, and the eighteenth-century rationalists held that all individuals must have the liberty to do whatever would not interfere with a like freedom on the part of others. This doctrine of laissez faire or noninterference was applied in economics by Adam Smith, the physiocrats, and others. It was not without influence in education. And the rationalists also tended toward utilitarianism, holding that nothing had any right to exist which could not demonstrate its present usefulness.

Education was less developed than politics or religion. The schools for the common people, where they existed at all, were narrow in their subject matter, formal in teaching methods, and harsh in discipline; and the Renaissance secondary schools were plainly decadent. The educators of the time were developing new interests in health and physical education, in science and the study of nature, in the use of the senses and the effort to teach pupils to think for themselves, and in the practical arts by which materials are made fit for human use. But the prophets of the new day were not well received and new practices were carried out in only a few schools and by small groups of innovators.

These innovators began to consider the nature of immature children and to adapt their teaching to the growing child, an idea which Comenius had begun to explore in the previous century. They attempted to determine the stages of mental development and to fit methods and materials to these stages. These efforts to base education upon child psychology, which are marked in Sulzer and Rousseau, reached a high point at the beginning of the following century in the attempt of Pestalozzi "to psychologize education." It was Pestalozzi also who tried to use the school to reform society and improve the lives and the living conditions of the common people. Finally, because of the growing nationalism of the eighteenth century, leaders began to see in the school an instrumentality for making the nation strong and great. But such ideas developed only gradually, and several of the leaders with whom we shall deal in the present chapter tended to take a cosmopolitan rather than a national attitude.

1. JOHN GEORGE SULZER

The intellectualist trend of the century showed itself more in John George Sulzer (1720–1779) than in the other educators whom we have mentioned. In Zürich, where he was born, he came under some of the same influences which shaped the youth of Pestalozzi. As a school reformer, he worked in Germany, where he became one of the savants attached to the court of Frederick the Great. His first book, The Essay on the Education and Guidance of Children (1745), is noteworthy for its emphasis upon child psychology. Sulzer divided childhood and youth into six stages. His plan included sports, work, manual skills, science by observational methods, and great attention to the development of accurate knowledge, clear concepts, and true judgments. To try to think without accurate knowledge, he said, is to attempt to erect a building upon insecure foundations. This emphasis upon thinking and the large place that he gave to mathematics, "A lordly science," he called it, reveal his rationalism.

He was also a realist. This is indicated by his broad curriculum at all stages but especially in the adolescent period. He wanted pupils to be given a certain amount of free time in which, with some guidance, they were to plan and carry out work of their own selection. At the age of fourteen, one-third of the day was to be given over to student-planned school activities. In his political attitudes, Sulzer was a cosmopolitan rather than a nationalist. This does not prevent him from proposing public tax-supported schools for the education, in common and without regard to social class, of all children from six to sixteen. The student will see that Sulzer, like Locke and Comenius, anticipated Rousseau in important respects

2. SENSATIONIST PSYCHOLOGY

Locke derived ideas from two sources, sensation and reflection; but Etienne Condillac (1715–1790) made reflection a product of sensation. The mind, according to him, is the product of sensation. But he did not draw the inference to which this doctrine would lead, namely, that the mind is completely determined from the outside. On the contrary, he declared his belief in the freedom of the will. Nor did he attempt to train the senses of the young Prince of Parma, whose tutor he was. The principle of training the senses was accepted by Rousseau, who did not follow Condillac's psychology, and more generally by the contemporary teachers of the blind and deaf. These teachers began to develop practical means of training the senses of their pupils. On the one hand, they invented raised print and taught the blind to read it, and on the other taught lip reading and vocal speech to the deaf. France was the leader in both fields and the first schools were opened there by Valentin Haüy for the blind and the Abbé de l'Epée for the deaf; but other countries were not far behind. Roderigues Pereira (1715–1780), a famous teacher of the deaf, drew pupils from great distances to his school in Paris.

The sensationist doctrine was accepted by Helvetius (1715–1771), who held that men are entirely formed and controlled by outside forces. This means that education, in the widest sense, is all-powerful, which is what Helvetius actually taught. Morality, he believed, is mere custom; and self-interest, founded upon the love of pleasure and the fear of pain, is the only effective motive of conduct. As evidence of the state of opinion in "enlightened" circles in the Age of Reason, we may quote the remark which was current at the time that "Helvetius merely said what everyone believed but was afraid to say." Rousseau opposed this deterministic view.

3. JEAN JACQUES ROUSSEAU

The educational doctrines of Locke were quickly carried to many countries by translations of his works and by schools founded upon his views; but their most inspired interpreter was Jean Jacques Rousseau (1712–1778). Contrary to the opinion sometimes expressed, he was much more than an interpreter of Locke. Rousseau differed from Locke at vital points and he added not only his style and enthusiasm but wholly new ideas to Locke's educational views. His system still influences a great many educators and, properly interpreted, would have value for others. The critical study of Rousseau is very necessary today when a current philosophy of education is based partly upon his ideas. To such a study, Rousseau himself invited us in the preface to the *Émile* where he said: "When I freely express my opinion, I have so little idea of claiming authority for it that I always give my reasons, so that you may weigh and judge them for yourselves; but though I would not obstinately defend my ideas, I think it my duty to put them forward; for the principles in which I differ from other writers are not matters of indifference; we must know whether they are true or false, for on them depends the happiness and misery of mankind." This invitation should be accepted by all young students of education for there is no better opportunity to cut one's philosophical eyeteeth.

Rousseau not only invited the reader to criticize him; he also provided some of the means to carry forward the critical process. He admits his debt to Locke and points out where he parts company from his master. Where Locke had discovered the individual with his personal traits, Rousseau discovered the child with its childhood traits. Some of the traits which he seemed to find were negative, namely, the lack of moral concepts and of the power of abstract thought; and others were positive, such as the ceaseless activity, trustfulness, curiosity, and interest in concrete problems which young children show; but the greatest difference between the child and the adult is that the former is growing while the latter is, at least relatively, mature. Education is growth may be taken to be the most important conclusion of Rousseau. Study the child, he commanded, for you may be sure that you do not know him. In the *Émile*, he attempts to study the child introspectively by recalling his own childhood and that of other children whom he had known and by forecasting the condition and development of his imaginary pupil, Emile, in specified situations. Rousseau had several short—short because unsuccessful—experiences as a tutor. He did not make systematic observations or psychological studies of real children and, except for a few observations by Pestalozzi, by the young duke of Württemberg, and by a few others, his call for such studies went unheeded for many years. In writing on education, he was greatly influenced by his own experiences; and since his experiences had often been unsatisfactory, his advice on the whole is: Do the opposite of what is customary and you will nearly always be right. Evidently Rousseau meant to be a radical reformer, and he was one. Describing his childhood, he wrote: "Tedium drove me at an early age to books. At six I happened to light on Plutarch; at eight I knew him by heart; I had read all the romances; they had drawn from me floods of tears before the age when the heart has awakened an interest in romance. From this source sprang my taste for the heroic and romantic, which has never ceased growing to the present time, and has ended by blunting my taste for everything which does not resemble my day-dreams."

We may grant that this early addiction to such books was a bad beginning for his education; but we do not therefore need to go to the opposite extreme and to say with Rousseau that children should have ro books of any kind before the age of twelve. A better selection of books and a less sentimental use of them would seem a reasonable alternative. There is also the question whether he could have been turned into the active, playful lad which he desired Emile to become. Perhaps Rousseau's dreamy and romantic imagination was the cause of his sentimental reading and not the effect of it. Throughout we must keep in mind that it is such a man who wrote the *Émile* and that, in spite of what he says in his *Confessions*, he supposes other people to be like himself.

In his celebrated *Confessions*, Rousseau has told the story of his life with great frankness, although not always correctly. He was the second son of a citizen of Geneva, the early capital of Calvinism. His mother died in giving him birth and this he called the first of his misfortunes. The father was temperamentally unfitted to care for his sensitive, neurotic child, and neither he nor an uncle to whom Jean Jacques was committed at the age of ten paid sufficient attention to the boy. While Jean Jacques was still with his father, the two frequently sat up all night reading tear-filled novels until, at the approach of dawn, the father sent the son to bed with the confession that he was the more childish of the two.

Rousseau's extraordinary talents received little systematic cultivation. For two years he was given some instruction in "Latin as well as all the insignificant twaddle" which goes by the name of education. A little later he had some tuition in drawing and the elements of geometry. He learned no vocation by which to gain self-support and a settled position. The resulting insecurity deeply affected his view of life. He attempted many sorts of occupations, etcher, lackey, secretary, tutor, music teacher and copyist, composer, dramatist, until finally at thirty-eight he became a successful writer. Before that time his philosophy had become fixed.

The want of a healthy family life had a similarly unsettling effect upon him. Never as child or man did he have a real home. We have seen the circumstances of his childhood. In his youth he was apprenticed to an engraver who mistreated him, although not without provocation, and he ran off wandering through the valleys of Savoy, intoxicated with the beauty of nature. From childhood his heart responded to natural beauty and his love of flowers and trees made him an enthusiastic amateur botanist. He developed an interest in many sciences but never acquired a close or accurate knowledge of any. It was only popular or salon science.

We shall not follow closely his journey after he left Geneva. It was marked by adventures, slight hardships, and at least one exhibition of utter meanness. Being employed as secretary to a lady of quality, he stole a ribbon and, when he was questioned, he put the blame on an innocent servant girl who thereby lost her position and probably, said Rousseau, had a hard time getting another. Nor does he attempt to excuse or explain this dastardly act. Almost immediately after leaving Geneva he had renounced his Protestant faith for Catholicism in return for food and the hope of further support. To establish him in his new religion, he was sent to Madame de Warens, who was however more deist than Catholic. He lived with her for a dozen years but was finally drawn to Paris by the idea of selling the plan of a new musical notation which he had developed. Nothing came of this but he made friends who helped him to earn a precarious livelihood. At thirty-two he took as his mistress Therese Levasseur, an ignorant servant girl, by whom he had five children. One by one these were all, against the tearful protests of the mother, committed to the orphan asylum.

Rousseau claimed to have felt endless remorse for these evil deeds, but the main explanation that he gave was that it would have been inconvenient to care for the children. In the case of the stolen ribbon he gave no explanation whatever. The fact is that present pleasure, or even a mere whim, bulked larger in Rousseau's conduct than the sense of duty or justice.

He was employed for about a year (1741) as tutor to the two small sons of M. de Mably, provost of Lyons, and wrote an account of his plan for his employer. This account shows that he was attempting to follow Locke and Montaigne, whom he read as early as 1737. The experience convinced him that he was unfit for the work of a teacher. He had an irritable temper and the unhappy faculty of getting on bad terms with his pupils. In the *Confessions*, where the whole story is told, he reported that, with patience and temper, he would have succeeded but wanting these qualities his pupils profited little. There is no doubt, however, that this experience gave him a permanent interest in questions of education.

On walking tours through France, he observed the oppression, the unjust and exorbitant taxation, and the poverty of the peasantry. The evils of his adopted country made him cherish the memory of the one he had given up and at the age of forty-two he returned to Protestantism in order to reclaim his rights as a citizen of Geneva. From this he received little practical advantage, for he was not permitted to live there for any long period. During much of his life, he suffered from a painful and incurable disease and in his latter years his mind became seriously unbalanced. Both church and state condemned his works and persecuted their author; but he also developed a persecution complex so that he accused his friends, one of whom was David Hume, of taking part in conspiracies against him. He died in 1778, on an estate which a friend had made available to him, eleven years before the outbreak of the French Revolution which he had foreseen.

Rousseau had many faults and was also the innocent victim of great misfortunes. His theory of education was his proposal for realizing his ideals for the individual and for mankind. The conflict between his life and his ideals is important because the faults of his life are sometimes charged against his teachings. So bad a man cannot be the author of good doctrines or wise policies, it is said. But this does not follow and cannot be defended as a principle of interpretation. The life may frequently explain how he came to hold certain views and may teach us to examine those views very critically. The facts to notice are that he was a man alienated from all the stabilizing institutions of society, without a country, without a real home or a settled vocation, and also without good health or sufficient self-control. The true principle of interpretation is that the theory shall be judged by its tendencies and results.

4. ROUSSEAU AS A WRITER

Rousseau first came into general notice in 1750 through his prize-winning *Discourse on the Sciences and Arts*, written in answer to a question set by the Academy of Dijon: Has the revival of learning led to purer morals? In this discourse, he maintained that culture and learning had made men luxurious and effeminate, to the prejudice of military qualities and moral virtues and to the neglect of their duties as citizens and parents. "I would as soon," said a wise man, "that my pupil spent his time in the tennis court for there at least his body would have been exercised." What should we teach children? This important question has an easy answer: Let them be taught what they are to practice when they are men, not what they ought to forget. His second *Discourse* (1754) on "The origin of inequality among men" did not win the prize but was much better reasoned than the first. He concluded that in a state of nature men were more equal than they are under civilization and that education greatly increases the natural inequality between men. This greater inequality is a positive evil, because it leads to slavery on the one hand and oppression and domination on the other. Both of these essays deal with the reform of society which he held to be easier than the reform of education in a bad society. The reform of society was to be accomplished by a return to a state of nature. The idea of a state of nature was not invented by Rousseau, and he doubted that such conditions as others imagined had ever existed. He therefore supplied his own content and made his idea of the state of nature into an ideal. What was the content of this ideal? While he sometimes speaks of "the noble savage," he did not contemplate a return to primitive or savage life. The state of nature which he desired was a simple farming community or state without the evils which he ascribed to large cities, corrupt rulers, social classes, and luxury. Such an ideal was shared by others including, it would seem, Thomas Jefferson.

In addition to the early discourses, the works of Rousseau which demand the attention of students of education are the *Discourse on Political Economy* (1755), the *New Héloise* (1761), the *Social Contract* (1762), the *Émile* (1762), and the *Considerations on the Government of Poland* (1773). Of these only the *Émile* deals with education as the main subject. The *New Héloise* incidentally considers family education but announces no ideas which are not found also, often expressed in similar words, in the *Émile*; and both books urge that education should, if possible, be carried on in the family and by the parents. The other three works named, the *Political Economy*, the *Social Contract*, and the *Government of Poland*, have passages dealing with state or public education.

5. ROUSSEAU ON PUBLIC EDUCATION

Rousseau proposed two complementary systems of education. His opposition to the autocratic state and luxurious society of his day and his poor opinion of the condition of family life, especially among the great, together with his proposal to return to an ideal state of nature led him to consider the two schemes: the one is a system of public and national education which he would apparently prefer if a state fit to carry it out could be found; the other is the private, individual education of the *Émile* which was to prepare the "natural man" to live as well as possible in the artificial society which characterized the eighteenth century. We present first his argument for public education.

Good public education can exist only in a good state; and a good state can be maintained only by good education. So said Plato; and so Rousseau also said. The great nations of the world no longer attend to

this, he declared, and, indeed, there appear to have been only three ex
amples of effective national education in all history: Crete, Sparta, and
ancient Persia. In the good state, the people must rule; and the primary
law of popular government is that all must obey the general will. The
distinguishing characteristic of the general will is that it establishes justice
and virtue; and it demands that the individual wills shall conform to the
general will. It is not enough to say to the citizens: Be good; they must
be "taught to be so by patriotism and by example." By example, for
courage should be taught by soldiers and justice by judges. And by patriotism, for education must give the souls of the people a national form
and must so shape their opinions and tastes that they become patriots
as much by inclination and passion as by necessity. We must teach
them, nay compel them, by education to love their country, its land
and life and liberties. Begin at birth. After egoism has been allowed
to develop it will be too late to begin. A child ought to look upon his
fatherland as soon as his eyes open to the light, and should continue to do
so till the day of his death. He must live only for his country. National
education is the privilege of free men who must be educated in schools that
are common and public. This further requires that our country shall show
herself the common mother of all her citizens. No patriotism without
liberty, no liberty without virtue, no virtue without citizens; create citizens and you have everything you need. This is Rousseau's ideal of a
national education. He nowhere develops a complete system and he shows
plainly that he has no concern for the lower classes, the peasants, and
the poor. Like Plato in this, he is similarly pessimistic about the possibility
of establishing such an education. This pessimism led him to develop an
elaborate program for individual education which is found in the *Émile*.

6. THE *Émile*

In form, the *Émile*, a work of five hundred pages in five books, is a story
or romance with four chief characters: Emile, the boy who is being educated; Sophy, to whom most of the fifth book is devoted; the tutor; and
Rousseau himself, who moves through these pages explaining, expostulat-
ing, eulogizing. Although Rousseau advised the simple life of the poor,
Emile was supposed to be chosen from the upper classes. "The poor man,"
wrote Rousseau, "has no need for an education; for his condition of life
forces one upon him, and he would not be able to receive any other." But
if a young nobleman is educated, there will be one man more, one knave
less. Book one deals with the two years of infancy, book two with the
child to age twelve; book three considers the youth approaching adolescence with rapid strides in the years from twelve to fifteen and book four

the adolescent from fifteen to twenty. Toward the end of the fifth book Sophy, after being educated or rather trained, is married to Emile with the intimation that they will live happily ever after.

Implicit in the work as a whole is the doctrine of the culture epochs, that is, it implies that the natural stages of individual growth and education run parallel to the stages of the growth of human civilization. The child on this theory begins life in a state of nature and in twenty years becomes a social individual just as mankind, in twenty or forty centuries, has progressed from a state of nature to a highly organized and cultivated society. Thus from the history of man's cultural evolution, which Lessing called "the education of the human race," hints and principles may be drawn for the education of the individual. Later in this book we shall see that other writers continued to use the idea of the culture epochs.

With the contrast between a state of nature as a simple society and a corrupt unnatural society we are now familiar. But in the opening lines of the Émile, where Rousseau declares that "everything is good as it comes from the hands of the Author of Nature" and that evil results from the perversion of Nature, he uses the word nature in a new sense. Here he means by nature, not a simple social order, but the inherited traits and abilities of the child. He means that the child's original nature is good and pure. But since the child is immature and unable to care for himself, education is necessary. The task of education is to preserve the child's goodness and purity without stain from the world and to provide the conditions in which it may grow and mature. The contrast now is between the good individual and evil society.

As the work proceeds, and especially in the third and fourth books, the author gradually introduces the notion that a good society is, at least theoretically, possible and that such a society would also be natural. He had already approached this concept in the New Héloise, where he described a harmonious family, and in the Political Economy and Social Contract, where he imagined a social order in which popular government and conditions of simple living, equality, and liberty characterize the natural society. We now have three uses of the word nature by Rousseau: the state of nature, the natural but fully developed man, and the natural civilization. But the latter two are thought of not only as conditions but also as goals, the goals of education which are accepted in the Émile. Then Rousseau falls into the common fallacy of personifying nature. Nature lays plans and would have things be other than they are. Finally, like everybody else, he also uses the word to designate the external world. We should keep in mind, as we read Rousseau, these distinct uses of the word. Even if we are not always able to distinguish the sense of the word because Rousseau is not always clear, it is well to be forewarned.

The idea of a rational, universal nature which includes humanity played a controlling part in the Stoic philosophy and was introduced into English thought by Hobbes. In France the physiocrats, a group of economists, based their system upon the same idea of a law-abiding nature which included society. A brief examination of this theme will show how much Rousseau was indebted to the ideas of his time. The leading physiocrat, François Quesnay (1694–1774), was writing about the time when Rousseau started to compose the *Émile*. Quesnay's theory rested upon the law of nature which governs human nature and the structure of society and which is discovered by the light of reason. It is a law of nature because, like the law of gravitation, for example, any attempt to violate it merely serves to illustrate it. The natural law, Quesnay said, gives everyone the right to the property which is produced by his labor. By the gift of nature each individual has abilities which enable him to produce goods; and in a just society, that is in a society which is based upon natural law, these goods are guaranteed to the producer. The first duty of society is to teach its members the laws of nature but Quesnay does not set forth a curriculum. Quesnay also held that agriculture is the only source of real wealth. Anyone familiar with his doctrines will see in reading the *Émile* that Rousseau's teaching on property and his favorable attitude toward agriculture, as well as his ideas on nature, were colored by the theories of the physiocrats. We now turn to the text of the *Émile*.

Education begins at birth and the nurse is the child's first teacher. When he has come to recognize her, he already has much knowledge. He should not be restrained by caps, bands, or tight clothing. Place him in a wide cradle, well cushioned, and leave his limbs quite free. As soon as he is able, let him creep about the room to get exercise. Bathe him frequently, at first in warm but gradually in cooler water until at last it may be quite cold. A thermometer should be used to get the proper temperature. Cold air and cold water tend to invigorate the child. Do not let him form invariable habits, in eating, sleeping, or physical activities. Simple wholesome food should be supplied. Vegetarian diet is to be preferred. The taste for meat is unnatural; and French cookery simply proves that the taste of the people is perverted. The natural man requires no such elaborate foods.

The hardening system of Locke is to be continued through childhood and youth. Emile is to live an active, vigorous, outdoor life both to develop his body and to train his senses while he also acquires a knowledge of natural objects and forces. In the physics class, boys of eighteen are taught the use of the lever; but every village lad knows that already. Emile must be as much at home on the water as on land. Carefully educated young men do not learn to swim because it is so inexpensive but instead they are taught to ride. Emile shall learn both and without attending a school for either.

Gradually accustom the young child to strange sights and noises so that he may learn by easy stages not to be frightened by masks, firearms, ugly animals, and other unexpected experiences. And do not give in to his whims. The tears of children must not be allowed to become commands. Never give way to obstinacy. If he cries because of discomfort or pain, he should be relieved, but without being caressed or rocked to sleep. Servants must not be allowed to tease or to irritate him. His playthings should be very simple, such as little branches with fruits and flowers, a poppy-head with seeds that rattle, but no gorgeous trinkets, no elaborate toys.

He should hear only simple, well-articulated words, and cheerful songs. It is a great abuse to be overhasty in teaching children to speak. Have you ever heard of a child who does not learn to walk and talk in the course of nature? A child needs words only for *his own* ideas. Teaching him to use words without clear ideas will establish a habit from which he will suffer all his life. He will not need to learn to read before the age of ten or twelve. Provide a proper motive and he will learn to read almost without help. In the *New Héloise,* he found such a motive by reading to the child half of a very interesting story which he will then wish to finish. In the *Émile,* he supposes the boy to receive invitations to children's parties which he will miss unless he learns to read. In both cases, Rousseau supposes reading to develop almost as naturally as walking and talking. This is an error into which no experienced teacher would fall unless, like Rousseau, he had a phobia against all persistent and systematic teaching and learning.

The danger to intellectual growth, which comes from the promiscuous use of words and symbols that are not understood, led Rousseau to develop some of his basic principles. It led him to distinguish between "the reason of sense experience" and "the reason of intelligence." Since everything that comes into the human mind, he says, enters through the gates of sense, man's first reason is a reason of sense experience. This serves as a foundation for the reason of intelligence, which is another name for Locke's "reflection." This "first reason" develops early and enables the child to deal with concrete topics; the second reason, which deals with abstract ideas and especially with moral and social concepts, does not develop until the adolescent period. It matures late and to appeal to it by attempting to teach a child rational conduct and social studies is not only futile but it builds up in the child the false notion that merely knowing words is real knowledge. Verbal "knowledge comes but wisdom lingers." Such teaching will tend to preclude the child's ever acquiring clear ideas about the most important subjects in the world, namely, human relations and morality.

Right and wrong are words which the child simply cannot understand. To do wrong means for him merely to do what is forbidden without understanding why. The true course is to give no commands, to prohibit nothing. Necessity must be his teacher. We merely set him free in situations in which he will not hurt himself and let him learn by experience and the results of his own conduct. If he falls, he will be bruised. He will be more careful the next time. Punishment must never be inflicted on children but should always come to them as the natural consequence of their own imprudence. This is the famous doctrine of natural punishment which was to be exploited by Herbert Spencer. If Emile breaks a window pane, let him suffer the resulting inconvenience, for it is better for him to have a cold than to be a fool. When he becomes an adolescent, his ability to reason will develop. Then we shall teach him the need for moral and social conduct and then he will obey willingly, not the tutor but society itself. Meanwhile we shall treat him according to his age. Childhood has its own way of seeing, thinking, and feeling. Nature would have the young be children before they become men.

From this flows a second more general principle which Rousseau calls the most important, the most useful rule of all education. It is that we should not try to gain time but to lose it. Early education should be chiefly negative. It should consist, not in teaching virtue and truth, but in shielding the heart from vice, the mind from error. This is why Emile is brought up in the country away from the evils and vices of the city and the bad manners of flunkeys. This is in harmony with Rousseau's basic principle that "Everything is good as it comes from the hand of the Author of Nature." A very useful outcome of this principle is that in practice it gives the tutor time to study the nature of his pupil. Each mind has a form of its own; but the traits of the child mind can be learned only by observation as they develop. A wise education proceeds by observing the child and adapting its measures to the individual capacities and needs.

A principle of curriculum making also follows from the law that the child is to be taught by experience and not by verbal lessons, by his own reason when it develops and not by the reasoning of adults. Memory and reason do not develop independently of each other. The former depends upon the latter. The child may indeed remember words mechanically but it is only through judgment that he will understand ideas and relations. I say then, declared Rousseau, that children, not being capable of judgment, have no real memory. They retain sounds, forms, sensations, but rarely ideas and still more rarely their combinations. Pedants think differently, for they teach nothing but words without the experience which would give them meaning. The study of languages is the rubbish of education.

In connection with this attack on the study of languages, we should notice that Rousseau assumes, contrary to fact, that Emile at twenty will be able to read Latin and Greek without having systematically studied them; and should compare his scornful attitude toward foreign languages with his inadequate treatment of the problem of learning to read the native language.

Not only languages but also history, fables, literature, and geography as usually taught are among the "inutilities" of early education. All studies learned from books and by means of language, signs, and symbols of every kind except the mother tongue, and drawings made by Emile himself, are to be postponed until adolescence or later. He must never learn anything by heart. Even the fables of La Fontaine, artless and charming as they are, must be omitted from this "natural" education. History should be taught only to older children. It is easy to put the words king, empire, revolution, or law into the vocabulary of children, but they will have no true ideas of the things intended.

There are, however, some general ideas which may be taught to the young child. One of these is the idea of property. This may be best done in a garden. Emile will see growing plants and this will interest him and he will wish to plant things for himself. The tutor now contrives to have the boy plant some beans on the spot where the gardener has recently planted some rare melon seeds. Naturally, the gardener is angry and reads the boy a lesson on disturbing valuable seeds with his miserable beans; and he ends by offering Emile a small plot where he may raise things which shall be his own. From the experience, the boy learns the meaning of mine and thine; but the reader should notice what Rousseau does not mention, namely, that there is also a good deal of language in this lesson, and that Emile will need to have more experiences and will have to assimilate more language before he can have a complete idea of property.

Geometry, drawing, and music should also be taught to the young child through experience, projects, and active doing. Geometry should be taught, not by demonstration, but inductively by drawing figures and by comparing and measuring them. "Draw accurate figures, combine them together, put them one upon the other, examine their relations, and you will discover the whole of elementary geometry in passing from one observation to another, without a word of definitions, problems, or any other form of demonstration but superposition. I do not profess to teach Emile geometry; he will teach me. Geometry means to my pupil the successful use of rule and compass."

Drawing, like geometry, is not to be taught but rather invented. Emile will never copy drawings but will learn to draw from natural objects. To give him an incentive, his drawings will be framed and hung on the wall so that he will have a record of his progress. Both geometry and drawing will teach him the art of seeing. His games and sports also will not only invigorate his body but will teach him to estimate, compare, measure, and to use his senses in becoming acquainted both with the world around him and with his own growing abilities. When a small child plays at shuttlecock or an older boy at ball games, his eye and arm are trained in accuracy. To spring from one end of the hall to the other, to estimate the bound of a ball still in the air and to send it back with a strong and steady hand, trains both the limbs and the senses. This is the necessary preparation for work in the natural sciences, and all that scientific instruments do is to sharpen our sense-observation. A large portion of book two is devoted to this subject, to which Rousseau's particular attention was probably directed by Pereira, the skillful and philosophical teacher of the deaf, who lived near Rousseau in Paris.

Music is a suitable subject for the young child. It is to be learned at first by hearing and by rote singing. The boy will easily catch simple melodies, and harmony may be gradually introduced into these exercises, the tutor taking the bass. Teaching him to read the notes may be postponed. "Moreover to learn music thoroughly we must make songs as well as sing them and the two processes must be studied together. First give your young musician practice in regular well-cadenced phrases; then let him connect these phrases with the very simplest modulations; then show him their relations to each other by a fit choice of cadences and rests. Use a simple tuneful air, with its bass so clearly indicated that it is easily felt and accompanied, for to train his voice and ear he should always sing with the harpsichord."

The third period of the boy's life, which extends from the age of twelve to the age of fifteen, is the period of intellectual education and is treated in book three. Because of the boy's mental immaturity up to this time, necessity has been our guide but now utility is to determine our course. The understanding of the physical environment and an introduction to social problems are to be our aims. In the next period, after the age of fifteen, we shall be concerned with moral and social conduct and with religion; and the studies of the third period will prepare the way for those interests. Necessity, utility, and morality form the three successive spirals of human development; and curiosity is the constant motive force in all of them. Emile's progress in geometry will serve as a ready test of his intelligence; but in any case human intelligence is limited and the years of man's life are few and those which may be wholly devoted to study are far fewer. Not only is man unable to know everything but he cannot even learn all that is known. Our first task, therefore, is to eliminate from our course those studies for which there is not time or need. We shall omit all that is false, all that is useless, all that is merely showy, all that requires a full-grown mind for its comprehension, and all that which, though true, might mislead the young. We are thus reduced to a circle much smaller than the whole of knowledge but one that is still immense with respect to the powers of a youth.

The most important part of what remains is geography and science, the knowledge of our physical environment. All these sciences are really one and should be taught in the same way, the senses being our guide. Let there be no book but the world. If your pupil is made attentive to natural phenomena he will soon be curious; but to nourish this curiosity never be in haste to satisfy it. Ask questions but let him solve them. He is to discover science, not to learn it. In science there is no room for authority. In teaching him geography, show him not globes and maps but the earth, the sky, the setting sun, and on the morrow the rising sun. We saw the sun set over there, you will say to him, now it rises here; how does that happen? We shall not be in any hurry for the answers. Before we have answered the question about the rising sun, we shall make another beginning. We shall choose the city where Emile's father lives and his country house and we shall trace the road connecting them. Let him make a simple map of all this, gradually filling in streams, villages, and roads, and enlarging the boundaries of our sketch as we explore the surrounding country. There is no need for carrying maps in the head provided he understands the art of making them and has a clear idea of what they mean. For our experiments in magnetism and other topics in physics and chemistry, we shall make all our apparatus. This should all be invented according to need and not prepared beforehand. Complicated apparatus from a shop might be neater and give more accurate results, but neither the operation nor the results will be so well understood. Besides, the construction of such equipment provides excellent training in manual skills. If the boy develops skill and scientific talent, he might learn to make mathematical instruments, telescopes, and other precision equipment. But we do not so much aim to teach him the sciences as to give him scientific tastes and an understanding of scientific methods. And yet the questions upon which Emile is employed should have coherence and follow a sequence, and the resulting knowledge, though elementary, should be systematic as far as it goes.

Before the age of fifteen, the time will arrive when Emile may begin the study of society; the industrial arts are the best introduction to such questions. The second half of book three is devoted to this topic, and we have suggested, in the preceding paragraph how the transition is to be made by means of manual skills. Rousseau also provides a more explicit introduction to social problems in a colorful passage on the story of Robinson Crusoe who, by his situation, was driven to practice "the natural arts" of self-preservation, which also provide the basis for social participation. Robinson Crusoe is "the happiest treatise on natural education" and indicates the best standards by which to judge the social education which is to follow. To show the boy how men depend upon each other, we shall not use moral problems but the industrial and mechanic arts. We shall go from shop to shop and, not content with seeing how the work is done, we shall take part in it. We shall prefer the basic industries, such as work in wood, iron, or agriculture, to engraving, gilding, or diamond cutting, which are merely decorative and superfluous arts. Of all the occupations which furnish subsistence to man, that which approaches nearest to the state of nature is manual labor.

Emile must have a trade which would be of use to Robinson on his island. He and his tutor will learn the trade together in an actual apprenticeship. Cabinetmaking or carpentry and not farming was the trade selected because it leaves the workman free to pick up his tools and leave if conditions become unsatisfactory. We must reflect that society is subject to revolutions. France is standing on the edge of a social cataclysm and, when the threatened revolution breaks out, Emile must be free. His trade will teach him how and why men work for each other. He will learn the need for specialized labor and the exchange of the fruits of labor and that money is simply a conventional standard of value and means of exchange. This whole passage in the *Émile* was doubtless inspired by a similar exposition of the bases of society in Plato's *Republic*.

Adolescence is treated in book four. Rousseau describes it as a period of storm and stress, when the passions rise in tumultuous power and put in jeopardy the whole fabric of education which has been built up. We are twice born, once as a child and now into manhood. Our basic passions are love of self, or the desire of self-preservation, and egoism, or the desire to dominate others. From the former, with wise guidance, love of others and all kindly feelings may grow. True love, whether of others or of the one preferred from the opposite sex, will always be held in honor by mankind. To be loved we must be worthy of love and this provides an excellent basis for moral education; but it may also lead to egoism and so to rivalry, jealousy, and hatred. The true method of moral education is to delay the growth of the passions until judgment and self-control have had time to develop. There are dangers in books, in low companions, and in obsequious servants who flatter the young at the expense of their morals. Rousseau, perhaps because of faults in his own character, does not seem to know how to develop self-control, and the education of nature does not provide an adequate basis for such education. On sex education, he has some good advice. When sex questions arise we must meet them frankly and honestly, and our replies should not raise more questions than they answer.

This is the time to study mankind, and we must do this before the young man is exposed to the pomp of courts and the evils of society. To show him the world before he knows men is to corrupt him. He must be able to estimate society at its true worth before you expose him to it. This may be done in part through history. The chief value of that study is that it teaches morality, and the best part of history for this purpose is biography. If, as John Morley says, Rousseau knew very little history, he nevertheless outlined some good criticism of history as it was written in his day. But few historians would agree that it is their function as historians to teach morals, although many would admit that history furnishes valuable materials to the moralist, the political scientist, and the educator. This is also the time to teach religion, and Rousseau shows, in his eloquent "Confession of the Vicar of Savoy," how he believed religion should be taught. He believed that the intelligence of a well-educated young man will find, in his own heart and in the world, convincing evidence of God, human freedom, and immortality, without making any appeal to revelation.

In the last book of the *Émile*, he shows how Sophy is to be educated, or rather trained, to charm and serve her Emile. In the education of women, Rousseau does not rise above the conventional ideas of the eighteenth century and he repeats the sentiments which he had already employed in the *New Héloise*.

7. LA CHALOTAIS ON NATIONAL EDUCATION

In France, where the Jesuits were in control of education, the idea of national education received little support until the latter part of the eighteenth century, when La Chalotais, Condorcet, and many others began to promulgate it. The *Essay on National Education* was written by La Chalotais in 1763. It was an attack rather than a program. It was directed against political and religious privilege and especially against the Jesuits and their schools rather than toward national education; but yet it contained an argument for a secular system of public schools and it offered a regular plan of studies. There was the usual attack upon the decadent humanism of that period and the charge that the Jesuits taught little but Latin and that ineffectively. Their pupils, he declared, cannot tell a bad argument from a good one, set forth the principles of their religion, or even write a letter. But more important still, the Jesuits, who are presuming to prepare citizens of France, give their allegiance to a foreign power, the pope in

Rome. He demanded, instead, a national system of education, because every state, he claimed, has the right and duty to educate its own citizens. Yet he was an educational reactionary, for he restricted schooling to the upper classes. As a mercantilist, he wanted to limit the number of the clergy and lawyers, whom he regarded as economically unproductive. Considering the opposite end of the social scale, he condemned any extended education of the working classes because it would make them discontented with their lot as laborers.

8. THE PLAN OF CONDORCET

In the generation following La Chalotais, interest in national education increased rapidly in France. Turgot, who was for a short time the capable finance minister of Louis XVI, proposed in 1775 the creation of a Council of National Education which should control all schools, including those of the primary grades. In the primary school, he proposed to have instruction given in manners and customs and the social duties of citizens, with a schoolmaster in every parish to teach the usual elements and also elementary geometry and the principles of mechanics. Diderot, in his plan of a university, proposed schools which should be open without distinction to all the children of the nation where publicly paid teachers should instruct them in an elementary knowledge of all the sciences. But it was Condorcet (1743–1794) who prepared the most careful plan for the education of the French people along modern lines in his *Report on Public Instruction*.

The Marquis de Condorcet was an original mathematician, a philosopher, and one of the leaders of the Revolution, an aristocrat by birth but a democrat by conviction. He was also one of the great exponents of the theory of historical progress. One of his finest achievements was a life of Turgot, whose plan for the financial rehabilitation of France he had ardently supported. Living in times of social upheaval, he was a friendly spectator of the drama of the American but a tragic actor in the French Revolution. He was chosen a member of successive national legislatures and was commissioned by one of them, the National Assembly, to prepare a report on education. This he presented in the spring of 1792. It was a document of about fifty pages containing a plan for a complete system of national education; but it was meant to be more than that, namely, a charter of freedom, self-realization, and happiness. Condorcet was possessed by two ideas: the idea of liberty and the idea of human perfectibility.

The aim of national education is a part of the larger aim of every social institution, namely, the general and gradual improvement of the human race. This desired improvement of all would be attained, he continued, by

offering to all individuals the means of securing their welfare and their
rights, of satisfying their needs and fulfilling their obligations; by giving
to each the opportunity of perfecting to the fullest extent all those talents
with which Nature has endowed him. Then each will be able to perform
his political duties; and only then will the political equality of the citizens
guaranteed by the law become a fact. The individualistic spirit and the
optimistic tone of this statement are apparent. The counterpart of this
interest in the individual was his cosmopolitanism and interest in the welfare of all mankind. The needs of mankind impose upon governments the
obligation to establish schools in which every individual may develop fully
all his natural talents; and this, given the opportunity, everyone will do.
The direction of such a view diverges at an angle of practically one hundred
eighty degrees from the usual nationalist position that governments should
support education for the sake of national unity, and economic and military
power. Condorcet would have the government serve the people; and the
people were to him, not a mass, but a group of individuals.

The outlines of his plan are clear and logical, as one would expect from
a mind like Condorcet's. His basic principles demand universal education
with equal opportunities for everyone and with curricula and facilities as
complete as money and time will allow; as much freedom as possible from
political control, from political propaganda, and from the political suppression of truth; and continued opportunity for adult education throughout life. He proposed four grades of schools: the primary schools, one in
every village to teach the elements including measurements, morals, and
some agricultural and industrial instruction; the secondary schools, one in
each town of four thousand inhabitants, in which the sciences and social
studies were to be taught; the institutes, one or more in each of the ninety
departments of France, in which the applied sciences such as agriculture
and the mechanical arts were to be taught; and the lyceums, corresponding
to the university in grade, of which there were to be nine in the whole
country. Education was to be free in the primary and secondary schools;
scientific, social, and civic studies were to be emphasized at the expense
of the languages and the fine arts; the courses in the institutes and lyceums
were to be elective; special attention was to be given by the teachers
to methods of teaching, the use of demonstrations and other illustrative
materials, the preparation of good textbooks, all for the purpose of making
the student as soon as possible independent of the teacher and school. In
his faith in the common man's desire for knowledge and enlightenment,
Condorcet was one of the most optimistic of all educational writers.
Comenius believed that the average man had great, practically unlimited
capacity to retain what he had been taught; but Condorcet believed that
the average man would ardently and persistently pursue knowledge, if

only the means were made available. Not only in the lower schools but even in the institutes, a certain number of chairs were to be reserved in each classroom for those citizens who had not been able to receive a complete education but who, while not being regular students, might yet wish to follow a course of instruction or even merely to be present at a few lessons.

To make it possible for poor but talented children to continue their education above the primary schools, Condorcet proposed to have about four thousand national scholarships created. Each of these was to maintain a national scholar for a year. The plan was to open to the poorer classes an "abundant source of prosperity and learning" and to society a "powerful means to maintain the natural equality of man." The plan has no provision for normal schools or teacher training.

The final proposition of Condorcet's plan was quite unrealistic. To protect the schools against political interference, he proposed to place the system under the control of a self-perpetuating board of scholars which he called the National Society of Sciences and Arts. It was to be their duty to supervise the schools, to perfect the sciences and arts, and to disseminate useful discoveries. We may applaud his purpose but surely no government would continue to support a full complement of national schools over which it was not allowed any sort of control. A nonpartisan board, either elected or appointed, would have been a more reasonable suggestion.

The actual French school system will be separately considered. The hopes of the Revolution were long deferred, but during that period there were drafted many, a score or more, plans for a system of schools for the French nation. For the most part they asked for publicly supported and controlled secular schools with a practical, civic, and largely scientific curriculum. Education was to be free and universal in the lower grades at least. In general they proposed a centralized system of state administration and some scheme of normal schools for the preparation of teachers.

The rationalism which the eighteenth century inherited from Descartes and Locke was followed by romanticism, in education as well as in literature. Both the evangelism of Wesley and the doctrine of fraternity, although differing in other respects, supported the growing humanitarianism which reformed prisons and asylums, created schools for the deaf and the blind, and improved the care of children. The natural right of the individual to liberty and equality was considered to justify the democratic revolutions against kings who claimed to rule by divine right.

The eighteenth century was a period of diverse trends in education. Humanism, although it had become traditional, was still dominant, but a young and vigorous realism was opposing it. The church schools for the common people were beginning to feel the hostility of democrats and nationalists demanding universal education for citizenship. Political and scientific advances led from the uncritical optimism of the writers of utopias to a definite but still uncritical theory of progress. Although the philosophers favored education, they did not fully realize the central place which the school should have occupied in this program. Civilization was expected to produce a perfected society easily and quickly.

Rousseau thought otherwise. He believed that man had been perverted and enslaved by a civilization which had fostered oppression, corruption, injustice, an artificial and extravagant urbanism, and "those ridiculous institutions called colleges." Men had been happier in simpler conditions. He also disagreed with his contemporaries on the nature of the world and man. Nature gave sufficient grounds for belief in God, freedom, and immortality. Man should guide his life not only by reason but also by feeling and conscience.

According to Rousseau, the first task of the teacher is to study the child. True education is self-education which is a dual process of growth in native capacity and the discovery of truth. It will be the teacher's function to provide the environment that will be best for the growth of the child's body and mind and that will stimulate in him the spirit of investigation. Growth and discovery can take place only where there is no constraint. The child's freedom must not be circumscribed and he must be placed in a rich and stimulating environment. Rousseau's key idea that it is the environment which provides the conditions for education is important and was influential. Through Pestalozzi and Froebel it influenced the schools which the Western nation-states were beginning to establish.

QUESTIONS

1. Who were the leaders of thought and action in France in the eighteenth century? How well did they agree?

2. Do Sulzer's ideas reveal any of the contemporary conflicts of opinion?

3. What is a deterministic view of man? Compare the views of Condillac and Helvetius with "behaviorism."

4. Consider the probable effect of Rousseau's errors, follies, and misfortunes upon his doctines.

5. Would Rousseau's scheme of state education allow any freedom or develop free men?

6. How do we learn the full meaning of words such, for example, as war or golf? Gradually, or all at once? Do we ever learn the full meaning? How do these questions bear upon Rousseau's theory that teachers should not use words that children do not understand?

7. Discuss, pro and con, the doctrine of natural punishment. See Herbert Spencer's *Education, Intellectual, Moral, and Physical.*

8. Consider the values and limitations of teaching by the method of discovery by the child.

9. What are the most serious defects of the educative environment proposed for Emile? Why did Rousseau leave out the additions which you are suggesting? Would you include other children, and family life? Why or why not?

10. Compare the main elements of Condorcet's plan with the basic ideas of public school systems today.

FOR FURTHER READING AND STUDY

Few writers have evoked as much discussion as Rousseau. All over the civilized world his ideas are still "living thoughts" which call out either the acclaim or the criticism of partisans. Among the following books, those of Babbitt, Davidson, and Maritain are critical if not hostile and in the same vein is Paul Elmer More's "Shelburne Essay" on Rousseau, which is not listed below. Rousseau is also considered in most of the collections of essays on "educational reformers" by Frank P. Graves, R. H. Quick, and others. These have been mentioned in the reading lists in previous chapters. The paper on Rousseau by Quick is especially illuminating. We do not list Rousseau's Confessions, but there are many editions in French, English, and other languages.

Aldington, Richard, Letters of Voltaire and Frederick the Great, London, George Routledge & Sons, Ltd., 1927, 395 pp.

Archer, R. L., Rousseau on Education, New York, Longmans, Green and Company, 1912, 278 pp.

Babbitt, Irving, Rousseau and Romanticism, Boston, Houghton & Mifflin Company, 1930, 426 pp.

Ballantyne, Archibald, Voltaire's Visit to England 1726–1729, London, Smith, Elder & Company, 1893, 338 pp.

Boyd, William, The Minor Educational Writings of Jean Jacques Rousseau, Glasgow, Blackie & Son, Ltd., 1910, 159 pp.; The Educational Theory of Jean Jacques Rousseau, New York, Longmans, Green and Company, 1911, 368 pp.; From Locke to Montessori, London, George G. Harrap & Co., Ltd., 1914, 271 pp. The collection of Rousseau's "minor educational writings" by Boyd should not be neglected. From Locke to Montessori has short passages on Pereira and on Condillac.

Cole, G. D. H., The Social Contract and the Discourses by Jean Jacques Rousseau, New York, E. P. Dutton and Company, 1950, 330 pp.

Davidson, Thomas, Rousseau and Education according to Nature, New York, Charles Scribner's Sons, 1898, 253 pp.

Fontainerie, F. de la, French Liberalism and Education in the Eighteenth Century. The Writings of La Chalotais, Turgot, Diderot, and Condorcet, New York, McGraw-Hill Book Company, Inc., 1932, 385 pp. Complete translations of four documents with introduction and notes.

Foxley, Barbara, Emile, New York, E. P. Dutton & Company, Inc., 1925, 444 pp. In the "Everyman's Library." Complete translation.

Graham, H. G., Rousseau, Philadelphia, J. B. Lippincott Company, 1883, 227 pp.

Green, F. C., Jean Jacques Rousseau, a Critical Study . . . , Cambridge, University Press, 1955, 376 pp.

Havens, George R., "Diderot and the Composition of Rousseau's First Discourse," New York, The Romanic Review, Vol. 30 (Dec., 1939), 369–381.

Hendel, C. W., Citizen of Geneva, Selections from the Letters of Jean Jacques Rousseau, New York, Oxford University Press, 1937, 405 pp.

Josephson, Matthew, Jean Jacques Rousseau, New York, Harcourt, Brace and Company, 1931, 546 pp.

Klinke, W., *Johann Georg Sulzer's pädagogische Schriften*, Langensalza, Beyer und Söhne, 1922, 211 pp. With introduction and notes.

Maritain, Jacques, *Three Reformers: Luther, Descartes, and Rousseau*, New York, Charles Scribner's Sons, 1929, 234 pp.

Morley, John, *Voltaire*, London, Macmillan & Company, Ltd., 1913, 365 pp.; *Diderot and the Encyclopedists*, London, Macmillan & Company, Ltd., 1914, 2 vols.; *Rousseau*, London, Macmillan and Company, Ltd., 1915, 2 vols.

Payne, William H., *Rousseau's Emile*, New York, D. Appleton & Company, 1914. An abridged translation first published in 1892 in the "International Education Series."

Rolland, Romain, *The Living Thoughts of Rousseau*, New York, Longmans, Green and Company, 1939, 185 pp.

Schaupp, Zora, *The Naturalism of Condillac*, Lincoln, Neb., University of Nebraska Studies in Language, etc., No. 7, 1926, 123 pp.

Tozer, Henry J., *The Social Contract*, New York, Charles Scribner's Sons, 1895, 247 pp.

Vaughan, C. E., Editor, *The Political Writings of Jean Jacques Rousseau*, Cambridge, University Press, 1915, 2 vols.

10 NEW SCHOOLS FOR OLD

THE NEW VIEWS OF NATURE AND MAN WHICH AROSE IN THE eighteenth century led to the creation of radically different schools: the Philanthropinum for the upper classes by Basedow and his disciples and the new elementary school by Pestalozzi and a long line of followers. Education became a more active process: observational methods and new studies were introduced, and old subjects were taught in new ways and for new purposes. The new purposes were central in the whole movement for it was intended that education should change the individual lives of the people and should promote the gradual but thorough reformation of society.

Even before the revolutions of the eighteenth century, autocratic but far-sighted rulers, who are sometimes called benevolent despots, had begun to foster national education for patriotic service to the state. They meant to use the schools to make the nation strong in peace and dangerous to its enemies in war but without developing liberal ideas among the people. Instead, feelings of loyalty to state, king, and church were instilled and care was taken that the lower classes should not be educated beyond the needs of their condition. The peasants were to be satisfied to remain peasants, hardworking, God-fearing, proud of king and country, and with no desire to move to the city. Such benevolent despots were the Hohenzollerns of Prussia, Maria Theresa and Joseph II of Austria, and Catherine II of Russia. Eventually, the democratic and revolutionary changes which created the new United States, overturned the government of France, and liberalized those of England and Switzerland, affected Prussia also but not until the nineteenth century. Meanwhile, in the more democratic countries with a free press, religious toleration, and civil liberty, the schools could develop along new lines. And even in autocratic countries private schools, which did not come under the inspection of the church or the civil authorities, were often allowed to experiment with new studies and methods. Three of the reformers whom we consider in this chapter,

Planta, Basedow, and Salzmann, developed private schools for future leaders, while Pestalozzi became the apostle of universal education for rich and poor.

1. A GREAT SWISS SCHOOLMASTER

An early pioneer in the development of new schools was the Swiss pastor and schoolmaster Martin Planta (1727–1772). The history of Switzerland in the eighteenth century sparkles with great names. The Bernoullis and Euler were mathematical geniuses; Albrecht von Haller was a poet and naturalist; and Bodmer and Breitinger, who were professors in Zürich, were critical scholars. Of the great Swiss educators of that time, we have already named J. G. Sulzer and Rousseau, and they were followed by Pestalozzi, Fellenberg, Wehrli, and Gregoire Girard. The economic life of the country was reviving and new industries were developing. Agriculture was in a depressed state but the agricultural societies which were established show the interest that was taken in its improvement. One of the new industries to which we have referred is sufficiently indicated by two facts: that the first Swiss guidebook was issued at this time and that Swiss engineers began to build the excellent roads which now connect the different parts of the country.

Martin Planta came from a peasant family in the Grisons. His older brother, who was a pastor, supervised his early studies and then sent him to Zürich where he learned mathematics, the sciences, languages, and divinity. He was ordained at an early age and was for a short time the pastor of a church in London. Before he was twenty, he began to plan a new kind of school which received government approval in 1760 and was established in the following year at Haldenstein. Pupils came even from foreign countries, and a number of prominent men received their early education there. One of these was Frederic C. La Harpe, statesman and tutor of Czar Alexander I. The aims of the school were to develop Christian and patriotic men of affairs thoroughly imbued with the need and desire for Swiss unity. The curriculum included three modern languages and Latin, arithmetic and advanced mathematics, physics, history, geography, drawing, dramatics, bookkeeping, music, and dancing. Observation and independent thought were encouraged and the curriculum and methods were adapted to individual capacity and need. Gymnastic exercises and mountain climbing in the Alps were features of the school. Excursions were taken to collect minerals and plants, and these collections were used in the school. There was a shop for work in glass, wood turning, and cabinetmaking. A system of student government was used to prepare the pupils for participation in democratic political life. Thus it is seen that

Planta developed a Philanthropinum more than a decade before Basedow. After the founder's untimely demise, no one could be found who was able to carry it on successfully and in 1777 it was closed.

2. BASEDOW AND THE PHILANTHROPINUM MOVEMENT

In a moderate and tentative fashion, Johann Bernhard Basedow (1724–1790) favored state control of education; but he took this position not so much to develop patriotism and a strong state as because he opposed the church and favored deism and secularism. The experimental school which he founded and named Philanthropinum cultivated international rather than national feeling and the love of mankind, as the name suggests. In this respect, Planta's school was not typical for it was both national and religious in spirit.

Basedow was a German and was born in Hamburg. In his time the idea of state education was no longer a novelty in Germany, but it was the idea rather than the fact that was common, although in the sixteenth century several German states, including Württemberg in 1559, established state systems, in the seventeenth Weimar and Saxe-Gotha did likewise, and in the eighteenth the large state of Prussia attempted to develop state education. Compulsory attendance was decreed in several countries. Basedow favored this trend and proposed to place education under the control of a Council of Public Instruction. And such a body was constituted, although not especially through his influence, in Prussia in 1787, but it continued to delegate the local management of schools to the clergy. Conditions, therefore, remained about as they had been. Basedow's work was necessarily done in a private school; and his own and later Philanthropinums had little direct influence upon the common schools.

No friendly star shone upon Basedow at home or at school. To escape harsh treatment in each of these he ran away and shipped for the East Indies, but the vessel went aground at Copenhagen and he was persuaded to return home. He became a tutor in a nobleman's family and a governess taught him French by conversational methods. He attended the Universities of Leipsic and Kiel and in 1752 received the doctor's degree from the latter. His dissertation dealt with language instruction and embodied several of the ideas which he later applied in schools. This was ten years before the *Émile* appeared and proves his partial independence of Rousseau who, however, also seems to have influenced him decidedly. He began to teach but his deism and his boastful and bombastic speech aroused the opposition of his colleagues and the public.

In 1768, Basedow issued an educational manifesto which in his inflated manner he called a *Memorial to the Friends of Mankind and Men of*

Means on Schools and Studies and Their Influence upon the Public Welfare, with an A. B. C. Book of Human Knowledge. The latter part of this title shows that the *Memorial* was to be the first volume of a series. The second in the series was his *Elementarwerk,* or elementary "Book of Knowledge." With a good book, said Basedow, anybody can be a good teacher, which is a piece of educational heresy not yet wholly extinct. The *Elementarwerk* was to be such a book. When completed, it comprised four volumes. The first volume was a *Book of Method for Fathers and Mothers* (1770). It deals with the education of the nobility "since reform must begin at the top." The whole work was finished in 1774, and included an atlas and many copperplate engravings by a famous Polish artist, Chodowiecki. This new *Orbis Pictus* of the Age of Reason, he claimed, had "a sufficient stock of all necessary knowledge for the instruction of youth, their elders, teachers, and tutors, and to make complete the information of every reader." Goethe said he liked the original *Orbis Pictus* of Comenius better.

The *Memorial* was also intended as a prospectus and brought its author the aid of Prince Leopold of Dessau. The school, which was founded with his help, was called a Philanthropinum, a name that was widely copied by similar institutions. From its location, Basedow's school was also known as the Dessau Institute. The teaching in the Dessau Institute did not follow the bookish line suggested in the *Elementarwerk.* Studies were selected for their utility or supposed utility. Languages were taught through conversational methods. There were regular and carefully graded physical exercises and games under a special teacher; drawing, handwork and training in skills and crafts, field excursions, and nature study were included; and the whole scheme was to be characterized by activity, observation, and thoughtfulness. Friendly relations between teachers and pupils were cultivated and the use of force was to be avoided. Pupils were to participate in the school government and group activities were emphasized. The school was to become a center for the preparation of teachers who were to spread the Philanthropinum ideas. Even in the Kiel dissertation of 1752, Basedow had proposed a normal school, facilities for practice teaching, and a school library. As we shall show, these ideas were given partial application at the University of Halle by one of his assistants.

The founder and friends of the school were disappointed that only fifteen pupils attended when the Dessau Institute opened in 1774. The number grew slowly, but it was never large, although pupils occasionally came from distant places. Great men praised the plan. Kant declared that only in Philanthropinums were teachers free to experiment. But the fault lay not so much in the plan as in its execution. Basedow's character was not admirable and, in a teacher, not tolerable. He was not himself a good teacher and his immoderate claims left a bad impression. To the author and philosopher J. G. Herder, the work of Dessau seemed superficial. Basedow died in 1790, and a few years later the Institute was closed.

Such success as the school had was due in part to Basedow's assistants. The one indispensable teacher was C. H. Wolke (1741–1825). Kant, who was greatly interested in this school, said of Wolke that he was unassuming, indescribably industrious, and not to be deterred by difficulties. He was in fact a gifted man, skilled in drawing, painting, and etching, and an independent thinker. J. H. Campe (1746–1818) was on the staff for a short time. In earlier years he had been the tutor of two boys who became famous, the scientist and diplomat Alexander Von Humboldt and his brother William Von Humboldt, a scholar who became Minister of Public Instruction of Prussia and played a leading part in organizing the University of Berlin. Campe was a voluminous writer. One of his books was his *Robinson the Younger*, an imitation of DeFoe's classic. *Robinson the Younger* outlived its hundredth edition and was read by children in all languages from Gibraltar to Moscow. The development of a literature for children was promoted by the Philanthropinum movement. Another Dessau teacher was E. C. Trapp (1745–1818) who worked with Wolke to develop a more systematic plan of lessons for the Dessau Institute. Afterward he became professor of pedagogy at the University of Halle and director of the practice school (1779). This seems to have been the first example of a university practice school for the training of teachers. He published a *System of Education* in which, like Sulzer, he took psychology to be the essential foundation for a science of education. The hostility of the rest of the faculty at Halle made his university career unhappy and after four years he resigned.

3. SALZMANN'S PHILANTHROPINUM

Although several attempted it, Christian G. Salzmann (1744–1811) was the only one of Basedow's staff who succeeded in establishing a permanent Philanthropinum. Like Pestalozzi, he was moved by ideals of social reform. He was for three years the chaplain and teacher of religion and other subjects at Dessau and always acknowledged his indebtedness to that experience. The school which he opened in the duchy of Saxe-Gotha with the help of its ruler, Duke Ernest II, celebrated its centennial in 1884.

Salzmann's first criticism of the Dessau Institute was directed against the teaching of physical education. He thought more attention should be given not to teaching about health but to the formation of health habits and cleanliness. The dancing, riding, running, jumping, and swimming which the school carried on were good, he admitted, but all this seemed to him to be mere play. Physical education should include work, hard and useful labor. Perhaps it would not be unfair to say that Salzmann wished to interchange the roles given to work and play in the old schools: the classroom lessons were to be taught through play; but in the physical education, work and the acquirement of manual skills were to be included. Shops with tools and materials were an essential part of the scheme. Every teacher was to have a skilled trade.

Every child, Salzmann said, is a born naturalist, and the streams and fields of the beautiful Thuringian land "offer us so many interesting things that we shall not have time to examine them all." Nature itself, he said, is my science cabinet. The school should have fields and gardens to satisfy the children's passion for activity. It must be located in the country for reasons of health, morals, and intellectual education. The pure air and the vigorous outdoor occupations of the country make for health. Life in the country avoids the temptations which the city spreads before youth. Only in the country are geographical and botanical excursions and the study of nature at first hand possible. Like all the philanthropinists, Salzmann was opposed to the rising "new humanism" with its emphasis upon Latin and Greek and its preoccupation with distant lands and ancient peoples. The immediate surroundings and the life of the present should engage the children's attention.

Salzmann gave advice to teachers as follows: Be healthy; always be cheerful; play and work with the children; strive to form clear ideas and to make them clear to the children; learn to use your hands skillfully; become well educated yourself and keep on learning; and, in all you teach, be an example. In the conduct of his school, he was aided by able assistants, among whom was C. F. Guts Muths, the organizer of school games and founder of systematic school gymnastics. The first pupil to be admitted to the school was Karl Ritter who became the founder of the "natural method" in geography and a famous professor of that subject at the University of Berlin. Salzmann was an important contributor to the children's literature which the Philanthropinum movement developed. In his *Carl of Carlsberg*, which appeared about the same time as Pestalozzi's *Leonard and Gertrude*, he painted a picture of the school evils of the time. He proposed to collect into a pile, which would reach the clouds, all catechisms and spelling books and into another, equally high, all rods and canes and to set fire to both at once. His once popular *Stories for Children and Their Friends* was begun in 1778 and was continued until the collection filled seven volumes.

It will now be clear that Pestalozzi, who was to carry out many of the preceding ideas, was born into an experimental age. The study of nature, the care of the body, the training of the hand, self-activity and pupil self-government, the appeal to thought and intelligence, naturalism and rationalism in morals and religion, were leading ideas of the reformers. In the new schools of that time, these ideas were put to work. Pestalozzi accepted these ideas and this experimental spirit, but he added to them love. His great heart went out to all mankind but especially to the poor and the oppressed. He was the true philanthropinist. He began, not at the top in the hope that some of the good things of the new schools would seep down, but at the bottom, among the common people. He turned his attention toward the reform of the schools for the children who lived in narrow homes among the mountains and even to the waifs who had no homes at all. He became the apostle of a new common school.

4. PESTALOZZI, REFORMER OF ELEMENTARY EDUCATION

Human nature is put together in a thousand ways and Pestalozzi, who received the *Émile* so enthusiastically and read it in his eighteenth year, was a very different person from the author of "that dream book." He had a warm and sympathetic heart and a calm and well-unified personality free from the inner conflicts that racked and shattered the soul of Rousseau. But they had one weakness in common; they were equally impractical. Rousseau retreated to the world of ideas; but Pestalozzi, during his whole life, attempted to make ideas work and with but indifferent success. A large school such as he developed at Yverdon requires money and financial management; it demands system and organization; and it calls for a personality which can bring into harmony and cooperative endeavor the divergent personalities of the staff. In the face of such problems, Pestalozzi was helpless; but in spite of that, he was a very great man whose influence reached far and whose fame will last.

It is one sign of his greatness that Pestalozzi understood himself as few understand their own nature, and another that he can use the first person singular, which he does constantly, with hardly a trace of egotism. We shall let him introduce himself by means of some selected and rearranged sentences from his book, *Views and Experiences*. "From childhood," he wrote, "it lay in the peculiarity of my character and of my home training to be benevolent and kindly and to have unlimited confidence in those about me. I came early into association with the suffering and the poor and, in a thousand experiences with them, came to feel the deepest sympathy with them and their many sorrows; and I likewise came to feel the urgent call to attempt to remove the multifarious causes of the evils which they endured. Nor was I alone in this for, in my time and in my Swiss fatherland, many of the pupils and the contemporaries of my teachers, Bodmer and Breitinger, were also trying to seek out the sources of the evil which kept the people of our fatherland from happiness and blessedness."

Johann Heinrich Pestalozzi (1746–1827) was born in Zürich, a city which was at that time, as it is today, famous for wealth, culture, and excellent schools. It is located on the shores of a beautiful lake in the German portion of Switzerland and the German language was his mother tongue; but his name is evidence that there was Italian blood in his veins. This was inherited from John Anton Pestalozzi who came from the southern slope of the Alps to Zürich where he prospered and became an adopted citizen. In Zürich, the Pestalozzis were business and professional people connected with some of the most eminent Zürich families. Henry's father was a physician. He died when the future educator was six years old, and thereafter the mother with her faithful servant, Barbara, devoted herself entirely to the care and education of her three children. It is often said that feminine influences were too strong in Henry's early life; and his natural tendency to self-sacrifice, generosity, and excessive trust in others were certainly not counteracted by his very kind mother and her gentle servant. This genial family circle was the basis of the vision which filled his mind and led him to consider a good home as the greatest of all means of education.

When we find Pestalozzi eulogizing the virtues of domestic education, we should recall that in his own case he recognized the deficiencies of such training. He admitted that the best of mothers brought him up as a spoilt darling, who never left the domestic hearth. In childhood he was allowed to see the world only from the sheltered confines of his mother's living-room and the equally narrow limits of the schoolroom. Experiences which would have developed manly vigor, sports, and work were largely excluded from his life. One window into the sorrows and sufferings of the real world was, however, provided by long residences with his grandfather, who was the minister and conscientious shepherd of souls in a village outside of Zürich. There, and in the poorer parts of the city, Pestalozzi saw enough of the poverty and oppression to lead him to become a social reformer. And it is as a social reformer that we must consider him. He saw that pity and charity were mere palliatives and that they indeed nourished the disease they were meant to cure. Education became for him the means by which society was to become first enlightened and then purified and elevated.

From his schooling under excellent teachers, Pestalozzi derived great inspiration and a varied if not very accurate knowledge. This does not apply to the elementary school which he attended, for that was poor and he learned little. But in the University, the Carolinum, he came under the stimulating instruction of men who were to influence him strongly. Bodmer was a professor of history, a literary critic who debated with Lessing, and the founder of the Helvetic Society for the spread of liberal political ideas. Pestalozzi's membership in this society had embarrassing consequences, as we shall see. Breitinger taught the ancient languages and edited an edition of the Septuagint. Both men leaned toward naturalism and romanticism and helped to restore the rights of the fancy and the imagination in German literature, and the rights of the people in Swiss political life.

The inspiration which Pestalozzi received from his education is well indicated in his own account of the results. He said that he seized quickly and avidly upon general ideas but failed in everything that demanded precise knowledge, trained skill, or practical competence. Realizing that this is a fair statement of the case, one is surprised to learn that he had acquired some facility in the Greek language. When one of his teachers published a correct but uninspired translation of some orations of Demosthenes, Pestalozzi handed in a more vigorous rendering of one of the eloquent and patriotic passages. Part of this school exercise was published and was the first item from his pen to see the light. Freedom, benevolence, and patriotism were the watchwords of the education which he received, but he was not taught how to achieve these ends practically in the Swiss cantons. His school education, in his opinion, was not more realistic than his home education had been; and from this conviction came his attack upon an education of words without experience and of ideals without deeds.

When he tried to realize his ideals for the fatherland, he promptly found himself in difficulties. The young men of Switzerland and Zürich, his contemporaries, were deeply affected by the revolutionary ideas of the eighteenth century, especially by the writings of Rousseau. Pestalozzi joined a small circle of "patriots" and when the Helvetic Society published a propaganda weekly, *The Reminder*, he contributed to its columns. About this time a friend, who was supposed to have taken part in some underground, possibly treasonable, activities, fled the country and Pestalozzi was arrested on the suspicion that he had helped in the escape. Although he was soon released, the experience probably led him to give up a contemplated career in the law and public affairs. Another plan to study theology and to follow in the footsteps of his grandfather was also given up.

The objective which he had in mind in considering those two professions was social, that is, moral, political, and economic reform, and especially the improvement of the condition of the destitute peasantry. The city of Zürich and especially certain patrician families had a practically feudal control over the lower classes and the country people of the canton. It would be a mistake to suppose that Pestalozzi changed his main purpose; in that, he was singularly consistent throughout life.

Agriculture was making rapid advances in various countries, and the first schools of agriculture had recently been established. The advances in the natural sciences, and the ideas of the physiocrats, also, led many to regard a perfected agriculture as the panacea for social ill-health. And some examples of the "new agriculture" were close at hand. Hans Hirzel, the city physician of Zürich and a zealous promoter of agriculture, had just written a popular book, *The Economics of a Scientific Farmer*, which was based upon an actual case, and this work may have been the deciding factor in leading Pestalozzi to undertake an agricultural experiment. Hirzel's opinion was that "the science of agriculture is worthy the attention of the wisest and best men for upon a well-ordered economy the happiness of the whole state depends." A short apprenticeship was arranged with the proprietor of a model farm and Pestalozzi spent the winter and spring of 1768 in attempting to learn the details of farm management by actual participation. Meanwhile he had become engaged to a young woman with excellent family connections, Anna Schulthess. And now this young man, bred in a large city, educated in a classical school with one winter's experience on a farm, purchased a hundred acres of stony land and erected thereon a beautiful but too-elaborate set of buildings. In September 1769, Pestalozzi and Anna Schulthess were married and took up their residence at Neuhof, as the estate was called. The marriage was a lifelong success but not so the farming. The venture failed; and the failure was very positive and came in an incredibly short time. Only the generous financial help of his mother and of his wife's relatives was able to stave off bankruptcy.

Neuhof was to become known, not for the plan to redeem agriculture, but for a partially successful effort to redeem waifs and outcast children by instruction coupled with industrial occupations. The custom of the time was to bind out orphans and poor children to farmers, who sometimes mistreated them and frequently exploited them. Pestalozzi's new institution was not conceived as a form of poor-relief but as an example of a new kind of education in which domestic and farm occupational training were joined with moral training and instruction. With help from friends, Pestalozzi was able (1774) to receive about fifty abandoned children, some of whom he had himself picked up in the streets. He neglected nothing that could give these children occupational, intellectual, moral, and religious education. They were taught the usual school arts, and also spinning, weaving, and farm work, and he especially tried to influence them along moral and religious lines. So large an establishment required a considerable staff which, in the spring of 1778, numbered about a dozen persons. From time to time, he made reports of progress in the newspapers and asked for further support.

The condition of many of the children was greatly improved, but some of them were already so tainted with vice or inured to begging that little could be done for them. Some of the parents also failed to cooperate and the institution developed increasing deficits. In 1780, after six years of successes and failures, it had to be closed. He was compelled to sell most of his land, retaining only his home and buildings and a garden. "For years," he wrote later, "I lived in the midst of fifty little beggars, sharing my bread with them, living like a beggar myself in order to teach beggars to live like men." The worst effect of the failure upon his own fortunes was that he was now discredited in Zürich where he had come to be considered a bankrupt and a hopelessly impractical idealist. But most of those who scoffed at his failure had done nothing and would do nothing to relieve the distress of their fellow men.

With the closing of the Neuhof Institute a new period opened in Pestalozzi's life. Outside his own family, almost the only supporter who remained was Isaac Iselin of Berne, municipal secretary and publisher. Iselin thought he saw a successful popular writer in Pestalozzi and he opened to him the columns of his paper, the *Ephemerides*, and thus introduced him to the literary world. Yet these were difficult years for Pestalozzi. He had begun to doubt, even more radically than before, his own powers but never his purposes. Practically, he had failed; the world of ideas was still beckoning to him. Much of what he then wrote, and he wrote a great deal, was not printed till long after; but what he published, in the two decades after Neuhof was closed, gave him a European reputation. His first successful writings were the *Evening Hours of a Hermit* (1780) and his educational romance *Leonard and Gertrude* (1781); and these were followed by *Swiss News, People's Weekly Review, Christopher and Elizabeth*, and the continuations of *Leonard and Gertrude*. Literary success brought him many correspondents, some from the highest social circles, and contact with the Illuminati, a secret society which played with reform ideas but never did anything more. He came to discover that nothing was to be expected from the dilettante reformers who applauded his ideas from a distance; and yet he continued to hope and work.

The story of *Leonard and Gertrude* was about the Swiss village life, which Pestalozzi knew inside and out from living with his pastor-grandfather. The heroine of the tale is a calm and loving mother who kept her children busy spinning while she taught them Bible verses and moral sayings and discussed with them the common questions of conduct as they arose. Her teaching of arithmetic likewise exemplified the plan of dealing with concrete experiences. They counted the threads in weaving, the steps across the room, the number of panes of glass in the windows, and they learned the meanings of common terms of quantity and form, such as "long," "narrow," "round." She taught them to observe carefully everything about them and to use their observations in practical work. Love led the way. And when the school in the village was established the same spirit and methods were employed. Gertrude taught that the school must be like a home but with wider interests. Through *Leonard and Gertrude*, Pestalozzi reached an audience that extended far beyond the borders of his own country.

He was a writer, but to what purpose? While the people everywhere were suffering and were sinking to ever lower depths of despair and dependence, he was spending his time in making books. What triviality! So he thought. To write merely for fame or money would have seemed to him a sin. To act, to do, to work positively, actively for the freedom, economic independence, and moral improvement of the people, that was life, a life which he was not permitted to share from 1780 to 1798. That was why these were diffcult years for Pestalozzi.

The French Revolution, more than anything else, cleared the air for him. He took part in the pamphlet war of the time but, unlike the young Schiller, he saw clearly the evils along with the good of the revolutionary movement. Even so he again burned his fingers. With Schiller, Washington, and others he was named a "Citizen of the French Republic." This close approach to the Revolution caused him to be still more suspected in Zürich and raised up enemies who never forgave him his liberal tendencies, especially his support of the peasant demands for political power and economic justice. His most philosophical book and one of the important works of the period appeared in 1797: *My Investigations into the Course of Nature in the Development of the Human Race.*

The Revolution gave him another opportunity to engage in teaching. Except for that, he would now be forgotten; because of that, he will always be remembered. In 1798, as a result of the French Revolution, Switzerland became the Helvetian Republic; and Philipp A. Stapfer, a distinguished intellectual, was appointed minister of arts and sciences. Stapfer determined upon a reform of the elementary schools and Pestalozzi submitted to him his plan of a school for poor children similar to the one described in *Leonard and Gertrude.* The Directory approved the scheme. Meanwhile Stapfer appointed Pestalozzi editor of the *People's News*, a government paper; but events spoke louder than his words and with more convincing arguments. In putting down an insurrection in the Forest Cantons, where the population was largely Catholic, the little town of Stanz was burned down and most of its ablebodied men were killed. As a result, the government had to undertake the care of about five hundred orphaned and needy children. Stapfer had previously offered Pestalozzi a political appointment which he declined with the declaration: "I want to be a schoolmaster." In the end, Pestalozzi had his wish when he was put in charge of about eighty orphans of Stanz and vicinity. A convent was made available and he became a schoolmaster in 1799 when he was already fifty-three years old. With the help of a single servant, he undertook to care for the physical, mental, and moral needs of his flock. The work was made more difficult because of the open hostility of the people, who regarded him as a heretic, and the almost complete lack of the usual instructional materials. It was at Stanz that he began to emphasize sense perception and to develop a psychological basis for teaching. There he developed his doctrine that there should be no impression without expression. He could employ manual work only slightly, but he came to see that the chief value of such work was educational, not economic. When he had succeeded in establishing paternal relations with them, he was able to do even more for the moral growth of the children than for their mental culture. For his own further development, it was important that at Stanz he came to see that children could be taught effectively in groups of considerable size. Great as was the success of this half-year it was fortunate for him that the progress of the war put an end to a task that was beyond any man's endurance. Stanz was again occupied by the troops and he went to Gurnigel for needed rest. Confessional differences and political complications prevented his return to Stanz; and instead Stapfer sent him to Burgdorf.

Pestalozzi's most important period as a teacher and school reformer began at Burgdorf in July 1799, and came to a close in 1804. At first, he taught in a school for the youngest children of the poor but later he was permitted to open his own school in the castle. There he developed his "new method" and secured his first collaborators, Krüsi, Tobler, and the drawing master, Buss. There he wrote his fundamental exposition of the new method, How Gertrude Teaches Her Children, "an experiment in teaching mothers how to bring up their little ones." With Krüsi, he prepared his Book for Mothers. His work was interrupted by a short trip to Paris where he was sent as a member of an official Swiss delegation. There is no evidence for the story about a meeting with Napoleon. In 1803, he secured a new disciple, Niederer, a gifted young man with whom he came to be very closely associated although afterwards violent opposition developed on both sides. At Burgdorf, the stream of famous visitors began, and there were always several foreigners who had come to study the school. Herbart, who had just completed two years as a tutor, praised the careful grading of the lessons and the thorough mastery of the elements which the pupils achieved. He also raised some questions. Gruner of Frankfort, who later established a Pestalozzian school in which Froebel found his life-work, gave an enthusiastic report of a moral lesson which he heard Pestalozzi give. Stapfer organized a Society of Friends of Education to solicit funds and to spread the fame of the school.

Emanuel Fellenberg (1771–1844), with whom Pestalozzi formed a brief alliance when he had to leave Burgdorf in 1804, had a plan for a system of agricultural schools for Switzerland. This plan, which he carried out on a large estate near Berne, included a school for the upper classes and a separate school for the poor. Industrial and agricultural, as well as literary, instruction was provided; and the students were organized into a school republic. Since Fellenberg was an able administrator, it might have been thought that the two men would admirably supplement each other. But it turned out that they were unable to cooperate. By August of the same year Pestalozzi had settled in Yverdon where he was given a lifetime lease of a castle as the home of his school.

The new institution in Yverdon increased in numbers and in reputation and became a Mecca for educators from Europe and America. Prussia annually sent groups of young teachers that they might "warm themselves at the fire of Pestalozzi's genius" and learn the details of his system. Nicolovius of the Prussian state department of education became an ardent admirer. Fichte called the attention of the whole world to Yverdon in his *Addresses to the German Nation.*

While his work was praised and imitated in foreign lands, a strong opposing party in Switzerland launched violent attacks against the school. Pestalozzi demanded an official investigation. The resulting report was not exactly hostile but it was cool and partly ironical in temper. They damned the school with faint praise; and no one read Niederer's long and heavy arguments in reply. These attacks from the outside were not fatal, but dissension developed within the staff especially between Niederer and Schmid. The harmony of the early, struggling days was destroyed beyond recovery. Schmid left in 1810 but had to be recalled because his administrative ability was essential. By vigorous measures, he rescued the Institute from imminent bankruptcy but he could not establish peace. Pestalozzi's wife died in 1815. Within two months, sixteen of the teachers sent Pestalozzi an ultimatum: "Dismiss Schmid or we will leave in a body." They left. Niederer, Krüsi, and Ramsauer remained for a time but finally they also resigned. An unedifying war of pamphlets and legal process followed. An effort was made to establish a new school for poor children at Clindy near Yverdon. There a young Englishman taught; and to him Pestalozzi addressed the thirty-four *Letters to J. P. Greaves* which were also published in German with the title *Mother and Child.* Finally, in 1825, Yverdon and Clindy, which had been combined with it, were closed and Pestalozzi returned to Neuhof.

The world had changed since the fall of Napoleon. Although he had suffered immeasurably from the conflicts of the last fifteen years, Pestalozzi continued to work to the end. In his last sad efforts, *Swan's Song* and *Life's Experiences,* in which he judged himself impartially and fairly, the faith in mankind of his early years still shone bright. The questions with which he had dealt were now more urgent than ever. How to educate the common people had become an exigent political question. Democracy was becoming an international movement. The greatness of the master's reputation in his last days is shown by the fact that Schmid was able to get a contract from a large publishing house and the promise of fifty thousand francs for a general edition of Pestalozzi's collected writings. Pestalozzi dedicated his share of the sum, one-half of the expected proceeds, to the furtherance of education. "Everything for others, nothing for himself," as his epitaph has it. In November 1826 he made his last public appearance to give an address on the education of small children. He died on February 17, 1827, and was buried in the churchyard beside the schoolhouse at Birr. In 1927, hundreds of addresses, papers, books, and memorial exercises attempted to do honor to his memory and to set the seal of world-wide approval upon his efforts.

5. PESTALOZZI'S METHODS

Pestalozzi's life was his work; but yet a systematic account of the "new method" is necessary. Beyond all theory, Pestalozzi meant to be a practical educator. Education was to be based upon experience and since the child did not already have it, the experience had to be provided in the home and school. This was to be done mainly through *Anschauung*, an untranslatable word for which we shall use Observation with a capital letter. The process of Observation begins with confused sense impressions. The world is for the child, as William James was to say, "a blooming, buzzing confusion"; or as Pestalozzi said: "The world lies before our eyes like a sea of confused sense impressions, flowing into one another." Through attention, the sense impressions grow definite and distinct. Objects, with their qualities, separate themselves out so that they become units and can be recognized, described, and finally named and classified. With naming and classification we reach a third and final stage of observation, the stage when objects, not merely sense impressions but objects, are seen in relation to other objects and finally to all objects. The idea of all objects, of a whole or universe, is an example of an intuition. The universe is something which we have never seen and cannot see except in a few of its parts but which we must assume intuitively. This, then, is the course of Observation: confused sensations, clearness and description, definition, and classification.

Several remarks on this bit of Pestalozzian psychology are necessary. Pestalozzi is here influenced, probably unconsciously, by the doctrine of Kant that in knowledge the mind supplies the "form" and the world the "matter" or content of knowledge. "Matter without form is blind; form without matter is empty." Completed observation is due not only to sense impressions but to the mind which by intuition contributes quite as much as the outside world to the total result. And the contribution is twofold. Attention selects what is seen; the mind is not a white sheet of paper or a photographic film which merely registers whatever appears. The mind selects and also contributes the final stage of Observation, the categories by which objects are defined and classified. Pestalozzi took the basic categories to be number, form, and language. The course of Observation is followed not only by the child but also by the adult. We all make our ideas clear by the same general process. The teacher has the responsibility of guiding observation. Pestalozzi did not merely turn the children loose to find their own way among phenomena; but he, more than Rousseau, emphasized the value of guided individual and social experience in directing the process of learning.

The project is one form of a complete Observation lesson. While it would be hazardous to attempt to name the inventor of the educational project and to decide whether he was Rousseau or Basedow or even Plato, it is clear that Pestalozzi used it. A good example of its use comes from a pupil at Yverdon in the following description. "The first elements of geography were taught us from the land itself. We were first taken to a narrow valley not far from Yverdon, where the river Buron runs. After taking a general view of the valley, we were made to examine the details, until we had obtained an exact and complete idea of it. We were then told to take some of the clay which lay in beds on one side of the valley, and to fill the baskets which we had brought for the purpose. On our return to the Castle, we took our places at the long tables, and reproduced the valley we had just studied, each one doing the part which had been allotted to him. In the course of the next few days more walks and more explorations, each day on higher ground, and each time with a further extension of our work. Only when our relief was finished were we shown the map, which by this means we did not see until we were in a position to understand it."

This example illustrates the large part which the teacher played in Pestalozzi's "new method," or Art of Education as he also called it. Some might doubt whether the exercise should be called a project because of the absence of student planning. This is a question of definition. On the larger question of the teacher's function in Pestalozzi's method one may further quote in modified form from *How Gertrude Teaches*, as follows: "If our development through nature alone is not sufficiently rapid and unhindered, the business of the teacher is to remove the confusion of first sense impressions, to separate the objects to make them distinct, to place those together which are related to each other or similar, making them clear in this way and thereby evolving definite ideas. Instruction accomplishes this when it presents confused sense impressions in units so that they can be counted; when it then places them in different positions so that we may perceive their forms; and when it brings them into the cycle of our previous knowledge and names them." Here Pestalozzi nearly or quite anticipates Herbart's famous doctrine of apperception but he does not develop it. The passage is quoted because it is a general description of *Anschauung* or Observation.

Using the method of Observation, Pestalozzi sought to expand the school curriculum, particularly along scientific and naturalistic lines. The spread of his doctrines and of the whole Pestalozzian effort was furthered both by the scientific movement and by the humanitarian movement of the nineteenth century. Nature study, physiology and hygiene, geography and the sciences were knocking at the school doors seeking admittance; and Pestalozzianism was both cause and effect of this condition. Science had heretofore been the concern of scientists; but it was now to be simplified and its elementary and practical phases were to be taken up in general education. We may show how this could be done in a single case.

Geography had already attained some standing as a school subject, but the older methods and content were generally unsuitable for small children. Locke had regarded it as a branch of mathematics and had based his method upon the globe and its circles. Another type of geography, almost the opposite of this, was purely informational, beginning with map study and lists of names, boundaries, and products. Basedow and Rousseau had proposed to teach the geography of the locality in which the pupils lived. But Pestalozzi actually did this in elementary education. It was Pestalozzi who introduced local geography, or home geography, studied by project methods; and who said that this subject should deal with the lives of the people, with the country in which they live and the resources from which they make their living. This was actually a new study and came to be called human geography. Its origin is traced to Pestalozzi and Karl Ritter (1779–1859) and their interpreters. Ritter, the founder of the modern study of geography, after a visit to Pestalozzi at Yverdon wrote: "I have seen more than the Paradise of Switzerland for I have seen Pestalozzi. Never have I been so filled with the sense of the sacredness of my calling and the dignity of human nature as in the days I spent with this noble man. Pestalozzi knew little geography but he taught me all that I know. In listening to him I first conceived the idea of the natural method. It was he who opened the way to me." Ritter began to publish his great work on human geography in 1817 and appropriately called it the *Science of the Earth in Relation to the Nature and History of Man*.

In his application of Observation to geography, Pestalozzi was guided by intuition, pupil interest, and purpose. But it seemed that in some subjects such as reading or arithmetic a different method should be used, and in these fields he turned for help to analysis and scientific technique. In all fields, however, the new method developed the use of oral teaching and the subordination of books to direct experience.

Direct experience in the school skills seemed to require that the pupil should build up each skill from its elements, as written language is constructed from the alphabet. Pestalozzi therefore went out in search of teaching alphabets. Each subject was to be reduced to its simplest elements, its ABC. Unfortunately, he went wrong at the outset, mistaking mechanical parts for psychological units.

We may illustrate his idea from the teaching of language. He correctly pointed out that speech comes before reading and writing and is psychologically fundamental to these; but he went astray when he analyzed language into syllables as the natural units of speech. Only an infant who cannot yet speak attempts to speak in syllables. When significant speech begins, a higher synthesis occurs and the idea, and later the sentence, becomes the psychological element. Perhaps he was misled by the age-old use of lists of syllables in schools, some of which lists have come down to us in the school exercises of the ancient Greeks and Babylonians. At all events the school child is far past the syllable stage of utterance, and Pestalozzi was mistakenly attempting to take the pupil back not forward. In connection with the syllables and the early language lessons, Pestalozzi also developed a form of concert recitation in which the children repeated his statements after him. This is in general the poorest of all forms of oral instruction and belongs to the list of errors of Pestalozzian practice. But his emphasis upon oral teaching, oral expression by the children, and the use of conversational methods was an advance. The teacher had to be better prepared, more skillful, and freer in the use of ideas than in the older book recitations. The children likewise had to depend upon their own eyes, minds, and speech faculties. Oral teaching called for activity and resourcefulness.

Oral and object teaching revolutionized the teaching of arithmetic, and Pestalozzi became the founder of what is essentially a new subject, primary arithmetic. Arithmetic had been mainly a commercial subject and was taught by formal rules and examples. Pestalozzi based primary arithmetic upon the process of counting. Here, for once, he was fortunate in his idea of the elementary units, the ABC of the subject. He began by having children count small objects like pebbles or sticks, arranging them in groups of two, five, and ten and in that way inductively building up the notion of number. Much of the work was oral, and this led to the development of primary arithmetic teaching without the use of pencil and paper, whence it was called "mental arithmetic." Books featuring "thought problems" with small numbers under the title *Mental Arithmetic* were issued by enterprising authors and publishers; and for a hundred years mental arithmetic and written arithmetic went their separate ways as independent subjects in schools. This was an educational excrescence for which Pestalozzi is not to be blamed, but he is to be honored as the founder of the elementary arithmetic of everyday life and of the arithmetic methods which have had an extensive development in our own day.

Speaking develops before reading, counting before calculation, and before children write they draw, according to Pestalozzi. He made the ABC of drawing consist of straight and curved lines in all possible positions, horizontal, oblique, vertical. Practice on these was to prepare for penmanship. The written letters were then analyzed into the various "strokes" and to each of these appropriate practice was assigned. Drawing was emphasized for its own sake also and not merely as a preparation for handwriting. Number, form, and language formed the categories of teaching, as we have seen, and drawing was one means of cultivating the sense of form. Geometry was another and this also Pestalozzi taught inductively in the manner of Rousseau. Even physical education was supposed to have its ABC. The elements were simple motions, which after being practiced separately were to be combined into the complex activities involved in games. All this will sufficiently illustrate what Pestalozzi meant by psychologizing education. He meant that the teacher should start with the elements of every subject and should follow the natural order of child growth and development.

In addition to the subjects mentioned, Pestalozzi included in his school manual and agricultural experiences, physical training and military drill, nature study, music, and moral and religious education. Literature, history, and the aesthetic side of life hardly received their due in his curriculum. He himself taught morals and religion although Niederer, who was a theologian, also gave religious instruction. Few if any teachers ever have so loved not only children but each individual child, or have been able to gain their confidence so completely as Pestalozzi. Love wins reciprocal love, he said. Pestalozzi, like Lincoln with whom he has some traits in common including the love of a good story, was an intensely religious man although it is not quite clear what his exact beliefs were. Much was made of the great holidays. At Christmas, the usual tree with apples and candles was set up in the middle of the chapel. New Year's Day was celebrated with a speech from Pestalozzi, a religious ceremony, and in the evening a grand dinner. But the great celebration of the year was January 12, Pestalozzi's birthday, for which preparation began immediately after New Year's Day. Often the pupils gave a play based upon the heroic history of Switzerland for which they made the costumes themselves.

For most subjects, special teachers were available. For music, these were Pfeiffer and Nägeli, both Swiss, who prepared popular collections of songs for the young. Music was taught by the natural method, beginning with rote-singing. Singing had a large place in the life of the Institute. Physical education was at one time taught by Joseph Neef, an ex-soldier from Napoleon's army who later attempted to establish Pestalozzian schools in the United States. At Burgdorf and Yverdon, carefully graded gymnastics were regularly taught and games were played. Target shooting was one of these games, and the older boys had military drill. Skating in winter, swimming in summer, and long mountain tramps at all seasons gave vigorous exercise. Pestalozzian physical education had wide influence in Spain and France and other countries, while Spiess carried it into Germany. After the industrial and farm school at Neuhof, it is surprising that not more was done on these lines at Yverdon. Manual work was on the program. It was not always systematically carried on, but some crafts like bookbinding and making geometrical models together with gardening were practiced.

Long hours were the rule in the Institute. Pestalozzi rose early and began to dictate to Ramsauer, one of the teachers who acted as his secretary. At the beginning and the end of the day, he held personal conferences with the pupils. There were ten lesson periods, each an hour long, with short intervals between, taking up the whole day from six to eight. But some of the lessons consisted of practice and work demanding little preparation such as drawing, gymnastics, and music. The last hour, from seven to eight in the evening, was free time when pupils were allowed "to work for themselves," in writing letters, drawing or modeling, or doing whatever they pleased in the room. Three times a week the masters handed in reports on the work and conduct of each boy to Pestalozzi. The younger teachers, many of them teachers-in-training, had the supervision of the pupils out of the classroom, played games with them, and slept with them in the dormitories. But the pupils always enjoyed great freedom. The two gates of the castle stood open all day and pupils could come and go as in a family.

We shall summarize the main features of the Pestalozzian system before we take up its spread and influence:

1. A good home is the ideal educational institution for it is a center of love and active cooperation for the common welfare.
2. Since the larger society requires a range of education which the homes cannot give, schools are necessary. In spirit and discipline, these should be modeled upon the good home. Personal love for the child must guide the teacher who stands in the parents' place. The discipline, though kind, must yet be strict and firm.

3. The harmonious development of all man's powers is the aim of education. We aim to produce men educated for manhood first of all and only secondly to train citizens and workers.

4. Because they have been most neglected and are in such desperate circumstances, the regeneration of the lower classes must receive first attention. This calls for an education which rouses the will and vitalizes their powers, for charity only makes bad conditions worse.

5. Education is to be social and universal.

6. Instruction is to be "psychologized," that is, it is to be based upon the psychological development of the individual and the race. This involves the grading of pupils, the presentation of subject matter in harmony with the stage of growth, and the enlistment of the child's purposes and self-activity.

7. Instruction is to be carried on by Observation and by graduated activities, beginning with the simplest elements of each area or skill.

8. The curriculum must be expanded along practical and scientific lines. Although he did not use these words his concept was that of an "activity and experience curriculum."

9. Teaching is a skilled occupation and a moral vocation. Teachers can best learn their occupation and vocation in experimental schools which are themselves seeking means of improvement.

6. THE INFLUENCE OF PESTALOZZI

The actual influence upon the schools was greatest in Germany. In his homeland, many citizens, the local authorities of Yverdon, and even the Swiss government rendered him aid and contributed to the support of his schools. Many of the teachers who were prepared in his schools taught in Switzerland and Hermann Krüsi, one of the most important members of Pestalozzi's staff, became principal of the normal school at Gais. But many Swiss leaders were suspicious of his aims and critical of his methods and his French sympathies. In Germany, his system was rapidly introduced after the defeat of Napoleon and became the basis of the new educational reforms. In the largest German state, the resulting organization was appropriately named the Prussian-Pestalozzian system. Many Prussian teachers and heads of teachers' seminaries were trained by Pestalozzi. One important philosopher, Fichte, and two great German educational theorists, Herbart and Froebel, were directly influenced by Pestalozzi. In the chapter on education in Germany, the Pestalozzian influence upon that country will be more fully treated.

Great Britain was moved through Pestalozzi to adopt object teaching and to develop her infant schools, but the Pestalozzian influence upon the training of teachers was most important in Great Britain. The Home and Colonial School Society established a model infant school which applied Pestalozzian methods and educated several thousand teachers in the new way. The English did not become fully aware of Pestalozzi's work until late. The famous writer Maria Edgeworth visited him early and again in 1820. Writing home on the latter occasion she said: "He recognized me and I him; he is, tell my mother, the same wild-looking man he was, with the addition of seventeen years. The whole superintendence of the school is now in the hands of his masters; he just shows the visitor into the room, and reappears as you are going away with a look that pleads irresistibly for an obol of praise." J. P. Greaves was an assistant in the latter years. And Charles Mayo, one of the founders of the Home and Colonial School Society, was at Yverdon from 1819 to 1822. It was partly due to this late acquaintance with Yverdon in its decline that English Pestalozzianism became formalized from the beginning. By this is meant that the forms of the method were followed without the spirit, without experiment, or taking advantage of new opportunities, or making special adaptations to particular needs. But after all, except for the monitorial schools, British teacher education owed its beginnings and some of its good features to Pestalozzi. Battersea Training College definitely followed Swiss ideas. It had a model school for experiment, demonstration, and practice; and Battersea introduced Pestalozzi's reforms in the teaching of arithmetic.

The movement reached the United States through several different channels and it is more fully considered in the chapters on American education. Joseph Neef, mentioned above, came in 1806. The early teachers' journals, Albert Picket's *Academician*, 1818–1820, William Russell's *American Journal of Education*, beginning 1826, Barnard's *Journal* of the same name, the *American Annals of Education*, and many others introduced Pestalozzian ideas. Official reports such as Cousin's, Stowe's, Bache's, and the *Seventh Report* of Horace Mann went into the matter systematically. Visitors to Europe wrote travel books such as John Griscom's *A Year in Europe*. There were really three periods of Pestalozzian influence upon American education. Neef came in 1806, established a school, and published his *Sketch of a Plan and Method of Education* but exerted little influence. The Fellenberg manual labor system was introduced as early as 1816 but went into a decline by 1840. Meanwhile, about 1830, the second Pestalozzian period helped to develop the idea of the universal elementary school, teacher training, a broader curriculum, and milder discipline. The American normal schools, and similar schools in all countries, were generally influenced by Pestalozzi. The third period showed English influence and introduced object teaching. Because of the leadership of the Oswego Normal School this is usually called the Oswego System. Although the contributions of the new education of the eighteenth and early nineteenth centuries to teaching practice were great, there were also great defects and these were due in part to a faulty psychology. We next turn to the efforts which were made to develop a more adequate view of human and child nature and of the process of learning.

Not all of the eighteenth-century trends of thought and feeling affected education immediately. Rationalism, which gave the period its name, the "Age of Reason," influenced the schools less than the romantic views and humanitarian ideals of the time. Nationalism, also, although it was growing stronger with every decade, did not gain control of the schools until the following century was far advanced. Only then did the governments establish the ministries of education which had been demanded by Basedow, Condorcet, and others; and only gradually did the schools become secular. Except in German countries, compulsory attendance was long deferred.

The schools of this chapter may be regarded as different varieties of one species whose characteristics were realism and democracy. The experimental spirit which also characterized them was connected with their realism and democratic liberalism.

Their debt to realism is clear from the broad, naturalistic curricula and the activity methods. Among the methods used were observation, excursions and the collecting of natural objects, handwork and construction projects, and simple demonstrations and experiments. There was a decided renaissance of physical education and a vigorous creative movement in this field.

The democratic liberalism of the time led educators to organize pupils into school legislatures, courts, and administrative bodies. The new schools attempted to develop not only knowledge and language, but also skills, moral character, and social conduct. To develop pupils along these lines, most of the new schools employed some form, and several of them an elaborate form, of pupil self-government. The purpose was not mere school discipline but political and moral education. They were to learn how laws are made and executed by making and executing laws and by governing themselves. Cecil Reddie, an English educator of a later day, expressed the idea by declaring that the school must be a smaller state and a larger home. Pestalozzi especially stressed the latter attitude. His school was to be a family, and was to aid in transforming society into a fraternal social order.

Pestalozzi's greatest idea was the conception that the common school should provide a liberal education for the common people. Through education the masses were to become true men and women, wise, free, and noble. Schools with such a task would require teachers who had the qualities that they were to instil. Pestalozzi's international influence upon teacher education and his promotion of educational experimentation were of lasting value to the cause to which he gave his life.

QUESTIONS

1.   What do you consider to be the meaning of the phrase "benevolent despot"? Examples? Are the ideas included in it self-contradictory?

2.   How fully does the school of Martin Planta answer the description of the new schools which concludes the present chapter?

3.   Criticize Basedow's principle, that with a good book anybody can be a good teacher. What truth, if any, does it express?

4.   Were there any entirely new ideas in Basedow's Philanthropinum?

5.   What were the values and what the shortcomings of the books for children which were written by the Philanthropinists?

6.   In what respects were Salzmann's school and doctrine an improvement over Basedow's?

7.   Arrange in the order of their importance the qualities that made Pestalozzi a great educator; and in the same manner his greatest defects.

8.   Why was the story of Leonard and Gertrude applauded not only by the poor but also by the rich and powerful?

9.   Trace the evolution of Pestalozzi's methods.

10.   What are the differences between Pestalozzi's curriculum and that of a good present-day elementary school?

11.   What seems to be intended by the statement that, by means of the common school, Pestalozzi meant to provide a liberal education for the common people?

12.   In what ways do the new schools imply a new conception of nature and of man?

FOR FURTHER READING AND STUDY

Many of the important books on Basedow and Pestalozzi are in German and have not been translated. The literature on these men, their contemporaries, and their period is very extensive and cannot be adequately represented in a short bibliography. Books dealing with the introduction of Pestalozzian ideas into the United States will be given in a later chapter. There are other good English biographies of Pestalozzi than those named below, and Quick's *Educational Reformers* should not be overlooked.

Anderson, Lewis F., *Pestalozzi*, New York, McGraw-Hill Book Company, Inc., 1931, 203 pp. Contains selections and an introduction.

Andress, James M., *Johann Gottfried Herder as an Educator*, New York, G. E. Stechert & Company, 1916, 316 pp.

Barnard, Henry, *Pestalozzi and his Educational System*, Syracuse, N. Y., C. W. Bardeen and Co., 1906, 751 pp.

Bosse, Richard, and J. Meyer, *Christian Gotthilf Salzmann's pädagogische Schriften*, Leipzig, A. Pichler, 1886–1888, 2 vols.

Channing, Eva, Translator, *Pestalozzi's Leonard and Gertrude*, Boston, D. C. Heath and Company, 1906, 181 pp. Much abridged.

Cooke, E., Editor, *Pestalozzi's How Gertrude Teaches Her Children*, Syracuse, N. Y., C. W. Bardeen and Co., 1898, 391 pp.; *Letters on Early Education, Addressed to J. P. Greaves*, Syracuse, N. Y., C. W. Bardeen and Co., 1898, 180 pp.

Dändliker, Karl, *A Short History of Switzerland*, London, S. Sonnenschein and Co., 1899, 322 pp.

Escher, Hermann, Chairman Editorial Committee, *Pestalozzi and His Times, a Pictorial Record*, New York, G. E. Stechert & Company, 1928. About 80 pages of text and 165 plates, several in colors, illustrating scenes and persons connected with the life and work of the great educator.

Fritzsche, Theodor, *J. B. Basedow's Elementarwerk mit den Kupfertafeln Chodo-wiecki*, Leipzig, Ernst Wiegandt, 1909, 3 vols.

Göring, Hugo, *J. B. Basedow's ausgewählte Schriften*, Langensalza, H. Beyer und Söhne, 1880, 519 pp.

Green, J. A., *Pestalozzi's Educational Writings*, New York, Longmans, Green and Company, 1912, 328 pp.; *Life and Work of Pestalozzi*, London, W. B. Clive and Co., 1913, 393 pp.; and by Warwick & York, Baltimore.

Guimps, Roger de, *Pestalozzi; His Life and Work*, New York, D. Appleton & Company, 1914, 445 pp. Translated by J. Russell.

Highet, Gilbert, *The Art of Teaching*, New York, Vintage Books, 1954, 259 pp. Originally published 1950, by Alfred A. Knopf, Inc., New York.

Hunziker, Otto, *Geschichte der schweizerischen Volkschule*, Zürich, F. Schulthess, 1881–1882, 3 vols. Contains an account of Martin Planta's school.

Krüsi, Hermann, *Pestalozzi; His Life, Work, and Influence*, New York, American Book Company, 1875, 248 pp. With accounts of Pestalozzi's associates in his schools.

Misawa, Tadasu, *Modern Educators and their Ideals*, New York, D. Appleton & Company, 1909, 304 pp.

Oechsli, Wilhelm, *History of Switzerland*, Cambridge, University Press, 1922, 480 pp. Translated by Eden and Cedar Paul.

Pinloche, Auguste, *La Reforme de l'Education en Allemagne au dix-huitème siècle. Basedow et le Philanthropinisme*, Paris, Librairie Armand Colin, 1889, 596 pp., (German edition, prepared by Pinloche and J. Rauschenfels, *Geschichte des Philanthropinismus*, Leipzig, Fr. Brandstetter, 1896, 494 pp.); *Pestalozzi and the Foundation of the Modern Elementary School*, New York, Charles Scribner's Sons, 1901, 306 pp.

Pollard, Hugh M., *Pioneers of Popular Education*, Cambridge, Massachusetts, Harvard University Press, 1957, 297 pp. May be used to supplement Chapter 15, also.

11 NEW SYSTEM BUILDERS: HERBART

A COMPREHENSIVE SCHEME OF EDUCATION MUST TAKE PROPER account of the nature of the child and the adult as well as the nature of the social structure in which life is to be lived. The founders of educational philosophy, Plato and Aristotle, fixed their attention upon the latter question and, although they did not overlook the fact that states are composed of men, they developed social systems; and the society they had in view was the Greek city-state. They agreed that a satisfactory education must be directed to the preparation of citizens, and being chiefly concerned with social issues they, but Plato more than Aristotle, tended to magnify the duties and to neglect the interests and needs of the individual and the child. This attitude was accepted by teachers for many centuries. The writers of the Renaissance, and after them Comenius and Locke, discovered the individual. Rousseau accepted their individualism and, indeed, pushed it to a dangerous extreme; but his greater contribution was his recognition of the difference between the immature child and the adult. Pestalozzi tried to redress Rousseau's individualistic imbalance without forgetting that children must be educated as children before they can become men. At that point John Frederick Herbart (1776–1841) and Frederick A. W. Froebel (1782–1852) began to develop their new systems of educational thought. The novelty consisted in the psychological bases of their philosophies. Each founded his program upon a psychology, Herbart upon associationism and Froebel upon activism; and each, because he selected fundamental factors in learning and growth, must be counted among the founders of educational psychology. We shall deal with Herbart in this chapter, and with Froebel in the next.

1. THE LIFE OF HERBART

John Frederick Herbart was born at Oldenburg, the only child of a civil official. His mother, who was the daughter of a physician, directed his studies at home and even accompanied him to the university. He was a precocious lad who read Kant at sixteen. From twelve to eighteen, he attended the classical school at Oldenburg and then entered the University of Jena where he came under the influence of Fichte and joined a student club called the "Free Men." For several years he served as tutor in a Swiss family at Berne, where he attempted to test Fichte's thought that the "self creates its own world." It seemed to Herbart, however, that the pupils did not make their world but instead were themselves made by the world of ideas which he presented to them. This is the key to his philosophy of education. Our minds are formed by the ideas that the world and our teachers impress upon us.

At the University of Göttingen, where he remained until 1809, he began as a lecturer and wrote his early books on education, ethics, and general philosophy. This activity led to his appointment at the University of Königsberg to the chair which Immanuel Kant had made famous. There he worked for a quarter of a century, lecturing, writing, and conducting a small practice and demonstration school for students who were preparing to teach. In 1811 he was married to Mary Drake, the daughter of an English merchant. At Königsberg he wrote his *Text-Book in Psychology* (1816), *Psychology as a Science* (1824), and several systematic philosophical works. That was the great Hegelian period in Germany and Herbart, although not without influence, failed to get the hearing for his philosophy which he thought it deserved. When Hegel died in 1831, Herbart hoped for appointment to the vacant chair in Berlin but he was disappointed; and two years later he returned to the University of Göttingen where he taught until his death in 1841 and where he wrote his most practical book, the *Outlines of Educational Doctrine*.

2. EDUCATIONAL PSYCHOLOGY BEFORE HERBART

The central topics of educational psychology are the topics of learning and growth. How we learn, how learning may be made easier and more permanent, how learning in one field may be applied to other fields, and how learning is conditioned by the age, the physical condition, the individual differences, and the motivation of the learners are its most important questions. The answers to such questions would go far to settle the question of how we should teach; and this is the question which most interested Herbart.

The answer Herbart gave was that we learn by association. This doctrine had a long history. Plato, for example, had noticed that a lyre will call to mind the one who had played upon the instrument. This is an instance of association by togetherness or contiguity. When any two ideas have been in the mind at the same time or in close succession, either one is likely to recall the other. Plato had also noticed that any idea or experience tends to bring back a like experience. This is associated by similarity. Continuing this line of thought, Aristotle added a third principle, association by contrast. Thus night may suggest day, up may suggest down, and love may suggest hate. The dynamics of the process also interested Aristotle. He noted that recall is not always accidental and that deliberate recollection takes place through a seeking and selecting activity. Starting with any one of a series of ideas, we follow along from term to term until we find the desired one, when the process stops. This self-active selectivity of the mind was not always accepted by later students who tried to explain mental functions in mechanical terms; but the three principles of association mentioned above, contiguity, similarity, and contrast, became the common property of later psychologists.

Associationism became an important doctrine in educational psychology and especially so to those who were seeking a mechanical or a physiological explanation of learning. Among the latter was David Hartley, a physician, who attempted to reduce all ideas to sensations, and all sensations to nerve vibrations. He attempted to show that all association is based upon contiguity, that is, he held that all associations occur because the associated ideas have been in the mind together. Of course they do; but this does not take us very far. Neither similarity nor contrast nor any other relation could be noted unless the ideas were in the mind at the same time. But this is not enough. The association has still to be made; and many ideas are in the mind together without being associated. The basic "laws" of association do not explain why certain associations are made and other possible ones are not. The conditions which they state are necessary but not sufficient.

The doctrine of Hartley was extended and modified by Thomas Brown and James Mill, two pupils of the noted Scotch teacher Dugald Stewart. Stewart revived Aristotle's doctrine that the mind seeks and selects what is remembered. He taught that the self, through its self-active power of attention, directs recall and that, therefore, the mechanics of association alone do not fully explain memory. Brown accepted his teacher's view of the unified and active self but he also made an important contribution to association theory. He tried to answer the question raised in the preceding paragraph, Why does night sometimes suggest day, at another time sleep, or again the darkness of a cave? Why, when two possible associations come into competition, does one win the spotlight of attention while the other recedes into the shadow? To answer this question, Brown proposed "secondary laws" of association, such as recency, frequency, duration, and liveliness. Accordingly, night should usually suggest day, but if we have recently visited a deep mine and especially if we lost our way and were thoroughly frightened, then the approach of night may recall the darkness of the dangerous underground.

To these secondary laws by Brown, James Mill added the law of primacy which says that the first association of a series tends to be stronger than the later ones. Concepts, said Mill, are formed through language which is itself formed by association. He held, further, that not only language but all human character is formed through the "universal Principle of Association" and that by the use of this principle the moral and intellectual condition of mankind may be improved without limit. The mind, according to Mill, is merely the sum of our sensations, feelings, and ideas, which association combines into groups and series. This was the general standpoint of Herbart also, but he did not accept the doctrine of human perfectibility which Mill had taken from Helvetius. Mill took education to include all the influences of life but even so he ascribed to it more power than it actually has. Education cannot overcome inherited differences for the good reason that men differ in the capacity to be educated. Herbart described this fact in terms of the differing plasticity of individuals. After Mill, association doctrine was transformed by the biological outlook of Darwin, Herbert Spencer, and Alexander Bain, but these writers came too late to influence Herbart.

Another persistent doctrine is that of the mental faculties. Like associationism, this also orginated with Plato and Aristotle. Both held that the rational faculty is the highest and should control the lower ones, while St. Augustine made the will supreme and ascribed to it the power of choice in action. The faculty psychology became especially prominent in the work of Christian Wolff (1679–1754) who divided the mind into will, feeling, and intellect, and the intellect into sensation, perception, memory, imagination, and reason. In the eighteenth century both association psychology and faculty psychology had important exponents; and, since a thoroughgoing association can leave no place for faculties, a conflict was unavoidable. Herbart, who was a thoroughgoing associationist, taught that the mind acts, through its most powerful ideas, as a unit; and that there are no separate faculties. As a consequence of this view, he held that there is no possibility of formal discipline or transfer of training.

Other influences came to Herbart through Locke and Leibnitz. Locke made out that all ideas, by which he meant all mental contents, come from experience. There are no innate ideas. The mind of the new-born child is a blank sheet upon which experience writes whatever will be found there. But perhaps he gave away his case by recognizing two kinds of ideas, those of sensation and those of reflection. Ideas of reflection, if they are really different from ideas due to sensation, seem to indicate that the mind has a pattern of its own and that not everything comes from the outside. Leibnitz attacked Locke at his weakest point, his failure to recognize the self-activity of the mind. The mind, he pointed out, is not so passive or so calmly logical as Locke made it; and he also declared that it is always active even in sleep. Here the unconscious mind enters psychology. Leibnitz called these unconscious activities *petites perceptions*, minute or slight perceptions. He used the word perception to indicate the more passive reception of ideas, and apperception to denote the active understanding of what is received. Herbart, in the same vein, used apperception to denote the assimilation of sense data and new ideas to those which are already in the mind. The knowledge which we have of plants enables us to understand a new specimen. Such clusters of ideas through which we interpret new ideas he called an apperception mass.

We have now reviewed some of the older psychological thought which influenced him. We shall notice that his philosophy, including his psychology, has the general character of natural science.

3. HERBART'S PSYCHOLOGY OF EDUCATION

The main difference between the educational psychology of Herbart and the older associationism is that ideas in his view are themselves dynamic. They are active forces and these form the substance of his psychology. Learning is the active assimilation of ideas; and the ideas already in the mind are not only active but selective.

Consistent ideas, said Herbart, will combine to form more inclusive ideas through fusion. The idea of a triangle is the result of the fusion of several ideas such as three, line, and plane. Ideas which have no necessary connection with each other but which do not conflict may also be combined. The ideas of color, form, texture, and taste may be combined to form the idea apple, or orange. This process he called complication. But ideas may be conflicting as in the case of round and square. Such ideas will compete and then the stronger will win and the weaker will be suppressed but not extinguished. The weaker ideas will be driven to the margin of consciousness or even over the threshold into the unconscious mind, from which, however, they may again emerge when the conditions are favorable. Among the terms Herbart introduced into psychology are fusion, complication, conflict, threshold, central and marginal consciousness, of which there was a hint in Wolff, and the unconscious mental processes, which he borrowed from Leibnitz. Most of these are still used by psychologists but sometimes in new senses.

Ideas have usually been considered as purely intellectual phenomena; but contrary to the usual practice, Herbart connected emotion and will with the relations between ideas. Pleasure results when ideas harmonize with each other and pain is the outcome of conflict between them. Pleasant idea relations lead to desire and will. The strongest group of ideas will lead to action. There is no separate will in Herbart's psychology, nor any other independent faculties, but only ideas and their relations.

When a new idea is presented, it can be interpreted only by means of other ideas. It is by the context that we understand a new word, a new acquaintance, or a new experience. The word bay means a body of water, a color, or a sound. The word plate has forty or more meanings all of which are clear when it is used in context. A forest is one kind of thing to the hunter, another to the lumberman, a third to a party of picnickers, and so on. To understand the Constitution, we have to study it in its context, including its entire history. This understanding of the new by means of its associates Herbart called apperception. An apperception mass is the name for the whole body of related ideas which enable us to interpret new ideas and to assimilate them. When they become assimilated, they form a part of the given apperception mass which may then be used to interpret further experiences. Thus knowledge is built up in the mind in a series of steps. Through his experience and knowledge of the human body in health and disease, the physician is able to make a correct diagnosis from facts which the layman does not notice and which he would not understand if they were pointed out to him. This is a case of apperception. The doctrine has important applications in teaching and these Herbart used in his theory.

The mind originally, and in essence, was for Herbart simply the ground on which ideas carry out their activities. It had little more to do with mental functions than Locke's blank sheet of paper. But Herbart opposed the passivity introduced by Locke and the associationists; and, therefore, he made the ideas active forces and the mind became the moving system of such forces. Such a mind is entirely formed by the ideas impressed upon it from the outside, and education, which presents the ideas, becomes as powerful in making the mind as any associationist could have desired.

4. HERBART'S EDUCATIONAL PRINCIPLES

To a systematic philosopher like Herbart, it seemed self-evident that a practical science like education must begin by stating its purpose. We realize that as a matter of method this has its dangers. A more empirical attack will deal with children, materials, processes, and will hold questions of ultimate purpose in suspense, well aware that good educational practices, like scientific chemistry, may be used for all sorts of purposes. The purposes are not part of the science; and there are some thinkers who are trying to develop education as a pure science unhampered by moral or political considerations. Herbart was, however, not only a scientist but also a practical teacher and the question of purpose was unavoidable.

To Herbart, it was clear that the aim of education is virtue. "As the highest purpose of man, and consequently of education," he wrote, "we universally recognize morality. He who should deny this could really not know what morality is; at least, he would have no right to take part in this discussion." And he also wrote: "The term virtue expresses the whole purpose of education. Virtue is the idea of inner freedom as a constant state of mind." That man has inner freedom in whom there is no longer any conflict between what he thinks he should do and what he actually does. Now what a man thinks he should do is determined by the ideas he has; and when these ideas are clear and comprehensive, or "many-sided," when full knowledge controls conduct, then a man is virtuous. "When volition has come into permanent accord with educated insight, virtue has been attained." But Herbart has defined education as the process of attaining virtue; and now we are told that virtue is education. Herbart tries to get out of this circle by redefining virtue in more empirical terms. He says, in effect, that virtue means, or points to, health of body and mind, good will (instead of malice, envy, cruelty, and such vices), active social cooperation, justice and the desire to avoid strife, and obedience to proper authority. Here he defines ethical conduct as that manner of life which society approves. He does not show how society itself could be improved.

Since Herbart is criticized because of the individualistic character of his educational doctrine, we should consider his view of the social virtues. When many conflicting wills come together the first need is that of preventing strife and maintaining peace. This demands a legal system of rewards and punishments. The welfare of each citizen demands a system of civil administration. The essence of welfare is found in the development of the capacities and the exercise of the powers of each person, which can be secured only in a cultural state, a civilization; and this in turn demands the "good community," to borrow a phrase from Josiah Royce. That is virtue, Herbart said, which by way of self-determination develops the good individual in a good society. This is not individualism.

Education, he said, has three phases, namely, government, instruction, and training. We shall consider the first two here and shall treat training later in this chapter. Education is possible because children are plastic, because they are able to receive and hold impressions; but this educability is limited by the age, the circumstances, and the individual nature of the pupil. And as the pupil's mind and character become mature, they become less open to external influences. While the child is still immature, there is need for government. The child, who has not yet developed a firm moral character, must be guided by others until he is able to guide himself. This phase of education is named government. It controls present conduct while instruction and training prepare for future conduct.

Government should be free from pampering but also from a too vigorous control. The secret of good government is found in keeping children employed. It is better to have children choose their own occupations; but, having chosen a task, they should be required to complete it. Teachers must be vigilant, and reasonable in their requirements, especially where moral insight is not yet developed, but resolute in imposing deserved penalties. Boys and girls must meet their responsibilities and take their chances if they are ever to become men and women. In a phrase, good government requires the exercise of reasonable authority.

Psychology shows, according to Herbart, that ideas are formed first and that desire and will follow. There is no independent faculty of volition. The will is the resultant of the struggle between opposing sets of ideas; and the strongest ideas finally determine choice, decision, and action. Since the will is the outcome of the struggle between ideas, the will and disposition may be formed by instruction. It is instruction which builds up effective masses of ideas leading to ethical conduct. Instruction is, therefore, not merely the importation of information but it is the building of character. To give educative instruction is the teacher's chief function and this is the foundation of Herbart's theory. This is also the point at which criticism is directed when his doctrine is charged with being too intellectualist. Men do not always act from knowledge.

Educative instruction demands interest; or, putting it differently, knowledge and ideas are not effectively assimilated nor do they lead to original thought or to ethical conduct unless the pupil takes active hold of them. This is the meaning of interest or attention, which are practically synonymous. Herbart analyzes these concepts. Attention may be voluntary, deliberate, not spontaneous; or it may be native, involuntary, spontaneous. In the absence of spontaneous interest, it may be necessary to induce voluntary interest but it is not to be a forced and artificial interest brought about by the use of marks, prizes, or competition. The truly psychological method of inducing voluntary interest is the method of association. The child who is not interested in measurement and arithmetic will develop these interests when he sees that they are essential in science, design, building, or anything in which he is already interested. Because all knowledge is interconnected and forms a "circle of ideas," it is always possible to find a path from what is known and therefore interesting to what is not yet known. It is the teacher's task to find this path and to lead the pupil in it. "The circle of thought contains the store of that by which gradually interest will lead to desire and desire to volition and action." And it is in action, in ethical conduct, not in knowledge by itself, that man's worth finally resides. Not only is it the teacher's task to find the path from one idea to another but rather to build up those groups of ideas which he hopes to make dominant and permanent in the life of the pupil. This he can do through the laws of association, using both the primary laws such as contiguity, similarity, and contrast and the secondary laws such as frequency and vividness.

Even in repetition, under the law of frequency, presentations are not merely repeated. Presentations must be supplemented by analysis and synthesis. Only that can be effectively presented which is similar to what has been directly observed. Herbart had learned from Pestalozzi the importance of observation and direct experience. Pictures, models, and descriptions must be used if the pupil has no sufficient background of experience. The principle which Herbart announced is that the presentation should be so vivid "that the pupil will imagine that he has a direct sense perception." Analysis proceeds by taking apart experiences or events, making them clearer by separating them into elements, and finding essential relations. Synthesis builds up from the elements new and ever more far-reaching combinations. Art, science, history are examples of such syntheses which the race has made inductively. In the same way the pupils, on a very small scale of course, may start from their own experience and by observation, experiment, reading, and in other ways may build up systematic masses of ideas by the process of apperception.

It is clear that this many-sidedness of interest requires time. The necessary ideas can be acquired only by successive efforts; and time is also required for combining ideas and for assimilation. Some teachers lay more stress upon explication, step by step, together with reproduction by the pupils, some teach by conversation, some ask for summaries and general statements, while others are not satisfied until the pupils engage in independent thinking. Various methods of teaching will thus arise and all will be valuable when appropriately used. Each may contribute its share in aiding the development of the pupil. Some teachers begin with (1) the explication and analysis of the material before the class and proceed through (2) a synthesis which was begun in conversation to (3) a simple generalization which will furnish opportunitiy for (4) independent thought by the pupil. Herbart called these steps clearness, association, system, and method.

5. THE DOCTRINE OF THE FORMAL STEPS

The systematic planning of lessons or larger units had been treated by many earlier writers. Creative workers in other fields than teaching also dealt with the sequence of steps by which they attained their results.

Cicero, for example, in the *De Oratore* dealt with the parts of an oration as these were outlined by his Greek teachers. This, he said, is not a very abstruse study, "for who would not understand without assistance, that nobody can make a speech unless he has settled what to say, and in what words, and in what order, and remembers it?" Herbart likewise threw out somewhat casually the suggestion of his four steps as an outline of the process by which the mind acquires knowledge and reaches conclusions. But the Herbartians seized upon this outline, expanded the four steps into five, namely, preparation, presentation, comparison and abstraction, generalization, and application, and made an utterly deadening rule out of this sequence. Herbart knew, as every good teacher knows, that teaching must not be stereotyped, must not lack the element of surprise. Cicero also divided the model oration into five steps. They were: winning the favorable attention of the audience, stating the case, presenting the evidence, making the argument, and stating the conclusion. It is not necessary to suppose that either Herbart or the Herbartians modeled their steps on the Ciceronian outline. Copernicus, who is not likely to have copied the *De Oratore*, gave a comparable series of steps in an account of the method of his great discovery. He said, as we explained more fully in Chapter 8, that he had become dissatisfied with the complexities of the Ptolemaic system; that he then gathered all plausible suggestions from the writings of previous astronomers; that, from all this body of knowledge, he formed his own hypothesis; and finally, that he verified it by fitting the known facts of the solar system to his theory.

With these examples before us we can better understand the relation between the Herbartian steps and John Dewey's steps in the process of a complete act of thought as described in his famous little book, *How We Think*. We may set the three series in parallel columns, as follows:

Herbart	Herbartians	Dewey
CLEARNESS	{ PREPARATION	{ COMING UPON A PROBLEM OR DIFFICULTY
	{ PRESENTATION	GATHERING DATA
ASSOCIATION	{ COMPARISON AND ABSTRACTION }	MAKING A HYPOTHESIS
SYSTEM	GENERALIZATION	DEVELOPING A THEORY
METHOD	APPLICATION	VERIFYING THE THEORY

It is obvious that Dewey's analysis of the act of thought deals with the process of investigation and discovery and resembles the Copernican account more nearly than the Ciceronian. Equally clear is the general similarity of the Herbartian scheme to Cicero's. It is evident that one group, Copernicus and Dewey, dealt with concrete problems in the natural sciences while the other group dealt with language, literature and logic, to which inductive trial and error methods do not so readily apply.

Herbart did not regard the steps as a fixed scheme to be invariably followed and, in particular, he did not propose to have this scheme carried through in each lesson. He indicated that with changes in the subject matter the teaching process must vary. Too often these warnings were not heeded. The formalizing tendency which lies deep in human nature, especially in second-rate human nature, came to the surface. The "five formal steps," which Herbart never framed or named, and "model lesson plans," an idea with which Herbart never had any connection, were introduced into the normal schools and taught as mechanical devices. Schools for teachers required inexperienced young candidates to make model plans and teach model lessons in the practice school as if the problem of Comenius, namely, how to teach all things to all pupils, had been solved at one stroke and as if a unique answer to such a question were possible. Herbart held no such misconception; but even more absurd is the error of writers who make the formal steps the chief feature or even the whole of Herbart's philosophy of education.

A corrective to that ignorant misconstruction can be found on a near-by page of the *Outlines of Educational Doctrine*. Herbart, the supposed intellectualist, dealt with teaching as an art, which is the true view. Teaching is an art and like other arts, such as good conduct or painting pleasing pictures, it can be taught and it cannot, it is based upon science or exact knowledge and it is not. The teacher, like any artist, can learn much from other artists in comparable fields but he must develop his own methods. The arts most closely related to teaching are the medical, psychological, political, and literary arts. Herbart, in the example to which we have referred, compares teaching with written exposition. He wrote:

The teacher should by all means study literary masterpieces for the purpose of learning from great authors how they escaped from these difficulties. [The difficulties to which he referred are such as monotony, sudden change of subjects, overly rapid pace, talking down to or over the heads of pupils, and similar teaching sins.] That the teacher may strike the right chord in the earlier stages of instruction, he should turn particularly to simple popular writers, Homer, for example. . . . Classic writers seldom take sudden leaps and never stand still entirely. Their method of unfolding consists in a scarcely perceptible, at any rate an always easy, advance. They dwell, indeed, long on the same thought, but nevertheless achieve, little by little, the most powerful contrasts. Poor writers, on the contrary, pile up the most glaring antitheses without other than the natural result—the antagonistic ideas expel each other and the mind is left empty. The same result threatens the teacher who aims at brilliancy of presentation.

The author of that paragraph did not intend to restrict teaching to any formal "plan," "system," or "steps," because he realized that it is an art.

6. HERBART ON THE CURRICULUM

The word interest may be taken to refer to a process, being interested; or to a condition, having interests. One is interested when he is actively pursuing; one has interests when he is the sort of person who, under given conditions and with a set stimulus, will actively pursue. Being interested leads, according to Herbart, to having interests; and having well-selected, manifold, permanent interests is the precondition to inner freedom and virtue. The selection of interests to be developed can be made from two fields, the external world of nature, and the inner world of human nature and social participation. Interests stemming from the external world are mainly matters of knowledge and practical skill but the interests in humanity are participatory interests, that is, interests not in making and controlling but in taking part, cooperating, and belonging.

The expansion of the pupil's interests is not to be haphazard and unconditional. The pupil's individuality is to be preserved and yet a reasonable balance is to be sought. The interests are not to be merely superficial and diffused but are to be organized and integrated as suggested in the previous paragraph. Instruction must guide and deepen experience, thus gradually overcoming the casual and accidental nature of unguided activity. And the pupil must not be allowed merely to mark time. To be tedious is the greatest of teaching sins; and tedium is avoided by a carefully adjusted but ever expanding and deepening course of study.

Since our ideas have two main sources, nature and mankind, the curriculum of the school must draw its materials from these. Herbart stressed the second or the humanistic side to a far greater degree than Pestalozzi and the naturalists. These had emphasized the practical skills but had not, of course, been able to dispense with language. Herbart placed the languages, literatures, and history on an even plane with mathematics and the sciences. He said that an education which neglects either the humanities or the sciences is lopsided. He emphasized the comparative study of languages but recognized that not all children have time for extended language study. He realized that the relative importance of Latin and Greek was decreasing. He said that "the labor implied in the study of the ancient languages pays only when talent combines with the earnest purpose to achieve the most complete scholarship." The study of the ancient languages should be based upon ancient history. He leaned toward Quintilian's proposal of beginning Greek before Latin. The study of history may begin with biography and stories; and the Odyssey is the best of all Greek stories. The young teacher of history must practice the telling of stories and must at all cost avoid prolixity and boredom. Teaching is a fine art and no cost of labor is too great in preparing for it. The stories of Herodotus should serve the teacher as models to be imitated in teaching. "In fact, they should be actually memorized," said Herbart, "in an accurate but fluent translation. The effect on children is surprising." All possible concrete helps in representing historical ideas to the senses, such as portraits, pictures, maps, and charts, are to be used. With history are to be taught geography, chronology, literature, and politics. A brief, well-proportioned history of inventions, arts, and sciences should be included. Cause and effect should be carefully traced, for, as Herbart said, "History should be the teacher of mankind; if it does not become so, the blame rests largely with those who teach history in schools."

The elementary teaching of mathematics and science must be inductive, objective, and practical. Mathematical study should begin with counting, measuring, weighing, training the senses in estimating distances, angles, and other magnitudes, and combining simple computations with these exercises. This work in mensuration, accompanied by plane geometry and algebra including quadratic equations, is to lead directly to trigonometry. The young student of the newer ideas of mathematics teaching may be surprised to learn that Herbart, over a century ago, stressed the need of "impressing far more deeply the concept of proportion, demanded even by elementary arithmetic, and also for developing early the idea of function." Herbart also dealt with the very important educational question, how far and for whom rigid demonstrations are necessary; and he concluded that only students who can become thoroughly familiar with the whole range of the concepts involved should bother with logical derivations and proofs. The practical student should be taught how to use logarithms without much attention to the underlying theory. After a comparison of arithmetical and geometrical series, practical application will immediately follow. Herbart recognized that it would not be too difficult to teach Newton's binomial theorem and the theory of logarithms but he doubted whether this would be worth while except for those who would continue in advanced mathematics. Along with elementary mathematics, a good deal of elementary science should be taught, some astronomy, physics, the construction and use of instruments, and manual training. "Every human being ought to learn how to use his hands. The hand has a place of honor beside language in elevating mankind above the brute." These examples will be sufficient to illustrate Herbart's treatment of the curriculum.

The student will have noticed that subject matter and methods of teaching are often treated together. They are always closely related. Geometry can be taught inductively or deductively but it will not be the same subject; and so every method affects the content and meaning of the material to which it is applied. Implied in a curriculum are not only methods and purposes but also organization and sequence of materials. Besides the logical ordering of the material and its usual adaptation to the age of the pupils, Herbart proposed three other principles for curriculum organization. These are correlation, concentration, and the culture epochs principle. Correlation has already been illustrated in the proposal to combine the teaching of mathematics with its application in physics, manual training, and other fields. Geography, as treated by Herbart and his disciples, provides another example of correlation and also illustrates concentration. He called geography an associating science. It brings together the sciences, the arts, politics, and history. Under concentration, he included the ideas which we now associate with a "core curriculum." The ideas of correlation and concentration are not to be too sharply distinguished, for concentration is merely a more systematic and closely knit correlation.

The culture epochs theory was not original with Herbart. In fact, it had a long history reaching back to Clement in ancient Alexandria and it attracted renewed attention after the Renaissance. Lessing, Herder and many others were captivated by the notion. Culture epochs are merely, as the name literally says, successive epochs or stages of cultural development from primitive conditions through nomadic, early agricultural, and other periods to modern civilization. One may call this evolution of culture, as Lessing did, an education, the education of the human race. By long and often disastrous trial and error man has learned to live in the way he lives now! That has been a racial education, the education of mankind. The culture epochs theory supposes further that each child coming into the world begins as a little primitive and gradually attains maturity and civilization by passing through a series of stages which parallel those of the human race itself.

The culture epochs theory, we have said, was not originated by Herbart; and while he referred to it, he made practically no use of it. But the Herbartians Tuiskon Ziller, Wilhelm Rein, and several Americans based whole curricula upon it. The culture epochs theory has been given up. Rousseau, Pestalozzi, Herbart, and Froebel were all attracted by the possible applications of the theory. It was the followers of Herbart who, in a period of enthusiastic Herbartianism, built imposing culture epochs curricula, but these have been taken down long since and stored in a dark closet in the basement.

7. TRAINING

We must recall that for Herbart education consisted of three divisions, government, instruction, and training. Training is largely a matter of tact and skill. Harsh methods of discipline and also the isolation of the child from all possible temptation must be avoided because the pupil is to learn self-direction and self-control. A firm will can be developed only by exercise. The opposite extreme must likewise be avoided for laxity and exposure to evil may lead to moral shipwreck, and hence the need for tact and skill in the teacher. It is his function to give enough of the right kind of direction to keep the right ideas in the center of the pupil's attention. Often also the teacher must awaken inspiration and resolution by some "rousing word," some noble ideal, or some appealing example. Argument is not to be recommended as a means of forming character. And the teacher cannot do everything. The pupil must also live with his equals in age and attainments and the school must provide a helpful social life. Herbart, without developing the idea, even suggests the establishment of a school republic, a rare but not new idea at that time. Children must be encouraged in the frank expression of their opinions however erroneous these may be. Children are often very positive and dogmatic in moral judgments which are mistaken, for the young have no idea of the variety of ethical views which have been held and disputed. The cure for such arrogant self-confidence is instruction, wider and deeper knowledge. The great function of training is to enable instruction to become effective in developing character.

We must notice that Herbart's pedagogy, like John Dewey's, did not emphasize physical education, although he recognized the need for exercise and recreation. But physical education cannot have a commanding place in a pedagogy so largely based upon ideas and the pure intellect as Herbart's and Dewey's systems are. This is a major point of attack upon the theory of Herbart, especially by those educators who emphasize the importance of physical training for the formation of character, the very aim which Herbart had chosen. To attack Herbart successfully one must lay siege to the foundations, his intellectualist psychology and conservative social principles; otherwise he is less vulnerable.

8. THE INFLUENCE OF HERBART AND THE HERBARTIANS

The activity of Herbart as a philosopher and educator fell into the Hegelian period. Hegel was only six years older than Herbart, and his system so completely lighted up the philosophical skies that all other stars were obscured. When Herbart's first general work on education appeared, in 1806, everyone was engrossed in the works of Fichte and Hegel, and Herbart somewhat plaintively wrote: "My poor pedagogy has not been able to lift up its voice." Thirty years later, he still felt that he had not obtained a fair hearing. And yet he had a number of important disciples, especially in

Austria but also in Germany. In Austria, W. F. Volkmann was doubtless the greatest. He did some work in the measurement of sensation and in 1856 published an important textbook of Herbartian psychology which remained for two decades the standard work and included not only a systematic treatment but an elaborate review of the literature and the history of its subject. Volkmann's slightly younger friend, Gustav Adolf Lindner, wrote (1858), and several times revised, a textbook of *Empirical Psychology*, which followed Herbartian lines. It was intended for young students of education and was long the standard text in teachers' seminaries and normal schools. The first American edition, translated by Charles De Garmo, was published in 1889, the year before James's *Principles*.

In Germany proper, the universities of Leipzig and Jena became leading Herbartian centers. At Leipzig, Moritz Drobisch attempted to develop the mathematical methods of Herbart's psychology. He helped to bring Wundt to Leipzig and taught Herbartian philosophy to G. E. Müller, who was to become one of the greatest of experimental psychologists. Drobisch had a colleague in Leipzig in Gustav Hartenstein who became the general editor of Herbart's *Works*, issued in ten volumes. A real renaissance of Herbartian doctrines occurred in Germany about 1865, and in the United States his greatest influence developed twenty years later. The American influence of Herbart will be treated when we come to speak of education in the United States. This chapter has dealt with one of the great educational system builders; and we shall next deal with another, Froebel.

Herbart was a practical schoolman and teacher and the value of his philosophy lies rather in its details than in its outlook. He regarded teaching as an art which was based upon ethics and psychology. The task of ethics was to define virtue, and virtue became the goal of education. Psychology explored the mental processes and explained the methods and conditions of learning and thus indicated both what the teacher should do and how he should proceed. The psychology which Herbart developed was a form of associationism. He modified the older account of a purely mechanical association by ascribing self-activity and force or assimilative power to ideas. At this point, he was under the influence of Leibnitz who also suggested to him the notion of the apperception mass.

Education, according to Herbart, has three phases, government, instruction, and training. Since the mind is really composed of ideas implanted by instruction, it will be evident that instruction is by far the most important educative function. This, in turn, leads to the charge that Herbart's system is an intellectualist and individualist system. His emphasis upon the social virtues and upon a full circle of interests including the humanistic and historical interests and upon social action and conduct refutes the charge of individualism. To repel the charge of intellectualism would be more difficult although he includes pupil self-government and manual education in his program.

The child can be educated only if he becomes active and interested. To develop a wider circle of interests we must begin with those which are already present. Through the laws of association those groups of ideas which are to become permanent may be built up from present ideas and interests. In this process of building up permanent idea masses we should follow the general steps of mental activity. These are called clearness, association, system, and method.

To develop individual and also social virtue the school must stress both scientific and humanist ideas. To keep these from developing in departmentalized groups, the principles of correlation and concentration should be followed in organizing the curriculum. Until the child's good tendencies are sufficiently strong he needs the support which comes from government by reasonable authority and from training which leads to firm habits.

QUESTIONS

1. Examining several books on educational psychology, make a list of the chief topics treated in them. How is the topic "learning" related to the others?
2. Does the doctrine of association concern itself mainly with memory? What function does memory have in the educative process as a whole?
3. Compare the psychology of Herbart with that of Rousseau. Does learning as a process of discovery imply the forming of associations?
4. Is the individual, as Herbart views the matter, completely determined from without, by the ideas which his environment implants? Compare Herbart on this point with Helvetius and Rousseau. Can he escape from this trap through his doctrines of virtue, of the self-activity of the ideas, or of interest?
5. How does the doctrine of association apply to teaching?
6. What are apperception, correlation, concentration, and culture epochs? Find illustrations and applications.
7. Why do writers independently listing the steps in a process of thought or in constructing a work of art usually arrive at similar conclusions?
8. What facts would you assemble to show that teaching is an art?
9. If teaching is an art, how should the "formal steps" be used?
10. How does the Herbartian curriculum compare with those of (a) Comenius, (b) Rousseau, and (c) Pestalozzi? In making this comparison do not omit consideration of physical education, manual skill, history, language, and literature.
11. How similar were the views of Locke and Herbart on what the latter calls (a) government and (b) training?

FOR FURTHER READING AND STUDY

Most of the following works are translations or paraphrases and they usually contain introductory and editorial matter in addition to the text. A general edition of Herbart's writings in twelve volumes was published at Leipzig (1850–1851), under the editorship of G. Hartenstein. The publications of the Herbart

Club and Society and the files of educational magazines issued between 1890 and 1910, especially the *Educational Review*, edited by Nicholas Murray Butler, contain a great deal of material on Herbart and the Herbartian movement in the United States.

Adams, John, *The Herbartian Psychology Applied to Education*, Boston, D. C. Heath and Company, 1906, 284 pp.

Bode, Boyd H., *Conflicting Psychologies of Learning*, Boston, D. C. Heath and Company, 1929, 305 pp.

Boring, Edwin G., *A History of Experimental Psychology*, Second Edition, New York, Appleton-Century-Crofts, 1950, 777 pp.

Cole, Percival R., *Herbart and Froebel; an Attempt at Synthesis*, New York, Teachers College, Columbia University, 1907, 116 pp.

Davidson, John, *A New Interpretation of Herbart's Psychology and Educational Theory Through the Philosophy of Leibniz*, Edinburgh, William Blackwood & Sons, Ltd., 1906, 191 pp.

De Garmo, Charles, *Herbart and the Herbartians*, New York, Charles Scribner's Sons, 1895, 268 pp.

Eckoff, William J., *Herbart's ABC of Sense-Perception and Minor Pedagogical Works*, New York, D. Appleton & Company, 1896, 288 pp. Reissued several times.

Felkin, H. M., and E., *The Science of Education . . . and the Aesthetic Revelation of the World*, by J. F. Herbart. Preface by Oscar Browning, Boston, D. C. Heath and Company, 1895, 268 pp.; *Letters and Lectures on Education*, by J. F. Herbart, Syracuse, N. Y., C. W. Bardeen and Co., 1898, 285 pp.

Lange, Alexis, *Herbart's Outlines of Educational Doctrine*. Annotated by Charles de Garmo, New York, The Macmillan Company, 1901, 334 pp. This is the best source in English for the practical parts of Herbart's views and its value is not only historical.

McMurry, Charles A., *The Elements of General Method, based on the Principles of Herbart*, New York, The Macmillan Company, 1903, 331 pp.

Miles, Susan, *Childhood in Verse and Prose, an Anthology*, New York, Oxford University Press, 1923, 408 pp.

Mulliner, Beatrice C., *The Application of Psychology to Education*, by J. F. Herbart, New York, Charles Scribner's Sons, 1898, 231 pp.

Murphy, Gardner, *An Historical Introduction to Modern Psychology*. Third edition, revised, New York, Harcourt, Brace and Company, 1932, 471 pp.

Randels, George B., *The Doctrines of Herbart in the United States*. No publisher, place or date. A dissertation written at the University of Pennsylvania, Philadelphia, 1909, 67 pp.

Smith, Margaret K., Translator, *A Text-Book in Psychology . . .* by J. F. Herbart, New York, D. Appleton & Company, 1891, 200 pp.

Ufer, Christian, *Introduction to the Pedagogy of Herbart*, Boston, D. C. Heath and Company, 1901, 123 pp. Translated by J. C. Zinser for the Herbart Club.

12 NEW SYSTEM BUILDERS: FROEBEL

FRIEDRICH FROEBEL WAS THE CREATOR OF A COMPLETE scheme of education which, beginning with the early years, extended through adolescence. This scheme was based upon an activist psychology. Because he was in his latter years so exclusively engaged in the development of the kindergarten, the rest of his contribution is sometimes forgotten. In this chapter we shall be concerned with the general history of the infant school, kindergarten, and nursery school movements but also with Froebel's broader theory of elementary and secondary education and with the underlying psychology.

Others had begun to deal with the education of small children. Comenius had written of the "school at the mother's knee" and had, at least to a slight degree, anticipated the kindergarten. The need for better child care had been noticed by Locke and Rousseau. In some poor districts of eastern France, the infant school was developed before the French Revolution. Pestalozzi instructed mothers on the education of their children. A new attack upon the problems of early education was made by Froebel, who may in this respect be called the greatest of the Pestalozzians. Thus three of the greatest modern educators, Comenius, Pestalozzi, and Froebel, each wished education to begin in the earliest years. Froebel declared that education should be based upon the psychology of the growing child. The kindergarten propaganda encouraged the genetic study of children; and kindergartners often became eager students of child development. Herbart and Froebel were both psychological thinkers, but while Herbart emphasized the psychology of instruction and conscious learning, Froebel directed his attention to the means for encouraging the natural growth of the whole personality.

Rousseau had pointed out a dualism between the individual as a man and as a citizen; and proposed to remove the child from society to protect it and preserve its personality from the evil and destructive influences of the world. The new movement for infant education followed Rousseau on the whole but without using his radical measure of withdrawing children from society. Froebel, at all events, intended to cultivate the personality and native traits of the child, holding that there is no necessary conflict between the individual and society. The founders of the great national school systems, on the other hand, thought otherwise, namely, that if there is conflict it must be resolved in the interests of the state. Education of the individual "for himself" had to wait for a later day.

With the attempt to educate very young children, a new problem was presented to teachers. When children were not admitted before the ages of six or eight years, many of their habits were already formed and they could be treated almost like adults. With the admission of three- to five-year-olds, the situation changed. For these a new kind of institution was required in which attention would be given to their inability to sit still and to deal with symbols, and to their lack of common social development. Obviously, a new kind of school was needed and one was gradually evolved. Historically, it passed through three stages, the infant school, the kindergarten, and the nursery school. We omit from consideration the dame school, and the crèche or day nursery, because these did not attempt to make any thought-out adjustment to children's needs. Schools like the kindergarten which did try to meet the demands of small-child nature developed new principles, methods, and materials and these have spread to other fields. The new education, called progressive in the United States, has been influenced by the kindergarten movement. Through the kindergarten, women gained a larger professional place in education and the alliance between home and school was strengthened; the elementary school was transformed; and the general philosophy of education was fundamentally modified.

1. INFANT SCHOOLS

The earliest type of school to make special provision for the needs of small children was the infant school. Literary anticipations of this institution began to appear frequently in the seventeeth century. Thus John Valentin Andreae in his *Christianopolis* (1619), John Amos Comenius in his *School of Infancy* (1633), and Samuel Gott in his *Nova Solyma* (1648), and in the following century the Edgeworths, Pestalozzi, and others conceived new ways and a new spirit in infant care and education. All, however, proposed plans that were to be carried out by the mother in the home. Many poor homes or ignorant parents were not able or anxious to introduce such plans; and in a peculiarly destitute locality, humanitarian feeling and evangelical piety led Jean Frederic Oberlin (1740–1828) to open an exemplary infant school at Waldbach in eastern France in 1769. Oberlin employed young women, first Sara Banzet and soon after Louise Scheppler, to teach the children to play and, the older ones, also to spin, knit, and sew. Pictures, nature study, collecting, singing, drawing, and simple handwork were introduced and the children were taken on walks to gather flowers and other interesting natural objects. Oberlin's work, although it was undertaken under great difficulty and against much local opposition, did not remain unrecognized. The French government awarded him a money prize and French and Germans paid him the sincere compliment of imitating his institutions. The *salles d'asile* of Paris (1801) and the infant school established at Lippe-Detmold by Princess Pauline and named after her, the *Paulinenanstalt*, are good examples. The humanitarian, Professor Wadzeck, of a Berlin classical school, opened an infant school in 1819. An even more famous instance was provided by Pastor Theodor Fliedner who opened an infant school at Kaiserswerth on the Rhine (1835), a normal school to prepare young women for work in such schools, and the first nurses' training school. Humanitarians roused by Pestalozzi established infant schools in many European countries and these paved the way for the kindergarten.

Oberlin is one of the heroes of the teaching profession. To compare him with Pestalozzi is an obvious thought. Both were social reformers, deeply moved by the miseries of the oppressed and the poor. More practical than his greater contemporary, Oberlin worked on a much smaller scale. He improved the agriculture of his mountain valleys, organized a farmers' club, introduced new plants and trees, imported better seeds from abroad, established a nursery for fruit trees, and developed the cultivation of the potato. He persuaded his parishioners to build a road and a bridge across a mountain chasm—the "Bridge of Charity"—to provide a way for wheeled vehicles out of the valley into Strassburg. In the French Revolution he was a wise and liberal leader of his flock in difficult times. Nothing was neglected that could improve the income, homes, and lives of his peasants. He dealt effectively with local problems, but his writings had no influence and have indeed never been collected and published. We have dared to compare him with Pestalozzi as one compares the small but excellent with the great. Pestalozzi is a world figure; Oberlin was the kind of wise and active leader that is needed in every community. By a curious circumstance and almost by accident, the name of this French educator and pastor, who was once on the point of emigrating to Pennsylvania, has been given to an American college. All teachers would do well to read and meditate the career of Jean Frederic Oberlin, the founder of the infant school in the valleys of the Vosges mountains.

The rise of the infant school under Robert Owen about 1800 may have been independent of the continental movement. One cannot be sure. Its spread to England and promotion by Samuel Wilderspin and its return to Scotland and propagation by David Stow followed. From a very favorable account of the Stow variety of infant schools, we gather that the physical health and habits of the children were carefully attended to; lessons were illustrated with objects and pictures which were preserved in the schoolroom; habits of cleanliness, order, and obedience were instilled gently but persistently; the children's duty to God was not neglected. All was joyous activity: short recesses with plays and games every fifteen minutes and one-third of the time spent in the playground in swinging, running, singing, or building castles out of wooden blocks. The infant school, we are told, made the schoolroom, a nursery and a playground.

In England the infant schools became especially popular because the early beginning made possible a little longer period of instruction before children were sent into the factory. And they also tended to emphasize the formal skills of reading, writing, and arithmetic. By 1870 when public school boards were established, the infant school had become a fixed part of the English system; and they usually became independent departments with a separate course of study.

Leadership in the British infant school movement soon passed to the Home and Colonial School Society. This brought the movement into close contact with Pestalozzian influences, which were then affecting education in all western countries. Accounts of such schools appeared in the *American Journal of Education* in 1827, but their greatest propagandist was Henry Barnard. His description in the first volume of the *Connecticut Common School Journal* admirably shows their Pestalozzian qualities. He wrote:

Infant schools, though they are very different from each other in a variety of respects, generally agree in a few material particulars. Low seats with backs are provided; healthful and pleasing physical exercises are practiced; singing is a frequent occupation; the study of natural history is pursued either by means of sensible objects, such as leaves, fruits, shells, or with pictures of them, or at least with books which give easy accounts of animals, plants, minerals, with questions adapted to recitations. Writing, and often drawing, on sand or slates, is generally practiced; the manner of teaching is generally more varied, enlivening and parental than in some of our other schools; and the discipline is commonly more mild; while religious and moral instructions are more frequent and familiar.

Probably no teacher ever entered an infant school for the first time without receiving hints of importance on some point of instruction or discipline.

The infant school was after all a school, not a nursery, but also not a playground or a children's garden, that is, its chief defect was that it was too eager to teach reading, writing, and arithmetic. That some of the best avoided this error is shown in Barnard's account but one must not miss the anticlimax of his description: from objects, to pictures, down to books with recitation questions. Truly, *facilis descensus Averno*. There was still something left for Froebel to invent.

The founder of the infant schools in Italy, Ferrante Aporti (1791–1858), was born in a small town near Mantua. He opened a school for little children in Cremona in 1827, about a decade before Froebel began developing his kindergarten. He tried to provide for the children's health and physical development, for gymnastics and recreation, and for daily occupations according to age. He aimed to cultivate the sentiments and emotions in a friendly, homelike setting, and devised many exercises to train the senses. Doubtless he was influenced by Pestalozzi, but much of his work was original. His schools were approved by the government of Milan and spread to other cities. In 1833 he issued a *Manual* which was to aid in the extension of his system beyond his personal influence. His fame spread to France where he was created a Chevalier of the Legion of Honor. For a time he held a university position at Turin. But his hopes for the reform of Italian primary education were not to be fulfilled. Reactionaries in church and state attacked him because they thought they discerned liberal tendencies in his infant schools, an experience which Prussia was to provide for Froebel also. Aporti fled to France, a sacrifice to the conservative reaction against the revolutionary movements of 1848.

2. EARLY EDUCATION OF FROEBEL

The creator of the kindergarten, Friedrich Wilhelm August Froebel (1782–1852), was the son of a pastor in a Thuringian village. The boy's life was somewhat lonely but the story of great unhappiness and cruelty is a myth. The poetry of nature early found its way into his romantic spirit and stimulated his interest in elementary science and natural history. His brother Christoph, to whom he stood in an especially close relationship, helped him to solve some of his puzzling questions. Still the boy was lonely and at the age of ten was taken to live with an uncle, his mother's favorite brother, where he had more freedom and more attention. He always looked back to these four or five years as one of the happiest periods of his life but school did little for him. He was not good at games, and was a bit lonesome even among forty boys. The teaching was abstract and over his head but he did well in arithmetic. This interpretation of Froebel's boyhood may be supported from his own words. "The kindly influences of my youth," wrote Froebel to his brother, "gave me a freedom which broadened my views, increased my strength, and developed my inner life." The opposing view of Froebel's early life, for there is an opposite one, seems to be a rationalization. The young Froebel was a dreamy, poetic, highly sensitive lad, in love with nature and inquisitive about natural phenomena, religious minded, and hungry for companionship and friendship. It was not surprising that some considered him lazy, although in later life he manifested great activity.

Confirmation over, he was apprenticed to a forester because his father could not afford to send another son to the university nor to pay the high premium which was demanded by a first-class agriculturist for taking him as an apprentice. The forester was to teach him his craft, including applied mathematics and the methods of appraising land and timber, but he did none of these things. Friedrich read books on geometry and forestry in his master's library, communed with nature, and became even more of a recluse. He made some observations on plants and insects which he, like self-taught men of all times, considered original and more important than they were. He found nature everywhere connected, every fact and phenomenon leading to some other, and all pointing to an underlying ideal and spiritual unity. At sixteen and seventeen his theistic, half pantheistic philosophy was developing. Later he was to find that this was similar to the views of Schelling and K. C. F. Krause. His study of mathematics developed a longing to work with the university teacher who had written these interesting books.

Almost by accident he found the opportunity to go to the University of Jena; and while he continued his study of mathematics, his interest now came to be centered on science. His most stimulating teacher was Professor A. J. Batsch, sometimes called the "German Huxley" because he taught comparative zoology and demonstrated the similarity in the plan of the skeletons of the vertebrates, fish, birds, and mammals, including man. The ideas of evolution which Froebel gathered in this study helped him to mature his theory of the unity of all things, of the organic nature of the world, and of the correspondence of part with part. His study at Jena came to a close with a nine-week term in the university prison for debt.

After some experience in teaching and an extended period with Pestalozzi, Froebel also studied at Göttingen and Berlin. At Göttingen he undertook to trace the culture epochs through the development of language but discovered that neither his preparation nor his linguistic ability were sufficient for this purpose. He continued to believe in the correspondence of individual development with the racial stages. Another unhappy outcome of those studies was his attempt to connect the sense and the sound of words. The resulting grotesque word plays which he included in the *Education of Man* spoil a number of its pages for the reader. After about a year at Göttingen, Froebel settled down at the University of Berlin in the summer of 1812. He was employed in a famous Pestalozzian school in the city maintained by Plamann, whose acquaintance he made through Father Jahn. Most of his time was spent in study, especially with Professor Weiss in crystallography, and he became curator of a museum of minerals. The regularity of the crystals, like the similarity of the vertebrate skeletons, further directed his mind to the idea of a universal plan and law of creation. Goethe's work on plant structure, Krause's and Hegel's philosophies also led him in the same direction.

Following analogies, and arguing that "if man is ever to fulfill his destiny he must be trained in accordance with the laws of his development," he finally evolved his law of human growth and education. This he called the "reconciliation of contrasts." Froebel regarded activity as life's essential characteristic and the human being as primarily an active organism; and, therefore, the contrasts which are to be reconciled had best be taken as opposing activities. Such activities are those in which we mutually work and share for group ends; and, on the other hand, those which are personal expressions of interests, urges, and ideas of the self. Harmonizing these divergent activities leads to individuality.

Between the beginning and the end of his university study, 1799–1816, Froebel engaged in many kinds of practical work. His education was by no means obtained in the lecture rooms and laboratories only. He carried on private study in German literature, in anthropology, and in architecture, he worked on a farm, he managed an estate, he served as private secretary and accountant to a large landowner, and in all these occupations, which he performed to the satisfaction of his employers, he met many stimulating people. One of these suggested that Frankfort-on-the-Main would be an excellent place to study architecture. He reached Frankfort in June 1804, and obtained employment with an architect; but he was not satisfied. He felt that he really wanted to work with people, to build not houses but men. Even his work in architecture appealed to him because it was a means to the aesthetic culture of the people; even as an architect he considered himself a teacher.

Opportunity to work with children was now at hand. A successful Pestalozzian teacher in Frankfort, Gustav Anton Gruner (1778–1844), asked him to take a class of boys, nine to eleven years old. In a letter to his brother he wrote that from the first day he felt as if he had always been a teacher. In the short holiday at the end of the term he visited Pestalozzi's school at Yverdon but he came away with conflicting judgments. The curriculum seemed to him to be a patchwork with many gaps, the teaching now good, now mechanical, often without system. When he returned from this vacation visit, a regular position with a contract for three years in Gruner's school was offered him (October 1805) and he entered upon a period of successful teaching which included also an important share in management. His nature study and geography became especially well known and not only within the school. Meanwhile, like Herbart, he became the tutor of the three sons of a wealthy family.

3. FROEBEL AND PESTALOZZI

Enthusiastic for his new calling, Froebel decided to make serious preparation for it. He mapped out a program which included a period at some university, an examination of the work of the great educators, and a year of residence at Yverdon to study the Pestalozzian system. Then he would establish a school for boys on new lines. This program, several times interrupted, required eight years but he completed it.

When Froebel came to Yverdon a second time the school was at the height of its renown. This time he came not for a short visit but for an extended stay. The parents of his pupils having consented, he took the three boys to Switzerland in the summer of 1808. He had conceived the idea of putting the boys into the school while he took general charge of their work and shared all their lessons. Pestalozzi wished to appoint him teacher of geography in the school; but he did not accept, perhaps because it would have interfered with his tutorship. He did teach handwork to a dozen boys who worked with his own pupils. He seems to have had frequent conferences with Pestalozzi. In a contemporary account, he praised the work in sense training and in language as well as the emphasis which Pestalozzi placed upon the part of the mother in the small child's education. Undoubtedly his stay at Yverdon directed Froebel's mind to infant development and had a most important influence upon his later work. Pestalozzi's system of early training and the happiness and industry which resulted would save children from many faults, he said. At this time some of the best work in music teaching was carried on at Yverdon and two of the teachers, Naegeli and Pfeiffer, published a song book for school use. Froebel learned a great deal from Naegeli's lessons and lectures on music. He gained the important idea that singing, movement, and speech are three correlative forms of expression. He made a careful study of the system of music instruction used by these two teachers and the effects can be seen in the kindergarten. He was also influenced by the work in drawing and in practical occupations. The school was, however, already suffering from dissension in the staff and Froebel was more and more anxious to continue his own advanced studies.

4. WAR AND FRIENDSHIP

Froebel transferred from Göttingen to Berlin in the summer of 1812. He secured sufficient income for his studies at the university in the Capital by teaching in Plamann's Pestalozzian school. Connected with the school staff was another of Germany's great educators, Father Jahn, founder of a famous gymnastic system, who was at the moment directing his outdoor gymnasium and cultivating the patriotic spirit of young Germany. He had indeed become so effective in the latter activity that he roused the suspicions of the French. One day, on the Hasenheide, Jahn spoke to one of his young disciples named William Middendorf about Froebel, an "odd chap" who spent his time drawing the "strangest conclusions from the study of stones and spiders' webs." After they were all in the army, it was Jahn again who introduced to Froebel the young scholar Henry Langethal; and a few days later, Langethal presented Middendorf. These three, Froebel, Middendorf, and Langethal, formed a historic friendship and spent their lives in closest association in the development of the new education.

The world was tense with anxiety and excitement during Froebel's first year in Berlin. Europe was gathering her resources for the great conflict with Napoleon. Hatred of the foreign master and patriotic enthusiasm were ruling passions in Berlin. Froebel was not affected as much as others for he lived a quiet, studious, and very busy life and, besides, he was no Prussian; but he reflected that he was after all a German who was expected to teach every boy that he must be willing to defend his country. Feeling that his example ought to square with the instruction he would give the young in the school which he hoped to set up, Froebel and a group of others including Jahn enlisted in a crack regiment which, as it turned out, saw some active service. His future life-work was always in his mind at this time, and the two friends who were to share in it were the most important result to Froebel personally from the war. His corps was mustered out in the spring of 1814 and he returned to Professor Weiss in Berlin.

5. KEILHAU

The opportunity to begin was now at hand. Froebel's favorite brother, Christoph, had recently died leaving three boys in need of a guide toward a good education. With these as a nucleus, to which he soon added two other nephews, and the younger brother of Henry Langethal, he opened his first independent school on November 13, 1816, at Griesheim. This was close to his boyhood home but the school was moved to Keilhau, still in the same general neighborhood, where it remained. "My plan," he had written, "is very simple; what I want is a happy family school, and a peaceful life with nature around me." The boys were to be taught by educative contact with external nature but also by developing their own individual and human nature through cooperative work and play. It had come to be one of Froebel's dogmas that there was no conflict but a pervading harmony between nature and human nature. He was a mystic seer who saw God in everything and all things in God. Learning was to occur through living and doing, living with others and doing with purpose. Holidays and celebrations, including the birthdays of the pupils and teachers, were used for educational purposes. The boys made gardens and planted them with the beautiful wild flowers with which Thuringia abounds. There was a form of student government, a sort of patriarchal democracy, with officers, a court, and constitutional forms. Any boy whose mischief or negligence caused property losses had to repair them. The curriculum was flexible and provision was made for boys who wished to enter business but others were prepared for the university.

Keilhau grew slowly in numbers, but the school secured a favorable verdict from a government commissioner who was sent to inspect it. Out of his philosophy and experience at Keilhau, Froebel wrote *The Education of Man* (1826). But difficulties were already threatening the whole enterprise. Froebel had married a well-educated and resourceful young woman, Wilhelmine Hoffmeister, who entered heartily into his plans. Middendorf and Langethal added a great deal to the effectiveness of the school. Langethal taught the boys correct speech and applied Herbartian ideas in the teaching of the classics. Drawing and handicrafts were taught. But new buildings and equipment were needed and the increased staff and facilities required more money. As at Yverdon, divisions appeared within the faculty. One of the teachers turned traitor and, after undermining Froebel at Keilhau, established a competing institution. It was a time of scarcity, almost famine, in Thuringia and the quality and scarcity of food on the dining tables came in for a good deal of criticism. The children had come from the most diverse homes, and pauper and prince were hard to weld into the harmonious school family which Froebel desired. Soon Keilhau was in financial difficulties. A younger teacher, Barop, saved the school from bankruptcy.

At this time Froebel turned toward a new project which had, among its novel features, one that pointed in the direction of the future kindergarten. This project was the ill-fated Helba plan which contemplated a complex institution including a school of art and industry, a higher school for boys for which Keilhau was to serve, an elementary school, a school for mothers, and one for orphan children of three to six years. Froebel in 1828, while the scheme was under consideration, wrote Barop that he had long been thinking of the education of small children and that he was going to include a school for them in the institution which the Duke of Meiningen seemed about to establish at Helba. He said: "I shall not call this an infant school, because I do not intend the children to be schooled, but to be allowed under gentlest treatment to develop freely." The Duke once placed his young son before Froebel and asked how the boy should be educated for his future position. Froebel answered: "With other children; and as a child, as long as he is a child." The inclusion of parent education was another new feature. In the school for mothers, Froebel intended to teach what the family must do to ensure the early and natural development of its children; and how the elementary school may continue this free, natural education. The third feature of the Helba plan was the inclusion of several kinds of handwork, art, and construction. These were to educate mind and hand in skills, industry, and practical judgment and to prepare children to become active members of society; but Froebel was throughout rather opposed to vocational and utilitarian education, at least as an end.

Froebel wished to use activity as a means of education, not merely for recreation or for vocational training. A half-starved junior lecturer at the University of Jena, J. G. H. Heusinger (1767–1828), had published a book with the title *Concerning the Use in Education of the Children's Powerful Impulse to Activity*, and Froebel's copy of this little work was well-thumbed and annotated. It is also significant that before he invented the name kindergarten Froebel called his embryo institution a "School Based upon the Active Instincts of Children." This is one of the modern roots of manual training and of the activity school; but the Helba plan remained only a vision because the Duke of Meiningen was persuaded by Froebel's opponents to withdraw his support.

Froebel's central idea of education through *Darstellung* is as hard to translate into unobtrusive English as Pestalozzi's *Anschauung*; but it means expression not of one certain kind but of many or all kinds. It means "living out" what is clamoring for utterance in the heart. One gives expression to ideas, emotions, beliefs, desires, and purposes by drawing, building, planning, inventing, and dramatizing, as well as by speaking or writing. Such expression demands cooperation and an audience and group activity. The child must learn to use many languages, the language of sports, of art, of algebra and geometry, and so on, if he would give expression to the world within and understand the world without. *Darstellung* means creative self-expression, and this idea that the child becomes educated through creative activity is Froebel's most important inspiration.

When the Helba plan was abandoned, Froebel went to Switzerland. After several years first at Wartensee and then at Willisau, the government of Berne in 1835 appointed Froebel director of a normal school at Burgdorf. A school of sixty teachers of all descriptions, young and old, father and son in some cases, was organized. There was also a demonstration school and, for the first time, Froebel was able to include classes of children as young as three years. Trying to meet their needs, he began to collect occupations, songs, stories, games, and other materials which would call out their active responses and lead to their natural development. He was influenced by Spiess who was developing his system of physical education in Burgdorf; but, more important, the ideas of the Helba plan again came to life. Froebel was seeking not merely new methods and exercises. He had caught the grand vision of a unified people in a harmonious commonwealth. The highest purpose of home and state, to which all other purposes were to be subordinate, was to be the development of mankind, that all men might live a "holy, pure and inviolate life." From early days Froebel had considered himself an "educator of mankind," as was already indicated by the title of *The Education of Man*. This education must begin in early childhood. In play, he believed, we have the fullest expression of child nature, and this should be the means of child education. "Play," declared Froebel, "is the great game of life itself in its beginnings." Home and school, on either side of the budding kindergarten, were each to be brought into conformity with his concept of play.

6. CREATION OF THE KINDERGARTEN

Froebel left Burgdorf in the spring of 1836 and was succeeded there by Langethal. The school at Willisau was at this time in the hands of Middendorf and Froebel's nephew, Ferdinand Froebel; and they continued to conduct it for several years longer. When Middendorf returned to the home base at Keilhau and Ferdinand Froebel went to Burgdorf, Willisau was taken over by Swiss teachers who carried it on along Froebel's lines. Froebel himself spent some months in Germany in visiting infant schools which had been founded as a result of the impulse given to the movement by Oberlin and his German disciples. He found the schools conducted by teachers without adequate training and often they were mere day nurseries whose chief purpose was to keep children out of harm's way while the mothers were at work. Eventually, he returned to Blankenburg in his native Thuringia which became the cradle of his new institution.

The problem was to find the best materials and activities and to organize them so that they should form a regular series which would call out and cultivate the children's powers of observation and understanding, and develop their self-activity and self-expression, the "living out" or expressing in life of the children's natural capacities, both social and individual. Froebel's early names for his institution, a "school for psychological education," a "school based upon the active instincts of children," were felt to be unnecessarily clumsy. He sought for a simpler and more expressive name. On May 1, 1840, on a walking tour in the mountains, the desired phrase came to him and he shouted, "Eureka! I have found it. The school is a kindergarten," a garden in which children may grow as naturally as a plant under the care of an expert gardener. It was a fortunate choice. The name has had a widespread acceptance and has been in-corporated into many languages as the title of Froebel's school and spirit.

As materials for the children's play, Froebel selected three forms, the sphere, the cube, and the cylinder. These are the basic Gifts, as he called them. The spheres of the kindergarten were balls which children rolled and tossed; the cubes were used as building blocks; and the cylinders, as a mediating form between the other two, could be used as either sta-tionary or movable elements in the plays. Many elaborate plays were worked out. Squares, triangles, sticks, and rings were included for use in construction. These objects were considered as typical of nature and art and Froebel held the view that nature and art form a unity and that the highest form of this unity is God. The child has in him a spark of the divine fire and is, in his small way, a creative personality as God is the great Creator. Education as self-expression, *Darstellung*, is a creative process through which and in which the child develops. This symbolism, which has been discarded, is best expressed by Froebel himself in numerous passages from which we select three, as follows:

I have not only forms for the child's eyes which are to make him acquainted with the outward world which surrounds him; I have symbols which unlock his soul for the thought or spirit which is innate in everything that has come out of God's creative mind. If the ripened mind is to know this thought, its em-bodied image must make an impression on the yet unconscious soul of the child and leave behind it forms which can serve as analogies to the intellectual order-ing of things. . . .

We must render perceptible to the child the unity of the world, absolute existence, the world within. . . . Such things we have to give the children through the system of ordered games and occupations which I have created. . . .

God clothed His own image in a mass of clay and was not ashamed of his creation; neither will I be ashamed to set forth in little blocks of wood my ideas upon the nature of man.

These passages are quoted in Susan E. Blow's *Educational Issues in the Kindergarten* (Appleton, 1908, pp. 52–53); and in regard to them even that loyal Froebelian asked: "What must any sane person think of an effort to render perceptible not only the unity of the world, but absolute existence? And is not any educator clearly daft who attempts to set forth in little blocks of wood his ideas upon the nature of man?" In our work-aday and secular civilization there is little room for mysticism, and Froe-bel's symbolism has disappeared from the modern kindergarten.

As the kindergarten developed, not only were features which Froebel had regarded as essential, such as symbolism, dropped out but also some new features which he would not have approved were introduced. Charles Dickens, as early as 1855, pointed out the dangers of formalism in the kindergarten. One type of formalism which Froebel would have opposed grew out of the mingling of Pestalozzian and Froebelian ideas. Froebel never intended that the stories, collections, and nature materials should be used for object lessons. His aim was not knowledge about things, especially not verbalism, but rather the use of things for the accomplishment of the child's or the children's purposes. Yet object lessons were introduced. Nor did Froebel intend that the kindergarten should develop free and unregulated play. His thought was the exact opposite of chance or chaotic self-expression. "In all things," God and man and nature, he had said in the opening sentence of his first book, "there lives and reigns an eternal law." This, one of his key ideas, would, if taken to heart, have prevented the "free play" which for a time characterized the American kindergarten. Free play is perhaps analogous to "busy work" in the elementary school.

7. SPREAD OF THE KINDERGARTEN

The Prussian government, through its Minister of Education, proscribed the kindergarten. The edict (August 7, 1851) was probably based upon a confusion in the official mind between Friedrich Froebel and his nephew Karl Froebel who held socialistic views; but once issued the prohibition was not withdrawn in spite of all that Froebel and influential friends could do. Even a direct appeal to the king was ineffective. Since Germany was not yet united, the prohibition did not apply to the other German states but it made the institution suspected everywhere. And from the Prussian official standpoint the suspicion was, doubtless, justified for the new school leaned toward democracy; and as Georg Ebers, a Keilhau pupil, remarked, in any German legislative assembly the Froebelians would have sat on the Left. Froebel died in the following year (1852) but there is no evidence that the blow, although he felt it keenly, shortened his life as has been asserted. The prohibition was withdrawn in 1861, and the new school for very young children spread rapidly.

The opposition at home may have aided the extension of the kindergarten abroad for its missionaries had to find open doors and sought for them beyond the borders of Prussia and even of Germany. The most famous of these foreign missionaries was Bertha von Marenholtz-Bülow, a titled and well-educated lady with fine personal qualities. She had made Froebel's acquaintance in 1849 and devoted the remainder of her life to the spread of his ideas. Her *Reminiscences of Friedrich Froebel*, translated into English by Mrs. Horace Mann, and others of her numerous writings were read in many countries, and her personal labors were almost as widespread. She worked in Germany for several years but in 1854 went for six months to England, where Mrs. Rongé had already established a demonstration kindergarten at Prince Albert's Exposition in London. These two women enlisted the support of Charles Dickens, who expressed his high approval of the kindergarten in a paper which he conducted, *Household Words* (1855). Eleanore Heerwart, who later aided in the founding of the International Kindergarten Union, and Adele von Portugall established kindergartens in Manchester. Bertha von Marenholtz-Bülow visited France in 1855, won the approval of the historian Michelet and other well-known French leaders, and through her addresses aroused interest in the kindergarten. The Low Countries had already received the message from other hands but, beginning at the Hague, she worked in Holland and Belgium also. In the latter country, she with others wrote a *Manuel des Jardins d'enfants* which had great influence. Henriette Breyman, who assisted in the preparation of this manual, was called to Switzerland in 1864 where the two cities of Lausanne and Geneva particularly became centers of kindergarten propaganda. The Baroness von Marenholtz-Bülow also worked in Italy where, at Florence, Elizabeth Peabody found her in the winter of 1871. Many of the leaders of the newly unified Italy, including Garibaldi, showed much interest in the new education. In several of the larger cities, Florence, Rome, and Naples, kindergartens and training schools were established.

After all, the kindergarten was first spread in the land of its birth. Froebel, we saw, left Switzerland in the spring of 1836 after establishing his schools at Willisau and Burgdorf. After four months at Keilhau, he moved into a house at Blankenburg where he collected and invented his gifts and handwork occupations, experimenting with the village children. This school was called a "school for the psychological training of young children." From 1837 he published a small weekly called the *Sonntagsblatt*, the Sunday sheet, to spread his ideas. During the following year, Barop and Adolf Frankenberg took some Keilhau pupils to Dresden on a trip and gave a demonstration of the future kindergarten exercises with some small children of Dresden. At Leipzig, where Langethal had prepared the way, they gave a further demonstration. Froebel himself gave demonstrations in Göttingen and Frankfort. Many visitors came to Blankenburg. In December 1838, Froebel and Middendorf helped Adolf Frankenberg open a "play school" at Dresden which he ably conducted for twenty years. The queen of Saxony expressed interest in the movement and asked for a demonstration; and a "christening" of the new institution was held in June, 1840, at which a "Women's Kindergarten Union" was formed. The well-known *Mutter-und Kose-Lieder*, actually suggested by seeing a mother carrying her child about the farmyard and singing to it, was published in 1844. It had been in preparation for years and the first edition, like the early kindergarten, had a bulky title, A *Family Book for Developing the Self-Activity of Children.*

Assistants, chiefly young women, began to leave Blankenburg to establish kindergartens of their own. There were a half-dozen of these before 1844 in different parts of Germany. Articles began to appear in journals. Diesterweg, the great educator, came and was convinced and his favorable influence was important; and Froebel's travels and addresses helped. Froebel's later years, after 1845, were mainly devoted to the education of young women as kindergartners. The kindergarten as a private institution was well established in numerous places of Germany during Froebel's lifetime.

8. FROEBEL'S PSYCHOLOGY

Many of the features of the kindergarten were based upon the observation of child conduct, but the observation was not systematic and Froebel was not a psychologist in the academic sense. Rousseau had demanded that teachers should study their children; Pestalozzi had tried to take him at his word and kept a record of his son's development for a short period; and Tiedemann had published (1787) observations on the development of the mental capacities of children. But scientific child psychology began in the nineteenth, not the eighteenth century. The doctrine of evolution and the experimental study of physiology formed the foundation stones for child psychology and Darwin himself (1877) published a "biographical sketch" of an infant; but this came after Froebel.

Although Froebel was not a psychologist, he had a psychology. His most fundamental ideas were (1) that education is a natural process; (2) that the child is an organism or organic whole, which through creative self-activity develops according to natural laws; (3) that the individual is an organic part of society; and (4) that the universe as a whole is an organism of which all lesser organisms are members. As the hand or eye is a member and organ of the body, so the individual is an organ of the human race and the race an organ of the cosmic consciousness, God.

The first point greatly interested Diesterweg because it is an essentially scientific standpoint. This concept, he declared, places Froebel among the originators in education. In Froebel's psychology this is, however, combined with the second point, the idea that man from the beginning of life is an organism which realizes its complete development through creative self-activity. The individual, he held, must rise to complete self-activity and full self-consciousness from partial and imperfect stages of both. Through participation in the developing achievements of mankind in their ascending culture stages, he gradually realizes his own full nature and makes his own contribution to the total human achievement.

Creative self-activity through social participation is the basis of Froebel's psychology. His concept of the individual is genetic. The child grows into maturity. He made out five stages, infancy, childhood, boyhood, youth, and maturity, but these are not sharply separated from each other. His concept of the individual is, secondly, an activist concept. The child is by nature a doer; and learning is secondary to doing, out of which it grows. Formal training of the senses, such as Rousseau or Pestalozzi approved, is to be discarded. The senses are used and perception is developed in the course of creative self-activity. Creativeness implies purpose. The individual is partly determined from without, else why a kindergarten, but he also has his own purposes which he works out as far as conditions permit. The child's purposes must not be too closely controlled, yet civilization, the achievements of the race, must guide the growing individual.

Froebel's psychology, therefore, is less analytic and less mathematical-mechanical than that of Herbart or Locke. Biological and evolutionary ideas were becoming prominent though Froebel lived before Darwin. The child, according to Froebel, is "replete with all the active tendencies of human nature" and, in John Dewey's phrase, is "spilling over with interests." These active tendencies and interests first manifest themselves as play.

9. PLAY IN EDUCATION

Little use was made of play in school until men accepted the premise that education should be adapted to the nature of the child. Since it is the nature of the child to love to play, if we can make play educative we shall have gone far in solving the basic problems of method and curriculum. But there are obvious difficulties.

Just what play is, it is hard to say. The word is a popular term for spontaneous activities carried on for pleasure. The activities may be solitary, competitive, or cooperative. The arts and the so-called "instinct of workmanship" as well as games and sports provide examples. In drama, "the play's the thing." In play children imitate adult activities; and in play men revert to the activities of childhood. Play is often defined as an activity in which one is interested and which is performed for the fun of it. Art, exploration, invention, and research may all be forms of play and Froebel, we recall, regarded children's play as the earliest form of the great game of life. This suggests the theory of play formulated by Karl Groos which is noticed below.

Several theories attempt to explain why we play. Four of these may be mentioned. All of them, being formulated by intelligent men, have some measure of truth and value. One of the oldest is the Schiller-Spencer surplus-energy theory. The poet Schiller, in the twenty-seventh of his "Letters" on aesthetics, said: "When the lion is not hungry, and no beast of prey challenges a fight, his unemployed strength finds an outlet for itself and he fills the resounding wilderness with his bold roaring; his exuberant energy rejoices in aimless display." Schiller's contemporary, the romantic novelist Jean Paul Richter, in *Levana* (1807) called play "the working off of the overflow of both mental and physical powers"; and this once-famous book on education had the most elaborate treatment of children's plays and occupations since Comenius. Herbert Spencer, in his *Principles of Psychology*, held a like view and introduced the phrase "surplus energy." Schiller, writing on aesthetics, directed particular attention to the "play of the imagination."

A second theory was devised by the Herbartian, Professor Moritz Lazarus, of the University of Berlin. When tired, he said, man turns to play for recreation. Play is the restorer of depleted energy. If such play is found in change of occupation, there need be no conflict between this theory and the previous one, although it seems to be a contrast to it.

In his widely read works on the play of animals and the play of man, Dr. Karl Groos regarded play as preparation for adult activities. This theory found the origin of play in instinct. Instincts appear in the child and young animal before he seriously needs them. Thus play is explained as a pre-exercise of native abilities and a preparation for mature life. Play includes those exercises which will develop into the skills that will be useful later.

There is, finally, a fourth theory, sponsored by G. Stanley Hall, who regarded play as recapitulation. When we play we are not preparing for life activities but, on the contrary, are repeating racial history. "The child brings out in play the actions of the cave-man. . . . He rehearses, in play, actions which were vital to the species, ages ago." This is a phase of the culture epochs theory. Again, this view does not necessarily contradict the theory of Groos. It may be that the fundamental activities of the present adult are so like those of his remote ancestors that racial activities may also prepare for life in the twentieth century.

The recapitulation theory has been outlined in the following table.

Cultural Stages	Play Stages
PRIMITIVE LIFE	CLIMBING, SWINGING, BABBLING
SAVAGE LIFE	CHASING, HIDING, HUNTING
NOMADIC LIFE	WANDERING, GANGS, FIGHTING
TRIBAL LIFE	THE ABOVE, PLUS TEAM GAMES
EARLY CIVILIZATION	IMITATIONS OF ADULT OCCUPATIONS

For such parallelism, there is no more than a trace of scientific or historical evidence; but it is, as we noticed in speaking of Herbart, a beguiling notion which has exercised great influence upon curriculum building. Actually little dependence is to be placed upon the periodizing of either the culture epochs or the play stages. The four theories have value in showing the complexity, variability, and highly modifiable character of play phenomena.

Froebel, although not wholly original, is the great exponent of play in education, developing both its theory and practice. He invented the kindergarten, going a long step beyond Comenius, Oberlin, and Aporti. His work has influenced education at all levels by a gradual interpenetration. He saw the child brimful and overflowing with outgoing impulses; and he also saw the child's need for new materials, for companions, and for direction and guidance. The distinction between play and educative work was erased by Froebel; these two are one. The activity of the senses and limbs of the infant comprises the bud, and games, building, song are the early blossoms of child development. Playful but serious activity in the production of some desired objective result is essential. Schools without working hours dissipate the precious energies of the child. Education must not be soft but it must be playful.

This play, which is also work, is important in Froebel's thought both for future industry and for religion; and both demand early cultivation. It is through religion and industry that personality is formed. Religion without industry, said Froebel, ends in visions and dreams; and industry without religion degrades man into a beast of burden and makes him a means, as Kant had said, when he should be an end. From the earliest years mother and father and child are to play together. "Come let us live with our children," and "for them." Speech and activity develop together and before the child understands words he can understand tones and gestures. For the next stage, Froebel prepared the "gifts," number games, rhythmic plays, dances and songs, drawing and geometric studies, and group games involving speech and cooperation. Boyhood is the third stage and its play shows greater complexity and continuity. There is to be more group work and long-time planning. Collecting, gardening, building play-shelters, and boats, exploring, and the owning of personal possessions are prescribed. The child should have his garden, his own room, tools, and books, as means to the development of his individuality.

As the child grows older, these play tendencies must be sublimated, as the psychologist calls it. They must become the attitudes of his normal life. Enterprise, exploration, purpose, and joy in performance are to characterize his later studies and his adult life. This doctrine of play, not invented but most fully developed by Froebel, has had the greatest influence upon educational practice and forms the center of the new education for it is implied in the project and in the whole range of experimental and creative activities which the modern school uses.

10. THE NURSERY SCHOOL

The purpose of the nursery school is sometimes stated to be to provide for the healthy physical and mental development of children over two and under five years of age. Nurture as well as education is, therefore, an essential element of nursery school function. The institution, like the early kindergarten, has often been considered as especially important for children of the poor in congested districts. Children of these young ages had been included in infant schools and day nurseries and some less than four years old in kindergartens; but the establishment of separate nursery schools did not occur until about 1900. The work of Dr. Maria Montessori in Italy and her books, such as the one translated into English under the title *The Montessori Method* (1912), have had considerable influence in developing the nursery school. She laid great stress upon natural development in wholesome and regulated surroundings. The medical and preventive features of her work are pronounced. She was a physician and had also been strongly influenced by Edouard Seguin (1812–1888). Much of her equipment, which seems somewhat formal, was devised for groups of low intelligence. Dr. Montessori emphasized apparatus which could be used by the children themselves without help from the teacher. Much of it is used for sense training and for individual occupation.

In terms of recent and rapid progress in nursery school education over previous conditions, Russia among all countries takes first place. In England and the United States, the nursery school is an evolution from the charity kindergartens such as Mrs. Shaw established in Boston and Dr. Felix Adler in New York. A British example is the one founded by Sir William Mather at Salford in 1873. This was equipped with kitchens and provided meals and baths for the infants and has been called the first nursery school in England. Aided by the new hygiene and preventive medicine, by the new biology and evolutionary doctrine, and by the increasing political power of labor, the nursery schools in England grew slowly until the end of the first World War when public grants were provided in the Fisher Act of 1918. The most noted of the earlier English workers in nursery school development were two sisters, Rachel and Margaret Macmillan, who established a school at Deptford in 1911. Margaret Macmillan's books have been widely read. One of them is *The Nursery School* (1919). "Educate every child as if he were your own," was Rachel Macmillan's principle.

In the United States, nursery schools were begun about 1920 in institutions for the preparation of teachers. Institutes of research in child development with nursery schools for laboratories were established. The New York Bureau of Educational Experiments and the Yale Psycho-Clinic made studies of the behavior and physical and mental growth of infants. Many agencies became interested, schools of education, private schools, public welfare agencies, and public schools. Within about a decade, the number of nursery schools in the United States increased from none to two or three hundred. Winnetka, Chicago, and Highland Park in Illinois, Pasadena and Los Angeles in California, Grand Rapids and Kalamazoo in Michigan, Rochester and Albany in New York are among the cities in which nursery schools were early introduced into the public school systems. The financial depression following 1929 curtailed many of these services.

Ever since the time of Plato men have said, at least occasionally a wise man has implied, that education should begin with the beginning of life and continue to the end of it; but Oberlin, Froebel, Montessori, the Agazzi sisters in Italy, and the Macmillan sisters in England have at least made a beginning. Assuming that we employ the best available brains and skill, can we think of any better principle to follow than to "Educate every child as if he were your own"?

After we have considered several national systems and the beginnings of American education, we shall see the influence which Herbart and Froebel exerted upon the American schools. Although Herbartianism as a cult had only a temporary importance, several elements of Herbart's thought have had permanent effects in the United States. The influence of Froebel has been more pronounced and more persistent in our country than that of any foreign thinker unless it should be Pestalozzi.

The Froebelian theory was to be a general system, applicable to children and youth of all ages. It was first applied in a school for adolescent boys; and that Froebel gave the most detailed application of his thought at the kindergarten level should not lead one to conceive it as adapted to that age only. Like Rousseau, he based it upon an activist psychology; but he did not propose to take the pupils out of society, as Rousseau did. On the contrary he made full use of group motives and activities in home, school, and community. From this standpoint, Froebel's system of education complemented Rousseau's by providing the richer and more stimulating environment which was denied Emile.

His home and university experience led Froebel to combine views that he had gained from religion, science, and the idealistic philosophy of the time. Especially from the study of comparative anatomy and from "stones and spiders' webs," Froebel drew the conclusion that all nature had a plan; and that the active, creative organism, which a man is, was part of nature. To fulfill this plan, man must be educated in accordance with the laws of his development. The present chapter, in its description of Keilhau and the kindergarten and in its analysis of Froebel's psychology, contains an account of his exercises and methods.

Froebel interpreted education in religious, that is, in theistic terms. The little child grows by discovering and creating, by expressing in the world and society what wells up in its heart. The child shares, not fully, of course, but really, in the divine nature and, like the Great Creator, it also creates and, thereby, develops.

He interpreted education, secondly, in scientific terms. Education is a natural process of growth through activity. The child is an individual organism but also an organic member of the social whole. It grows by interaction with the physical and by active participation with the social environment.

He interpreted education, finally, in historical and evolutionary terms. The child, the youth, the man contribute to the resources of the race; and the resources of the race are the materials with which the education of the race is carried on. By discovery, invention, and transmission, child, youth, and man build civilization and thus in a historical process, by natural scientific methods, fulfill the divine plan which is the Will of God.

QUESTIONS

1. How did the three types of educational institutions for the smallest children differ in nature and function?

2. To what degree do Froebel's experiences and times account for his views? Is this a significant and answerable question?

3. Compare the relations of Pestalozzi's and Froebel's theories to that of Rousseau.

4. What are the differences between using activities as a means of recreation, of training for a vocation, and of education?

5. Why did Froebel, in developing the kindergarten, collect songs, games, and other materials that were used by the common people instead of inventing appropriate activities?

6. How is Froebel's Darstellung related to Pestalozzi's Anschauung?

7. If education is growth, what place do knowledge, facts, have in the process of becoming educated? According to Froebel we learn in doing and by doing. Is the converse also true, that by abstract learning we are enabled to perform, to do? Find examples to illustrate these principles.

8. Are some kinds of play more educative than others, and which kinds?

9. How do the theories which explain why people play help to explain the functions of play in education?

10. Was Prussia, considering her theory of government in 1851, well advised in closing the kindergartens?

FOR FURTHER READING AND STUDY

The extensive and still expanding periodical literature on Froebel and the kindergarten can not be noticed here but the Reader's Guide, Education Index, and other indexes will open the way to some of the American items. There is a considerable biographical literature on American kindergarten leaders. There are many old and new books on Froebel in German but for these the student must go to the library catalogue, and special bibliographies.

Barnard, Henry, *Kindergarten and Child Culture Papers*, Hartford, Office of Barnard's Journal of Education, 1890, 799 pp.

Blow, Susan E., *Symbolic Education; a Commentary on Froebel's "Mother Play,"* New York, D. Appleton and Co., 1894, 251 pp.; *Letters to a Mother on the Philosophy of Froebel*, New York, D. Appleton & Company, 1899, 311 pp.; *Educational Issues in the Kindergarten*, New York, D. Appleton and Co., 1908, 386 pp.

Bowen, H. C., *Froebel and Education by Self-Activity*, New York, Charles Scribner's Sons, 1899, 209 pp.

Davis, Mary Dabney, *Nursery Schools, Their Development and Current Practices in the United States*, United States Office of Education, Bulletin No. 10, 1932, Washington, Government Printing Office, 1933, 92 pp.

Dwight, Fannie E., and J. Jarvis, *Mother-Play and Nursery Songs*, Boston, Lothrop, Lee and Shepard, 1906, 192 pp.

Ebers, Georg, *The Story of My Life*, New York, D. Appleton & Company, 1893, 382 pp.

Fletcher, S. S., and J. Welton, *Froebel's Chief Writings on Education*, New York, Longmans, Green and Company, 1912, 246 pp.

Foster, Josephine C., and Neith E. Headley, *Education in the Kindergarten*, Cincinnati, American Book Co., 1936, 368 pp.

Franks, Fanny, *The Kindergarten System*, London, S. Sonnenschein and Co., 1897, 253 pp. Although the title does not indicate it this is a biography of Froebel and a good one. The book is an abridged translation of the German work by A. B. Hanschmann, given below.

Froebel, Friedrich, *Die Menschenerziehung*, Leipzig, Philipp Reclam Verlag, 1926, 477 pp. With introduction and notes by Hans Zimmerman.

Hailmann, William N., *Kindergarten Culture . . . A Complete Sketch of Froebel's System of Early Education*, Cincinnati, Wilson, Hinkle and Co., 1873, 119 pp.; *The Education of Man*, by Friedrich Froebel, New York, D. Appleton & Company, 1898, 340 pp. Translated and edited by Hailmann.

Hanschmann, Alexander B., *Friedrich Fröbel. Die Entwickelung seiner Erziehungsidee in seinem Leben*, Dresden, Bleyl und Kaemerer, 1900, 535 pp.

Heinemann, Arnold H., *Froebel Letters*, Boston, Lee and Shepard, 1893, 182 pp.

Jarvis, Josephine, *Froebel's Education by Development*, New York, D. Appleton & Company, 1900, 347 pp.

Kilpatrick, William H., *Froebel's Kindergarten Principles Critically Examined*, New York, The Macmillan Company, 1916, 217 pp.

Lockhead, Jewell, *The Education of Young Children in England*, New York, Teachers College, Columbia University, 1932, 226 pp.

Marenholtz-Bülow, Bertha M., *Reminiscences of Friedrich Froebel*. Translation by Mrs. Horace Mann, Boston, Lee and Shepard, 1877, 359 pp.

Michaelis, Emilie, and H. K. Moore, Editors, *Autobiography of Friedrich Froebel*, Syracuse, N. Y., C. W. Bardeen and Co., 1889, 167 pp.

Müller, Maria, *Frauen im Dienste Froebels*, Leipzig, Felix Meiner, 1928, 187 pp.

Snider, Denton J., *The Life of Frederick Froebel*, Chicago, Sigma Publishing Co., 1900, 470 pp.

Vandewalker, Nina C., *The Kindergarten in American Education*, New York, The Macmillan Company, 1908, 274 pp.

[Young, Robert Fitzgibbon], *Infant and Nursery Schools*. Report of the Consultative Committee, London, His Majesty's Stationery Office, 1933, 282 pp.

13 NATIONAL EDUCATION IN FRANCE

W E HAVE NOW REACHED THE GREAT DIVIDE IN OUR HISTORY, which separates the older education, ancient, medieval, and early modern, from those schools and forms of educational control which are familiar to us by personal experience. The institutional mountain range which divides the older past from the present is Nationalism, and its individual peaks and great plateaus are the nation-states which use the school as an instrument of Nationalism. We see around us inclusive educational systems that are maintained and directed by the states. These form a close network of related and connected agencies which cover the entire area and embrace the whole population of the country. All of us as children were compelled, in the absence of legal exemptions, to attend such public schools. In the western countries, and not in them alone, these schools are now so firmly supported by public opinion and established by statute that other possible arrangements hardly come to mind. Yet they are a new phenomenon in history. Inclusive and powerful systems of public schools did not exist anywhere in the world even two centuries ago; and now those earlier conditions have passed away so completely that some historical knowledge and a vigorous use of the historical imagination are needed to understand the transformation caused by the rise of Nationalism.

We may at this point, then, with profit briefly recall how children were educated and how schools were managed before the national era. In all the classical world except Sparta, education was the concern of the family and was conducted according to custom, not law, by tutors in the home or in private schools. State aid was sometimes given, especially in the higher branches, in the Roman empire, but no general attempt was made to promote the education of the people or to regulate the schools. The Emperor Julian during his brief reign attempted to eliminate Christian teachers and teaching; and two centuries later, the Emperor Justinian decreed the closing of non-Christian schools. But in general the ancient laws and decrees merely served to offer inducements or privileges to teachers and to provide salaries for a very few or to regulate school hours or the conduct of pupils. Roman cities established chairs of letters, rhetoric, and law; but neither the cities nor the empire developed a general system.

With the dominance of Christianity, cathedral, monastic, and other church schools came into being. The church was far more active in the establishment of schools than the state was or had ever been. Charlemagne, however, harbored a conception of the civil importance of education and he even attempted to spread the benefits of church schools to the lay public. His efforts were not permanently or deeply effective but they may be considered to have been a slight anticipation of the later collaboration of state and church in education.

After Charlemagne and particularly after 1100, the church greatly expanded its educational efforts. Important cathedral schools developed in the cities and, in the thirteenth century, universities operating under charters and struggling for freedom from external control helped to make an epoch in the competition of state and church for the support of the rising intellectual classes. Schools under municipal, gild, and other corporate auspices also multiplied. And in the Renaissance-Reformation era, a new period of cooperation and competition between church and state for the promotion of education was begun. The growing nations and their national churches developed joint policies for the support and regulation of schools, not only for the ruling classes but also for the common people. This was the era of parochial schools, of semipublic secondary schools, and of the territorial-confessional universities.

The next step in this evolution no longer involved collaboration between state and church but instead led to the displacement of the church as a main educational agency. Schools became public, that is, they were established and controlled by the state; and to church-controlled schools there was reserved only a minor place in the whole system. In this and the following chapters we shall first very briefly point to the rise of nationalism and shall then trace the evolution of the state systems of several countries.

1. THE RISE OF NATIONALISM

Nationalism developed out of community of custom, feeling, belief, and the sense of a common origin and history; and its most effective carriers are language, religion, and education. In the medieval universities the students who came from particular regions organized themselves into "nations." In more recent times nationalism has added to the older foundations a common political organization and political patriotism, and these have led directly to the nation-state. States based upon nationality hardly existed in ancient and medieval times. The loyalty of the ancient Greeks was given to a city-state, not to Greece. The Roman empire was not a nation but an imperial system imposed upon peoples of many nationalities. The Middle Ages had little sense of nationality; and they could not have it because of the dominance of a universal church and a universal language, and the lack of a cultivated vernacular language and a common culture.

To understand modern education, it is important to realize that nationalism is a cultural product which is developed by propaganda and education. The nation and the state are objective facts but nationalism is a condition of the mind. A nation is a people connected by real or at least accepted racial unity, such unity being shown by language, religion, customs, and apparent destiny. The Poles form a nation. The individuals who compose a nation are sometimes called its nationals. A state is a sovereign political body, occupying a definite territory and having a central government. The Swiss state includes nationals of the Italian, French, and German nations. Nationalism, in contrast with these concrete terms, means devotion to national interests and unity, and a nationalist is such a devotee. The height of nationalism would be reached if each nationality constituted an independent state that commanded the complete obedience and loyalty of all its nationals. It is such extreme nationalism which Hitler, Mussolini, and the "one hundred per centers" of all nations have had as an ideal. Nationalism, therefore, implies patriotism, and it is the joining of an accented patriotism with nationality that is new. This is a state of mind that is developed by propaganda and education; and this is the reason why nationalism is an important issue in education. Modern states have used the schools, not merely to cultivate loyalty and patriotism, but also to develop chauvinism and an aggressive militarism.

Modern nationalism developed first in Europe. The Crusades, in which Frenchmen took a most active part, helped to develop a sense of solidarity in the West, particularly in France. The wars of the Christians against the Moslems in Spain stimulated a strong nationalist feeling among Spaniards, especially in the time of Ferdinand and Isabella. The strong monarchy which the Conquest of 1066 introduced into England was modified by the Magna Charta which the nobles extorted from King John, and in the struggle of Parliament with the Crown a high degree of nationalist sentiment was generated. These three countries were among the first to become great nation-states.

It was in France that nationalism developed most rapidly and reached the highest point. Intellectual and political forces aided its growth. The revival of the study of the Roman law had a considerable influence upon the French judicial system. The position obtained by a body of professional lawyers who derived their powers from the king increased the growing

Francis Bacon

Thomas More

Cicero,
Author of *De Oratore*
and Other Books on Roman Education

Comenius,
Portrait Ascribed to
Juriaan Ovens,
a Pupil of Rembrandt

Marc-Antoine Jullien,
Who Supported Pestalozzi and
Suggested the Idea of Comparative Education

Statue of Vittorino da Feltre,
in His Native City
(Courtesy of Professor Flaud C. Wootc

Pestalozzi and Grandson

Jean Jacques Rousseau

A

YEAR IN EUROPE

COMPRISING

A JOURNAL OF OBSERVATIONS

IN

ENGLAND, SCOTLAND, IRELAND, FRANCE, SWITZERLAND,
THE NORTH OF ITALY, AND HOLLAND.

In 1818 and 1819.

BY JOHN GRISCOM,

PROFESSOR OF CHEMISTRY AND NATURAL PHILOSOPHY IN THE N. YORK INSTITU
TION; MEMBER OF THE LIT. AND PHIL. SOCIETY OF NEW-YORK, &c.

IN TWO VOLUMES.

VOL. I.

New-York:

PUBLISHED BY COLLINS & CO. AND E. BLISS & E. WHITE, N. YORK;
H. C. CAREY & J. LEA, PHILADELPHIA; AND
WELLS & LILLY, BOSTON.
Printed by A. Paul, 72 Nassau-street.

1823.

Early Report on Education in Europe
for the Information of Americans

Jacob Steiner,
Pupil of Pestalozzi,
Assistant-Teacher at Yverdon,
Later Professor of Mathematics in Berlin

Georg Kerschensteiner, Superintendent of Schools, Munich, Germany, Leader in Vocational Education (From Erich Hahn, *Die Pädagogik der Gegenwart in Selbstdarstellungen*, Leipzig, Felix Meiner, 1926, p. 45; *Alle Rechte vorbehalten*)

John Dewey

Gymnasium of Bruchsal, Baden, Germany
(By Permission of Ohler, Bruchsal)

Lycée Montaigne, Paris, 1957
*(Courtesy of Professor
Flaud C. Wooton)*

Fellenberg School, Hofwyl, Switzerland, 1957
(Courtesy of Professor Flaud C. Wooton)

Tecumseh High School, in Ohio, U.S.A.
(Courtesy of Superintendent Lawrence Pflaumer)

The School of Education, Stanford University, 1938, from *Cubberley of Stanford,* by Jesse B. Sears and Adin D. Henderson *(Courtesy of Stanford University Press)*

Home of the National Education Association, Washington, D.C., 1958

Ella Flagg Young, First Woman Chosen President of the National Education Association, also Professor of Education, University of Chicago, Superintendent of Schools, Chicago

School of Athens,
with Plato and Aristotle the Central Figures, by Raphael,
the Vatican
(Courtesy of the Bettmann Archive)

Monastery School in the Middle Ages,
during the Reign of Charlemagne, after a Woodcut by Scheer
(*Courtesy of the Bettmann Archive*)

Visual Education according to Basedow
(Courtesy of the Bettman Archive)

Monitorial School *(Courtesy of the Bettmann Archive)*

Above: Kindergarten Children of Kiev on a Walk
(From *Education in the USSR*, U.S. Office of Education Bulletin,
1957, No. 14)

Below: Fifth-Grade Botany Class, Moscow
(From *Education in the USSR*, U.S. Office of Education Bulletin,
1957, No. 14)

Rehearsal at High School of Music and Art, New York City
(Courtesy of Wide World Photos)

Accent on Excellence in High School Chemistry,
Monroe, Louisiana
(*Courtesy of Wide World Photos*)

might of the monarchy. During the same period, the right of the king to impose taxes without the consent and against the will of the papacy was affirmed by the Estates General, and that body, and the system of national taxation which they ratified and the standing army which was then created, were all instruments of centralization. This tendency became much stronger during the Hundred Years War. If the Estates General had seized the opportunity during the anarchy that followed the French defeats at Crecy and Poitiers, they might have developed into an institution able like the English Parliament to set limits to the power of the crown; but they were unable to do this and the French monarchy continued in its course toward absolutism. Louis XIV admitted with royal candor that the love of glory took precedence over everything else in his soul. His ministers sought to stimulate the intellectual life of France for the exaltation of the crown, to encourage art, literature, and science, and to refine the civilization and culture of the nation. In this period France occupied the center of the European stage as the leader in thought and action. At last, the centralizing process reached such a point that Louis XIV could pertinently declare "L'état c'est moi"; and the cultural eminence of that state was likewise unchallenged.

Absolutism, although it both fostered and was fostered by nationalism in France, is not a necessary stage in the development of national patriotism. It may even be a hindrance to unity when the government becomes, as the French government in the eighteenth century became, high-handed, capricious, and extravagant. The result was the French Revolution, the First Republic, and a messianic enthusiasm in spreading world democracy.

The essential relations between nationalism and democracy are not altogether clear. No patriotism without liberty, said Rousseau. And it would seem that a people which governs itself would have a more intense loyalty to state and nation than one which is governed by a class, a party, or a dynasty; but the intense nationalism of National Socialist Germany and the devotion of many nationalities to Soviet Russia perhaps tend to refute this notion of a natural alliance between democracy and nationalism. In France, however, it was the Revolution which blazoned to the world the doctrine of national democracy and threatened the thrones of half of Europe. John Locke had developed the theory of popular government and he was followed by the American patriots of 1776. Rousseau performed a like function in France and the French Revolution swept away the autocratic monarchy, class privileges, and local provincialism and united the French-speaking people into a democratic national state which undertook the task of spreading democracy throughout Europe and the world. And it was the Revolution which called out the Report of Condorcet and other schemes for universal, secular education.

2. FRENCH EDUCATION TO 1830

The programs of the revolution could not be put into effect immediately. The disorder of the times, the lack of resources and of an effective tax system, the lack of professional lay teachers, and the absence of a national educational consciousness delayed the establishment of universal free education for almost a century. Meanwhile, France was working at this task. The actual achievements of the Revolution were in secondary and higher education. A radical bill by Lepeletier de Saint-Fargeau to create a system based upon that of ancient Sparta was not adopted. The law of Lakanal to establish elementary and secondary schools was ineffective. One of his proposals led to the brief opening in 1795 of the École Normale Supérieure and this, when it was re-established by Napoleon, became permanent and is still a part of the University of Paris. It has always been a higher school of science to prepare teachers for lycées. Another law of 1795, named for Daunou and sponsored by the middle class, led to the organization of some primary schools and more especially of secondary or central and higher schools in which the bourgeoisie was particularly interested. The Central Schools which this law established had a distinctly modern and practical curriculum and were later patronized by Napoleon but they were too few in number and too poorly organized to compete with the lycées. Daunou's law might have been more effective but for the foreign wars in which France became involved, but its failure also shows the bankruptcy of revolutionary radicalism which had demanded elementary, not secondary education. The same conservative trend is shown by the dozen or more technical schools, bureaus, and conservatories that were opened in Paris by the Convention. The Convention also adopted the newly devised metric system of weights and measures. From these revolutionary beginnings a national system of education was developed in the course of the nineteenth century.

The interest of Napoleon was in secondary and technical, not in primary education. One of his first acts was the creation of four military schools out of the endowments of the sixteenth-century humanistic school, the Collège of Louis le Grand. He also instituted a system of collèges and lycées and within a few years more than four hundred of these were opened or reopened in the whole country. These taught about fifteen subjects including Latin, French, science, and mathematics. They were boarding schools, and while the law defined their curriciulum the state, beyond providing the buildings, gave little financial help.

Yet, although private schools continued, this was the beginning of modern secondary education in France. The noted chemist, Fourcroy, was made Director-General of Public Instruction with three superintendents of secondary studies. The same law of 1802 established special schools of medicine, law, and science. And Napoleon created a School of Arts and Trades and fostered two schools of engineering and mining which had been opened earlier. French engineering schools took first rank under Napoleon, and the American West Point and Rensselaer Polytechnic were indebted to them. The same is true of the Paris schools for the deaf and blind which became models for American schools at Hartford (1817) and Boston (1832). For primary education, Napoleon did little more than to re-enact Daunou's law and to enjoin that teachers should not carry their instruction beyond the rudiments. The state did not support them, and after the Concordat of 1801, by which Napoleon made his peace with the Catholic church, the Brothers of the Christian Schools again came in as teachers of the primary schools.

The most spectacular and influential work of Napoleon in the whole field of education was the creation of the University of France, at first called the Imperial University. This is not a school but an administrative system to direct and control all grades of schools. The decree which created it, with a Grand Master at the head and a Council of twenty-six members, was issued in 1808. Its functions were to govern the schools, appoint the teachers, disburse the funds, and set the school examinations. "No school, no establishment of instruction whatsoever," the decree declared, "may be set up outside the Imperial University and without the authorization of its head." With various changes of powers and even of name, this highly centralized system of educational control lasted until 1940 and may be re-established. The nearest American analogy is to be found in the University of the State of New York.

Napoleon considered education to be a primary function of the state. He declared that education is of all political questions perhaps the most important. Unless there is a teaching body with definite principles, unless the child is taught from infancy whether he is to be a republican or a monarchist, a Catholic or a freethinker, the state will not be a nation but will rest upon shifting foundations constantly exposed to disorder and change. He saw clearly the political use that could be made of national education. In creating the University he said: "It was necessary for me to create a civil profession, disinterested, grave, which would work in the interests of science and letters. That is the ideal of my University. . . . Above all I insist that it shall devote itself to letters. I love the mathematical and physical sciences; algebra, chemistry, botany are excellent though partial applications of the human spirit; but letters are the human spirit itself. The study of letters is the general education which prepares for everything; it is the education of the soul." By letters he meant French and Latin literature. In this ideal of classical education as in his centralizing system of control, Napoleon expressed the spirit of France, and these two ideals have been dominant in French education from that time to the present.

During the period of the Restoration (1815–1830), French industry and agriculture prospered; but little was done for education. The very small annual appropriations were gradually increased and by 1830 somewhat more than half of the thirty-seven thousand communes (or townships) had established primary schools. An effort was made to improve the qualifications of the teachers by requiring certification, but the Brothers of the Christian Schools resisted this demand and were excused from the requirement. Thirteen normal schools for primary teachers were established. The monitorial system was introduced from England and, as in the parent country, it aroused great enthusiasm. The infant schools, first developed by J. F. Oberlin in the previous century in eastern France, were now modified to follow the English pattern. In the next reign they were accepted by the government as part of the public system.

3. UNDER THE JULY MONARCHY

The Restoration government fell because the king, Charles X, like a true Bourbon, attempted to alter the Constitution to increase his own power. The middle classes, who had been partially disfranchised by royal ordinance, with the help of the Paris workingmen overthrew the government in July 1830, and Louis Philippe of the House of Orleans became king. The July Monarchy was not a popular but rather a businessman's government. The working classes, who had ensured the success of the July Revolution, went unrepresented. But the country increased in wealth and population. Industry was fostered. The state aided in the building of roads, canals, and railroads; and agriculture was rapidly improved. The "internal improvements" of France paralleled those of the United States in the same period; and in both countries the increasing wealth provided the economic foundation for the extension and improvement of schools. The French Revolution had developed the theory and created the demand for national education and the Industrial Revolution created the means which made it practicable.

The greatest educational achievement of the July Monarchy was the Primary School Law of 1833. The primary and higher primary schools which the law created were intended for the common people; and the old collèges and lycées continued to furnish secondary instruction for the upper, the wealthy, and the professional classes. There was no attempt to combine the primary and secondary schools into a ladder system which would have enabled the children of the common people to enter the secondary schools and to prepare for a profession. The July government was conservative and bourgeois and was the friend of popular education to this extent and on these lines only. It did not intend to open the higher professions to common people.

The new government immediately increased the annual appropriation for primary schools; required all teachers to hold a certificate from the state, even those who belonged to religious orders; and opened thirty new normal schools. To find a model for the new primary school system which was proposed, they looked to Germany which had recently reformed its schools. Victor Cousin was sent as a special investigator to gather the results of that country's experience. His *Report on . . . Public Instruction in Germany . . .* was issued at Paris in 1831 and an English translation appeared in London and New York. This was one of the important educational documents of the century. Cousin favored local school control, but the centralizing tendencies of France were too strong to permit the use of this idea. He did not recommend compulsory attendance because he was sure the French people were not ready for it. He insisted that every commune must have a primary school and proposed the establishment also of higher primary schools. These ideas were adopted.

By the law of 1833, the primary schools were required to teach the French language and this teaching was to include work in reading, writing, spelling, grammar, and composition, the elements of arithmetic, and the metric system of weights and measures. Church schools were to be allowed if the teachers held legal certificates and if the schools submitted to state inspection. Other important concessions were made to the church. Religious bodies were to be represented on the local school committee, but any child was to receive religious instruction only when it was approved by the parents. These provisions show how the religious difficulty was solved and they reveal the extent to which France had receded from the secularizing tendencies of the Revolution. The schools were allowed to charge fees, but these were to be remitted to poor children. The teachers' salaries were guaranteed and the cost of the schools was to be met, according to a formula written into the law, by the communes, the departments, of which there are ninety in France, and the state.

The administration of the schools was apportioned among the same units. There was to be a local committee of the commune with slight powers; and a committee of the arrondissement with more general powers. The arrondissements are the largest political divisions of a department and are themselves divided into cantons and these into communes. The committee of the arrondissement appointed the teachers and reported to the national ministry on the condition of the schools. The power of the central government was supreme. Through inspectors, the minister could control the schools, the teachers, and the officers of the arrondissements and communes. By the end of the reign of Louis Philippe about one hundred and fifty inspectors were in service and were exercising delegated powers similar to those of an American superintendent of schools.

The law required the establishment of higher primary schools in the chief cities. These admitted pupils who had completed the work of the lower schools. They taught practical mathematics, including the elements of geometry, drawing, design, some measurements and surveying, some physical and biological science, singing, and the history and geography of France. Where possible, instruction in a modern language and other additional subjects might be offered. But the higher primary schools were primary rather than higher, for they did not prepare their pupils to enter a university. Adult classes were organized, and by 1848 a hundred thousand persons were receiving post-primary instruction. Despite this auspicious beginning, the higher primary schools soon began to decline. Their greatest success was achieved after they were revived by the Third Republic.

The infant schools which had been established under the Restoration were accepted as a part of the public system in 1837. The industrial development of France and the employment of women in factories made them a useful adjunct of the primary system. They were placed under the management of the existing school committees. They admitted children up to the age of six and taught singing, needlework, and manual activities, together with some work in the elementary school subjects.

Within a few months after the passage of the law, the Minister of Public Instruction, Guizot, sent a body of special investigators to report upon the condition of primary education throughout the country. The reports were compiled by P. Lorain and published as *A Survey of Primary Education* (1837). This survey called particular attention to the educational ills of the poorer rural districts and showed that whole communities were illiterate and many communes entirely without schools. Where schools existed, they were often poorly housed and conducted by teachers whose main business might be the selling of liquor or the mending of shoes. Some teachers were paid in provisions which they collected by going from house to house. These were only the worst cases and it would be easy to point to similar conditions in other countries. The purpose of the report was to arouse the French people to the need for immediate improvement. France in 1851 had sixty-one thousand primary schools, but there were even at that time twenty-five hundred communes without schools; the number of normal schools for men had been greatly increased, and a parallel system of normal schools for women had been begun.

The secondary schools, lycées and collèges, remained under government supervision. They were the classical schools which prepared for entrance to the universities, admitting students at the age of eleven and graduating them as *baccalaureates* at eighteen. By 1850, France had about fifteen hundred public and private secondary schools with a total enrollment of eighty-five thousand pupils. From these the future civil servants and professional classes were drawn, opportunities which to the parents justified the considerable expense involved. These facts perhaps sufficiently explain the initial failure of the higher primary schools which could offer no such privileges.

4. UNDER NAPOLEON III

The Second Republic lasted from 1848 to 1853, but during the last of these years Louis Napoleon was actually in power and in December of the latter year he was proclaimed Emperor of France and took the name Napoleon III. The revolutionary year of 1848 was followed in France, Germany, and other countries by a strong reaction from liberalism toward autocracy; and the French education law of 1850 was a reactionary statute. Carnot, the Minister of Public Instruction under the provisional government, had appealed to the primary teachers to work for the election of liberal-minded representatives. Looking back to the great Revolution, he declared: "It is not now a matter, as it was in the time of our fathers, of defending the Republic against foreign foes, but rather of defending it against ignorance and deception [from within]; and that task belongs to the teachers." We do not know whether the teachers followed Carnot's suggestion and electioneered for liberal candidates; but the conservatives won. And a noted English observer, Matthew Arnold, remarked that "the conquerors of the Revolution of 1848" did not fail to remember that Carnot and his party had made the schoolmasters their missionaries.

It is perhaps not hard to see why teachers should and why some of them do in fact support a liberal political policy. They usually come from the lower and lower middle classes and have a great deal to gain from a wide distribution of power and from liberal policies. One ought to expect also that teachers would be liberal-minded and liberally educated persons. If this was the attitude and disposition of the French teachers, they were disappointed. Both Carnot's bill and that of Saint-Hilaire, which was substituted for it, had provided for a full complement of infant, primary, higher primary, normal, and trade schools with liberal curricula, free tuition in part, and compulsory attendance to the age of fourteen. But such a program had no chance of adoption in the legislature, with its strong monarchist majority. An education committee of the new government led an attack upon the normal schools and their curriculum. They declared that the outlook of the primary teachers should be limited to the local school and community; and that they did not desire, as teachers in French primary schools, the budding scholars who had been coming from the normal schools. They limited the courses in history and geography in the normal schools and made them strongly nationalist in tone. They objected to normal students' browsing in libraries. Broadly educated teachers with liberal ideas were not wanted. In France, as in Prussia at this time, political reaction came into power and circumscribed the outlook of the teachers and their pupils. A slighter but similar trend was noticeable in Massachusetts and other American communities.

The Law of 1850 made numerous concessions to the church, in both primary and secondary fields. It also combined the administration of both levels of schools under a Minister of Public Instruction and an advisory Superior Council of twenty-eight members, who represented all the educational interests of the country. It increased the force of inspectors and established the academy as a unit for the administration of secondary and university education. France was divided into sixteen, later with the inclusion of Algiers into seventeen, academies. Since then the chief administrative units for the administration of education have been the whole state, the academies, the departments, and the communes. Only minor functions were given to the arrondissements and the cantons.

Under Napoleon III the power of the University of France became almost absolute, and the new ruler an autocrat. The press came under complete governmental control. Teachers were allowed to read only *The Monitor*, the official newspaper. An official order required them to shave off their moustaches so as to remove from "their faces, as well as their minds," every trace of the Revolution of 1848. By the Organic Decree of 1852, the emperor through the minister could name and dismiss teachers and practically all educational officials. Teachers were required to take an oath of loyalty, and prominent university professors were dismissed "in the interest of public peace." This centralized system, the University of France, was taken over by the Third Republic but its powers have not been exercised as tyrannically as in the days of the Second Empire. As the Revolution of 1848 receded into the past, educational support became more bountiful and educational administration more liberal even under Napoleon III. France was prosperous, the salaries of the teachers were raised, many new schools were opened, and many primary schools were made tuition free. Under a famous minister, Victor Duruy (1811–1894), the normal schools were improved and given a greater degree of freedom, and education became more professional. Under Duruy, who was a noted historian, much attention was also given to the advancement of higher studies.

5. NATIONAL EDUCATION COMES OF AGE

The defeat of France in the short Franco-Prussian War once again trans-formed the government into a republic. The Third Republic was pro-claimed on September 4, 1870, when the news of the disaster of Sedan reached the capital; but the danger that a monarchy would after all be re-established was great and in fact the National Assembly, which was elected to make the peace, was sharply royalist in composition. The Socialists and Jacobins of Paris feared that one of the Bourbons would again be en-throned. Then came the Commune, an insurrection of the poverty-stricken masses of the capital, which was put down, after a siege of two months, in seven days of ferocious street fighting, the "Bloody Week." In the summer of 1871, the hard treaty with Germany was signed and France was again at peace except that an army of occupation remained and would remain until the heavy indemnity should be paid. The most repugnant part of the treaty required the cession of the two provinces of Alsace and Lorraine to the harsh conqueror, who at once proceeded to Germanize them. Ger-man, which was a foreign tongue to many, was made the official language of the courts and the schools. It was this change which gave Alphonse Daudet the setting for a pathetic little story, *La Dernière Classe*, the last French lesson. It is not without meaning to a study of nationalism in educa-tion.

The difficulties of the first days of the Republic were staggering. Twenty-six departments were occupied by German troops, the horrors of the Com-mune were fresh in mind, the public services were disorganized, and party intrigue hampered the new government. The first task was to get the enemy out of the country; and under the leadership of Thiers, the chief executive, this was done so speedily that victor and vanquished were both surprised. The last German soldiers were evacuated in September 1873. The opponents of the Republic hoped to establish a monarchy, but they were divided among themselves and could not agree upon who was to oc-cupy the throne. As Thiers said, "Those who want a monarchy do not want the same monarchy"; and, "There is only one throne but three claimants." The three were a grandson of Charles X, a grandson of Louis Philippe, and the son of Napoleon III. Thiers used his influence in favor of democracy, and by applying the principle of "divide and conquer" he saved the Republic.

The new government adopted the parliamentary system. The President was elected for a fixed term, but the ministry remained in power only while it retained the support of the lower house, the Chamber of Deputies. This was essentially the English system. As a result of this plan, coupled with the unstable party alignments in French politics, the ministries changed frequently. The average term of the Minister of Public Instruction was less than a year. But because the laws did not change with the ministry and since the details of school administration were carried out by permanent civil servants, these changes did not affect the schools as much as one might suppose. The Republicans came into power in the elections of 1878. They celebrated their victory by repealing much restrictive legislation against the freedom of the press, the right to form labor unions, and the right to hold public meetings.

One of the great leaders in the new order was Jules Ferry (1832–1893), who was a member of several ministries and was twice prime minister. The Republicans were especially eager to nationalize primary education, to consolidate the administrative system, and to reform secondary education. As the state was now based upon manhood suffrage, primary education acquired a new importance and the most significant new legislation dealt with the primary schools. A law of 1881 made these schools free; and another law of the next year made attendance compulsory between the ages of six and thirteen and prohibited the teaching of religion. Increased financial support was provided. A law of 1883 required every town and village to erect and maintain public primary schools and, two years later, the government granted state appropriations to support them more adequately. The main laws of this period are often called the "Ferry Laws" after Jules Ferry, the statesman mentioned, who was Minister of Public Instruction from 1879 to 1880 and again in 1882. The educational activity of this creative period was also extended to the normal schools. Each department was required to establish two such schools, one for men and one for women, for the preparation of primary teachers. Two higher normal schools were created at St. Cloud and Fontenay-aux-Roses for the education of teachers of the departmental normal schools, but these have not been as well patronized as it was hoped. Public lycées and collèges for girls were established. The Higher Council of Public Instruction was reconstituted and provision was made for the inspection of the schools. The system of administration of the French schools will be more fully explained below.

The dominating idea of Jules Ferry was that education, especially in a democracy, is a function of the state. "Let it be understood," he said in an address on July 4, 1876, "that the first duty of a democratic government is to exercise control over public education." His nationalism did not go so far as to prohibit private schools, but these were to be subject to state inspection and regulation and he held that any delegated educational power must be revocable at the will of the state.

Such principles were certainly not accepted by the Catholic church, which had been officially recognized by the French state ever since the Concordat of 1801 between Napoleon and the pope. According to that agreement, the state paid the salaries of the clergy in return for the privilege of nominating them for appointment to their positions. The new leaders were now becoming more and more dissatisfied with this century-old settlement of the religious difficulty. The Catholic party had from the beginning opposed the Republic and joined forces with the Monarchists. On the other hand, in 1871 the fiery republican orator, Gambetta, had declared "Clericalism, that is our enemy." Three decades later, Waldeck-Rousseau, the prime minister, declared that the church was a rival power, hostile to the state. He claimed that unauthorized orders of monks and nuns had increased until their membership exceeded a quarter of a million and that they held property in excess of a billion francs. But the most serious element in the situation was their teaching, which he said was hostile to the principles of liberty and equality, the very foundations of the Republic. This was a new version of the argument of La Chalotais in his *Essay on National Education*. Waldeck-Rousseau in 1901 secured the passage of a law which made all religious orders illegal unless they were specifically authorized by Parliament. In 1904 the members of even authorized religious orders were excluded from teaching in public schools, and in the following year, the separation of church and state was made absolute and complete. The French state schools, like the French state, became entirely secular.

This does not mean that private schools were outlawed. It must not be forgotten that France is still a Catholic country and that the private, mainly Catholic, primary schools are still formidable competitors with the public schools. This fact is best exhibited by a few figures. In 1886 out of a total of five and a half million French primary school children nearly two million, or about one-third, attended private schools. In 1906 the proportion had dropped down to about one in five but has again increased. Due to the falling birth rate, the whole number of children in all primary schools dropped from five and a half million in 1886 to less than four million in 1926, a decrease of about thirty per cent. The French call their private schools "free schools," which is to indicate freedom from government control; but they are after all not entirely "free" in this sense. Their teachers, the curriculum, and their textbooks must meet all the state qualifications. They may teach religion, but even the catechisms that are used must be approved by the Minister. As a result, the private schools are largely patterned after the state schools, and set the same examinations.

The following table (from Carlton J. H. Hayes' *France, a Nation of Patriots*) shows the curriculum of the public primary schools.

Table of Studies, Primary Schools, 1938
(hours per week)

	Ages			
	6 and 7	8 and 9	10 and 11	12 and 13
MORALS AND CIVICS	1¼	1¼	1¼	1½
READING FRENCH	10	7	3	2½
WRITING FRENCH	5	2½	1½	¾
LANGUAGE STUDY		5	7½	7½
FRENCH HISTORY AND GEOGRAPHY	2½	2½	3	3
FRENCH SONGS	1¼	1	1	1
PHYSICAL AND MILITARY EXERCISES	1¾	2	2	2
MATHEMATICS	2½	3½	4½	5
SCIENCE	1¼	1½	2½	2½
DESIGN	1	1	1	1
MANUAL TRAINING	1½	1	1	1½
GAMES	2	1¾	1¾	1¾
	30	30	30	30

6. THE UNIVERSITY OF FRANCE

The organization of education in France is of particular interest to citizens of other democracies because it is so highly centralized in comparison with their agencies of control. The present description applies to conditions as they were under the Third Republic. The President of the Republic appointed a Minister of Public Instruction and Fine Arts as a member of his Cabinet. He was a member of Parliament, qualified to address either House, initiate educational legislation, prepare the budget, and issue regulations within the law. Because he was responsible for educational policy and had many legislative and ceremonial duties, he did not concern himself with details and this limited the powers with which he was legally and theoretically invested. The actual work of administration was carried on by a permanent civil service staff organized in four divisions: higher education, secondary education, primary education including higher primary and teacher education, and finance. There were also two sections which dealt with physical education and vocational education. This staff further served to limit the actual exercise of ministerial power. And the Higher Council of Public Instruction formed a third limiting factor. The members of the Council represented the several branches of education and the larger number were elected by their colleagues in the teaching profession. The advice of the Council on such subjects as courses of study, methods, examinations, textbooks, and supervisors was regularly given and almost always followed, though there have been exceptions. There was also a Consultative Committee which dealt especially with appointments and promotions. And there was, lastly, a staff of twelve national inspectors who supervised the field inspectors and reported on the conditions of education throughout the country. The general effect of this distribution of functions was that the several parts of the central organization served as checks upon each other and that each function was carried out by experts in the field.

The remainder of the system was largely an extension of the same pattern to the subdivisions of the country. For educational administration only, all France including Algiers was divided into seventeen academies. At the head of each was a Rector appointed by the President. He was responsible for the whole educational system of his academy, but in practice he dealt mainly with the university, the secondary schools, and the normal schools. An Academic Council advised the Rector, and a group of inspectors supervised schools and reported upon their work. Actually, the academy inspectors dealt mainly with the secondary schools. Another group of primary school inspectors dealt similarly with that level of education. They made recommendations on appointments, discipline, attendance, buildings, and similar matters.

In each of the ninety departments, the prefect was the head of the primary school system. He was aided by an elected departmental council. With their advice he appointed or transferred teachers, supervised expenditures, and located schools. The departments provided the normal school buildings and contributed to the salaries of the primary inspectors and the cost of education in the commune.

There are in France, as we have said, about thirty-seven thousand communes or townships. Each was administered by a mayor and a council, but except to supervise the school buildings, maintain a school census, and encourage attendance, there was little left for them to do. The communes had no authority over the teacher of the area. The system was nearly as national and centralized as possible. There was no opportunity for direct action or influence or even representation of the people themselves.

This is the nature of the University of France. First established by Napoleon I, re-established and clothed with autocratic powers by his nephew Napoleon III, taken over by the Third Republic and equipped with various "checks and balances," it has been the prevailing system of school administration in France through most of the nineteenth century and down to 1940. The French believe that education should be national and should be administered by experts and not by laymen who would represent either the local community or the people at large. The French are noted for orderly organization and for the clear definition of the functions of officials and institutions, and the University of France reflects French character or at least the character of the French intellectual classes. The American system, on the contrary, reflects our localism, our individualism, our regard for the wishes of the parents and the pupils, and our feeling that government should not interfere more than is necessary in social and educational matters. Our schools began as local and private institutions and, although centralization has made great progress in the last hundred years, the schools are still close to the local community. Under the laws of the states, the cities, counties, or other districts, each headed by one of our one hundred twenty-seven thousand American school boards, directly elected by the people, still control our schools. There is no greater contrast in the field of educational administration than that between France and the United States. Even in France there has been opposition to the uniformity of the system and a demand has been voiced that local and community interests should be considered. An organization of reformers, called *Les Compagnons de l'Université Nouvelle*, favored greater adaptation of the schools to local and individual needs but, as shown below, without marked success.

7. SECONDARY SCHOOL REFORMS

We should recall that the French system is a dual scheme of primary and higher primary schools, for those pupils who have no intention of attending or at least no opportunity to attend a university, and of secondary schools for those who are to be prepared for university entrance although not all do in fact enter. By the age of eleven the matter has to be decided, for at that age secondary studies proper begin. Two characteristics of French secondary education must also be singled out for special mention. Ever since the Renaissance it has been strongly classical; and it has been devoted to the preparation of a relatively small class of intellectual leaders and to the maintenance of a high level of culture.

Criticism of both of these features began to appear long before the Revolution. In the opening pages of his *Émile*, Rousseau referred to the "ridiculous colleges" of his time and, except for the contemptuous tone of his reference, he merely repeated what Descartes and the Abbé Fleury had said before. La Chalotais attacked not only the Jesuit control of the schools but also the absence of French, modern languages, science, and industry from the program of studies. Five years later Rolland proposed a state system of secondary schools which were to give attention to the history and language of the French nation and people, and to include also modern languages, mathematics, and physical education. The authors of the cahiers of 1789 and Talleyrand, Condorcet, and others favored and attempted to introduce similar changes. An unsuccessful effort to do this was made through the decree of 1852 which established a common course of three years to be followed by two parallel series of studies, the one classical, the other scientific. Each was to lead to the university. But such a program was only actually achieved in 1902. Within a decade the compromise of 1852 with the modern, practical world was again abandoned because it did not really meet the demands of that world. It merely directed toward the university a group less well prepared than the graduates of the classical course to do what the conservative higher schools required. The reform had gone too far for the classicists and not far enough to prepare for business, industry, or agriculture.

The demand for reform did not grow less, meanwhile, but instead was fast becoming irresistible. "Authority does all that can be done in favor of the old classical training," said Matthew Arnold after a study of secondary education on the continent. "Ministers of state sing its praises. Still in the body of society there spreads a growing disbelief in Greek and Latin, at any rate as at present taught, a growing disposition to make the modern languages and the natural sciences take their place." This was a correct analysis of public opinion. The demand for reform came from the lower and middle classes, not from the secondary teachers or the "ministers of state." But at this point the demand for reform struck a second snag. For centuries the French secondary schools had been not only classical but also highly selective and devoted to the preparation of an intellectual elite. The people themselves were now asking to be allowed to share directly in the benefits of this education.

Under the Third Republic six successive reforms of the curriculum were undertaken. Since all of these turned upon the question of the classics versus the modern subjects, it will be possible to deal with them somewhat generally without going into the details of each one. Jules Simon, Minister of Public Instruction under Thiers, increased the time given to modern language and reduced the amount of grammar and composition in the classical studies in favor of a broader reading program. "Modern languages," he held, "are to be spoken and dead languages to be read." This lasted about three years. Jules Ferry, in the important reform of 1880, made a radically different attack. He postponed the beginning of Latin by several years in order to make it possible for pupils from primary schools to enter the secondary schools later; and he also increased the attention given to the sciences. The time of the special classes in modern subjects which were taught in some of the lycées and collèges was increased from three to four and even to five years; but these classes were not part of secondary education proper. These efforts were, however, made to increase the opportunities of the common people.

The Ribot Commission of 1898 was appointed to study the whole question of secondary education. It concluded that the classical tradition should be maintained and even strengthened. But to do this it was declared essential that only suitable pupils, those with linguistic ability, should be enrolled in the classical courses and that a parallel modern course with equal rights and privileges should be set up. This was done in the reform of 1902. The new scheme provided for four sections of seven years, from the age of eleven to that of eighteen, in all full secondary schools. These may be designated as Latin-Greek, Latin-modern languages, Latin-scientific, and modern languages-scientific. Each of these, when successfully completed, led to the university. In all sections great attention was given to the study of the mother tongue. Modern foreign languages were to be taught by direct methods and in Latin the emphasis was to be placed upon reading and literature rather than grammar. Thus in 1902 the modern subjects won their long struggle for equal treatment and recognition in comparison with the classics. They did not succeed in winning equal prestige among the French people.

There was after all some question about the conclusiveness of the victory. It will be noticed that three of the four parallel courses included Latin and two included or might include Greek also. Only one had no classical requirement but this one did give all the rights and privileges of university admission. Except for the abortive attempt of Minister Bérard in 1923 to bring back compulsory Latin and Greek, the reform of 1902 stood until 1925. It was not satisfactory to all classes or perhaps to any in all respects. One of the most valid criticisms of the scheme was that it required a too early and too complete specialization, that the classical student did not get enough scientific and the scientific student did not get enough literary education. The reform of 1925 attempted to remedy this. The studies required of all secondary students by this act may be best exhibited in the following table, which is taken from Carleton J. H. Hayes' *France, a Nation of Patriots.*

Table of Studies Common to All Pupils in Boys Secondary Schools (1931) (hours per week)

	VI	V	IV	III	II	I
			Year			
FRENCH	4	4	3	4	3	3½
HISTORY	1½	1½		2	2	
GEOGRAPHY	1	1	3½	1	1	3½
MODERN LANGUAGE	3	3	3	3	1½	1½
MATHEMATICS	2	2	3	3	4	3½
NATURAL SCIENCE	1½	1½	1	1		
PHYSICS AND CHEMISTRY					3	4
DRAWING	2	2	1½	1		
ART				½		
	15	15	15	15½	14½	16

But the table shows only a part of the requirements. The boys took six or seven additional hours per week in language and literature. For this work they were divided into three groups, according as they elected to study Latin and Greek, Latin and a modern foreign language, or two modern languages. For the seventh and final year all the boys were divided into two sections, a philosophy section and a mathematics section. In the former they studied principally philosophy, history, and literary subjects, and in the other, principally mathematics and the sciences. The total program involved twenty-one hours of class work in each week in the early years and twenty-three to twenty-five in the later years of the course. There were also private secondary schools, but their curricula and work were very similar to those of the public ones. Boys, whether from private or public schools, had to pass the same state examinations for "graduation" and again later when, as men, they wished to be allowed to practice their profession.

Until within our own generation, secondary education in France remained a privilege of the ruling and the upper middle classes. And, since secondary education provided the only avenue to the university, the same statement applies to higher education. France carried on two separate school systems within one centralized administration, a primary system for the millions and a secondary-higher system for the elite, though there were scholarships for the brilliant among the poor.

In World War I, the *Compagnons de l'Université Nouvelle* was formed to secure for all classes of children the privileges which had been restricted to a few. They succeeded in 1925 in establishing the *école unique* or common school on the elementary level although only in a few towns. Preparatory classes for secondary schools continued to exist, but fees were gradually abolished and children were admitted from the *école unique*. In 1933 the number of scholarships in the secondary schools was increased and fees were abolished. But with few and unimportant exceptions the curricula remained as they had been. The reform had not gone far enough. It had opened the secondary-higher education to many poor and brilliant children but it had not diversified the offerings. Secondary and higher education still led only to the professions and the professions were already overcrowded.

When Jean Zay became Minister of Education in the middle thirties an attempt was made to correct this condition. He proposed to develop technical and industrial schools on secondary and higher levels to enable large numbers of young people, excluded from the professional and purely intellectual fields, to serve France in practical vocations and to provide means for personal advancement. He realized that a democracy must provide opportunity for all kinds of abilities. Guidance classes were established in the secondary schools and handicrafts and extracurricular activities were introduced, but the war in 1939 stopped all these efforts to make French education more fully democratic.

8. FRENCH NATIONALISM AND EDUCATION

Devotion to the nation and the state is always, in any country, a product of the contemporary culture. It is not inherited. It can be transmitted only as the knowledge of arithmetic is transmitted, by teaching each generation and individual; but, unlike arithmetic, it is not a matter of knowledge and skill only but of a knowledge that is highly charged with emotion. Love of country is a fit and frequent theme of story, poem, and drama, and it is taught not only in set lessons but also through popular works of literature and history, through songs, ballads, slogans, national holidays and ceremonials, by service in the army and the offices of the government, and through the activities of patriotic societies and deliberate propaganda of many kinds. Many of these means are employed in schools. Competent students have reported their conclusion that the French people were more nationalistic than most of their neighbors but this is a view that in the nature of the case cannot be demonstrated. Certainly this love of France was not able to produce unity in politics and national policy. It will, nevertheless, be useful to see how the schools contributed to French nationalism.

The national system of primary schools brought about one result, at least. The schools taught nearly everyone to read and write the national language. Illiteracy is a word of various meanings but, if it means some ability to read and write, then illiteracy in France was reduced from forty per cent in 1850 to about three per cent in 1940. The schools did their utmost to bring about this result. No nation has given more, or more careful, attention to the teaching of its national language. Since about 1880 French primary school children have received about thirty hours of instruction per week, and two-fifths of this time has been given to language instruction, to the reading, writing, and study of French. But there were also pockets of non-French nationalists who resisted these efforts of the schools. There were the Germans of Alsace, which had been returned to France after World War I, the Basques north of the Pyrenees, and the Bretons of the northwest. The autonomist movement in Brittany was at first purely cultural in character. A group of loyal Bretons agitated for the preservation of their ancient language and for its cultivation in the schools. Before the outbreak of the war in 1939, each of these three regions became centers of anti-French propaganda.

Not only the language instruction but also the history, geography, civics, and the French songs were made vehicles of nationalist influence. Nearly all the history taught in the primary schools was French history and almost all the heroes who were held up for admiration by the children in the lower grades were French heroes. Columbus, Franklin, and Livingstone were included and may seem to be exceptions and the only exceptions; and of these, Franklin as United States Ambassador was the friend and idol of France and Livingstone was the explorer of the African continent where France's most extensive colonial possessions lie. This leaves Columbus who discovered America, which was once the seat of a great French empire and is still the home of many who speak French. The history textbooks, including those used in Catholic schools, were all approved by the Ministry of Public Instruction and were so far official. Not all of them were equally nationalist but in the main they taught that the glory of France had been dearly bought and that all her children should early learn to love her and to sacrifice for her so that she might continue to hold her position in the world as the leader and champion of civilization. Except for the claim in this last clause this seems to be a reasonable patriotism.

Patriotism was also one of the main topics in the books on morals and citizenship, and many of the school songs were patriotic and nationalist in character. As early as 1883 the Minister of Public Instruction issued a circular on the then new branch of civics. He urged the teachers to teach it in a simple and concrete way through examples and illustrations. The children were to be taught good habits, respectful manners, and such virtues as obedience and loyalty in the home and school. The personal virtues of cleanliness, honesty, temperance, were extolled and the dangers of alcoholism were explained. The religious teachings were to be such only as would not offend the leading faiths, the Catholic, the Protestant, and the Jewish, that is, they were to be general and nondoctrinal. There were also lessons on the greatness of France and her claims upon the youth. A wide variety of books written on these lines was prepared. They generally stressed French nationality, the republican government, and the duties of the citizen to the nation. The necessity for a large army was explained and the children were taught that it would be their duty to pay taxes for its support and for the security which it would provide.

Both the history and civics books in later times went much farther. The wrongs of France in the war and peace of 1870 and 1871 came to be emphasized and a hatred against Germany was sometimes instilled. This tendency was greatly increased by World War I. Many of the newer books taught that Germany had deliberately caused the war and had waged it in a barbarous manner. The largest of the teachers' associations of France defended this account of the war. In a statement on the question of chauvinistic teaching which they made in 1927, the teachers declared that

Germany, without question, had wanted, prepared for, and begun the war and had indulged in barbarities and atrocities as long as she thought that she could win. Not all French teachers agreed with this verdict and the government itself on several occasions undertook to discourage chauvinism in the schools. But patriotic societies and some of the influential newspapers, including *Le Temps*, denounced all attempts to moderate the language of the textbooks as "school pacifism." The table on page 306 shows that from one-half to two-thirds of the work of the primary schools was admirably adapted to promote nationalism. And, while this cannot be in equal degree asserted of the secondary curricula, the product of these schools, the secondary school *bacheliers*, were even more nationalist than the average French citizen.

The effect of the teaching should be examined from a broader standpoint. Nationalism was not enough. While the school system helped to unite the people in their admiration for their language, history, and culture, it did not sufficiently unite them in other respects. The conditions in France preceding the disaster of 1940 would embarrass anyone who should assert the irrefragable unity of the nation. There were numerous groups and parties, communist, fascist, industrial, proletarian, Catholic, royalist, socialist, and republican, which in the latter years of the Third Republic fought with each other for control. Most of them were ready to shout for the *gloire de la belle France* but each of them wanted a different France. After 1936, the Republic was further undermined by a vicious German propaganda supported by Berlin and directed from Paris itself. Nationalist the French people were; but they were not united in support of their government.

The French school system will always be a profitable subject of study and especially so for those who live under so different a plan and organization as do the Americans and the English. From the foregoing it is evident that France did not have any profound influence upon American education. Particular institutions, such as Jefferson's university plan, several military and engineering schools, schools for the blind, deaf, and mentally defective, and certain devices such as the Binet tests have been borrowed or modeled upon French antecedents. But in school administration, in contrast with the French policy of central control, we began at the other extreme, with the local community, and we have not yet attained any very high degree of centralization. From the next country to be studied, Germany, we have borrowed a great deal more.

Before the rise of nationalism, schools were usually conducted either by private or by church agencies. The imperial and municipal schools of the Roman empire form only apparent exceptions, for they were not controlled by the state or specifically intended to promote its interests. In the later Middle Ages and after the Reformation, newly founded municipal schools became numerous and state activity became pronounced; but only in the last two centuries have the great national states created public schools for the education of all. Since the French Revolution had the most far-reaching effects in spreading an aggressive nationalism, we have considered the French national school system first of all.

To reduce the theoretical educational proposals of the French Revolution to practical form and to incorporate them in the political system of France required almost a century. Napoleon outlined the administrative system, the University of France; the government of Louis Philippe laid the foundations of primary education; and in the Third Republic, primary, secondary, and higher education became secular and nationalistic, well supported and efficient, and centralized in administration. Both primary and secondary education became free and the former became practically universal. The French schools have become especially effective in teaching the national language; and also in instilling nationalistic sentiment. The French child learns to write well and to believe in French culture and its civilizing value to Europe and the world. France is a Latin country and its secondary schools tend to emphasize classical education. An elaborate system of public professional schools for teachers has been developed. With all these public provisions, one-fourth of the primary and two-fifths of the secondary school pupils attend private, usually Roman Catholic, schools; but these are also required to meet state standards.

Although the schools and other institutions of France succeeded in developing a strongly nationalist sentiment, this was not able to prevent internal disunity or to repel foreign propaganda in the years before 1940.

QUESTIONS

1. Why has nationalism become strong and aggressive in recent times, when it was almost unknown in earlier days? Consider changes in economic conditions, in modes of communication, in science, invention, and the conduct of war, and the complementary effects of nationalism and education upon each other.
2. Why is French educational control highly centralized?
3. Why was it logical for the July Monarchy to develop primary and higher primary schools?
4. Compare the meaning of the phrase "secondary education" as this term is used in France and in the United States.
5. Why were the French primary school teachers more likely to be politically liberal than secondary school teachers?
6. Compare the plan of Condorcet with the system developed by the Third Republic.
7. Why would a unitary (ladder) system be more appropriate for a republic than the parallel system which France retained after 1870?
8. What objections do you see to an administrative organization such as the University of France? What advantages may it have?
9. Does French education seem more nationalistic than American education? If you think it is, how may this be explained?

FOR FURTHER READING AND STUDY

The present chapter and the following list deal in the main with education in France since the eighteenth century but a few works on the history of nationalism are included. In the brief introduction to his *French Liberalism and Education*, La Fontainerie contributes important information on conditions before the Revolution; and if to the four documents which he has translated we add the *Émile* we shall have the materials for a fair understanding of educational thought in the *Ancien Régime* and the Revolution. The *Yearbooks of the International Institute* are essential for the period between the two World Wars.

Allain, Ernest, *L'instruction primaire en France avant la Révolution*, Paris, Société Bibliographique, 1881, 304 pp.

Autin, Albert, *L'École Unique*, Paris, Librairie Felix Alcan, 1933, 158 pp.

Barnard, Howard C., *The French Tradition in Education. Ramus to Mme. Necker de Saussure*, Cambridge, University Press, 1922, 319 pp.

Brown, Rollo Walter, *How the French Boy Learns to Write; a Study in the Teaching of the Mother Tongue*, Cambridge, Harvard University Press, 1915, 260 pp.

Buisson, Ferdinand, *Dictionnaire de Pédagogie et d'Instruction Primaire*, Paris, Hachette et Cie., 1880–1887, 4 vols.; *French Educational Ideals of Today; an Anthology*, Yonkers-on-Hudson, N. Y., World Book Company, 1919, 326 pp.

Compayre, Gabriel, *The History of Pedagogy*. Translated and edited by W. H. Payne, Boston, D. C. Heath and Company, 1891, 598 pp.; *Histoire Critique des Doctrines de l'éducation en France*, Paris, Hachette et Cie., 1911, 2 vols.

Dickinson, G. Lowes, *Revolution and Reaction in Modern France*, London, George Allen, 1892, 300 pp.

Farrington, Frederic E., *The Public Primary System of France*, New York, Teachers College, Columbia University, 1906, 303 pp.; *French Secondary Schools; an Account of the Origin, Development, and Present Organization of Secondary Education in France*, New York, Longmans, Green and Company, 1910, 450 pp.

Gay, P., and O. Montreux, *French Elementary Schools: Official Courses of Study*. With an introduction by I. L. Kandel, New York, Teachers College, Columbia University, 1926, 270 pp.

Hassall, Arthur, *Louis XIV and the Zenith of the French Monarchy*, New York, G. P. Putnam's Sons, 1925, 444 pp.

Hayes, Carleton J. H., *Essays on Nationalism*, New York, The Macmillan Company, 1926, 279 pp.; *France, a Nation of Patriots*, New York, Columbia University Press, 1930, 487 pp.; *The Historical Evolution of Modern Nationalism*, New York, Richard R. Smith, 1931, 327 pp. The second work above is an important study of nationalist education as conducted by schools and other agencies.

Huddleston, Sisley, *France*, New York, Charles Scribner's Sons, 1927, 613 pp.

Hyslop, Beatrice Fry, *French Nationalism in 1789, According to General Cahiers*, New York, Columbia University Press, 1934, 343 pp.

Kandel, Isaac L., *The Reform of Secondary Education in France*, New York, Teachers College, Columbia University, 1924, 159 pp.; *Comparative Education*, Boston, Houghton Mifflin Company, 1932, 922 pp.; *History of Secondary Education*, Boston, Houghton Mifflin Company, 1930, 577 pp.; Editor, *Educational Yearbook of the International Institute of Teachers College, Columbia University*, New York, Teachers College, Columbia University, 1934, 564 pp. Under the title "The Educational System of France," this contains (pp. 1–290) a translation of the *Atlas de l'Enseignement en France*, prepared by the *Commission française pour l'Enquete Carnegie sur les Examens et Concours en France*. It has an extensive bibliography. The *Yearbook* has been published annually since 1924 and each volume to and including that for 1932 contains material on French education. See especially the volumes for 1929 and 1930.

La Fontainerie, François de, *French Liberalism and Education in the Eighteenth Century; the Writings of La Chalotais, Turgot, Diderot, and Condorcet on National Education*, New York, McGraw-Hill Book Company, Inc., 1932, 385 pp.

Reisner, Edward H., *Education and Nationalism since 1789*, New York, The Macmillan Company, 1922, 575 pp.

Walsh, Henry H., *The Concordat of 1801: a Study in the Problem of Nationalism in the Relations of Church and State*, New York, Columbia University Press, 1933, 259 pp.

14 NATIONAL TRENDS IN GERMAN EDUCATION

THE HISTORY OF GERMANY PROVIDES THE MATERIAL FOR A second study of the national trends which characterize education today. That country was a loose confederation of states until Bismarck welded them into an empire but even then the states retained their autonomy in education. Complete unification and subordination resulted when the National Socialist party came into power in 1933.

After the Reformation, each state gradually developed its own school system; but the church, the Lutheran state church in the north and the Catholic church in Bavaria and the south, remained strongly entrenched in educational matters. Cooperation between state and church marked the earlier systems but the actual management of the schools long remained in the hands of the clergy, who did not favor strong civil control of education and who were in intimate contact with the people.

1. IN THE EIGHTEENTH CENTURY

Although the Reformation inspired the organization of elementary schools, it was the eighteenth century, and partly the influence of Frederick the Great, which laid the foundations of the Prussian and other state systems that were later held up for our admiration. Compulsory attendance had been proposed by Luther and was enacted into law in Weimar in 1619 and a century later Frederick William I of Prussia issued an order requiring attendance at school. His son, Frederick the Great, in 1763 prescribed a detailed Regulation for rural schools. This decree marked an educational milestone. Compulsory attendance from the age of five to fourteen was ordered and arrangements were made to relieve the poor from excessive financial burdens. The school year, the hours of the school day, and the curriculum were fixed. Supervision was prescribed but was left in the hands of the clergy. There were other difficulties. Funds and means of enforcement were lacking. Similar but somewhat broader regulations covering the urban schools also were made for Catholic Silesia. And a parallel code for normal, secondary, and elementary schools in Austria was prepared by J. E. Felbiger (1724–1788), who had been appointed minister of education by Maria Theresa. The "normal schools" were model practice schools in which teachers were to be prepared.

Prussia took further measures in the eighteenth century. A national board of education or *Oberschulkollegium* was instituted in 1787. The Prussian code of 1794 included the principle of state control of education, declared schools to be state institutions, and established local school committees. Supervision was still left to the clergy and even the members of the *Oberschulkollegium* were taken from the same profession. No religious discrimination was to be permitted. But these advanced measures were mere paper reforms. Frederick the Great had revealed his real intention when he said that "in country places a little reading and writing will be enough, for if the peasants learn too much they will want to move into town and become clerks." The schools were not much improved and this explains why neighboring countries paid so little attention to Prussian education until the next century. When progress began in earnest, not only in the law books but in the actual schools, Victor Cousin of France, Henry Brougham of England, and Alexander Bache, C. E. Stowe, and Horace Mann of the United States made the world acquainted with the new developments.

The eighteenth century was the period of the "benevolent despots," Frederick the Great, Catherine II of Russia, and Maria Theresa and Joseph II of Austria. They all understood the educational strategy of autocracy which is based upon the cynical observation that highly educated officials do not easily become revolutionaries but that to educate the poor spells danger. Frederick the Great, like Napoleon after him, was most interested in the education of leaders. He reformed the old knightly academies, a task which he committed to J. G. Sulzer, and, also, the classical gymnasiums. Upon the advice of Frederick Gedike (1755–1803), the gymnasial leaving certificate was introduced. This certificate, which was granted after a comprehensive examination and which admitted its holders directly to the university, raised the level of instruction and guaranteed its quality. The measure had far-reaching effects upon both the gymnasium and the university.

If the government had provided financial support, the lower schools also might have been improved. Under existing conditions, reform in elementary education often depended upon the initiative of humanitarian landlords. Such a landlord was Eberhard von Rochow (1734–1805). In the preface to his *School-Book for Country Children* he said: "I live among country people and I pity them for the wretchedness of their condition and their ignorance and prejudices. They neither know how to make good use of what they possess nor how to give up cheerfully what they lack. They are not at peace with either God or king." This condition he ascribed to defective education. On his estate he demanded and attempted to supply educated teachers, good buildings, and adequate salaries, and set up a curriculum that included arithmetic, nature study, letter writing, and enlightened religious teaching. He was personally acquainted with Basedow and accepted his aims of happiness, utility, and reasonableness and his principle that schools should be public institutions. His reforms and ideas did not spread and the effort to introduce them in Brunswick in 1786, with J. H. Campe as superintendent, was wrecked by the opposition of the clergy and nobles. The ideas of Basedow and the Enlightenment were adopted in private schools and affected national education when it actively developed in the Napoleonic era. The real beginnings of modern public education must be placed in the nineteenth rather than the eighteenth century, and only a generation before similar measures were taken in France and the United States.

2. BIRTH OF THE FATHERLAND

Napoleon routed the German armies in the battles of Jena and Auerstedt in October 1806, while Hegel, with the thunder of the guns in his ears, continued to write his philosophy. The incident may be taken to mark the lack of nationalist feeling of the greatest Germans then living, Hegel, Goethe, Beethoven, and others. Nine months after the defeat, France imposed the severe peace of Tilsit upon the humiliated Germans. Prussia lost vast territories, assumed a heavy indemnity purposely left indefinite, and agreed to support the armies of occupation and to limit her own army to forty-two thousand men. When Napoleon later needed soldiers for the Spanish campaign he was compelled, fortunately for Prussia, to withdraw many regiments from the occupied areas.

The defeat and the drastic peace treaty aroused the patriotism of the Germans. Fichte, who in his lectures of 1805 had declared himself a citizen of the world, now became a nationalist. His *Addresses to the German Nation*, delivered while French soldiers patrolled the streets of Berlin, were a call to regeneration and as one means he recommended a Pestalozzian education. It might be easy to overemphasize the influence of Fichte but not of these ideas which many held in common with him. Within eight years after Tilsit, the allies were in Paris and Napoleon was on his way to St. Helena.

The German Fatherland was a creation of the youth under the lead of von Stein, Hardenberg, Scharnhorst, and Gneisenau. The collapse had revealed the fault of the state to von Stein: it was built from the top downwards. He saw new forces arising from below, from the common people, and he turned to them. If the state could develop and enlist their talents, it would become invincible. This was von Stein's program for the regeneration of the nation: "To bind everyone to the State by conviction, sympathy, and cooperation in the affairs of the nation, to give the forces of the nation free play and direct them towards the common good." And if this sounds like the voice of revolutionary France, the answer is that von Stein was not deaf. Nor were the principles of the French Revolution altogether French or new. Government by the people was a principle of Calvinism that had been asserted in the English Commonwealth, the English Revolution of 1688, and the American Revolution of 1776.

The first law of von Stein freed the serfs and he attempted to provide land for the peasants. Civil rights were promoted and internal improvements were begun. When the French secured von Stein's dismissal, Hardenberg carried on. He abolished gild monopolies and developed commercial freedom and he annulled the restrictions on the Jews. Scharnhorst created a citizen army by evading Napoleon's limits upon its numbers. Greater than any specific measures was the moral renewal of the nation.

The political and social reforms implied educational reforms and of this the leaders were well aware. Education, said von Stein, must develop love of country, of fellow-men, and God, and must avoid all merely decorative, borrowed, artificial culture. Such an education, the Pestalozzian, was waiting to be adopted and it was in this period that Pestalozzi's ideas became fruitful in Germany. Ernst Moritz Arndt (1769–1846), the patriotic writer, was to some extent a disciple of Rousseau and Pestalozzi. Friedrich Ludwig Jahn (1778–1852) was the founder of a propagandist German physical education. He was at this time a teacher in Plamann's Pestalozzian school in Berlin, as was Froebel. Eighty-four gymnasiums of the Jahn type were established in Prussia and most of the young men who attended them enlisted in the War of Liberation.

The reorganization of the central educational administration and the founding of the University of Berlin testify to Prussian concern for education. The old *Oberschulkollegium*, a sleepy and reactionary body, was abolished and a new bureau was set up in 1808 as a division of the Ministry of the Interior. William von Humboldt (1767–1835) was the first chief of the division. He was a scholar whose appointment to a government post was about as remarkable as that of Henry Barnard to a similar position at Washington in 1867. With others, Humboldt organized the University of Berlin. He secured for Prussian students the right to study

at non-Prussian universities, introduced a state examination for all prospective secondary school teachers, and reformed the gymnasium on a
more thoroughly humanistic plan.

3. FOUNDERS OF SCHOOLS FOR THE COMMON PEOPLE

The greatest changes in education occurred in the elementary schools.
Prussia in the north and Bavaria in the south were the leaders, but all
states became active. Two of the officials in the Prussian bureau of education were G. H. L. Nicolovius (1767–1839) and J. W. Süvern (1775–
1829). Nicolovius met the young Pestalozzi while he was still at Neuhof
and wrote: "I have made the acquaintance of a man who is really a man,
Henry Pestalozzi, the author of *Leonard and Gertrude*." The great Swiss
was equally drawn to the young visitor. Upon returning home, Nicolovius
was advised by the philosopher, Kant, to devote himself to education and
to aid in adapting the schools to the new needs of the nation and people.
Nicolovius and Süvern were able to persuade the government to send young
men to study with Pestalozzi, expenses paid, in order that they might
acquire a similar zeal for the education of the common people. These young
men, when they returned, became the nucleus of a corps of Pestalozzian
teachers. Pupils of Pestalozzi were put in charge of seminaries for teachers. One of these was Karl A. Zeller (1774–1840) who, as principal of the
teachers' seminary in Königsberg, educated hundreds of young elementary
teachers. Another great leader was William Harnisch (1787–1864) who
had come into intimate contact with Jahn in Plamann's Institute in Berlin. He published his first work, *Schools for the People, on Pestalozzian
Principles*, in 1812. "I have been inspired," he wrote, "by the ideal of a
popular education for the development of a community which shall include the whole nation and all the people." Because no one else has written
on this subject, therefore, he declared, "I write upon it." Jahn found him
a kindred spirit and Walt Whitman, if he could have known him, would
have acclaimed him.

His book made Harnisch, at twenty-five, head of the teachers' seminary
at Breslau, but officialdom and the aristocracy did not share his views.
When the reaction caught up with him, the *Turnplatz* which he had
opened was closed, his nature study excursions were suspended, and he
was moved to another seminary at Weissenfels which he also made into a
model institution. It was this second seminary which he directed that was
visited and praised by Bache and by Stowe from the United States. During
the next period of reaction in 1840, he was permanently retired. His influence was continued by his writings and by the teachers' association he
had founded at Breslau.

The extension of the Prussian-Pestalozzian system was largely due to the one who gave it this name, F. A. W. Diesterweg (1790–1866). Diesterweg was a teacher and successively director of two teachers' seminaries, but it was as a liberal educational publicist and a champion of the common schools and their teachers that he was most significant. He campaigned for improved teacher education and for better salaries, and he organized educational associations, directed conferences, delivered speeches, and conducted institutes. He fought for professional and against clerical administration, and opposed the teaching of sectarian religion in the schools. On these latter points he had against him the full weight of the church, the government, and the Holy Alliance. In his later years he made the acquaintance of Froebel and became a promoter of the kindergarten. His services to Froebel were of doubtful value because he was suspected of socialism and the Prussian bureaucracy retired him. Even then he was not completely silenced for he continued to write and speak for the cause of broader and freer education.

The success of the new schools was retarded by the opposition of the officials, the clergy, and the landlords who had the legal privilege of selecting the teachers of schools on their estates. We have incidentally referred to several waves of reaction. The first came in 1819, the year when Süvern proposed an education law that outlined a ladder system which would have opened the way for even peasants' sons to pass through the elementary schools to the gymnasium and into the university. This was the plan of Comenius come to life and shows the height to which educational liberalism rose after the defeat by Napoleon. Such a scheme might have received serious consideration a decade earlier when the government was in desperate straits, but it had no chance after the danger passed and the princes breathed freely again.

4. REVOLUTION AND REACTION

We have seen how liberals such as Harnisch and Diesterweg were moved from one position to another and finally retired from active service during periods of conservatism. We must look a little further into the revolutions of 1813, 1830, and 1848. During the hundred days before Waterloo, the thoroughly frightened Prussian king promised his people a constitution and popular assembly. This pledge was forfeited after Napoleon was interned. A national association of students, the *Burschenschaft*, was founded at Jena in 1815 and chose for its motto, "honor, liberty, and fatherland." Two years later, meeting at the Wartburg to celebrate the third centennial of the Reformation and to claim its liberties for themselves, they burned the writings of a reactionary university professor. But when in 1819 a student killed Kotzebue, the dramatist and journalist, the government seized the opportunity to suppress all student associations and all liberal movements. Teachers charged with liberalism or socialism were thrown into prison. One of the victims was Father Jahn. He was arrested in his child's sickroom and, although the accusations against him could not be proved, he was carried from prison to prison, and shut off from communication with his friends until even his tenacious spirit was broken. The reactionaries were in complete control.

The Greek revolt against Turkey (1821) aroused anew the "liberal conflagration" which had been damped down by the Holy Alliance. Free peoples everywhere sent sympathy and aid. In 1830 the revolution broke out in France and the Bourbons were for the last time driven from the throne. When the storm passed through Germany, many of the princes were compelled to grant constitutions to their people but a few years later some of these were again revoked. When this occurred in Hannover, seven Göttingen professors, including the historians Gervinus and Dahlmann, and the Brothers Grimm, protested against the arbitrary act. All seven were removed by the Duke of Hannover and some were banished. A Prussian cabinet minister declared: "It is not becoming for subjects to judge the actions of the Head of the State by the measure of their limited understanding." This cause célèbre should not be forgotten when we hear of the boasted Lehrfreiheit of the German universities.

Some of the objectives of the liberals in the revolution of 1848 were free speech and a free press, the right of assembly and petition, and popular representation in government. Although the army soon had complete control of the situation, the king was irresolute because he swayed between a romantic desire to be regarded as the father of his people and a firm faith in the divine right of kings. His promises were worth no more than those of his father had been. The common school teachers were in general of peasant or working-class stock and were on the side of freedom; but the common schools had not prepared the people for participation in politics. As a result, there was no cohesion among the liberals and they were unable to work out a plan which the majority would support. Frederick Engels called it "playing at revolution." Much of the social legislation which was proposed in the Frankfort Parliament (1848) was, however, enacted later.

The authorities demanded changes in the work of the elementary schools as early as 1840. In December of that year a beginning was made in the effort to curb liberalism by placing restrictions upon teachers' seminaries. Teachers were not to instil in the children hopes that could not be realized. The schools should emphasize religion, a modest vocation industriously pursued, simplicity, and loyalty. Future teachers were to read only "safe" books. Horace Mann visited Germany in 1843, and the student can read in his *Seventh Report* not only his praise of the schools but also his criticism of the government of that period.

During the revolutionary movement of 1848, the teachers took fresh courage. They attempted to return to the earlier program of Süvern which proposed to frame the lower schools, town schools, gymnasia, and universities into an educational ladder; and they urged the establishment of continuation and infant schools. Nothing came of it at the time. The king appeared before a meeting of the teachers' seminary leaders to threaten and scold. All the misery of Prussia, he said, was due to the false and godless education of these schools. "As long as I hold the sword-hilt in my hand," he boasted, "I shall know how to deal with such a nuisance." The king won; but one suspects that it was after all a somewhat nervous hand that grasped the royal weapon. A new minister, a bureaucrat who knew how to govern by edict and decree, Karl von Raumer, was placed over the schools. He prohibited the circulation of the writings of Diesterweg and Froebel and proscribed the kindergarten in Prussia. In the October Regulations of 1854, he prescribed the curriculum of the teachers' seminaries. Broad cultural education was to be avoided. Educational theory was a powder keg for which school management had to be substituted. The elementary curriculum was to be similarly limited and was to aim at the development of loyal, submissive subjects who were not to have or to expect political influence. Thus it becomes evident that in Prussia each liberal movement was curbed by an autocratic reaction which laid its heavy, repressive hand upon the schools and teachers.

5. THE UNIFICATION OF GERMANY

The unification of the German states, with the exception of Austria, was accomplished through the Franco-Prussian War in 1871, and the king of Prussia became the head of the new German empire. Neither in the violent methods used nor in its outcome was it such a unification as the liberals had proposed. They had worked for a union under a democratic constitution; but the constitution of the empire gave Prussia the controlling voice in foreign affairs, and even in domestic questions the representatives of the people had little power.

The empire was a union of the governments of twenty-six states. Its chief administrator was a chancellor who was responsible only to the emperor and not to parliament. The imperial parliament was composed of two bodies with very unequal powers. The upper house or *Bundesrath* represented the states of the federation and had extensive powers over foreign affairs, the army and navy and the issue of peace and war, and

over commerce and communications. The members were appointed by
the governments and Prussia sent nearly one-third of the whole number,
far more than any other state. Action on important questions including all
constitutional changes could be blocked by fourteen votes and Prussia had
seventeen. Theoretically the *Reichstag*, the lower house, which was elected
by the people, had a veto in legislation, but the efficiency of this was
greatly limited by the condition that the Cabinet, that is, the active government, was not responsible to the people's representatives. It was proposed
during the process of unification to make the Ministry responsible to the
Reichstag. This would have given the people powers similar to those exerted in Britain through the House of Commons; but the princes, governments, and Bismarck would not consent. Since the empire was a federation,
many matters of local concern and internal administration were, as in the
United States, left to the state governments. Education was one of these
political functions which were left to the direction of the separate states.

In her economic and industrial development, Germany in 1870 was
almost a century behind England. It was in 1874 when Queen Victoria
took the title of Empress of India and when England reached out for the
Suez Canal; but in Germany at that time only the first signs of colonial
ambition and the earlier stages of the industrial revolution were to be
observed. Bismarck declared Germany to be "a satiated state," for he
needed peace to consolidate the recent gains. Industry developed with
unexampled rapidity after 1871. The output of coal, a good index, quad-
rupled between 1860 and 1880 and increased to six times the 1860 output
by 1890; and this rate of expansion was maintained for two decades longer.
Within the single year of 1872, nine thousand miles of railroad were under
construction in Prussia alone and, instead of importing it, the rolling
stock was now manufactured within the country. A part of this huge expansion was financed from the indemnity which France was forced to pay
after the war. The chemical and electrical industries showed similar vigor.
The good times were interrupted by a severe business depression, partly
caused by the flow of French gold into Germany. Bismarck declared that
"next time" he would insist upon paying the indemnity instead of receiving it. Although the panic of 1873 brought severe losses and great
disillusionment to workers and capitalists alike, German industry recovered and with few setbacks continued to expand until 1914. This industrial
expansion led to a pronounced and increasing emphasis upon vocational
education.

Administration under the empire was bureaucratic, that is, it was carried out by appointive officials and boards who were not directly responsible to the people. This, taken with the extensive social welfare and relief legislation which was passed, makes it an apt comparison to say that

the policy of the empire was a continuation of the patriarchal and benevolent despotism of Frederick the Great and his contemporaries. An aggressive nationalism developed and led to German colonial expansion and to competition for world markets. And nationalism had important domestic consequences, for it brought the government into conflict with all agencies that competed with it for men's loyalties, and especially with the Catholic church. The Lutheran church, being a state institution, was more amenable to pressure from the government. The struggle, known as the *Kulturkampf*, began about 1850 and was resumed in an intensified form under Hitler, although the same name was not applied. In the earlier phase of this German cultural war, Bismarck secured legislation which drove the Jesuits from Prussia (1872), suppressed the Catholic bureau in the ministry of education, withdrew all schools from church control, and provided for their inspection by qualified, nonclerical officers of the state. These are known as the "May Laws" of 1873. They were given a moderate interpretation. Falk, the minister of education of Prussia, removed only a minority of the clerical inspectors. Ultimately, Bismarck had to give way. When Leo XIII became pope (1878), Bismarck opened negotiations with him and the cultural war ended in a truce with the church.

Nationalism was also attacked from the opposite side by the radical socialists. Although socialism of many kinds had existed for centuries, the Marxian form which developed in Germany in the Bismarckian period was new, vigorous, and hostile to the nation-state and the church as well as to private capital. There were some considerable social evils. Some of these resulted from Bismarck's policies, the hegemony of conservative Prussia, royalism, a strong army not subject to the will of the people, and bureaucratic government; and others, as in all countries, were the evils growing out of the industrial revolution. The factory divided the work of each laborer into the smallest possible fraction and robbed him of all joy in it. Every boom period drew a new labor supply into the towns which enabled the employers to cut wages, increase hours, and employ women and children. Stupefying drudgery and inhuman living conditions in the best times alternated with periods of unemployment when only the soup kitchens barely prevented starvation. There was no adequate provision for illness and old age. These conditions contributed to the development of socialism in Germany. Ferdinand Lassalle (1825–1864), a revolutionary of 1848, founded the Socialist Party; and Karl Marx (1818–1883) promoted the international working-class movement and a somewhat different brand of socialism. In 1875, a fusion was effected; the platform, adopted at Gotha, demanded public ownership and control of industry. The Socialists insisted upon universal suffrage of men and women by secret ballot, a free press, a progressive income tax, health legislation, the prohibition of child labor, and other social reforms. The socialist vote increased rapidly between 1880 and 1890.

Bismarck replied to the socialists with the weapon he had already used against the church, repressive legislation. A murderous attack upon the life of the emperor gave him the needed opportunity. He dissolved the Reichstag; and the newly elected house agreed to a law prohibiting all socialist meetings and publications with severe penalties. Yet the socialist vote kept on increasing in successive elections. Then the attempt was made to draw the teeth of the opposition by extensive social legislation. Old age and disability insurance, government aid in sickness and accidents were voted but without conceding the main point, that the people should have a greater voice in government. The state benevolently relieved distress but its authoritarianism prevented it from securing the loyalty of the laboring class. And the greatly extended social legislation after Bismarck also suffered from the same basic defect.

6. EDUCATION UNDER THE EMPIRE

In educational legislation also the attitude was similarly paternal, cautious, and restrictive. The effort was not to make people critical and independent but on the contrary to make them orderly, vocationally efficient, satisfied with conditions and their position in life, and submissive to the authorities. In vocational education, especially, Germany became a leader. There were already, from 1850 and earlier, a great many local vocational schools and classes and most of the new vocational schools were developed by the towns, the employers, and the local authorities in general, not by the empire or even the states. In the later nineteenth century, the vocational continuation or part-time school for young people who already had jobs became widespread. Even before the formation of the empire, the old North German Confederation made it compulsory for workers under the age of eighteen to attend continuation schools for a specified number of hours a week, and for employers to release them from work for that purpose. This law was retained by the empire.

One defect in the situation was that there was no law requiring the establishment of vocational continuation schools, and even in 1918 about half of the states had only permissive laws on this subject. Where there were no schools with classes in the particular trade in question, the young workers could not, of course, be required to attend. Most localities had some schools but few had so full a complement and so extensive and effective a system as the one developed by Georg Kerschensteiner, about 1898 in the South German city of Munich. Kerschensteiner was one of the leading educators of Europe in the period before World War I. In 1913 he visited and lectured extensively in the United States. Upwards of fifty somewhat distinct trades and vocations, including the commercial vocations, were taught in the public schools of Munich. Besides the trade schools there were others for preparing foremen, superintendents, and personnel workers in general. A second defect of these schemes was that they continued class education.

Meanwhile higher vocational education in science and its applications had an extraordinary development. The universities, beginning with Liebig (1826) or earlier, gave more and more attention to the sciences and, through their emphasis upon research, made many fundamental discoveries. German medical education was world famous and, at a time when our medical schools were undeveloped, they served as examples for the United States. Besides the universities, Germany also had great technological schools in agriculture, engineering, mining, and other applied science fields. The industrial growth and technical competence of Germany rested squarely upon an excellent system of education for the learned vocations and professions.

Teaching in the lower schools was one of the vocations to which special attention was given in the legislation of Prussia and other states. The Prussian general regulations of 1872 dealt with the curriculum of the seminaries in which the future teachers of the elementary schools received their professional and much of their general education. In comparison with the regulations of 1854, these were liberal and enlightened but in making the comparison we must remember that the earlier rescript had been an angry response to the revolution of 1848. Under the regulations of 1872, the reading of the students was broadened to cover general history followed with German history, the classical German literature including such un-Prussian authors as Goethe and Schiller, and the great educational classics. There were courses on logic, psychology, and the history of education. The German language, grammar and composition, were studied thoroughly; and foreign languages, including French, were offered as electives. The work in science and mathematics covered what would be included in a good American high school in these areas. The biology and earth science had a considerable resemblance to general science. Religion, since it was one of the subjects in the common school curriculum, was taught in the teachers' seminaries. Bible history, the gospels, the parables, hymns, and church history were stressed and, while the instruction was less confessional than it had been, the emphasis upon memory work was retained. There is a diverting but unfriendly account of the work of the teachers' seminary in the autobiographical works of the schoolmaster-author, Otto Ernst.

At a later date the curriculum was further extended, but the teachers' seminaries were not made a part of the secondary-higher education of Prussia. Common school teachers were kept a race apart from the higher professional class of society and, except in Saxony, had no opportunity to attend the universities. A boy who wished to teach in the elementary schools was first sent to these schools, then to a seminary for six years and, after a trial year as an assistant, was installed in his own school. Now and then one left this employment to attend the secondary school and the university—Kerschensteiner is an example—but in that case he never returned to the lower schools unless, like Kerschensteiner, he became an administrator.

Until the establishment of the Republic (1918), Germany had a dual system of schools, one path for the common people down in the valley and another on the heights in the bright sunlight for the professional and official classes. This was, evidently, a necessary element in the system of caste and privilege which had been written into the imperial constitution.

One small dent in this armor of the privileged classes was made by the pressures of social democracy. The general regulations of 1872 permitted the erection of a new type of expanded and elevated common school, called the Middle School. While the common schools were entirely free, the Middle Schools charged a tuition fee. The name was doubly appropriate because, educationally, the Middle School occupied an intermediate position between the lower and secondary schools and, socially, it was the school of the lower middle class such as minor officials and retail businessmen. The schools provided for these a more extensive and socially exclusive education than the common schools, but it had other qualities to commend it. The course varied in length from three to nine years. In the former case, children transferred to it after a certain number of years in the common schools. In the upper years of the Middle School courses, work more advanced than that of the lower schools and, in particular, English, French, and Latin, was offered. It was this which made possible the pupils' transfer from a middle to a secondary school and thence to the university. Few took this path, so difficult for the children of the poorer classes; but boys who completed the full Middle School course, having studied two foreign languages, got off with one year in the army and had access to skilled and semiprofessional occupations. These schools were found only in larger cities and before 1914 about one child in twenty-five in Prussia attended a Middle School.

By the end of the nineteenth century, three types of secondary schools had been developed. All were boys' schools although there were also comparable schools, much fewer in number, for girls. Coeducation on the secondary level was practically unknown in nineteenth-century Germany.

Each of the boys' schools had a nine-year course and their graduates were admitted to the university without examination. The oldest type was the *Gymnasium*, an early example of which was established by John Sturm in 1538. We have seen that Humboldt had helped to standardize this type in the second decade of the century through a leaving examination and certificate. A second type was the *Realgymnasium*, a Latin-scientific school which in some cases taught Greek as an elective, never as a required subject. The time saved by the omission of Greek was given to modern foreign languages. The *Realgymnasium* was more popular in southern Germany than in Prussia. It was an intermediate school between the gymnasium and a third type, the *Oberrealschule*. This latter school, in which neither of the classical languages was studied, emphasized mathematics, science, and modern languages. The type goes back historically to 1747 when a *Realschule* was opened in Berlin. This was only a six-year school and when the type was changed to a full nine-year school the word *Ober*, or higher, was prefixed to the name.

All of these types also existed as part-course or six-year schools, with slight changes of nomenclature which we need not specify. The reason for these part-course secondary schools will appear in a moment. In addition to the major subjects we have named, all of the schools taught religion, German, history, singing, handwork, physical education, and other subjects, twelve to sixteen in all. The average weekly schedule comprised about thirty recitation periods, but not all of these subjects required outside preparation. The course, however, was stiff beyond the dreams of the average American high school boy.

After three years in a common school or in a public or private preparatory school in which elementary subjects were studied, the boy at the age of nine entered a *Gymnasium*, or a *Realgymnasium*, or an *Oberrealschule*, and at eighteen he was ready to enter the university. This assumes that he completed a year's school work in each year without repeating. None of the ten or twelve subjects assigned to the year could be omitted, nor were substitutions allowed, although if a pupil stood high in the major subjects, German, foreign languages, mathematics, and science, the staff would exercise some leniency in its rating of the minor subjects. But the promotions were annual events and the pupil who was considered to have failed was compelled to repeat the work of the whole year. Let us note again that all subjects were prescribed. Electives, if any, were extras and were not required for graduation. As a result of this system, the pupils at graduation were on the average about twenty years old. Pupils who completed the first six years of a secondary school course were required to spend but one year in military service, instead of the customary two or three years. A large number of pupils who had difficulty with their studies, or who were poor, or who for other reasons could not go to the university, consequently left school at the end of the sixth year. This was one reason for the popularity of the six-year school; and another reason was that many towns were too small or too poor to support a nine-year school.

7. EDUCATION UNDER THE REPUBLIC

The constitution of the German Republic, adopted after World War I at Weimar, contained (Art. 1) this declaration: "The German Reich is a Republic, the political power emanates from the people"; and this admirable general statement (Art. 148) on education: "In all schools effort shall be made to develop moral education, a sense of responsibility for the public welfare, personal and vocational competence in the spirit of German nationality and reconciliation with the nations." Unfortunately, "the nations" and powerful sections within the country did little to promote this reconciliation. Germany had lost her colonies and her markets; economic conditions were unpropitious; and the German people soon became so divided politically that it was difficult for the nation to pursue a progressive policy. The constitution went on to say that the central government "may define the guiding principles for the educational system, including higher education; that the public school system is to be developed as an organic whole, and the middle and higher, that is secondary schools, are to be extensions of a common school."

These sections provided, for the first time, the basis for a national school system on the plan of an educational ladder which should open the universities to the common people and to the teachers of the elementary schools. The most liberal among the educational leaders tried to revive Süvern's proposal of 1817 for the development of a single school system which should provide a common education throughout the elementary school years and should open freely the various vocational, liberal, and professional doors to the young adolescent. This program, which would have abolished the dual system, was not to be realized. The general school law of 1920 did, however, provide for a four-year public elementary school that was to be common to all children. The new institution was called the foundation school (Grundschule). The public preparatory schools to prepare the children of the wealthy for entrance to secondary schools were closed in 1924; and the private schools of the same kind were to be abolished in 1929. This would have lengthened the course for secondary school pupils from twelve to thirteen years, and in 1925 the general school law was amended to permit capable children to transfer to the secondary schools after three years in the Grundschule.

Although the constitution prescribed that the education of youth should be carried out in free public institutions, it permitted the establishment of private schools which should fully meet the standards and appointments of the public schools; private elementary schools were allowed only for experimental or conscientious reasons, and all private schools had to be approved by the state. The constitution both guaranteed religious freedom and decreed that, except in the comparatively few secular schools, religious instruction must be a part of the regular curriculum. This suggests the fact that there was a serious religious problem in education. Several unsuccessful attempts were made, the last in 1927, to authorize the establishment of sectarian, interdenominational, and secular schools as a community might decide. But comparatively few parents exercised their right to withdraw children from all religious instruction. The right to inspect schools was taken away from the clergy. Attendance was made compulsory for eight years full time; and, beyond that period, for four years part time at free continuation or vocational schools. The lack of schools and of money for their establishment prevented the enforcement of the latter clause in many communities. The constitution provided that the central government, the states, and the local units were to cooperate in the promotion of education; but, actually, each of the states developed its own system as in the United States although, also as in the United States, there was considerable similarity in these systems.

In Prussia the Ministry of Public Education had the general direction of the schools and also of the cinema, stage, public museums, and the fine arts. Some phases of child welfare and other activities related to education were controlled by other departments. The spirit of educational administration was greatly liberalized. Instead of authoritative decrees, the ministry now set up standards, offered guidance and suggestions in matters of curricula and methods, and gave opportunity for local adaptation to community and individual needs. Within this pattern a new type of secondary school, the six-year *Aufbauschule*, was organized for those gifted children, chiefly from the lower classes, who were unable to begin secondary classes at the age of nine and to carry them on for nine years. Through the *Aufbauschule* such pupils, entering the secondary school at the age of twelve and finishing at eighteen, were enabled to prepare for the university in six years. Finally there was also created a fourth type of nine-year secondary school called the *Deutsche Oberschule*. Some schools of this type were established in all the states except, apparently, Bavaria. These schools based their curriculum upon German culture rather than upon classical or mathematical-scientific subjects; and they were given a coordinate place in the system beside the *Gymnasium*, *Realgymnasium*, and *Oberrealschule*.

The training of teachers was to be conducted according to the principles which applied generally in higher education and teachers were to have the status of public officials. These provisions of the constitution were intended to apply particularly to teachers of the elementary schools. It was intended that future elementary teachers should first complete a secondary school course and that their further and professional preparation should be completed in the university; but economic conditions and party politics prevented the realization of this ideal. In those states where a liberal party was in power for a time after the Revolution of 1918, the necessary transformation of the teacher education program was begun but all this was swept away later when the conservatives returned to power. In some states teachers were prepared partly in the university and partly in a teachers' seminary. In general the attempt to make teacher education a part of the secondary-university system was not successful.

The productivity of German writers in the fields of psychology, philosophy, and history of education and of methods of teaching is well known. No other language has so extensive a literature of books, monographs, and magazines on these subjects. Several of the factors which were at least partially responsible for this educational ferment were the bureaucratic management of the schools, the decline of interest in school and university work among the students themselves, the German youth movement, progressive education, and the collapse which eventuated in the formation of the Republic.

During the late nineteenth century, it was frequently noticed that pupils in the secondary schools and students in the universities no longer had the enthusiasm for study which had characterized their fathers and their grandfathers in 1830 or 1870. The reasons were found in the formalism of the schools and the academic and the purely intellectual and abstract nature of their work. Music, the arts, social problems, manual and constructive activities, and the development of the will and of individual responsibility were neglected. Rigid standards and great overpressure militated against the development of personal interests. When the students entered the university, they found themselves completely free from all control and even guidance; and the tendency grew among them to waste their time during the early years of the university course and to attempt to make up for this by cramming for a few semesters before the final examinations. Alcoholism and other vices had made great inroads among students.

There was also an economic-vocational problem. Thousands of young men after achieving a doctor's degree found that they could not find a secure place in the professions or could do so only after many years of waiting. The country had become oversaturated with "learned" men and an academic proletariat was forming. This body of the disillusioned and discontented formed fertile ground for social revolution and radical measures of many kinds. Even the elementary schools, although they were set apart as the schools for the lower classes, tended to become authoritarian and to be guided by the intellectual aims of the higher schools. German education, so highly admired by much of the outside world, was ill with a complication of maladies. Industrialism, the great cities with their luxury and their slums, the insecurity, not only of the poor, bureaucracy and repression, and the worship of material success, which plagued other countries also, were basic causes of social ill-health.

The German youth movement was one of the most spectacular protests against these conditions. It was begun by Karl Fischer, a pupil in a Berlin gymnasium, with the organization of the Wandervögel in 1896. The Wandervögel was a hiking club whose members wished to come into close contact with nature and the peasants. They attacked the compulsions of the school with its Wissensballast of dead information and its success philosophy. They opposed themselves to the social and secret associations which were analogous to American Greek letter societies. They stood for simplicity, physical health, wholesome human associations. Other societies were formed on similar lines. The Hamburg Wanderverein of 1905 cultivated folk songs and dances, conducted walking tours to come in contact with peasant life, and held discussion meetings. Most of the youth societies in one way or another stressed the simple life and fostered a "back to nature" movement.

When the first Liberal Congress of German Youth was held (1913) on a mountain top near Cassell to form a closer union and to celebrate the centennial of the liberation of Germany (1813), the delegates from thirteen youth associations numbered several thousand. The Congress declared that youth must chart its own course without adult interference, although most of the speakers and leaders were adults, some of them teachers. One of the most influential was Gustav Wyneken, founder of a radical progressive school. Physical fitness, self-control, community spirit, and love of the Fatherland were set up as goals, and a pledge against alcohol and nicotine was exacted.

Under the Republic, political purposes came to play an increasing role. Girls had come into the movement early and a great many girls' associations were formed. The German youth movement spread throughout the country but became less and less harmonious as political activity grew within it until 1933, when all the various societies were by command merged into one, the Hitler Youth.

In scouting and in the gradually developing youth hostels and trails, we have the slight beginnings of a similar movement in the United States. We have no autonomous youth movement, however, although in the colleges there are a number of associations with political aims. The German youth movement might well be studied by us, as a symptom and in its outcome as a warning.

An attempt to show how some of the defects of the schools might be overcome was made by the founders of experimental schools. Hermann Lietz, one of the pioneers of the new education in Germany, was much influenced by Herbart and directly by Cecil Reddie at whose school, Abbotsholme, in England, he taught for one year. Returning, he developed his own "country home schools," Ilsenburg first (1898) and others elsewhere. Manual labor, music and the fine arts, hiking, projects, a varied curriculum, comradeship between teachers and pupils were some of the features. Teachers whom he had trained established other schools. One difficulty, the matter of expense, kept such an education from spreading.

Most of the recent educators of Germany have been concerned with the place of the individual in the social order. Most of them have been individualists, even those, like Spranger and Litt, who derived their values from a theory of culture and those who began with the demands of society and community as Gaudig and Kerschensteiner did. Friedrich Paulsen, the beloved teacher of many American students at the University of Berlin, was for a generation the most uncompromising foe of bureaucracy and was bold enough to brave the wrath of Kaiser William II. More recently and far more radically, Paul Oestreich has preached the complete freedom of the child from all prescription. All this was wiped out in 1933 and Germany returned to uniformity and authoritarian control of the most extreme kind. In Chapter 21, we deal with the failure of National Socialism and the return to more democratic practices.

One victory for democratic education was won by the Republic through the establishment of the Grundschule, which brought all classes of the people together for four years in their early childhood and which led to the closing of the separate preparatory schools for future secondary school pupils. And this was the only important victory. The Aufbauschule and Deutsche Oberschule were to make secondary education more accessible to the people, but few of these were successful. Fees for secondary education were not abolished. Most of the secondary school teachers were hostile to the principles of the Republic. While many more pupils attended the secondary schools than before, they were, as in France, prepared only for the already overcrowded professions. The secondary schools did not offer a cultural and vocational education for practical life.

The result was inevitable. It has been estimated that in 1932 there were fifty thousand unemployed professionals in Germany, and many of this intellectual proletariate accepted the promises and assumptions of Hitler. Neither Germany nor France did enough to bring culture and vocation together and to open a way for people of all classes to raise themselves to the level appropriate to their abilities. Both were hampered by the philosophy and institutions of a stratified society. A democratic system should unite the people and not set them against each other. To do this it must be flexible, enabling those who may have made wrong vocational choices to correct their errors, assisting those who are poor but capable to raise themselves to higher levels, and aiding the adventurous and the gifted instead of suppressing them. In these respects the German system, even under the Republic, was not sufficiently democratic.

8. GERMAN INFLUENCE UPON AMERICAN EDUCATION

German immigrants brought new educational ideas and institutions to the United States, such as the outdoor gymnasium, the *Turnkunst,* and the kindergarten. They also provided a tough Americanization problem which is not yet altogether solved. Other influences came through books and magazines, through visitors, either Americans visiting in Europe or Germans spending some time in the United States, and most of all by American students returning after a period of study at a German university. We should remember that Alexander Dallas Bache, Calvin E. Stowe, and Horace Mann wrote influential reports of their visits to German schools, that many important American chemists were trained in German laboratories, that the historical seminar and the doctor of philosophy degree were imported from Germany, that the German language was for many years the modern foreign language most studied in our high schools and colleges.

The *Turnkunst* has been carried on chiefly in the greater German centers in large cities. There were, however, a few examples of Jahn's system and outdoor gymnasiums introduced early into New England by refugees after the revolutionary movement of 1830. The names of Charles Beck and Charles Follen are connected with this effort, which aroused great enthusiasm for a short time and then came to an early end. The same can be said of the private secondary schools in New England which were modeled on the German *Gymnasium.* Among these were the Round Hill School established by George Bancroft and others and Sereno and Henry E. Dwight's New Haven Gymnasium. Our four-year college and the public high school precluded the wide adoption of a nine-year secondary school.

The German teachers' seminary affected the American normal school by its example, but its program and curriculum were not closely followed. The effectiveness of the German teachers' seminaries became known in the United States through Cousin and several American investigators, and that knowledge clearly furthered the establishment of the state normal schools, but without affecting their curricula or administration to any marked degree. The normal school was an American institution. But, through Horace Mann, the methods of the elementary schools and, through S. G. Howe and Mann, the education of the deaf, were influenced by German example. Early state administration of schools and the centralization of educational authority in the state were frequently attacked by American publicists on the ground that they were borrowed from autocratic Germany. This argument was used in 1840 in Massachusetts against the State Board of Education and has often been confused with the contemporary attack upon the normal schools. The chief charges against the latter were that they were ineffective, unnecessary, and expensive, not that they were foreign importations. The American elementary school organization owed little or nothing to Germany; but the methods of teaching were affected somewhat by German example and much more by the theories and demonstrations of Pestalozzi, who was an Italo-German-Swiss, and of Herbart and Froebel, who were wholly German. The playground movement, physical education, and music education show German influence; and the kindergarten was a direct importation from that country. The American kindergarten, however, soon diverged from the path marked out for it by Froebel.

Of all our educational institutions, Germany had the greatest influence upon the college, for it was to a considerable extent German example and teaching which transformed our colleges into universities emphasizing advanced study, investigation, economic and technical applications, and the development of research and independent graduate work. A new and great era of university history was opened by the establishment of the University of Berlin in 1810; and it was at that moment in their evolution that the influence of the German universities upon American education began.

German influence was introduced by students returning from German universities, where they had been welcomed and accorded all the available educational facilities. And the American students seem to have done very well, although they lacked the severe training which the German gymnasium provided. The results of that rigorous course were sometimes criticized even by the Germans themselves. One such criticism was reported by a young American, James Henry Breasted, who studied at the University of Berlin about 1890. Writing home, Breasted said: "Yesterday, I heard Virchow's inaugural speech as Rector of the University. His intensely interesting address touched German education in general, and disapproved of many features. One statement especially interested me: he said that many foreigners have come into the universities without having had the benefit of the severe training of the German gymnasium and have done just as good work as the Germans. Something, he therefore argued, is wrong with the gymnasium."

The influence of the German universities upon the American when it got fully under way was potent, widespread, and in the main beneficial. It was transmitted by students who went to Germany, one in 1799, another in 1811, four about 1820, and ten thousand altogether in the course of the century; and these, after shorter or longer periods of study at one or more institutions, returned home, many of them with a doctor's degree, to become college or university research workers, scholars, and professors. Besides the higher degree, they came back with a fund of knowledge, with new methods of work in investigation and teaching, and with a devotion to learning and its uses in private and public life such as our own meagerly equipped institutions were unable to give or to call out.

Several hundred Americans had studied in Germany before 1850 and the numbers increased very rapidly decade by decade until 1890; they then began to decline and, with the outbreak of World War I (1914) and the American entry in 1917, dropped to zero. The University of Berlin enrolled the largest number, with Leipzig, Heidelberg, Halle, Bonn, Munich, and Göttingen, in about that order, attracting smaller but still considerable contingents. Several of the early migrants, George Ticknor for example, studied literature and languages; but the development of Liebig's laboratory at Giessen, opened in 1826, and Wohler's and other laboratories elsewhere attracted some young American chemists soon after 1830. The younger Silliman and others of the School of Applied Chemistry at Yale followed German examples. The doctor of philosophy degree, first granted in the United States at Yale in 1861, was imported from the same source. Eventually, all the liberal arts and sciences and the old professions, theology, law, and medicine, drew American students. As a temporary but important phase of this migration, the Herbartian pedagogy attracted about fifty American students, chiefly to Jena and Leipzig.

There were no graduate schools or advanced and research courses in American institutions before the nineteenth century. These were to a great degree a result of German influence. The first well-organized and adequately staffed graduate school was Johns Hopkins, opened in 1876, although Yale and Harvard had been making efforts in the same direction. Through the example of Johns Hopkins, aided by the vast expansion of higher education, the increase in the number of colleges, and the development of the state universities, the field for collegiate and graduate instruction in the United States expanded at a phenomenal rate. The German university seminar, research work, the doctor of philosophy degree, the expansion of laboratories and libraries were all introduced or greatly stimulated by students returning from Berlin, Leipzig, or their sister institutions. One of the fields of study which was entirely transformed and rapidly expanded by the movement was the field of psychology. Shortly after

Wundt opened his psychological laboratory at Leipzig in 1879, American students flocked to it. G. Stanley Hall and J. McKeen Cattell were among the first, and they and their contemporaries developed new phases, such as educational, differential, and functional psychology, and founded psychological laboratories and journals.

American students attended German universities because they were freer, more accessible, and had more to teach us than those of other countries. Academic freedom, however, was never as unqualified as has sometimes been asserted. On political and social questions, the professors usually agreed with the state. The faculties and the state usually saw to it that unsafe men were not appointed to professorships. But outside this danger zone, *Lehr-* and *Lernfreiheit* were great indeed. Not only was there freedom of teaching, but the professors were qualified to teach by their learning, industry, and capacity in their fields. When George Ticknor, after graduating from Dartmouth and living under the shadow of Harvard among some of the best American scholars, went to Germany, he was astounded by the depth, breadth, and originality of the scholarship of his Göttingen professors. The same experience was repeated by many of Ticknor's successors. Many Americans went to secure special training in research or to use the great European libraries and laboratories; some to secure the advanced degree and prestige of foreign study; and some merely combined study with travel and a period of residence abroad. An important item is the fact that residence at German universities was less expensive than at Oxford and Cambridge; and the English institutions did not offer the advanced work nor the degree of doctor of philosophy which was becoming a prerequisite for appointment to an American professorship. Before World War I, the United States had learned many of the lessons which Germany had to teach us and our facilities in scholarship and equipment had in many fields begun to rival and even to excel theirs. Even so it is still true that foreign study in England, France, or elsewhere provides stimulation and a broadening experience.

The German states began to take an interest in the schools at the Reformation; and did so to a greater extent in the eighteenth century, when the benevolent despots began to direct education toward national purposes. But it was in the nineteenth century that they created universal, public education in Prussia and Germany. Accepting many of the principles of the French Revolution and Napoleon's policy of universal military service, the youth of the country united to repel the conqueror and to create a liberal Germany. In education their success was hardly greater than it was in politics, yet something was accomplished. Taking Prussia as our example, they formed a central educational administration, established the University of Berlin (1810), reformed the secondary schools, and, most important, remodeled the common schools and the teachers' seminaries on Pestalozzian principles. There was a galaxy of democratic leaders that rivaled the American group of the same period (1810–1850); but the first conservative reaction (1819) came within a decade, and the subsequent history of German education oscillates between successive waves of liberalism and autocracy.

Under the empire, the May Laws (1873) made the schools more secular and repressed Catholic and, in general, clerical influence. In that period of rapid industrialization, Germany became the leader in vocational education. This development was aided not only by the demands of industry but also by the sharp division into social classes which made it easy to direct working-class youth into a definite vocation at an early age. In the nineteenth century also many secondary schools were opened and the *Realgymnasium* and *Oberrealschule* acquired the right to prepare pupils for the university. A new type of school, called the Middle School, was established in some cities. This made it somewhat easier in the favored localities to transfer from the common school to the secondary school.

The Weimar Republic took the creation of a unitary, or ladder, system as one of its goals; and it actually established a four-year common school for all children. This school, the *Grundschule*, brought all classes of children together for a short period, after which they were separated as in previous times. Beginning as early as 1850 and continuing under the Republic, education was agitated over many serious problems: bureaucratic administration, overpressure of pupils, decline of interest in school, increased youthful vice, the overcrowding of the professions, and the hostility of many secondary school teachers to the Republic.

Through German literature and official reports, through immigration, and especially through the thousands of Americans who studied in Germany, that country has exercised a potent influence upon education in the United States. This influence has been greatest at the extremes of our system, in the lower grades and in the university; the high school has been much less affected.

QUESTIONS

1. Why did the German states introduce compulsory attendance requirements earlier—and how much earlier—than other states?
2. How does the "educational strategy" of autocracy differ from the policy of democracy?
3. Compare the educational conditions and policies after military defeat, in Prussia after 1806, in France after 1870, and in Germany after 1918.
4. Consider the complementary effects of education upon politics and of politics upon education during revolutionary crises.
5. Why was it easier to carry out a scheme of compulsory vocational education in Germany than it would have been in the United States?
6. Using Russell's *German Higher Schools*, or Kandel's *Comparative Education*, compare the amounts of work demanded in the German secondary school and the American high school. How do you explain Virchow's judgment quoted on page 338.

7.   Why, in your opinion, were German secondary school boys of 1900 less interested in school work than their fathers and grandfathers had been?
8.   In what respects, if in any, do you agree that German influence upon American education was beneficial? Was this due to the excellence of the German schools, to the weakness of ours, or to our wisdom in borrowing?
9.   Study and evaluate the educational experience of George Ticknor in American and European schools and universities.

FOR FURTHER READING AND STUDY

There are many German encyclopedias of education which cite the literature on each important topic. We shall name only two of the more recent ones, as follows: Ernst M. Roloff, *Lexikon der Pädagogik* (Freiburg-im-Breisgau, 1913–1917, 5 vols.) and Hermann Schwartz, *Pädagogisches Lexikon* (Leipzig, 1928–1931, 4 vols.). *The History of Secondary Education and the Comparative Education* by I. L. Kandel, and E. H. Reisner's *Nationalism and Education since 1789*, which were given in the preceding chapter, apply also to this one and to the chapter on England. We include below some works by Kandel, Kneller, Lindegren, and others which deal with recent phases of education in Germany; and this subject will be further noticed in Chapter 21.

Alexander, Thomas, *The Prussian Elementary Schools*, New York, The Macmillan Company, 1919, 511 pp.; and, with Beryl Parker, *The New Education in the German Republic*, New York, The John Day Company, 1929, 387 pp.

Barnard, Henry, *German Educational Reformers*, Hartford, Conn., Brown, Russell and Gross, 1878, 724 pp.

Fletcher, Arthur W., *Education in Germany*, Cambridge England, W. Haffer and Sons, 1934, 61 pp.

Heman, Friedrich, *Geschichte der neueren Pädagogik*, Leipzig, A. W. Zickfeldt, 1921, 588 pp. Revised edition.

Henderson, Ernest F., *A Short History of Germany*, New York, The Macmillan Company, 1902, 2 vols.

Hillard, George S., *Life, Letters, and Journals of George Ticknor*, Boston, James R. Osgood and Co., 1875, 2 vols.

Kandel, Isaac L., *The Making of Nazis*, New York, Teachers College, Columbia University, 1934, 143 pp. Also found in the eleventh *Yearbook* (1934) of the *International Institute of Teachers College, Columbia University*. A bibliography is given. Each volume of the *Yearbook* from 1924 to 1934, excepting that for 1930, contains one or more articles on Germany.

Kneller, G. F., *The Educational Philosophy of National Socialism*, New Haven, Yale University Press, 1941, 299 pp.

Kotschnig, Walter M., *Unemployment in the Learned Professions; an International Study of Occupational and Educational Planning*, London, Oxford University Press, 1937, 347 pp.

Learned, W. S., *The Oberlehrer; a Study of the Social and Professional Evolution of the German Schoolmaster*, Cambridge, Harvard University Press, 1914, 150 pp.

Lexis, W. H., A General View of the History and Organization of Public Education in the German Empire. Translated by G. J. Tamson, Berlin, A. Ascher and Co., 1904, 182 pp.

Lilge, Frederic, The Abuse of Learning; the Failure of the German Universities, New York, The Macmillan Company, 1948, 184 pp.

Lindegren, Alina M., Education in Germany, Washington, Government Printing Office, 1939, 145 pp. Bulletin No. 15, 1938, Office of Education. Useful for its collection of secondary curricula as well as its brief treatment of National Socialist education.

Moog, Willy, Geschichte der Pädagogik: die Pädagogik der Neuzeit vom 18 Jahrhundert bis zur Gegenwart, Leipzig, A. W. Zickfeldt, 1933, 540 pp. This is the second volume of a general history of education from the Renaissance; but it is especially complete on German education.

Paulsen, Friedrich, Geschichte des gelehrten Unterrichts, Leipzig, Veit and Co., 1896–97, 2 vols.; German Education, Past and Present. Translated by T. Lorenz, New York, Charles Scribner's Sons, 1908, 310 pp. Paulsen was an educational liberal and the inspiring teacher of many Americans who studied at the University of Berlin. His little book on German Education is a classic in the field. He also wrote several important philosophical works and was a constant contributor to periodicals.

Pinnow, Hermann, History of Germany; People and State through a Thousand Years. Translated by Mabel R. Brailsford, New York, The Macmillan Company, 1933, 473 pp. A good short history in English giving special attention to social and popular developments.

Russell, James Earl, German Higher Schools; the History, Organization and Methods of Secondary Education in Germany, New York, Longmans, Green and Company, 1899, 455 pp.

Samuel, R. H., and R. Hinton Thomas, Education and Society in Modern Germany, London, Routledge and Kegan Paul, Ltd., [1949], 191 pp.

Scott, Jonathan French, Patriots in the Making, New York, D. Appleton & Company, 1916, 262 pp.

Thwing, Charles F., The American and the German University. One Hundred Years of History, New York, The Macmillan Company, 1928, 234 pp. Sketchy but containing information not otherwise readily available.

Walz, John A., German Influence in American Education and Culture, Philadelphia, The Carl Schurz Memorial Foundation, 1936, 79 pp.

15 EDUCATION IN ENGLAND

ENGLISH EDUCATION HAS BEEN LESS CONSCIOUSLY NATIONALIST than that of France or Germany but, as in the continental countries, it has suffered from the division of the people into social strata. The English have achieved the difficult task of forming a stable society of such conflicting elements as social and economic aristocracy, political democracy, and religious freedom. It is especially remarkable that they have done this in a situation which has shielded them from direct attack. But the political democracy and religious freedom of England have not been altogether favorable to the development of schools and to free and generous provision of education for all.

Education was long considered to be the province of the home and the church. Religious toleration and the growth of large bodies of dissenters made the religious question in education a difficult problem. Traditionally, the English have held that the activity of the government should be restricted to essential matters of state and should not interfere in such a social, church, or private interest as they conceived education to be. This traditional feeling, although now declining and perhaps disappearing, was strong within recent times. Finally, the considerable, although partial, success of private and philanthropic agencies in providing schools operated to restrain vigorous public effort. As a result of all these factors, England trailed the continental countries by as much as a half-century in the development of public schools.

1. EARLY BEGINNINGS

The first schools were probably established in Roman times. Roman Britain sent three bishops to the Council of Arles in A.D. 314 and since there were churches there were, no doubt, also schools. These were destroyed after the Romans withdrew from the island; but before A.D. 800 Christian schools had again been established and had become notable.

They produced such scholars as Aldhelm, in the seventh century, and Bede and Alcuin, in the eighth. The red ruin of the Danish invasions interrupted progress again, but King Alfred encouraged the founding of schools. Schoolbooks in both Anglo-Saxon and Latin were prepared by English scholars in that and later times. Testimony to the flourishing condition of learning a century after Alfred is furnished by Ælfric, a teacher of about the year 1000, whose schoolbooks, including a glossary, a Latin colloquy with an Anglo-Saxon gloss, and a Latin grammar in Anglo-Saxon, provide first-hand evidence of the educational vigor of that time.

The advent of John Wycliffe in the fourteenth century marked not only a religious reformation but also a democratizing movement. The Black Death and the heavy taxes made necessary by the foreign wars of Edward III helped to produce a social revolution which gave greater privileges to the laboring classes. In religion itself we may see the contrast between an England that was building great cathedrals and a second England that listened hungrily to Wycliffe's "poor priests." The common people were becoming a social force, and the English language, after a long period of neglect which had begun at the Norman Conquest, was again coming into use not only in common life but also in law and in religion.

To reach the common people, teachers and propagandists had to give up the Norman-French and use the vernacular. That is what Wycliffe did. The evidence also shows that many of the common people were sending their boys to school; and that "low-born" Englishmen were claiming this privilege as a right is indicated by the petition of 1391 which asked the king to ordain that no villein should be allowed to send his children to school. The object of the petition was to prevent such children from rising in the social scale "par Clergie," that is, by becoming priests. The king denied the petition; and the Statute of Artificers in 1406, which may be called the first education law in England, confirmed his denial. That law said: "Every man or woman, of whatever state or condition he may be, shall be free to set their son or daughter to take learning at any school that pleaseth them within the realm." The student can follow the subject further in the third volume of Bishop Stubbs' *Constitutional History*.

In the fifteenth century Lollardry, as the Wycliffe movement was called, was crushed and in the process many schools were destroyed and the effort to democratize education came to an end. Instead, the great Public Schools for the privileged classes were established in those years. Among the most famous of these are Eton, Harrow, Shrewsbury and Winchester. Many schools which had been intended for the poor were taken over by the rich. An example would be the hospital school of St. Anthony's which was attended by Thomas More and John Colet. The revival of classical learning in the following century led to the founding of new grammar schools and the reform of others. Some were founded by businessmen and several were placed under the control of lay boards. St. Paul's was one of the most famous of the schools which were reformed in the classical direction and placed under a lay governing board. This was done by John Colet, the dean of the cathedral; and this fact will enable us to view Colet, as school reformer, in truer perspective than is sometimes done. He introduced into this ancient cathedral school "clean and chaste" authors both classical and Christian but he was not a radical innovator, although it is somewhat remarkable that the dean of a great cathedral should establish a secular governing board.

The educational influence of the English Reformation has been described in Chapter 7. There was a certain slight impulse toward elementary education and Mulcaster urged universal education in the common tongue. The change from a Latin to an English church service was an important result. The Bible and the catechism were introduced into schools, even into grammar schools. John Colet prepared an English catechism for St. Paul's School. But neither the church nor the state actively promoted elementary education; and on the secondary level, the Reformation did not increase but rather reduced the facilities for learning. The Reformation did little for the education of the ordinary poor and for a time less than nothing for the well-to-do; but through the apprenticeship laws it accomplished something for the poorest of the poor.

The second English Reformation, which was carried out by the Puritans in the seventeenth century, promised an educational revival. The Puritan Parliament of the Commonwealth proposed to educate the children of the nation. In 1649 it voted twenty thousand pounds for elementary education. But political conditions prevented the execution of the program and the Restoration (1660) put an end to all efforts in this direction for nearly two centuries. The Restoration laws which were passed to suppress all nonconformist teaching were partly undone by the Acts of Toleration under William and Mary, which again gave the dissenters religious freedom under certain conditions. The court cases of Bates (1670) and Cox (1700) further loosened the hold of the Church of England, and a law of 1719 removed the last restrictions from dissenting teachers of elementary schools. But the people still occupied opposing educational camps, the Puritans and other dissenters fighting the Anglicans. This made agreement upon a unified national system difficult and delayed the establishment of such a system. It has been truly said that three promising opportunities to establish national education in England were blighted and destroyed, the first after King Alfred, the second in the time of Wycliffe, and the third, by the reaction against the Puritan movement.

2. PHILANTHROPIC EFFORTS

An extensive system of charity schools developed in London and surrounding towns and suburbs near the beginning of the eighteenth century. These provided free education for poor boys and girls, furnished clothing, and helped them to find work. It seems that the charity schools of London were influenced by the similar work of Thomas Gouge (1609–1681) in Wales. Gouge had been a clergyman in London but, having turned Puritan, he lost his pastorate as a nonconformist in 1662. Ten years later, with the permission of the bishops, he began to evangelize and educate the people of a section of Wales. The costs were met by subscription, and a society to spread the schools was formed. Schools on this plan developed in many parts of the country, but their later history is somewhat obscure.

In Anglican circles a similar but more active agency, the Society for the Promotion of Christian Knowledge, was formed by Thomas Bray and associates in 1698. The S.P.C.K. aided members "to set up catechetical schools for the education of poor children" in reading, writing, and especially in the principles of religion. It is almost certain that the founders were influenced by the work of Gouge and that of the German pietist, August Hermann Francke of Halle. In a charity sermon of 1706 by Dr. White Kennet, it was asserted that the schools were directed not only against indifference in religion and dissenting faiths but also against Roman Catholicism. Every charity school was to be "a fortress and frontier garrison against popery." A secondary aim was to prepare children to earn a livelihood; and girls were taught to sew, spin, and knit, and boys were apprenticed to trades. The schools, like those of Gouge, were supported by subscriptions and from the proceeds of annual "charity sermons." They grew rapidly in numbers and had forty thousand children under instruction by 1740. Joseph Addison called them "the glory of the age we live in." Bernard Mandeville, the cynical Dutch physician of London, thought differently. In his *Fable of the Bees* he argued that "To make society happy and people easy under the meanest circumstances, it is requisite that great numbers of them should be ignorant as well as poor." Mandeville's attack is a witness to his belief that the schools were effective. Francis Place (1771–1854), the London tailor who became a utilitarian reformer, condemned the charity schools because they "taught poor children next to nothing, and nothing likely to be useful to them." All of these were prejudiced witnesses and the true verdict seems to be that the schools were a useful agency at a time when a national system or even good private schools were not yet possible.

To carry on the same work in the British Dominions a daughter society, the Society for the Propagation of the Gospel in Foreign Parts, was formed and Thomas Bray came to America to found schools and to provide libraries for the clergy, the teachers, and their pupils. Although thousands of children in New York and the southern states received at least the elements of an education in the charity schools, the work of the S. P. G. aroused the antagonism of many who had come for religious freedom. Fear of an American episcopate and an established church was one of the factors in the Revolution, and the S. P. G. helped to keep alive that fear. The society remained active in the American colonies until the close of the Revolution. A further extension of elementary education was made by the Sunday School movement which was widely publicized by Robert Raikes, a newspaper publisher of Gloucester, England, and was more directly promoted by the Methodists, the Friends, and other religious bodies. Many, who might have had no teaching otherwise, learned to read in Sunday Schools. Attendance at Sunday Schools, also, carried no stigma of pauperism; and the Bible, as interpreted by workingmen, became an important introduction to social democracy.

3. TOWARD A PLANNED EDUCATION

Public opinion was becoming more favorable to the idea of universal education as the eighteenth century unrolled. At the beginning of the century few were interested; at the end, it was becoming a national question. The whole argument had moved into a new phase. Earlier generations had asked whether the poor should be educated but now the leaders, at least, were asking how the common people, not merely the very poor, could be educated. Not all had arrived at this point. Many still feared that education would make the "industrious classes" discontented with their lot, disobedient, extravagant, and politically radical. In spite of these prophecies of doom, humanitarian and libertarian opinions came to prevail, partly because of the increase of industry and greater material welfare. Although England was gaining the conviction that the people should be educated, she was not yet ready to lay taxes for that purpose. And education was not to be secular or to violate anyone's conscience. How could this be done?

The answer seemed to have been found about 1800 when Joseph Lancaster published a new method of conducting schools cheaply by having the older boys teach the younger. The system was not new, having been brought from Madras, India, by a British army chaplain, Dr. Andrew Bell; and it had also been used by the Jesuits, by John Brinsley, and others; but it seemed novel and as simple and inevitable, once it had been thought of, as the discovery of America or the invention of the steam engine. Indeed, its similarity to the mechanical operation of power machinery and the factory system was one of its chief recommendations to a practical, industrial people. Actually, it was only the first of the modern "plans" which have so often promised short and easy solutions.

Bell was imitated by Joseph Lancaster. When he was a boy of fourteen, Lancaster was prevented from sailing to Jamaica where he intended to teach the slaves of the sugar plantations. He therefore determined to gratify his passion for teaching in his native country and opened about 1796, when he was sixteen, a school for poor children in his father's house. There he taught reading, writing, and arithmetic for a weekly fee of fourpence. He soon had sixty children and twice that number in the summer. Members of the Society of Friends, which he joined about this time, aided him with funds and his school prospered. About the year 1800 he read a pamphlet published in 1797 by Dr. Andrew Bell, entitled *An Experiment in Education made at the Male Asylum of Madras, suggesting a System by which a School or Family may teach itself.* In the absence of competent teachers, Bell had used those pupils who knew a little to teach those who knew less and now Lancaster enthusiastically adopted the same scheme and vigorously advertised it. The pupil-teachers were called monitors and the scheme the monitorial system. Lancaster's schools were nonsectarian and Bell's Anglican; and that was the chief difference.

By this plan the teacher met his monitors each session and taught them in a class the lessons of the day which each of them then relayed to the small group of perhaps ten children to which he had been assigned. The school was carried on in a single large room equipped with benches, black-boards, and other materials. Lancaster collected and invented a good deal of simple equipment and many devices for use in instruction and discipline. Competition and rewards were used to excess. The schools were organized along military lines. The monitors received for their reward only the lessons which the head of the school gave them and, sometimes, the hope of becoming masters of other schools. They were not paid in money. A large school could be maintained for a whole year for the rent and heating cost of a building and a single salary, the master's. The annual cost per pupil might be as low as one pound or even ten shillings.

A witness from Dr. Bell's schools testified before the Brougham Committee (1816). The following colloquy ensued:

How many can one master superintend, according to your system? I conceive I do not exaggerate when I say 1000. What would be the expense? The room being given, the expenses are, salary to the master, and the expense of books, which is a mere trifle, say £80 a year. The room being given I conceive, 4s. 2d. ($1.00) a head abundantly sufficient for 500 children. What is the longest time that you take a boy for education? I conceive two years abundantly sufficient for any boy.

Such was the cost and such the conception of education in high quarters.

Though the instruction was mechanical, it succeeded in teaching children the elements of reading, spelling, and arithmetic. Apparent efficiency and the low cost explain the enthusiasm with which the system was received. Henry Holman, a critical historian of English education, has described the reception that was accorded the monitorial system as follows:

The greatest popular enthusiasm was aroused. If it were possible to teach poor children next to nothing for next to nothing—a reasonable equation—by all means let it be done. The king, members of the royal family, nobles, gentry, all subscribed to so pleasing a project. Lancaster was a public hero, and almost every city erected a monument to him, in the shape of a Lancasterian school.

Lancaster had solved, or appeared to have solved, the question of the cost of popular education. He was not so successful in dealing with the religious question. The religion which was taught in his school was too undogmatic, Holman said, too purely religious, for some members of the Church of England. Some became obsessed with the notion that Voltairean ideas and a covert attack upon Christianity lay concealed beneath the smooth surface of Lancaster's system. When the schools began to spread, Dr. Bell, who had taken little interest in the matter, was drawn out of his retirement and whipped up to lead a campaign for monitorial schools in which the catechism and formularies of the Church of England were to be taught. A controversy over originality and priority also arose. Was Lancaster or Bell the inventor? Which one had stolen the other's idea? The controversy may have had a good deal to do with the spread of both systems, but it was a dispute which should never have arisen. Neither was the inventor. Dr. Bell had seen the monitorial system in operation at Madras in India. Lancaster had acknowledged his debt to Dr. Bell in the first edition (1803) of his *Improvements in Education as It Respects the Industrious Classes*. After the fight became hot, he not only ignored his indebtedness but claimed to have invented the monitorial system. Really, he had only "improved" it; and some of his additions, such as the excessive use of emulation, of rewards, medals, and decorations, and of humiliating punishments, were serious defects, not improvements.

Improvements in Education was an important book because it discussed a scheme for a national system of popular education. The education of the people as a whole is a matter of national importance and the greatest obstacle, he believed, was the proselyting spirit of the religious bodies. This could be removed if people would consent to have only "general Christian principles" taught in the schools. Such an education could be made universal; but he was opposed to compulsion. To make the system universal, public funds would be required. Although each sect was permitted to maintain its own schools, a compromise similar to the one which Lancaster had suggested was actually adopted and followed by the government down to 1870 when the public school boards were instituted by the Forster Act.

The monitorial schools performed a useful function and even the controversy over the discovery was fruitful. Combining forces with the S.P.C.K. and Sunday School movements, the monitorial systems prepared the public for the final step toward public education. Two societies were set up to promote the two systems: the British and Foreign Society (1810) to establish Lancasterian schools; and the National Society to spread those of Dr. Bell, also called the Madras system. Each set up a model school and provided some training for its teachers, but as the courses were short, averaging only about three months for each prospective teacher, the training dealt chiefly with the organization and management of schools. By 1835 the National Society had trained about two thousand teachers and had about three thousand schools under its nominal charge. The British and Foreign Society had far fewer, perhaps not over five hundred schools, but many of these were large schools in London. The National Society had established schools in rural parishes, had introduced the Madras system into Sunday Schools, and had taken over some of the S.P.C.K. charity schools. While there are no accurate statistics, it has been estimated that all three of these types, the S.P.C.K., the Sunday, and the monitorial schools, in 1835 enrolled about sixty, perhaps only fifty, per cent of the children of the working classes of England.

The Lancasterian system was introduced into New York City in 1806, whence it spread to most of the larger and many of the smaller cities of the United States, including those as far west as Cincinnati and Detroit. Joseph Lancaster himself came to the United States and an idea of the honor accorded him is to be found in the fact that he was invited to address the two Houses of Congress in a joint session and did so. Philadelphia in 1818 established a city training school for teachers on the Lancasterian principles. The monitorial system remained in use in New York City until 1853, but its active life was much shorter in most American cities. In both England and the United States the system did a great deal to spread the ideal of education for all.

4. INFLUENCE FROM ABROAD

From the beginning of the nineteenth century English educationists began to study the developments which were taking place on the continent. Robert Owen visited Switzerland and established at his mill town of New Lanark the first British infant school (1815), which received children "at one year or as soon as they could walk" and retained them until the age of six when they were transferred to the elementary school. Within four years, Henry Brougham and others opened an infant school at Westminster; and in 1824 the London Infant School Society was founded and Samuel Wilderspin became its superintendent. Through his activity, infant schools were rapidly established in England and they have remained a permanent part of the English system. Later the infant school was also influenced by Froebelian ideas but it has, with some notable exceptions, remained comparatively formal, more like a school in its emphasis upon reading and other school skills than like a kindergarten.

About the same time, David Stow of Glasgow was working out his system of preparing teachers; and other students of popular education were introducing the ideas of Pestalozzi and Fellenberg, and of their German disciples. The *Quarterly Journal of Education* (1831–1835) performed for England a function similar to that of W. C. Woodbridge and later Henry Barnard in the United States in acquainting the English with new developments in France, Switzerland, and Germany. The *Quarterly Journal* showed particularly that the elementary curriculum in England was meager and formal compared with that of the best schools abroad and that English teachers lacked the professional preparation which was becoming usual in progressive countries. One who was soon to become the real founder of national education in England, Dr. James Philips Kay (1804–1877), later known as Sir James Kay-Shuttleworth, visited many European schools where he made the acquaintance of Father Girard of Fribourg, of Fellenberg, and of Wehrli, who had conducted Fellenberg's school for poor children before becoming the principal of a Swiss cantonal normal school. Through Kay-Shuttleworth's work in developing teacher training, the ideas of David Stow and of Wehrli were embodied in the English system. From Stow he learned the virtues of the "criticism lesson" in which a skilled teacher taught a class while normal school pupils observed the work which they later analyzed for the purpose of deriving principles. Wehrli taught him that future elementary teachers should develop habits of frugality, patience, and sympathy by sharing the conditions of life of the pupils whom they were later to teach. The Battersea Training School for teachers was founded on these lines in 1839.

Pestalozzian methods were introduced into England and the United States about the same time. In England, Elizabeth Mayo published a book on Pestalozzian object teaching in 1830, the famous *Lessons on Objects*; and her brother Charles Mayo had spent three years at Yverdon following 1819 and upon his return established a Pestalozzian school. The Mayos and others in 1836 organized the Home and Colonial School Society, which brought a famous Pestalozzian, Hermann Krüsi, Jr., to England. Krüsi later taught at Oswego, New York, but he was not responsible for the Oswego method which was a direct importation (1860) of English Pestalozzianism.

5. RISE OF THE NATIONAL SYSTEM

Education in England as elsewhere had long been the function of the church and the family. To propose now in the nineteenth century that the government should establish and support schools for all the people represented a radical break with this tradition. And, in the second place, not only education but other social matters were considered to be outside the sphere of government and contrary to the individualism expressed in such phrases as "government is a necessary evil," and "a man's house is his castle." English democracy, because it had to create a public opinion in favor of education, made slower progress than highly centralized governments such as the Prussian. And the very success of the voluntary efforts by the S.P.C.K., the monitorial schools, and other private agencies in some cases delayed national education by raising the hope that additional similar efforts might be able to provide opportunity for all without governmental action. Finally, there was no easy solution of the religious question. For all these reasons, national education was achieved a generation or perhaps a half-century later in England than in the advanced countries on the continent.

Some of the steps were the following. The Factory Act (1802), called the Health and Morals of Apprentices Act, limited the daily hours of labor for apprentices in textile mills to twelve, prohibited night employment, and prescribed that "every such apprentice shall be instructed, in some part of each working day, for the first four years of his or her apprenticeship, in the usual hours of work, in reading, writing, and arithmetic, to be paid for by the master or mistress of such apprentice." The law was evaded by refusing "to apprentice" the child workers; but it was a beginning in the area where there was a precedent, established by the old apprenticeship legislation.

Further advance was blocked for thirty years. One cause was the fear that the education of the masses would lead to a wave of radicalism, such as had engulfed France. The Napoleonic Wars occupied the attention and emotions of the country until 1815 and after Waterloo came the conservative reaction led by the Duke of Wellington. The Lords rejected Whitbread's Parochial Schools Bill of 1807, which would have provided two years of free education for every child. In the year after the final defeat of Napoleon, as frequently happens after a war, the people were for a moment willing to give serious attention to education. Henry Brougham was in 1816 appointed chairman of the committee to investigate the condi-tion of the poor in London. Witnesses testified that they lived in a "very dreadful state" from overcrowding and lack of sanitation, that large masses of children received no education, and that those who attended school re-ceived little benefit. But in spite of this evidence, Brougham's education bill of 1820, a tax measure, had to be withdrawn.

Not until 1833, one year after the passage of the Reform Bill which abolished the "rotten borough" representation and extended the franchise to the middle classes, did Parliament vote any money for schools, namely, twenty thousand pounds for building schoolhouses, to be used by the two monitorial societies, the National, and the British and Foreign. It was a time of serious financial difficulty, but in the same year England pur-chased and freed all slaves in the British Dominions at a cost of two million pounds. The education grant became an annual one and the yearly amount was from time to time increased, to thirty thousand pounds in 1839, to one hundred thousand in 1846, and to eight hundred thousand pounds in 1860. The year 1839 was also memorable because it was then that a Com-mittee of Council was created which was to function as a department of education. The chief function of the Committee of Council was to allo-cate the government money grants. In 1846 the further policy was adopted of appointing school inspectors upon whose reports the allocation of funds could be based. It will readily be seen that the powers of the Committee were expanding. From allocating money to inspecting schools is itself a big step. Matthew Arnold was for most of his life one of Her Majesty's Inspectors of Schools.

The first secretary of the Committee of Council was a man whom we have named, James Kay-Shuttleworth. He was educated as a physician at Edinburgh and his fellow student, Charles Darwin, later recorded admir-ing regard for his ability and particularly for his skill as a public speaker. As an administrator he was discreet and self-sacrificing but energetic and progressive. Matthew Arnold, who had every opportunity to know the basic facts, called him the founder of the system of public education in England. Kay-Shuttleworth, like Horace Mann, began as soon as possible to make provisions for the education of teachers. The first effective appro-priation for training colleges was made in 1841, five thousand pounds to the Borough Road College, named above, and smaller amounts to two other new schools.

Following the Chartist agitation and the increasing strength of the labor movement, the demand for a local tax for schools kept growing, but the opposition of the friends of the voluntary system and of those who would have to pay heavily was too strong. Meanwhile, without a clear plan or national decision, the school system kept forming itself. English democracy has always laid great store by fact-finding and publishing, believing that the facts when known will convince the public and lead to well-informed action. Thus in 1858 the first national education commission was appointed to study the "state of popular education in England, and to consider what measures, if any, are required for the extension of sound and cheap elementary instruction to all classes of the people." It was called the Newcastle Commission, for the Duke of Newcastle who was its honorary chairman, and made its report in 1861.

The Newcastle Commission reported on all sorts of elementary schools, dame, infant, Sunday, evening, and day schools, and both private and public schools in any of these classes. Public in this case means conducted by a society or board and not managed by an owner for his personal support or profit. The Commission recognized the public day schools as the most important provision for the education of the poor; and they recognized too that the quality of any school depends most upon the capacity and education of the teacher. They found also that schools of some sort, often of a very bad sort, existed everywhere and that there were very few children in 1860 who did not attend school at some time in their lives. On this point the Commission was probably much too optimistic, since it was shown ten years later (1870) that in Liverpool one-fourth of the children attended no schools at all. Less than half the children were in schools that were receiving the government grants. The Commission report also showed that in England and Wales, thirty-two training colleges for teachers were in operation.

The Commission did not recommend any organic change in the system which was growing up; but one matter which might seem a detail had striking consequences. This was the scheme of "payment by results," which provided that the government grants were to be allocated to schools on the basis not only of average daily attendance but also on the basis of the number of pupils who annually passed a state examination in reading, writing, and arithmetic. The system of payment by results was apparently first suggested, long before, by Dr. Andrew Bell and used in his monitorial schools. The plan was, of course, an unfortunate experiment. It placed a premium upon the bald teaching of facts by cramming and drilling for examinations and it tended to restrict the curriculum essentially to reading, writing, and arithmetic, for no grants could be earned for work in geography, history, or drawing, however excellent, because these subjects were not included in the examinations. Kay-Shuttleworth argued against the adoption of "payment by results," declaring that it would be "ever remembered with shame." So it has been, although it remained in use in English schools until the middle eighties when it was gradually abandoned; it was completely abolished in 1890. A suggestion by Archbishop Ireland that "payment by results" should be introduced into American schools was brilliantly answered by B. A. Hinsdale (*Studies in Education*, Chicago, 1896).

The next great step, and the greatest yet taken, came in 1870 with the passage of the Elementary Education Act of 1870. This law is also known as the Forster Act after the author W. E. Forster. The Reform Act of 1832 had extended the vote to the middle classes, but it still left the numerous working class and the poor generally without the ballot. A new Reform Act passed in 1867 extended the suffrage further and formed the foundation of a long campaign which led to manhood and, after World War I, to adult suffrage. The return of the Liberal Party in 1868 was the opportunity for a great deal of social legislation: laws on child labor, on hours of labor, on sanitation, and on accident prevention, an act permitting trade unions to hold property, and another introducing the secret ballot. It was the influence of the workingmen when they were given representation in Parliament that formed the balance of power between the dissenters and churchmen and enabled the Forster Act to pass.

The central provision of this act was that it established school districts and elective school boards for the purpose of providing and supervising elementary schools in all places where the existing supply was insufficient. The school boards had the power to levy taxes for schools in their districts. The government continued to aid private schools; but it now could and did establish its own public schools for the education of the "schoolless multitude," of children, as Matthew Arnold called them, whom the private schools had not reached. Acts of 1876 and 1880 introduced compulsory attendance; and in 1891, elementary education was made free. By that time, where elementary education was not supplied by voluntary bodies, it was public, free, and supported by local tax and government grant. Everywhere attendance was compulsory. The Committee of Council was not an efficient agency, and in 1899 Parliament created a national Board of Education with a President as the executive officer directly responsible to Parliament. The Bryce Commission of 1895 reported in favor of public secondary schools closely connected with the elementary schools, and this recommendation was embodied in the Balfour Act of 1902.

By 1910 there were nearly twelve hundred secondary schools supported by local tax or government grant or both, in addition to the old grammar school and Public School foundations. The Fisher Act of 1918 attempted to weld into one system all the public educational agencies, all the elementary, secondary, technical, and higher schools under public control. And in 1944, in the midst of another war, England was again engaged in further democratizing its educational provisions. To this we shall return immediately.

6. PRESENT PUPILS AND SCHOOLS

About two-thirds of England's children attend public or "provided" elementary schools and the rest attend the "nonprovided" or private and voluntary schools, which are conducted by the Church of England, the Catholic church, or other smaller denominational bodies. Many of the nonprovided schools are located in rural England and have smaller average enrollments than the public schools. Religious instruction is sectarian in the nonprovided schools, while, in accordance with the Cowper-Temple clause of 1870, in the provided schools, only nonsectarian Scripture knowledge, in which "no religious catechism or religious formulary which is distinctive of any particular denomination," may be taught. Bible reading without comment, and prayers, are permitted.

The infant schools for children between the ages of five and seven are separately organized. Above these ages the elementary school proper, with seven or eight classes, may enroll either boys or girls or both. It was usually organized into the junior, intermediate, and senior grades, but some schools had only one or two of these departments. Until recently most children did not continue in school beyond the elementary period. Compulsory attendance ended at age fourteen after which there were opportunities in evening classes and adult education. As will be seen, the Butler Education Act of 1944 changed these conditions. Earlier attempts to raise the compulsory attendance age had failed.

England has made two recent attempts to reconstruct its educational system. The Fisher Act of 1918 contemplated raising the compulsory age to fifteen but, for financial reasons, it was not possible to bring it into operation. The same fate overtook the provision for compulsory continuation schooling. In the years between the two World Wars the question of improved education for England was under continuous study. This is best shown by the issue of the Hadow Reports on *The Education of the Adolescent* (1926), on *The Primary School* (1931), and on *Infant and Nursery Schools* (1933) and the Spens Report on *Secondary Education* (1939). The student of English educational history cannot afford to neglect these Reports which are valuable not only for their recommendations but also for their historical sections written by Robert Fitzgibbon Young, the learned and judicious secretary of the Consultative Committee which conducted the extended hearings upon which the Reports were based.

The Hadow Reports defined the limits of infant and nursery, primary, and secondary education in England more clearly. Secondary education was to include all schooling between the ages of eleven-plus and eighteen years. Many English people understood secondary education to include only pre-university training that was given in the Great Public Schools and the more prominent public and private grammar schools (see p. 360). These schools were selective and offered an extensive classical curriculum in which only very bright youth could succeed. Because the complete curriculum occupied the pupils to the age of about eighteen years, only the leisure classes were able to take full advantage of it. Others had to go to work several years earlier.

There were various stopgap measures to provide some post-primary schooling for those who were excluded from the grammar schools or who needed a more immediately useful education. The public central schools, an institution somewhat like the junior high schools of the United States, were the most widespread examples of these. For reasons that will now be apparent the Hadow Report of 1926 carried the phrase "Education of the Adolescent" in its title instead of the words secondary education. Its purpose was to draw a plan for the education of all English youth. This report had a great effect upon educational discussion and was a major step toward the formation of the Butler Education Act of 1944. This Act will be considered in Chapter 21.

The elementary schools all taught religious knowledge, English, physical education and hygiene, arithmetic which received one-fifth or one-sixth of the total time and attention, nature study and geography, history which received little emphasis, writing, drawing, and practical subjects such as manual or domestic instruction. Each school made its own schedule which, however, had to meet the regulations of the Board of Education, and each school was given considerable freedom in arranging its courses and determining its methods of teaching. There was and is little effort to use the schools for nationalist indoctrination.

This last topic is of great and growing importance in the world. The English people seem to be no less loyal and patriotic than those of other nations, of France, for example, where great efforts are put forth in the primary schools to instill nationalist sentiment. Do the situation of France and the history of her relations with her neighbors explain and provide the motives for her nationalist indoctrination? Is nationalist feeling more effectively instilled in adult years than in childhood and through public communication and ceremony than through schoolbooks? These questions merit study. If schools have ever tended to increase chauvinism they should do so no longer.

Above the elementary schools there were the central schools, already mentioned, which gave advanced elementary and prevocational courses and were public and free, and a great variety of public and private secondary schools. The secondary schools gave a general liberal education and usually charged fees, but to receive government aid they had to provide a certain number of free places, usually one-third of the enrollment. Entrance to the secondary schools was obtained through the free place examinations which were taken at the age of eleven. The examinations covered English and arithmetic, and frequently history and geography. Intelligence tests were sometimes also used and consideration was given to the pupil's school record. Because there were not enough free places to accommodate all the children who might qualify, the examinations were made rigorous and became, in fact, not qualifying but competitive. It was said that only ten per cent of the children were able to pass the free place examinations. Those who did not pass with the highest averages might be admitted to a central school.

The central schools provided a considerably lower and easier form of education than the secondary schools which prepared for the university. They were called by this name because each central school served a number of the surrounding elementary schools. Because the best of the senior pupils from the elementary schools attended the secondary schools the work of the central schools was often further lowered in quality. This was a weakness of the system. And another problem arose from the variety of schools and curricula which made transfer and promotion from school to school more difficult. The central schools offered general, industrial, commercial, domestic, and fine arts courses. These were four years in length, and some pupils were permitted to remain an additional year. It was often possible to enter a secondary or technical school from a central school.

The reader will remember that in England the terms elementary and secondary were not clearly defined. Some schools for girls or boys took pupils from the primary grades to the door of the university. Some secondary schools admitted pupils between the ages of nine and twelve and retained them to sixteen or eighteen. From twelve to eighteen was regarded as the secondary period; and to be eligible for government grants, a secondary school was required to have a stated proportion of its pupils in continuous attendance between twelve and sixteen. But the Board of Education said only that a secondary school was one in which most of the work is secondary, which is not a model definition. Usually English secondary schools, like those on the Continent and unlike the American high school, have offered only academic and not activity and vocational curricula; but this does not apply to the experimental schools, then or now.

The English secondary schools were of four kinds. Established under the Education Act of 1902 there were public secondary schools maintained by counties and county boroughs. These were required to teach the English language and literature and at least one foreign language unless there was special provision to give adequate linguistic and literary training by means of English only. Most schools taught two foreign languages, and, in that case, one was to be Latin. By permission a second modern language could be substituted for Latin. These provisions reveal the flexibility of the controls over secondary curricula. The other required subjects in the public schools were geography, history, mathematics, science, drawing, and physical, manual, and musical instruction. In girls' schools domestic studies had to be taught. In some schools Greek, German, French, Spanish, or Italian were offered. In subject matter and in the percentage of the adolescents attending, the English public secondary schools before World War II were similar to the American about 1890. They did not offer the technical, industrial, and commercial courses that were common in the larger American high schools; but one must remember that of the subjects just named only the commercial course was almost universally offered in the American high school.

The second class of English secondary schools was composed of local, day schools managed by a private board like an American academy. Many of these are old grammar schools. They have a classical curriculum. Because they are local, day schools, they are somewhat responsive to local demands. These schools charge fees.

The Great Public Schools form the third class. Only nine such schools were originally recognized, but the definition has been broadened and new ones have been founded so that the *Public Schools Handbook* includes about two hundred, many of them nineteenth-century foundations. These are expensive schools for the richer and upper classes. They are managed by private boards.

There is, finally, a wide variety of wholly private secondary schools that are conducted by the owners. Some of these are conservative, but included in this class are some of an experimental or "progressive" type. A once-famous school of this kind was established early in the nineteenth century by Thomas Wright Hill at Birmingham but it did not become permanent. Abbotsholme School was founded by Cecil Reddie in 1889 and it has inspired numerous other schools with a modern activity curriculum. Bedales is a coeducational school established in 1893 by J. H. Badley, who had been an Abbotsholme teacher. Abbotsholme has other daughters in France and Germany. Schools of this type usually have a flexible curriculum and emphasize the physical, manual, intellectual, moral, and aesthetic development of their pupils. The curricula are broad as well as flexible and are intended to promote the development of the children rather than to transmit a set body of knowledge. Since these schools are experimental and have the most various facilities no simple description will apply to all of them; but like other secondary schools they prepare some pupils for admission to the university and others, perhaps the greater number for practical life. (See p. 359 ff. for further account of the English secondary schools.)

The variety of the English schools is the result of freedom and group planning. The Education Act of 1944 made the system more uniform without changing its basic character. English education like English life and history is the result of compromises and changes introduced as new classes of people came into the programs. It will not be possible, in our limited space, to give a precise outline of a system which contains so many irregularities, but I. L. Kandel's *Comparative Education* (Boston, Houghton Mifflin Company, 1933) from which also much of the above information is taken, shows the general relations of the schools.

English educational freedom is even embodied in the legislation which has consistently sought to protect existing institutions and to preserve existing interests. Schools have grown up or have been provided by law to take advantage of opportunities and local needs or to fill gaps in the arrangements previously made. It was on this basis that the Education Department and the Department of Science and Art were created in the nineteenth century. Their functions were at the turn of the last century assigned to a single body. Thus, England in 1899 created a central authority for education, the Board of Education. Its power consisted in the fact that it distributed and allotted the public money to the schools; but it did not control the schools through rigid and general regulations, as is done in France and Germany. Instead, it called upon the local authorities to submit their programs and to make reports and it also inspected the grant-receiving schools. There are general regulations on buildings, class size, the number of days when the schools must be in session, and other physical matters, but the prescriptions on what should be taught and how it should be taught are flexible and are couched in terms of suggestions and minimal essentials merely. The Board of Education and the schools have generally cooperated and exchanged views on the best ways of using the available resources. This ideal plan permits a maximum of local planning and adjustment to local need.

7. THE SPREAD OF ENGLISH INFLUENCE TO AMERICA

English education has influenced the schools of foreign countries and of the British Colonies and the Dominions. The views and practice of Rousseau and the philanthropinists were shaped by the doctrines of John Locke. The English cooperative movement played a part in the development of the Folk High Schools of the Scandinavian countries. The Hazelwood School of the Hills was copied in Sweden; and Cecil Reddie's Abbotsholme became a model for both French and German school reformers. But the British dominions feel that influence most strongly. In Canada, Australia, and South Africa and in the British Colonies, one finds modified extensions of the English system. A comparison of these shows family like-nesses which stem from the education of the mother country.

Similar resemblances stemming from common centers of origin can be traced in other parts of the world. Latin-American systems are similar to each other and different from the English because the Latin-American countries borrowed the outlines of their civilization from Spain and Por-tugal. The Scandinavian countries are so closely united by language and religion, and by the similarity of their political and economic systems and ideals that their school systems also have developed along similar lines. And, to give only one more example, it is well known that schools in the countries within the Russian bloc have taken on many of the character-istics of the education of the dominant nation. Modern education is car-ried forward on national lines as the last three chapters have shown. Since we are next to take up American education it will be appropriate to close this chapter with a brief survey of English influence upon American educa-tion. This is especially pertinent since we were colonies of the British empire in its early stages.

In Virginia and Massachusetts, the early schools were established by Englishmen and followed the pattern of education which prevailed in Eng-land in the seventeenth and eighteenth centuries. The English language be-came the language of the American people, government, and schools, and has so remained. The early text-books were written in England and many of the teachers for two centuries came from England. The Latin grammar school was imported from England. The English S.P.G. was active in the colonies, especially in those in which the Anglican church was established. The *Thoughts* of John Locke were widely read; and they impressed even so original a man as Benjamin Franklin when he came to promote the establishment of the academy. In other ways, also, the American academy was affected by English writings, and by English experience with a similar institution; but it did not entirely follow its English model or Franklin's idea. It became, as we shall say later, the first important educational inven-tion to be developed in America.

Other English influences were of a local or temporary character. The monitorial system of Lancaster and the English variety of Pestalozzian object-teaching have already been mentioned. The mechanics institutes developed by George Birkbeck about 1820 and the scheme promoted by Albert Mansbridge, early in the present century, for the education of organ-ized labor were both copied in the United States but never attained the success which they had in England. The nursery school is an even more recent importation. It remains to be seen whether it will become a general feature of the American system.

The American colleges also were at first modelled upon the colleges of England. Harvard College was founded by graduates of Emmanuel College,

Cambridge, and was named for one of them, John Harvard. Even the town in which the new college was opened was named for the city on the Cam where its promoters had studied. William and Mary College, Yale, Princeton, King's College, in New York, and others followed. But the wide dispersion of our people did not permit the association of these colleges into a university of the Cambridge or Oxford type. Religious diversity also divided them. Some were Anglican, others Congregational, Presbyterian, Baptist, or Dutch Reformed. Because there was no overarching university to hold them together and direct their ways they each gradually developed into independent universities. One important feature of the English college we have retained, namely, the idea that there should be a period of broad, liberal education interposed between the secondary school and the specialized study and investigation of the professional and graduate schools. The continent of Europe and Latin-America do not have any institution resembling the American or English college.

The examples that we have already given illustrate a general truth about the diffusion of culture and its institutions. It is this. Unless the conditions in the borrowing country are very similar to those in the lending country, the culture and institutions which are imported either fail to take root or are quickly and often radically modified. One or both of these results followed in most of the cases named above. Even our language is no longer quite the language of England. The Latin grammar school, although imported, was not suited to American conditions. The academy never closely followed its English prototype. And so with most of the other importations.

American democracy was one of the conditions that tended to limit the introduction of English schools and educational practices or that transformed them when they were brought over. By democracy we here mean merely the greater equality in the social status of the American people, the absence of an aristocracy and of great landed estates and the extension of the suffrage. Even in England the aristocracy was not a caste but there were ruling classes. Her Prime Ministers were not like Jackson or Lincoln, drawn from the self-educated "common" people. Her educational leaders were drawn from the Public Schools and the old universities. The open frontier, and the scattered population were other American conditions that tended to transform borrowed institutions. Our rapidly expanding economy made necessary the extension of elementary and some secondary education to the general public. This need in its turn promoted the education of girls who in many cases became teachers in our fast growing school systems. The separation of church and state and the development of schools from which sectarian instruction was banned, eliminated from American public education much of the religious dissension that long hampered the development of public education in England. These American conditions will be considered further in the following chapters. Those chapters will show that, although we borrowed from England and many other countries, the American people have developed their own system of education.

The development of national education in England makes an especially interesting historical study because conditions hindered it which, abstractly considered, should have promoted it. English individualism, a restricted view of the functions of government, political democracy which could not use compulsion or royal fiat, religious freedom, the growth of a class of wealthy and influential dissenters, all tended to delay nationalization. We must add to this that the English, like other Western peoples, had to overcome a tradition of family and church education, and that the partial effectiveness of philanthropic efforts often made public education seem less necessary.

The monitorial schools of Bell and Lancaster played an important part in demonstrating that universal education would not be too expensive. They also developed methods of administering large schools, of grading the classes, and of organizing and teaching the subject matter. They convinced many that teaching was a skilled, if not a professional, occupation for which some preparation and training were necessary. They formed an important stage in the movement for universal education.

The early nineteenth century was notable for a fruitful interchange of educational ideas with the continent. While the monitorial system was being introduced into France and other countries, the English and the Scotch schoolmasters borrowed and spread the infant school, the teacher-training school, and a series of Pestalozzian practices and ideas. The English variety of object lessons was widely spread in the United States.

After three failures at widely separated intervals, in the time of King Alfred, of Wycliffe, and of the Commonwealth, the English government in 1833 adopted the promotion of education as a public policy. Parliament granted a sum of money for building schoolhouses to be used by the two monitorial societies; and it shortly instituted the inspection of private schools, and established training colleges for teachers. The Newcastle Commission drew the map locating the evils of English elementary education in 1861 and added another to a chapter of errors, "payment by results." The Act of 1870 established local elective school boards and assigned them the power to levy taxes for schools in their districts. Compulsory attendance followed a decade later. The elementary curriculum has been greatly expanded, health services, vocational, and technical courses and schools have been developed, and an extensive system of partially free secondary schools has been created. The Act of 1944 was passed in the midst of war to unify, extend, and modernize the comprehensive system of national education which England has developed.

QUESTIONS

1.   Why was it difficult for the English to agree upon a national system of education?
2.   Compare and contrast the philosophies of philanthropic and of public education, as these were developed and held in England.

3.   Do you agree with the statement in the text that the charity schools were useful; and why or why not? Would the period to which this question is taken to refer influence your answer?

4.   If Napoleon's plan to invade England had succeeded, would public education have developed as rapidly as it did in Prussia?

5.   Why did the monitorial schools develop in England rather than in Prussia, Switzerland, or France?

6.   Examine Lancaster's *Improvements in Education* and estimate its significance in its own time and country.

7.   Compare the methods and stages of educational progress in England and France.

8.   Why was "payment by results" a mistake? Give other examples in which public money payments had, or have, to be "earned."

9.   Private secondary schools have occupied a strong position in English education. Why has this been true? Has it been advantageous to England or to the English people?

10. Examine C. Reddie's *Abbotsholme*. How do you account for the fact that this early "modern progressive" school arose in an educationally conservative country like England? Why may England be called educationally conservative?

FOR FURTHER READING AND STUDY

The literature on the Great Public Schools must be omitted here, but this note will apprise the student of its existence. There are special volumes which deal with individual schools and also more general treatments. The histories of the English universities must likewise be passed over. The following list is intended to amplify the history of national, popular education in England. Particular mention should be made of the extended series of Board of Education reports, including the *Special Reports on Educational Subjects* which began in 1897. Recent noteworthy publications include the Hadow Reports on *The Education of the Adolescent* (1926), on *The Primary Schools* (1931), and on *Infant and Nursery Schools* (1933), and the Spens Report (1939). The Year-Books of the International Institute of Teachers College, Columbia University, have many articles on English education.

Adamson, John W., *English Education, 1789–1902*, Cambridge, University Press, 1930, 519 pp.

Archer, R. L., *Secondary Education in the Nineteenth Century*, Cambridge, University Press, 1921, 363 pp.

Arnold, Matthew, *Reports on Elementary Schools, 1852–1882*, London, Macmillan & Company, Ltd., 1889, 306 pp. Nineteen reports on elementary schools by the poet and critic who was also one of Her Majesty's inspectors of schools.

Birchenough, Charles, *History of Elementary Education in England and Wales*, London, University Tutorial Press, 1938, 572 pp. Second edition.

De Montmorency, J. E. G., *State Intervention in English Education; a Short History from the Earliest Times down to 1833*, London, Cambridge, University Press, 1902, 366 pp.; *National Education and National Life*, London, Swan Sonnenschein and Company, 1906, 287 pp.

Dobbs, Archibald Edward, *Education and Social Movements, 1700–1850*, London, Longmans, Green and Company, 1919, 257 pp.

Dressler, Bruno, *Geschichte der Englishen Erziehung*, Leipzig, B. G. Teubner, 1928, 340 pp.

Field, Louis F., *The Child and His Book. Some Account of the History and Progress of Children's Literature in England*, London, W. Gardner, Darton and Company, 1895, 358 pp.

Greenough, J. C., *The Evolution of the Elementary Schools of Great Britain*, New York, D. Appleton & Company, 1903, 265 pp.

Holman, Henry, *English National Education: a Sketch of the Rise of Public Elementary Schools in England*, Glasgow, Blackie & Son, Ltd., 1898, 256 pp.

Kelly, Thomas, *George Birkbeck, Pioneer of Adult Education*, Liverpool, University of Liverpool Press, 1957, 380 pp. Illustrated.

Leach, Arthur F., *English Schools at the Reformation, 1546–1548*, London, Constable & Company, Ltd., 1896, 346 pp.; *The Schools of Medieval England*, New York, The Macmillan Company, 1915, 349 pp.

Lochhead, Jewell, *The Education of Young Children in England*, New York, Teachers College, Columbia University, 1932, 226 pp.

Mansbridge, Albert, *An Adventure in Working-Class Education, being the Story of the Workers Education Association, 1903–1915*, New York, Longmans, Green and Company, 1920, 73 pp.

Newton, Alfred W., *The English Elementary School*, London, Longmans, Green and Company, 1919, 299 pp.

Ogilvie, Vivian, *The English Public School*, London, B. T. Batsford, Ltd., [1957], 228 pp. Illustrated.

Parmentier, Jacques, *Histoire de l'Education en Angleterre; les doctrines et les écoles depuis les origines jusqu'au commencement du XIXe siècle*, Paris, Perrin et Cie, 1896, 302 pp.

Reddie, Cecil, *Abbotsholme*, London, George Allen, 1900, 640 pp.

Snell, Reginald, *Progressive Schools, their Principles and Practice*, London, L. and Virginia Woolf at the Hogarth Press, 1934, 197 pp.

Truscott, Bruce, *Red Brick University*, a Pelican Book, 1951, 375 pp. On the English provincial universities. The author is said to have been Professor E. Allison Peers of Liverpool University.

Ward, Herbert, *The Educational System of England and Wales and its Recent History*, Cambridge, University Press, 1935, 256 pp.

Watson, Foster, *The English Grammar Schools to 1660: Their Curricula and Practice*, Cambridge, University Press, 1908, 548 pp.; *The Beginnings of the Teaching of Modern Subjects in England*, London, Sir Isaac Pitman & Sons, Ltd., 1909, 554 pp.

Webb, Sidney, *London Education*, New York, Longmans, Green and Company, 1904, 219 pp.

Wilson, J. Dover, *The Schools of England; a Study in Renaissance*, Chapel Hill, University of North Carolina Press, 1929, 388 pp.

16 AMERICAN BEGINNINGS

THE EARLY COLONIAL PERIOD WAS AN ERA IN WHICH THE colonists copied European schools as closely as American conditions permitted. We sometimes call it the period of transplantation. But even so the schools were gradually adapted to the needs and circumstances of the frontier. The break with tradition which resulted from the migration, and the mingling of many peoples, gave occasion for innovation. The first great innovation was the development of the American academy. In this chapter, we shall treat of education in the British-American colonies from the settlements down to the Revolution.

Thirteen colonies, extending from New Hampshire to Georgia, were founded in this period of one hundred and eighty years. By hard work a living was obtained from the soil, the sea, and the forests. In savagely fought wars, the Indians were driven inland and the strip of English civilization along the Atlantic was gradually widened. By 1750, in Pennsylvania and Virginia where the strip was widest, the settlements reached up into the Alleghenies and were spilling over the crest. The French and Indian War (1755–1763) assured the frontiersmen that the Ohio Valley would be English and not French. By 1770, the people of the thirteen colonies numbered two and a quarter millions and, from natural increase and continued immigration, they grew so rapidly that, as Burke said: "While we spend our time in deliberations on the mode of governing two millions, we shall find that we have millions more to govern." This growing body of people became ever more restive under English control, especially after the French menace was removed; and in 1776 they declared their independence and their intention to build up a separate American civilization.

1. THE EARLY SETTLEMENTS

The period when the British formed their early American settlements was a time of low wages, unemployment, and social unrest. The famine of

1595 was the beginning of a long depression. Many people were obliged to find new ways of making a living and some of these turned toward foreign lands. The destruction of the Spanish Armada in 1588 had established the sea power of England, and the East India Company was founded in 1600. Others looked westward to the little known lands across the Atlantic. How little the English knew of America, even after the voyages of Hawkins and Drake and after Raleigh's attempted settlement, is shown by the account of George Weymouth who visited the coast of Maine in mid-summer of 1605 and thereupon reported a climate suitable for tropical fruits. Much of the difficulty that the early English settlers encountered came from mistaken notions about the resources and conditions of the country.

The band of one hundred and five colonists who landed on the banks of the James River in 1607 did not find the gold and immediate wealth for which they had hoped. Starvation and disease carried off half of them in six months and would have destroyed the rest but for supplies and replacements supplemented by greater attention to agriculture. A few years later, when the Puritans came into control of the company which promoted the settlement, they sent over a new governor with instructions to hold an election for members of a representative assembly in Virginia. This first American legislature met in the church in Jamestown in 1619. The new government lasted only five years, for Virginia was made a royal province in 1624.

The Virginia settlements became permanent through the discovery of a profitable crop suited to the climate, tobacco. The tobacco plant rapidly exhausted the soil so that new land had to be constantly brought under cultivation. The plantation system which developed demanded a supply of cheap, unskilled labor. This demand was met by transporting debtors and criminals from English jails, children from English poorhouses, and persons kidnaped in London alleys. English paupers came as redemptioners and paid for their passage by a term, usually four years, of labor in the tobacco fields. Some of the redemptioners were skilled mechanics, book-keepers, or schoolmasters. The first shipboard of slaves from Africa was brought over in 1619, the year of the first legislative assembly. Thus there were two classes in Virginia, one consisting of the planters, the clergy, and a few other professional people and the other the working class, many of them employed at forced labor as slaves or redemptioners. There was no large middle class.

The population of Virginia was widely scattered on the plantations fronting on the rivers. There were no cities, few villages, roads, industries, or stores. Cooperation and the assembling of people was difficult. The center of the planter's life was still in London where he disposed of his crops and purchased his clothes, furnishings, and implements. The planters' families were frequently refined and their homes were furnished with books, musical instruments, and English furniture. The children were educated by the parish clergy or in schools maintained on the plantations. There were a few Latin grammar schools and some of the boys in wealthy families were sent to English schools. For the poor, neighborhood or "old field" schools were established, in which itinerant teachers taught upon occasion. The system of apprenticeship provided opportunity for vocational train- ing. Many children received little or no schooling.

The first settlements in northern Virginia, or New England as it came to be called, were made at Plymouth in 1620 and at Boston in 1630. In the latter year the great emigration of Puritans began, for civil war was im- minent in England. In that single year more than a thousand and within ten years not less than twenty thousand colonists came to Massachusetts. No such peaceful mass migration had taken place in historic times. The colonists settled in compact villages, and the New England town, that is township, became the center of their political life. There was no large- scale agriculture and no plantation system. Diversified farming which de- manded varied knowledge, skill, and business ability became the rule. And since New England could not maintain her growing population by agricul- ture, she turned to industry and fishing. Cod and herring from the waters between Marblehead and Newfoundland were exchanged for the products of the West Indies and Europe. Fishing boats and seagoing ships were needed. There were great forests of timber and the resourceful colonists readily learned to build their own vessels. Within twenty years of the settlement of Boston, more than a thousand boats were engaged in the fishing industry. Masts for the royal navy were frequently exported to Eng- land. Thousands of skilled workmen were employed in shipbuilding and in navigation. The New England system of farming and industry was built upon the skilled and semiskilled labor of a dominant middle class.

Economically, New England was democratic. By industry and intel- ligence it was usually possible for the poor to become landowners, artisans, shipowners, or merchants. Scores of trades developed. The wealthy class were often alarmed because of the high wages which enabled artisans to own houses and gardens and which threatened to break down the social classes. There were few slaves, but the slave trade was profitable and many slave ships were owned by New Englanders. Business and the town meetings provided training for democracy.

Political democracy developed very gradually. In the beginning, society in New England was neither democratic nor tolerant. But Puritanism was a leavening influence, a transition movement, tending to dissolve the medieval system of class and status and to produce free and equal individuals. A dozen men held all the powers of government in Massachusetts in 1630. The next year one hundred and sixteen others were admitted to the company. The leaven was working; but the freemen were still only a small part of the population. Thomas Hooker, who founded Connecticut, declared that "to leave power in the hands of rulers who are not responsible to the people is to invite tyranny." The numbers of the freemen were increased and a form of representative government was worked out; but it was in the annual town meetings and by serving on town committees that the people received the most useful political education.

Tolerance also developed slowly. The Puritans had chosen a post of danger in the wilderness, instead of their quiet homes in a civilized country, to establish a "godly commonwealth," free from error; and now they were dismayed to find error both springing up within and assailing them from without, threatening ruin to their "holy experiment." They tried to defend by mistaken means that for which they had sacrificed home and native land. Their executioner burned heretical books; they censored the output of their printing press which, established in 1639, remained for a generation the only one in America; and they did worse in driving Roger Williams into the wintry forests and in banishing Ann Hutchinson. But the persistency of the Quakers, whose opposition to a regular clergy made them especially obnoxious to a theocracy, led to the strongest measures. Four were hung.

The theocracy could not continue on this road. Sympathy for the victims, a growing sense that ideas can not be destroyed by force, and a growing fear of interference from England put an end to the killings. Charles II did interfere; and the "glorious revolution" of 1688 further strengthened the principle of toleration throughout the English world.

The most advanced position was taken by Roger Williams. In 1631 he became pastor at Salem and ascended the pulpit to denounce the union of church and state and to declare that the civil authorities had no right to punish violations of religious commandments, Sabbath-breaking for example. This was the position later taken by John Locke. Williams founded his colony in Rhode Island on civil equality, the separation of church and state, and complete religious freedom; and these principles became foundation stones of government and public education in the United States. Close approaches to religious liberty were also made in the colonies of Maryland and Pennsylvania.

2. COLONIAL MELTING POT

The settlers of the Middle Colonies, with their confused intermingling of languages, faiths, and nationalities, were much more diverse than those to the north or the south of them. New Amsterdam, before the English conquest in 1664, was a mere village, yet in its streets more than a dozen languages were heard. The Swedish and Quaker settlements on either side of the Delaware attracted men from the British Isles and almost every country of western Europe. The Dutch, after winning their struggle for independence from Spain and after the decline of Spanish sea power, turned even more vigorously than before to commercial and maritime pursuits. They became enterprizing traders rather than colonizers. Because they found religious toleration and reasonable economic opportunity at home, they did not emigrate in large numbers. New Netherland was governed not by the mother country and not in the interest of the colonists but by the Dutch West India Company for the financial enrichment of its members. The fall of New Netherland and its occupation by the English seems to have been welcomed by most of the inhabitants. In the last quarter of the seventeenth century the colony, favored by its excellent location and by the development of representative government, began the rapid growth which early in the nineteenth century made New York the largest American city. During the eighteenth century, however, Philadelphia, not New York, was the largest city in British America.

The active settlement of the Middle Colonies to the south of New York was held back by Dutch claims and Dutch control of that region until 1664. After that the vacant spaces on the Atlantic coast between the southern and the northern colonies were rapidly filled up. The great increase in population which took place in the two decades following 1690 was due in considerable part to the new immigration into Pennsylvania, New Jersey, and other colonies and in part to the high birth rate in colonial families everywhere.

The people who were coming into the Delaware Valley in those years were of many stocks and faiths. Small settlements of Swedish Lutherans and Dutch Calvinists had been there long before. The Dutch social reformer Plockhoy established a small colony far south on Delaware Bay in 1663. Puritans, escaping from the unfriendly England of Charles II, English and Welsh Quakers, and Welshmen who were not Quakers to the number of several thousand, had come before William Penn arrived in the ship Welcome in 1682. Some of the Welsh moved out into the country and Welsh names like Brecknock and Caernarvon are found far from Philadelphia in Pennsylvania. A small number of Huguenots came in the same year (1683) as did Francis Daniel Pastorius and the Mennonites who founded Germantown. Pastorius was a scholar, university bred, and a Pietist. He was for several years a teacher of a Friends' school in Philadelphia and later a teacher and town officer of Germantown. The statement is sometimes made that he was the most learned man of his time in America, not excepting Cotton Mather. Among the half-dozen languages of which he had a command was the English, and he prepared a little primer, *The True Reading, Spelling, and Writing of English*, which was printed by William Bradford of New York in 1697. German and Swiss and some Dutch Mennonites came in large numbers into the counties of southeastern Pennsylvania. Twenty families of Dunkards, now the Church of the Brethren, arrived in 1719 and others followed. Influenced by John Huss, Caspar Schwenkfeld, a nobleman of Silesia, founded the sect which bears his name. In the first half of the eighteenth century, some Schwenkfelders settled in eastern Pennsylvania where they much later founded the Perkiomen School. The Moravians, who were the direct disciples of Huss and who had settled in the new colony of Georgia, were aided by George Whitefield in moving to Pennsylvania where they settled at Nazareth and Bethlehem about 1740. They have been noted for their work as missionaries to the Indians, for their activity as founders and teachers of excellent schools, and for their devotion to music, especially the music of Bach. The Scotch-Irish, grievously oppressed in Ulster and cordially hating their English oppressors, began to arrive sometime before the German and Bohemian groups and settled in the mountain valleys of Pennsylvania and Virginia. They were mainly Presbyterians and they played an important part in the Revolution and in the politics and education of America. Catholics, both from Germany and from Ireland, also migrated to the Middle Colonies; and Maryland was for a time a haven for English Catholics. Episcopalians came in large numbers into New York and Pennsylvania. Many of these groups developed their own church schools so that the Middle Colonies became a parochial school region.

3. EDUCATIONAL TRANSPLANTATION

Many motives served to send people across the Atlantic. Redemptioners came because they were out of work. Ship captains could sell the time of a healthy and especially of a skilled immigrant for more than the regular passenger fare, and even found it profitable to delay transportation, holding emigrants at embarkation ports until their savings were used up, when they could be taken as redemptioners. Some were transported from English jails where they had been confined for debt, for political offences, and for many worse crimes. Others came voluntarily to escape political or economic or domestic involvement, some for travel or adventure, some to Christianize the Indians. Many came to escape religious persecution, especially during the horrors of the Thirty Years War; others, such as the Puritans, the Quakers, the Moravians, and Roger Williams, intended to found an ideal church. As in other conditions of human life, economic motives were usually also involved: to find gold or work at high wages and to return; to engage in trade or to develop a new country and to make a fortune; but perhaps the most frequent reason for the great migration, which to the majority meant a complete severing of all ties with the old country, was a keen desire to found quiet and comfortable homes under easier conditions than Europe could offer.

None came for educational advantages for these were not to be found in a wilderness, except that in a negative sense the new world might help them to escape some of the disadvantages of the traditional, and at that time decadent, schools of the old world. But apparently they had no idea of the shortcomings of the schools of the seventeenth century. It is a striking fact that none of the colonists were dissatisfied with the educational institutions or with the opportunities which would have been theirs in those institutions if they had remained in Europe. They were seriously dissatisfied with their religious, political, and economic opportunities, but for the schools of their mother countries they expressed the sincerest admiration by imitating them and attempting to transplant them to the new soil.

With some exceptions they were satisfied with a moderate degree of education for their children. Some of the planters of the South, some of the official class, and those who looked forward to professional careers for their sons demanded secondary and higher schooling. But the vast majority of American settlers were less ambitious. Women and the mass of unskilled laborers were at best taught little more than reading and writing. The slaves expected no education and received none. The Puritans, the Presbyterians, the Quakers, the German sects, and all those aroused by the Reformation to a living sense of religious issues demanded literacy and a knowledge of the catechism and Bible. Some, but not all of these, also required an educated ministry. The small businessmen and skilled artisans and even the farmers needed some arithmetic, practical measurement and calculation, and elementary training in drawing up legal documents. The land surveyor was an important functionary in every community in the seventeenth century; and a knowledge of navigation had to be acquired by ship captains and of handwriting and bookkeeping by merchants. The general effect of frontier life was to reduce both the demand and the supply of schools. By 1700 or soon after, the lands nearest to the coast and to the larger rivers were pretty well occupied and the Indians less menacing. The peace of Utrecht in 1713 coincided with the conquest of the Tuscarawas by the Carolinas. Soon the strong Scotch-Irish immigration was to begin. As a result of all these factors, a broad and spreading band of frontier settlements began to develop to the westward. In seventeenth-century America the real frontiersman, like the unskilled laborer and most women, was likely to be illiterate.

4. THE TRANSPLANTED EDUCATIONAL INSTITUTIONS

Four main types of educational endeavor characterized the seventeenth century: apprenticeship to the manual vocations; reading and religious instruction directed by churches and missionary societies, or obtained in dame schools, field schools, or otherwise; the formal secondary and higher education of the Latin schools and colleges, although until near the end of the period Harvard was the only college; and practical schooling in mathematics and its applications to accounting, navigation, and surveying together with supplementary work in English. Only the first three of these were transplanted. The last was in the main a native development. Every one of these four types of education was found in each of the colonial regions, New England, the Middle Colonies, and the South. The cultural similarity of all the early colonies, in spite of their economic differences, has not been sufficiently noticed and has even been denied; but it is a true statement that the educational differences between the different social classes and the different regions of any one colony were greater than those between the different colonies.

5. APPRENTICESHIP

In the laws and the practices of apprenticeship training, English legislation and precedent were directly followed. The English laws on apprenticeship education were from the first closely related to poor relief. The first such act was voted in the reign of Henry VIII, and the series of enactments came to its climax in the code of 1601 just as the colonizing trend was beginning. The English gilds were declining. The state, therefore, took over some of the most necessary of their activities, including the relief of the poor and the vocational education of poor children. The laws in England provided for the compulsory apprenticeship of such children at public expense and made it the obligation of the local government to supply the necessary materials and facilities. Those laws were copied by the colonies. Apprenticeship was one of the most widespread forms of education in colonial America and all the colonies passed laws to facilitate it.

The word "apprentice" comes from an old French verb that even in the Latin from which it was derived meant "to learn." An apprentice is one who is bound to a master to learn a trade. The legal instrument, which specified the duties and privileges of the master and the apprentice, was called an indenture. The indentures frequently contained a clause that required the master to provide opportunities for a small amount of schooling, sometimes in an evening school. In such cases we have a combination of two of the four types named above, trade training and elementary literary education.

One of the early acts of the Virginia legislature ordered that the English "statute for artificers and workmen" should be published in the colony. A law of 1646 further provided for a workhouse school to teach spinning and knitting to young children. A third Virginia act in 1661 required the justices of the peace to apprentice poor children. Various other acts dealt with the same subject and with the literary and religious education of poor and orphan children. The repeated reference to orphans in the laws demands a word of explanation. All youths and minors whose parents remained in England, as well as those whose parents were no longer living and all illegitimate children, were by law classified as orphans, and for the education of these the state attempted to provide. Others were voluntarily apprenticed by their parents if they were to learn a trade. The apprenticeship system was most widespread in the northern colonies but it was found in Virginia, as indicated, and in the other southern colonies also. The system was frequently abused. Masters sometimes exploited their apprentices, employing them at common labor without teaching them the specified trade. In such cases the laws provided redress through fines or by reassignment to more responsible masters. The laws of New York introduced a new element by providing that the completion of an apprenticeship should entail the right of full citizenship.

The first general education law in New England, that of Massachusetts in 1642, was in part an apprenticeship law. The law was passed to remedy "the great neglect in many parents and masters in training up their children in learning and labor and other employments which may be profitable to the commonwealth." A later clause in the law explains that by "learning" was meant "ability to read and understand the principles of religion and the capital laws of the country." Any parents or masters who neglected to teach these abilities together with a trade were subject to a fine; and the selectmen of the town were commanded to remove children or apprentices from the custody of neglectful parents or masters and to commit them to the care of others who would perform their duty under the law. In this "first New England school law," as it is sometimes called, schools are not mentioned. It was not a school law but a law on the proper upbringing of children among the poor and the lower middle classes. We should notice particularly that it required training in "learning and labor," joining apprenticeship to reading and religion as many indentures also did. Court records in the several colonies show that the apprenticeship laws were sometimes enforced but not how constantly or how strictly this was done.

The power of legislation in colonial times was in the hands of the rich and well-to-do. The apprenticeship laws were therefore an example of one class legislating for another class, the rich for the poor, partly for the benefit and the control of the poor, and also partly for the benefit and relief of the rich. These motives may be best exhibited in a summary of the arguments for such laws and for the apprenticeship system. Apprenticeship, it was held, tended to reduce the burden of poor relief and to prevent pauperism and crime; to avoid probable distress; to prepare capable workmen for employers; to teach the elements of learning and religion in addition to a trade; and to aid in maintaining the traditional, or as they would have said the natural, order of society. Obviously apprenticeship and the legislation related to it were not wholly, perhaps not even chiefly, intended to benefit the apprentice and his social class.

Apprenticeship declined in importance in the colonial period and even more rapidly afterward. The abundance of land, the mobility and freedom of the people, the willingness of the frontiersman to do with makeshift implements and furnishings, and the immigration of mechanics and craftsmen who had been trained in Europe all worked against the apprenticeship system. The heaviest blow was delivered by the factory in the nineteenth century, but the system had been declining in colonial days.

6. SCHOOLS FOR READING AND RELIGIOUS INSTRUCTION

Everywhere in the colonies the common people were seriously concerned that children should be taught reading and the principles of religion; but frequently their interest in education did not go much further. Everywhere, education was still accepted as one of the functions of the church although it was felt that other agencies, such as private bodies or the state, might properly support or at least supplement the church in the performance of this duty. The Virginia statute of 1631, which required the clergy to instruct the youth in the catechism and the *Book of Common Prayer*, also laid an obligation on the parents and all those who had the charge of children: that they should send them to the church to receive this instruction. Many of the Virginia churches established parish schools and a few maintained charity schools. In the eighteenth century the Church of England missionary body which was called the Society for the Propagation of the Gospel in Foreign Parts established charity schools, imported orthodox schoolmasters from England, opened libraries, and provided wholly or in part for the support of these institutions.

The interest that parents took in the education of their children is proved by the wills of the period. Many testators provided not alone for the education of their own but also for the children of others. There were Virginia wills bequeathing funds for the education of "six poor children";

or for the schooling of the poor children of the testator's county; or giving five hundred pounds in trust for the salaries of schoolmasters; and providing for the maintenance of a free school in the County of Lancaster. Wills and letters also show that indentured servants were employed in teaching. From the very end of the colonial period we have the diary of John Harrower, an indentured servant from the islands far north of Scotland, who served as teacher in the Daingerfield family near Fredericksburg. The last entry of the diary, made after the news of the Battle of Lexington had reached Virginia, speaks not of teaching but of getting a supply of lead, perhaps for bullets, from the roof of one of the buildings on the estate.

Families with means frequently employed a tutor or established a family school in the mansion house or in a separate building erected for the purpose. It would not be possible to distinguish clearly between the tutorial plan and the family-school plan. The one merges into the other, but in the latter there was often a separate building close by the residence, especially erected for school purposes, and the children of the plantation and those from neighboring plantations were taught together. Graduates of northern colleges or Scotch schoolmasters were sometimes employed. There is an excellent account of such a family school, as it was at the end of the colonial period, in the diary of Philip Fithian. Fithian was a graduate of Princeton and taught for a year in the Carter family in eastern Virginia. The boys of the school followed an English and classical course, including some Greek, but the girls were given merely an English education. Fithian described not the school alone but also the social life of the period and region.

Another nonchurch type of school was the neighborhood or, as it was usually called, the "old field" school. The historian Beverly speaks (1705) of the habit of the people of Virginia of joining together to form little schools for their children; and Jones in The Present State of Virginia (1724) says that "in most parishes there are schools, little houses being built on purpose where English and writing are taught." The latter of these passages almost certainly and the former probably refer to the old field school. In these buildings, usually located on some plot of abandoned or waste land, whence the name, itinerant teachers "kept school" when they were able to gather a sufficient flock of pupils. Such teachers were good, bad, or indifferent in ability and character. Their reputation in history is certainly not high but some historians think injustice has been done them, pointing out that almost every advertisement for a teacher demands one of sober and correct life and good character. But even this evidence is really ambiguous. The unanimity with which such qualities were demanded may actually mean that they were hard to find. We know that some of these itinerant teachers were learned and reputable men and that some were not, and this seems to be all that we do know.

In Pennsylvania, and the Middle Colonies generally, educational conditions were not so different as they have been painted from those of Virginia and the South. There was no established church, there were many sects, and the people lived in more compact settlements. They engaged in diversified farming and in the towns in a great variety of occupations. The middle class of free and independent workmen, farmers, and small businessmen formed the bulk of the population. In this region also the locally organized and democratic neighborhood school was a familiar and frequent institution; and it was most frequent where, as in Pennsylvania, the settlers were divided into many sects and where the number of any one sect was too small for a church school. In Philadelphia and other large towns, in the southeastern part of the colony, and wherever whole communities were composed of a single denomination there were church schools. Elsewhere the neighborhood schools predominated and served the children of all faiths. They were commonest in the region toward the Susquehanna and beyond in the valleys of the Cumberland and Juniata rivers and in the region across the Alleghenies. There a common school, established by the people themselves, religious in its tone but undenominational in its teaching, grew up on the frontier and formed the basis for the public school when the time arrived. Wickersham has estimated that in 1834, when Pennsylvania voted to adopt the public school system, there must have been at least four thousand schoolhouses in the state built by the contributions of the people themselves. They were not closely modeled upon any previous institution but were the simple response of farmers and frontiersmen meeting a need with the resources at hand. The fact that the Scotch-Irish settled in the central and western parts of the state aided the movement because, although interested in education, they did not usually favor church schools.

From the historical accounts of several county superintendents in Pennsylvania, the historian Wickersham has presented descriptions of the way in which these neighborhood schools came into being. We select the one prepared by the superintendent of Delaware County because it is in the southeastern corner of the state where, if anywhere, the so-called parochial system would be expected. This is what he wrote:

"The reader will understand that in the times thus far noticed, there was no system of public instruction, but the education of children was almost wholly a matter of private concern. The family school was succeeded by the neighborhood school. The establishment of such a school was usually effected by the voluntary and united action of the people of the neighborhood who desired it. Certain persons were made trustees, who had charge of the school property, and who mostly appointed the teacher and had the general management of the schools. The teachers were paid by their patrons at the rate of two or three dollars a quarter for each child, and sometimes something additional for wood and ink." Such a plan had many defects. The school was not free although the cost was low. Where money was scarce the fee was often paid in corn or pelts. The school terms were short, usually three months, and there was no assurance that even this minimum of opportunity would be available every year. Some of the teachers were without sufficient learning or proper habits, but the usual quality of the instruction was probably as good as that of the district schools in New England. The schools were established and maintained by the voluntary efforts of the people and were in that sense democratic; and although not public they were almost as well adapted as the district schools to provide a foundation for the free, public, and universal education of the nineteenth century.

The Dutch of New Amsterdam had a school in 1642 when Jan Stevenson began a term of service as master of the parish school of the Dutch Reformed Church. They may have had one as early as 1638, taught by Adam Roelantsen, but a long controversy has made it clear that there is no real evidence for a school in 1633, as had been held. The early schools in New Netherland were conducted under a system of joint support and control by both state and church, which had long been in use in Holland and was now transplanted to America. The support which in the old country would have been provided by the government actually came from its American representative, the Dutch West India Company, whose directors bought the schoolbooks and drew up the rules for the schoolmaster's daily life and work. The church supplied the schoolmaster, making sure of his orthodoxy and literary competence. The school taught the four R's, namely, reading, writing, arithmetic, and religion, and the teacher served as assistant to the minister. He frequently led the singing in church or read the service and sometimes he officiated as sexton and bell ringer. The same plan was followed in all the Dutch villages. When the English came into permanent control of New York, the school had to be supported by the church but it was the state that authorized the church to collect school rates. These, although levied and collected by the church, were gathered by authority of the civil law. This principle, inherited from Dutch rule, made easier the establishment of public schools in the State of New York in 1795.

New York was also the scene of vigorous missionary efforts by the Church of England through its Society for the Propagation of the Gospel in Foreign Parts. Trinity Church was the first Anglican congregation to be organized in New York City (1697) and it supported the school of a Mr. Huddlestone. A few years later the S.P.G. began to support Mr. Huddlestone and required him, after 1710, to teach forty-four children free. As a result nearly all the paying pupils were withdrawn by their parents, leaving only the charity pupils; and then Trinity Church again established a separate parish school. Most of the schools of the S.P.G. were charity schools; and, since they were missionary enterprises, the school-master had to be an orthodox member of the Church of England. These schools were established in the villages about New York and in the Hudson and Mohawk valleys. The usual subjects were the four R's, and the methods were formal and wholly memoriter. Church schools were maintained by many denominations throughout the colonial period in New York.

In Pennsylvania the Friends made an effort to set up an educational system as the Dutch had done in New York. The deep interest which they felt in the practical and religious education of children is shown by the frequent appeals and resolves of their meetings, by the doctrines promulgated by their leaders, and still better by the schools which they established. The London yearly meeting sent appeals to all Friends to care for the education of children, to assist young Friends to prepare themselves as teachers, and to attend particularly to the education of the poor. Local monthly meetings regularly appointed overseers to carry out these directions. Many Friends both in England and among the early settlers were educated men. It is true that the Friends laid more emphasis upon religion than upon learning and, because they did not demand education as a qualification for preaching, it was often thought that they depreciated education. This is an error, but being mainly middle class working and business people they stressed practical and religious teaching rather than classical education. It has, however, never been easy to find anywhere an illiterate Friend.

William Penn, one of the truly great men of our colonial period, was a democrat in politics and a pious but liberal mystic in religion. In education, although schooled in the classics and the Church Fathers, he was a realist. Any people is free, he held, whatever the form of their government, if they are governed by laws of their own framing. But we are not content that government shall be merely free. We demand also, he said, that it shall be wise and good; and that it may be so we need not only good laws but also good men. If we would preserve our government after it is established, he continued, we must teach the people to love it and this must be done by educating the youth who will conduct the government when we are gone. The young while they are still children are the wards of the commonwealth, which has the high duty of providing a sound education for them. The realism of Penn also appears in a letter to his wife advising her to spare no cost in the education of their own children for "by such parsimony all is lost that is saved"; but he requests that they should be taught useful knowledge such as applied mathematics, shipbuilding, and agriculture.

Holding such principles, Penn in his Frame of Government (1682) ordained that the governor and council should establish and direct all "public schools"; provided for a committee on manners, education, and the arts; and decreed that children from the age of twelve should be taught useful trades. Article thirty-five of Penn's Frame guaranteed in the strongest terms the rights of conscience and the separation of church and state. The first Assembly of Pennsylvania (1681) ordered that the laws of the province should be taught in the schools. The second Assembly passed a statute very similar in its provisions to the "learning and labor" law of 1642 in Massachusetts. The fine imposed upon parents or masters for failure to teach reading, religion, and a trade was five pounds. Numerous cases under this law appear in the court records of early Pennsylvania showing that the statute was needed. Universal education was the aim both in Massachusetts in 1642 and in Pennsylvania in 1683 but it was not attained in either colony. A school was established by the Council of Philadelphia in 1683 when Enoch Flower was employed to teach reading, writing, and bookkeeping and to provide board and lodging for pupils from a distance. Fees were charged and the rate was set by the Council. A Friends' Public School, now the William Penn Charter School, was opened in 1689 and chartered in 1697. It was a classical institution like the Boston Latin School (1635) and the School of the Dutch Reformed Church of New York (1638), now called the Collegiate School. These three seventeenth-century schools are still in operation. Included in the plan of the Penn Charter School was a system of charity schools which for almost two centuries taught the elements of reading, writing, and religion to the poor children of Philadelphia. They were abandoned when the public schools took their place.

While the first Frame of Government contained liberal provisions on education, the second, called the Charter of Privileges, which Penn granted in 1701, omitted all of these. The Charter remained in force for three-quarters of a century, until the Revolution, and during that time church, charity, and neighborhood schools held the field in elementary education in Pennsylvania. There was no effort to develop state activity. The Friends had established sixty or seventy meeting houses before the Revolution, and near many of them there were schoolhouses. The Germans of the Lutheran and Reformed churches carried over from Europe a well-developed parish school tradition and practice and were very industrious in teaching their children after the most severe frontier difficulties had been overcome. One of the Lutheran leaders in church and school was Henry M. Muhlenberg who came from A. H. Francke's schools at Halle. A Pennsylvania college has been named for him. The Episcopalians and the one or two thousand Catholics who came to the province before the Revolution established parochial schools. The Moravians at Nazareth and Bethlehem established important schools and together with the Friends were among the early pioneers in the education of girls in America. The Presbyterians, who more than others favored universal education under public auspices, often established private schools in Colonial times. The Catholics, Episcopalians, and Lutherans favored parochial schools. On the other hand, the Baptists, the Seventh Day Adventists, the Methodists, who were only beginning to grow rapidly at the Revolution, the Mennonites, the Amish, the Dunkards or Brethren, and the Schwenkfelders, while they built some schoolhouses or taught classes in their churches, were more likely to cooperate in building and maintaining neighborhood schools, or to teach their children in the family.

Towards the middle of the eighteenth century, Germans were migrating into Pennsylvania in such large numbers that their English neighbors began to think of them as a serious political problem. Many of the German immigrants were poor and, under frontier conditions, until the land was cleared, crops planted, and permanent buildings erected, education must frequently have been neglected. The English, unable to understand their language and ignorant of their past history, looked upon them with distrust. They even feared that, in the imminent war with France, the Germans might support the enemy. It was in such a time that Rev. Michael Schlatter of the German Reformed Church came to America (1746). After a five-year preaching mission among the Germans on the frontiers of Pennsylvania, Maryland, and Virginia, he sent to Europe a highly unfavorable report of American religious and educational conditions. This was printed in Holland, translated into English, and widely read. The Episcopalian provost of the College of Philadelphia, Dr. William Smith, wrote a long letter confirming and commending Schlatter's report although he had no first-hand knowledge of the facts. Dr. Smith proposed that an effort should be made to Anglicize the Germans, teaching them the language, customs, and laws of the English colonies and colonists. This was, of course, an early Americanization proposal. He argued from the sound principle that without education it is impossible to preserve a free government; but he had little understanding of these Swiss and South-German political and religious refugees. He professed to believe that they were in danger of "degenerating into a state little better than that of wood-born savages!" As a result of these and other appeals, some noblemen and wealthy gentry of England organized a Society for Propagating Christian Knowledge among the Germans in America. This title itself and still more the offer of charity aroused opposition and the Germans thought they also saw political and sectarian purposes in the program. Nevertheless, about fifteen schools were established in Reading, York, Easton, Lancaster, and other places and at one time they had a total attendance of seven hundred and fifty pupils; but they never became popular and by 1763 this early attempt at Americanization had ended in failure because the leaders did not take the trouble to understand those whom they attempted to teach.

New England developed the public school more easily and sooner than other parts of the country. There were several reasons for this such as the compact settlements, the prevalence of skilled and business occupations, the town meetings and town control of local affairs, Puritan and Calvinistic interest in education, and the close cooperation between state and church. Where church and state were as closely joined as they were in New England, it was a comparatively simple matter to secure state support of the church's educational program. This was what Luther had proposed in the early years of the Reformation; and in some of the German states, and in Holland and elsewhere, forms of church and state cooperation which looked toward public education had already been developed.

The Massachusetts law of 1642 attempted to institute compulsory education but not compulsory attendance. And again in 1647 in her second general law on education Massachusetts voted, not compulsory attendance but the compulsory establishment of schools, ordering every town, that is, township, of fifty households to establish an elementary school and every town of one hundred households a secondary school as well. One teacher qualified to teach the secondary subjects, Latin and Greek, could satisfy both requirements since the second might well include the first. A town was fined five pounds for failure to comply. This was too small an amount because, at a time when teachers received a greater amount for a year's work, recalcitrant towns found it cheaper to pay the fine than to maintain a school. The fine of five pounds was increased to twenty pounds in the course of the century.

Throughout the colonies schools were supported in the most varied ways, such as by income from lands or other endowments, local taxes, rates, appropriations, contributions, tuition fees, lotteries, liquor license fees, and bank and theater taxes. Combinations of several of these were often used at the same time, as was the case in Virginia and Massachusetts. For three centuries a great historical experiment in the means of school support has been carried on in colony and state. The first problem was to eliminate tuition fees and rates, to make the schools free of cost to parents, in order that education might cease to be a special privilege and become a public service, open to all. The schools were made tuition-free about the time of the Civil War, although Massachusetts took this step in 1827, Pennsylvania in 1834, and Vermont in 1850. The second part of the problem was to find an equitable, dependable, and sufficiently flexible source or combination of sources of funds to maintain, in good times and bad, the education of a whole people. This also was accomplished, but only gradually and at a later time.

Cities and towns generally secured free schools before the country districts. The Pennsylvania free-school law of 1834 was anticipated by more than a decade in some cities; and some of the large cities of New York had provided free schools a full generation before the state enacted the free-school law of 1867. Not every gain by the free-school interests was permanently held. Connecticut passed a law in 1700 requiring each town to levy an annual tax of two mills for the support of the schools; and in 1750 that state established a state common school fund. From the proceeds of the sale of the land of the Western Reserve a large fund was built up, and in 1821 the two-mill tax was repealed and the schools were wholly supported from the income of the state fund. The people, however, lost interest in schools for which they were not required to pay, and the schools themselves rapidly declined in efficiency. School costs increased and the schools of neighboring states, especially those of New York, forged ahead. For a time Connecticut employed cheap teachers and maintained schools only until the proceeds of the fund were exhausted. Rural school terms in the state during this period were often as short as three months. Many districts returned to the rate bill to eke out the meager support provided by the fund. Henry Barnard, Noah Porter, and several of the governors attempted to rouse the people from their slumber. In 1856 a one-mill tax for schools was passed but the rate bill was not abolished. The Connecticut public schools were not again made free until 1868. This passage from the history of school support in Connecticut illustrates several principles: that a cause such as the support of free schools by public tax may be won, and lost, and only by strenuous and long-continued effort again regained; that the people tend to lose interest in schools which are provided for them and for which they do not themselves help to provide; and that fixed endowments, permanent endowments as we incorrectly call them, do not form a dependable support for growing institutions since the funds may be lost, the rate of yield may decline, and costs are very likely to increase.

A further significant development in the town schools of New England was the separate school board, usually called the school committee. First the town meeting itself, then a special committee appointed to carry out a particular task, such as the employment of a schoolmaster, thirdly, an annual standing committee on schools appointed by the town meeting, and finally an elected school board, made mandatory in Massachusetts by the law of 1789—these were the steps by which the evolution took place.

The schools of New England, unfortunately, did not keep pace with this administrative progress. Many factors tended to lower the tone and hamper the conduct of the schools. The district school and the dame school came to take the place of the town school; and as a result, elementary education in the eighteenth century became less effective than it had been in the seventeenth. This is shown in the town records and other writings of the two periods. The Indian wars had been destructive and costly and the money spent on arms could not at the same time be used for schools. In King Philip's War half of the ninety New England towns were involved and many villages were destroyed. After the war a large debt remained to be paid. With the removal of the Indian danger, the colonists set up separate farmhouses instead of rural villages and moved farther and farther into the wilderness where the school could not easily follow them. On the frontier, also, a literary education was less needed and therefore less desired than in the eastern towns where shopkeepers, mechanics, ship captains, and those of other skilled vocations demanded arithmetic, bookkeeping, and literary skills. Before the end of the seventeenth century the Puritan church was divided into liberal and conservative branches; and a good deal of the religious fervor which had supported education at first had been dissipated. Toleration, admirable though it is, does not favor unity and in New England it gave entrance to many sects. All these changes led to a decline of education on the frontiers of all the colonies. In New England they produced the district school, which is first cousin to the neighborhood school of colonies farther west and south.

The separation of the people into small and isolated settlements led to the separation of the township into small neighborhood districts for school purposes and the establishment of the district system. The word district is ambiguous when used in education without qualifying explanation. We may speak of city districts, supervisory districts, and other types, but when we speak of "the district system" we refer to a one-teacher school that is controlled by a board which administers this one school only. This obviously is to reduce the school to its lowest terms, to bring it as close as possible to the people, to make it, in that sense, as democratic as possible. The district system was peculiarly adapted to the frontier which created it. It is historically important because it moved from New England westward with the advancing frontier so that almost all regions of our country were at some time under the district system. It is historically important because once firmly established, supported by the sentiments of the neighborhood, it became a formidable obstacle to educational progress. The shortcomings of the district school, as compared with the consolidated or city school, were such as the short terms, the low salaries, and the lack of uniformity between neighboring schools, of supervision, of equipment, and of sufficient enrollment for efficient group work.

7. SECONDARY AND COLLEGE EDUCATION

Our early secondary schools were Latin grammar schools which prepared boys for college and which were closely connected with the colleges. Some Latin grammar schools were public, others were private. Most of them were independent but some were merely the preparatory departments of colleges. The curriculum was always classical, but the role of the Greek studies had shrunk so greatly that only the simplest elements of the language were taught. The instruction in Latin was more extensive and consisted of drill in grammar and composition and the reading of Cicero and other authors. Rhetoric, declamation, and ancient history were sometimes added.

Many of the American Latin schools were local day schools which enrolled the children of the community, but there were some boarding schools. Obviously the boarding school, a little world in itself which shuts out the great world beyond its walls, erects a greater barrier between its pupils and those who are excluded than the day school. The day school is not so far removed from everyday interests; and after school hours the children of the whole neighborhood mingle freely with each other. The typical colonial grammar school was a small day school in a middle class community; and it frequently taught the common branches to one group and Latin to another and smaller group who intended to go to college. To cite just one example: the school of Roxbury, Massachusetts, at the end of the colonial period had eighty-five pupils, and only nine of these were studying Latin. The rest were enrolled in the common branches. Only in the largest towns were there many Latin pupils. In small places the master was compelled to teach reading and arithmetic to ten boys before he had the chance to introduce a single one into the mysteries of the Latin tongue. The aristocracy of the Latin grammar school of which we sometimes read was a good deal of a myth; but educationally it was not well adapted to the frontier. Before the end of the colonial period a new institution, the academy, began to take its place because it was a more flexible institution and better adapted to a new country. Very few of the colonial Latin schools remain, but among these are the Boston and the Roxbury Latin Schools and the William Penn Charter School.

As early as 1621 a free school called the East India School was planned at Charles City, Virginia, but perhaps it was never opened because the whole settlement was wiped out in the following year by an Indian massacre. The Symms school, endowed by a will of 1634, and the Eaton school were not in constant operation, but there is a slender thread of continuity leading to the present Symms-Eaton Academy, a public school at Hampton in which the two old foundations have been merged. Several other private and endowed schools offered classical education in Virginia. The school at Norfolk was a public school controlled by the town council. Thomas Jefferson prepared for William and Mary and James Madison for Princeton in private grammar schools, and such schools became numerous in the later colonial period when Scotch schoolmasters migrated to Virginia. One of these was Donald Robertson who maintained a prosperous school in the period from the French and Indian War to the Revolution. The College of William and Mary, named for the sovereigns brought in by the "glorious revolution," was the only colonial college south of Philadelphia; but this section rapidly developed new colleges after 1776.

Several efforts were made by the legislatures of North Carolina and of Maryland to encourage the founding of grammar schools but conditions were very similar to those in Virginia. As Governor Calvert of Maryland said, "the remoteness of the habitation of one person from another" was the great obstacle. The government of North Carolina aided several grammar schools with grants of land and funds; and Maryland provided for a school at Annapolis, which later developed into St. John's College, and also a county system of Latin schools, each county school system to be governed by a board of trustees. Only a few of the twelve schools projected by the latter act were successful.

The Penn Charter School, already mentioned, was the first permanent Latin school in Pennsylvania. Several elementary charity schools were connected with it; and the central school itself was in two divisions: a Latin school and an English and mathematical school. The former was strictly classical throughout the colonial period and long after; but the latter was a practical school which taught a range of subjects, arithmetic, bookkeeping, trigonometry, navigation, surveying, and others. The French and German languages were taught from 1742. This early school differed from Franklin's Academy in that it was conducted by a religious society and was not connected with a college; but otherwise the two were very similar. Eastern Pennsylvania had many private grammar schools in the eighteenth century. Several of these, which were designed to prepare young men for the ministry, were established by Presbyterians and resembled the Puritan academies of England. They taught the classics, which received the main emphasis, but also included mathematics, some of the sciences, and theology. There were grammar schools conducted by several of the churches, and there were a few neighborhood grammar schools managed by groups of interested citizens. Most of these were classical but from the Penn Charter school and some of the schools of the Presbyterians we gather a hint of an important truth, that even in colonial times grammar schools in the Middle Colonies tended to introduce modern subjects. This statement applies to the schools of New York and New Jersey as well as those of Pennsylvania. Life was less ecclesiastical west and south of New England and medical and scientific interests were more widely diffused.

The settlers of Massachusetts began to set up grammar schools in the first years of the Bay Colony. Because conditions were more favorable than in the other colonies, their success was much greater. Seven or eight grammar schools in the towns of Boston (1635), Roxbury, Ipswich, Dorchester, Cambridge, and others were begun within a few years of the settlement; and the law requiring every town of a hundred families to maintain a school where boys could prepare for college was passed in 1647. Connecticut enacted a similar law in 1650, although a few grammar schools had been established earlier. Two of these were located at New Haven (1641) and Hartford (1642). The bequest of Edward Hopkins was applied in aid of these two schools and of another one at Hadley. The Hopkins Grammar School of New Haven is still in operation. In most of New England the zeal for grammar school education declined in the late seventeenth and eighteenth centuries. According to the Massachusetts court records, some towns which had been favorable to education neglected their schools and deliberately incurred the penalty of the law of 1647 because it was cheaper to pay the fine than to pay the master. Many grammar schools also became mere elementary schools because there were no advanced pupils.

8. ACADEMIES IN THE MAKING

The schools in America made numerous adjustments to the special conditions of the new country but in the eighteenth century they effected an invention, a distinctly new institution, which developed into the American academy. Among the adjustments which have been mentioned were public control, the district system, the neighborhood schools and, contrary to the English practice of grouping colleges in universities, the distribution of our colleges in widely separated population centers. The new invention was the incipient academy, often called "the private school in the city," or "the advertised school." With the increase in population, new business and construction needs arose, and the gap between what the grammar schools taught and what practical life demanded became constantly wider. Enterprising teachers sought to satisfy these growing needs where they were most insistent, namely, in the towns of Boston, Newport, New York, Philadelphia, and Charleston. Such teachers opened evening and day schools, offered practical subjects, and advertised their programs in the papers. Evening elementary schools had appeared in New Amsterdam before 1650, but these practical evening or day schools on the secondary level did not become very numerous until 1725. Philadelphia alone had one hundred and sixty teachers of such advertised schools between 1722 and the end of the Revolutionary War. City directories tell a similar story. In the period following the Revolution, New York City had one private teacher for every ninety families. About one-fourth of these teachers were women. Many of the advertised schools for girls were well stocked with ornamental branches but those for boys were more likely to offer mathematics and its applications. The schools usually followed the quarter-plan; and being without endowments, if they were to prosper they had to meet the needs and wants of the pupils.

To show the emphasis upon mathematics and the variety of the branches and topics in that field, we give a list made by combining the offerings of several of the schools. Each of the subjects named below was taught or at least advertised by one or more private schools in eighteenth-century America. The list is as follows: algebra, geometry, mensuration, logarithms, plane and spherical trigonometry, fluxions (also called calculus), the quadrant, navigation, astronomy, surveying, dialing, gauging, geography, maps, use of the globes, bookkeeping; and also engineering subjects such as leveling, hydraulics, hydrostatics, pneumatics, optics, perspective, architecture, fortification, and gunnery. Bookkeeping was advertised to be taught according to "the Italian method of double entry." The modern languages were not omitted. There were teachers of French, German, Spanish, and other subjects which the grammar schools and colleges of that time ignored almost entirely. These were new schools meeting practical needs.

9. THE EARLIEST ACADEMIES

The foundations of the American academy were laid by the private schools which we have described. The academy is distinguished from these by the fact that its control was vested in a board of trustees which often operated under a charter from the state. In the present account both the chartered secondary schools with a realist curriculum and those without a state charter will be included under the term academy. It was a more flexible and variable institution than the English academy. It frequently admitted girls and sometimes was open to girls only. In the latter case the term female seminary was often used. The English academy was a boys' school and usually taught theology to ministerial students, while in America the academy frequently had no church connections. Many American academies prepared teachers for the common schools and indeed these institutions became the models for both the normal schools and the public high schools. The Americanism of the academy is suggested by its development during the movement for independence and its general acceptance during our first national period. The prerevolutionary period belonged to the Latin grammar school; and soon after the Civil War the high school became dominant; but during the intervening century from 1770 to 1870 our needs for secondary education were served mainly by the academy.

The chief defects of the academies as institutions in a democracy are that they were not free and were not controlled by a public board. Many tended to become expensive and exclusive boarding schools, but in the beginning they furnished educational opportunity to the boys and girls from the farms and villages. They were not free, but in the thousands of country academies the costs were low. To maintain themselves these schools had to teach what the public demanded at a cost they could afford. The curricula were broad and flexible and included many courses in mathematics, the sciences, English, and history. Logic, ethics, geography, and civics were offered. The great subject fields were divided into short courses. The English branches might include reading, elocution, grammar, composition, rhetoric, word study, declamation, debating, literature, and literary history. Mathematics and the sciences were likewise divided into short courses. As many as one hundred and fifty distinct courses were offered although most of these were subdivisions of a few large fields. Like the "advertised schools" from which they stemmed, the academies taught many subjects which led to engineering or business employment; but the idea of a general, liberal education was also present. Gradually, as the weaker academies were displaced by the public high school, those which survived tended to become college preparatory schools.

School equipment had not yet become extensive in the age of the academy. Libraries and laboratories were lacking in most cases, although there were usually little-used cabinets of minerals and apparatus. Most of the courses were taught from textbooks and the spread of the academy must have greatly encouraged the writers of the flood of schoolbooks which came from the press after 1800. Many of the academies were small, one- or two-teacher schools, and textbook recitation was the usual method, although field work and simple experiments were not entirely unknown. It should be remembered that the boys and girls of that rural age had more direct contact with nature and more knowledge of her ways than the city-bred youth of today; but, in itself, academy education was both bookish and discursive, even superficial.

Secondary schools were sometimes called academies early in the eighteenth century if not before. There was a South Carolina academy in 1712; the "log college" of Pennsylvania, opened in 1726 by Reverend William

Tennent, was not only sometimes given the name but it had the characteristics of the English dissenting academies. As early as 1743, Franklin "drew up a proposal for establishing an academy" in Philadelphia. Six years later he returned to the project, secured the help of a number of active supporters, wrote a pamphlet entitled, "Proposals relating to the Education of Youth in Pennsylvania," and started a subscription for funds. A board of trustees was agreed upon, and in November 1750 they ordered "that the Academy be opened on the seventh day of January next," and it was opened on that day. Although not incorporated until 1753, it may have been the first chartered academy in America. It was Franklin's intention to found a wholly nonsectarian school and one in which modern subjects, especially English, history, and mathematics, were to have the chief places; but he was disappointed in both objectives, as it was inevitable that he should be. Of the twenty-four trustees about two-thirds were Episcopalians. And after the College of Philadelphia was established in 1755, an active clergyman of the same church, Reverend William Smith, became provost. Neither the original academy charter nor the new charter of *The Trustees of the College, Academy, and Charitable School of Philadelphia in the Province of Pennsylvania* mentioned the religious affiliations of the trustees or staff and the nonsectarian character of the school was, in the legal sense, preserved; but at any rate some very prominent Episcopalians felt that the school leaned to their side. The academy, like the old Penn Charter School, was divided into a classical and an English school and the chief teacher of the classical division became the administrative head of both classical and English schools with the title of Rector and a salary which was twice that of the English master. Perhaps these were the best terms that even the diplomatic Franklin could get from the board for his cherished English school; but it is not surprising that the Philadelphia Academy laid more stress upon the classics than upon the modern subjects, especially when we consider its close affiliation with the college. It was in the public high school that Franklin's educational ideal finally came to prevail. As the high school developed many academies were closed, others were turned over to the public school boards, and the rest became a minor but not unimportant agency in the whole field of American secondary education.

10. THE COLONIAL COLLEGES

Four colleges were established in the New England colonies: Harvard, Yale, Dartmouth, and Brown; four in the Middle Colonies: the College of New Jersey, now Princeton, King's College, now Columbia, the College of Philadelphia, which grew out of Franklin's Academy, now the University

The Colonial Colleges

Timeline: 1600 — 1620 — 1636 — 1640 — 1660 — 1680 — 1693 — 1700 — 1701 — 1720 — 1740 — 1746 1754 1755 — 1760 — 1764 1766 1769 — 1780 — 1800

THE VENERABLE NINE

1636 HARVARD	1755 PENNSYLVANIA	
1693 WILLIAM AND MARY	1764 BROWN	
1701 YALE	1766 RUTGERS	
1746 PRINCETON	1769 DARTMOUTH	
1754 COLUMBIA		

IN NEW ENGLAND — HARVARD, YALE, BROWN, DARTMOUTH

IN MIDDLE COLONIES — PRINCETON, COLUMBIA, PENNSYLVANIA, RUTGERS

IN SOUTHERN COLONIES — WILLIAM AND MARY

EARLY TIME SCHEDULE, HARVARD

CLASSES	8:00–9:00	9:00–10:00	10:00–11:00	1:00–2:00	2:00–3:00	3:00–4:00
M FRESHMEN / JUNIOR SOPHS / SENIOR SOPHS	Logick, Physicks	Ethicks, Politicks	Arithmetic and Geometry	Disputations[3]	Disputations[3]	Disputations[3]
T FRESHMEN / JUNIOR SOPHS / SENIOR SOPHS	Logick, Physicks	Ethicks, Politicks	Arithmetic and Geometry	Disputations[3]	Disputations[3]	Disputations[3]
W FRESHMEN / JUNIOR SOPHS / SENIOR SOPHS	Greek Etymology and Syntax	Greek Prosody and Dialects	Greek	Greek Grammar	Greek Poetry Disputation	Greek Composition and Verse
TH FRESHMEN / JUNIOR SOPHS / SENIOR SOPHS	Hebrew Grammar	Chaldee	Syriack	Bible	Ezra and Daniel	Trostius on New Testament
F FRESHMEN	Rhetorick[1]	Declamations[2]		History (in winter) Botany (in summer)		
F JUNIOR SOPHS	As Above	As Above		As Above		
F SENIOR SOPHS	As Above	As Above		As Above		
S FRESHMEN	Divinity	Commonplaces				
S JUNIOR SOPHS	As Above	As Above				
S SENIOR SOPHS	As Above	As Above				

[1] Collectively.   [2] Everyone, once a month.   [3] Each in his art.

of Pennsylvania, and Queen's College, now Rutgers; and one in the southern colonies, William and Mary, at Williamsburg, in Virginia. For fifty years after the settlements, Harvard was the only American college and it was long a small and mediocre institution. It began to grow in numbers and importance in the eighteenth century and especially after the Revolution. Something of its early scope and purpose can be gathered from the accompanying diagram. Evidently its early curriculum was composed of three historical strata of materials taken respectively from the Middle Ages, the Renaissance, and the Reformation. The diagram also reveals the significant fact that six of the nine colonial colleges were founded within the last thirty years of the colonial period.

The colonial colleges were regarded as societies of ministers and prospective ministers. The only profession for which they specifically prepared was the clerical. Many destined for other callings, however, attended and only about forty per cent of the graduates of the colleges became ministers. Only the College of Philadelphia was to any great degree independent of church affiliation; but the head of that school throughout the colonial period was a clergyman and was accused of teaching Episcopalian and Tory doctrines. Besides the clergy, lawyers and physicians became intellectual leaders in the years before the Revolution. No colonial college maintained a law school; but the College of Philadelphia, located in the city which had become the greatest medical center of America, established a medical school in 1765.

The plantation system of Virginia and the South was much less favorable to school development than the compact settlement, skilled industry, and town government of New England. Both of these sections were settled by Englishmen; but the Middle Colonies had a mixed population of many languages and faiths. As a result of these differences, three types of school administration were developed. The South depended largely upon private education, New England upon a simple form of semi-public schools under the legal and extra-legal control of both church and town, and the Middle Colonies largely upon parochial and neighborhood activity. The South, therefore, followed the ancient classical custom, the Middle Colonies the medieval practice, while New England adopted the rising idea of state action. Examples of all these types of school administration existed in Europe and, in fact, in the British Isles. Religious toleration and freedom and political democracy, as they slowly developed, gave increasing support to the growing public school idea.

The schools themselves, like the administration, were transplanted. There were four main types of schools and educational effort, namely, apprenticeship, the elementary school of the four R's, the secondary and collegiate scheme which was carried on by the Latin schools and colleges together, and practical schooling to prepare youth for simple engineering and business occupations. A noteworthy achievement of the period was the development of the American academy. Each of the main types of institutions was found in all sections.

In retrospect, the colonies are seen to present almost every variety of educational systems and institutions, all competing for social acceptance and survival; parochial, sectarian missionary, private, neighborhood, town, district, and still other elementary schools; medieval, humanist, and realist secondary schools; schools and apprenticeship for vocational preparation; and Old World colleges in the towns; and to maintain all these educational endeavors, various kinds of administrative devices, numerous forms of financial support, and several ways of securing public attention and interest were employed. It was as though some educational Francis Bacon had set up a giant experiment to determine which types of schools and of school management could best survive and prosper in a wilderness developing into the United States of America. One of the most conclusive phases of this experiment is that which had to do with modes of support; but, although much has been learned from this and the other phases of the whole great adventure, it is important to notice that the "experiment" has not ended. It is still in process and the evaluation is continuing.

In the colonial period, then, the foundations were laid for our public school systems, for our numerous types of private schools, and for the public policy which permits private education to continue and to compete with public. Only the foundations were laid upon which the next period began to build.

QUESTIONS

1. Educational differences between colonial New England and the South are supposed to have been due to different physical, economic, political, and religious influences in the two sections. What effects can be assigned to each kind of influence?

2. How did the diversity of religious faiths affect early education in Pennsylvania?

3. American education is justly proud of its success in helping to "Americanize" foreign immigrants. Why is Pennsylvania Dutch, an anglicized German dialect, still widely used in eastern Pennsylvania?

4. Civil control of schools, support by public taxation, and nonsectarian (or, perhaps, secular) teaching may be considered as cornerstones of public education. How much progress toward achieving each of these was made in colonial days? What would you choose for the fourth cornerstone? Would it be compulsory attendance, or some other feature, and why?

5. Evaluate the apprenticeship laws and practice in the colonies.

6. What were the advantages and defects under colonial conditions of the neighborhood schools?

7. Using Wickersham's *History of Education in Pennsylvania*, consider the statement that William Penn was a realist.

8. Why did American education tend to become less rather than more effective in the latter seventeenth century?

9. Why was it easier for New England than for other parts of the country to approximate public education?

10. Why did the district system develop and why was it found unsatisfactory? What is a district school?

11. Compare educational opportunity about 1770 in Philadelphia with that open in the country (a) to a boy and (b) to a girl. Was the difference between city and country greater for a boy or a girl? Why?
    (Town, date, and distance in this question may be varied to fit available data. Other considerations, such as cost and religious requirements, may be included.)

12. Why must the academy in late colonial and early national times be considered an important development?

13. Using Woody's *Views of B. Franklin*, show why the Academy of Philadelphia did not accomplish what its chief promoter intended.

14. Using Pauline Holmes's *History of the Boston Latin School*, trace and explain the curriculum changes in that school in colonial times.

15. The early settlers merely "transplanted" European institutions. How much progress did their successors achieve before 1775?

16. What are the conditions that aid, and the others that hinder, educational borrowing by one country or culture from another? Consider the chief examples mentioned in this book.

FOR FURTHER READING AND STUDY

About ten per cent of the fourteen thousand sketches in the *Dictionary of American Biography* (New York, Charles Scribner's Sons, 1928–1936) deal with educators, teachers, scholars, and others whose "lives" form a part of the history of education. The work, in twenty-one volumes and an index volume, was edited by Allen Johnson and Dumas Malone. Volume 21 (1944) is a supplementary volume edited by Harris E. Starr. Colonial educators, such as Francis Alison, the presidents of Harvard and other colleges, Ezekiel Cheever, David James Dove, Michael Schlatter, Ebenezer Kinnersley, and many others, are included. The *Dictionary* will be useful for all periods of American education as will Barnard's *Journal* and Monroe's *Cyclopedia*, which have been mentioned before. The *Circulars of Information* issued by the United States Bureau of Education, between 1887 and 1903, as "Contributions to American Educational History" cover all of the thirteen colonies but give the chief emphasis to higher education. A list of the *Circulars of Information* is found (pp. 253–254) in Donald W. Tewksbury, *The Founding of American Colleges and Universities before the Civil War* (New York, Bureau of Publications, Teachers College, Columbia University, 1932, 254 pp.). The colonial colleges are, of course, treated in this latter work and there is an extensive bibliography. An illustrated list of arithmetic texts and other mathematical books, published or reprinted in the American colonies is found in Louis Charles Karpinski, *Bibliography of Mathematical Works Printed in America through 1850*, (Ann Arbor, University of Michigan Press, 1940, 697 pp.).

Adams, James Truslow, *Provincial Society, 1690–1763*, New York, The Macmillan Company, 1927, 374 pp. In the "A History of American Life" series.

Bridenbaugh, Carl, *Cities in the Wilderness; the First Century of Urban Life in America, 1625–1742*, New York, The Ronald Press Company, 1938, 500 pp.

Burr, Nelson, *Education in New Jersey, 1630–1871*, Princeton University Press, 1942, 355 pp. Useful for Chapter 17 also.

Clews, Elsie, *Educational Legislation and Administration of the Colonial Governments*, New York, 1899, 526 pp. A Columbia University dissertation, also published in "Columbia University Contributions to Philosophy, Psychology, and Education," Vol. 6, Nos. 1–4.

Earle, Alice Morse, *Child Life in Colonial Days*, New York, The Macmillan Company, 1899, 418 pp. Mrs. Earle has written many other popular books that would furnish useful background. Among them are *Costume in Colonial Times, Curious Punishments of By-gone Days, Home Life in Colonial Days*, and others.

Eggleston, Edward, *The Transit of Civilization from England to America in the Seventeenth Century*, New York, D. Appleton & Company, 1901, 344 pp.; *The Hoosier School-master, The Hoosier School-boy, The Circuit Rider, Roxy* and other novels.

Fithian, Philip Vickers, *Journal and Letters of Philip Vickers Fithian, 1773–1774: a Plantation Tutor of the Old Dominion*. Edited by Hunter Dickinson Farish, Williamsburg, Va., Colonial Williamsburg, Incorporated, 1943, 323 pp.

Ford, Paul Leicester, *The New England Primer*, New York, Dodd, Mead & Company, Inc., 1899, 78 pp.

Holmes, Pauline, *The Tercentenary History of the Boston Public Latin School, 1635–1935*, Cambridge, Harvard University Press, 1935, 541 pp.

Jernegan, Marcus W., "Compulsory Attendance in the American Colonies," in *The School Review*, Vol. 26, 731–749 (Dec., 1918); and Vol. 27, 24–43 (Jan., 1919). See also other articles by this author in *The School Review*, 1918–1920.

Johnson, Clifton, *The Country School in New England*, New York, D. Appleton & Company, 1893, 102 pp.; *Old-Time Schools and School Books*, New York, The Macmillan Company, 1904, 381 pp.

Kilpatrick, William Heard, *The Dutch Schools of New Netherlands and Colonial New York*, Washington, Government Printing Office, 1912, 239 pp. Bureau of Education, Bulletin, No. 12, 1912.

Kraus, Michael, *Intercolonial Aspects of American Culture on the Eve of the Revolution, with Special Reference to the Northern Towns*, New York, Columbia University Press, 1928, 251 pp.

Morison, Samuel Eliot, *Three Centuries of Harvard, 1636–1936*, Cambridge, Harvard University Press, 1937, 512 pp.

Mulhern, James, *A History of Secondary Education in Pennsylvania*, Philadelphia, published by the author, 1933, 714 pp. This detailed study covers the colonial and later periods.

Schneider, Herbert W., *A History of American Philosophy*, New York, Columbia University Press, 1946, 646 pp. Applies to this and the later chapters.

Seybolt, Robert Francis, *Apprenticeship and Apprenticeship Education in Colonial New England and New York*, New York, Bureau of Publications, Teachers College, Columbia University, 1916, 121 pp., Teachers College Contributions to Education, No. 85; *Source Studies in American Colonial Education: The Private School*, Urbana, Ill., University of Illinois, Bureau of Educational Research, 1925, 96 pp.; *The Evening School in Colonial America*, Urbana, Ill., University of Illinois, Bureau of Educational Research, 1925, 68 pp.

Thwing, Charles Franklin, A History of Higher Education in America, New York, D. Appleton & Company, 1906, 501 pp. The first six chapters deal with the colonial colleges.

Updegraff, Harlan, The Origin of the Moving School in Massachusetts, New York, Bureau of Publications, Teachers College, Columbia University, 1908, 186 pp., Teachers College Contributions to Education, No. 17.

Weber, Samuel E., Charity School Movement in Colonial Pennsylvania, Philadelphia, W. J. Campbell, 1905, 74 pp.

Wells, Guy F., Parish Education in Colonial Virginia, New York, Bureau of Publications, Teachers College, Columbia University, 1923, 95 pp., Teachers College Contributions to Education, No. 138.

Wertenbaker, Thomas J., The Golden Age of Colonial Culture, New York, New York University Press, 1942, 171 pp.

Wickersham, James Pyle, A History of Education in Pennsylvania, Lancaster, Pa., Inquirer Publishing Co., 1886, 683 pp. This work contains material on the educational views of William Penn and on private and neighborhood schools in an important colony.

Woody, Thomas, Early Quaker Education in Pennsylvania, New York, Bureau of Publications, Teachers College, Columbia University, 1920, 287 pp., Teachers College Contributions to Education, No. 105; Quaker Education in the Colony and State of New Jersey; a Source Book, Philadelphia, published by the author, University of Pennsylvania, 1923, 408 pp.; A History of Women's Education in the United States, Lancaster, Pa., The Science Press, 1929, 2 vols.; Editor, The Educational Views of Benjamin Franklin, New York, McGraw-Hill Book Company, Inc., 1931, 270 pp.

"State School Finance Systems," National Education Association Research Bulletin, Vol. 20, No. 5, pp. 149–195 (November, 1942).

17 UNDER THE NEW CONSTITUTION

URING THE REVOLUTIONARY WAR, THE COMMON DANGER led to a certain unity among the states; but when the war was over, sectionalism and state sovereignty again strongly asserted themselves. The period between the close of the war and the adoption of the Constitution was an era of political confusion when the new sovereign states competed among themselves and on several occasions threatened armed hostilities within the confederation. Even before the Constitutional Convention, education was proposed as an important means of forming a more unified nation. With the establishment of the federal government, the need for education to promote national unity and citizenship became apparent to all thinking men. Washington and other leaders argued that education should be fostered and employed to overcome sectionalism, to prepare the young for the duties of citizenship in a republic, and to maintain the spirit of liberty. Many urged also that practical education would aid agriculture and commerce and would in this way promote the general welfare. Nor could the individual need of education be neglected in a country which claimed to be the land of opportunity for the common man. In this chapter we shall treat the period between the Revolution and the Civil War.

1. EDUCATION FOR A MORE PERFECT UNION

The Constitution was framed to strengthen the central government, to bind the states together, and to overcome sectional feeling, and the preamble proposed, as the first aim, the development of a more perfect union. Other aims would, indeed, become possible only if this one were attained. Many of the framers of the Constitution believed, with Washington, that education would be an additional means of drawing the people together. There were, however, obstacles to closer union which neither the Constitution nor the school was able to reach. Such obstacles were the wide dis-

persion of the population, poor roads, difficult communication, and property qualifications for the suffrage. These tended to divide the people and,
since they were hindrances to the development of schools, they tended
to keep the people apart by hindering the formation of agencies that would
have drawn them together. We shall illustrate some of the above statements.

About the year 1800 the whole population of Great Britain was fifteen
millions, that of France almost twice that number, while the United States
with its vast area had only five and one-third millions. Manhood suffrage
existed in only four states, and the one million voters of the republic were
fewer in number than the slaves. Many felt that the new government gave
them no more voice than the British had done. The center of population was northeast of the city of Washington; but there were already a
half-million settlers in the Ohio valley, separated by a hundred miles of
mountain and forest from the civilization of the East. Transportation,
everywhere, was slow, costly, and laborious, and the West found it easier
to reach her markets through New Orleans than by crossing the mountains.
There was a good deal of sentiment and some intrigue, fostered by Spain
and by Great Britain, for a separate nation in the Great Valley.

Communication was equally unsatisfactory. Franklin had organized an
intercolonial postal system in 1753, but in 1800 it still required twenty days
to cover the one main mail route from Maine to Georgia. Letter postage
varied with the distance, and the cost of sending a letter from Boston to
Philadelphia was twenty-five cents. As a result few letters were sent, in the
year 1800 fewer than one per white inhabitant. The triweekly stage from
Boston to New York took three days to reach its destination and the daily
stage from New York to Philadelphia two days. Stage-coach travel with
hotel charges cost about twenty cents a mile. These were the conditions
where roads existed; that is in the neighborhood of towns and between
the cities. In many settled parts of the country there were no roads. Jefferson wrote to his Attorney-General that five of the eight rivers which had
to be crossed between Monticello and Washington had neither bridges nor
boats.

The people and the government realized that improved communication and transportation were essential to the success of the union. They
did not foresee the steamboat or the railroad, but they set about building
the Cumberland Road from the Potomac to the Monongahela, another
road southwest toward Knoxville, and a third from Philadelphia to Pittsburgh. The era of the canals also was just beginning. Towns were still
small in 1800. Philadelphia, the largest, with seventy thousand people and
New York with sixty were about three times the size of Boston, Baltimore,
or Charleston. Educational facilities in these and even in much smaller

towns were far better than among the dispersed rural population. Rural education in Europe is village education, but the American farmer lives in an isolated home at some distance from all neighbors. This dispersion, greatest in the new West and the South but a basic fact also in the East, was one of the most difficult of educational problems. It is one that has not yet been solved, for the country school is still the weakest link in our educational system.

In the period of eighty years covered by this chapter, the cities with a population of more than eight thousand increased in number from five to one hundred forty-one; and the percentage of the total population in cities of the size stated increased from three per cent in 1780 to sixteen per cent in 1860. After the War with England (1812–1815), American industry developed rapidly. Cotton spinning became a New England industry and Pennsylvania became the center of iron and steel production. The steel, in turn, made possible the construction of the railroads and manufacture of the newly invented farm machinery. In 1844, when the telegraph was invented, there were about eight thousand miles of railroad lines in operation.

With the increasing demand for labor, immigration rose to a flood. Most of the newcomers found homes and work in the cities of the North and on the prairies of the West. The children of the migratory workers who built the railroads, canals, and telegraph lines and those of the new immigrants who did not speak English made difficult educational problems. As in England, slums and various social maladies such as pauperism and juvenile delinquency marred life in the factory towns, and, to mitigate such evils and provide a little education for the children before they entered the factory, first monitorial and charity, and then public schools were established.

More important in determining the future of the nation than the industry of the East was the westward migration of the people. Between 1800 and 1820 the population of the country increased nearly two million, and the extending frontier presented a staggering educational problem. It was a problem not solved in one generation, for illiteracy in the United States as a whole increased rather than diminished in the middle decades of the century. Frontier life was without luxuries and scanty in comforts. The frontiersmen were or became self-reliant and self-assertive individualists. The period of nationalism (1815–1825) was followed by the revival of sectionalism and the rise of the grass-roots democracy which characterized the party of Andrew Jackson. Before the Civil War, thirty-one states, six of them beyond the Mississippi, had been admitted into the Union. To a moderate degree at least, the educational needs of this empire were met through its increasing wealth and the resurgent democracy of its people.

2. EDUCATIONAL LEGISLATION

Education became a matter of popular and public concern after the Revolution; popular as shown by a growing volume of writing on the subject; and public through the action of state and national legislatures. Even during the war Pennsylvania, Massachusetts, and other states introduced

6	5	4	3	2	1
7	8	9	10	11	12
18	17	16	15	14	13
19	20	21	22	23	24
30	29	28	27	26	25
31	32	33	34	35	36

FIGURE 5

PLOT ALLOTMENT FOR SCHOOLS UNDER THE ORDINANCE OF 1785

sections on public education into the new state constitutions adopted at the time. The old Congress of the Confederation also acted. The Ordinance of 1785 provided that "there shall be reserved the Lot No. 16 of every township for the maintenance of public schools within said township." Ohio became a state in 1803 and was first to benefit from this clause. One section for schools for each township became the rule as new states were admitted into the Union; but some of the later states were given two sections and the last few states, four sections for each township. In each state the people through their legislatures were the ultimate custodians of the school lands. In some states, especially the new ones which profited by the mistakes of others, the lands were carefully managed and yielded large endowments for public education; but in many the lands were dissipated through inefficiency and dishonesty, both the results of a too easy public morality. Even when this was not the case, land was plentiful and cheap in early times, and the financial returns were meager. Even after 1860 the standard price of public lands was only a dollar and a quarter per acre. Yet there was some return and some aid to schools; and one may argue that, if the lands helped to make a beginning in public education, an important service was rendered. Later generations could provide for the support of schools more easily than the early pioneers could establish them.

Another far-reaching act was passed by the old Congress. The Ordinance of 1787 for the organization of the Northwest Territory excluded slavery from the entire region north of the Ohio River. This ordinance also included what may be called a charter for public education in this large area from which five states were to be carved. The charter is in Article Three and is expressed in these words: "Religion, morality, and knowledge, being necessary to good government and the happiness of mankind, schools, and the means of education shall be encouraged." This is intended to mean, and it is so stated in the sentence that follows, that the government shall encourage education, for the ordinance was a scheme of government.

State governments also took action. Their aid to the academies has been mentioned. Their constitutions frequently included clauses on education. By an act of 1787 the legislature of New York set up a permanent Board of Regents to charter all secondary schools and colleges and to control the education, on these upper levels, of the whole state. This idea of the centralized control of education, especially of secondary and collegiate education, cropped up about the same time and later in several of the states including Georgia, Louisiana, and Michigan. As noted in Chapter 12, the University of France was established by Bonaparte. In the United States, however, the nation was not yet ready to undertake an educational program. The only educational discussion in the Constitutional Convention concerned a proposed national university, which was to promote national unity. The Constitution does not mention education, but its adoption profoundly, though indirectly, fostered educational progress.

3. THEORIES OF DEMOCRATIC EDUCATION

The utilitarian individualism of Franklin which presaged the practice of the academy was met by a vigorous opposing current of social and political thought. The new theory was that education should serve not individual but state ends. In America an interest in educational principles can hardly be said to have existed before 1776. Except for William Penn and Franklin, both of whom introduced European ideas in language that the common man could understand, educational theory was almost a total blank until we come to the writings of Jefferson, Benjamin Rush, Robert Coram, Samuel Knox, S. H. Smith, and Dupont de Nemours; and the last of these was a Frenchman living in America.

Jefferson in 1779 prepared a bill for the more general diffusion of knowledge which is our best source for his views on this subject. In reading it we should remember that it was not a statement of what he might have ideally wished to have, but a bill to be hopefully laid before the legislators of Virginia as an outline of what he expected to get. Even so it asked for more than they were willing to grant. The bill implied that a popular government can be maintained only if the people are intelligent and well informed, particularly on history, with emphasis on the history of popular liberty. It provided for free public schools everywhere to assure universal education, and which all children could attend without cost for three years and longer by paying fees, for a secondary school in each county, with free education for a few of the ablest boys, and for a state college also giving free education to a limited number of selected students. Others could attend by paying the usual fees. The last part of this scheme, the state college or university, was realized on a grand scale nearly fifty years later by the opening of the University of Virginia. Madison agreed with Jefferson that popular government cannot exist without popular information or the means of acquiring it; and he also supported the idea of school taxation. John Adams wrote the liberal and eloquent paragraph on education in the Massachusetts constitution of 1780.

Writers on education became numerous after the Revolution. They drew plans for public schools to be established and supported by the people for the preservation of liberty, democracy, and citizenship. They were not able to outline all the details of such an education. Benjamin Rush developed an argument and a plan for a national university and a plan of schools for Pennsylvania. The special preparation of teachers was urged, apparently by Elisha Ticknor and by Samuel Knox. Many urged a more utilitarian education in which science should show how natural resources might be developed. Robert Coram declared that education should be a state function and all children, in a public system of schools, should have the same opportunities. He was particularly insistent that country children should have the same opportunity as city children. As in the French Revolution, so in America a strong prejudice grew up against higher education as being undemocratic and tending to the growth of privileged classes. Coram was one of these egalitarians who thought it a shame that any should be sent to college where they would merely "learn to cheat the rest." Fortunately the country did not agree with him and a great many academies and colleges were founded in the two decades which closed the eighteenth century.

A centralized national school system was in the minds of several. Three of the writers named, Knox, Smith, and DuPont, proposed a national board of education which, as Knox said, should develop a uniform system for the whole country, able to unify the diverse peoples which made up "the citizens of this extensive republick." Knox and DuPont suggested a national board composed of members from each state, but S. H. Smith proposed a plan which may have been taken from Condorcet. Smith proposed to vest the national control of education in a board of scholars and scientists. How visionary, at that time, all such ideas of a uniform and highly centralized national system were is made clear by one historical fact, and that fact is this. For a hundred and fifty years powerful centralizing forces have been consolidating the national government, whose power like a snowball has been growing every time it has moved; but these forces have not yet been able to overcome our localism, particularism, and individualism sufficiently to create a federal department or a national system. The problem was in men's minds. Many thought in 1800 that education should be used to form a more perfect union. They did not agree on the methods or the next steps to be taken to aid the children on the farms and in the villages.

4. THE LANCASTERIAN SCHOOLS

The actual next step did not tend to help the rural children directly. They had to wait another century until the modern elementary and high school, scientific agriculture, good roads, and the autobus were developed. The next step was an effort to aid city children by the introduction of the Lancasterian monitorial system. The main agencies of this movement were private; and for decades after 1800 progress continued to be made chiefly not through state action but through the labors of private persons or groups, incorporated societies, and churches. The Lancasterian schools were promoted by each of these; but one result of the movement was to further public education. In many cities the Lancasterian schools led directly to the establishment of public schools. Cincinnati, Louisville, and Detroit, in the far West of that time, and New Haven, Albany, and Baltimore, in the East, were only a few of the scores of cities which welcomed the Lancasterian monitorial schools. The system continued in use in many places until 1830 or later; and we must not, because it was finally discarded, suppose that it had no value.

About 1805, New York outdistanced Philadelphia to become the largest city in the country; and there the first Lancasterian school was opened in 1806 and there the monitorial system received its most extended trial. A small group of Friends and others formed a Free School Society, later called the Public School Society, and secured a charter for the purpose of providing schooling for children "who do not belong to, or are not provided for by any religious society." They developed and operated a number of monitorial schools; but although active for almost half a century the society was never able to reach all the children, nor could any other system, without a compulsory attendance law, have reached all the children of a rapidly growing city. For a time the Society attempted to charge those who were able to pay a very moderate fee, but this proved to be a mistake. The attendance immediately declined because the poor refused to "confess their poverty." For a time, the Society received financial aid from both the state and the city, but this also led to difficulties. Various churches insisted on sharing the funds on the ground that the Lancasterian schools were also sectarian. They argued that if the state or city supported the schools of one sect it should also support the schools of every other sect. As a result in 1842 New York City established a Board of Education and laid the foundation of a public school system. The Public School Society continued to operate monitorial schools until 1853 when it transferred its property to the city school district and ceased to exist.

Elsewhere the monitorial schools had disappeared twenty years earlier but not before they had taught several useful lessons. They were, first of all, cheap. In New York City the per pupil cost was one dollar and twenty-two cents per year in 1822; but by reason of higher prices and greatly reduced classes the per capita cost rose to almost six dollars in 1852. The Lancasterian schools convinced many doubters that the cost of universal education would not need to be prohibitive and they accustomed many parents to pay something at least for the education of their children. The schools were fully organized and prepared the way for grading and class management. Lancaster used sand tables, charts, slates, and slate pencils, even setting up a factory to make this and other equipment, and he familiarized teachers with the idea that schools should not depend exclusively upon books. The *Manual of Instruction* he prepared was a teacher's handbook. Teachers in the system were usually given a short course of instruction and apprenticeship before being given charge of a school. The idea of professional training was fostered in this way. In Philadelphia, where the Lancasterian schools were received with as much enthusiasm as in New York, a city normal school grew out of the Lancasterian training classes. In Philadelphia and in many other cities free public schools resulted directly or indirectly from the Lancasterian movement. These were useful services to education, but the schools themselves, as compared with the best schools even of that time, were poor. The routine, the rigid organization and semimilitary discipline, the mechanical instruction and a curriculum restricted to the formal elements of the different branches were all bad features. Yet the general influence of the monitorial schools was favorable to the extension of education; and both their introduction and their early disappearance after they had made their contribution were forward steps in the path of progress.

5. VOCATIONAL EDUCATION TRENDS

A similar verdict may be passed upon the Fellenberg manual labor schools which taught practical agriculture and handwork by a sort of apprentice system. The students were employed for a part of the day in the productive work of a school farm or shop while the rest of the time was devoted to study. The purpose was in part vocational, to educate working farmers. The same plan with a similar vocational emphasis was also introduced into reform schools. In some of the academies, colleges, and theological seminaries, the manual labor system was introduced to enable students to earn their way; and also, in the absence of school athletics, to provide physical exercise.

Manual labor education aroused great enthusiasm about 1820, reached its peak in the early thirties, and declined rapidly thereafter. Vigorous propaganda for it was carried on by the *National Intelligencer*, a Washington paper, the *Albany Cultivator*, the *American Farmer*, and the *American Annals of Education*. Woodbridge, who edited the *Annals*, had studied the Fellenberg institutions at first hand in Switzerland and seems to have had a share in bringing one of Fellenberg's disciples, F. A. Ismar, to the United States where Ismar delivered speeches, wrote articles, and helped to establish a combined manual labor and classical school in Pennsylvania. He proposed a normal school to prepare teachers for manual labor and other schools; but he seems not to have had any great influence. The agricultural and rural press was interested in the vocational aspects of the schools, and in the efforts to unite "labor and science." The editors held that all schools should give a portion of each day to the "teaching of some useful mechanical branch, such as practical agriculture, or horticulture." Many held the optimistic belief that boys could pay their way in college by simple routine labor such as caning chairs, making boxes, or working on a college farm. And this can indeed be done, but most schools found that to balance their books required an ability in marketing and management which they did not have at command.

Many colleges and many academies which later became colleges introduced the manual labor scheme. Among these were Oberlin, Denison, Wabash, Knox, Western Reserve, Davidson, and Wake Forest. A society for promoting manual labor education was formed in 1831, but it lapsed after one annual report by Theodore D. Weld, its general agent. The movement had an influence upon the growing interest in agricultural education. And it should be noticed that the land-grant colleges about 1870 introduced similar plans and that there is a family resemblance between the Fellenberg idea and those cooperative education plans which have been developed more recently at the University of Cincinnati in technical education and for more general purposes at Berea College, Antioch College, the high school of Fitchburg, and many less widely known instances.

Two schools which were directly affected by the manual labor plan must be particularly mentioned: the Gardiner Lyceum, an agricultural school which was opened in 1821 near Portland, Maine, and the Rensselaer School of Troy, New York, which began in 1825. The Gardiner Lyceum was established to prepare "scientific farmers and skillful mechanics." The school rendered excellent pioneer service for a decade but it did not become a permanent institution. It has been called our "first agricultural school" and the title may be justified although a few earlier attempts to teach agriculture had been made. The great campaign to "do something for the farmer" was, however, beginning and henceforth the subject was not allowed to lapse until the Morrill Act was passed in 1862.

The Rensselaer School was originally formed to prepare teachers and science lecturers for rural schools. After a brief trial the manual labor feature was discarded and a highly original combination of laboratory, project, and field work was substituted. Amos Eaton was the head teacher and he conceived and carried out the idea of having the pupils lecture to each other, explaining and demonstrating the observations and investigations of the field and laboratory. Eaton was one of the most inventive of our earlier teachers and his plan worked almost too well, for many of the early graduates of the school became distinguished scientists and did not devote themselves to rural school and agricultural improvement. As state geologists, agricultural chemists, and founders of agricultural experiment stations, their work ultimately aided the farmer, but directly the rural school benefited little.

With the coming of the railroads, Rensselaer became an engineering school. Many other schools, academies, and colleges also began to teach civil engineering about 1835. John Millington's *Elements of Civil Engineering*, which may have been the first American textbook in its field, appeared in 1839. At first it was the new and marginal schools and colleges that offered engineering courses, but before the Civil War the old and rich institutions also began to establish schools of applied science. From about 1840 attempts were made to secure federal aid through land grants for agricultural and engineering education; and these efforts, as we have suggested, succeeded in 1862 when the Morrill Act was passed. This will be more fully considered later.

Another important beginning in vocational education was made by the rise of the private business colleges about 1820. These taught commercial arithmetic and English, penmanship, bookkeeping, and other subjects. The private business college was itself a small business, carried on for profit by teacher-owners. They were not colleges but were partly elementary, partly secondary schools. Although the new field attracted many reputable, qualified teachers there were no external standards and no supervision to keep out charlatans. Edmund J. James, a leader in higher business education who was later president of the University of Illinois, considered the business college a peculiarly American institution. Nothing like it, he said in 1893, was found in other countries. It embodied, he believed, the defects and excellences of the American character in its spontaneous development, its rapid and wide diffusion, and its rough adaptation of primitive materials to urgent needs. Among the early pioneers were James Gordon Bennett, Peter Duff, and R. M. Bartlett. When the typewriter was invented shortly after the Civil War, typing and shorthand became two of the most important subjects. The private business college was in control of the field until about 1880 when the public high school began to introduce commercial courses. Forty years later the high school had largely driven out the business colleges, although many of the stronger ones are still active today. The field has greatly expanded and many collegiate and graduate schools of business have been established. The first of the collegiate schools of business was the Wharton School (1881) of the University of Pennsylvania.

6. THE TEACHING OF HANDWRITING

Several changes in school writing materials came in the period. Slates were introduced by the monitorial schools and wall blackboards were used after 1820 in many schools. About 1830 the steel pen began to displace the quill pen, a change which greatly affected the work of teaching. While quill pens were in use the teacher had to spend a large amount of time in school and after school hours in making and mending pens. The lead pencil and inexpensive paper displaced the slate; and the fountain pen, invented before 1700, was so greatly improved that it came into general use by 1900. Several systems of teaching penmanship, the English system of Joseph Carstairs, the American system of Platt R. Spencer, and the modification of the latter by A. N. Palmer were tried in succession. Vertical writing about 1890 and manuscript writing about 1915 were tried for a short time and discarded. The typewriter has greatly altered the place and reduced the importance of penmanship as a school subject; but a "fair hand and swift" is still, as Benjamin Franklin said, "useful to all."

7. SCHOOLS OF BOSTON TO 1820

Educational conditions can be studied by taking a selected example and tracing the development of the schools of a particular city. We shall choose Boston, which was far in the van and was breaking new paths on many occasions but which was also extremely traditional on others. We shall go back to the beginning. The citizens of Boston on April 13, 1635, at a "general meeting upon public notice" agreed to ask Philemon Purmont to become their schoolmaster, but it is not known whether he complied with the request. Either then or in the following year the school was opened and perhaps Latin was taught from the beginning, as it certainly was a little later. It is clear that from an early day reading, writing, and arithmetic were also taught in the school; and this was in harmony with the custom in England that the smaller Latin schools should teach the ABC's to little boys as well as Latin composition to the big ones. This practice, which Hawthorne in a story in *Grandfather's Chair* associates with the teaching of Ezekiel Cheever, was probably in vogue from the beginning. Eventually the school was called the Boston Latin School. It was and is a public school. Private schools also began to appear in the seventeenth century and at times, as we shall show, these enrolled more pupils than the city schools. In 1666 an assistant to the master of the Latin School was appointed to teach writing and probably other subjects also; but when the curriculum became more strictly classical, the boys of the Latin School were sent to private schools to be instructed in reading, writing, and arithmetic, at the parents' expense.

Although a common English education and preparation for college were given in the same school and by the same teacher, these were not considered equivalent or even comparable types of schooling. As soon as Boston was able, the city provided for separate "free schools to teach the children of poor people"; and in providing these the selectmen hit upon a curious plan which was known as the "double-headed system." Under this plan separate reading schools and writing schools, each under its own principal and management, were established. The former taught reading, English grammar, and at a later date, geography; and the writing schools taught penmanship, arithmetic, and bookkeeping. One-half of the pupils attended a reading school in the morning and a writing school in the afternoon; and the other half reversed this order, attending a writing school in the morning and a reading school after the midday meal. This double-headed system was continued until about the middle of the nineteenth century.

New schools were established as the local demand or the state law required. The North Latin School was opened in 1712 in obedience to a law which had been passed in 1683 and which required towns of five hundred families to have two Latin and two writing schools. Only boys were admitted to either type of school. The two writing schools were created at once, but the city took twenty-five years to comply with the Latin school requirement; and the North Latin School was again abolished as soon as "the new system of education," which permitted this to be done, was adopted in 1789. There was slight need for two Latin schools since the two together in 1785 enrolled only sixty-four pupils. This decline from one hundred fifty-nine pupils in 1741 was probably caused by the Revolution. A third writing school had been established in 1720 and two more were added later.

The new system of education, a local application of the Massachusetts School Law of 1789, was devised by a committee of eminent Bostonians, including Samuel Adams, which presented its report to the town meeting in the same year. This provided for only one Latin school, three writing, and three reading schools. The "new system" of 1789 also provided, for the first time, for the education of girls in the public reading and writing schools. They were to attend during the summer months from April to October. The rule adopted in 1785, that no children could be admitted into the public reading and writing schools below the age of seven and not until they were able to read, was continued in force. This preparation in reading they were expected to receive in the private dame schools. Under the "new system" a regular school committee or school board of twelve members, elected annually by wards, was given charge of the schools. Obviously the purpose of Samuel Adams and the committee was to "democratize" education. As the need developed other schools were added until in 1845 Boston had nineteen reading and the same number of writing schools.

At the beginning of the Revolution the schools were closed and continued so for a year or longer. When they were reopened many families had left the city, many children were occupied otherwise, and the attendance long remained below the previous figures. There were, for example, 823 pupils in the schools in 1772, and in 1785 only 564; and of the latter, as we have seen, only 64 were in the Latin schools. Not until near the end of the century did the public schools enroll 900 pupils, while the private schools of Boston at the same time had 500. Furthermore, the private schools were gaining on the public institutions. Twenty years later (1817) Boston with a population of 40,000 had only 2356 pupils in her reading and writing schools while 4132 pupils were taught by 162 private teachers at an annual cost of fifty thousand dollars. At the same time there were between 500 and 1000 children of school age who did not go to any school whatever.

After having enjoyed the benefits of public education for a century and three quarters, Boston was able to enroll only one-third of her school-age children in her public schools. Two-thirds were in private schools or on the streets. This was the sad result of two conditions. The public reading and writing schools were considered and treated as schools for the poor. And secondly, as indicated, no child could be received in a public reading school until he had learned to read in the Bible sufficiently well to keep his place in the book as the classwork proceeded. To acquire this minimum of knowledge, children had to be taught at home or sent to private schools. Boston might have removed this defect by increasing the number of public schools and ordering them to admit children at the age of six or earlier. The city chose instead to establish a whole new system of primary schools to be taught by women at much lower salaries than the masters of the reading and writing schools received. Financial economy was doubtless one reason for this plan. The year 1817 was the last of the old regime and 1818 the first of the new when Boston began to open public primary schools to teach young beginners to read.

We shall trace the progress of this revolution. The introduction of Sunday Schools into Boston in 1816 accidentally touched off an explosion by revealing that the city had a large number of illiterate children. A citizens' organization spurred the selectmen to appoint a committee to investigate conditions; and they admitted finding over five hundred children of school age who were not attending school. This was later shown to have been a gross understatement, for parents did not like to confess their poverty nor the committee to report large numbers of illiterates. But even five hundred was more than one-fifth of the public school enrollment at the time, yet it was by the complacent committee "deemed to be a very small number" in so large a city with many "foreigners and strangers, who are ignorant of our institutions, or have not learned to value them." It did not occur to them to suggest that the public schools should be used to acquaint the newcomers with our institutions.

The report was signed by Charles Bulfinch, a noted architect, who had prepared at the Boston Latin School for Harvard College from which he graduated in 1781. And the document betrays a view of public education that must be noticed because it was common. Mr. Bulfinch reminded his fellow citizens of the heavy school tax which was assessed upon their property and expressed the opinion that they ought not to expect public schools to be as good as private schools, because "from their public character there must arise some disadvantages which are not felt in private schools." Among the disadvantages which were considered inherent in public education were large classes, a narrow curriculum, and limited aims. This adverse report was not laid before the people in town meeting but was at once printed and distributed as if to close the issue. But Elisha Ticknor, James Savage, and others immediately reopened the question in the newspapers and presented a new petition in town meeting. Then the selectmen and school committee still further showed their hostility to the extension of public education by enlisting the services of prominent Bostonians, including a United States Senator, to fight the public primary school movement; but they were signally beaten. A separate primary school committee was constituted and the sum of five thousand dollars was voted for the first year. Thirteen hundred children applied for admission to the eighteen schools that were established in 1818.

The new primary schools for children between the ages of four and seven years were so successful that the awkward system of separate management by a special committee was continued down to 1855 when the primary schools were merged with the grammar schools in a unified system. The primary schools were reading schools pure and simple. The instructor began with the alphabet and, after dealing with the spelling of syllables and easy words, ended in the reading of English prose. There was no connection with the infant school movement of Robert Owen; and when a few years later some liberals attempted to introduce the infant school ideas they were vigorously repelled by the primary school committee.

The schools, of which eighteen were in operation the first year, thirty-six the third year, and so on in ever mounting numbers as the city grew, were invariably taught by women. The annual wage or salary was two hundred dollars or two hundred and fifty when the teacher provided the schoolroom. After the primary system became well established, no Boston child was debarred from the public schools of the city because his family was unable to send him to a private school to learn to read. The "resurgent democracy" of which we shall speak in the next section was doubtless influential in the promotion of the primary school movement in Boston.

Within a few years after the opening of the primary schools, realizing that her system was still incomplete, the city of Boston opened the English Classical School (1821). This was a free public secondary school that emphasized the English language and practical mathematics. It is considered to be the first high school, a name that was adopted when Boston in 1824 voted to call its new institution the English High School. The word English was used in both of the early titles to indicate the absence of ancient and all foreign languages from the curriculum; but later high schools soon began to teach the languages to prepare pupils for college. For a long time the high school competed for public favor with the academy, and it did not become the leading secondary school until after the Civil War. Its spread and internal development will be considered in Chapter 20.

8. RESURGENT DEMOCRACY

The age which followed our second war with Great Britain was an era of expansion, accompanied by strong democratic and humanitarian movements. The tide of immigration was flowing toward the United States and there was a marked urban and industrial development. The growing practice of providing national aid and encouragement to internal improvements, including canals, railroads, and manufactures, was called the American System. The daily newspaper with paid reporting was crowding out the weekly and circulations were mounting in geometrical progression. Gas for lighting was just coming in to aid study and reading in the evening. John Griscom, a school teacher already becoming known and later to become eminent, was engaged on January 26, 1816, in demonstrating the new light to the mayor, aldermen, and businessmen of New York City. He showed that it was cheaper, cleaner, and more brilliant than candles. The application of steam power, inventions, and manufacturing were developing rapidly. We were becoming an industrial nation. From the mountains of Vermont the movement for manhood suffrage spread along the western frontier and finally overcame the resistance of the conservative East. It was a combination of frontiersmen and workingmen in the cities that elected Jackson and gave to Jacksonian democracy a more popular trend than the older democracy of Jefferson had exhibited.

Liberal and humanitarian reformers became so numerous and insistent that Emerson declared that every thinking man had a plan for a new society in his vest pocket. Some of those designs, it must be confessed, were European dreams which fitted even less well into the new society of America than into the old one of their origin. Fourierism, after elaborate publicity by the *New York Sun*, was briefly tried in several places including Brook Farm where Emerson was a cool and collected spectator, but it was not a lasting influence. New Harmony in Indiana harbored Robert Owen's brief unsuccessful attempt to reform the world quickly. Of the one or two hundred ideal communities founded in the nineteenth century, not one left any permanent impress upon American society or had any important message for education. The humanitarian movements accomplished far more. The reforms of prison management and criminal law, and of the asylums and their treatment of the insane and defective, the building of hospitals, the discovery of anesthesia, these were positive gains.

Religion and religious controversy were to occupy a large share of the attention of Americans in the nineteenth century. Protestant foreign missions, starting from a famous meeting at Williams College, were just beginning to develop American missionary interest in China, India, and Africa, and led eventually to the establishment not only of native churches but also of educational institutions such as Robert College in Constantinople, the University of Beirut, and Yale-in-China. The arrival of many Catholic immigrants aroused the fears and prejudices of Protestant leaders and incited them to support both the public school movement and the foundation of denominational colleges as means to forestall what they regarded as a threat that the West would become Catholic. At the other end of the religious spectrum, Unitarianism was developing and also affecting the religious views of many who did not become Unitarians but either remained in the orthodox communions or on the other hand moved beyond Unitarianism itself into complete secularism. A philosophical version of Unitarianism was the movement known as transcendentalism, a sort of popular Platonism. But the great moral and economic question of the day was slavery, abolitionism, and on this the churches, which in early days had opposed slavery, became hopelessly confused and divided, once the issue was sharpened. Only the Friends, the Mennonites, and other unpopular sects stood by their earlier convictions. The Quaker Poet, Whittier, in whose works antislavery poems fill a hundred pages, hailed William Lloyd Garrison as the "Champion of those who groan beneath oppression's iron hand," and dared to ask:

> Is this the land our fathers loved,
> The freedom which they toiled to win?

Certainly it was not an accident that American education, democratic and widespread, first became an ideal and gradually a fact in the period of Andrew Jackson, of the abolition movement, of religious liberalism, and of moral and social reform. Universal public education, like those great causes, gave new hope and opportunity to the common man.

9. EDUCATIONAL PROMOTION

The educational renaissance was not the work of a few leaders, although there were great leaders, nor the achievement of any one class or narrow section of the people. Professional men and mechanics, labor leaders, and social reformers cooperated with teachers and political leaders, especially the state governors, in raising the issues and informing the people. Yet the victory was not an easy one. The opposition was powerful, and in the older states there was a bitter struggle over state control, over the school tax, over religious as against secular education, and over other questions. Conservative religionists, private school interests, men of property, and those who fancied themselves aristocrats are said to have opposed public education. But no sharp lines can be drawn. It would be easy to name exceptions; and when exceptions become numerous they no longer prove but tend to annul the rule. Certainly many successful private school teachers like Albert Picket, many rich men such as James Wadsworth (1768–1844) of New York, and clergymen like Bishop Potter of the same state fought vigorously for public schools.

The country was still rural, the demand for manual labor was insistent, and parents felt that their children were needed on the farm. Because of parental pressure, business conditions, and the lack of convenient schools many children left school early or perhaps never attended any school. From the most illiterate class also there was opposition. There were those who considered that any who had an education beyond the three R's were likely to be proud, or were afraid to work, and were trying to live by their wits. But the growing native population, the rising flood of immigration, and the cityward trend created a need for new schools, better schools, and a more diversified education, a need which no private agency would have been able to satisfy.

From the birth of the nation, as we have said, public men began to urge the development of education for civic and political ends. In the new republic, it was agreed, citizens must be taught to value their new freedom, to understand their government and the questions with which it had to deal, and to serve their country both patriotically and ably. "In proportion as government gives force to public opinion," declared Washington's Farewell Address, "it is important that public opinion should be enlightened." Economic and social arguments were often added to the political one. It was pointed out that the vast resources of our country could be developed only by trained men and that this implied the need for more advanced schools. The need to conserve our human resources was indicated in the phrase of Horace Mann, who held that "the more schoolhouses we build the fewer jails we shall need."

The educational obligation of the government was constantly pressed by the governors of the states. Selecting from scores of parallel statements by the governors of most of the states we present one made in 1826 by DeWitt Clinton of New York. He wrote: "The first duty of the government and the surest evidence of good government, is the encouragement of education." Some of the governors in their messages went into the education question in great detail. Governors Worthington of Ohio (1817) and Edward Everett of Massachusetts (1838) urged the establishment of state normal schools; and Everett had an important share in the founding of the first such institution.

Although labor organizations were not yet numerous or powerful, they expressed themselves strongly in favor of public education, urging particularly that a democracy should provide equal opportunity for schooling all citizens, the poor as well as the rich. The extension of manhood suffrage led the early labor groups to work for public education although this was not their foremost aim. The ten-hour day, and the abolition of mechanics liens and of imprisonment for debt were among the earliest objectives of organized labor, but the demand for free, tax-supported public schools was not far behind.

The factory system was yet in its infancy in 1825, but an education committee of the Massachusetts Senate found that in most industrial towns of the state the children employed in factories were receiving no schooling. After the customary twelve-hour day there was little time or will to study. Illiteracy was common. A writer in the *Mechanics Free Press* estimated that not more than one-sixth of the youthful textile workers of Pawtucket and Philadelphia were able to write their names. Some of the manufacturers professed to believe that schooling for factory children was not desirable. Some employers refused to release a child for school attendance under threat of dismissing the whole family from the mills. A contemporary writer said, "We have even known these threats put into execution." The Massachusetts Senate Committee thought protective legislation should be enacted but they were not prepared to submit a bill; and it was not until 1842 that Massachusetts, first of the states, passed a child labor law and provided that every small child must be given opportunity for twelve weeks at school annually. Massachusetts was also the first state to enact a compulsory school attendance law (1852).

The organized workingmen of Philadelphia, before the election of 1828, asked the candidates for public office for their views on an equal and general system of education. In the following year a committee of workingmen reported upon the schools of Pennsylvania. They pointed out the defects of the private schools and the "venal administration" of the law of 1809; they referred to the decay of apprenticeship and the associated provision for schooling; and they urged the admission of small children to schools so that they might obtain a little education before they became employable. They explained that many parents were too poor to clothe their children for school, to buy books for them, and to meet the individual expenses of any school, even a free school. As a solution for these difficulties they proposed a manual labor school in each county. The New York Working Men's Party contended for free schools supported by public funds as a right, and they attacked the custom of appropriating money to private colleges and academies which benefited chiefly those who did not need such help. A more radical program for national public boarding schools was rejected by the party. The government was to furnish not only education but also board and clothing in order that poor children might have opportunities equal to those of the rich and that "the spirit of democracy which Jefferson labored for half a century to plant in our republican soil" might become universal. Although repudiated, this radical proposal of 1830 is significant of the mind of a section of the working class.

Many newspapers of the day were opposed to the movement for public schools. Schemes of universal education were called socialistic, economically unsound, and, in a competitive society, undesirable. The advantages of the prevailing plan of competitive private education, in which the schools had to be good in order to survive, were painted in glowing colors. They expatiated on the serious defects of the existing public schools in Connecticut and Massachusetts as "proof" that the whole idea of a thorough education in public schools was utopian. These editorial views in the press of the country show that the workingmen's propaganda was having some effect but it is easy to overemphasize its importance. Organized labor was still too weak to exert a preponderant influence and the crisis of 1837 scattered its forces. Public education was achieved by the combined action of men and women of all professions and social classes under the leadership of idealists, humanitarians, teachers, and publicists. The laws which were necessary for the creation of public school systems were passed upon the persistent demand of a majority of the public.

A second phase of the propaganda effort dealt not so much with the establishment but rather with the improvement of schools. And it was correctly judged that a chief need lay in finding and preparing better teachers. Early in the century the Lancasterian monitorial system had been regarded as the ready-made solution of the two connected problems of universal education and teacher training. It did not solve either but it succeeded in arousing public interest in them. The academies also did something to raise the general level of education and to prepare teachers for both elementary and secondary schools. A few of them also attempted to teach the elements of psychology and of school management. An example was furnished by Samuel Read Hall who taught at Concord, Vermont, in 1823 and a few years later published his *Lectures on School-Keeping*. James Gordon Carter also worked at the same task before the advent of state normal schools. In the third place, the incoming Pestalozzian doctrines and a growing acquaintance with German teacher-training gave renewed and stronger emphasis to the demand for professional education.

New instruments to carry these ideas to the people and the teaching profession were invented. Two of these were the educational magazine and the teachers' association. Educational journalism was born in 1818 when Albert and John W. Picket of New York brought out *The Academician*, a sixteen-page semimonthly at three dollars per year. This ran for only twenty-five numbers. It presented a psychological theory of education based upon the doctrines of Bacon and Locke, it reviewed for its readers the ideas of Pestalozzi, Fellenberg, and Lancaster, all of whom were then living, it gave practical advice to teachers, and it published school news. It was a sensible and wise, but not very lively, paper. A few years later, William Russell founded the *American Journal of Education* and this was continued under the title *American Annals of Education* by William C. Woodbridge. The state journals of education emerged soon after. *The Common School Assistant* (1836), edited by J. Orville Taylor at Albany, was privately supported but was distributed to public school teachers. *The Ohio Common School Director* (1838), edited by Samuel Lewis, was circulated at public expense. A little later in the same year Henry Barnard began to issue the *Connecticut Common School Journal* and Horace Mann the *Common School Journal* for the teachers of Massachusetts. Besides spreading educational information and plans of teaching and school management, the state journals served as means of communication from the state office to the public school teachers. By 1850 more than three score educational magazines had been founded, but many were short-lived.

The earliest associations of teachers were founded for the protection and advancement of their members rather than for the improvement of education. One of these, founded for social and benevolent purposes and to collect unpaid tuition fees, was formed by the private school teachers of New York City as early as 1794, and one of its few public acts was to welcome the famous refugee, Joseph Priestley. Similar societies were organized in other cities. By 1830 a great change had come about. Teachers developed a keen public spirit and looked forward to the establishment of state systems of public schools and the creation of a profession of teaching. These later societies welcomed men of many callings into their membership. Two of the most influential early associations of this kind were founded at Boston and Cincinnati about the same time (1831). These were, respectively, the American Institute of Instruction and the Western Literary Institute and College of Professional Teachers. The latter held its last meeting in 1845, but the former still survives. Both were regional associations, one affecting chiefly New England and the other the West of that day. The American Lyceum attempted to perform similar functions on a national scale. These societies were in turn followed by state associations of teachers and in 1857 a national association was formed out of which the present National Education Association has grown.

10. THE AMERICAN LYCEUM

Scientific societies, called lyceums, whose purposes were to collect natural history specimens, to study the natural resources of the country, and to provide lectures on such subjects, were founded in several localities before 1820. It was only a short step from these lyceums to the local "associations of adults for mutual education," which were proposed by Josiah Holbrook in the *American Journal of Education* for October 1826. Holbrook listed as the chief aims of these associations the opportunity for cheap, practical education, and for the application of science to the domestic and useful arts and "to all the common purposes of life." He is considered the founder of the lyceum movement for he made the important suggestion that the local groups should be organized into county and the county into state organizations, and indicated in his first proposal that it might be advantageous to form a general board for all the associations in the whole country. For several years Holbrook devoted all his time to the extension of the lyceum movement.

The local lyceums, which spread rapidly in the northern states and reached into the far West and the South, carried out the adult education which the promoter intended; but the state and national associations undertook a task which he had not mentioned, namely, the promotion of public education and the development of state school systems. The lyceums reached the number of eight hundred within five years, and three thousand within ten years; and these were united into numerous county associations and state associations. As a means of instruction for adults and a system of forums for the best speakers in the whole country, the local lyceums had great value.

The national association, called The American Lyceum and composed of delegates from the state lyceums, held its first annual meeting in New York City in 1831. While the American Lyceum gave attention to the spread of local lyceums, a consideration of the main topics which were brought before the national meetings shows that the national body was mainly occupied in promoting public education. The association was a means of arousing public interest in education and, although there is no exact measure, it undoubtedly helped to create sentiment for the state departments of education which were established during its time.

11. RISE OF STATE SYSTEMS

The Constitution guarantees a republican form of government to each state; it was not thought necessary to guarantee to each a democratic system of education. Although certain beginnings had been made early, it was in the second third of the nineteenth century that our system of democratic education began a vigorous growth. It was then that the states actively undertook to educate their children for democracy.

From early times the colonies, and later the states, passed a large volume of laws dealing with education; but the administration and enforcement of this legislation were left to the courts and the ordinary officials. As public education grew the need came to be felt for a state agency to interpret school laws, to spread ideas and information, to supply professional leadership, and to exercise some supervisory and administrative functions. Such duties were assigned ex officio to an officer, usually the secretary of state, or to a newly chosen officer who was variously styled superintendent of free schools, or of common schools, or, in a few states, superintendent of public instruction.

Strong traditions impeded the development of the powers and prestige of the new office. The old historical tradition that the education of children should be directed first by their parents and then by the church was against public education and still more against state administered education. But a second party, that of the frontier democracy, held that if education were not to be private then the local community should be allowed to manage it without state control. In several states the superintendency, after having been established at a politically favorable moment, was again abolished when its enemies had mustered their strength. The arguments against the office were sometimes opposed to each other and frequently contradicted the facts. The office was declared to be too expensive for a state which may have counted a half-million people, or too ineffective when the officer was given almost no powers, or Prussian in origin or tendency, although it was, with slight exceptions, American in both respects.

New York, which had long before placed a Board of Regents over secondary-higher education, was in 1812 the first state to create the office of State Superintendent of Common Schools. The first and only appointee under this law was Gideon Hawley who, after an able and successful administration, was for political reasons removed from office in 1821. The secretary of state acted as superintendent until 1854 when a separate office of Superintendent of Public Instruction was again created. Fifty years later in 1904 the administration of elementary and of secondary-higher education was combined under one executive with the bulky but historically interesting title of President of the University of the State of New York and Commissioner of Education.

Maryland established the office of state superintendent in 1826, abolished it in 1828, and re-established it in 1864. For Ohio the corresponding dates are 1837, 1840, and 1853. The history of the office in Connecticut, Rhode

Island, Iowa, Missouri, and other states shows similar advances and retreats, and finally permanent establishment. Elsewhere, as in Illinois in 1825, Louisiana in 1833, and in other states at other times, ex officio officers were provided before the state superintendency as a separate office developed. But Michigan in 1836, while it was still a territory, Massachusetts in 1837, and Kentucky in 1838 created state school superintendencies which have continued to function without a break. This list could be extended. Of the thirty-six states and organized territories existing in 1861, thirty had provided state school officers.

The movement was far broader than we have indicated. The decades before the Civil War were marked not by the revival but by the birth of public education as we know it today—a broad and generous extension of educational opportunity to "all the children of all the people" in a school system created by the people themselves. This was the ideal at least, and on this plan the states proceeded. We should honor our colonial forefathers for their efforts to provide schools but of such an educational ladder they had no conception; this is a program developed in the nineteenth century, not the seventeenth. The development of the state school office may be regarded as an index to the growing will of the American people to develop public education.

12. SECURING PUBLIC SUPPORT FOR EDUCATION

Public education is usually financed through local taxation, state appropriations, and federal aid. Small amounts, less than ten per cent of the total in most states, are obtained from other sources such as income from permanent funds, fees, and donations. The process by which the public has educated itself to consider taxation and the appropriation of public funds as the fairest, most dependable, and most adaptable method of educational support may be regarded as an historical experiment which has now been carried on with varying success for more than a century.

A century ago there was no such agreement upon the best methods of supporting schools. Most schools were private then and charged tuition or depended upon contributions from the wealthy or from organized groups such as churches. Usually there were also numerous special charges, for firewood, for supplies, for candles in evening schools; books were provided by the pupils or their parents. Lotteries were a common source of support for schools and colleges, and were frequently authorized by state legislatures. As we learn from sober history, and not only from school stories and poems such as the *Hoosier Schoolmaster*, *Ichabod Crane*, and Whittier's *Snow-Bound*, many teachers "boarded round" among the families of their district. Boarding the teacher was a form of school support, and it was not the only example of "payment in kind." An Ohio teacher in 1825 contracted to accept Indian corn at thirty cents a bushel; and a governor of Massachusetts paid the expenses of his son at Harvard College in the same commodity. Rents from lands or fish weirs, income from herds of cows, contributions, bequests, license fees collected from banks, theaters, liquor sales, and marriages, occupational taxes, the rate bill, and other items were among the sources of funds applied to schools before taxation was fully accepted. Clearly such financing did not assess the costs fairly and such sources were not dependable or readily adaptable to changing needs.

The monitorial schools rendered a service by demonstrating that a little education could be provided very cheaply to large numbers. Another effort to support a general system of education was based upon the federal land grants. The initiation of these was contemporary with the introduction of the monitorial schools. It was soon discovered that the land grants were also inadequate, although this was already well known to those who were familiar with the history of rents and land endowments for schools from early colonial times down to the period in question.

Those states which had come into the Union before Ohio did not share in the federal land grants for schools, and many of them formed state school funds from other revenues. Connecticut in 1795 sold her vast and rich "Western Reserve" of nearly four million acres for the trifling price of about thirty cents an acre and through this transaction added over a million dollars to a school fund which had been established almost fifty years earlier. As a result the state was for a time so wealthy that she could pay for the simple and meager schools of that time without taxation. The people, consequently, almost forgot the existence of their schools, neglect bred contempt, the "better people" patronized private schools, and it required the statesmanship of Henry Barnard to teach them their duty to provide good schools for all the children. Most of the permanent school funds in the older states were established in the first third of the nineteenth century. By themselves they were everywhere inadequate; and if as in Connecticut they were sufficient to pay for a short annual term of school, the unfortunate result was that the people went into an educational coma. One can perhaps state it as a principle that when people regularly pay at least a substantial portion of the cost of a public service they will take a more active interest in its management.

The early idea was that schools and especially public schools should be cheap. When improvements were made, even poor schools whetted the appetite of the people for good schools and then for better schools, and their willingness to pay for improved education for their children grew with their experience. A very slight tax, often left to the option of the districts, was the entering wedge to a low mandatory tax and this to heavier and more adequate taxation. Cities, because of their concentrated wealth and population and the greater need for highly educated men, were more willing and better able to raise taxes than the rural districts. The example of the wealthier cities exerted a potent influence upon their neighbors and from this competition better support for all schools emerged. A special stimulus was also deliberately applied. The states offered aid to local areas on condition that these should levy a specified tax or on condition that the district should out of its own funds maintain the schools for a specified number of months in each year. Such aid then enabled the district to keep its schools open longer or to pay better salaries or otherwise to improve its educational program. By these means the principle was eventually established that property taxation was the most equitable, dependable, and sufficiently flexible method of supporting public education. This essential lesson was learned gradually and at different times in the several states but it may be said to have been well driven home by about 1870. By that time the public schools not only were supported by local taxes and state appropriations but also had become generally free.

Important improvements in the application of the principle have been made. The standards which districts must meet before state aid is granted have been made more inclusive and the levels have been raised. The idea has been accepted that state aid should be used to assure a basic minimum of educational opportunity to every child and also to stimulate the further improvement of the schools. Not the equalization of education but the greatest opportunity for all is the ideal. To assure to each the basic minimum of opportunity, the state may, after the district has met its obligations, guarantee a certain amount of money per child per year. The details of such "foundation programs" vary in different states. The contribution of the federal government, except for the early land grants, has generally been given in support of vocational and technical education.

13. DEFECTS OF THE OLD SCHOOLS

Without the support of an enlightened and united public, the schools of the pioneers could not have become the instruments of democracy. And although this unity of the public was never completely attained, yet as sentiment became more favorable the schools were given increased funds; but they needed, more urgently even than money, systematic organization and scientific administration. These advantages were lacking in the district schools which prevailed in the Jacksonian era.

The district system was widely employed even in the cities until the middle decades of the century and much longer in sparsely settled regions.

By definition it required an individual trustee or a separate board of trustees for each one-room school, and until about 1830 or 1840 almost all schools were one-room schools. To these district boards the broadest powers were allowed. They had the right and duty to levy the school tax, to fix the length of the term, to make all contracts for buildings, repairs, and equipment, to select textbooks, to determine the curriculum, to certificate and employ the teacher, and to settle upon and pay his salary. But they did not always carry out all these functions. The standards of school administration were so low that many of the powers committed to the district boards were neglected through default. And when they were exercised, practice varied from district to neighboring district because each board was an independent agency. One school might, therefore, have a three- and another a six-month term, and similar variations were to be found in salaries, books, and other elements of the school program.

Because the district schools were small and the pupils were frequently not classified the teaching was carried on by individual recitation. True, the graded-class system was coming in here and there before 1840, and skillful teachers in larger schools had been using it for some time, but it was not in vogue where most of the people lived, that is, in the country and small towns. Not only were the schools generally small, but the attendance was very irregular also. Starting in the fall with a few pupils, a school might swell to fifty or more during one or two winter months after the corn had been husked and the hunting season had ended. A single teacher was expected to care for the whole number; and against truancy or simple absence he was helpless. Under such conditions individual teaching, or rather individual reciting, was practically unavoidable.

School discipline was authoritarian, sometimes capricious, and often harsh, even according to the standards of that time. The punishments which included sentence to occupy the dunce block and other forms of school disgrace, and corporal punishment in several forms and all degrees, reached a maximum in expulsion from school. The pupils retaliated by insubordination and by breaking up the school. Edward Eggleston's *The Hoosier Schoolmaster* is not the product of a novelist's imagination alone but was based upon actual conditions. In New England it was found advisable to have cases of flagrant disobedience and violence in schools reported in open town meeting, naming names and giving the facts. There are few boys, said Horace Mann, who will not recoil from such a public report. Repeated and gross infractions of school discipline were to be finally entered upon the public record that the pupil's ignominy might be transmitted to future ages. It was a great satisfaction to Horace Mann to be able to report in 1842 that the number of schools broken up by the insubordination of the pupils was not more than one-tenth of what it had been for the preceding year; but the record for that preceding year seems to have disappeared. A century ago the district schools were frequently disorderly, badly organized, and educationally ineffective. One should not be surprised to learn that the "better people" refused to send their children to such schools and, therefore, took little interest in their improvement.

The teachers themselves knew no better way. There were no normal schools, teachers' institutes, or summer schools for professional education. Even the necessary academic education for teaching could not be obtained in public schools but had to be secured in academies or colleges. More than one-half of the teachers of Massachusetts and probably a larger proportion in other states were allowed to teach without any examination whatever, and of course without a certificate. Teachers' wages, too, were low, being about on a par with the wages of farm laborers. Accurate statistics are not available but about 1830, men teachers, who "boarded round" with their patrons, received about fifteen dollars per month and women from one-third to one-half of that amount. Farm hands were earning ten to fifteen dollars with board, lodging, and other services such as washing and mending, although in the haymaking and harvest season the wages of day-laborers were higher. Mill hands earned rather more than teachers or farm laborers but not as much as skilled artisans. Henry Barnard in 1842 reported that men teachers in Connecticut received seventeen dollars per month. The wages of the same class in Michigan were slightly below and in Pennsylvania and New York slightly above the Connecticut level; but men teachers in Massachusetts were in 1842 receiving rather more than twenty-five dollars per month. This latter group of figures all represent cash wages. In addition, teachers often received board and room by "boarding round."

Another great and almost universal evil of the common schools was the variety of the schoolbooks that the children brought into the schools. The diversity of textbooks was itself reason enough for the individual methods and the absence of grading. Simply because such action was likely to give offense, school boards did not perform the function of prescribing the books. *The North American Review* in 1841 proposed to solve the difficulty without demanding uniformity by persuading the publishers of approved books to furnish them at reduced prices. The same writer remarked upon the very general absence of apparatus, blackboards, maps, globes, and the means to illustrate the common weights and measures. The schoolhouses, as will be explained in a later section, were often quite unfit to shelter the children.

The natural result of the poor condition of the public district schools followed, namely, the establishment of numerous private schools which gave instruction in the same branches that the public schools taught or were expected to teach. To these private schools, the minister, the doctor, the lawyer, and others who could afford it sent their children; and in this way they reduced still further the prestige and standards of the common school. Horace Mann estimated that, in 1840 in his state, thirty thousand pupils making one-sixth of all the children between the ages of four and sixteen were attending private elementary schools; and he figured that the cost of teaching those thirty thousand children in private schools was six to eight times what it would have been if all had together attended the common schools. He showed from enrollment figures that by reason of this division of the children and the funds both the private and the public schools were too small for economy, and also too small to provide the socializing advantages of a good school.

All of this was no doubt true and discouraging, but there is another side. Some of the private schools and their teachers served as models and provided leadership for the common schools. Such men as Ebenezer Bailey, George B. Emerson, and G. F. Thayer were far in advance of the district schools and provided excellent examples for imitation; and we know that they were imitated. The proverb about the ill wind applies here yet it remains true that the private schools were both effect and cause of the unsatisfactory condition of the public district schools. The obvious solution was to improve the public schools, to raise them to such a level that private schools could no longer compete with them; and since the resources of the whole public must always be greater than those of a few, this would seem to be a general solution, applicable in a democracy at all times.

14. COMMON SCHOOLS FOR DEMOCRACY

It was in these circumstances that Horace Mann became Secretary of the Massachusetts Board in 1837; and the greater part of his notable achievement was the overcoming of the defects of the district system. But to gain the true perspective upon his work and upon the whole period, it is necessary to see that the improvement was due not to individual effort alone, whether that of Mann or Barnard or another, but to the increasing density of the population, the industrial and commercial revolution, the growing wealth and the rising standard of living of the American people; and it is important to see, secondly, that the reform of the schools had already begun years earlier and was spreading, in 1837, from widely separated centers of influence, such as New York, Pennsylvania, Ohio, Indiana, and Michigan.

Horace Mann carried forward a program which had already made great progress in Massachusetts under the leadership of James G. Carter and many others. The law of 1827 had been in operation for a decade before Mann took any interest in public education. Gideon Hawley had for a quarter of a century served public education in New York, first as superintendent of common schools and then as secretary of the Board of Regents. State school officers were being chosen in the East and the West as we have already noted, the governors in their messages were urging legislatures to attend to public education, and teachers and citizens were beginning to organize in the interest of this cause. Education had a long road ahead but it was making progress. If we will keep this background in mind we shall be able to understand better the development of the common schools for democracy and the work of Horace Mann.

Mann began to attack along the whole front. His first task was that of informing and educating not only the teachers but the people. Most of the citizens had themselves been educated in district schools alone and knew of no better system of education. Mann traveled from county to county holding educational conventions in the more important towns. He spoke often and secured the aid of other speakers, including John Quincy Adams, Daniel Webster, and Edward Everett, to arouse interest in school improvement. Upon returning to Boston after covering the state for the first time he wrote in his journal that, in spite of weariness and some irritation caused by a few "miserable, contemptible, deplorable" meetings, the tour had been successful. He had on the whole met with unexpected and extraordinary encouragement. This, he wrote, shall be only a beginning. "I confess life begins to have a value which I have not felt for five years," he declared. He also knew the value of printer's ink. He established the *Common School Journal*, writing much of its contents with his own hand, and he prepared twelve annual *Reports* in which he took up the defects of the schools and proposed remedies.

During his term (1837–1848) great changes occurred in the schools of Massachusetts and the country. In some of these he played an important part. He was a reformer and a prophet but like some other prophets he was without much aesthetic feeling or a saving sense of humor. He had great faith in the common man and a very practical understanding of the value of useful knowledge in such fields as physiology, bookkeeping, drawing, surveying, and applied sciences. For science beyond its more immediate uses, for history, even the history of his own country, for ideas as ideas he had little use in his educational scheme. He was a man of action, a propagandist, and a publicist; but in judging his achievement one must consider not only his own gifts and defects but also the difficulties of his office. For years he was hardly ever free from attack and had to fight to maintain his position. A more sensitive and less devoted man would have retired from the storm. Mann fought on for twelve years and by that time the amount of money appropriated for schools by the state was double that of 1837, the average school term was longer by a month, teachers' salaries had risen fifty per cent, four normal schools and fifty high schools had been opened, the latter without direct help from Horace Mann, and the private schools were improving in equipment, curriculum, and teaching. Pestalozzian ideas and a growing faith in American institutions and in our national destiny had begun to build schools for democracy.

The Pestalozzian influence was brought in through official reports, accounts by travelers, and the personal contributions of European teachers such as Agassiz or Guyot. To American teachers, Pestalozzi represented two principles. The first was that the child should be governed by love and not fear, that whoever was unable to gain the affections of a child was unfit to teach. The second principle was that lessons should as far as possible be concrete and objective and the child should be led to understand what he was asked to learn.

The *Common School Journal* as early as 1840 published a series of model object lessons. It also proposed the "elliptical method" which had a curious history. According to this Pestalozzian "elliptical" manner of teaching, the pupils had to supply words that were omitted from the sentence which was given them. Thus the teacher, referring to an object before the class, might expect the child to supply the italicized word in, Glass is *brittle*, or, Water is a *liquid*. A further step was taken when language books incorporated composition exercises which required the pupils to complete the sense by providing the missing words. Then Ebbinghaus in 1897, and other psychologists who followed his lead, devised "completion tests" using the same idea. Unfortunately several words could often be used to complete a sense, for glass is not only brittle, but also transparent, useful, hard, and so forth. But by controlling the recognized completions as in the item, Northern flowers that bloom in the spring include, 1. asters, 2. tulips, 3. golden rod, 4. chrysanthemums, an objective test could be constructed. Thus a device used by Pestalozzi contributed, after a century of development, to a purpose which was much in his mind and which he called "psychologizing education," or, as we should say, making education scientific.

Along with object lessons, the Pestalozzians, as we have just noted, stressed composition through both oral and written language lessons and with reduced attention to formal grammar. The attack upon formal grammar was not at once successful, and indeed the schools of the early nineteenth century were a grammarian's paradise. Webster, Lindley Murray, and Kirkham wrote several of the most popular school grammars used at that time. The Pestalozzians also favored oral teaching and an expanded common school curriculum including local geography, nature lessons, drawing and modeling, mental arithmetic, and music. Mental arithmetic was so called because the problems were to be solved without the use of a pencil and the pupil was asked to explain the reasoning he followed in the solution. Warren Colburn's *First Lessons in Arithmetic on the Plan of Pestalozzi* (1821) went through numerous editions. Mental arithmetic became a fad which lasted in some parts of the country until 1890 or later. Perhaps it is unfortunate that it has died out. It seems reasonable that all arithmetic teaching, whether with a pencil or "in the head," should be "mental." Pestalozzi's demands for the systematic teaching of music and a direct approach to music through singing were accepted by those who introduced the subject into the common schools.

How far Pestalozzian ideas penetrated the American educational frontier, and what their permanent influence was, it would be hard to say. The normal schools were few and the institutes, which by 1850 reached a great many teachers, were in session for very short periods. Besides they were likely to be of the "Do as I say and not as I do" variety. Through magazines, teachers' meetings, and all the intangible ways by which ideas spread and especially through textbooks, Pestalozzianism was diffused. Horace Mann judged that Pestalozzi's "influence has been felt where his name even has not been heard."

Professional supervision of education had begun to develop before the Civil War, the grading of schools was under way, and our school system with, in many cases, an eight-year elementary school leading to a four-year free public high school was beginning to take form. Among the notable city superintendents of schools in the nineteenth century were William T. Harris (1835–1908) of St. Louis and William N. Maxwell (1852–1920) of Brooklyn and Greater New York. At first the schools were loosely graded, often into four levels of three years each, and these levels were sometimes called the primary, secondary or intermediate, grammar, and high school grades. Many of the early high schools were three-year schools. The elementary school years also varied, being at one time six in Newark, New Jersey, seven in Rochester, nine in Oswego, and ten in Louisville. In the South and in Kansas City the elementary school was usually a seven-year, and in Maine it was a nine-year, school. The most frequent number was eight.

Closer grading began to develop and the result in the cities was the familiar year by year grading. On this plan each elementary teacher was put in charge of a room in which all the children were doing the same work and aiming to complete a specified year's course in each school year.

In a later chapter we shall see how this iron-clad system of grading, which was called the "greatest invention in education in several centuries," came into conflict with the new ideas of the twentieth century.

With the formation of the new nation, education to overcome sectionalism and to promote citizenship became important. Educational needs became greater also from the rise of industry, the growth of cities, the westward movement, and the increasing immigration. Even before the adoption of the Constitution, land was granted for the support of elementary schools; and the encouragement of schools by the government was demanded by the Northwest Ordinance. The states gave their adherence to the theory of public education but delayed effective action. A favorable public opinion was developing, however. Beginning in the Revolutionary War, many writers, from Thomas Jefferson and other distinguished men to the most obscure, drew plans and declared that without general education no republic could survive. A few, convinced that national education was essential to political salvation, proposed a centralized system on the French model.

Instead of the French system, we introduced the English monitorial plan. All the cities along the coast and inland as far as Cincinnati welcomed the Lancasterian schools because they were cheap. These schools also taught us something about grading subject matter, classifying children, equipping classrooms, and preparing teachers. Although the education they provided was somewhat meager, they helped to convince the people that universal schooling was feasible. Educationally, as in other fields, the time preceding the Civil War was a creative era. Besides the Lancasterian schools, this period introduced the manual labor education of Fellenberg, made a beginning in business, agricultural, and engineering education, developed the lyceum system, which was an adult education scheme, and by modifying the academy created first the high school and then the state normal school.

The most important educational achievement, however, and the most notable reform of that reforming age, was the free, public school system in the northern and western states. There was a great wave of propaganda in favor of more schools and better schools. Teachers' magazines and teachers' associations, promotion societies of citizens, the Workingmen's Party, legislative lobbies, and the favorable section of the press urged the creation of the state school office and the passage of laws for the establishment, support, and administration of public schools. New York led the vanguard, to be followed later by Michigan, Ohio, Massachusetts, and other states. Even with state action, the most serious defects of the private schools were only gradually overcome. But in the more progressive sections of the most advanced states, and especially in the cities, there were better curricula, some use of the Pestalozzian methods, higher salaries, longer terms, and better textbooks in 1860 than in the preceding decades. Education was beginning to aid in forming a more perfect union.

QUESTIONS

1. How may the adoption of the Constitution have influenced education?
2. How may Art. IV, Section 4, and Amendments I, X, and XIV, of the federal Constitution affect education?
3. Why, in your opinion, is there no direct reference to education in the Constitution?
4. What educational provisions are found in the constitution of your state?
5. In what ways did the influence of science, and economic and practical demands affect education in this period?
6. Does "demand" tend to call out "supply" in education, as it does in economic matters; or, more specifically, did the growing need for education in the period 1780 to 1860 tend to promote more and better schools? Illustrate.
7. Why may Amos Eaton be considered one of the most ingenious and original of American teachers? Use the works of P. C. Ricketts for material on this question.
8. How was the cause of public education related to the several tendencies which are mentioned in section eight under the heading "Resurgent Democracy"?
9. If you have access to early teachers' journals, study the issues of two or three consecutive years between 1820 and 1840. What topics and problems are most frequently treated? Have these been solved or are we still debating them?
10. Compare the present school publicity methods with those used a century ago.
11. Why was Pestalozzianism probably less evident in America at this time than in Prussia? Read Horace Mann's *Seventh Report* (1843) on this question.
12. Had education by 1860 succeeded in binding the people together to any great degree? Had it succeeded in doing so at the North?

FOR FURTHER READING AND STUDY

Educational journals began to appear in the period covered by this chapter. They contain a great deal of first-hand information on conditions, ideas, movements, and text-books. The most important early ones are William Russell's *American Journal of Education* (1826), W. C. Woodbridge's *American Annals of Education* (1831), Henry Barnard's *Connecticut Common School Journal* (1838), and Horace Mann's *Common School Journal* (1839). Volume Nineteen of Barnard's *American Journal of Education* contains a study of curricula, especially those of the early high schools (pp. 463, 465–576), and of illiteracy between 1840 and 1860 (pp. 802–835). Educational leaders including Albert Picket, George B. Emerson, Jacob Abbott, A. B. Alcott, Ebenezer Bailey and others can be studied in the *Dictionary of American Biography*. Some of those omitted from the *Dictionary* are included in Barnard's *Journal*.

Anderson, Lewis F., "The Manual Labor School Movement," *Educational Review*, 46: 369–388 (Nov., 1913).

Barnard, Henry, *School Architecture*, sixth edition, Cincinnati, H. W. Derby and Co., 1854; *Pestalozzi and His Educational System*, Syracuse, N. Y., C. W. Bardeen and Co., 1936, 751 pp.

DuPont, Bessie Gardner, *National Education in the United States of America by DuPont de Nemours*, Newark, Del., University of Delaware Press, 1923, 161 pp.

Fitzpatrick, Edward A., *The Educational Views and Influence of DeWitt Clinton*, New York, Teachers College Bureau of Publications, Columbia University, 1911, 157 pp., Teachers College Contributions to Education, No. 44.

Griscom, John, *A Year in Europe*, New York, William Collins Sons and Company, Ltd., 1823, 2 vols. Contains an early American account of Pestalozzi and other European men and movements that were influential in this period.

Hansen, Allen Oscar, *Liberalism and American Education in the Eighteenth Century*, New York, The Macmillan Company, 1926, 317 pp.

Hayes, Cecil B., *The American Lyceum; Its History and Contribution to Education*, U. S. Office of Education, Bulletin No. 2, 1932, Washington, Government Printing Office, 1932, 72 pp.

Herrick, Cheesman A., *Meaning and Practice of Commercial Education*, New York, The Macmillan Company, 1904, 378 pp.

Hinsdale, Burke A., *Horace Mann and the Common School Revival in the United States*, New York, Charles Scribner's Sons, 1900, 326 pp.

Hubbell, George A., *Horace Mann, Educator, Patriot, and Reformer; a Study in Leadership*, Philadelphia, W. F. Fell Co., 1910, 285 pp.

Jenkins, Ralph C., and Gertrude C. Warner, *Henry Barnard, an Introduction*, Hartford, The Connecticut State Teachers Association, 1937, 118 pp.

Lancaster, Joseph, *Improvements in Education*, London, Darton and Harvey, 1805, 211 pp. Editions are several and various.

Mann, Mary, *Life and Works of Horace Mann*, Boston, Walker, Fuller and Company, 1867, 5 vols. Republished, Boston, Lee and Shepard, 1891, 5 vols. Volume one is a life of Horace Mann by his wife and the other volumes contain his writings and official reports.

Regier, Charles G., "Beginnings of the Commercial School," *Education*, 42:133–144 (Nov., 1921).

Reigart, John Franklin, *The Lancasterian System of Instruction in the Schools of New York City*, New York, Teachers College, Columbia University, 1916, 105 pp., Teachers College Contributions to Education, No. 81.

Ricketts, Palmer Chamberlain, *Rensselaer Polytechnic Institute; Amos Eaton, Author, Teacher, Investigator*, etc., Troy, N. Y., Rensselaer Polytechnic Institute, 1933, Engineering and Science Series, No. 45, 32 pp.; *History of the Rensselaer Polytechnic Institute, 1824–1934*, New York, John Wiley and Sons, Inc., 1934, 293 pp. Third edition.

Shoemaker, Ervin C., *Noah Webster, Pioneer of Learning*, New York, Columbia University Press, 1936, 347 pp.

Steiner, Bernard C., *Life of Henry Barnard, the First United States Commissioner of Education, 1867–1870*. U. S. Bureau of Education, Bulletin No. 8, 1919, Washington, Government Printing Office, 1919, 131 pp.

Stevens, Neil Everett, "America's First Agricultural School," *Scientific Monthly*, 13:531–540 (Dec., 1921). On the Gardiner Lyceum, and including a bibliography.

Warfel, Harry Redcay, *Noah Webster, Schoolmaster to America*, New York, The Macmillan Company, 1936, 460 pp.

Wightman, Joseph M., *Annals of the Boston Primary School Committee from its First Establishment in 1818 to its Dissolution in 1855*, Boston, G. C. Rand and Avery, City Printers, 1860, 305 pp.

Williams, E. I. F., *Horace Mann, Educational Statesman*, New York, The Macmillan Company, 1937, 367 pp.

Wright, Arthur D., and G. E. Gardner, editors, *Hall's Lectures on School-Keeping*, Hanover, N. H., The Dartmouth Press, 1929, 192 pp.

18 THE AMERICAN SYSTEM

B Y THE CLOSE OF THE CIVIL WAR MOST OF THE NORTHERN states had developed the outlines of their systems of public schools. Progress in that section had not been easy or uniform, but those states generally were committed to the program of developing a state-wide common school. The South had made similar but more tentative beginnings; and there a period not of reconstruction but of primary organization and educational construction paralleled and followed the political and economic phases of the Reconstruction era. Beginning not much before 1873, the state school office, the school tax, and laws for the organization of common schools were generally introduced in the South. That section also demanded a dual system, one set of schools for the white and another for the Negro children, and this made the problems of finance and organization extremely difficult.

In the North the period from 1865 to 1900 was marked by the rapid development of common schools, high schools, and normal schools, the grading of the schools, the expansion of their curricula, the passage of compulsory attendance laws, and a great increase in expenditures for buildings and equipment. The foundations for this expansion, which formed the subject of the preceding chapter, were laid in the three or four decades which came before the outbreak of sectional strife. The kindergarten was introduced into the public system after 1873, and at the other end of the ladder, the state universities, then for the first time aided by regular appropriations, and the new land-grant colleges established through the Morrill Act, completed the system. The junior high school and the junior college developed later, but they are only links inserted into the chain. The system, or rather, each of the state systems when fully formed, comprised the kindergarten, the elementary school, the high school, the teacher education school, and the state university and land-grant college; and it offered the pupils opportunity, at public expense, for a complete education beginning in the preschool years and continuing to the attainment of a graduate or professional degree.

1. PROBLEMS OF THE SOUTH AFTER THE CIVIL WAR

We do not have the space to describe the effects of the war and its terrible consequences. Time was needed to heal its wounds, to revive the spirit of the people, and to lay the foundations for future progress. Four years of conflict had ruined industry and agriculture and demoralized the labor system. The political evils of the congressional plan of reconstruction increased the sectional hatred aroused by war; and the fear of Negro control, the burning issue of mixed schools, and outright opposition to Negro education even in separate schools tended to paralyze the agencies which might have developed public education.

The agencies that first attempted to provide education for the South were private and church associations; and they wrote a chapter that we are likely to forget but ought to remember. Even before the end of the war, northern teachers in large numbers went into the occupied sections and established schools for Negroes or for both races. Others followed after the war until many towns had schools for the freedmen. There were nine thousand teachers in these schools by 1869 and more than half of them were from the North, sent and supported by freedmen's aid societies and educational associations. Two of the latter were the American Freedmen's Union, composed of Unitarians and other religious liberals, and the American Missionary Association, which had been founded by the Methodist and other orthodox churches. The two bodies did not cooperate with each other because the former insisted upon secular and the latter upon religious schooling. The Freedmen's Bureau, which was created by Congress in 1864, was a public agency to provide medical and hospital services, to supervise labor contracts, and to establish schools in cooperation with the private associations. The head of the Bureau, General O. O. Howard, believed that education was the most urgent need of the freedmen.

The emotional force which abolitionism had generated furnished a part of the motive power for the education of the Negroes. They would not really be free, it was held, until they had been equipped to take their places as full citizens of the Republic; but there were also partisan and economic and, as we have seen, religious motives. Many of the teachers came from the centers of abolitionism and former stations of the Underground Railroad. Others who had strong political interests attempted to lead their pupils safely into the fold of the Republican Party. And much of the support came from northern industrialists who hoped to develop markets for their products by educating the freedmen.

The quality of the schools varied, but very poor schools seem to have been the most numerous. The buildings and equipment were inadequate.

At first the pupils were eager and not only children but older men and women attended. The attainment of an education proved to be a long and tedious process, however, and in a few years the enthusiasm declined. The southern whites were at first helpless against the new invasion but they soon became violently hostile to the "Yankee schools." They refused to board the teachers or to rent them buildings for schools and frequently they engaged in real persecution. The attempt to establish mixed schools for the two races, as the American Freedmen's Union tried to do, especially provoked southern ire. By 1870 the northern teachers had begun to withdraw, and by 1873 radical reconstruction had lost the day. There are those who see in the work of the northern teachers and politicians the origin of the public school system of the South, but this contention cannot be supported by sound evidence.

The presidential plan of reconstruction from 1865 to 1867 attempted to enlist the cooperation of the white citizens of the South; but under the congressional plan from 1867 to 1876, the freedmen and northern carpetbaggers controlled the attempted reconstruction. Under presidential reconstruction at least five states had made efforts to re-establish schools; but these attempts were nullified by the radical members of Congress who in 1867 passed the Reconstruction Act over President Johnson's veto. This act formed the southern states into military provinces under martial law. As the state governments were reconstructed, educational clauses were included in the state constitutions, boards of education and state and local supervision were provided, and state appropriations and the property tax for schools were authorized. Much of the legislation was taken from the laws of the same states before the war, although it was made more mandatory and more detailed. By 1870 public school systems had again been created in outline, but the financial difficulties and the hostility of many of the people prevented the effectual administration of the laws.

The extent to which some northern elements were willing to go in order to force educational reconstruction upon the South was shown by the attempt to institute a federal system of education in those states. Representative Hoar, in introducing a bill with this purpose, dwelt upon the failure of the South to provide free public education before the war. The Hoar Bill (1870) was written to apply to all of the states of the Union, but its terms would actually have applied to the southern states only. The bill provided that the President should appoint a state superintendent of national schools for any state which did not provide an approved system of schools for all children between the ages of six and eighteen; and that the Secretary of the Interior should appoint division and local superintendents of national schools for each such state. All textbooks were to be prescribed by the state superintendent and the United States

Commissioner of Education. Local, division, and state superintendents were to report to the federal government. And the schools were to be supported by an annual, direct tax to be collected by federal agents. The bill failed to pass. Superintendent J. P. Wickersham of Pennsylvania, reviewing this bill, in an address to the National Education Association, in 1871, declared that the country could not endure half republic and half despotism any more than it could endure half slave and half free. The Association passed resolutions favoring national aid for schools with local autonomy in educational administration.

There was agitation for national aid for some years after the failure of the Hoar Bill, but without tangible result. It was proposed to create a national school fund from the sale of public lands and to divide the income among the states for the support of public schools. When this plan also failed the Department of Superintendents formulated principles which were embodied in a bill that was introduced by Senator Blair in 1881. The Blair bill provided for the distribution of seventy-seven million dollars to the states in proportion to the number of illiterates in each. This would have given large proportional amounts to the southern states. The bill allowed each state almost complete freedom in the application of its share. The Senate of three successive Congresses passed the bill, but each time it failed in the House. For many years thereafter there was no revival of the proposal to secure federal aid for general education.

Private funds were, however, devoted to this purpose in the South, and these were used to stimulate self-help in certain sections and cities. The first great donation was made by George Peabody who provided two million dollars to be managed and applied by a board of trustees. The first general agent of the Peabody Fund was Barnas Sears who had followed Horace Mann as Secretary of the Massachusetts State Board, and who, therefore, came with large experience in educational promotion; and he was succeeded after some years by an able Southerner, J. L. M. Curry. The income of the Peabody Fund was used to cooperate with state authorities in aiding free public schools for either race, especially in communities where the people were already doing all that they could to help themselves. Since the annual income from the fund was only from ninety thousand to one hundred and thirty thousand dollars, it was deemed better to give considerable help in a few places which could become models for neighboring towns or schools rather than to give small amounts to a large number of places, in which case the effects would hardly be seen. The Peabody Board also followed the policy of aiding normal schools for both white and Negro women teachers. The agents of the Board spent much of their time in developing sentiment for education, allaying antagonisms, visiting schools, and conferring with state departments of education. One of the schools for teachers that was aided was the Nashville Normal School which with this help developed into the George Peabody College for Teachers, incorporated in 1909. A few years earlier (1898) the Conference for Education in the South had been organized, and the Southern Education Board developed out of this conference in 1902. The General Education Board (1903) and a number of other privately endowed boards cooperated with these agencies.

The conquest of illiteracy, the development of high schools, the improvement of living conditions and health, and the raising of the economic level through a more scientific agriculture were among the leading aims of the southern educational revival. One effort to reduce illiteracy in the country was begun in eastern Kentucky by Cora Wilson Stewart through her "moonlight schools," first established in 1911. Although greatly reduced since then, illiteracy has not been stamped out; the rate per thousand is still high in the rural parts of the South. The public high school also developed slowly in that section. Apparently no southern state had as many as one hundred four-year rural or small-town high schools in 1910. This number has been increased manyfold, the standards have been raised, and the curricula have been greatly enriched. Many consolidated schools have been developed and some states have numerous public junior colleges. But this does not mean that all sections are served by adequate schools. Indeed in the last half-century, educational progress in the South has not everywhere kept pace with that of the rest of the country.

The Negro schools have been improved and they have had the support of some of the great foundations; but even now, except for specially aided schools, they are often in very poor condition. Advanced schools and colleges for Negroes likewise trail far behind the best higher schools and teachers' colleges for whites. The Negro land-grant colleges, which will soon complete their first half-century, have developed slowly because of lack of funds and for other reasons. They have not always received their equitable share of the funds. During 1940, it is credibly asserted, sixteen southern states spent for agricultural extension work among Negroes above two million dollars less than a proportionate division of the funds would have allotted to them. Some of the private colleges, such as Hampton Institute and Booker T. Washington's Tuskegee Institute, have done important work for Negro education. But private agencies cannot carry the burden of the higher education and teacher education of Negroes.

A few figures will indicate the magnitude of the differences which have been mentioned. We shall use as a base the year 1900 which is the middle point between the Civil War and the present. The average school term in the South in 1900 was less than one hundred days as against one hundred and forty-five days in the country as a whole; and in North Carolina it was seventy days a year. Today no state has less than seven months of schooling a year. The showing with respect to teachers' salaries is much less satisfactory. The average annual salaries of teachers in the South actually declined after the Civil War and were little more than half of the national average in 1900. In comparison with northern salaries there has been no improvement since. The Mississippi teachers of both races combined earn less than five hundred dollars a year on the average, those of Arkansas less than six hundred, and those of three other southern states only a little more than half of the national average, which is thirteen hundred and seventy-four dollars (1940). The earnings of Negro teachers are at the bottom of the salary range. Negroes constitute a fourth of the population of the South, and nearly three-fourths of the Negroes of America live in that section. The salaries of the Negro teachers must be doubled and tripled before their schools can command adequately prepared staffs. North Carolina has, however, just passed a law (1944) providing for equal salaries for the teachers of the two races.

If the national government should aid education in the South, this would be only the application of a principle which many states have long applied to their poorer districts. Some federal control, and at least a federal audit of the moneys spent, should doubtless be required. It has been estimated that twenty-five million dollars annually would be required to bring Negro education up to the present level of white education. But many white schools also need the stimulation and the financial aid which the wealthier sections should supply through a federal aid law.

2. THE LAND-GRANT COLLEGES

The land-grant, or agricultural and mechanical, colleges were created as the result of the Morrill Act which was passed by Congress and signed by President Lincoln in 1862. We must distinguish between the state universities and the land-grant colleges, especially since in several states the land-grant colleges have been incorporated in the state universities. The state universities were formed to provide a liberal higher education and preparation for the old professions, especially those of law and medicine, under public, that is state, auspices. The land-grant colleges are also administered by the states but they receive national support; and, as they have developed, they furnish a higher education in agriculture, engineering, and many of the newer professions and vocations. In those states in which the older and newer functions have been combined in one institution, the name state university has usually been adopted but the second group of functions is subsidized by the national government under the provisions of the Morrill and supplementary laws. In such states the name land-grant college, or agricultural and mechanical college, or state college is not used. We shall briefly trace these developments.

Even the colonial colleges, although they were private corporations, were frequently given public aid in money or land. Such an investment of public wealth was understood to impose a responsibility, but the nature and limits of the obligation were not clear. In the Revolution and intermittently for a period of forty years, several attempts were made by different states to secure control of private colleges and to transform them into state institutions. Such efforts were made in the cases of Yale, William and Mary, Pennsylvania, Columbia, and Dartmouth. At that time all maintained their private status. The last attempt occurred between 1815 and 1819 in New Hampshire and led to the celebrated Dartmouth College case before the Supreme Court of the United States. The decision (1819) reached far beyond the immediate issue to declare that a charter is a contract which a state legislature is not competent to annul. This decision gave legal protection to private property and business agreements in general; and, in particular, it guaranteed the endowments and chartered rights of private colleges. The New Hampshire state legislature was compelled to return Dartmouth College with all its former rights and property to its old board, and the college has continued as a private institution. The decision may have stimulated the founding of private colleges by assuring their continued private status; and it has been asserted that it convinced the public authorities that they would have to establish their own state colleges and universities in order to complete the public school systems. This they proceeded to do.

They had already begun. Nine state colleges and universities had been established by the year of the Dartmouth decision: by Georgia in 1785, by North Carolina in 1789, by Virginia in 1819, and by other states. Twelve more state universities, making twenty-one in all, were founded before the Civil War. Most of them did not at once acquire the later characteristics of state universities. The early institutions were hardly of college grade, were not secular, and were not given regular support by the parent states. The University of Virginia (1825) and the University of Michigan (1837) became the leaders in developing university standards of scholarship and teaching. Eventually, the state universities and the land-grant colleges became what the Constitution of Indiana in 1816 had indicated that they should be, the top rung in our education ladder, or, in the language of that document, the highest stage in a "general system of education ascending in regular gradations from township schools to a State University wherein tuition shall be gratis, and equally open to all." These phrases well describe the ideal of the American state systems of education. It should, however, be noticed with great concern that state universities and land-grant colleges, by charging fees and often by piling one fee upon another, have come more and more to violate this early principle of gratuitous instruction. This is a policy that cannot be harmonized with the ideals of free, public education.

We turn now from the early state universities to the land-grant colleges. The Morrill Act had a distinct purpose, to provide advanced education for working farmers and mechanics and other members of the "industrial classes." The older colleges and the state universities prepared students for the older professions; the land-grant colleges for scientific agriculture, engineering, homemaking, and the growing industry and commerce of the country. The Act required each state which accepted its benefits to maintain "at least one college where the leading object shall be, without excluding other scientific and classical studies, and including military tactics, to teach such branches of learning as are related to agriculture and the mechanic arts . . . in order to promote the liberal and practical education of the industrial classes in the several pursuits and professions in life."

For this purpose the Act made available to the states, in proportion to population, about ten million acres of public lands. As a result of the gift, almost every state established such a college. They developed slowly at first because they lacked the prestige of older types of institutions and because both the sciences and the teaching of agriculture, home economics, and engineering were not well developed at that time. Not until about the end of the century did they begin to grow rapidly both in size and effectiveness. Nine of them have developed into state universities, and the rest are usually designated as state colleges but many of these are also universities in fact. This latter development was natural because advanced technical and vocational education cannot be imparted except to those who have the necessary basic preparation in the arts, languages, mathematics, and sciences. Meanwhile, these institutions have exercised great influence upon the high schools by preparing teachers, developing new sciences and materials, and enabling the schools to serve the common people's needs. We have fought against early vocational stratification, by means of comprehensive high schools, state universities, and liberal land-grant colleges, by educating future lawyers, teachers, and physicians in the same schools and up to a point in the same classes. The Morrill Act in these and other ways has been a powerful democratizing force that has been felt throughout the American System.

In the Congressional debates on the Morrill Act, it was freely predicted by its opponents that the initial appropriation would be only the first of a series of "raids on the treasury." One may object to the words and to the philosophy underlying them, but this was a true forecast. Not only are the land-grant colleges receiving regular support from the national treasury but a whole series of supplementary acts, all carrying further appropriations, have been passed. The agricultural experiment stations were created in 1887, and at present the annual appropriations to these amount to an average of about one hundred thirty-five thousand dollars for each state. A "Second Morrill Act" in 1890 provided fifteen thousand dollars a year for the maintenance of each of the original institutions and this amount has now risen to an annual average of ninety-nine thousand dollars for each college. An act was passed to provide seventeen separate land-grant colleges for Negroes in the southern states. Other national acts that may be considered to be supplementary to the original Morrill Act because they are intended to carry out its purposes among those whom the colleges could not reach directly are the Smith-Lever Act of 1914 for the extension teaching of agriculture and home economics, the Smith-Hughes Act of 1917 for vocational education in high schools, and the George-Deen Vocational Act of 1936. The Smith-Hughes and George-Deen Acts carry appropriations of twenty-one million dollars a year for agricultural, home economics, and vocational education, in the states.

That this series of laws would raise many questions is evident. Three of these problems will be mentioned. When the Morrill Act was passed in 1862 it was widely believed that the new colleges could directly reach their object, the teaching of agriculture, home economics, the mechanic arts, and the related subjects, by enrolling future farmers, homemakers, and industrial workers in their campus classes. This was a double error. It was soon discovered that the required teaching methods and means and to a great degree the sciences themselves were undeveloped and often were still to be created. Hence the need for experiment stations, experimental laboratories, shops and research workers to discover and to organize the knowledge and techniques that were to be taught. In two or three decades considerable progress was made in solving this problem and scientific agriculture, home economics, and the several technologies were developing their present forms. In the second place the colleges did not reach the working farmers and mechanics in large numbers. Those who completed the college courses went into technical and government employment rather than to the farm or factory. Hence the need for simplification and the extension of the new practical knowledge to those who would directly apply it. Much of this was done through the publications of the United States Department of Agriculture; and much also through the Smith-Lever (1914), Smith-Hughes (1917), and George-Deen (1936) Acts and the resulting high school and extension teaching, and the county agents, the Four-H Clubs, and other organizations. The whole complex program is an instructive example of popular education and can be studied by educators in all fields with profit.

A third problem concerns national educational administration: if we are to develop a national system of education, what parts in the total scheme are to be played and what controls exercised by the local community, by the state, and by the nation? Only a part of this whole question has been raised by the legislation supplementary to the Morrill Act. The original act provided for national aid to the states for a specified purpose, the foundation of new colleges. But it did not supervise state plans to carry out the purpose. The Smith-Hughes Act for the first time introduced a measure of national supervision over the expenditure of national funds for education. That law provided that the money assigned to a state under the Act must be matched by an equal amount of state funds; and it created a Federal Board for Vocational Education with the power and duty to examine the state programs of vocational education. A state may be required to modify its program to meet the judgment of the Board before it is allowed to draw upon the federal funds. We have called this a measure of national supervision over vocational education. There is evidence that it has not worked to the satisfaction of all. The proper integration of national aid and supervision with state and community interests is a more inclusive problem to which the future may be required to find a satisfactory answer.

3. FEDERAL AID BILLS

Federal aid for vocational and technical education is now a well-established policy. Every year Congress appropriates large sums, more than twenty millions of dollars, for vocational education and an average of nearly a quarter of a million for each land-grant college; and so far there has been little evidence of any undue federal influence. But federal aid for the improvement of general education in the elementary and secondary schools is a different matter. When it is proposed to use federal funds to equalize educational opportunity among the states, the cry of states' rights is raised and the fear of possible federal interference or control is expressed.

An example in World War II was Senate Bill 637 which was debated in 1943 but did not come to a vote. The bill would have appropriated annually two hundred million dollars to the states to meet educational emergencies caused by the depression and the war and an additional one hundred million for equalizing elementary and secondary school opportunities among and within the states. The bill was only one example of several in a series of similar bills which have been before Congress periodically since World War I. The need has long existed and was recognized more than a third of a century ago when the Smith-Towner Bill, the first of the series, was introduced. State inequality of educational opportunity arises from the fact that the states vary in wealth and in the number of children for whom they have to provide. Those states with the highest proportions of children of school age, many of them in the South, are also the states with the lowest per capita wealth.

Federal aid for general education in elementary and high schools would be a means to resolve the paradox indicated above; and this would be merely the application of a principle which many states have long applied to their poorer districts. Such grants would probably lead to a degree of federal regulation. Such regulation should be carefully circumscribed, but if the national government is to furnish money for general education it should have the power and duty to require that the money will be used by the states for the intended purposes. In the past the state governments have amassed power over education; and it is a fair question whether reasonable regulation by federal agencies is less necessary or desirable than state regulation. It is in the local community where citizens and parents can influence the school directly. Such educational democracy as we have —and we have a great deal more than the people of most nations—resides primarily in the local community. But some governmental regulation of public education there must be, and it should probably be distributed between the community, the state, and the nation. It should not be too difficult to devise a scheme of federal and state cooperation that will give each unit its proper share in the direction of public education. In this matter the nation is moving slowly but it does move.

4. THE FEDERAL OFFICE OF EDUCATION

A third effort by the national government looking toward the development of a more truly national system of education was made by the creation of the Federal Office of Education. This movement also attained its early form shortly after the Civil War. The national government conducts some special schools of its own and renders important services to schools in the states. The Military Academy at West Point, conducted since the early years of the nineteenth century, and the Naval Academy, founded in 1845, are national schools. Many of the departments of the government, such as the Department of Agriculture, carry on extensive educational activities. The Smithsonian Institution and the Library of Congress are national agencies. The Federal Department of Education, later called the Bureau, and since 1933 the Office, of Education, was established in 1867 to promote education by collecting and disseminating information. The first Commissioner was Henry Barnard who had been active in securing the establishment of this agency. Further duties have from time to time been assigned to it. The Office of Education promotes vocational education and

aids in the administration of the funds set aside by Congress for this purpose, conducts investigations including fundamental research studies, issues
numerous periodical and occasional publications, and maintains in Washington a national library of education. Upon request the Office of Education conducts educational surveys of national, state, or local scope. An example is the National Survey of Secondary Education whose findings were
published about 1932 in a series of monographs. The Office issues about
thirty bulletins a year and publishes a monthly magazine, *School Life*,
that for the duration of the war was called *Education for Victory*. Its
Biennial Survey of Education is a primary source on education in the
United States for each two-year period, and it also prepares and publishes
many studies of education in foreign countries.

5. FROM NORMAL SCHOOLS TO TEACHERS' COLLEGES

Public schools for the preparation of teachers are an essential part of the
American System. A few public normal schools had been established before the Civil War, but the period of expansion began with the conclusion
of that struggle. In earlier times, it was often considered that teachers were
sufficiently prepared when they had completed the work of the school in
which they were to serve. Of the principles of school administration, of
educational psychology, and of the real functions of the profession which
they were entering, they knew almost nothing, and knowing little they
were doubtless hardly aware of their professional ignorance. The special
schools for teachers have improved these conditions, at least as they relate to elementary and secondary teachers.

Lacking special schools, other means had already been used in Europe
to acquaint prospective teachers with their future duties. Handbooks and
some forms of cadet teaching were used by the Jesuits, the Brothers of
the Christian Schools, Joseph Lancaster, and others. The educational works
of the great writers were not very suitable for this purpose because they
were not practical handbooks but broad, theoretical treatments. With the
rise of systems of public education, teachers were gradually expected to
show competence in teaching as well as knowledge and moral character.
Professional schools and the modern systems of universal education have
developed together. The elementary normal schools of France, from which
we apparently derived the name of the American schools for teachers,
were first established during the Bourbon Restoration (1815–1830). A
normal school is literally one which maintains or sets forth a norm or standard of teaching ability. The American normal school is a native institution,
and this applies to the similar schools in other Western countries also.
They were all similar in purpose, closely associated with the elementary

schools, and formed of native materials. The one international influence which affected them was the influence of Pestalozzi. His methods and spirit, although variously interpreted, permeated them all.

The American normal school did not come without preparation. It was exactly fifty years from 1789 when the idea of such a school was first proposed by a writer, probably Elisha Ticknor, to the opening of the first state normal school at Lexington, Massachusetts, in 1839. During this half-century many plans and propaganda articles appeared. One of these by Thomas Hopkins Gallaudet in 1825 anticipated the most essential features of the schools as established, including the idea of a practice and demonstration school. Travelers returning from Europe published their observations of such schools in books, magazines, and official documents.

There had also been more concrete anticipations. The academies had long been preparing teachers in the knowledge of the common and more advanced branches and a few had begun to give some attention to the principles and practice of teaching. The well-known schools for girls established at Troy, New York, by Emma Willard and at Hartford, Connecticut, by Catherine Beecher prepared many women for teaching but they did not give courses on methods. A course of three years for the preparation of teachers, in which the common branches were reviewed and special lessons in the art of teaching and class management were given, was instituted by Samuel Read Hall in a private academy in Concord, Vermont, in 1823. He also published his *Lectures on Schoolkeeping* (1829), an elementary work on teaching which was based upon the lessons that he gave in his normal-academy. The report of the principal of the Canandaigua Academy in New York for 1829 shows that prospective teachers in that school were formed into a class to study Hall's *Lectures* until the book had been "finished and thoroughly reviewed." The defects of common schools, the methods of teaching the several school subjects, the making of pens, the government of schools, the construction of schoolhouses, the formation of lyceums and school libraries, and "Pestalozzi and his mode of instruction" were among the topics of the teachers' class in this New York academy in 1829. In New York also an act appropriating funds to promote the education of teachers in the academies was passed in 1827; and this act was followed by a stronger law in 1834. These laws seem to have been the first legislative provisions by an American state for the professional education of teachers. But they fell short of establishing a special institution for that purpose.

The first state normal school was opened in Massachusetts in 1839. It combined instruction in the common branches with work in methods and management and in a practice school. The same year a second, the following year a third, and a few years later a fourth, state normal school were opened in Massachusetts. The state of New York, influenced by the report of a committee of its legislature upon the Massachusetts schools, abandoned its academy program and opened a state normal school at Albany in 1844. But less than a dozen similar schools were established in all the states before the Civil War. The first thirty years of the schools formed an experimental period; but after the close of the Civil War, state normal schools were established at the rate of about twenty-five in each decade until nearly every state had one or more. Populous states, such as New York and Pennsylvania, each had ten or more so located that the various sections of the state would be served. By the end of the century more than a hundred state normal schools were in operation.

Meanwhile the normal schools developed internally, in number of students, in the qualifications of the staffs, and in their courses of study and equipment. The typical state normal school of 1860 was carried on in a single building which contained the dormitories and also housed the model school. There was a staff of five teachers and less than a hundred students who were seventeen or eighteen years old and whose only preparation was a common school education. The one-year curriculum included reviews of the common branches, methods of teaching, class management, some elementary psychology, and some work with children in the model school. Twenty years later the typical school of 1880 had two hundred and forty students, and the model school was conducted in a separate building. The curriculum had been increased to three years and the staff had grown to ten or twelve. Some academy and college preparatory subjects were usually taught, and this led to an unexpected result. Many of the students were no longer preparing to teach but were in preparation for college instead. The normal school which had evolved out of the academy tended to turn back toward its earlier academic functions, and this tendency continued until the state normal schools became teachers' colleges. But meanwhile other changes had made this development seem natural and indeed necessary. To this we shall come back.

From the first many of the normal schools were led by able men, most of whom have not received the attention which their work for American education merits. Cyrus Peirce, the first principal of the Lexington school, David P. Page, of the Albany school, James Pyle Wickersham, Nicholas Tillinghast, Richard Edwards, and Joseph Baldwin are only a few of the great leaders of that heroic age. With few resources and against great odds they succeeded in building serviceable institutions.

Meanwhile other means were tried to improve the services of those who were already engaged in teaching and who, for the most part, had no professional preparation. One of these means was the teachers' institute which was a teachers' meeting conducted for professional instruction and continuing usually for a week. The normal institute had the same general character but continued for four or six weeks. Henry Barnard organized a normal institute in Connecticut about 1846 and J. S. Denman of New York apparently first developed the short period teachers' institute. Another medium with the same purpose was the summer school for teachers. One of the first and most famous was conducted by Louis Agassiz on the Island of Penikese on the coast of Massachusetts in the summer of 1873. One with a more distinctly professional purpose was conducted at Martha's Vineyard about ten years later. The universities of Wisconsin, Indiana, and Cornell instituted summer schools about 1890. The Summer School of the South at Knoxville was established in 1902 by Charles W. Dabney and enrolled two thousand students. Thereafter, many other colleges and universities throughout the country began to conduct summer schools and a large proportion of their students were teachers or prospective teachers.

Professional courses for elementary teachers were given in some of the midwestern state universities before the Civil War. These were usually of the normal variety and were administered in special normal departments. The standards were low and the universities, at that time weak, marginal institutions, were competing with the state normal schools. The competition was frequently effective. At the State University of Iowa the teachers' courses for many years had a larger enrollment than the collegiate departments.

When the attendance and the support of the universities increased they abandoned their normal departments, and after an interim of ten or fifteen years, during which they gave no professional work, they began to offer courses for high school teachers in "the science and art of teaching." At the State University of Iowa, which was first in the field, the transition to education courses for secondary school teachers was made in 1873. At the University of Michigan, courses for elementary teachers had been given at intervals from the opening of the university in 1841, but in 1879 a new "chair of the science and art of teaching" was established to prepare school administrators and high school teachers, to develop teaching as a profession, and to promote cooperation between the secondary schools and the university. These purposes acquire special meaning when we notice that they were framed only a few years after the university began to accredit high schools and after the Kalamazoo decision. These matters will be further noticed in Chapter 20. By the end of the century, one-half of the recognized colleges and universities reported that they were teaching education courses, and today almost all are doing so.

As the departments of education grew in size and importance in the large universities, they were reorganized into university Schools or Colleges of Education. Teachers College in New York was chartered in 1889 and became affiliated with Columbia University in 1898. A School of Education was established at the University of Chicago in 1900 with a famous educator, F. W. Parker, as director. Similar developments occurred in the growing state universities between 1890 and 1920. Bureaus of educational research were frequently established as divisions of the Colleges of Education. At Indiana University this took place in 1915, at the University of Illinois in 1917, and at many other universities in the following decade.

During the same period it became a marked tendency for the stronger state normal schools to develop into four-year degree-granting teachers' colleges. About one-fourth of the previous two- or three-year normal schools had become teachers' colleges by 1920, and one-half of them by 1925. There still are county, city, and state normal schools and a number of private normal schools, but rising standards of certification, competition with university and college departments and schools of education, and rising teachers' salaries after World War I practically compelled the normal schools, especially in the more opulent sections of the country, to raise their facilities and standards to the college level.

With all this progress teacher education is still very defective. One major difficulty is the condition that teachers' colleges, universities, private colleges, and indeed all institutions which prepare teachers are in competition with each other for students and are therefore unwilling to apply any strict selective principles in the admission of students. Nor is there any accepted prognostic scheme which will with certainty or near certainty predict future teaching success. Secondly, there is too little relation between supply and demand as teacher training is now conducted. Under war and postwar conditions there is likely to be a serious shortage and in periods of economic depression a vast oversupply of teachers. This is, of course, due not only to the numbers being graduated from teachers' schools but also to conditions of appointment and terms which the professional schools do not control. The schools do in a large measure control their own courses. It is admitted by almost all, faculty and students, that the courses are too theoretical and that in any given institution there is unjustifiable duplication of content between courses with widely different titles and professed aims. There are, on the other hand, large gaps in the curriculum. Practical questions in school management, in planning lessons, courses, and programs, in guidance, and in personal relations are often treated briefly, theoretically, or not at all. The courses also deal with conditions in large schools and metropolitan centers, although some graduates spend the first years of their teaching in small schools in rural or village surroundings. Finally, not to make this arraignment too long, there is often a lack of scholarship in the faculties, not only a lack of present knowledge and training but also a lack of the investigative spirit and the scientific scholarly interest which would fill up gaps and remove present deficiencies. But it would be unfair to end on this critical note. Teacher education has been created in the last hundred years, has improved greatly in quality and scope in the last fifty years, and is still developing. It must continue to improve if it is to serve the future well.

6. COMPULSORY ATTENDANCE

The United States very gradually developed the conviction that an educated citizenry could be developed only if all the children attended school. This conclusion was not accepted until the later decades of the nineteenth century. It was seen that no country had attained universal education or even general literacy by merely setting up schools and encouraging the parents to send their children to school. The church schools, the philanthropic and neighborhood attempts, the Lancasterian schools, and the public schools had all failed at this point. It came to be recognized that only an agency such as the state which includes everyone and which can act directly upon individuals can secure general school attendance, and then only by specific legislation. Some degree of the increased attendance and greater regularity of attendance at school which we have attained is certainly due to the growing recognition of the need for education in modern life; but wherever society has concluded that universal schooling is a necessity, it has been found necessary to enact compulsory attendance legislation in order to attain it. Most of the more democratic states long resisted this necessity and it was not until the latter nineteenth century, about fifty or sixty years ago, that France, England, and the United States began, as Guizot, French Minister of Public Instruction, phrased it, to exercise "this coercive action of the state upon the domestic economy of the family."

Nearly one-half of the states of the union enacted compulsory attendance laws between 1870 and 1890, and within thirty years after the latter date the other half had slowly and somewhat reluctantly followed their example. One state, however, anticipated the rest by more than a decade. Massachusetts as early as 1852 passed a law that embodied the essential features of such legislation; and that law may be used here as a convenient illustration. These features were the age limits, the annual period of attendance required, the necessary exemptions and allowance for alternative instruction, the provision for enforcement, and a penalty for noncompliance. According to the Massachusetts law of 1852, all children between the ages of eight and fourteen years were required to attend school for twelve weeks a year, and for six of the twelve weeks the attendance had to be consecutive. The legal exemptions were specified. Children who were too poor, or too weak in body or mind, or who were otherwise receiving instruction, or who had already completed the school course were not required to attend. The selectmen and the "truant officers" were to examine the merits of each case and, if any refused to obey their summons, a set fine was to be imposed upon the parents. This law with its easy requirements was a beginning, but even these moderate demands were not rigidly enforced.

The compulsory attendance laws provide an excellent illustration of the general truth that in education the American states while following similar historical patterns are, at any one time, at very unequal stages in the evolution of their program. Every state has now for more than twenty-five years had some kind of compulsory attendance law, but the provisions of the laws are not alike in any two states. Massachusetts and Mississippi, and even two adjoining states like Ohio and Kentucky, differ in the provisions and in the enforcement of their laws. This unfortunate diversity in our compulsory attendance requirements is the natural result of the differences in the past history of the states, in their economic and industrial condition, and in the character and distribution of their people. The industrial states and the new western states were the first to pass such laws: Massachusetts, Connecticut, and New York led in the industrial East; and in the West, Washington, while yet a territory, Nevada, and California, all fell into line before 1875. The southern states were the slowest. The last twelve states, one-fourth of the whole number of states, were all south of the Mason and Dixon line and all but two were east of the Mississippi River, that is, in the "Old South."

The general tendency of the growing legislation has been to strengthen both the compulsory attendance and the related child labor laws and the means of enforcement. By 1890 Massachusetts was requiring seven and one-half months of schooling each year between the ages of eight and fourteen; but apparently no other state then demanded more than five and some only three months a year, while one-half the states still had no laws on the subject. The trend since then has been to lower the age when attendance must begin, to raise the leaving age, to increase the number of months of attendance per year, to stiffen the requirements for work permits, and to improve the methods of enforcement. Ohio now requires children to be in school from age six to eighteen, a twelve-year period extending from the first year of the common school to the normal age for graduation from high school. This is at present the longest period of required attendance in any state. One-half of the states demand attendance for nine years and some for less time.

The laws allow reasonable exemptions. Children who are ill and whose physical-mental condition is such that they cannot profit from school work, or who live at a distance from the nearest school, or who are receiving adequate instruction otherwise are, in most states, not required to attend the public schools; but the exemptions vary from state to state as the attendance ages and other provisions of the laws also do. The last-named exemption, which permits parents to send their children to private schools, has been challenged. A referendum in Oregon, actively supported by the Ku Klux Klan and adopted March 7, 1922, would have required all children between the ages of eight and sixteen to attend the public schools whenever they were in session. This act would have had the effect of permanently closing all elementary private schools in the state, and this was no doubt the object of the referendum. The Supreme Court declared this act unconstitutional. A somewhat analogous attempt was made, about the time of World War I when a wave of "Americanism" swept the country, to legislate upon what private schools may teach. Laws were passed in several states prohibiting the teaching of foreign languages in elementary schools, both public and private. The Supreme Court declared these laws unconstitutional in the case of Meyer vs. Nebraska. In the third case, the state of New Jersey has held that home education cannot be accepted in lieu of school attendance. These cases have both a practical and a historical interest because they mark the present frontier between the power of the state and the liberty of the family in the matter of education and school attendance.

7. SCHOOL PLANT IMPROVEMENT

The state may clearly be taken to assume a corresponding obligation when it passes attendance laws, namely, the duty of providing good schools. It would be against public policy to require children to attend a school where health might be endangered, character corrupted, or learning time wasted. Through the normal schools and colleges of education and by certification and curriculum legislation, an effort was made to guarantee good teaching. Several of these efforts will be more fully treated in the two following chapters.

The health and comfort of the children and the facilities for teaching were also safeguarded and improved by the provision of better buildings and equipment. Here and there some physical improvement had been made earlier, but the greatest progress occurred after the Civil War. A picture of the deplorable conditions which existed is shown by the report of a survey of school buildings, made in New York State in 1841. Overcrowding, lack of ventilation within, of playgrounds without, and of appropriate seating and desks were common. Nine schools out of twenty-two in a single township were maintained in log cabins. Many schools had no conveniences whatever, not even toilets. Drinking water from an open spring was provided in a bucket, and all the children drank from a common tin cup. The fact that the New York school boards were asked to make this survey is evidence that the bad conditions were attracting attention. The leaders in education, including Horace Mann and Henry Barnard, had recently begun to agitate for better buildings and Barnard's *School Architecture* was several times revised, enlarged, and republished.

Even the cities continued to build one-room school buildings. As the number of children increased another room, laid out exactly like the first, was provided by adding a second story. Cincinnati extended this plan by erecting four-room buildings with two rooms on each floor and a central corridor between them. The Latin and English High School of Boston was erected in 1844. It was three stories high and had six classrooms. As the schools grew and the science of school architecture developed, better plans were used. In 1881, Boston built a new Latin and English High School which followed the plan of the academic gymnasium of Vienna. It was built around a central court, had fifty-six rooms, including a gymnasium and a chemical laboratory, although not the first in the country, and some fireproof construction was used. With the introduction of manual training and home economics into the curriculum, schools began to include shops, kitchens, and cafeterias. Offices and teachers' rooms became standard features.

Conflicts often arise when it is attempted to embody several individually good features in the same structure. Thus in 1867 the principle of durability was adopted in the regulations of the school board of Philadelphia. So obvious a consideration was, of course, not new but its official adoption brought it into conflict with the idea that buildings should be easily extended or adapted to new uses. From the idea of durability, it is only a step to that of fireproof construction. As buildings increased in size the demand for safety developed. This question was tragically emphasized by the Collingwood school fire of 1908 in which one hundred eighty children lost their lives. After this, most states began to pass or to strengthen legislation against fire hazards. The difficulty was increased by the growing height of the buildings. While early school buildings had been low, by 1900 they had risen to three and even four stories above the basement. Thomas H. Burrowes in his *Pennsylvania School Architecture* had protested against this trend as early as 1855. Henry Barnard declared that economy is the only argument for high buildings since "sky costs nothing"; but he added that a schoolhouse is never really economical unless it meets the requirements of health, convenience, and safety, and in all these respects "the four-story plan is decidedly inferior." Since 1900 one- and two-story plans have again become popular.

School furniture has likewise gone through an evolution which paralleled the school's evolving functions. In the earliest schoolhouses wooden pegs, driven at a steep slope between the logs, supported the writing desk; and there, facing the dark wall, the pupils sat on high benches without backs. Later long benches and desks made by a carpenter and nailed to the floor with cleats formed a second stage. This was followed by the double and then the single desk. Factory-made desks with cast-iron standards were in general use about 1900. These were cheap but they were also noisy and easily broken and they were not adjustable. Movable chairs and desks had been designed before 1850, but they did not come into use until school work became more intimate and informal. The Moulthrop movable desk designed by a school principal of Rochester, New York, popularized the idea; but, even now, school furniture is usually "made for listening."

Not only the furniture but the teaching equipment, maps, charts, bulletin boards, laboratories, shops, gymnasiums, and a long array of other inventions have helped to make our schools qualitatively different from the simple school of the last century. There is a close relation between the building and equipment and the educational efficiency of a school. We should be more healthful and happier in the modern type of schools, but many buildings are not to be so classified. We should not be content until all children have, not luxurious, but healthful, convenient, and educationally favorable buildings, equipment, and grounds.

8. FORMING THE SYSTEM

The school attendance movement was closely related to two parallel developments in the organization of the schools. These were, first, the classification and grading of the children according to their progress in school; and, secondly, the articulation of the schools themselves. By articulation is meant the fitting together of schools and courses so that pupils may go in a regular progression from the lowest to the highest. The public kindergarten, elementary schools, junior and senior high schools, the teachers' college, and the state colleges or state university form such a closely articulated series of institutions because the completion of a properly selected course at each level is the necessary and adequate preparation for undertaking an appropriate course at the next higher level.

Both the grading of the children and the closer articulation of the schools came about gradually in the United States; and they developed together. Evidently when the student body becomes large and the courses of study complex, grading becomes necessary; and the increase in population and compulsory attendance produced these conditions. It was in the cities where the graded school first attained its full development. Conditions varied so widely that the organizing process followed various patterns in different cities. One or two illustrations will show this. An irregular but very minute grading of pupils was introduced into the Lancasterian schools of New York City where the reading classes were divided into nine stages and the arithmetic classes into seven. This minute division was not retained when the public schools were established in 1853, but yet the public board maintained thirteen grades. The highest of these, however, included some secondary school work. In Chicago, a fully graded course of study was adopted in 1861. The elementary schools of the city were organized in ten grades which together with the high school course, established in 1856, made a fourteen-year system. Kansas City developed a seven-year elementary school which with the high school created an eleven-year system. These examples show the fact that there was no uniformly graded system at the mid-century and for some years thereafter. To this point we shall return when we consider the history of the high school.

Almost as soon as the schools had become fully although variously graded there arose a chorus of opposition to the system. Teachers and citizens protested against the school-machine, the lock-step, and the consequent retardation of children in school and their elimination from school by the rigid grading, the fixed curriculum, and the stiff promotion examinations at the end of each year of work. The opposition really arose, in part, from a new theory of education. Close grading had been satisfactory in monitorial times; it became unsatisfactory later because there had occurred a shift in psychology and educational principles. The new views had been derived from many sources, but they came to us from Pestalozzi and Froebel. They placed greater weight upon the children's interests and needs and demanded a more flexible organization to provide for these individual variations. They helped to prepare the way for the new elementary school which is described in the following chapter.

The outlines of the American System were practically complete by the end of the nineteenth century. It consists of the kindergarten, in many cities, of a practically universal elementary school, of a widespread public high school, sometimes divided into junior and senior schools, of many public junior colleges very unevenly distributed, of teachers' colleges, and of state universities and land-grant colleges. There are also several municipal colleges and universities. The outlines were practically complete by 1900, but the kindergarten in the United States, because of its influence in developing a "new elementary school," and the junior high school and the junior college, because they are mainly twentieth-century institutions, will be treated in later chapters.

The American System is a ladder system. Its aim is to provide appropriate education for all, at all levels, and to require the regular attendance by children at the lower levels at least. The aim is also to provide these opportunities at public expense and without fees; and to articulate the schools so that there may be a series of easy transitions from the kindergarten and the elementary school to the professional and graduate studies at the top. Education for teachers, in this system, has been articulated with the rest of the system and is no longer set apart as it was in the early normal schools.

The American System permits the operation of private schools and welcomes their contributions. They have made many important contributions in the past and will doubtless make new ones in the future. The Catholic church and other churches and many secular agencies operate a large number of schools in the United States. Many adult educational services also are outside the public system. Many private organizations of parents, teachers, and citizens, who do not maintain schools, contribute their wisdom and energy for the improvement of the system.

From the administrative standpoint the American System is not yet unified. There is instead a series of state systems, but all of these bear a strong family resemblance to each other. The educational branch of the federal government which would be the logical head of the system has so far concerned itself most actively with technical and vocational education rather than with general elementary and secondary education.

In the last seventy-five years, the public institutions which had grown up independently, each to meet a specific need, were joined together to form the American System, a unitary scheme to provide educational opportunity under public auspices from the kindergarten to the graduate school. Besides this public system there are in all states numerous private schools also. After the Civil War northern efforts to impose a system upon the South having failed, that section gradually developed public school systems on the common plan; but for emotional and financial reasons, they have not attained the standards of some other sections. Federal subsidies, planned to meet southern needs, have been proposed as a means of raising the level of southern education quickly. None of the bills providing such subsidies has been passed by Congress.

The Morrill Act of 1862 led to the creation of an entirely new type of school, the land-grant state colleges of agriculture and the mechanic arts. These, and the complementary experiment stations, have aided in developing the sciences and their practical uses, have furnished aid to farmers, homemakers, and engineers, and have prepared teachers in these areas for the high schools. Meanwhile, the state universities, which originated earlier, had developed and in some states the land-grant college and state university were combined in one institution. Seventeen Negro land-grant colleges were established in the southern states. A series of laws was passed, supplementary to the primary purposes of the Morrill Act, and to achieve its purposes more completely. Among these laws are the Smith-Lever, Smith-Hughes, and George-Deen Acts.

The Federal Office of Education is mainly an information gathering and disseminating, and a promotion agency. But it also administers the allotment of federal appropriations for education. It does not have the power of some foreign Ministries of Education, but neither do they exercise the democratic leadership of our Office of Education.

The state normal schools began in 1839, but they were not established in numbers until after the Civil War. The earliest normal schools were mainly advanced elementary schools with a few professional courses added; but later they were raised to a secondary school or junior college level and recently they have become degree-granting teachers' colleges.

The public kindergartens and elementary schools, the high schools, the state normal schools and teachers' colleges, the state colleges and universities, and the public junior colleges and special schools were gradually joined together in a sequence which presents an unbroken highway to the student. The formation of the American System also involved legislation on administration and especially on attendance and on school plant and equipment. Other essential phases were the classification of the children, the better articulation of the schools, the elevation of standards, and the distribution of schools among the people in order that educational opportunities may be extended to all as fully as possible. This American ideal is the objective of the American System.

QUESTIONS

1. What do you take to be the meaning of the title of this chapter?
2. What are the chief points of dispute in the interpretation of the educational history of the South?
3. Why was the Hoar Bill an educationally unwise measure?
4. Why did the high school have a slow growth in the South? Find several reasons.
5. If the federal government should subsidize elementary and secondary education, is it probable that federal control will develop? Is state control to be preferred to national control, and why? What is meant by democratic control of education; and why is it to be desired?
6. Which should be most jealously preserved, local control or state control of education? What does history have to say about the defects of each?
7. What important lessons have been learned from the development of the land-grant colleges?
8. Does the early history of the normal schools justify the claim that they were intended as part of the working-class schools while preparatory schools and colleges were intended for professional people? How was this incipient dualism overcome?
9. Why did the early western state universities establish "normal courses" for elementary teachers?
10. What changes in American teacher-education that have taken place in the past do you regard as improvements; and what are its remaining defects? How can these be removed or lessened?
11. Would it be desirable to extend the compulsory attendance requirement in your state, and to what extent? Why? What are the limits of desirable compulsory attendance?

12.   Should private schools be abolished as intended under the Oregon law of 1922, or rigidly controlled as in France, or allowed considerable freedom as in most states of the Union?

FOR FURTHER READING AND STUDY

On Negro education and race questions the *Journal of Negro Education*, issued since April, 1932; and on school buildings, the early *Proceedings* of the American Institute of Instruction and the issues in 1831 and later of the *American Annals of Education* should be consulted. Considerable attention has recently been given to the systematic study of school law. *The Colleges and the Courts*, an important work on the law of higher education in the United States, by E. C. Elliott and M. M. Chambers appeared in 1936 and several annual supplements have been added. The list below contains two manuals on school law, one by Edwards, and the other by Hamilton and Mort. The case, *Meyer v. Nebraska*, mentioned in the text, was argued before the United States Supreme Court February 23, 1923, and decided June 4, 1923. See *U. S. Reports*, Vol. 262, pp. 390–403. The Oregon Compulsory Attendance Case, *Walter M. Pierce, Governor of Oregon, et al. v. Society of Sisters, and Hill Military Academy*, was argued March 16, 17, 1925, and decided June 1, 1925. See *U. S. Reports*, Vol. 268, pp. 510–536.

Agnew, Walter D., *The Administration of Professional Schools for Teachers*, Baltimore, Warwick and York, 1924, 262 pp.

Barnard, Henry, *School Architecture; or Contributions to the Improvement of School-Houses in the United States*, Cincinnati, H. W. Derby and Co., 1854, 464 pp.

Boyden, Arthur C., *The History of the Bridgewater Normal School*, Bridgewater, Mass., Alumni Association, 1933, 156 pp.

Dabney, Charles William, *Universal Education in the South*, Chapel Hill, University of North Carolina Press, 1936, 2 vols.

Edwards, Newton, *The Courts and the Public Schools; the Legal Basis of School Organization and Administration*, Chicago, University of Chicago Press, 1933, 591 pp.

Finegan, Thomas E., *Teacher Training Agencies*, Albany, University of the State of New York, 1917, 439 pp. This is volume two of the Eleventh Annual Report of the New York State Department of Education.

French, William Marshall, and Florence Smith French, *College of the Empire State. A Centennial History of the New York State College for Teachers at Albany*, Albany, N. Y., New York State College for Teachers, 1944, 271 pp.

Frothingham, Paul Revere, *Edward Everett, Orator and Statesman*, Boston, Houghton Mifflin Company, 1925, 495 pp. As scholar and teacher, Governor of Massachusetts, and President of Harvard College, Edward Everett had considerable influence in educational matters.

Hamilton, Robert R., and Paul R. Mort, *The Law and Public Education, with Cases*, Chicago, Foundation Press, 1941, 579 pp.

Hampton Normal and Agricultural Institute, *Twenty-two Years' Work of the Hampton Normal and Agricultural Institute*, Hampton, Va., Normal School Press, 1893, 520 pp.

Hanus, Paul H., *Adventuring in Education*, Cambridge, Mass., Harvard University Press, 1937, 259 pp.

Harper, Charles A., *Development of the Teachers College in the United States with special reference to the Illinois State Normal University*, Bloomington, Ill., Macknight and Macknight, 1935, 384 pp.; *A Century of Public Teacher Education. The Story of the State Teachers Colleges as they evolved from the State Normal Schools*, Washington, D. C., American Association of Teachers Colleges, 1939, 175 pp.

Hubbell, Leigh G., *The Development of University Departments of Education in Six States of the Middle West*, Washington, D. C., Catholic University of America, 1924, 125 pp. A doctoral dissertation.

Hutchins, Clayton D., *Federal Funds for Education, 1954–55 and 1955–56*, U. S. Office of Education Bulletin, 1956, No. 5, 163 pp. With notes on history and legislation.

James, Edward Janes, *The Origin of the Land Grant Act of 1862 . . . and Some Account of Its Author, Jonathan B. Turner*, Urbana-Champaign, Illinois University Press, 1910, 139 pp.

Judd, Charles N., and S. C. Parker, "Problems Involved in Standardizing Normal Schools," U. S. Office of Education *Bulletin*, 1916, No. 12, Washington, D. C., Government Printing Office, 1916, 141 pp.

Loomis, B. W., *The Educational Influence of Richard Edwards*, Nashville, Tenn., George Peabody College for Teachers, 1932, 213 pp.

Matthews, J. C., *The Contributions of Joseph Baldwin to Public Education*, Nashville, Tenn., George Peabody College for Teachers, 1932, 184 pp.

Norton, Arthur Orlo, Editor, *The First State Normal School in America; the Journals of Cyrus Peirce and Mary Swift*, Cambridge, Mass., Harvard University Press, 1926, 299 pp.

Parker, William B., *The Life and Public Services of Justin Smith Morrill*, Boston, Houghton Mifflin Company, 1924, 378 pp.

Potter, Alonzo, and George B. Emerson, *The School and the Schoolmaster*, New York, Harper & Brothers, 1842, 552 pp.

Rice, John Andrew, *I Came Out of the Eighteenth Century*, New York, Harper & Brothers, 1942, 341 pp.

Russell, James Earl, *Founding Teachers College. Reminiscences of the Dean Emeritus*, New York, Teachers College, Columbia University, 1937, 106 pp.

Scott, Emmett Jay, and Lyman Beecher Stowe, *Booker T. Washington, Builder of a Civilization*, Garden City, N. Y., Doubleday, Page & Company, 1916, 331 pp.

Swint, Henry W., *The Northern Teacher in the South, 1862–1870*, Nashville, Tenn., Vanderbilt University Press, 1941, 221 pp.

Tewksbury, Donald G., *The Founding of American Colleges and Universities Before the Civil War*, New York, Bureau of Publications, Teachers College, Columbia University, 1932, 254 pp.

Washington, Booker Taliaferro, *Twenty-five Years of Tuskegee*, New York, Doubleday, Page & Company, 1906, 18 pp.; *Up from Slavery; an Auto-*

biography, Garden City, N. Y., Doubleday, Page & Company, 1913, 330 pp.

Westfield State Normal School, *Semi-Centennial and other Exercises of the State Normal School at Westfield, Mass., June 25, 1889.* Boston, Wright and Potter, 1889, 79 pp.; *The State Teachers College at Westfield*, compiled by workers of the Writers' Program of the Works Progress Administration in the State of Massachusetts and sponsored by the State Teachers College at Westfield, 1941, 114 pp.

Woodson, Carter Godwin, *The Mis-Education of the Negro*, Washington, D. C., The Associated Publishers, 1933, 207 pp.

Wright, Arthur D., and G. E. Gardner, *Hall's Lectures on School-Keeping*, Hanover, N. H., Dartmouth College Press, 1929, 192 pp.

19 TRANSFORMING THE ELEMENTARY SCHOOL

THE NEW ELEMENTARY SCHOOL OF WHICH WE SHALL SPEAK IN this chapter is the school of the twentieth century and of today; but since our treatment is a historical one, we must recognize that the newest institution of any age is never wholly new. The old elementary school was the school of the three R's and of Whittier's *In School Days*:

> Still sits the school-house by the road,
>   A ragged beggar sunning;
> Around it still the sumachs grow
>   And blackberry vines are running.
>
> Within, the master's desk is seen,
>   Deep scarred by raps official,
> The warping floor, the battered seats,
>   The jack-knife's carved initial.

The old elementary school was the school of Ichabod Crane and *The Hoosier Schoolmaster*, the school of rote memory and brute strength. With honorable but not very numerous exceptions, the new school began to supersede the old little more than a century ago.

The elementary school of the present differs widely from that of a century ago both in its external relations and management and in its internal conditions and teaching. The transformation began about 1830 and has continued to the present day. It is still continuing and the future will certainly see great improvements in elementary education. Externally, the elementary schools are now organized into a network that reaches all parts of the country. There are new teachers equipped with professional preparation; and professional administration and supervision are provided. The school term has been extended from three months to eight or nine. Systematic methods of financing the operation of the schools and laws to secure the regular attendance of the children are in force. Better buildings and more adequate equipment are provided for child and teacher. These matters have been considered in earlier chapters. Efforts are being made to draw school and community into a closer alliance and a more helpful relationship. All of this progress has occurred within a century.

There have also been many internal changes, brought about by a new philosophy, new methods of teaching, and a new curriculum. It is these changes that we propose to describe in the present chapter. For the old doctrine that mere literacy, an education in the elements of reading, writing, and arithmetic, is sufficient, there has been substituted the Pestalozzian view that the elementary school, by providing a rich and stimulating curriculum and intelligent teaching, can develop a genuine popular culture even among those whose regular school attendance ends at fourteen or fifteen.

The elementary school has come to draw its materials from the resources of science, literature, history, and the arts. The industrial and the expressional arts have been made to yield their contributions. Instead of merely verbal exercises based upon formal textbooks the schools teach children to investigate, to gather knowledge and ideas from many sources, to think and evaluate, and to take an active part in their own education. For the old rigid grading of fifty years ago a more flexible organization has been substituted. Equipped with tools, shops, kitchens, well-planned auditoriums, medical aid, playgrounds, and libraries, the better elementary schools carry on work of a quality that was not possible in earlier days. S. R. Hall, writing a little more than a hundred years ago, stated, and this was the almost universal fact, that the teacher would not even have a dictionary to aid him.

We shall deal first with the influence which was originally derived from Pestalozzi and then also with those influences which stemmed from Froebel and Herbart. But we must not assume that American education is merely an application of European ideas. Every borrowed idea was quickly changed to fit local conditions and our elementary school is a thoroughly American institution. Our curricula and our methods are our own, but we eagerly and wisely adopted promising suggestions wherever we found them.

There were three Pestalozzian movements, or rather three phases of one movement, in the United States. The earliest efforts to introduce the practice of the great Swiss educator, which center about Joseph Neef on the one hand and the manual labor education concept on the other, were only slightly effective. The second Pestalozzian development, which occurred in the three decades preceding the Civil War, was locally effective but did not spread widely. It was in the period which followed the Civil War that Pestalozzianism made its greatest impression, not only through the object teaching of Oswego but also through nature study. We shall begin with the second of these three periods.

1. THE INTRODUCTION OF ELEMENTARY SCIENCE

Elementary science, object teaching, and nature study were widely introduced after 1860, but there were earlier beginnings in the use of such subjects. The ideas of Pestalozzi had been filtering into the United States since the first decades of the nineteenth century. There were parallel influences such as that of the *Orbis Pictus* of Comenius which was republished in New York in 1810, and the writings of Bacon and Locke. There was a growing interest in agriculture and in the applications of chemistry to practical life. That theories should be based upon facts, that real things should be studied along with words and ideas, and that children should learn to understand as well as remember were doctrines that had long been familiar but the time for their more general application had now arrived. Teachers were coming to realize that children should acquire meanings from words, and that expressionless oral reading is a sign that the passage is not understood. They began to introduce the word or sentence method and to discard the usual alphabet and spelling method in teaching beginning reading. Arithmetic was now to be developed intelligently by the pupil, where before the memorizing and mechanical application of uncomprehended "rules" had been in vogue. In grammar there had been a like slavish adherence to rules, and a more inductive, active, and intelligent method of teaching language and composition came to prevail. A beginning had been made when teachers came to see that pupils cannot learn effectively what they do not understand; and when they began to analyze the pupils' difficulties, to illustrate their lessons, and to provide exercises and applications. This was a considerable part of the Pestalozzian message.

Another part of that message concerned the use of objective materials, concrete things, pictures, and drawings. When Horace Mann returned from Germany he was more than ever convinced that skill in drawing and sketching was a necessary acquirement for teachers. David P. Page condemned mere book-learning in which the pupil was a "passive recipient." The teacher, he said, must inspire the pupil with the desire to know and to find out for himself and not from books alone but also from nature and life. He proposed to have the children observe nature, question their parents, review their own experiences, and also to read books and to report to the class what they had learned. This was a phase of Pestalozzi's doctrine of learning through observation and it came into use in American schools about 1830.

A third Pestalozzian influence of the period concerned the teacher's relations to the pupils and the spirit of the school. By 1830 and 1840 many educational leaders insisted that the school should be a pleasant and harmonious company. The old harshness was to be outlawed. Only teachers who could inspire love and cooperation were to be considered worthy of their office. There was a close connection between this notion of "discipline" and concrete, intelligible teaching; and both together made some headway in the better schools a century ago.

Teachers were urged to deal with concrete things, to teach orally and visually, and to avoid the tyranny of the textbook. Henry Barnard urged schools to provide "cabinets of real objects as subjects of oral instruction in the field of the pupils' everyday observation and experience." Horace Mann had given many similar suggestions by word and pen. Warren Burton, an early institute lecturer and the author of a quaint little book, *The District School As It Was* (1833), urged that the school should no longer fasten the child to his chair or offer him mere words, "little black images that he can not get his fingers under." This book has recently been reprinted (New York, T. Y. Crowell and Co., 1928, 213 pages). Louis Agassiz, addressing a class at a teachers' institute in Massachusetts, said to the young women before him: "I see before me many bright eyes, but alas! these eyes cannot see!" He then began to explain some natural object, a grasshopper, for example, and every member of the class held a specimen in her hand while she followed his instruction.

The authors of *The School and the Schoolmaster*, which was mentioned earlier, pointed out that a great part of infancy is spent happily in learning the names, properties, and uses of common things. This, they said, should be a cue for the teachers in the school. The teacher should aid the children in doing better what they were already doing and what they loved to do. Listen, they advised, to the questions that children ask, such questions as these: Why do the birds come back in the summer? What makes the rain? Why does the smoke go up in the sky? They said teachers should be familiar with elementary science so that they could answer such questions and could teach children to observe correctly, to draw, and to measure. They gave a list of sixty subjects for lessons in easy science, agriculture, physiology and health, and the useful arts.

The Massachusetts normal schools at Westfield and Bridgewater began to build up science collections and to employ demonstrations and object teaching. This Pestalozzian drift was supported by the natural interest of their rural pupils in the problems of the farm and the household. These normal schools developed what they called the "analytic, objective method" by which pupils were taught to observe, to analyze, and to think. John W. Dickinson (1825–1901), who became the secretary of the Massachusetts Board of Education, had been connected with the Westfield State Normal School for a quarter of a century and he believed that this school was "the first to show that all branches of learning can be taught by the same objective method."

This early form of elementary science and nature study is also revealed by the children's literature of the time. Elementary science books and books giving common-sense information about nature, rocks, plants, animals, and the farm were prepared for use in school and home. Such titles as *The Young Chemist*, or *Familiar Lessons* in one or another subject field, were numerous even twenty years before the Civil War. An example is David Blair's *Catechism of Common Things* which was in its fifth edition in 1825. Most of the books of this type were by undistinguished authors. One of the writers, however, was David A. Wells, later a prominent economist, who had studied under Agassiz and who in his earlier years wrote *Familiar Science* and the *Science of Common Things*. The flood of such nature and easy science books can only be suggested here but even this brief notice shows that in the literature for children and schools a scientific current was then beginning to flow beside the older moralistic and patriotic streams. The Pestalozzian influence, as we have already indicated, was also seen in the school subjects of arithmetic, geography, and music. The growing interest in nature and in children led to the development of inductive and object teaching. We shall now show that these sound early methods were perverted by the introduction of a less flexible and less natural method, the Oswego system of object teaching.

2. THE OSWEGO SYSTEM

The highly formalized scheme of object teaching which was developed and spread by the State Normal School at Oswego, New York, was an importation from England. At least two earlier efforts to introduce it had been unsuccessful, one by Horace Mann, who in 1840 had published some of the English object lessons in his *Common School Journal*, and another by A. J. Rickoff, the superintendent of the Cincinnati public schools. Both efforts failed. But a similar attempt by Edward A. Sheldon, founder of the Oswego Normal School, was successful. Sheldon was an enthusiastic promoter for whom difficulties were steppingstones. Having already established a "ragged" school for Oswego's neglected children and served as superintendent of schools in Syracuse, he was in 1853 recalled to a similar position in Oswego. There he established Saturday classes for the teachers and these developed into a training school. He felt that the schools were too mechanical and that the children were asked only to memorize, not to observe and reason. The work, he thought, should be more objective. "For this purpose," he wrote, "we wanted collections of objects of all sorts, charts of color and form, natural history, pictures, objects for teaching number, and reading matter in quantity, suited to the ages of the children."

In his search, Sheldon in 1859 visited Toronto where Egerton Ryerson, the well-known Canadian educator, had placed a full set of the lesson materials and teachers' guide books from the English Home and Colonial School Society. These materials, it should be noticed, were not in use and had not been introduced into the Canadian schools; but to Sheldon they seemed to be exactly what was needed.

By convincing his board of education that the venture would "not cost the taxpayer one cent" he was permitted to bring an English critic-teacher, Margaret E. M. Jones, to Oswego to introduce the Home and Colonial version of Pestalozzianism. Sheldon secured the necessary one thousand dollars by dispensing with the services of one teacher, by charging the teachers a fee for the lessons which Miss Jones gave, and by soliciting contributions from his teachers. Miss Jones remained only one year, but that was sufficient time to establish in Oswego the formal object teaching which she sponsored. Because it was formal it was easily transmitted by means of outlines, lesson plans, and manuals. Object teaching became a fad. In 1866, Sheldon was able to secure recognition of his training school as the second New York state normal school. The first had been established at Albany twenty-two years before.

Oswego graduates carried its system into nearly every state during the twenty-five years (1861–1886) when it was in favor. They were to be found in large numbers in New York and all the states north of the fortieth parallel, but few entered the Old South or the West. Other normal schools also spread the system including those at Trenton, Kirksville, Terre Haute, and Winona. But object teaching was not approved by everyone. In the methods of the Home and Colonial School Society, and of Oswego, the objects were such things as leaves, colors, and geometric forms. These were selected and arranged by the teacher, and frequently there was only one object before the class. It could not be handled and could hardly be "observed" by each child; and it was even more unfortunate that no real motive for dealing with this object was established in the child's mind. The description was abstract and usually confined to the number, shape, size, color, and the parts of the selected objects. Stilted language was standard in the Oswego system, which had copied the errors rather than the inspiration of Pestalozzi. Most important of all, the teachers often knew too little science to deal intelligently with the materials they employed.

The faddism of the Oswego movement seems to have irked Henry Barnard. He remarked that educators had for a quarter of a century urged that school work should be based upon the pupils' own observation and experience. Now, he said, within two years (1860–1861) a host of model object-lesson books have been published with such titles as *Manual on*

Object Teaching, Lessons on Objects, Primary Object Lessons, Outlines of a System of Object Teaching, and *Child's Book of Nature.* The danger now, he said, is that teachers will copy the methods of some manual without understanding the principles, without considering the ages and attainments of the pupils, and without adapting the work to the pursuits of the people. Object teaching, said Barnard, can be made as verbal, mechanical, and monotonous as any other teaching. And it often was.

3. NATURE STUDY

While the British object lessons were spread from Oswego, the older and more informal study of nature continued in many schools. William T. Harris prepared a syllabus of oral science lessons for the schools of St. Louis. Agassiz continued to teach until 1873 and during his last year he conducted his famous summer school at Penikese. Two years later Francis W. Parker began his work at Quincy, Massachusetts, which is treated below and H. H. Straight, who is sometimes regarded as the founder of organized nature study, had been a student at Penikese and was to be a teacher under Parker at Chicago. Several of the normal schools were carrying on the earlier tradition which has already been described. New influences also came into play. The kindergarten and child study which had begun independently reinforced each other in opposition to formal object lessons and in favor of more active and more natural methods. A wave of interest in the rural school, which was set in the midst of nature, and in the improvement of agriculture fostered the new movement. Out of all these tendencies a new nature study which greatly improved elementary instruction was born.

Nature study is not altogether easy to define. It is allied to the older natural history. It is simpler and less formally organized than science and attempts to consider the children's interests more. The sciences of that day often concerned themselves with classification and names and with the structure of animals and plants. They emphasized laboratory methods and dissection and paid little attention to the questions children ask about natural objects. Nature study, which tried to correct these trends in elementary instruction, was directed toward a more informal science. It dealt extensively with living things, both plants and animals, and with their environment and it attempted to answer the children's questions somewhat as an old field naturalist would have done.

Several phases of nature study may be distinguished. One was a humanistic and literary interest in nature, its color and poetry, its seasonal rhythms and the interdependence of its living forms. This type had a tendency to become a sentimental study rather than a scientific one. The practical study of nature formed a second phase, and here the purpose was to introduce the children to agriculture, home economics, health studies, and the conservation of natural resources. And, thirdly, there were those who used nature study as an introduction to science, or as a kind of general science; and books proposing to deal with physics and chemistry or with elementary biology by homemade apparatus and simple experiments were called nature study books. Although the subject is hard to define, it will be most helpful to think of it as elementary school science and as closely allied to the natural history of earlier times.

If we leave that earlier period out of consideration, Henry H. Straight (1846–1886) may be regarded as the founder of nature study. He was born near Chautauqua, New York, grew up on a farm, and began to teach at sixteen. As a student at Oberlin, then still in its frontier stage, he became interested in languages. To earn money to study these subjects in Germany, he took a position as principal of the public school in the small town of Galena, Ohio. Experience in teaching object lessons led him to substitute lessons in elementary science and natural history; and his whole life program was changed by his success and by the growing conviction that scientific knowledge and training were essential in fitting children for life. Instead of going to Germany, he continued his studies at Cornell University where he received a strong scientific and educational impulse.

After a year as principal of a new state normal school at Peru, Nebraska, Straight resigned to take the more congenial position of science teacher in the same school. There he developed a plan of education based upon science and the industries, a scheme which he attempted to work out more fully in later years. The following year he was first on the list of Agassiz's students at Penikese (1873) and he continued to work with N. S. Shaler and other Harvard scientists, and at Cornell University, until in 1876 when he became professor of natural science at the Oswego Normal School. He had at Peru turned the basement of the school into a number of laboratories; and Agassiz had made it clear that it was feasible to handle large numbers of students in experimental work. But at Oswego he attacked another problem. He tried to transform the old formal object teaching into the study of living plants and animals in their natural habitat. He believed that laboratory work was not suitable for children and instead substituted nature study, especially field excursions to the woods, swamps, and lake shore, where his young naturalists used the pencil and brush rather than the forceps and scalpel. Although some members of the Oswego staff, Hermann Krüsi, for example, valued his work, he was not able to make his ideas prevail. The decadent object lessons had become too firmly entrenched. Meanwhile, at the Martha's Vineyard summer school for teachers where he lectured, he came under the notice of Francis W.

Parker who in 1883 invited him to the Cook County Normal School. He accepted and there he spent his remaining years. Parker credited his own use of the principle of correlation to Straight, who stressed the connections of natural science with geography and other subjects. This principle, independently developed by Straight, was an outgrowth of his great theme, the unity and interdependence of all nature.

After Straight's death, one who is even better known, Wilbur S. Jackman, was chosen to succeed him. Jackman's *Nature Study for the Common Schools* (1891) was a teachers' guide, not a book for pupils although, since it was composed mainly of questions on direct observations and experiments, it could have been used as a laboratory and field manual. The "lessons," drawn from nine different sciences, consisted of the regular gathering of materials and the discussion and systematic arrangement of them, followed by the reports of the pupils' observations. The subjects were arranged in a month by month series throughout "the rolling year." Like Pestalozzi, he placed great stress upon the expression of the children's observations and conclusions; and he proposed varied reports by means of gestures, music, modeling, drawing, painting, as well as oral and written language.

Before the end of the century the nature study movement had spread far and many higher institutions had begun to prepare teachers for work in this field. Cornell University and the Illinois Normal University were prominent in the promotion of the agricultural phase, and Clark University and the University of Chicago were also important centers. Interest in nature study for farm boys and girls grew out of the severe agricultural crisis of the early 1890's when many farm families became destitute and the agricultural colleges considered plans for the relief of the rural population. It was agreed that the improvement of the rural school was an essential step in the program and that one means for the improvement of the rural school was nature study pointed toward farm life, and farming as a vocation. Among the leaders in nature study at Cornell were Liberty H. Bailey in the administration of it, Anna B. Comstock in the preparation of materials, and John Walton Spencer in the development of nature study clubs. Bailey was also important as a writer. In his *Nature-Study Idea* (1909) he declared that, if anyone were to plan schools for a rural section which had no schools of any kind, he would certainly include something about plants, animals, fields, and people. He could not conceivably plan purely academic rural schools in which the work of the children had no visible connection with the habits of the people and the immediate needs of the community. Yet the purely bookish elementary school was not only conceivable; it too often was a fact.

One of the outstanding books produced by the entire movement was prepared at Cornell by Anna B. Comstock. Its title is *Handbook of Nature Study*. Originally issued in 1911 as an outgrowth of her leaflets for teachers, this work attained its twenty-fourth edition in 1939. In that form it contains 900 pages, 1100 illustrations, and an extensive bibliography. Part One is pedagogical, dealing with the teaching of nature to children. The remainder of this important work treats of animals, plants, earth, sky, and weather, and presents materials from which exercises and courses of study may be developed by the teacher. While it is a teachers' book it can easily be read by upper-grade children. A more vocational presentation of the same idea developed in the black-soil country of the Middle West. This was the *Practical Nature-Study and Elementary Agriculture* (1909) by Coulter and Patterson of the Illinois Normal University. The title was accurately descriptive, for it deals with trees, insects, weather, weeds, pollination, plant breeding, and rural school gardens. "In an agricultural community," the authors said, "the lessons must be primarily agricultural." The general movement also gave rise to a national and many local nature study societies and to magazines such as the *Nature Study Review* which was started in 1905.

As formulated by Straight, the new subject developed as a reaction against object lessons. It was clear to him that nature study should be elementary science and this was in the main the view of Jackman also. In Jackman's writing one may notice the influence of the kindergarten and the child study movement. To others nature study appeared to be especially appropriate for the rural school and the children from the farms, and had special importance for agriculture and life on the farm. By 1900 a more sentimental phase had begun. A critic of this "effeminate" nature study put his judgment in these words: "Nature study is science. The idea that it is not science leads to serious results. The responsibility for accuracy seems to disappear and much of the nonsense and sentimentalism that has brought discredit on the subject is due to this fundamental error." There can be no doubt that where nature study was seriously pursued, either as a subject with practical applications to agriculture or as an easy natural history introduction to science, it was a valuable addition to the work of the schools. It was easily possible to link it with geography and with elementary handwork and this was often done.

4. THE KINDERGARTEN IN THE UNITED STATES

The founder of the kindergarten considered his system and philosophy to be of general application to education at all levels and not to be confined to the education of small children; and in the course of time the new institution has come to influence the work of most of the elementary grades. Perhaps the first Froebelian to work in the United States was Caroline Frankenberg who came to Columbus, Ohio, in 1838. According to a family tradition which it is difficult to verify, she in that year established "a school based upon the active interests of children." This title which had been chosen by Froebel for his new institution was discarded in 1840 when he thought of the name, "Kindergarten." At any rate, Caroline Frankenberg had been in the Froebel circle for some time before coming to America; and after a year in this country she returned to Dresden to help her brother in developing the kindergarten there. Her brief early American visit had no influence.

A notice of Froebel's "infant-gardens" was printed by Henry Barnard in his *American Journal of Education* in 1856. He described the Froebelian gifts and a kindergarten which he had seen at the London Exposition. He declared the new institution to be "by far the most original, attractive, and philosophical form of infant development that the world has yet seen." At the same time (1855) Mrs. Carl Schurz opened a small family kindergarten for her own child and the children of her neighbors at Watertown, Wisconsin. A native American, Elizabeth Peabody of Boston, opened a kindergarten in 1860 upon information furnished by Mrs. Schurz. In her own opinion this effort was a failure and she left for Germany to study the kindergarten in its native land. She later declared: "It was Emma Marwedel who in 1867 first introduced me to Froebel's genuine kindergarten in the city of Hamburg and inspired me with the courage to make the extension of the kindergarten in my own country the main object of my life." In this decision she persevered. The kindergarten became for her a sacred cause. By editing magazines, writing books, and delivering addresses she became an important propagandist for the new education.

When Elizabeth Peabody returned from Germany in 1868, she found that a school to prepare teachers for kindergartens had just been established in Boston by Matilda and Alma Kriege. Mary J. Garland who became another kindergarten promoter was educated in this school; and she and her own pupils found a patron in Pauline Agassiz Shaw who aided not only the kindergarten but also the manual training, vocational guidance, and other educational movements.

The foundations for the spread of the kindergarten in America were laid by the schools for kindergarten teachers which the disciples of Froebel established here, by the Krieges in Boston (1868), Maria Boelte and John Kraus in New York City (1872), and Emma Marwedel in Washington, D. C. (1872). All of these were German immigrants who had been prepared by the immediate pupils of Froebel. Maria Boelte (1836–1918) was the most successful of all and in the course of a long life she sent out about twelve hundred kindergartners from her school. With Dr. Kraus she published an important early book, *The Kindergarten Guide* (1877). William N. Hailmann (1836–1920) came from Switzerland and was judged by G. Stanley Hall to have been "by far the most eminent of all men in this country devoted to the interests of the kindergarten." Hailmann made the well-known translation of Froebel's *Education of Man* in 1887.

The crucial step of incorporating the kindergarten into the public school system was taken in St. Louis in 1873. Before that the kindergarten had been a private institution promoted by philanthropists, churches, and welfare agencies. In New York the Ethical Culture Society under the leadership of Felix Adler established a kindergarten in their school for workingmen's children. Mrs. Shaw supported thirty or more private kindergartens in Boston until the city finally took them over. Great industrialists sometimes supported the new institution in the belief that it would make children more skillful with their hands and thus develop skilled workers. Many were supported as a means of providing social relief and moral training. But in St. Louis the kindergarten was made a part of the public school system. The initiative was taken by Susan E. Blow (1843–1916). Having secured the support of Superintendent Harris, she prepared for her work under Maria Boelte and opened a training class and one kindergarten in a public school building. By 1880 there were fifty-two in the schools of the city.

The public kindergarten spread slowly at first but more rapidly after 1885. As early as 1880 there were reported to the United States Bureau of Education more than two hundred public kindergartens which enrolled nine thousand children in fourteen states. Five years later the numbers of the institutions and their pupils had doubled and were found in thirty-five states. Between these two years Milwaukee, perhaps influenced by the large German population, sent a committee to study the St. Louis arrangements. Upon receiving a favorable report from its investigators, that city introduced the new institution into its public school system. Boston established the public kindergarten in 1888 by incorporating the large number which had been privately supported in the city. This rapid progress continued at an even greater rate throughout the cities of the country until the early nineties. As a result of the financial depression of 1893 many were again abandoned. Then and in every financial crisis since, the kindergarten has been one of the services which school systems have sometimes been too easily persuaded to give up. The kindergarten has never become common in the rural sections; but in the cities it has maintained itself quite well. According to recent official figures, only a little less than one-half of all five-year-old children are enrolled in the kindergarten, and the proportion is still increasing. This does not support the opinion of some otherwise well-informed persons that the kindergarten is losing in popular estimation. It is, however, true that it is not getting enough financial support. The classes are too large, the salaries too small, and the space and arrangements often inadequate.

When the National Education Association in 1884 organized a kindergarten department, William N. Hailmann became its first chairman and was several times re-elected to that position. The topics considered by this department provide an index to the questions which interested kindergartners in those pioneer days. Some of the most frequent topics were the following: child study, education for parenthood, how to fit the kindergarten into the primary school system, handwork and industrial education, and the physical development and health of small children. Consider the third topic. The integration with the elementary school has not always been successfully carried out. The kindergarten has often remained apart. Where integration has taken place, its methods have often to a startling degree modified the primary school. Even where the kindergarten remained apart, and in spite of its insecure position in American systems, the kindergarten influence has been one of the main agencies in the development of the new education.

5. ELEMENTARY HANDWORK

The close connection between simple work with the hands and child development was emphasized by Froebel in his writings and in the kindergarten. And he carried on this manual activity into the higher grades of the school. He had in mind not mainly the economic results of handwork but its educative and expressional value. He wrote: "The debasing illusion that man works, produces, creates, only in order to preserve his body, in order to secure food, clothing, and shelter, may have to be endured [apparently because it was so common and widespread] but it should not be diffused and propagated." He meant to use work and play to cultivate the mind and elevate the spirit of man. A man's vocation, it seemed to him, could offer no difficulty to one who was generally well-educated.

This view was accepted by some of Froebel's American disciples. Felix Adler in founding the workingmen's school said: "We are seeking to apply the principle which ought to be at the foundation of every modern scheme of education: namely, that, as experiment conjoined with observation is necessary to the discovery of truth, so object-creating must supplement object-teaching in the rediscovery of truth which it is the purpose of all education to facilitate. Therefore, work-instruction is not something outside of regular instruction; it is an organic part of regular instruction.

. . . It becomes the means of making the hand a wise and cunning hand by putting more brain into it. But, on the other hand, it makes the brain a clear and vigorous and enlightened brain, by giving it the salutary corrective of the demonstrations of the hand." Adler's views were later supported by Wilbur S. Jackman, F. W. Parker, and by many of the exponents of kindergarten theory who combined observation and object study with drawing, painting, modeling, and building.

One form of manual work was brought into the schools from Sweden, where it was called sloyd. Sloyd means sleight-of-hand or skill and as introduced here it was a simple form of woodwork. The sloyd-knife was the most important tool, and the pupils made common articles such as penholders, picture frames, racks for holding various objects, or wooden mixing bowls. All objects were to be well-designed but without meretricious ornamentation. They were to be useful, made wholly of wood, and finished by the pupils themselves. Sloyd was introduced into the schools of Boston under the patronage of Pauline Agassiz Shaw by an able teacher from Sweden, Gustaf Larsson, and by others elsewhere. About the same time domestic activities, such as sewing and simple weaving, drawing, woodwork with carpenter's tools, and wood turning on the lathe were introduced. Samuel Love, superintendent at Jamestown, New York, was one of the first to develop a full course of such activities. Teachers equipped to carry on such work were prepared by the New York College for the Training of Teachers, later Teachers College of Columbia University, and by some of the land-grant colleges of agriculture. Even at that time construction work was sometimes connected with nature study and geography.

Another group also connected with the kindergarten movement stressed vocational or prevocational purposes. Manual training introduced after 1876 frequently had this technical purpose. It was employed in engineering schools and colleges of agriculture and was taught in the new manual training high schools. But some professed to see in such work, even down in the kindergarten and the primary grades, an opportunity to prepare more skillful apprentices; and with this in mind a high official of the Standard Oil Company gave a large sum for kindergarten promotion. The vocational argument was chiefly employed in the effort to promote manual training in the high schools and beyond.

Elementary handwork was more correctly conceived as a new educational means and an opportunity to develop the capacities and the interests of children. Children love to plan and to execute if proper opportunities are not denied them. In the process of creating and constructing objects of use and beauty they acquire skill, knowledge, and valuable new interests. They grow, they become better educated, and they learn to understand the material and the social world. These were the purposes of elementary handwork.

6. CHILD STUDY

The call to study the child had come from Rousseau. "Begin," he said in the preface to the *Émile*, "by making a more careful study of your scholars for you may be sure that you know nothing about them." This was sound advice, but as in so many other cases, he was unable to provide an example and his advice went unheeded. Yet it was not altogether lost for Pestalozzi wrote his *A Father's Journal* describing the development of his son, Jean Jacques Pestalozzi. Charles Darwin, without having Rousseau in mind, prepared *A Biographical Sketch of an Infant*, and the French writer Taine gave a similar account. More important for future child study than the *Biographical Sketch* was Darwin's doctrine of evolution and the closely connected interest in individual differences.

A beginning in child study was made in the United States in 1883 when G. Stanley Hall published his work upon "the contents of children's minds upon entering school." The research upon which this paper was based was carried out by some teachers of Boston and vicinity with the financial support of Pauline Agassiz Shaw, a generous promoter of educational innovation in that period and region. The teachers asked beginning school children individually a series of questions which Hall had prepared. There were about a hundred items covering their knowledge and understanding of common things, what they knew about plants and animals, about number, about games, what things they could do, and what were their ideas about religion. "The results seemed almost to suggest a new science of ignorance." Teachers learned from this study that there was very little that children of six could be safely assumed to know. A similar study with similar results had been made by a well-known Herbartian educator, Moritz Lazarus, of Berlin. And the publication of Hall's paper led many other Americans to make similar inquiries. Hall's results may be conveniently found in his *Aspects of Child Life and Education*.

The peak of the child study movement came after 1890. In the two decades after 1895 about two hundred investigations were carried out by Hall's students at Clark University alone, and many hundreds of others were completed elsewhere. Various methods were used, the questionnaire, the child biography, and the controlled experiment. The results were very uneven. Millicent Shinn, using the biographical method, produced her classical *Notes on the Development of a Child* (1893), which was also published in popular form as the *Biography of a Baby* (1900). Many investigations were published in the *Pedagogical Seminary*, the *Child-Study Monthly*, and the kindergarten magazines. Many child study organizations were formed. One of the most active of these was the Illinois Society for Child Study (1894) which enrolled F. W. Parker, John W. Cook, and John Dewey among its members. A close connection can be made out between this society and the Herbartian movement which is treated below. Child study was not confined to the United States, having originated in Europe as we have seen; and it enlisted such men as Sully in England, Binet in France, and Meumann in Germany. It was in fact a phase of the new study of educational psychology. In 1896 Lightner Witmer at the University of Pennsyvania established a "psychological clinic" for the study and remediation of the handicaps and maladjustments of children. The child study movement called attention to the defects of the old school, the rigid grading system, the faulty school equipment and furniture, the formal teaching, the narrow curriculum, and in general the failure of the schools to adjust their work to the needs of the children. The work of Stein and Piaget, of Watson at the Phipps Clinic in Baltimore, of Bird T. Baldwin at the State University of Iowa, of Arnold Gesell at Yale University comprises a more scientific child study and is continued in many universities.

7. THE QUINCY METHODS

The Quincy methods were named after a suburb of Boston where Francis W. Parker (1837–1902) was superintendent of schools in the latter seventies. The methods of teaching favored by Parker at Quincy and afterward were based, like the Oswego system, upon observation, and Parker acknowledged his indebtedness to Sheldon; but they were also influenced by the new movements which we have just been considering, nature study, child study, and the kindergarten. At Quincy, observation was to lead to further experience because the classes were to be more active and informal and the materials were to be more appropriate and interesting to the children than in the Oswego object teaching. And Parker succeeded in this. The textbook-recitation routine was overcome; but in steering away from the precipice of formalism, the Quincy schools sometimes sailed close to the whirlpool of triviality.

A product of the American frontier democracy, Parker was to a great degree self-educated. Except for the Civil War period when he fought in the Union armies, he had been from the age of sixteen a teacher and a schoolman. "I do not remember the day," he once said, "when I did not believe that I should be a teacher." From the war, which made him a colonel, he gained a fierce hatred of war and militarism. From the hardships and narrow opportunities of a pinched boyhood in rural New Hampshire he derived his love of nature, his interest in the common people, and his militant democracy. He was a part of the developing new education at home but for three years he also studied at the University of Berlin (1872–1875).

The "selfish aristocracy" which attempted to subject the common people to the domination of the few was Parker's greatest enemy, and he never ceased to assail it. He hated the dual educational systems of Europe and all schemes to confine people in fixed classes and by class education to keep them in ignorance and thereby in subjection. He held that in building a democracy we must begin with the children; we must give them both freedom and responsibility; and, therefore, we must make the school a working democracy. And the freedom of the child, in his view, implied the freedom of the teacher; but with the possible conflict which is implicit here he did not deal. There were to be no fixed course of study, no numerical records, no inflexible classification of pupils. Instead of report cards the children's drawings, compositions, and models were themselves taken to the parents. The "social factor" he declared is the greatest factor of all, more important than the subjects taught, than the methods, than the school itself. That which children learn from each other in play and work is the highest that is ever learned. Altogether in the spirit of Lincoln, he insisted that in school the strong and clever must serve the weak, for the sake of the social education of the strong and not only that the weak might be served. In democracy, he held, there can be neither masters nor slaves.

It appears, however, that Parker's analysis was inadequate. He nowhere dealt with the basic economic questions, nor with race, nor apparently did he realize that the lessons learned in a school democracy may be all too quickly forgotten in the stress of practical life and business. Like Horace Mann he hoped for an easy victory over the devils of our modern society. If such criticism, sixty years later, is easily made and unfair it is nevertheless important that we make it in order that we may see our own duty more clearly. Our duty is to attempt to use the school more effectively to build democracy; and we shall not be able to do so if we ignore economics, racial discrimination, and the power of ordinary human selfishness.

Parker returned from his European studies in 1875 and was chosen superintendent of schools in Quincy, Massachusetts. The changes which he made in the elementary schools of the city are indicated in a well-known book by Lelia Patridge, *The Quincy Methods Illustrated* (1885). Mindful of the formalism which had developed in object teaching, Parker wrote: "These lessons should not be copied. Imitation never leads to creation."

The basis of the Quincy methods was, however, a new form of object teaching in a more natural setting and using a much greater variety of materials from common life and the sciences. The elementary curriculum of the Quincy schools was greatly enriched and much greater emphasis was placed upon the activity of the children, upon counting, measuring, calculating, drawing, coloring, modeling, conversation, and written composition. Indeed, so much emphasis was placed upon activity itself that some of the projects became, and were in fact called, "Quincy Busy-Work." This was one of the diseases that afflicted the new method. To find time to make the teaching more personal the children in each class were divided into smaller groups; and while the teachers then worked with one of these groups each of the other groups worked upon its own exercises. Some of these activities with pegs, splints, or beads were merely ways to keep the hands occupied. The children sometimes complained that they "had beans" in every room.

The curriculum was reformed. The schools paid more attention to physical education, for the harmonious development of the child was, according to Parker and Pestalozzi, "the guiding principle of the New Education." A combination of local and human geography was introduced. The plan of concentrating as much of the instruction as possible around a geographical core was developed. This was similar to Herbart's idea whether obtained from him or, as Parker thought, from H. H. Straight. The concentration of studies no doubt resulted from the attempt to unify the materials of an enriched program. Parker agreed with the Pestalozzi-Froebel emphasis upon varied self-expression, not only through speech and writing but also through drawing, modeling, and other means. Like Froebel he introduced the principle of the culture epochs and used primitive industries, myths, and folk lore as bases for manual work, history, and literature.

At the same time the course of study was flexible in the hands of the teacher, who was given freedom to experiment in selecting and arranging the materials. Textbooks were little used, subjects were fused, and the school skills such as writing and arithmetic were taught through use and not in separate classes. But there was an excess of recitations. The teacher was so much the center in the Quincy methods, there were so many questions and answers, that the children had too little chance to think and work consecutively. The object lesson had come back in a revitalized form. And as we have already indicated, the greatest significance of Quincy lay in its emphasis upon education for democracy and upon cooperation between the school and the home. Parker's best phrase was, "The ideal school is the ideal community."

For a brief period, Parker became supervisor of primary schools in Boston. During these years he gave several series of lectures at an early summer school for teachers at Martha's Vineyard, which had perhaps grown out of Agassiz's school. There Quincy and Oswego met. One day in 1882, after an enthusiastic lecture on Pestalozzi, in walked Hermann Krüsi, Jr., who had been for twenty-five years an Oswego professor and was the son of Pestalozzi's first assistant. Parker was just ready to begin a lecture. Krüsi who reported the incident wrote: "The enthusiastic man at once introduced me to his whole class with great warmth, and I was pleased to find that my work on Pestalozzi had found so many intelligent readers." Krüsi referred to his then recently published biography of the Swiss educator. Parker's lectures were published under the title *Talks on Teaching* (1883). He also wrote *How to Study Geography* (1889); and he was one of the most favored speakers at the meetings of the National Education Association. The last twenty years of his life were spent in Chicago as head of the Cook County Normal School and finally of the School of Education of the University of Chicago. Parker was not a technical philosopher but, more than anyone else before John Dewey, he was the spokesman for the "New Education."

But if child development, "free child, free teacher," and education for democracy were to be widely followed as principles in American education, it gradually became clear that the organization of the school would have to be changed. To many it seemed that the rigid promotion system of the graded schools was the greatest of all hindrances in their efforts to promote the welfare and growth of individual children.

8. EFFORTS TO BREAK THE LOCKSTEP

In the graded school with its fixed curriculum and annual examinations there were frequent failures. The failing pupils were required to take over not only the studies in which they had failed but all the work of the year. Many pupils were stopped completely, perhaps at the fifth or sixth grade, and continued to repeat the work until they could leave school forever at the end of the compulsory attendance period. Few people thought to inquire what proportions of the pupils failed and why; nor did they ask what were the effects of the failures upon the personality of the pupils or how they would respond in the future, when as voters and parents they had to do with public education.

Questions were however raised, after a while, by a well-known educator, Calvin M. Woodward of St. Louis. He published a study of "the age of withdrawal from school" (1878), based upon the figures provided by the St. Louis school report of that year. His indictment received little notice until the subject was revived in the nineties and his study was republished. Then Woodward returned to the inquiry with a new paper on "When and why pupils leave school; and How to promote attendance in the highest grades." His answer to the latter question was that attendance in the upper grades would be promoted through free textbooks, an enriched course of study including domestic science and manual training, and regional high schools making it unnecessary for pupils to travel across town to attend. He also showed that the problem was much more acute in some cities than in others. The facts which Woodward presented had long been known in a general way, but no one knew precisely what was happening and very few had stopped to think that things might be improved. There was no real child accounting in education at that time.

To show how pupils of a given city at a given time were distributed by school years and chronological years, a new instrument, the age-grade table, was devised. Such a table was published in a book by Preston W. Search, *An Ideal School* (1901). The table shows that the schools of the city in question consisted of a one-year kindergarten, a nine-year elementary school, a four-year high school, and a year of "postgraduate work." The table also shows that in almost every grade a majority of the children were over age. This falling behind the normal rate of progress in the course is called "retardation." Reading the totals in the bottom line of Search's table we notice that there were five hundred ninety six-year-olds but only three hundred ninety fourteen-year-olds; and after the age of fourteen the numbers drop abruptly although the new entrants into the high school partly cover up the facts. This dropping out before the course is completed is called "elimination from school."

Within a few years the reports of city superintendents began to present such facts and in less than a decade a group of young statisticians started to deal with them much more comprehensively. E. L. Thorndike's study of *The Elimination of Pupils from School* (1907) was followed by *Child Accounting in the Public Schools* (1909) by Leonard P. Ayres and the same author's *Laggards in Our Schools* (1913). Ayres directed special attention to "the money cost of the repeater" and to the extraordinary difference in degree of retardation between comparable cities. George D. Strayer's *Age and Grade Census* had appeared in 1911. These statistical publications together with J. M. Rice's "Spelling investigation" (1895) and other studies of teaching efficiency may be taken to mark the American beginnings of the "science of education."

Attempts to overcome the evils of rigid grading had been made before accurate information was available: by Parker at Quincy through the formation of homogeneous groups in each room and by W. T. Harris at St. Louis by a plan of frequent reclassification and promotion. Harris, about 1868, had the pupils reclassified every six weeks so that none was compelled to remain long in a class doing work that was far above or below his level or capacity at that time. Several other cities introduced modified forms of this frequent reclassification scheme.

Other individualizing schemes were the Cambridge and the Batavia plans, supervised study, and the platoon school. The Cambridge "multiple-track" plan allowed pupils to take a longer or shorter time to complete a standard course of study. The plan requires each pupil to do all the required work of the course but permits him to vary the rate. In other systems bright pupils were permitted to skip a half-year or a year of the course; or they were given extra work to do, thus asking them to complete an enriched or amplified course. Both the double promotion and the enriched course plans assume that the curriculum is adapted to the average pupil but that some adjustment should be made for the keen and aggressive pupils. On the other hand, the Batavia plan and supervised study as well as various forms of remedial instruction are intended to help the slow and the unwilling. Supervised study was very widely introduced about 1915, especially in high schools, but its equivalent was also used in the elementary grades. The Batavia plan was a form of supervised study in the elementary school devised by Superintendent John P. Kennedy of Batavia, New York. Under this plan two teachers were assigned to each room, one to help the pupils in their preparation and the other to conduct the group and class exercises. We have now mentioned three kinds of plans to adapt the school work to the varying abilities of the pupils: to vary the rate of the pupils' progress, to vary the total amount and kind of work, and to aid weak pupils to overcome difficulties which they could not master alone.

The most extreme position against rigid grading was taken by Preston Willis Search (1853–1932), who developed the scheme of individual instruction which is usually called the Pueblo plan after the city in Colorado where it was fully developed. Search varied all three of the factors named above, the rate of work, the amount of work, and the help given, in accordance with the apparent needs of each pupil. He turned the classrooms into laboratories, studios, and workrooms, and abolished all regular class work except in music and physical education. He did not individualize the course of study. Each pupil followed a regular course, and in each subject such as algebra, history, or Caesar the pupil prepared the same series of exercises, but he did this at his own gait, going as far as his abilities permitted in the allotted time. The teacher helped the pupils with difficulties and suggested methods of attack.

After Search, the most active exponent of "individual instruction versus the lockstep in education" was his disciple, Frederic Burk (1862–1924). As superintendent of schools, research worker under G. Stanley Hall, and Principal of the State Normal School at San Francisco, Burk wielded considerable influence. Like Search, he considered repeating and retardation the cardinal evils in education and individual instruction the effective remedy. His example and his pupils spread the method, especially Carleton Washburne who devised a modified form, the Winnetka plan. The Dalton Laboratory plan, which Helen Parkhurst developed about 1915, was indebted to Burk but also to Dr. Maria Montessori of Italy and to Edgar J. Swift and his widely read book *The Mind in the Making* (1908). The Dalton plan was intended to give the pupil greater freedom, and also greater responsibility for "budgeting his time and fulfilling his contract." Both the Winnetka and the Dalton plans provided some opportunities for group activities and for cooperation along with the individual programs.

This combination of individual and group work also characterizes the platoon school or work-study-play plan which was carried out at Gary by Superintendent William J. Wirt. The more complete and economical use of the school plant is another major objective of the platoon plan. The school day is divided into three equal periods, and in any given period one-third of the pupils are engaged in "work," another third in "study," and the rest in "play." In this way all the facilities of a school will be in constant use. Many cities employ the work-study-play plan or some modification of it.

All of these plans have some merits, but none is a panacea and not one has lived up to the early claims of its sponsors. Some of them have been generally abandoned, including the Cambridge, Batavia, Pueblo, and Dalton plans, and the Winnetka plan has never been widely adopted. The present tendency is to use individual and group projects within the class system and the usual social organization of the school. We have learned from all this experimentation to provide for a moderate degree of freedom and responsibility and to increase both as children learn to use them wisely. Schools have not been able to dispense with the judgment and the leadership of the teacher. Teachers, in general, still believe that they should teach their pupils as well as guide them and should use class as well as individual methods.

We may appropriately close this section with a word from F. W. Parker who in answer to Search said: "The ideal school is the ideal community, an embryonic democracy. The child is not sent to school to acquire knowledge only, but to learn to live. Education is not so much preparation for life as it is real living. The teacher must be the leader in this community in which the child and teacher must learn to live not only for themselves but for others." Words such as these were accepted and have indeed been repeated by Dewey who continued the Parker doctrine of democratic education in a democratic school; and of this we say more in a later section of this chapter.

9. THE HERBARTIANS

The effort to develop a science of education was promoted by the Herbartian doctrines which were introduced in the early nineties. Herbart's psychology, his curriculum program, his methods, and his social aim all gave support to that endeavor. A short notice of Herbart and Beneke was published by Henry Barnard in 1873 and another by W. H. Hailmann the following year. Louis Soldan gave a brief exposition of Herbartianism before the National Education Association. Nobody followed up these suggestions at the time, and it was not until 1883 that Charles De Garmo announced to the National Education Association that he was on his "way to Germany to spend some years in the study of pedagogy." He went to the University of Jena and when he returned he became the Herbartian leader in the United States. He had many followers, for by 1900 fifty Americans had been to Jena to study Herbartian theory and practice. De Garmo returned in 1887 and two years later published his *Essentials of Method* and a translation of a psychology text by G. A. Lindner that was in the Herbartian tradition. For some time thereafter every year saw the publication by different writers of Herbartian books, either new or translated.

Associations were formed to propagate the new ideas. The National Herbart Club was organized in 1892 to facilitate their spread and application. Lange's original work on *Apperception* was translated by the members of the Herbart Club, and the American edition bears the names of the translators on the title page and thus forms an index of some of the leaders. In 1895, to overcome the doctrinal implications of its title, the Herbart Club was renamed; and still later, it became the National Society for the Study of Education. This was a not unimportant result of the Herbartian movement.

Although there were few if any strict disciples in the United States, those who accepted the Herbartian label made great changes in the schools. The greatest change was accomplished by renewed emphasis upon one of the eternal ideas, that children should understand what they learned instead of merely committing it to memory. But new ways of accomplishing this were devised. Studies were better organized around correlation centers, subject lines were passed over by integrating the materials, and the interests of the children were considered in the reorganization. Prominence was given to the type of lesson in which large units of connected, meaningful materials were taught according to a systematic five-step lesson plan. In fact the "steps" became far too prominent. Emphasis was also laid upon right social attitudes and conduct; and the social studies of literature, history, and civics were brought in to supplement the Pestalozzian nature study. Closely connected with these changes was the socialized recitation emphasizing the free cooperation of pupils in developing a topic on their own initiative while the teacher remained in the background as a guide. Lesson planning, apperception, correlation, and concentration, the culture epochs, and the social aim compelled the reconstruction of the elementary school. No one should think Herbartianism unimportant in its influence.

At no period were the Herbartians allowed to have things all their own way. W. T. Harris, who was a partisan of Hegel, attacked Herbart with great vigor. Herbart's psychology was constantly under fire. Quite outside the question of its truth was the fact that it was difficult to understand. And it became fashionable to assure those who complained of its abstruseness that Herbart's psychology and his educational doctrine were quite independent. But this is clearly incorrect. Actually, Americans passed over Herbart's psychology because they were busy developing a psychology of their own, the evolutionary psychology of adaptation which was worked out by James, Angell, Dewey, and others. With the psychology they also discarded much of Herbart's educational system. But not everything. As a movement Herbartianism had run its course within a decade and a half, but many even of its opponents continued to bear the impress of its influence. The most notable example is John Dewey, who began as a Hegelian and therefore a critic of Herbart. But Dewey made industrial activities, in their historical and social development, the center of the curriculum and grouped the rest of the studies around this center. This is an example of the Herbart-Ziller theories of the culture epochs and concentration. Dewey's own steps in a complete act of thought are, as he pointed out in *How We Think* (1910), a transformation of the Herbartian steps. And his general aim of education has a fascinating resemblance to the moral aim of Herbart. Not all of Dewey is to be found in Herbart. One does not find there Dewey's use of the doctrine of evolution, his deeper socialization, or his vision of an industrial democracy, or, of course, his later instrumentalism.

10. PROGRESSIVE EDUCATION

The term "progressive education" has been in common use for more than two decades but, since the complex movement which carries this label has changed from time to time, its various meanings must be gathered from the narrative and description which follow. There is no acceptable, short definition. There were progressive teachers before John Dewey and Francis W. Parker. One may name Amos Bronson Alcott, G. F. Thayer, David

P. Page, and H. H. Straight, without exhausting the list. Not everything that these great teachers did was "progressive," but neither is everything progressive that the present progressives do. Some of the trends of the "common school revival" fall within the progressive category. All of the movements which have been described in the present chapter have some elements of progressivism; and the manual training movement, which is more fully treated in the following chapter, formed one of its introductory stages. The student should have in mind the doctrines of Rousseau and the work of Pestalozzi and Froebel, and should read the section on school activities in Chapter 20 in order to see the scope of the present topic.

Manual training and kindergarten education were combined in two new departures which took place in New York City about 1880. One of these experiments was made by Felix Adler when he organized a free kindergarten for workingmen's children in 1878. In this undertaking he proposed to form a new type of school "in which the reformed system begun in the kindergarten might be continued through all the higher grades of instruction." The next year the Workingmen's School was organized with handwork, artistic and constructional activities, object lessons, and light gymnastics, in addition to the usual school subjects. Adler was most of all interested in practical ethics or improved social conduct, and his school became the Ethical Culture Schools or system, which today is one of the leading progressive centers. Unfortunately the schools had to charge fees and they are no longer maintained for workingmen's children.

The other new departure in New York commenced with the effort of Emily Huntington to adapt kindergarten methods to the education of older girls. She substituted domestic utensils and occupations for the kindergarten gifts and developed a curriculum based upon household activities. The society formed to promote these classes was called the Kitchen Garden Association; and it was later combined with the Industrial Education Association which was formed to prepare manual training teachers. The outcome of these movements, as noticed earlier, was Teachers College of Columbia University, with the Horace Mann School and later also the Speyer School as demonstration centers. The early work of Felix Adler and Emily Huntington was contemporary with Parker's work at Quincy, and the three are examples of the new education about 1880. Parker's later work in Chicago brought him into contact with John Dewey who in 1896 established his laboratory or experimental school at the new University of Chicago. The University Elementary School was the official title.

Several of the current trends in elementary education were integrated in Dewey's new school. The chief of these were the ideas of Froebel and Parker that the school should be a community and that learning should be an active and cooperative process involving investigation, construction, and artistic creation; and these were supported by the biological and functional psychology of James, Angell, and Dewey himself, by the manual training and nature study movements, each of which underwent important changes at Dewey's hands, and finally by the effort to relate the school to the outside community. This laboratory school thus compounded of earlier elements was Dewey's first great contribution to what was later called progressive education. This was also the beginning of Dewey's philosophical development which found expression in a long list of works, including *Democracy and Education* (1916). We should premise that for Dewey philosophy and education are identical. Each of these familiar but even now still cryptic words means the practical experimental study by man of man himself and of his world. Dewey's philosophy gradually developed into experimentalism.

An excellent account of the school appeared in a series of nine monographs that were published in 1900 under the title *The Elementary School Record*. In one of these, Dewey deals with his debt to Froebel as follows:

One of the traditions of the school is of a visitor who, in its early days, called to see the kindergarten. On being told that the school had not as yet established one, she asked if there were not singing, drawing, manual training, plays and dramatizations, and attention to the children's social relations. When her questions were answered in the affirmative she remarked both triumphantly and indignantly that that was what she understood by a kindergarten, and she did not know what was meant by saying that the school had no kindergarten. The remark was perhaps justified in spirit, if not in letter. At all events, it suggests that in a certain sense the school endeavors throughout its whole course—now including children between four and thirteen—to carry into effect certain principles which Froebel was perhaps the first consciously to set forth. Speaking still in general, these principles are:

1. That the primary business of the school is to train children in cooperative and mutually helpful living.
2. That the primary root of all educative activity is in the instinctive, impulsive attitudes and activities of the child, and not in the presentation and application of external material. . . .
3. That these individual tendencies and activities are organized and directed through the uses made of them in keeping up the cooperative living already spoken of, taking advantage of them to reproduce on the child's plane the typical doings and occupations of the larger, maturer society into which he is finally to go forth; and that it is through production and creative use that valuable knowledge is secured and clinched.

So far as these statements correctly represent Froebel's educational philosophy, the school should be regarded as its exponent.

The Chicago school was experimental in two senses. It was experimental in its constant use of experiment and inquiry as the children's method of learning; and also in its purpose to serve as a laboratory for the transformation of schools and of their relation to society. According to Dewey, investigation begins with a difficulty or problem. What was the basic problem which called the Chicago school into being? It was the Hegelian idea of conflict. There were the old oppositions between interest and effort, child and curriculum, and school and society. These phrases are the titles of some of Dewey's early writings. In *School and Society*, he directed special attention to the educational changes which had resulted from the industrial revolution. The school which he desired was to be a miniature society, in the closest relation to the larger society around it, and an agency for resolving social and intellectual conflicts.

Into such a school the occupations of common life and industry were to be introduced, not as special subjects or for vocational purposes but as the center of the general curriculum and the model for teaching-method. This core-curriculum-and-method idea was characteristic of the Chicago laboratory school. Children at the age of six began with home activities involving simple domestic and industrial tasks, materials, and implements. Thus manual training became industrial arts. In the following school years, using the culture epochs concept of the Herbartians as the organizing principle, the historical development of industry, invention, and group living was followed. The dependence of man upon nature and upon society led the pupils to the study of science and history. Nature study and simple experiments were introduced. Mechanical devices such as the spinning wheel and loom were used. The study of cotton, for example, was carried through all stages from the seed and growing plant, the matured fiber, spinning and weaving, to the uses of the finished cloth. Thus the old nature study in new forms was combined with industrial and social studies. Old and new inventions were studied. Clocks and telephones led directly to the consideration of communication and social cooperation. Blind effort, formal drill, recitations, and overt discipline were eliminated by guiding the children in self-education through discovery, construction, and cooperation in engrossing work. The school was in existence for only eight years, not long enough to realize its full promise. Even so it is unfortunate that we do not have a study of the influence it may have exerted upon its pupils. The usual assumption, therefore, that this was the ideal elementary school is after all only an assumption. It is, however, one that has been used in many situations by the disciples of Dewey.

There were other "new schools" at this time. Preston W. Search in *An Ideal School* (1901) named several of the progressive schools of that day: among the European, Abottsholme and the École des Roches; and among the American, the George Junior Republic, Felix Adler's Ethical Culture School, The Tome School, and the Casa de Rosas of Los Angeles, as well as several public school systems. But for admission to Search's list it was rather imperative that a school should be a promoter of individual teaching, and this may explain why he did not mention the University Elementary School. Two new schools which may have been influenced by the Dewey experiment were the laboratory school of the University of Missouri, which was organized in 1904 by Junius L. Meriam, and the Speyer School of Teachers College, Columbia University, into which a strong Herbartian element was introduced by Frank M. McMurry. McMurry developed a curriculum composed of primitive life activities, domestic occupations, nature study, and construction work. Reading and writing were closely related to these activities. Arithmetic was separately organized but it was also connected with the activities as far as seemed feasible. The correlation of materials from different subjects was stressed and problems were employed, but there was provision for drill and subject mastery. The Speyer School under McMurry, therefore, followed a program that was intermediate between the activity and the conventional schools.

The schools named, although all contain new features, were based upon the doctrines of Herbart or Froebel, more especially the latter. The School of Organic Education opened in 1907 by Mrs. Marietta Johnson at Fairhope, Alabama, was a still more radical departure from current practice, and it closely resembled the plan of Rousseau. It was, however, a school, not a tutorial scheme. In an ideal school, said Mrs. Johnson, there should be tables and chairs, no desks, and not more than twenty pupils to a teacher. Money would be needed to reduce the size of schools to this number, but we have money for cut glass and silver. One may remark that some people have money for these desirable items. No reading or writing should be taught before the age of nine or ten and "infinite materials" for the children's work and play should be provided. There must be no acceleration and no specialization in the early years, that is, we must, as Rousseau held, lose time, not gain it. Interest, spontaneity, joy, and mental grasp, not knowledge or skill are the goals. There must be no recitations and no assigned lessons, no examinations, grades, failures, or promotions. The children should be outdoors in the midst of nature, but nature study makes children hate nature and is taboo. Music, dancing, singing games, and handwork, together with stories, are to be the main elements of the early curriculum. All children should be admitted to high school at fourteen and to college at eighteen without examination. This summary of her program is from Marietta Johnson's *Youth in a World of Men* (1929) and is an example of left-wing progressive education.

About the time of World War I and since then, numerous elementary and secondary progressive schools were founded and many older schools turned in the progressive direction. The Country Day School movement of that period was evidence of dissatisfaction with the conventional mass education of the public schools. Wealthy or at least well-to-do parents in many of the large cities cooperated in the establishment of private day schools in the suburban or near-by rural districts. The Shady Hill Country Day School was opened in Germantown, Pennsylvania, in 1912; the City and Country School under Caroline Pratt in New York in 1914; the Walden School in New York and the Shady Hill School of Cambridge, Massachusetts, in 1915; and similar schools were established in other large cities. Many boarding schools and academies with elementary classes developed progressive philosophies and practices. Activity and project methods and core curricula were also introduced more widely in some of the large city systems, including some schools in New York, Denver, Des Moines, and elsewhere. The Progressive Education Association was organized in 1919 by a group of educators and interested citizens for the purpose of uniting those who were experimenting with the new schools and of securing the interest of a wider public for them. At first the Association was mainly concerned with elementary education but later, as we shall see in the next chapter, it moved into the secondary field also. In 1932 the Association became an affiliate of the New Education Fellowship, which carries on similar work in Great Britain, Europe, and other parts of the world.

At the time of its organization the Progressive Education Association declared that its aims were to encourage the free and natural development of children and for this purpose to study their physical and mental development and to base the education of children upon their interests. Many progressives later modified the latter principle to say that education should be based upon children's interests and needs. Even this did not satisfy everyone and some within the progressive ranks urged that social needs should also be considered; but one might raise the question whether these were really progressive. On the physical side the Association demanded small classes, expanded and improved health teaching and services, and better and more varied equipment for teaching and learning. They proposed to develop cooperation between the school and the community and to promote the freedom of teachers, two aims, each good in itself, but not always easy to harmonize. The progressive teacher, however, was to guide and stimulate rather than to control the child or to hear recitations. One of the leaders of progressive education, Vivian T. Thayer of the Ethical Culture Schools, wrote a book called *The Passing of the Recitation* (1928).

The first honorary president of the Progressive Association was Charles William Eliot, president of Harvard University and promoter of the college elective system. He was succeeded in office by John Dewey. For a time the Association conducted two magazines, *Progressive Education* and *Frontiers of Democracy*. The latter journal was discontinued in 1943 and shortly thereafter the Association took the new name of American Education Fellowship. It would seem that the Fellowship took a defensive position to try to hold ground already won and gave up further pioneering. Progressive education had been under attack from the time of Francis W. Parker and the opposition seems to have increased after 1930. It was reported that the change of name was due to influences stemming from World War II and it is a fact that the membership declined sharply after the American entry into the struggle. War always reveals the real or reputed shortcomings of the schools. Similar charges were made in World War I, but the United States participated only a short time in that conflict and the accusations were quickly forgotten after our early return to "normalcy." In World War II, the continued existence of many remediable physical defects, lack of discipline, inability to write effectively, and great deficiencies in elementary mathematics and science were blamed upon the schools. But even if this arraignment is justified, the defects can hardly be attributed wholly to progressive education because our schools had not become widely and generally progressive. The accusers, however, assert that even conservative schools had become soft and flabby through the infiltration of progressive ideas. On the other hand the facts may be quite otherwise. It may be that in our attempt to provide free access to educational opportunity for all, we have everywhere, in the conservative as in progressive camp, placed too little emphasis upon accuracy and thoroughness.

Attempts have been made to evaluate the results of the work of the conflicting types of schools by scientific methods. J. Wayne Wrightstone's *Appraisal of Newer Elementary School Practices* (1938) and J. Cayce Morrison's *The Activity Program* (1941) are two of these. Both agree that in the "fundamental subjects" the pupils in the new schools do about as well as those under the older types of teaching and recitation. Pupils from progressive schools may do a little better in reading and writing English and a little worse in spelling and arithmetic, but there is little to choose between them. In more intangible matters such as breadth of knowledge and interests, social activities, initiative, and skill in dealing with new problems, the progressive school pupils excel those from the conventional schools, but again the differences, while significant, are not very great. These results must be profoundly disappointing to both parties. Neither the expert teachers, small classes, rich curricula, varied equipment, and new methods of the one, nor the more rigid standards, drill, and examinations of the other have solved the problem of securing a high level of universal literacy, critical intelligence, scientific knowledge, democracy, tolerance, and social cooperation. This does not mean that our schools have failed but it does mean that there is no easy road to a high level of national education. It must be the task of the next few years to learn all we can from the great and instructive experiment which progressive education is conducting and has conducted for the last seventy-five years. And our results should also be compared with those of other countries.

As is implied in the title of this chapter, the elementary school of the present day whether progressive or more conventional is a new school. Its instruction has a far richer content, its physical facilities and educational materials are better, its teachers have a more scientific preparation and clearer conception of their task, and its treatment of children is more humane and is based upon a fuller understanding of child nature than was the case one hundred years ago. The progress of the past is a guide and an incentive to further improvement in the future. But we must always remember that many of our schools in large areas have hardly been affected by the progress in other areas. Although the general level has been raised, many schools are even now poorly equipped and badly staffed, and have narrow, highly traditional curricula. Such uneven conditions set a great challenge before our educational statesmanship.

The old school was almost purely intellectual and bookish, even textbookish. The new elementary school has a far more varied, richer, and better balanced program than the old school employed. Nature study, health care and instruction, domestic activities, handwork, music, drawing, literature, history, and other materials have been added. Child study and educational psychology have supplied a valuable body of knowledge on growth, nutrition, interests, emotional stability and instability, group versus individual conduct, and other school and child conditions and problems. A great deal of knowledge is now at hand for the teacher's use. Social conditions have also, since the time of Pestalozzi and in the first instance through his influence, aided in transforming the old authoritarian relations between teachers and pupils. The older attitudes have largely vanished, and instead one finds greater cooperation and more scientific understanding. Teaching has become more informal and is more directly related to the lives of the pupils. New methods involving investigation by the pupils, group work, projects, and activities have come to be more widely employed. At this point, however, many students of education and prospective teachers sometimes develop a mistaken conception of the actual conditions in the schools. They think progressive education is more widespread than is the case. The activity curriculum, the child-centered school, integrated learning without subject divisions, freedom for the child within the school have become familiar phrases in descriptions of the new conditions, and these can all be found in actual schools here and there but they are not general. They are still ideals rather than achieved conditions, and many responsible educators do not accept them as ideals. Most of our schools are likely to remain fairly conventional for a long time.

One of the permanent issues that was sharpened by the depression and also by World War II is that between social orientation and individual interests and development. On the one hand we have those who would stress the demands of society, the problems of American life and culture or education for democracy; on the other hand those who consider that the personal interests of children, recognized and accepted by them, provide the only sound basis for a school program. It seems that in the last twenty years the social aims have been given greater attention than they were between 1920 and 1930. Radical progressives would call this a reactionary trend and it may be in part a reaction against their program; but it is also a recognition that the elementary school needs to teach the duties and the values of citizenship in a democracy more effectively than either the old school or the new has done. The whole school, not only history or the study of current problems, should contribute to this end.

Considerable interest in school improvement developed even before the elementary schools had become fully established. A part of this concern was due to the influence of Pestalozzi. Emphasis was laid upon comprehension in reading and arithmetic, upon the use of illustrative materials such as pictures, drawings, and objects, upon the introduction of geography and elementary science into the course of study, and upon friendlier relations between teachers and pupils. Many children's books and schoolbooks, dealing with nature and giving practical and scientific information about things in the home and on the farm, were written. The Oswego system of object teaching was introduced into all the northern states but it was often merely another memory exercise.

The elementary science movement of the early part of the century led to nature study and back again to elementary science. The two are, indeed, hard to distinguish from each other for one form of nature study was simply elementary science; but there were also a sentimental or poetical study of nature and a utilitarian study with application to health, the home, and other practical matters. An extended literature was called out by the nature study movement, and schools were made more interesting and informative.

The kindergarten, the child study movement, and handwork and industrial activities came into elementary education together; and this is natural, for they have much in common. They have greatly modified the philosophy and practice of elementary education. It was these three trends, all of them embodied in the Quincy methods, that have done most in creating the new elementary school; but Parker at Quincy and elsewhere was important not only as a promoter of the "new education" but also as a vigorous protagonist of democracy in school and in society. Thus Parker laid the groundwork for progressive education for which John Dewey provided the philosophical justification. Dewey's early writings were an interpretation of Herbartian and Froebelian doctrines; but he soon developed his well-known pragmatic and instrumentalist philosophy. Future historians may find that, in his case as in that of Parker, it has been his Americanism, democracy, and spirit of social reform rather than his technical philosophy that have most deeply affected American education.

QUESTIONS

1. Did the rise of science and of democracy provide a favorable condition for the introduction of Pestalozzianism? Compare with conditions in Prussia.
2. What is an educational fad? Did the Oswego system of object teaching have some of the characteristics of a fad? What part did propaganda play in the movement?
3. What characteristics are most necessary to an effective teacher? Make a simple scale and rank Henry H. Straight on it. Also F. W. Parker.
4. What forms of nature study would be most appropriate for a particular school with which you are well acquainted?
5. How has the Froebelian kindergarten been changed in the United States, and why?
6. Examine the literature on the subject to see whether children who attend the kindergarten benefit measurably from the experience.
7. How were the Quincy methods related to previous and contemporary educational theories and practices?
8. Would P. W. Search be accepted today as a progressive? How does his program differ from that of the child-centered school?
9. Is Dewey's idea developed in *School and Society* of basing the elementary curriculum upon the evolution of industry and society any less far-fetched than the culture epoch theory?
10. There are said to be thirteen varieties of pragmatism. How many varieties of progressive education can you distinguish?
11. What variety of progressive education do you prefer, and why?

FOR FURTHER READING AND STUDY

Many of the sources for this chapter have been given in the text and these will not be repeated. The final references in the preceding chapter, those on the normal schools at Westfield and Bridgewater, are useful in connection with the present chapter as well. Several magazines are of special interest here. Such are *The Nature Study Review* (New York, 1905 and after), *Progressive Education* (Washington, D. C., 1924 and after) and, for numerous child-study papers and the history of the movement, the *Pedagogical Seminary* (Worcester, Massachusetts, 1891 and after). The *Yearbooks* of the National Herbart Society provide data on the Herbartian movement in the United States. Paul Monroe's *Cyclopedia of Education* (New York, The Macmillan Company, 1911–1913) has articles on the development of "Child Study," "Kindergarten," "Manual Training" and "Object Teaching." Several object teaching manuals are listed below as evidence of the nature of the subject and of the aims assigned to it. The *Educational Review*, edited by Nicholas Murray Butler, and the *Proceedings* of the National Education Association contain important historical materials.

Berkson, I. B., *Education Faces the Future. An Appraisal of Contemporary Movements in Education*, New York, Harper & Brothers, 1943, 345 pp.

Brueckner, L. J., and others, *The Changing Elementary School*, New York, Inor Publishing Company, 1939, 388 pp. This is a volume of the Regents' Inquiry into the cost and character of education in the State of New York.

Calkins, N. A., *Primary Object Lessons for Training the Senses and Developing the Faculties of Children. A Manual for Parents and Teachers*. Fortieth edition, New York, Harper & Brothers, 1870, 448 pp.

Case, Roscoe D., *The Platoon School in America*, Stanford University, California, University Press, 1931, 283 pp.

Culkin, Mabel L., "The Contemporary Kindergarten," *The Educational Record*, 24:345–357 (October, 1943).

Curti, Merle, *The Social Ideas of American Educators*, New York, Charles Scribner's Sons, 1935, 613 pp. Studies of Harris, Bishop Spalding, F. W. Parker, G. S. Hall, William James, and others.

Dearborn, Ned H., *The Oswego Movement in American Education*, New York, Teachers College, Columbia University, 1925, 189 pp., Teachers College Contributions to Education, No. 183. Has a bibliography.

Kennedy, Millard Fillmore, *Schoolmaster of Yesterday, A Three-Generation Story, 1820–1919*, New York, McGraw-Hill Book Company, Inc., 1940, 359 pp. Written in collaboration with Alvin F. Harlow. This excellent story deals more with the old school than with the new but is valuable as a corrective to idealized history of education.

Krüsi, Hermann, *Recollections of My Life, an Autobiographical Sketch . . .* edited by Elizabeth Sheldon Alling, New York, The Grafton Press, 1907, 439 pp. Contains materials and judgments on the Oswego System and other topics in elementary education.

Monroe, Walter S., *Development of Arithmetic as a School Subject*, Washington, D. C., Government Printing Office, 1917, 170 pp. U. S. Bureau of Education Bulletin, No. 10, 1917.

Monroe, Will S., *History of the Pestalozzian Movement in the United States*, with nine portraits and a bibliography, Syracuse, New York, C. W. Bardeen, 1907, 244 pp. One questionable generalization in this book is that New England was less influenced by Pestalozzian doctrine than other parts of the United States.

Niemeyer, N., *Children and Childhood*, New York, Oxford University Press, 1921, 206 pp. Contains selections from child study literature.

Otto, Henry J., *Elementary School Organization and Administration*, New York, D. Appleton and Co., 1934, 652 pp.

Patridge, Lelia E., *Notes of Talks on Teaching, given by Francis W. Parker at the Martha's Vineyard Summer Institute, 1882*, New York, E. L. Kellogg and Company, 1885, 182 pp.; *The Quincy Methods Illustrated*, New York, E. L. Kellogg and Company, 1886, 660 pp.

Randels, George Basil, *The Doctrines of Herbart in the United States*, Philadelphia. No publisher given, 1909, 67 pp.

Schatzmann, Iman Elsie, *The Country School at Home and Abroad*, Chicago, University of Chicago Press, [1942], 233 pp.

Search, Preston Willis, *An Ideal School*, New York, D. Appleton Century Company, Inc., 1901, 357 pp.

Swift, Fletcher H., *Emma Marwedel, 1818–1893, Pioneer of the Kindergarten in California*, Berkeley, University of California Press, 1933, 66 pp., a reprint.

Tharp, Louise Hall, *The Peabody Sisters of Salem*, Boston, Little, Brown and Company, 1950, 372 pp.; *Until Victory: Horace Mann and Mary Peabody*, Boston, Little, Brown and Company, [1953], 367 pp.

Unsigned articles on "Object Lessons," in the Massachusetts *Common School Journal*, 2:179–185 (June 15, 1840); 193–204 (July 1, 1840).

Vandewalker, Nina C., *The Kindergarten in American Education*, New York, The Macmillan Company, 1908, 274 pp.

Weller, Florence, and Otis W. Caldwell, "The Nature Study and Elementary Science Movement." *School Science and Mathematics*, 33:730–745 (October, 1933).

Woody, Thomas, "Historical Sketch of Activism," *The Thirty-Third Yearbook of the National Society for the Study of Education, Part II*, pp. 9–43. Bloomington, Ill., Public School Publishing Co., 1934.

20 CREATING THE HIGH SCHOOL

I N OUR EDUCATIONAL RENAISSANCE THE COMMON SCHOOL DE-
veloped with a speed and vigor which the high school for
a long time could not match. It did not become the leading institution in
the secondary field until almost the closing decade of the nineteenth century. Its growth was hampered by the competition of the academies, the
pressure of college entrance requirements upon its program, the tradition
that secondary education must be selective and restricted to the few, and
the limited popular interest in secondary education and its high cost.
Although many high schools had developed out of elementary schools, even
these tended to become preparatory schools and there was justification for
the criticism that they were selective. Like the common school, the high
school finally won its victory by convincing the common people that it
would become their school and would serve their interests.

1. DEFINITIONS

The most distinctive feature of the American high school is this, that together with the common school it provides a continuous program of general education which enrolls a greater proportion of the youth and retains
more of them to the age of eighteen than the schools of other countries.
Although its main function is to give general secondary education, this
does not preclude the schools from giving specialized courses. Under the
Smith-Hughes law, agriculture is taught even in many small schools. It
stresses opportunity for youth rather than artificial standards. It is a day,
not a boarding school, it is usually coeducational, and the instruction is
free to the youth of its district. It is a public school, for under state law it
is controlled by a local board elected by popular vote. Other countries also
have developed great secondary school systems, but none has gone as far
as the United States in providing free general education for its youth. In
most countries the secondary schools have been, and to a degree still re-

main, distinct and separate from the common schools. In the United States the successive levels have been joined into an unbroken ladder leading from the kindergarten to the university.

2. FROM GRADED SCHOOLS TO HIGH SCHOOLS

We have already dealt briefly with grading in considering the American System, and in other connections, but the subject is so important to an understanding of high school development that further examples will be given. In most states the high school developed without legal authority, but laws permitting graded schools to be formed were frequently enacted: about 1850, in Iowa, "central grammar schools" and schools of higher grades; in New York, "union free school districts" with "secondary departments"; and in Pennsylvania, graded schools and the teaching of "higher branches." Many similar examples could be selected. The quoted phrases suggest the fact that the high school developed gradually and that its growth depended upon the grading of the schools. After the movement had progressed for several decades, that is, about 1870 or 1880, the character of the high school became clear. It was seen to be a separately administered and publicly controlled free school which offers general education to adolescent youth.

Even the famous Massachusetts law of 1827 was hardly a high school law. It was a re-enactment in somewhat broader terms of a still more famous statute, "the old deluder Satan" law of 1647. The new law prescribed that American history, bookkeeping, geometry, surveying, and algebra were to be offered in districts of five hundred families; and in districts of four thousand people, the employment of a teacher who was competent to teach Latin, Greek, history, rhetoric, and logic was demanded. This is a Latin grammar school law, and indeed the subjects named, excepting only the bookkeeping, surveying, and logic, are the exact subjects included in the curriculum of the Boston Latin School at that time. But while in 1647 every town of one hundred families was required to establish a Latin school, in 1827 a like provision was not demanded until the town had reached a size about eight times as large.

That graded schools formed the necessary base for the public high school must have been clear to many, but it was perhaps clearest of all to Henry Barnard. In 1838, when he had just become secretary to the Connecticut Board of Commissioners of Common Schools, he reported that the state had practically no graded schools, that so much was attempted in ungraded schools with all classes and ages intermingled that nothing was done well, and that the younger children were often neglected. Upon his recommendation, Connecticut passed a graded school law in 1839, and in the following year a rudimentary but, as it turned out, permanent high school was established at Middletown.

The young city of Cincinnati also furnishes an early example of grading. An Ohio law of 1829 had made that city an independent school district, but the first public schools were not graded and were conducted in rented rooms. Seven years later in 1836 the first public school buildings were erected, and the schools were divided into two "grades," called primary and secondary, each comprising several years of work. Albert Picket, who had been one of the advisers of the first staff of public school teachers in Cincinnati, was in 1840 a member of the school board. With the help of another member, James H. Perkins, he prepared a course of study with five grades extending from the alphabet and "teaching pupils to use their eyes as well as their ears" to high school mathematics and "rural economy" in grade five. The plan could not be fully carried out at once, but by 1847 the system was far enough advanced to permit the opening of the Central High School. Four years later the Hughes and Woodward funds became available and two high schools bearing those names were established. Many other high schools were opened in Ohio, Pennsylvania, and other states before the Civil War. It has been calculated that New England had one hundred and eighty-five high schools by 1865, but some of these were public Latin schools and others offered only partial courses of two or three years.

Secondary education, both private and public, entered upon a period of rapid expansion about the time of the Civil War. In the older states the sparse population, hard living conditions, and a great demand for manual labor had persisted for two centuries from the early settlements, but this pioneer period was progressively shortened as new states developed in the West. Even in the heavily wooded sections, such states as Ohio and Michigan quickly felled their forests and built cities, whose employments gave an opening for secondary education. Ohio, within a half-century after attaining statehood, passed her Akron law (1847) which permitted the grading of schools and the creation of "central schools." In Iowa this step took not half a century but hardly more than a decade. And in the far West many territories provided for general state school officers, public elementary and high schools, and a state university even before they were admitted into the Union. Through the migration of settlers from the older states and the optimism of the pioneers, the new states often started with plans which were in advance of those in operation in the regions from which the people had come. The North Central and Western states, which did not have as strong a prior allegiance to academies and private schools, accepted the high school more easily, developed it more experimentally, and supported it more ungrudgingly than the East and the Old South.

To report the number of high schools at a given time, say in 1860, is difficult because exact information is wanting and definitions vary. Henry Barnard, using a definition which involved a very high standard, estimated that there were only one hundred sixty. This left out hundreds of small schools, many with partial courses. In New England one investigator, as we have seen, counted one hundred eighty-five high schools by 1865, and two-thirds of these were in Massachusetts. In New York several academies had been taken over by the public boards; and union schools and high schools to the number of thirty or forty were in operation by 1860. Pennsylvania had as many. In Ohio, a student found evidence of twenty or more. We may reasonably estimate that by that time there were five hundred public high schools with a separate organization, each offering two or more years of work above the elementary school. But the academies were more numerous and more influential than the high schools until about 1880 or even later.

3. EARLY HIGH SCHOOLS AS ILLUSTRATIONS

The cities first established high schools, then the smaller towns, and not until after 1900 did the rural high schools develop rapidly. Boston opened its English Classical School in 1821, and this is considered to be the first high school. Philadelphia in 1838 was another large city to erect such a school. Each of these was a creation at a given time and place rather than an evolution such as we have described in the preceding sections.

Public opinion in Boston, having been awakened in the fight for primary schools, was ready to extend public education upward to the age of fifteen in order to make good the deficiency which arose from the fact that the city did not have an academy. A subcommittee of the school board reported that the elementary school curriculum was too easy for bright boys and that it encouraged habits of easy-going idleness instead of preparing them by vigorous study for the mercantile and mechanical occupations which they were to follow. Many parents could not afford to send their sons away from home to an academy. There was some fear that a new school might injure the Latin School and the upper classes of the elementary schools, but the town voted it in May 1821.

Boys only were to be admitted and only upon examination in the elementary branches including grammar. The age of twelve was set as the lower limit, and a three-year curriculum of English, mathematics, social studies, and sciences was formed. All subjects were required. The first principal was a noted teacher, George B. Emerson, and he was given three assistants. More than a hundred pupils entered when the school opened. The name, English Classical School, was later changed to English High

School. The term "high school" was probably introduced from Scotland and was not at once accepted by ultrademocrats who had no love for "high" institutions.

The charge of "aristocracy," really selectivity, which was leveled at the American high school was not without foundation. The later history of the Boston school furnishes some evidence. Comparison of the curriculum of 1821 with that of 1867 shows that at the latter date a fourth year had been added and a wholly different philosophy had been adopted. At the beginning the freshman studies were chosen to meet the needs of those boys who were unable to stay for the full course. But in 1867 it was declared "that it is for the best interests of the school, on the whole, to make the instruction of the first year conform more precisely to the requirements of a systematic course." In other words, freshmen who could stay only a year were to study the same subjects as those who would stay four years. We may anticipate to say that this untenable position was also taken by the Committee of Ten, twenty-five years later. But why should "the best interests of the school, on the whole" be preferred to the best interests of each particular student? The answer to this question and other obvious questions is found in the fact that in 1867 the English High School began to prepare its students for the then recently opened Massachusetts Institute of Technology. Thus a school founded for the sons of sea captains, small merchants, and artisans, forgetting its original purpose, was drawn into the net of higher education. Educational standards had won a victory over educational opportunities.

A high school for girls was opened in Boston in 1826 but this experiment had an unhappy ending. After two years under an able principal, Ebenezer Bailey, the school was closed because there were so many students that the city refused to provide the money which would have been required to continue it. The attack upon it was led by the Mayor, Josiah Quincy, who hotly denied its usefulness; but this was a point upon which opinions differed. In 1852, Boston established a normal school for girls which was later converted into a combined high and normal school.

When the Philadelphia Central High School came to be established in 1838, the high school idea had already undergone considerable development. The Massachusetts law of 1827, as we have seen, demanded the teaching of the ancient classics by public schools in the larger towns. The high school in Philadelphia included these studies and it was from the beginning a four-year school. And, also, it was influenced by the practice of the German *Realschulen*. Some plans and schools for teaching boys in preparation for the higher mercantile and mechanical pursuits had already been proposed or were in actual operation in Philadelphia. One of the latter was the private high school of the Franklin Institute under Walter R.

Johnson. Public interest was shown by the enactment of the Pennsylvania law of 1836 which authorized the opening of public high schools; and within the year, beginnings were made in Norristown and in Carlisle. The Philadelphia school board after receiving the report of a committee on the subject opened the Central High School in October 1838. The cities of Lancaster and York opened high schools in 1840. We shall use the Philadelphia school as another example of a growing movement.

In Philadelphia as in Boston, admission was by examination. Alexander Dallas Bache, who had recently returned from a study of European schools, was in 1839 chosen "president" of the new school. Bache organized three courses, a principal course, similar to the work of the German *Realschulen*, a classical course, and an English course. The principal course included work in English, modern languages, geography, mathematics which covered trigonometry, analytics, and descriptive geometry, and in addition physics, natural history, drawing, and the "evidences of Christianity." In the classical course, Latin and Greek were substituted for the modern languages, but in the two-year English course all foreign languages were omitted. By means of these parallel courses in a comprehensive high school, provision for three classes of students was made: those who wished to prepare for college, those who would enter business pursuits, and those who had time for a short course only. The two-year course was not popular and was later discontinued. Two-thirds of the pupils elected the principal course. The Philadelphia Central was one of the most fully developed, equipped, and staffed of the early high schools.

4. OPPOSITION TO THE HIGH SCHOOLS

Although the high school developed as a result of popular demand, it was not a universal demand and there was opposition. The early history of the Norwich Free Academy is instructive in this connection. A strong movement to establish a public high school in Norwich, Connecticut, developed in 1846, but the opposition proved even stronger and after a delay of eight years the present academy was founded as a private tuition school. In this and similar cases the establishment of an academy prevented or delayed the founding of a public high school. Later, by an arrangement with the school board of Norwich, the tuition of the local pupils was paid out of public funds, and this plan still continues in force. Elsewhere, many academies were from time to time transferred to the local boards and became public high schools. The Utica Free Academy and the Elmira Free Academy, both in New York, illustrate this process. A list has been compiled of about seventy New York academies which before 1874 became public schools.

In the Kalamazoo case of 1872 the Supreme Court of Michigan declared that a school district could legally use public money to teach branches above those of the elementary schools and to pay the salary of the superintendent. The case became famous because of the eloquent opinion written by Justice Cooley in which he supported the decision of the court by the historical, rather than strictly legal, argument that since the legislature had established public schools and a state university, the legislature must have intended that pupils should be prepared for the university by the lower schools. He argued that, since the university demanded a knowledge of a foreign language or languages for entrance, the schools below the university had the legal right to teach these and other preparatory branches. Although this decision has been frequently quoted and cited, its effect has probably been exaggerated. Within a decade after the Kalamazoo case, eight or nine other cases against the high school reached the supreme courts of other states and were decided in favor of the legality of the new schools. One of these which originated in St. Clair County, Illinois, bears a close resemblance to the Kalamazoo case. The main question was on the teaching of foreign languages in public schools. It was decided affirmatively in 1875, and there also the court based its decision upon the history of school legislation in the state. Some public controversy over the establishment of high schools has been traced in the same period in thirty or more states.

The opposition to the high school stemmed from various sources. The comparatively higher costs of high schools over elementary schools were frequently cited. The supporters of the high school pointed out that the comparison should be made between the costs of education in high schools and the costs in academies and attempted to show that the former were less. Other economic issues were also raised. The opponents argued that the heavy taxation which the high school required tended to discourage business. They also declared that a high school education caused children to despise manual labor. It was argued and denied that the high school courses were superficial, that they benefited only a small part of the population, and that the academies were more adaptable to the needs of the pupils and more thorough in their teaching. The private school interests seem to have mustered their forces against public secondary education for a special effort about 1885. At that time the high school enrollment in the country passed the total enrollment in private secondary schools; and the United States Commissioner of Education expressed the opinion, which history has confirmed, that the public high school would be the dominant institution in its field. By the end of the century the high schools were far in the lead and at present they enroll more than ninety per cent of all secondary school pupils.

5. EXPANSION OF THE PROGRAM OF STUDIES

The high school began with the somewhat broad curriculum of the academy, and this was further expanded as the schools developed. In 1820 the Boston Latin School offered seven subjects, including Latin and Greek; but the English Classical School of 1821, without offering Latin or Greek, taught twenty-one subjects. The Massachusetts law of 1827 specified sixteen subjects and this number rose to twenty-seven in the law of 1858. The high school of Providence, to take another example, in 1855 offered twenty-eight subjects. And Alexander Inglis listed seventy-three subjects as taught in different high schools in Massachusetts in 1861, although no one school offered all of these.

The Boston high school at the beginning offered only a single curriculum, but before long other schools began to organize two or more parallel curricula, and one of these was usually a college preparatory curriculum. The Philadelphia high school began with three curricula. Frequently in the early high schools a "normal" curriculum for teachers was also provided. This was usually similar to the general curriculum but included several professional subjects. As the movement developed the comprehensive high school, offering several kinds of curricula rather than the specialized school giving only a single one, such as the commercial, the manual training, or the college preparatory curriculum, became the typical American high school. The Central High School of Philadelphia, as was indicated, was an early example of this important trend.

The colleges had a pronounced effect upon the high school program. The great variety of curricula in most colleges in the latter part of the nineteenth century is indicated by the creation of new degrees such as bachelor of letters, of science, of philosophy, and of music. This bloated condition of the college offerings was paralleled by a similar distention of the high school program which now included several modern languages and Latin, many English subjects such as rhetoric, composition, literature, and the history of literature, several varieties of social studies including modern and American history and civics, and the sciences which gradually came to be taught by laboratory methods. The high school did not give degrees but it created a large number of curricula with such titles as English-Latin, Latin-scientific, English-scientific, in addition to the older general and college preparatory curricula. In 1900 a total of thirty-six curricula each leading to high school graduation was observed in different schools. Not many subjects were dropped from the high school program, but Greek was offered less and less frequently. Indeed it never secured a foothold in the smaller schools and was soon confined to the large city high schools. Logic, astronomy, and the "evidences of Christianity" often given in the early high schools also disappeared. It will be noticed that the expansion up to 1880 mainly involved what are known as academic subjects such as literature, languages, mathematics, the sciences, and the social studies; but beginning about that time a new period of further expansion set in and this involved "things to do" as well as things to learn.

6. ENTRANCE OF THE ACTIVITIES

The earlier high schools had devoted themselves to a literary and intellectual program, but before 1900 several imaginative and expressional and several semivocational subjects were introduced. The high school began to emphasize not only knowing and understanding but also doing. Agriculture, commercial studies, home economics, manual training, and music were now taught. Such a classification into knowing and doing is, however, not at all absolute, for language and literature involve speaking and writing as well as reading; mathematics, and science, especially when taught by laboratory methods, also involve activity. Yet it will not be denied that the new subjects stress training in skill and physical performance more than the older. We shall not have space to include the development of all the new activities; but as music was one of the earliest we shall take it first.

Music instruction books were written in colonial times, one by Thomas Walter in 1721. Private singing schools began about the same time and continued for a century and longer. These were classes meeting periodically for the purpose of teaching the students to read music, to give them practice in singing, and to cultivate familiarity with hymns, songs, and choral works. It was a form of adult education. Until music was taught in the public schools, the singing school and the church choir were the chief means of music education open to the people.

Music was introduced widely into the public elementary schools in our educational renaissance even before 1830. Boston began to give such instruction regularly in 1838 when Lowell Mason, one of our great teachers, became supervisor of music in the schools of that city. From the elementary schools, music spread to the high schools and an early text, the *High School Choralist*, was prepared by Charles Aikin (1818–1882). Graded series of books for music study were developed after the Civil War, and the normal schools and some colleges began to prepare teachers and supervisors of public school music. The Commissioner of Education in 1886 reported two hundred and fifty cities in which music was regularly taught; and so rapidly was it spreading that three years later eighty others were added to the list.

During the years that have passed since 1890, much of the emphasis has shifted from vocal to instrumental music and an extraordinary development has taken place, first of the school orchestra and in the last two decades of the school band. Indeed the band, and the marching rather than the concert band, has tended to win the greatest applause; but the high schools also continue to do not less but more choral and orchestral work. The phonograph and the radio, and the great artists and organizations of national fame, have given music a place in the life and the schools of the United States that could not have been imagined even fifty years ago.

The teaching of drawing as a useful study and especially as an aid in mechanical vocations was urged by Benjamin Franklin and Henry Barnard. To this Horace Mann added that this skill is of value to the teacher in illustrating his lessons. The high schools of Philadelphia and Baltimore offered work in drawing about 1840, and in the former school Rembrandt Peale was for a few years the teacher. Drawing textbooks began to appear. Massachusetts by a law enacted in 1870 became the first state to develop an effective program of drawing instruction. Few states followed this example, but many of the larger high schools in all parts of the country introduced the subject without a mandate from the state.

For a long time drawing was taught to serve industry and this is still an important purpose, but more recently new ideas and a broader program have developed. Free-hand drawing, sketching, illustrating, commercial art, modeling, and even home decoration and home planning have been given a place. Art appreciation in schools may perhaps be dated from a campaign of Ross Turner about 1892 for schoolroom decoration. The aims of appreciation subjects include the cultivation of the taste and of talent and the enrichment of life and leisure. Recent efforts have been made to relate the arts to everyday living and to join usefulness with beauty as well as to teach the best of both old and new art. The teaching of commercial and industrial art has kept pace with these more personal and expressional trends; but American education has not yet become art conscious to the degree that it has become music conscious.

The early purposes of manual training and of drawing instruction were the same, to serve industry; the methods of teaching also were similar, and the two subjects were often taught in close association with each other. In both, a formal method was developed. Both emphasized imitation, exact representation, and a step-by-step procedure. Experiments with shopwork courses were carried on by Calvin M. Woodward of Washington University in St. Louis shortly after the Civil War. Businessmen, hoping to find a substitute for apprenticeship, supported the venture and a manual training school was erected in 1880. The prospectus declared that "the interests of St. Louis demand for young men a system of education which shall fit them for the actual duties of life." This was a repetition, in almost the same words, of the aims of the first high schools opened sixty years earlier. Manual training was now to aid in doing what the older schools had not fully accomplished.

To indicate that he was interested in manual training not only for industrial purposes but also for its value in general education, Woodward used, and perhaps coined, a phrase which swept over the country. He said that manual training made it possible "to put the whole boy to school." Woodward also showed that the high schools were not holding their pupils, that too few of those who entered remained to graduate. He attributed the loss to the narrow academic curriculum and thought the remedy lay in the introduction of manual training, home economics, and other practical studies. This was twenty years before Preston W. Search in *An Ideal School* in 1901 published an age-grade table, and thirty years before Edward L. Thorndike made his pioneer study of retardation and elimination from school.

Private manual training schools were opened in a number of the large cities. The public elementary and high schools rapidly took it up. When the Children's Industrial Exhibition was held in New York in 1886, it displayed the work of all school grades and from many localities including some as far west as Chicago. A public manual training high school had been opened in Baltimore in 1883 and other cities followed this example. A few higher institutions had introduced shopwork even earlier. The Illinois Industrial University, now the University of Illinois, had prepared an exhibit of shopwork for the Philadelphia Centennial Exposition of 1876. Eventually the land-grant colleges became extremely effective agencies for the promotion of shop and laboratory work, industrial and practical arts, applied science, home economics, and agriculture, but this influence came only after several decades of experimentation. The most prominent early introduction of manual training into a higher institution was made by the Massachusetts Institute of Technology. This was the Russian system of the Imperial Technical School of Moscow. It consisted of formal drill exercises which never produced any finished objects; but its defects were not seen until later. Its value lay in setting up graded series of class exercises to develop shop skills, which could be easily administered in a school. Only in 1894 in the naming of the Macy Manual Arts Building at Columbia University was the word "arts" substituted for the word "training," to embrace the ideas of beauty, utility, and skill in one concept.

The United States Commissioner of Education in 1900 noted "a steady increase from year to year in the enrollment in the schools devoted especially to manual and industrial training." There were then about one hundred such schools and some of the largest high schools in the country were in this class. The new Technical High Schools gave considerable emphasis to vocational education without becoming trade schools, but many public trade schools were founded also. The trend, however, was toward the general high school in which the manual training curriculum ran parallel to the home economics, general, classical, and other curricula. The whole great movement toward activities had developed as the result of the convergence of many forces including the demands of a society which was rapidly becoming urban and industrial, the decline of apprenticeship, the introduction of science teaching, the kindergarten and child study movement, and the growing high school enrollments of which manual training was partly cause, partly effect.

7. THE RISE OF INDUSTRIAL ARTS EDUCATION

The ideas of Froebel that the school should be a community and that learning should be an active and cooperative process were applied in the elementary school which John Dewey directed from 1896 at the University of Chicago. These ideas had already been given considerable emphasis by F. W. Parker and they were now to be further supported by the biologically functional and evolutionary psychology of "the Chicago school" of psychologists of which Dewey and James R. Angell were prominent members. In Dewey's "experimental school," the industrial occupations were not special subjects but became the center of the curriculum. They were also considered to embody the most effective method of teaching; and, accordingly, subject matter and method were regarded as complementary phases of all learning situations. Weaving, for example, studied through the construction and use of a simple loom would involve a different content from weaving studied from a book, a lecture, a film, or even a demonstration by the teacher. The school was "experimental" in the sense that the children, under guidance, "experimentally" determined their own curricula and methods. Dewey in 1899 explained the theory and practice of the school in a book, *School and Society*, which quickly attracted wide attention.

Occupations were selected that were considered "real" for children and not merely those which were typical of adult activities. These were to serve as means through which the school was to become an active community instead of a place set apart for learning lessons. Dewey held with Parker, Froebel, and Rousseau, that through these direct modes of exploring, manipulating, investigating, and constructing, there would arise "plenty of opportunities and occasions" for the use of number, reading, writing, and spelling. These were no longer to be "subjects," but rather organic phases of the child's continuous experience. The natural activities of the child in following out his purposes would effectively correlate all his experiences, thus making unnecessary any special efforts at correlation such as the Herbartians of the same period tried to introduce. The phrase industrial arts was made necessary by the development of mechanized industry, and was coined by Charles R. Richards about 1904; and he and Frederick G. Bonser became leading interpreters of Dewey's conception of industrial arts. In the modern high school the work of the industrial arts department has since 1900 become more and more industrial and scientific and has come to use a wide variety of materials. In the high school, however, integration with other phases of schoolwork is often very slight. The aims are turning toward teaching for wise production and consumption in an industrial society.

8. VOCATIONAL EDUCATION TRENDS

Active interest in vocational education paralleled the rise of industrial arts education. The report of the Douglas Commission to the legislature of Massachusetts, the founding of the National Society for the Promotion of Industrial Education by Richards, David Snedden, and others, and the study of the same field by the New York State Department of Labor all came in the first decade of the twentieth century. A few technical schools for boys of sixteen or eighteen had already demonstrated what can be done in teaching the skilled trades. Efforts were now to be made to develop vocational schools either full-time or on a part-time cooperative basis. To study the questions further and to secure public support for the movement, state vocational commissions were appointed in several states about 1908 and 1910. Laws were also enacted authorizing cities to establish vocational schools. The most complete and detailed act of this kind was adopted by Wisconsin in 1911. This law helped to create a dual system since the state and local boards of vocational education which it established were separate from the local school boards and state education departments which had charge of the ordinary public schools.

Vocational education raised several problems which call for continued attention. The gulf between vocational and general education was widened by the increased activity of the federal government which resulted from the Smith-Hughes (1917) and later acts with similar objects. The recent war-training programs looked in the same general direction. The possibility that we are turning toward a national and state system of vocational education which will come into competition with the public school system which has been built up by a century of thought and effort is unfortunately a real possibility. Competition for funds is only one phase of this problem. Another stems from the conviction of public school leaders that young boys who have not completed their high school education are quite unprepared to choose their life-work wisely. This phase has led to the vocational guidance movement which has been growing vigorously since the early years of the present century. A related issue divides capital and management against labor. Labor leaders are disturbed by the prospect of the free and unregulated preparation of skilled and semiskilled mechanics and fear that this would seriously depress that area of the labor market. On the other hand, the lack of trained mechanics assumed almost crisis proportions in the war emergency of 1942 and 1943. Laborers also desire for their children the opportunity to prepare for the white-collar occupations, and in consequence they tend to favor general and academic courses. Further, the rapid mechanization of industry and agriculture is making it more difficult for young workers to secure employment and this social fact is one of the chief reasons why the compulsory school age has been raised, the average period of school attendance lengthened, and the enrollment in high school increased so rapidly in recent years.

Space limitations preclude a complete account of the high school curriculum expansion. Commercial studies have been briefly treated in an earlier chapter. The omission of agriculture and physical education leaves big gaps unfilled. Home economics also has made an important addition to the program. Progress in home economics education occurred in three periods: a long early stage when chiefly needlework was taught; a middle stage when, through philanthropic, health, and welfare movements and the establishment of the state colleges of agriculture, the foundations were laid; and the present period which began about 1914 and in which the field of home economics teaching has been expanded and diversified. Textiles and clothing, foods, cooking, nutrition, and housing are still the basic subjects, but in this third period other areas also have been cultivated. These include home management, furniture, decoration, fuels, health and home nursing, consumer education, child care and development, and the study of personality and home relationships. In a report of 1939 covering fourteen thousand high schools, it was found that about three-fourths of these offered home economics and that the largest enrollments were in the ninth and tenth grades.

Enough has now been detailed to show that a revolution in high school facilities, personnel, and purposes occurred in the latter nineteenth and the twentieth centuries through the introduction of activities and practical subjects. An administrative transition accompanied the changes in the program of studies. In this transition the high school was gradually freed somewhat from domination by the colleges. The early examinations for admission to the high school had long been given up. Now the control which the college entrance examinations exercised upon the high school itself was also to be relaxed. We shall turn back to trace the progress of this trend.

9. ACCREDITING SCHEMES

Admission to college had always been granted upon examination by the individual college itself. About 1870 the University of Michigan and a few years later Indiana University began to admit the graduates of accredited high schools without an entrance examination. The University of Michigan sent visitors who inspected and accredited the individual high schools, but Indiana University accepted the graduates of those schools which the State Board of Education certified as standard schools. These arrangements proved so satisfactory to both the schools and the universities that they were adopted by other institutions; and within thirty years similar accrediting systems were accepted by about two hundred colleges and universities, chiefly in the newer states. The new plan did not relieve the schools from preparing their pupils in the specific subjects which were demanded by the particular college which they wished to enter. The scheme was otherwise unsatisfactory because both the required standards and the required subjects varied from state to state and the subjects often differed among neighboring colleges in the same state. To correct this condition and to develop a more uniform policy for secondary education, the Committee of Ten was appointed and later regional associations of colleges and secondary schools were created to perform the accrediting functions. The latter came to be known as standardizing associations.

10. THE COMMITTEE OF TEN

The Committee of Ten was appointed by the National Education Association in 1892 with Charles William Eliot as chairman, and it made its report the following year. In preparing its report it had the assistance of numerous subject committees. The Committee in its report agreed that college preparation is not the main function of secondary schools, but what was thus granted was again withdrawn by the declaration that the same subjects taught in the same way form the best preparation for both college and life. Each subject was to be considered equivalent to any other that was pursued successfully for the same length of time. But they set up sample curricula in which the academic subjects were strongly emphasized. And they urged that for purposes of "mental training" each major subject must be pursued for a considerable period of time. This would be desirable for the mastery of a field also but if each subject is to be studied thoroughly the number of subjects that any one pupil could take will be clearly limited. Such a program also, like that of the College Entrance Board, did not encourage high schools to experiment with nonpreparatory kinds of work and services. As if to counteract some of the effects of the previous recommendations, the Committee proposed to reduce the elementary school to a six-year program in order that foreign languages and high school mathematics and science could be begun earlier. They also favored some degree of subject election by high school pupils.

The work of the Committee of Ten seemed, at that time, to be much more important than it actually was. Even within the Committee there was disagreement, and a minority report was prepared by the dissenters. These demanded a larger place for the activity subjects, opposed the doctrine of the educational equivalence of different subjects even for college preparation, and demanded a very different selection of subjects for the ninety per cent of the pupils who would not go to college. There were similar disagreements among schoolmen at large and it was charged that the Committee had been overstaffed with college and private school teachers and executives. A study of the effect of the report of the Committee of Ten, made by Edwin G. Dexter about 1905, found that the expansion of the high school program of studies had been little affected. Indeed the report was immediately followed by a brief trial of the elective system in many high schools. The rising opposition in the country to the doctrine of formal discipline may have been another reason why the report had no greater influence. In fact this outcome was foreseen by Chairman Eliot who predicted that the American high school, as he expressed it, would "diverge from the academy and endowed school, the first working on an information programme, the latter on a training programme."

11. FORMAL DISCIPLINE CONTROVERSY

The doctrine of general mental discipline which the Committee of Ten accepted was widely held. In its broadest form this is the view that learning develops a general mental capacity which may be turned to any mental task, much as the sun's energy can be diverted to many kinds of work such as to cook a meal, to warm a house, or to light a city. When this general mental capacity is supposed to result from the form of a study, we call it formal discipline. The study of plane geometry was, in this sense, supposed to develop the power of deductive reasoning and the study of botany to cultivate power in classification. When skill acquired in one field, say telegraphy, is supposed to make it easier to acquire another skill such as typewriting, we call the mental process transfer of training. These terms, formal discipline and transfer of training, are not always used consistently but they always imply that acquired mental capacities spread to cases and situations in which there has been no, or little, practice. Such views were used to support an academic curriculum such as the Committee of Ten favored.

An attack was launched against this doctrine by the early Herbartians who returned from their study in Germany about the time when the report of the Committee of Ten appeared. The question was also raised in a notable address by B. A. Hinsdale before the National Education Association in 1894. And an inconclusive experiment to test the doctrine was reported by William James in his *Principles of Psychology* which appeared in 1890. Other experiments were made before 1901, the year when Woodworth and Thorndike reported a famous study which had given a few negative results and a larger number of cases of small positive transfer. At the moment it seemed to many that the idea of transfer of training would have to be given up altogether, but this was an error. It seems obvious as a matter of sense and experience that mental abilities have both a specific and a more general phase; that when a boy has learned to add he will be able to add numbers which he has never added before; and that when he has acquired a more general concept of number he will be able to add negative and positive numbers with little further training in addition.

Today, with many hundreds of experiments completed, we know that transfer does occur but there is not complete agreement upon the amounts nor any single explanation of the way in which it may be secured. In about ninety per cent of the experiments, positive transfer has been found, but it has usually been in small amounts ranging from almost zero to as much as twenty per cent of the improvement in the trained function or skill. It seems also that the amounts are greater with young and very intelligent pupils; that they are greater when the training materials and the testing materials are similar; and that the amount can be increased by teaching and studying for transfer. The pupil who searches for principles and generalizations will be able to make a broader application of his acquired knowledge and skill than one who does not. We no longer suppose that a skillful student of Latin, mathematics, or science is by such study fully prepared for every emergency of life and we do not base high school curricula upon a theory of easy and universal transfer of training; but neither does the wise teacher neglect to develop principles, draw comparisons, and find varied applications of the work of his pupils. President Eliot was mistaken in supposing that the high school will merely purvey information. The outcome of the formal discipline controversy has made teachers wiser in this matter than their predecessors.

12. THE STANDARDIZING ASSOCIATIONS

To secure greater uniformity in entrance requirements voluntary standardizing associations were formed in several sections of the United States, thus performing by agreement what in some countries was done by government dictation. The associations of colleges and secondary schools were usually formed at the instance of the colleges and were largely directed by them. The New England Association of Colleges and Preparatory Schools (1885) was the first, and it is significant that the term "preparatory" instead of secondary or high schools is used. Others were the Association of Colleges and Secondary Schools in the Middle States and Maryland (1892), the North Central (1894), the Southern (1895), the Northwest (1918), and the Western Association (1930). The associations in their meetings considered not only uniform entrance requirements but also means of improving secondary and collegiate education and of developing helpful relations between secondary and higher institutions.

The North Central Association in 1900 recommended that member colleges should admit only those students who had completed the equivalent of a four-year course of sixteen units, a unit being defined as "a year's work in a subject for four or five periods a week." Included in the sixteen units there were to be two units of English, two of mathematics, one of science, and one of history. The same idea was a little later accepted by the Carnegie Foundation for the Advancement of Teaching, hence the term "Carnegie units." The North Central and other associations undertook the inspection of schools. Those schools which upon inspection met the standards of their associations were accredited. As late as 1940 less than six thousand out of a total of about twenty-five thousand secondary schools in the whole United States had met the standards of their regional associations and had been accredited. The standards set up by the different associations varied among themselves so that although the North Central Association set the pattern and some standards were common there still were no uniform national standards of college admission. The recent cooperative study of secondary school evaluation and standards by these associations will be treated below.

A second mode of college admission, through uniform entrance examinations, was developed by the Association for the Middle States and Maryland from a suggestion by President F. A. P. Barnard of Columbia University; and this led to the formation of the College Entrance Board. This Board, established in 1901, soon became an independent body. Its examinations are held annually at several hundred points in the United States and in foreign countries. The Board has endeavored to bring about "an agreement upon a uniform standard as to each subject required" by the colleges as well as agreement upon methods of teaching and the desired preparation of secondary school teachers. It has obviously not tended to encourage high schools to experiment with new types of high school work and services.

13. THE JUNIOR HIGH SCHOOL

The reorganization of the schools into elementary and junior and senior high schools is often said to have begun in Columbus, Ohio, in 1908, and Berkeley, California, in 1909. And it was about that time when the idea began to attract attention; but the Committee of Ten had suggested it, the curriculum of the schools of Springfield, Massachusetts, in 1867 partly embodied it, and even the English Classical School of Boston in 1821 might be claimed as a junior high school. The Boston school was a separately organized, three-year high school which included the ages from twelve to fifteen and followed a shortened elementary school course; and it offered an enriched curriculum which was supposed to be adapted to young adolescents. Considering still further the date of origin, Thomas H. Briggs in his *The Junior High School* (1920) reports two junior high schools before 1900 and five others before 1909 but without giving the locations.

It is often supposed that we had a fairly universal 8–4 organization before the coming of the junior high school, but this, as we have seen, is an error. There were elementary school courses of six, seven, eight, and nine years, and high school courses of two, three, four, and five years as well as other course-lengths and almost every possible combination of these. More than one-fourth of the larger cities did not have an elementary school of eight years followed by a high school of four years. So much for the uniformity of our 8–4 plan; although widespread, it was not universal.

The arguments for the reorganization were numerous. Some of the committees of the National Education Association, such as the Committee on Economy of Time, urged a readjustment of the elementary curriculum to enable pupils to prepare for college at an earlier age. This result has not been achieved, for pupils still finish the junior-senior high schools at eighteen in most systems. Bright pupils in the upper grades of an eight-year elementary school, it was claimed, were merely marking time. This "sauntering," as John Locke called it, and the resulting habits of idleness, which the Boston subcommittee of 1821 deprecated, could be overcome by an enriched course. There were precedents for this. In European secondary schools and in good private schools, the pupils at the age of eighteen were one or two years ahead of most American children in their educational advancement. Some subjects such as foreign languages, algebra, and prevocational work should be begun earlier. Pupils above the sixth grade needed broader opportunities and differentiated curricula. This result has been attained in many schools.

The program of studies for youth, it was pointed out by Nicholas Murray Butler, should be based upon the nature and the stage of development of the pupils, and children between the ages of twelve and fifteen are in a transition stage between childhood and full adolescence. The program should be adapted to them. This is seemingly a reasonable proposal, but there are difficulties in settling upon the stage of child development which a given pupil has actually reached and in showing in practical terms how the curriculum may be adapted to the young adolescent. Pupils, it was said, would stay in school longer if the end of the compulsory attendance period, frequently at the age of fourteen, and the completion of the elementary school course did not come at the same time. Costs would be reduced, congestion in elementary schools relieved, and the junior high school would be located nearer to the homes of the pupils than the senior high school. The last was an important factor, for experience has shown that many more pupils will attend if schools are made more accessible. Perhaps the most frequently used argument was that the junior high school would help to bridge the gap between the elementary school and the departmentalized high school by providing exploratory courses, by giving more attention to the individual pupil, and by introducing departmentalization gradually.

The junior high school spread slowly after 1910 and more rapidly after 1920. Many grade combinations have been tried and are in use but the 6–3–3 and the 6–6 plans are the most common ones. The reorganization increased the enrollments, especially of boys, it retained pupils in school longer, and it has succeeded in furnishing more varied programs for young adolescents. Most of the large cities and many smaller and rural systems have adopted the new plan. But the factors that give vitality to the junior high school are appropriate methods, courses, equipment, and skillful teachers, not mere reorganization.

14. THE JUNIOR COLLEGE

About the time when the junior high school was developing, and even earlier, several junior colleges were established. These are institutions which offer two years of work or more above the senior high school and which, therefore, cover somewhat the same ground as the first two years of the university or college course. Some of these regard themselves as terminal schools and offer vocational as well as academic courses; others are preparatory to the upper division of a college. There were junior colleges before 1850 but as the result of a self-conscious movement the institution must be placed in the latter decades of the nineteenth century.

Two ideas were basic. The first was the idea that the university should not dissipate its strength in teaching the elementary subjects of the freshman and sophomore years, but should devote itself to advanced studies and graduate and professional work. This is, of course, the practice in Europe where the secondary schools do the work of the early college years in the United States, and where the university student begins at once to specialize if not in a narrow subject then at least in a field. President Henry P. Tappan of the University of Michigan in 1852 urged that institution to transfer its lower division work to the high schools. This was not done, but in 1883 the university began to differentiate the work of the first two from that of the last two years and to permit specialization in the upper division. Similar developments took place in Minnesota and elsewhere, but the first real separation of the two divisions was effected at the University of Chicago under President William Rainey Harper who is sometimes called the "father of the junior college."

The second idea was that many high school graduates who would not attend a college or university should have the opportunity to do one or more years of work beyond the high school. This they would do, it was evident, if local institutions for that purpose were available. President Harper fostered this idea and urged the stronger high schools to establish junior college departments. Such extensions of the work of the high school, though for preparatory purposes, were carried forward in Michigan where the state university began in 1895 to accept one year of college work from the better high schools of the state. In response to the proposals of President Harper, junior colleges in affiliation with the University of Chicago were opened in Joliet, Illinois, and Goshen, Indiana, and elsewhere. Long before this time also a few private academies and seminaries began to offer one or more years of college work; and some struggling four-year colleges reduced their offerings to two years of work. The latter process was especially common in Texas, Missouri, and the Old South. In 1907 the state of California passed a law to permit high schools to offer "postgraduate courses of study" for their own graduates or those of other high schools; and the city of Fresno in 1910 took advantage of this law to establish a public junior college. Many others have been opened in that state, and California is now the home of seventy-one such institutions, enrolling more than 300,000 students. In the entire country, over 600,000 students were enrolled in 1958 in 580 junior colleges. The great majority and the largest of them are public institutions. In facilities and staffs they resemble the high school more closely than a university and form an admirable bridge between them.

15. VOCATIONAL GUIDANCE

Schools took little interest in vocational guidance before 1900, and as an organized effort it began in 1908. The essential features are self-analysis, occupational knowledge, and expert advice both upon the choice of a vocation and upon the necessary preparation for entrance upon the work and for progress in it. The choice must be the student's, for vocational guidance is a democratic process. Finding jobs for people is not vocational guidance and still less is the mere assignment of people to jobs. Yet in many countries youth is given little freedom or consideration in the choice of suitable careers. It is significant that in Poland, Germany, Austria, Italy, and Rumania, instead of vocational guidance in the schools, the state has set up vocational bureaus or exchanges in the departments of labor. The purpose is to use the "human resources" to build up the economic and military strength of the nation rather than to enable individuals to find and prepare for satisfying careers. The greatest progress in true vocational guidance has been made in Great Britain, France, Switzerland, and the United States.

More than most movements, vocational guidance in the United States was the idea of one man, Frank H. Parsons (1854–1908), who organized the Boston Vocation Bureau in 1908. The financial support was provided by Pauline Agassiz Shaw, who had already subsidized the kindergarten and the manual training instruction of Boston. Paul H. Hanus of Harvard University served as chairman of the board of trustees and introduced courses in vocational guidance into the Harvard Summer School. Vocational counseling was introduced into the Boston schools in 1909, and this helped to launch the movement as a phase of public education. Even in this case, the originator, Parsons, had been anticipated by George A. Merrill, who had organized a manual training school in San Francisco, and by Eli W. Weaver, the principal of the Brooklyn Boys High School. But, while these men had provided counseling services, it was the work of Parsons that led to the spread of vocational guidance. The first city-wide organization was established in Grand Rapids (1912) where Jesse B. Davis, the principal of the high school, was the leader. A National Vocational Guidance Association was formed in 1913. In the first number of the *Vocational Guidance Bulletin* in 1916, the editor listed fourteen cities which had special vocational guidance officials. The depression of the thirties and the war that followed have emphasized the need for guidance, but it is still true that many high schools offer little or none and also give little postschool attention of any kind to those who graduate or those who drop out. Several states have passed vocational guidance laws.

The Federal Board of Vocational Education was in 1918 given the responsibility for a Rehabilitation Division of Disabled Soldiers, and two years later civilian rehabilitation was also assigned to it. The rehabilitation of disabled soldiers became one of the most significant achievements in education and guidance in any country. More than one hundred thousand men completed the training and were immediately placed in useful positions. The National Youth Administration (1935) had a section on vocational guidance. The American Youth Commission (1935) made an extremely important survey of youth and employment, upon which Howard M. Bell reported in *Youth Tell Their Story* (1938). The Commissioner of Education has ruled that funds appropriated under the Smith-Hughes and George-Deen Acts are available for vocational guidance; and a Chief of Occupational Information and Guidance Service has been added to the staff of the Office of Education. The Office has also published a great deal of vocational information.

The social outlook of vocational guidance is a key problem. Many counselors believe that they have obligations to society as well as to the advisee. Teachers, whether directly delegated to give vocational information and guidance or not, will need to study the movement and the work of their own schools. The time when guidance could be left to chance or wholly to an expert or a bureau is past. It is one of the main functions of a school to aid pupils in understanding not only vocations but social forces and especially economic ones. And the schools should also follow the careers of their pupils after graduation, records should be kept, and the schools should use their resources of knowledge and understanding of the pupils and of life to aid them in their early years as workers.

16. NEW GOALS AND FUNCTIONS

The present high school has developed far beyond the ideas of 1890 and in a direction that diverges more and more from the European concept of the secondary school as a selective institution for the preparation of an intellectual elite. By 1910 the high school had come to the smaller towns and the automobile was facilitating the building of strong rural high schools; the junior high school was developing; the program of studies was still growing; and a broader, more democratic, and more practical education was gaining in favor. These trends were supported by the departments and schools of education, by the land-grant colleges and state universities, and by the social-educational philosophies of Francis W. Parker and John Dewey.

A reformulation of high school objectives was made by the Commission on the Reorganization of Secondary Education which reported in 1918 under the title *Cardinal Principles of Secondary Education*. They decided that secondary education should be based upon the needs of society, the natures and capacities of the pupils, and professional knowledge of education. They pointed out that only one-third of the elementary pupils reached the high school and that of these only one in nine remained to graduate. They approved the junior high school and declared for the comprehensive senior high school rather than one specialized along technical, commercial, college preparatory, or other particular lines. They proposed the following as objectives: health, command of fundamental processes, worthy home membership, vocation, civic education, worthy use of leisure, and ethical character. As an aid toward the attainment of these aims, they proposed that the curricula should be composed of constants, to be taken by all, variables, and free electives. In language that is reminiscent of Condorcet they declared that in a democracy education "should develop in each individual the knowledge, interests, ideals, habits, and powers whereby he will find his place and use that place to shape both himself and society toward ever nobler ends." Whereas the Committee of Ten had made college preparation primary, the Commission in planning the work of the high school made preparation for life the primary purpose.

The Commission somewhat unaccountably did not call attention to the contemporary movement for the supervision of study in the high school. It had been noticed that high school pupils often did not know how to take notes on their reading, how to make a systematic outline, how to use the dictionary, or the encyclopedia, effectively. They were unable to translate problems into algebraic language or effectively to attack a passage for sight reading. In literature they did not sense the mood or the purpose of the writer. In a word they did not know how to study. It was now proposed that the teacher should teach not only in the class but also by supervised study.

Several plans were used. One was the unprepared lesson. This was a period set aside for the preparation of a detailed assignment with the help of the teacher. A second plan was that of the divided period, one-half of the usual class period being given to preparation and the rest to group consideration of the material. This had the advantage that it did not interfere with the established daily schedule. Still another plan used double periods, this longer space of time being used as in the divided period plan. If these plans, which were much used about 1920, helped to emphasize teaching instead of mere reciting and if they enabled pupils to become independent students able to work on their own account they must have been salutary.

Both vocational guidance and supervised study, as well as the Commission Report of 1918, are evidences and effects of the change that was taking place in secondary education. The vast increase in high school enrollments changed the composition of the student body and led to a transformation of the philosophy of high school education. In 1890 there had been less than three thousand schools and slightly over two hundred thousand pupils. The Commissioner of Education reported thirteen thousand, nine hundred and twenty-two schools of secondary grade for the year 1915, and eleven thousand, six hundred and seventy-four of these were public high schools enrolling one and one-third million pupils. In the quarter-century the high school enrollment, having doubled each decade, had increased to six times the 1890 figure. Whereas in earlier times only the best of the elementary pupils even considered attending a high school, now the least academic often enrolled. During the transition period from 1890 to about 1910, the schools still took the position that it was their first duty to uphold academic standards. If the pupils came ill prepared and if they did not succeed in the studies the high school offered, these facts merely showed that they should not have come to the high school at all. But the public now felt that the high school should serve their children, and taking them as they were, it should teach them what was best for them. School administrators, who were in direct contact with the public, and later the teachers also came to take this view, and thus the high school gradually became a higher common school for all adolescent children who presented themselves.

The program expansion continued and curricula were multiplied. In 1929 the Commissioner of Education reported that the high schools of the country were offering two hundred fifty subjects or branches of subjects. The nomenclature and the makeup of the curricula varied, but the most frequently offered were the college or technical school preparatory, the commercial, the general, the industrial arts, and the household arts. Other less frequently offered curricula were named the English, modern languages, fine arts, music, and agriculture curricula. The practice of free election had disappeared, but a similar result was secured by allowing many substitutions and by counting subjects of the most diverse character as equivalent in educational value. Social demands and administrative considerations had driven the old and really vital question of educational values into the background. Extracurricular activities had secured a strong position in the school if not always in the formal program.

Extracurricular activities have sometimes been considered as mere diversions, the froth of student life. On the other hand there is a tendency to give them an increasing part in the work of the school, and in some ultraprogressive schools student-directed activities are tending to displace the formal curriculum. The problem everywhere is to make all activities, whether work or study or play, serve valid educational purposes.

School athletics and student government are two forms of extracurricular activities that have a long history. Vittorino incorporated games and physical exercises in his fifteenth-century school. Sports have formed a part of English upper class education from early times. In his school in Silesia, in the sixteenth century, Trotzendorf developed a school republic so that boys by learning to administer and obey laws of their own making might later rule and serve according to law. More elaborate forms of student government were found, early in the nineteenth century, in the Hazelwood School in England, in Froebel's school at Keilhau, and in Fellenberg's school at Hofwyl, examples which may have been due to the rise of political democracy in Europe and America. More or less highly developed forms of student government have been widely introduced in more recent times. Literary societies, debating, public speaking, and dramatics were early cultivated in the schools of many countries. Comenius tried, though unsuccessfully, to embody a whole curriculum in dramatic form.

High schools do much in promoting and guiding extracurricular activities, and teachers who are especially prepared to direct athletics, dramatics, musical organizations, and debating are often employed. The school assembly, which was formerly given over to speeches by the principal and teachers, or to persons brought in from outside the school, is now often conducted by the students themselves and sometimes involves active participation by the audience. Clubs, which take a great variety of forms, and social events are fostered. School authorities often frown upon the secret societies which creep into many high schools in imitation of the Greek-letter fraternities of the colleges and try to ban or regulate them. State laws have sometimes been invoked against them. Many activities, which were formerly considered outside the curriculum, have now been incorporated with it and almost all if skillfully directed may be used to support educational purposes. The greatest significance of these interests comes from the fact that they are the concerns of the pupils themselves, voluntary expressions of their desire to lead, to cooperate, and to create.

17. RECENT TRENDS

The responsibility of the high school principals to their pupils and communities frequently impressed them with the need for more power to resist unwholesome local interference; and, on the other hand, the old question of high school-college relations, which in spite of many efforts had never been settled to the satisfaction of the principals, was becoming more rather than less irritating as the high schools became stronger. These two conditions were the chief reasons for the formation in 1917 of the National Association of Secondary School Principals. How urgent the latter problem seemed may be gathered from the proposal of one of the founders who said: "I believe in the principle of inspection so firmly that I would extend it even to the inspection of the colleges by the high schools. The colleges inspect us to see whether our product is good enough for them to work with. Now let us inspect the colleges to see whether they are good enough to have the care and direction of our boys and girls." And Jesse B. Davis, a past president of the Association, in a review of its history declared: "Twenty-five years ago the National Association of Secondary School Principals was conceived in rebellion." The rebellion began in the Middle West where the high school was most powerful.

One would expect to find extended consideration of high school-college relations in the meetings of the Association, but this did not happen. Instead they were practically ignored and the Principals' Association dealt instead with problems of organization and administration, with the curriculum, student government, extracurricular activities, teaching problems, ability grouping, educational and vocational guidance, character development, the junior high school and junior college, and the function of education in a democracy. Although it may have been "conceived in rebellion," what really interested the Association was the question how the high school may best function as a higher common school. One of its important achievements has been the creation of a National Honor Society of high school students for the encouragement of character development, leadership, scholarship, and service.

An important study was made by the Association through its Committee on the Orientation of Secondary Education of which Thomas H. Briggs was chairman. The Committee began its work in 1932 and made its final report in 1935 during the tercentenary celebration of the founding of secondary education in the United States. The summary of the Committee's findings is embodied in the ten "issues" and ten "functions" of secondary education which they formulated. These were submitted to forums of schoolmen throughout the country for consideration and application. The functions are statements of the main tasks of secondary schools, a new and more elaborate set of "cardinal principles." Only once do they even by implication recognize that the high schools are preparing some of their students for college.

The ten "issues" on the other hand raise a whole series of questions, some of which the trend of our history for more than forty years has been answering. Whether public secondary education shall be given to all youth or only to some, whether it shall work for the welfare of both society and the individual, whether it shall provide differentiated curricula, whether it may offer vocational education, whether it shall be concerned only with knowledge or also with attitudes, whether it has a distinct field of its own

—these are hardly issues any longer. The answers which the history of the high school has given to these questions are hardly any longer in doubt. But they have certainly not yet been universally accepted and they may need modification in the future. The purpose of the formulation was doubtless to have them critically examined, especially by those of the profession who had not already accepted them.

The ninth issue asked: "Shall secondary education seek merely the adjustment of students to prevailing social ideals, or shall it seek the reconstruction of society?" Clearly all education, even if it does not intend it, actually does something to reconstruct society. But asked, as it was, during the economic depression, this question was doubtless intended to raise the alternative between the current economic system and some degree of greater social control. In this sense it was a living issue. The seventh "issue" will serve as a transition to our next topic. It contrasted the usual organization of secondary school work under the conventional subjects with a proposed organization into "functional" topics or fields such as the social-civic, the economic, the vocational, and other large interests. This was also a central issue in the "Thirty Schools Experiment" of the Progressive Education Association.

The Progressive Education Association was formed in 1918 to work for the improvement of both elementary and secondary education; and in 1930 it appointed a Commission on the Relation of School and College. The main question which it was to answer was significantly framed thus: "What would secondary schools do if they were completely freed from all detailed college entrance requirements?" Accordingly, several hundred colleges were pledged to accept the graduates of the selected schools on their records without special examinations, and without demanding the usual work in specified academic subjects. The schools were set free to teach those materials and in those ways which they considered best for the development of boys and girls, whether they intended to go to college or not. Several University High Schools and many private schools participated, and some of these usually sent eighty or ninety per cent of their graduates to college. But the public high schools of Tulsa, Denver, Des Moines, and Altoona were also included. Several of the schools were known as "progressive," but not all aspired to that designation and some were fairly "conventional." It is best to say simply that about thirty schools and systems of mixed character were set free to try what their staffs, students, and clientele wished to attempt.

The "experiment" began in 1933 and continued for eight years until 1941. It touched upon practically all phases of secondary school work, but curriculum reorganization was particularly involved. Curriculum study was not new. It had been carried on in American high schools for more than a decade before 1930 and less intensively for fifty years. Many methods of study had been tried: analyses of textbooks, of educational aims, and of life needs, job analysis, studies of the interests and capacities of youth, and comparative measures of school achievement. The chief difficulty was not in getting facts about youth, life, and the school but in finding any generally accepted principles which could be scientifically applied.

The Thirty Schools tried out a variety of nonsubject curriculum organizations. These might be named the fluid or experimental, the contemporary problems, the unified studies, and the cultural period curricula. The experimental curriculum is made cooperatively by pupils and teachers from day to day and is changed and redirected as the work is going forward. It contains little previously organized subject matter, no formal lessons, and no set recitations. This resembles the practice of the Dewey Experimental School at Chicago.

The contemporary problems curriculum deals with a living issue. The question of "housing" would be an example of somewhat restricted scope, while "a planned society" would be one of very wide scope. Any such problem will be studied from many standpoints. A study of the home would have to cover family income, housing, home equipment, food, servants, child care, personal relations, reading materials, and other topics. Usually several teachers cooperate in developing such a "core" curriculum. This is also done in teaching a unified studies curriculum in which several subjects such as English and the social studies, or mathematics, the sciences, and the industrial arts may be combined into a single field of study. The cultural period curriculum finds its "core" in some epoch or race such as ancient Greece, the Arabs, or Anglo-Saxon civilization. All phases of the period or culture are studied such as the art, politics, literature, science, work, and commerce of the Greeks, for example; and the purpose is to understand the life of today by the comparative and philosophical study of an epoch upon which somewhat definitive verdicts have been pronounced, as they cannot be in the case of contemporary civilization.

The students who entered college from the Thirty Schools made records that were a little better than those made by equally able students from other schools. They excelled their paired competitors somewhat more in extracurricular and social activities. The methods used in pairing students have been questioned. And one is surprised that the differences were comparatively small when the students from the Thirty Schools had the advantages of a particularly stimulating school environment and excellent teaching. Perhaps college success while significant is after all a crude measure of the value of the preparatory work. Given the required mental caliber, it seems that anyone who has studied earnestly in either a progressive or a conventional secondary school can succeed in college. We should now have a careful study of the success in college of students from small and substandard high schools. Do they also do acceptable college work?

In a little more than a century the high school has become more widely distributed and accessible than the elementary school was in 1830. It has also become more firmly entrenched in the good will of the people than the common school was at that time, but this acceptance was not easily won. The colleges, the private schools and their partisans, the business world, and the general public have kept up a fairly continuous fire of criticism. In no period of its evolution has it been free from attack, but it continued to flourish because it continued to give youth opportunities which no other country had provided in equal measure and which we could provide by no other means that were proposed.

The vitality of the high school is shown by its ability to profit from criticism and to adapt itself to changing demands. Again and again it has taken over the work of private schools and incorporated their services in its own program. When manual training was developing under private auspices, it was quickly adopted by the public school. When an aggregation of business colleges spread throughout the country, the high school established commercial courses. When laboratory science teaching, agriculture, home economics, music, and physical education programs developed, the high school adopted them. When the need for social education, student activities, and guidance came to be seen, the high school incorporated them in its program. But it is only the large and well-equipped school which can perform all these and other functions of a comprehensive high school, and many American high schools are small and are compelled to do the best they can do with their limited resources.

The high school has developed as a public school, a local school, and a day school. These three are among the most obvious and also most important of its institutional characteristics. It is a local, day, and not a state or national boarding school because it is intended to serve the great body of the people who cannot send their children away from home for purposes of education. It must, therefore, be located close to the homes of the children. As a result of this wide distribution many high schools are small schools. How small they are may be shown by a few figures. Three-fourths of all the schools are located in towns of twenty-five hundred people or less or in the open country. A few states are closing the very small schools, but many of the remaining schools have an enrollment of less than one hundred pupils, and another twenty per cent have between one hundred and two hundred pupils. A very large proportion of the smallest schools are not accredited by their regional standardizing associations. President Conant's judgment on these may be seen in his report of 1959 (see bibliography). The present condition of a school may be, in the long run, less important than the vigor and intelligence with which it is going forward and trying to improve its work. It was this view which led the standardizing associations to seek better ways of stimulating high school improvement.

The Cooperative Study of Secondary School Standards was carried out by a committee which began as early as 1928; but the study was formally begun in 1934. The committee was aided by advisory members from the American Council on Education and other bodies, and the study was jointly financed by the associations themselves and the General Education Board. Dissatisfaction with the rigid and mechanical standards that had come into use had been felt for some time. These standards usually covered such points as the amount of preparation which teachers had received, teacher loads, finances, the number of books in the school library, and laboratory and athletic equipment. The purpose of the study was to discover the characteristics of a good school, the best means of evaluating these, and the best methods by which a school can be stimulated to improve.

By a process of formulating evaluative criteria, trying these experimentally in a number of schools, and criticizing and reformulating them in the light of the experience gained, a definitive scheme for the cooperative evaluation of secondary schools by the staff and with the help of external committees was perfected by 1940. The scheme of evaluation uses both judgments made by teachers and competent investigators, and objective measures obtained from the use of tests and scales. More than a dozen phases of the school and its work are covered in a complete evaluation, and a definite program for improvement is the finest result. Among the phases covered are the school's philosophy of education, the pupils and the community, the program and courses of study, pupil activities, the library and its use, guidance, instruction, the staff, the plant, and the administration of the school, and also the outcomes of the school's work. Evidently a survey of a high school made on these broad bases will be more qualitative than an inspection which uses the older quantitative standards; and since the evaluations are made cooperatively by teachers, administrators, and outside experts, they serve an important purpose as means for the professional re-education of the staff and the improvement of the work and services of the schools. The stimulus which such an evaluation can give may be far more valuable than its standardizing function.

18. POSSIBLE FUTURE DEVELOPMENT

Current social conditions are certain to influence all education and especially secondary education. World War I, the centralizing tendencies in government, the depression that followed the business collapse of 1929, and World War II which began just ten years later are among the most ominous of these events and conditions. Some effects are already evident. There were in 1940 about seven million pupils in the high schools and about half as many adolescents in the country who had not yet been reached. The hope of providing secondary education for all the children of a great nation has long been considered chimerical by European and some American skeptics; and autocrats have even considered it highly undesirable. Present and imminent financial stringencies will make it more difficult. It is certain that to achieve such a goal we must accept it as a goal and must work to attain it.

There is today a deep concern that youth shall be better prepared to deal effectively with questions of public policy and the problems of democracy. It is altogether probable that foreign policy will in the future occupy the people more and more. Social studies have long been emphasized in the high school and in college. Almost one-third of the college students whose records were examined in the Thirty Schools experiment specialized in these fields while the next most popular fields of English and of the physical and mathematical sciences each attracted less than one-half as many. But while the social studies are popular, there is great disagreement on what should be taught in this field and how it should be taught. There are still those who think that the schools should "teach the facts" and the "known truth" of history and economics, avoiding controversial questions; others who would indoctrinate the pupils in what they regard as the best answers; and also a third class who doubt whether high school students can think to any purpose about such issues as the tariff, sovereignty, and the relations of capital and labor. But if young people by the age of eighteen, when they have been in school for twelve years, do not have the knowledge and training to deal with public questions, then it is hard to see where and how they will be equipped to perform the duties of citizens in a democracy. This applies particularly to that large group whose schooling ends with high school graduation. The Social Studies Investigation which was sponsored by the American Historical Association between the years of 1929 and 1933, the *Fourteenth Yearbook* (1936) of the Department of Superintendence, and a whole library of volumes by individual authors have dealt with this problem. While no final solution has been found or will probably be found, it is reasonable to hope that the teaching of the social studies is becoming more effective in developing political and economic understanding among high school students. This is certainly an urgent need. The high school must learn to teach democracy by democratic processes. As one phase of this task it must establish closer contact with its local community; and as another phase it must teach its pupils to read, to handle evidence, and to think independently.

Thirty-five years ago, as we have seen, there was a vigorous supervised study movement, but it did not fully achieve its main object which was simply to teach children to read and to think. That task must be continued more vigorously, intelligently, and persistently; and it is not a question of double periods or divided periods or other forms of organization but of stimulation and effective teaching. Reading is not a simple, mechanical skill but a series of highly complex skills which become progressively more difficult as the topics studied become broader, more technical, and more controversial. The high school of the future will teach reading in every year and every field by helping children to make use of the knowledge and the ideas which they gain in solving real and urgent problems. The high school teacher of the future will use the recent studies of the psychology of reading which have thrown much light upon the processes which are involved.

The depression of the thirties taught us much about the sad dilemma in which youth in an industrial society find themselves in such a period. The high school of the future will give more attention to vocational guidance and to vocational education. It is not enough to give courses which describe occupations and to supply occupational guidance through counselors. The school must provide work experience in school and community. It must teach working skills and attitudes, both as bases for the choice of an occupation and preparation for the pursuit of the occupation that is finally selected.

In these and other ways the high school of the future must be closely related to its community if it is to be effective in teaching citizenship, vocations, and economic cooperation. It must use the educative resources of its community more fully than it has done. And it must also aid the continuing education of the parents and other adults of its locality and serve as an effective agency for the improvement of community life. Taking advantage of these and other opportunities to serve, the high school as a still young and adaptable institution has before it the promise of extended development and usefulness.

The high school is our third effort to develop a serviceable secondary school. It followed the Latin school and academy. It is a public secondary school, closely articulated with the elementary school and offering a general course to practically all adolescents who wish to attend. Generally, the high school was an upward extension of the graded elementary school, but some early high schools were transformed academies. The high schools, early in their evolution, became college preparatory as well as terminal schools. College preparation tended to make them selective; and the effort to serve the community as a terminal school made them comprehensive and coeducational. The cost of the new schools, their selective character, and the vested interests of the academy were the occasion for strong opposition to high school expansion. After about 1880 or 1890 the schools gradually broadened their programs and began to serve a widening constituency; and the public in turn began to defend and support them more heartily.

The program of studies was expanded first along academic lines; then vocational and skill studies, and last extracurricular activities were added. Except for bookkeeping and surveying which were taught in the early high schools, the vocational courses did not develop until late in the century and vocational guidance began about the period of World War I. The junior high school movement developed at the same time. The public junior college, which has also shown its most rapid growth in recent decades, provides a favorable opportunity for educational expansion.

High school principals long felt that their schools were tightly wedged in between the elementary schools which directed the children for eight years and the colleges which restricted the high school program through their entrance requirements. By developing the junior high school below the tenth grade and securing a very considerable degree of freedom from college control, the high school has carved out an area of secondary education that is reasonably free from external domination. But a public demand for greater emphasis upon and better work in languages and science is now exerting great pressure upon them. Through the National Association of Secondary School Principals, the "Briggs Committee," the Thirty Schools experiment, the standardizing associations, and the leadership of state departments of education, the high school has attempted to decide upon a progressive plan for future operations. The task of the high school and junior college will be to provide solid foundations in language, mathematics, science, and social understanding, to give effective vocational preparation and guidance, to establish the character and physical and mental health of its pupils, and to prepare them to deal effectively with questions of public policy and problems of democracy, including world democracy. To do this, or any large part of it, is a challenging task for the high schools of today and tomorrow.

QUESTIONS

1.   What are the ten most essential characteristics, such for example as co-education or public control, of the high school?
2.   Study a number of these characteristics to determine why and how they developed. In this process it is useful to compare the American with some foreign secondary schools.
3.   Why may the graded school be regarded as a necessary preliminary to the high school? Why not also to the academy and the Latin grammar school?
4.   Why did the high school develop more rapidly after the Civil War than before?
5.   Why did the country decide in favor of the comprehensive rather than the specialized high school? Find as many examples as possible of specialized high schools and why they were created and still survive.
6.   Did the high schools reap any benefits from "college domination"?
7.   Compare the meaning of the terms: manual training, industrial arts, vocational education, technical education.

8. How could high schools serve their clientele better by keeping in touch with their graduates? Would you include the "drop-outs" in your proposals?

9. What are the advantages and disadvantages of voluntary accrediting and standardizing schemes as compared with governmental ones?

10. How well has the junior high school fulfilled the claims made for it in the reorganization period?

11. "Shall secondary education seek merely the adjustment of students to prevailing social ideals, or shall it seek the reconstruction of society?" This is the ninth of the Briggs Committee "issues."

12. Shall the high school abandon the ordinary subjects and institute core curricula and "functional" studies? What is "functional" education?

13. What conclusions may be drawn from the Thirty Schools experiment? Do all of your fellow-students agree with your summary of the results?

14. Analyze the conditions and services of the high school that you attended; and show how its work could be improved. Your proposals must be practicable and not mere dreams.

FOR FURTHER READING AND STUDY

Numerous articles dealing with the development of the academy and the high school have appeared in leading educational journals including Barnard's *American Journal of Education,* the *Educational Review,* and the *School Review.* Only slight hints can be given here of the variety of these materials. Volume Nineteen of Barnard has a table showing the frequency of fifty-nine subjects in the curricula of thirty high schools about 1867 (p. 463); and a section dealing more fully with the curricula themselves (pp. 465–576). The *Educational Review* and the *School Review* carried numerous articles on the work of the Committee of Ten between the years 1893 and 1895. Special attention is due to an article on this topic in the former journal for December, 1896, and another in the latter journal for April, 1906. A few other articles of special importance are included below.

Briggs, Thomas H., *The Junior High School,* Boston, Houghton Mifflin Company, 1920, 350 pp.; *The Great Investment, Secondary Education in a Democracy,* Cambridge, Mass., Harvard University Press, 1930, 143 pp. The latter volume is the Inglis lecture for 1930.

Broome, Edwin C., *A Historical and Critical Discussion of College Admission Requirements,* New York, The Macmillan Company, 1903, 157 pp.

Brown, Elmer Ellsworth, *The Making of Our Middle Schools,* New York, Longmans, Green and Company, 1901, 547 pp. First published in the *School Review* between 1897 and its appearance as a book. Frequently reissued in later years but not revised.

Burrell, B. Jeannette, and R. H. Eckelberry, "The American High School Question before the Courts during the Post-Civil-War Period," *School Review,* 42:255–265 (April, 1934); 333–348 (May, 1934). The second instal-

ment has a bibliography; "The Free Public High School in the Post-Civil-
War Period," same journal and volume, 606–614 (Oct., 1934); 667–675
(Nov., 1934), with bibliography.

College Entrance Examination Board, *The Work of the College Entrance Examination Board*, 1901–1925, Boston, Ginn and Company, 1926, 300 pp.

Committee of Ten, *Report*, Published for the National Education Association, New York, American Book Company, 1894, 249 pp.

Conant, James B., *The American High School Today, A First Report to Interested Citizens*, New York, McGraw-Hill Book Company, [1959], 140 pp.

Counts, George S., *Selective Character of American Secondary Education*, Chicago, The University of Chicago, 1922, 162 pp.; *The Senior High School Curriculum*, Chicago, The University of Chicago Press, 1926, 160 pp.; *Secondary Education and Industrialism*, Cambridge, Mass., Harvard University Press, 1929, 70 pp. This title is the Inglis lecture for 1929.

Douglas, C. H., "The Status of the High School in New England," *Educational Review*, 5:27–34 (Jan., 1893).

Edmonds, Franklin Spencer, *History of the Central High School of Philadelphia*, Philadelphia, J. B. Lippincott Company, 1902, 394 pp.

Edwards, Newton, *Equal Educational Opportunity for Youth: A National Responsibility*, Washington, D. C., American Youth Commission, 1939, 189 pp.

Fine, Benjamin, *Admission to American Colleges, a Study of Current Policy and Practice*, New York, Harper and Brothers, [1946], 225 pp.

Gaumitz, Walter H., *The Smallness of America's Rural High Schools*, Washington, D. C., Government Printing Office, 1930, 78 pp., Bureau of Education Bulletin, 1930, No. 13.

Gifford, Walter J., *Historical Development of the New York State High School System*, Albany, J. B. Lyon Co., 1922, 202 pp.

Grizzell, Everet Duncan, *Origin and Development of the High School in New England before 1865*, New York, The Macmillan Company, 1923, 428 pp.

Hillway, Tyrus, *The American Two-Year College*, New York, Harper and Brothers, 1958, 276 pp.

Inglis, Alexander J., *The Rise of the High School in Massachusetts*, New York, Teachers College, Columbia University, 1911, 166 pp. Contributions to Education, No. 45; *Principles of Secondary Education*, Boston, Houghton Mifflin Company, 1918, 741 pp. Chapter V of the latter volume deals with the history of secondary education in the United States, and Chapter VI with that of foreign countries.

Kandel, Isaac L., *History of Secondary Education*, Boston, Houghton Mifflin Company, 1930, 577 pp.; *The Dilemma of Democracy*, Cambridge, Mass., Harvard University Press, 1934, 79 pp. The first title deals with Europe and the United States, the second is the Inglis lecture for 1934.

Miller, George Frederick, "The Academy System of New York," *Fifteenth Annual Report* of the New York State Department of Education, Vol. II, 76–246, Albany, New York State Department of Education, 1922.

Mulhern, James, *A History of Secondary Education in Pennsylvania*, Philadelphia, Published by the Author, 1933, 714 pp.

Spaulding, Francis T., O. I. Frederick, and Leonard V. Koos, *The Reorganization of Secondary Education*, Washington, D. C., Government Printing Office, 1932, 423 pp., Bureau of Education Bulletin, 1932, No. 17, and Monograph No. 5 of the National Survey of Secondary Education.

Stout, John E., *The Development of High School Curricula in the North Central States, 1860–1918*, Chicago, The University of Chicago Press, 1921, 322 pp.

Stuart, Milo H., *Organization of a Comprehensive High School*, New York, The Macmillan Company, 1926, 127 pp.

Wharton, G. W., "High School Architecture in the City of New York," *School Review*, 11:456–483 (June, 1903). An illustrated article. Public high schools in old New York proper were first established in 1897.

Woody, Thomas, *A History of Women's Education in the United States*, Lancaster, Pa., The Science Press, 1929, 2 vols.

21 WAR AND PEACE

MEN, WOMEN, AND CHILDREN OF ALL AGES AND CONDITIONS suffer in the violence and chaos of war. The children suffer most because they are robbed of nearly the whole of life and of the opportunity to work in building a world of order under law. War destroys the means of learning. Libraries, laboratories, shops, and whole cities are reduced to rubble, and treasures are destroyed that can never be replaced. The world will forever be the poorer because a bomb was dropped in a given place. War scatters teachers and pupils, damages bodies and morals, and destroys the peace of mind needed for fruitful study. It is not news that the educational devastation of World War II is a part of the history of our time. Since the young cannot delay their education until times improve, the war losses set for nations some of their most urgent tasks.

We shall not deny that war can also stimulate educational reform or at least can drive nations to give effect to improvements already planned. This was the result in England and, in a smaller degree, in France. We shall describe the changes in those two countries. In Germany conditions and results were different. Twice in one generation the Western democracies and Russia have combined to defeat Germany, and after a period of punishment the West, at least, has helped to build her up again. It is a wasteful process. Education and re-education in a divided and occupied Germany will be treated in this chapter.

Troubled minds are among the most unyielding of the evils caused by war, but measures have been taken to restore hope and opportunity to survivors who were defrauded of them. Education has two further postwar tasks: to prepare the young for participation in the new industrial and political sphere, and to educate them for the preservation of the peace by building a world of order under law. This is peace; and the framing of such an order is its price.

1. EDUCATION AND WORLD WAR II

The Germans found it much more difficult to Nazify the people of their conquered countries than they had expected. The people and the teachers of Norway formed a brilliant example of refusal to take orders from the enemy. The Quisling government on February 8, 1942, promulgated a law requiring all teachers to join a new teachers' association that was specially designed to promote Nazi principles. Dismissal from their positions was to be the penalty for refusal to join. Twelve thousand of the fourteen thousand teachers of Norway refused, and within two months two thousand of them had been put into concentration camps. Five hundred were deported to the shores of the Arctic Ocean. From time to time school strikes broke out in Oslo and elsewhere. Children refused to take German as their foreign language and elected English instead. The Norwegian Church supported the teachers and pupils in their opposition to the foreign invaders (Höye, Bjarne, and Trygve M. Ager, *The Fight of the Norwegian Church against Nazism*, New York, The Macmillan Company, 1943, 180 pp.). After continued failure to secure a pliant teaching staff, the Nazis (1942) closed the schools on the grounds of a fuel shortage. They actually closed them because of the resistance of the population. There were some native collaborators in Norway and others in the coastal countries of Denmark, Holland, and Belgium. France had its Vichy government but also a vast resistance movement. In these countries the Germans frequently resorted to the abduction of children from the streets and then shipped them to Germany to be converted into Hitler Youth. In the words of Professor Walter Kotschnig, the Nazis held that "slaves need no leaders"; and they intended not to leave any among their subject peoples.

When the bombing raids over Great Britain developed, both England and Scotland devised plans to evacuate school children, teachers, and also mothers with infants from London, Glasgow, and other large cities. The movement was voluntary, but large numbers from the poorest sections of the towns streamed into villages and country districts. In this way the "two nations" of which Disraeli spoke came face to face with each other. The meeting was not always a mutually agreeable one. Many people were shocked to find that some of the slum children brought with them vermin, bad manners, and the speech and morals of the street.

City schools and homes had, meanwhile, in some cases been bombed. Other schools had been taken over for war purposes, and the available school buildings became overcrowded when the children drifted back, as they soon did. Many of the returning children simply returned to the streets. The problem of the waifs plagued England and all the war-torn countries. The authorities tried to provide schools, and they set up hostels for troublesome youngsters. Youth benefits which had been started in the nineteenth century were expanded. Health inspection, medical and dental care, play facilities, and food for the hungry and underfed were supplied through the schools.

On the Continent also there were large-scale evacuations toward the East and away from the cities and military installations. Food was often hard to obtain and the evacuees' diet was lacking in milk and other sources of calcium. As the war developed, many of such ordinary necessities of life, as fuel, soap, shelter, and medicines, became scarce. People, and especially children, became more subject to infectious diseases. In 1945 the children of France were on the average three and a half inches shorter and weighed ten pounds less than the comparable young people of 1939. Before the war ended and as the Russian armies approached, many thousands of those who had fled eastward came back and escaped into western Germany. These and the constant stream of those who continue to escape from Communist countries have burdened West Germany with vast numbers of displaced persons. In these and many other ways the children of Britain and the Continent have been deprived of what in a peaceful world would have been considered the normal opportunities of youth.

From the reminders of war's effects we turn to the program of some French leaders for the reform of the education of youth.

2. FRENCH EXPERIMENTS

Recent French educational experiments have concerned the secondary schools and vocational education chiefly. These are the phases of the French system which, as we saw in Chapter 13, have been long and severely criticized. They are indeed two of the phases of education that have been vigorously attacked in many countries. In France the *Compagnons de l' Université Nouvelle*, which came after and in part out of World War I, were the active proponents of free secondary education. They worked also for orientation classes in the early years of the secondary programs. These classes have aims that parallel some of the purposes of the American junior high school: to study the capacities and interests of individual pupils, to introduce more modern studies, and to provide educational guidance.

After the recommendations of the Commission for Educational Reform (1944) failed to win general approval, the government appointed a new Commission headed by Paul Langevin, a famous physicist, and Henri Wallon, an eminent psychologist, with other noted scholars as members, to bring in a new report. This, the Langevin plan, was published in 1947. It proposed raising the leaving age to eighteen. The educational system was to consist of three cycles: basic cycle, ages six to eleven; orientation cycle, eleven to fifteen; and determination cycle, fifteen to eighteen. Americans would call the third cycle the period of specialization. Economically, the most ambitious part of this proposal was the raising of the leaving age for all children to eighteen years; and the three-year orientation cycle was the most striking educational innovation.

The plan included new proposals for the preparation of teachers. Elementary teachers were to complete a secondary school course and two years of pedagogical study. More active teaching methods were recommended, and all external examinations were to be postponed to the end of the secondary school course—a radical change from practice. The Commission was able to agree upon the content of the syllabus for moral-civic education—an achievement. Adult education was to reach out to the villages and farms.

The Langevin plan implied that too many had been excluded too long from proper educational opportunity. In the opinion of the Commission, other forms of education, such as technological studies, were as good for their own purposes as the classics and were equally necessary in modern society. The plan may have threatened the social prestige of the classicists who form a large part of the educated public in France; and the plan, if adopted and fully carried out, would have tended to erase the line between those who read Euripides and those who build steel and concrete bridges. This thought was not acceptable to educational conservatives, and they launched a vigorous attack against the whole program. Across the Channel the papers reported that the Langevin reforms were tabled and spoke of them as being "ambitious" (*Times Educational Supplement*, London, November 15, 1947, p. 613). We shall see that the supporters of the English grammar schools were similarly exercised over the new views and provisions on secondary education in the Hadow Report and the Education Act of 1944.

Although the Langevin plan was not adopted, it was not without influence. Many of its proposals were not new, but it was of value because it gave the support of distinguished men to previous demands for improvements. The violence of the attacks upon it showed that it was gaining support.

The new trends which received most support were (1) the extension of the opportunity for secondary school education to pupils from the primary schools; (2) the improvement of teaching in secondary schools; and (3) the introduction of technical education on the secondary school level. After World War II the urban higher primary schools, mentioned on page 300, were transformed into modern secondary schools, *collèges modernes*, parallel to the *collèges classiques*. In theory this change enables a child of thirteen who has taken only the common school subjects to complete a secondary school course in modern languages, the sciences, and technical studies. Even village schools with only the one-year extension known as the cours complémentaire, instead of the higher primary school, can fit a pupil for transfer at age fourteen to a neighboring collège moderne where he can complete a secondary school course. The new collèges have been taken out of primary school administration and added to that of the secondary schools.

The second improvement was a reform in teaching and the internal administration of secondary schools. It will be necessary to say that in France there has been much complaint of overpressure in the secondary schools. Children in some lycées are in school nine hours a day and as many as forty-eight hours a week; and they do a great deal of homework. The teachers are officially given the title of professeur; and most of the teaching is done by means of lectures. The teachers have no out-of-class duties and few face-to-face meetings with the students. Examinations are difficult, and many pupils fail. It is perhaps not necessary to say that the teachers have had no training in child study, or psychology. The effort to improve these conditions is carried out in what are known as classes nouvelles, new classes.

The new classes are the outgrowth of a movement that began before World War II. The Ministry of Education began in 1937 to promote the use of school exercises and activity methods, including some slight elements of pupil self-government, and to advise the correlation of subjects such as history, literature, and geography. "Centers of interest" with projects are used. "Forests" might be one such center from which the work would go out toward biology, art, industry, and other topics. The classes were limited to twenty-five pupils. A school psychologist equipped with tests and interview charts made a study of the aptitudes and progress of each pupil. The experiment was started in the first year of the secondary school course and was moved up one year at a time for four years. The three upper classes were left untouched. The Ministry was careful from the first not to let this experiment get out of hand. The number of new classes was limited to eight hundred; and in recent years the program has been much diluted. It is doubtful that there will be further progress for some time.

The proposal to teach psychology and education to those preparing for secondary school positions has not been carried out. Educational guidance has been introduced into some of the lycées, and there are school psychologists in Paris and other cities to investigate cases of maladjustment among pupils. There are ways of enlisting the cooperation of the parents when their children do not do well at school. Vocational guidance is in the hands of the state, which requires tests and an interview before a child is assigned to a center of apprenticeship or given a job. Educational guidance was demanded by the Langevin Commission, but in the land of Rousseau and Binet it is not yet well developed.

The promotion of technical education is the third of the postwar movements. There are two phases, the creating of *collèges techniques* and the development of centers of apprenticeship. The former has made great progress, and apprenticeship was expanded in the rearmament effort of the thirties. The centers embody plans very similar to the scheme introduced into Munich by Georg Kerschensteiner. According to the scheme, the young person spends a part of his time on a job, a part in school, and the rest in whatever way he pleases. Boys and girls may choose any available trade. Some learn the fundamentals of several trades and become capable of independent work in one. This provides insurance against trade obsolescence. Each apprentice also pursues academic study in French, mathematics, civics, and geography. This scheme was recommended in the Langevin report, but in its essentials it was not new.

The continued high birth rate has given France another problem, that of finding schools and places, teachers, and books for the growing body of youth. We have seen (p. 304 f.) that the struggle of the state against "clericalism" and for a secular school system was fought out and won in the nineteenth century. The separation still exists, but conditions are not the same as they were even twenty years ago. Today one-fourth of all primary and two-fifths of all secondary school pupils attend private schools, mostly Catholic. The Church is asking the state for financial help in maintaining and operating her schools and is getting it.

The Vichy government in 1941 passed a law granting aid to private schools, up to three-fourths of the cost where needed. In 1945 this arrangement was sharply condemned by the Consultative Assembly. Catholics, liberals, anticlericals, and Communists fought over the issue for years. Radical Socialists and Communists advocated a single, entirely secular school system and the banning of all private schools. This is the Russian policy. It would obviously not be acceptable to the French. In 1950 the Minister of Education appointed a new Commission to bring in still another report on the position of the nonpublic schools. The Catholics explained once again that they found it difficult—especially so in the postwar inflation—to pay for their own schools and also the state school tax. They presented figures on the number of children for whom they care. They pointed to some parts of France, wholly Catholic, where the state had provided no schools. It was doubtless not the strength of these facts and arguments but the weakness of the postwar governments of a badly divided France that caused the state to yield. France has adopted the plan, also followed by England with its much smaller Catholic population, of giving financial aid to private schools. What effect this will have upon the public system we cannot tell now; nor do we know whether a stronger government may return to the old or find a new solution.

3. PROGRESS IN ENGLAND

Two world wars and the Education Act of 1944 were the most important educational events in England in our century. They were not unrelated. Ever since World War I the English people have tried to improve their schools. National committees worked over the problems and proposed solutions, the people were informed and aroused, and World War II presented the final unanswerable argument for reform.

If it should seem strange to speak of wars as educational events, a brief glance backward will help. The Boer War and the Balfour Education Act of 1902, World War I and the Fisher Education Act of 1918, and World War II and the Butler Education Act of 1944 were directly connected in pairs. In each case a war revealed deficiencies and impelled people and Parliament to seek remedies. But this is a costly and otherwise undesirable method of achieving educational progress. In fact, today's wars are more likely to destroy than to improve education.

The way to improve public education is to secure the moral support of the people. The Butler Act of 1944 was adopted and has been fairly, although not completely, successful because the people were gradually informed of the needs by means of a series of able and readable official studies and reports (p. 357), and by newspaper and professional discussion. The Fisher Act had failed. Mr. R. A. Butler, President of the Board of Education, and his colleagues were skillful strategists; all parties were represented in the government; the rural people saw that many of their schools could not go on without public aid, and some of them had come into contact with the slum children of the evacuation; business and industrial leaders were convinced, as they had not been in 1918, that a nation which depends upon industry and trade cannot survive without effective schools. For all these reasons the new bill was enacted into law in 1944 (Chapter 15).

The Act was intended to achieve the purposes which follow: (1) to provide stronger central direction of education while preserving local initiative; (2) to make each administrative district large enough to supply all kinds of educational services; (3) to raise the leaving age by one or more years as a condition of effective secondary education; (4) to treat secondary education as a continuation of primary education, and to supply appropriate kinds of secondary education, free, to all youth; (5) to offer "further education" for working youth; (6) to preserve church, voluntary, and independent schools insofar as they could be made efficient.

The law provides for a Minister of Education and empowers him "to control and direct," new language in English educational administration. The early ministers have been discreet, but there has been some partisan criticism of their official acts and language. The local school districts, as they would be called in the United States, were reduced to the number of 146 for the whole of England and Wales with 44,000,000 people.

The law extends the compulsory attendance period to age fifteen and permits further increase. Extension to fifteen years had been a provision of the Fisher Act and was re-enacted in a law of 1936 but had not been generally enforced. Enforcement after the war was made especially difficult by the extraordinary increase in the number of children to be accommodated. The increase in the birth rate during the war years was the reason why an unusual number of new five-year-olds was ready for school in the later forties. At the other end of the school years there were the thousands whom the law kept in school one more year. Each of these "bulges" required additional buildings and teachers, the two most expensive elements in the operation of schools.

This time the nation was determined to raise the leaving age. The Prime Minister's statement in Parliament on November 12, 1946, was applauded for its courage. He said, "We are straitened in our manpower. We must make up in quality what we lack in quantity. We are, therefore, raising the leaving-age." On April 1, 1947, the Minister set it at fifteen years.

In England, as in many other countries, elementary education is more fully developed than secondary. In England it consists of three stages: the nursery school, before the age of five; the infant school, from five to seven; and the junior school, from seven to eleven. The nursery school which was mentioned in Chapter 12 has grown during and since World War II, but many children under five are enrolled in infant schools. The compulsory period begins at age five. This seems to be an inheritance from the industrial revolution when children were put to work at early ages. The infant school has been much influenced by the Italian educator, Dr. Maria Montessori. The American student is surprised to learn that there is an active Montessori Society in England. Montessori influence was slight in the United States and died out about the time of World War I.

The junior school enrolls children of the ages seven to eleven. In American schools these would be in grades two to six. There is no nationally required curriculum, but language, arithmetic, geography, elementary science, history of England, local history, and community and home-making studies are common fare. The last three of the list were products of the evacuation and the war.

After the war the school-building problem and the teacher shortage troubled England and other warring countries. The International Con-ference on Public Education held in Geneva, July, 1957, twelve years after the last gun was fired, was devoted to the world-wide school building shortage. By using temporary buildings and starting a one-year training program for teachers, England was able to meet the 1947 deadline for the raising of the leaving age. All the children at age eleven or over were to receive secondary schooling. Even before the introduction of the bill to reform the general system it was secondary education that received most attention, and it was most radically changed by the Act. In deciding to have it begin at age eleven and to include all youth, England assumed a liberal position. Conservatives favor a long elementary school course to age fourteen or beyond and a secondary school for a different and socially privileged class of people; or if they cannot retain this oldest plan, they will move for a short elementary school course for all, preferably not over four years, and a division of the whole body of children about age ten into two groups, one of elementary and the other of secondary school pupils.

In England all the children are directed at eleven-plus into three kinds of secondary schools, the academic or grammar school, the technical, and the modern. This tripartite system is not in the law, but was proposed by the Norwood Committee (1943). It is not followed everywhere. Psycholo-gists have opposed this early division, on the ground that there is no scien-tific way of forecasting at that early age what capacities may develop. They cautioned the local authorities against erecting buildings for these three types of secondary schools without fuller assurance that the plan would work.

About the same time, many Englishmen made an old discovery over again, namely, that the intelligence quotient can be improved by coaching and that intelligence test scores reflect the subject's experience, not his native ability alone. Two other ways of classifying the eleven-year-olds were available: a selective examination, and the pupils' elementary school records. The examination plan was attacked as leading to cramming and coaching, and to anxieties and tensions. Both parents and teachers, it was said, concentrate too much upon it, and this perverts the children's sense of values. Both failure and success have unfortunate effects. Some writers in the press proposed copying the American comprehensive high school (*Times Educational Supplement*, London, February 8, 1952, p. 113). There are multilateral schools, that is, schools with a number of parallel courses, in London and elsewhere, but England is proceeding with the tripartite scheme. According to this plan the brightest and most literary children are selected for the academic or grammar school; those endowed with mechanical and scientific abilities are chosen for the technical school; and the rest, about sixty to seventy per cent, are gathered into the modern school.

The law looks toward the division at age eleven without competitive tests by using school records and teachers' opinions. Research groups and teachers' associations also stress guidance in all periods of schooling and a general review of all factors at the time when children are to be assigned to the special schools.

The program of the modern school will be handicapped if its pupils are to be merely those not chosen for the other two schools. Under good conditions, however, the modern schools should have a wide field for experimentation. If they were provided with facilities for group activity, practical exercises in shop and garden, community projects, drawing, music, and drama, these less academic children might find schoolwork interesting and rewarding. Teachers who will cautiously experiment, and small classes, varied equipment, and freedom should be the appropriate formula.

There is also political objection to the tripartite scheme. The Labor Party favors the comprehensive school and objects to schools that tend to preserve the class structure of society. Labor holds that the prestige of the Public Schools and grammar schools is unwarranted; and even some friends of those schools admit that school influence is exaggerated, that Etonians gain high office not because of Eton's virtues but because those who go there come from great and influential families. The Labor Party wishes to explode this so-called artificial prestige, and Labor is not alone in that wish.

School prestige is, however, built up over the years and will not be quickly overcome. Only when the pupils from other schools receive equal treatment with classical students at the universities and equally desirable positions in life will the prestige of the grammar schools be overcome. No one can say how much time this will take. It required a century in the United States where the classical tradition had not become firmly rooted. A better example is found in Prussia, where the modern language *Oberrealschule* established in 1885 was officially given equal status with the ancient classical *Gymnasium*. The pupils of each were admitted to the universities. The middle classes who had demanded the *Oberrealschule* continued to send their sons to the *Gymnasium*. The General Staff of the Army in 1905 had one hundred officers with a *Gymnasium* education but only four from the *Oberrealschule*. This example (from R. H. Samuel and R. H. Thomas, *Education and Society in Modern Germany*, London, 1949, p. 45) speaks for itself.

An idea of the degree of selection exercised by the grammar schools may be gained from a review of the examination system. At eleven-plus the children of the elementary schools take an examination that may determine their future. About one-third will pass with marks that will permit them to go to a grammar school or a technical school if one is available. The technical schools are not yet organized in all places. The other two-thirds will go to modern schools if these are available; otherwise, they will remain in the elementary school until age fifteen. At fifteen another examination of the third which passed at eleven-plus will eliminate all but about twenty per cent, who then enter the sixth form for specialized training. Two or three years later there is an examination that qualifies for university admission and, if passed with high grades, may earn a scholarship. Very few reach this goal. In proportion to population there are two and one-half times as many university students in Scotland as in England. This is an indication of the relative selectivity of the English and Scottish universities. At the end of the English university course there is a last examination requiring a three-hour paper each day for ten days. It is competitive, and a First Class or a high Second is required of those who hope for a civil service appointment or any high academic position. That is a map of the ten-year journey marked out for the brilliant grammar school boy who enters upon it at the age of eleven.

The proposal to establish large numbers of modern schools aroused the fears of the grammar school masters, although the new schools were to cater for a body of pupils whom the grammar schools would not take—not a generous position. The charge was made that Mr. Butler was willing "to jettison the traditions of the grammar school for the sake of uniformity." The fact is that he appointed the Fleming Committee to report on the place of the grammar schools in the system. The report (1945) was not unfavorable to those schools. The upper-class English view is that classical education is the best and that other forms are good in the degree to which they resemble the classical. In the debate over modern versus classical education for "the academically most gifted pupils," the grammar schools had an able spokesman in Doctor (now Sir) Eric James, High Master of the Manchester Grammar School. He argued that a grammar school education fits gifted pupils equally for the university or for their life-work. This formal discipline argument was also used by the American Committee of Ten in 1893. In the intervening years it has been shown that formal discipline is a reality, not a myth; that it is often small in amount and conditioned by circumstances; and that even gifted students of any age will still have to acquire the arts and crafts of their business after they leave school.

English independent schools and especially the Public Schools are now in a difficulty that has little to do with their virtues. They have always been expensive. With reduced fortunes and rising living costs, many who would wish to send their sons to exclusive schools are no longer able to afford the expense. How this may affect English politics may be gathered from the fact that Prime Minister Macmillan is an Etonian and all but two of his eighteen-member Cabinet are Public School men.

As noted above, the law gives the Minister "control" over education; and the central government is increasing its financial contribution so that it now pays two-thirds and the local authority one-third of the whole cost of education in a local area. Americans will be apt to ask whether this will lead to greater central control and even dictation. Judging the future by the past and present will cause almost everyone to doubt such an outcome. England has a long history of central and local cooperation in education.

Each local authority prepares a development plan to be submitted to the Minister. This shows how the local authority intends to meet its obligations and promote education in its area. After review and approval, this becomes a program. The Ministry has been quite lenient with localities which have been slow in submitting their development plans.

4. EDUCATION IN OCCUPIED GERMANY

In Germany at the end of the most destructive of all wars (1945), education had to be started afresh and under the direction of the military governments of the conquering nations. The new authorities had to work with a system which had been reorganized twice in a generation. The National Socialists had integrated the whole school and university system into a vast military and propaganda organization; and, contrary to all German history, they created a national, or Reich, Ministry of Science and Education to control all the schools. Under the preceding republican constitution and the still earlier empire the separate states had been the chief educational agencies. The existence of the numerous political parties and distinct religious groups had caused the development of school systems with general similarities and many individual peculiarities.

Religion had always been an important element in German life and education. It stood first on any list of the elementary or secondary school studies, and yet educationally and politically it was often a divisive influence. The people grouped themselves into Evangelical, Catholic, and Jewish confessions with many smaller faiths and unfaiths. There were many denominational schools, and these have been re-established and continue to form exceptions to the even structure of the system. Politically also, education has gone back to the pre-Nazi status. Each of the states has a long political past of independence or semi-independence, but all were politically dominated by one master-state, Prussia. Her school system was at times an example, but she did not impose it upon other states.

The Republic proposed a Reich education law but did not succeed in adopting it. Only the Nazis did that, and Germany has now gone back to the separate state systems.

Germany was one of the most literate nations of Europe and the world; but she lacked an active and powerful middle class. German localism did not lead to democracy. Even in the Republic, convinced democrats were doubtless in the minority. It may be this distrust of popular rule and also self-distrust by the common people that make them unwilling to shoulder responsibility for the enormities of the Nazi regime. They really feel that they could do nothing about the matter. And who in the democracies can say that he has done all that he could have done for peace, justice, and decency? At any rate, the roots of National Socialism, often not recognized, were deep in the soil, and the economic collapse of 1929 gave them the opportunity to grow.

German education had long been celebrated, and frequently admired by the rest of the world; but obviously the new masters of occupied Germany would not wish to restore the Nazi or the pre-Nazi system. They did not have a clean slate to write on. The war damage created a difficulty. It had come gradually, but at the end the destruction was, in many places, complete. Schools had continued in the usual way for several years, but in 1943 a sudden decline began. The difficulties were both material and spiritual. In Hamburg the schools were closed in July, 1943, and remained closed for exactly two years. By the end of the war, schooling in Germany had practically ceased.

Physical facilities were, as we have noted, lacking when the war ended. Great numbers of school buildings and all but nine of the universities had been damaged. The destruction of the University of Giessen, which is in the Russian Zone, was almost total. The University of Jena and the famous University of Berlin, now one hundred and fifty years old, are also in the Russian sector of the city. To make good the loss of the latter, a Free University of Berlin was founded in 1948 in West Berlin, but about forty per cent of the student body comes from Soviet parts of Germany. Frankfurt, Munich, and Würzburg had half of their buildings damaged. Heidelberg, the oldest German university, was intact. Many libraries and laboratories were destroyed. Large parts of the cities had been rendered uninhabitable, and usable structures were needed to shelter the homeless and fugitive or were requisitioned for military or hospital use. Schoolwork had to be conducted in shifts for lack of rooms to house the pupils.

In the American sector of Berlin, one-fourth of the more than six hundred school buildings had been demolished. Ninety per cent of the schools of Cologne were hit and many were totally destroyed. Even in semi-rural Schleswig-Holstein there were great losses. Everywhere there were shortages.

The lack of light bulbs was unimportant because there was no electric current. Coal was lacking as were housing, shoes, soap, and other necessities. The food shortage reduced the effectiveness of both teachers and pupils.

Despite such difficulties, the schools in the British Zone were reopened in July, 1945, and those in the American Zone the following October. There were many mental blocks and difficulties. The children were listless and purposeless. Like the older people they had no feelings of remorse. "What could we have done?" they said. They lacked power of concentration and decision. At the once progressive Odenwald School, one-third of the pupils were refugees. They had already been in several, some in as many as five, schools. The principal reported that they were thin, constantly hungry, and could not be quickly restored to a normal condition.

War had for several years been the main business, and as the British and American bombers had become more effective many people had been moved from the target cities to places of greater safety. Women, children, and the aged fled eastward, and from the cities to the country. Toward the end they were again driven back by the approach of the Russian armies. The chaos which resulted hampered the re-establishment of the schools. With one matter that might have been judged a probable cause of difficulty there was none. Compulsory school attendance is so much a part of German life that it was easy to get the children back into the schools.

The Potsdam Agreement (August, 1945) of the occupying powers declared: "German education shall be controlled so as completely to eliminate Nazi and militaristic doctrines and to make possible the successful development of democratic ideas." The powers did not all understand this in the same way, but the British and Americans made a strong effort to dismiss National Socialists from their teaching staffs. Two-thirds of the 36,000 elementary teachers in the American zone and eighty per cent in some districts were disqualified. Their places were taken by retired teachers or imperfectly trained persons. As a result the age of the staff exceeded fifty years. Many of these older teachers were like other Germans in holding a low opinion of democracy, and they had no stomach for an active crusade to make the schools democratic. Yet this was demanded of them. Schoolbooks, especially those in history, were filled with Nazi propaganda. Even arithmetic had been slanted in the Nazi direction. The process of de-Nazifying the books consumed time, and paper to print new editions was almost unobtainable. For a time, photographic reproductions of pre-Nazi books were used. With the return of the children and the arrival of refugees the schools became overcrowded. Classes averaged about seventy members, and the teachers were constantly overworked.

Schools in West Germany in general follow the organization developed after World War I. The *Grundschule*, or common school, which was instituted at that time is now accepted, but the length of this common school course varies from state to state. It is always given at least four years, ages six to ten, but the liberals and socialists who favor a one-class society want a longer course. A long common school course naturally reduces the time that can be devoted to secondary education. Those of the political right wing and Roman Catholics usually favor the short course. The states of North Rhine-Westphalia, which are mainly Catholic, transfer the pupils to the secondary school at the age of ten; the farmer-socialist state of Schleswig-Holstein keeps all pupils in the common school for two years longer; and the socialist administration of West Berlin has completely integrated elementary and secondary education, deferring the choice of the academic courses until the pupils are fourteen years old.

Where the short common school course is in vogue, pupils who are not planning to stay in school beyond the leaving age are transferred at age ten to an advanced elementary school course of four years. This takes them to the age of fourteen and the beginning of an apprenticeship or a vocational school program, or, more often, a combination of these two. Pupils who can remain in school longer may enter a middle school with a six-year course including a modern language. Those destined for a profession or an upper social status will attend a secondary school, with a course of eight years, which prepares for a university.

There is a variety of vocational schools and adult educational opportunities. Apprenticed youths must be excused for attendance at part-time schools. There are nearly two hundred folk high schools which provide opportunity for a combined liberal and vocational education part-time, for older youth and adults.

Russia in the eastern zone and sector of Berlin is imposing her own form of one-class school system. All private schools and all religious teaching are suppressed. The state is the only educator, and the school system is uniform in all phases from the kindergarten through the university. Study of the Russian language is required. The rigid control and the Communist ideology are deeply resented by many Germans, and they continue to flee to the West in great numbers. West German education for refugees will be treated in the following section.

Democratic processes were not emphasized in the schools of old Germany. Under the Republic some efforts were made in that direction, and parent councils and student government were tried. In some localities, such as Hamburg, they had a fair success. Where they had none or little it was frequently because the public, teachers, and pupils had not been prepared for the change and because new organizations, abruptly introduced, were given too much power and too free a hand at the outset. The Nazi government killed whatever democratic growth had taken root.

In the occupation a new beginning has been attempted and something has been accomplished; but few general statements will apply to the whole country, because education is again administered by the separate states (*länder*). The Reich, or All-German, Ministry of Science and Education which the Nazis erected has been abolished and each state in West Germany has its own laws, institutions, and practices, but there are naturally many similarities. Practice varies also between the American, British, and French zones; and the Russian Zone of East Germany is entirely different.

Although the states manage their schools, there is a Basic Law of the German Federal Republic (West Germany), and Article 7 deals with education. It provides that all schools are to be supervised by the state, but private schools which satisfy state requirements are permitted. There are reservations about private primary schools. The second main provision of Article 7 says that parents and guardians may decide what religious teaching, if any, the child is to receive. Private primary schools may be established if they are necessary to provide the desired religious instruction or if they are likely to make a contribution to the science and art of education. In any case all schools must satisfy state demands before they may be licensed.

The laws in the German states are much more explicit on the aims, methods, and curricula of the schools than are English laws. England leaves such matters to the teachers and the local authorities. We shall underscore this. The Act of 1944 says nothing about what must be taught, does not require a democratic or patriotic school, and is generally careful not to infringe upon the prerogatives of teachers and masters.

American school legislation is more like the German laws, and like those it tends to make teachers subordinate rather than professional public servants. For example, two or three years ago in a great and "sovereign" American state it was discovered that by a copyist's mistake the law was made to say that the elementary schools "may" teach reading. A rectification campaign was at once started, resolutions were adopted, and the legislature passed a new statute, using the word "shall" with respect to the teaching of reading, which was put on the books instead of the old. A lawyer led the campaign for this unnecessary law.

The educational directives of the American Military Government were framed in similarly specific terms, but there was more cause. They directed that the states were to provide equal educational opportunity for all, to stress education for civic responsibility and the democratic way of life, and to provide opportunity for the people to cooperate in the reform of education. The Germans correctly interpreted this as a criticism of their former practice.

The introduction of social studies into the schools, even into the vocational schools, is one of the new trends in West Germany. The teaching of citizenship and the cultivation of civic interests and skills are stressed. After much hesitation and some hostile objections, discussion groups have been organized in some schools. New teaching methods involving pupil activity are encouraged. Moving pictures showing how elections are conducted in Britain and the United States have been shown in the schools. For many years there has been a radio broadcast for schools. Aid has now been given for the further development of broadcasting, and radio receivers have been supplied to schools that had none. Encouragement has been given to the organization of student councils and a new youth movement.

School counseling and guidance, almost unknown in old Germany, have a special importance because they will doubtless moderate the authoritarian school discipline which has been traditional. They also have a particular use in a dual school system. At the end of the *Grundschule*, the child must choose between preparation for the university, the middle school, or continuance in the upper elementary grades. This choice has usually been made without scientific information about the child's abilities, interests, health, and other qualities, and with insufficient consideration of the vocational or professional opportunities for which he might qualify himself. In Europe the so-called vocational guidance is not real guidance but a mere assignment to an apprentice's job. It is done by the government, not the school, and is, therefore, poisoned at the source. Seminars and workshops on both social studies and counseling have been held and were opened to West Germans as well as others. They have been well attended.

An exchange of persons has been carried on between the occupying powers and Germany. Thousands of Germans, including many teachers, have traveled and studied in the United States, Britain, and France. The hope is that on their return home they will influence their friends and neighbors to support a more democratic school, one without fees for tuition, books, or supplies, one that offers an open road to all. This will take time, especially the open-road idea; the direction of the change is important now. The universities are even more conservative than the secondary schools.

Secondary school teachers were from the eighteenth century prepared in the universities. Under the Republic several states began to send also their elementary teachers to the higher institutions. The Nazis promised to continue this policy, but, as in many other matters, they failed to honor the arrangement. Anti-intellectual as they were, they even shortened the long-established secondary school course and limited the attendance of all classes and of women at the universities. Under the military occupation, teacher training has tended to go back toward the practice of the nineteenth century.

Elementary teachers are again prepared in pedagogical institutes, secondary teachers in the universities, thus reopening the social and intellectual gap between them. Secondary school teachers receive an exacting scholarly preparation, and they study their teaching fields intensively. Their pedagogical study is, however, wholly theoretical, containing little that will have immediate application to their work. Both elementary and secondary school teachers must take two state examinations, one upon completing their period of study and another after several years of teaching in a regular school. After these alternating periods of study, teaching, and passing examinations, they become eligible for permanent appointment. The requirement of a trial year or years is not new and surely has merit.

The educational system in the Russian Zone has a compulsory attendance period of twelve years, two more than in Russia itself. The German period of a Grund or foundation school of four years (or six in some states) has also been lengthened. It is eight years. As in Russia, every child has to study the Russian language, and the secondary school is continuous with the elementary. There are various types of vocational schools which lead off from the elementary, some part-time, some full-time. The curriculum emphasizes native and foreign languages, mathematics, and science. Religion is omitted and the treatment of the church and religious groups is becoming more harsh and intolerant. All prospective teachers must qualify for entrance to the university, and they are prepared at the university.

The de-Nazification process was much more thorough in the Russian Zone than in the others. The Russians made a clean sweep by dismissing all university teachers and then reappointing those deemed satisfactory. The authorities in West Germany temporized, dismissing only flagrant Nazis at first; and they found difficulty in getting rid of the rest. Hardly any action was taken in the French Zone. We must also notice that some anti-Nazis are as undemocratic as former members of the Party.

The effort to democratize the German universities gradually and by an internal process alone reveals in the authorities a certain blindness to the realities of the case. Only when Germany becomes democratic and develops an active and vocal middle class can the universities become democratic. They may be among the last institutions to resign the Prussian authoritarian spirit. And the secondary schools also have not been greatly transformed in the occupation. Japanese schools likewise have not changed radically under American tutelage. There are some clear lessons in these negative experiences.

Schools are conservative institutions. In fact the conservation of a way of life is one of the chief reasons for schools. The public often tends to resist the efforts of native leaders to "improve" the schools. And a nation resents much more the interference of a foreign and conquering power in its institutions. Also the Americans have for one hundred years praised German education, studied in German universities, and copied their methods. It is really not surprising that the Germans did not readily abandon their own educational program for the American, which they have never greatly admired.

5. MINISTERING TO TROUBLED MINDS

Many of the minds of Europe's scrambled people have been the victims of racism and war. They are the refugees, waifs, and delinquent youngsters. The refugees are still coming. The daily paper reports a steady stream of farmers, engineers, doctors, and teachers, including one former rector of a university, coming through barbed wire into West Germany. The first eight months of 1958 brought 130,000 because the Communist Party of East Germany had new orders to crack down on nonconformists. These are people who were long tolerated because they were needed; but they will not be longer tolerated unless they submit. Refugees began coming westward before the war ended and have continued ever since.

Figures tell only the least part of the story. The children among the refugees are not like the calmly self-confident youngsters whom one sees in school in times of peace and prosperity. They are the survivors from a much larger number of the victims of brutality and near-starvation. Many are marked in body and suffer from deficiency diseases. They have been hiding in cellars and ruined buildings by day, fleeing by night, foraging for food, stealing whatever seemed of value. Numbers had joined the underground, thus gaining the chance to retaliate upon their persecutors. They had acquired the immoral code of war, and after the war their teachers had difficulty in again instilling the morals of peace.

Those who escaped, leaving parents and friends behind, often developed feelings of guilt. They felt that they should atone for their desertion. Many who survived persecution, the disappearance of friends, the experience of deception by those whom they had trusted developed nervous and mental disorders.

Suspicion showed itself in peculiar ways in young refugees. They were not disposed to place confidence in their fellows, but they distrusted the camp management even more. When a new arrival came it was customary for two or three to accompany him when he was interviewed for assignment. They wanted to be assured that he got a square deal.

Although the numbers were so large that a severe burden was laid on the government, the psychiatrists and teachers, and the communities, they formed only a small proportion of the whole body of refugees. The report of the United States High Commissioner for 1953 said: "One of the most serious problems in postwar Germany is posed by the refugees who form one-fifth of the Federal Republic's population." The High Commissioner might have added that they composed a political force strong enough to gain respectful consideration from the government for their demands.

Many of those who would now be in middle age were killed in the prison camps and in the war, and, therefore, the old and the young are most numerous among the survivors. The child-refugees in the schools in 1956 numbered about 1,300,000, and they composed about one-fifth of the nation's entire school population. They are found in all types and at all levels of schools, including the technological institutions and universities. They are helping in the restoration and development of the country.

Many countries, including America, have gained excellent citizens through the admission of those who were not wanted elsewhere. The Pilgrims of early New England were refugees. Mrs. Carl Schurz, who introduced the kindergarten into the United States, was the wife of a refugee who became a national figure. The Revolution of 1848, the two World Wars, the Nazi coup of 1933, and the Hungarian revolt of 1956 caused many to flee to more hospitable countries, and among these there were scientists, scholars, and physicians. Canada and other American countries have given asylum to many, but probably no country in modern times has admitted as many in proportion to its population as West Germany.

The wars have, doubtless, also increased juvenile delinquency. This has, in any event, been growing in many countries. Some would say that programs exhibiting violence on television have contributed some cases. Guns and narcotics are too easily obtainable. The lack of jobs and recreation for youth in the cities must be other causes. The National Education Association has launched an investigation into the causes which are certainly not well known. Russia has not escaped. Her young hoodlums are ridiculed in *Krokodil* and castigated in the newspapers. England suffers from the "Teddy Boys" who were the instigators of race riots in 1958. In the United States, vandalism in school and church buildings and crimes of violence, gang warfare, and even murder, are reported in the press. Early diagnosis and special schools are being tried, but the rate of delinquency is still rising.

Many countries have large numbers of people who have no permanent homes or who can spend very little time in their homes. Such are the migrant workers, some theater people, gypsies, and others. The children of the workmen who built the early railroads of Massachusetts troubled the conscience of Horace Mann. Today the fruit-pickers, weeders of the onion fields, the circus people and gypsies, the "children of the roads and rivers" make a difficult educational problem. The solution is not easy but a scheme of national registration and boarding schools with scholarships might provide the answer. But few countries care enough, it seems, to make such provisions.

Waifs, gamins, and hooligans seem to form a more or less permanent element of society, but the numbers have increased in the postwar years. A psycho-educational study made in Italy lists parental neglect, poverty, mistreatment of the children, and family dissension as the chief reasons why children take to the streets of the less respectable parts of the cities. They live by begging, pilfering, trading, shining shoes, and doing odd jobs. The study showed that most of these adolescent wanderers were practically illiterate and had been badly corrupted by lawless associates. They were very suspicious but could be won over by amusements, games, companionship, and, finally, by offers of a home. An extended description of children of this class has been prepared by a noted Russian educator, A. V. Lunacharskii (1875–1933) who was the first Commissar of Education for the Russian Republic (RSFSR), which is by far the largest of the sixteen republics composing the Soviet Union. His book, *The Waif* (New York, Pantheon Books, Inc., 1955, 292 pp.), seems to be a synthetic account from the early Communist period. It is told in the first person by a "waif" and was published as the work of one, named Nicholas Voinov. Lunacharskii was a cultivated person, and it was he who persuaded Lenin to save the art treasures of Russia. He was removed from office in 1928.

6. THE PESTALOZZI CHILDREN'S VILLAGE

Pestalozzi, it will be recalled, had great success in dealing with orphans and strays at Stanz. It is, therefore, appropriate that a living monument to him has been established near his own city of Zürich. This is the Pestalozzi Children's Village, an international home and school for war orphans. The story of this splendid enterprise will conclude our account of the help given to war-damaged children. The Pestalozzi Children's Village was proposed by Walter Robert Corti, a Zürich editor, under the heading, *Ein Dorf für leidende Kinder*, a village for suffering children. It was to be a home and school and city, all in one, for destitute war orphans from many nations. The war was to be forgotten. No one was to remember who had been friend, who enemy. The children were to receive loving care and a chance to grow mentally, spiritually, and physically, under freedom, responsibility, and tolerance. Publicity brought support and also opposition, but in two years (1946) a beginning had been made.

The cottage or family plan was adopted. There are now eighteen houses, each with fifteen or more children, presided over by a married couple, who serve as house parents; and all members of each "family" are from the same country. There is a British house, a French, an Austrian, an Italian, and so on. Children are received at the age of six or a few years older, and they may remain until they are fifteen or sixteen. Each house has a large living room with a schoolroom above and a workshop below it. As Pestalozzi in his time advised, the living room is the center of the family life. The national language is spoken there, but the school is conducted in German. This is the language of the surrounding region, and the children learn it by means of songs, games, and plays. They may also, more formally, acquire a second foreign tongue. The school is of the type which some would call progressive. There is a community hall for general meetings; it is a gift from Canada's UNESCO and the city of Zürich. Interdenominational Christianity is the religion of the Village.

The legal control and government is made up of adults, but the children have a voice in the internal management of the community's affairs. They elect a Village Council and administrative officials. The residents over whom they rule are between two and three hundred in number. When the children are to be repatriated in their homelands, the Village aids in finding places and positions for them. The student of Cecil Reddie's Abbotsholme (p. 360) may see several resemblances between the early progressive school (1889) and the Pestalozzi Children's Village. Clearly, good schools are good medicine for troubled minds; and where homes are wanting or faulty, boarding schools may be best.

7. INTERNATIONAL EDUCATION

In professional books and papers, international education is a term of several meanings and indefinite scope. A few of the meanings will be indicated and illustrated in the following paragraphs. And by "the plain historical method" we shall try to show that one definition should have preference over others. This definition says that international education is education for peace, the education of nations not to learn the arts of war any more.

This idea will not be universally accepted, but it is at least not new. As World War II was drawing to a close, George F. Zook of the American Council on Education wrote that "a major responsibility for preventing future wars" rested upon education, and he claimed that American educators believed that the failure of the League of Nations to stress education for peace was partly responsible for World War II. Every effort should be made, he said, to bring to the world and the framers of the new world organization, the United Nations, the information and ideas that can be used in leading the world to a lasting peace. It was this line of thought, held by many, that led to the establishment of the United Nations Educational, Scientific, and Cultural Organization.

This latter view also is not shared by everyone. Friedrich Schneider, noted German educator, and founder and editor of the *International Review of Education* (The Hague), believes that the setting of a practical goal for international education will turn it into a biased or prejudiced kind of propaganda. Usually, we commend teachers when they develop definite aims and state them plainly; and in the search for peace a certain degree of prejudice may be excused.

International education as frequently understood is a formless sort of concept. From the earliest times education has tended to spread across both natural and social barriers. Neither mountains and seas nor the differences in the languages and customs of tribes and nations have been able to contain it. Soldiers, merchants, travelers, and missionaries have both incidentally and deliberately carried ideas, knowledge, and practices to those whom they have touched. This is plain from the earlier chapters of this book.

The Christian church through its propaganda of the faith has transmitted much besides its religion. The Moslems, who in the eighth century and afterward conquered portions of Europe, introduced new concepts in arithmetic and trigonometry, chemistry, medicine, architecture, and education. All modern nations use the schools to instill their way of life and to justify their policies before the world. International Communism is one of the most assiduous promoters of so-called international education.

The distinction is that such education is directed by the agent and imposed upon the learners. They do not seek it; it seeks them. To call it propaganda is not useful because the line between propaganda and education is too faint. The means to carry on this kind of propaganda-education has been greatly increased by modern inventions, including printing, the post office, and all the newer kinds of communication. Francis Bacon could today take all knowledge for his province if he had the capacity to absorb all of it. It could all be put before him.

The contrasting form of international education in this broad view requires inquirers and students to seek out notable centers and teachers. Such centers were ancient Athens with its Socrates and Alexandria with its library; medieval Europe developed its universities; in the Renaissance the cities of Italy attracted the students of classical learning. Such a center was Germany for the young scholars of the United States in the nineteenth century. The direction of the movement is not, however, the chief difference between this form and the preceding. The difference is that in this second form the students are the seekers and they are free. In the former case the teacher seeks the students, corrals them, and instructs them. We must not completely separate the two forms for they often coexist, but the difference between them is real and important.

A special example of the second form must be particularly noticed because writers have described it as an important phase of international education. This phase is the study and importation of foreign educational philosophy and practice. As an example we may take the schools of Pestalozzi. These drew from various countries many inquirers who spread his philosophy and methods. His books, especially *Leonard and Gertrude*, made him known; but it was visitors and students of his work at Burgdorf and Yverdon who in some cases converted practically whole nations to the Pestalozzian system. The early visitors inspired the later ones. Thus, Anton Grüner's assistant, Froebel, followed his master in visiting Pestalozzi and then went to live for a few years at Yverdon. Froebel in his turn became the leader of a succession of admiring disciples in Germany, Switzerland, England, and the United States who carried the kindergarten into the most distant lands. Americans have usually been borrowers instead of lenders of educational programs, but the views of John Dewey have been widely disseminated by his books, by foreigners studying in the United States, and by his activity as educational adviser abroad. Other Americans have been influential in foreign countries, but we need not list them.

International congresses, conferences, associations, fairs, and expositions spread both educational and other knowledge, through formal meetings, through exhibits, and by conversation in the corridors. The three ways are arranged in what is often the order of increasing importance. It was at the international exposition at London in 1851 that Henry Barnard saw his first kindergarten demonstration and realized that the new institution was an improvement over the infant school which he had promoted. The International Kindergarten Union was formed a little later. Gradually education won a recognized place in the programs and exhibits of international expositions such as the one at Paris in 1867 and the World's Fair at Chicago in 1893. There are international student federations, a World Federation of Educational Associations, and in the United States the Institute of International Education (1919) and the International Institute of Teachers College, Columbia University (1923). Further listings would not lead us to our goal, a definition of international education.

8. COMPARATIVE EDUCATION

We must, meanwhile, look at another subject which is sometimes equated with international education, the subject of comparative education. This is not a new field. A French scholar, Marc-Antoine Jullien, in 1817 published a *Sketch and Preparatory Survey of a Work on Comparative Education*. This pamphlet has only recently been translated into German, and only in part into English. It contains a plan for collecting and disseminating educational information. Fifty years later the United States created the Bureau of Education with just these functions, to be exercised, however, in and for the United States. The first head of the Bureau was Henry Barnard who was giving large space in his *American Journal of Education* to the school systems of Europe.

At least fifty years ago courses on comparative education were offered in the larger American universities by professors of the history of education. Classes were usually small and good textbooks were not available. But gradually some of the large publishing houses such as Longmans, Green and Company and The Macmillan Company provided series of volumes on English, German, French, and other national systems of education. The comparison had to be supplied by the teacher and the students; otherwise, the real subject of the course was not comparative education but foreign school systems. Twenty-five years ago Professor I. L. Kandel, the leading American authority in the field, brought out his *Comparative Education* (Houghton Mifflin Company, 1933, 922 pp.) which, although now quite old, is still excellent if suitably corrected by later publications.

But what is comparative education? A short answer is found in the title of another book, namely, *Contemporary Education, a Comparative Study of National School Systems*, by J. F. Cramer and G. S. Browne (Harcourt, Brace and Company, 1956, 637 pp.). Comparative education usually deals with national school systems, as they presently are, and "contemporary" is a more truly descriptive word for it than "comparative." Perhaps the chief question which such a book or course tries to answer is: What "makes the systems 'tick'?" Comparison must be based upon knowledge of the forces which propel and direct each of the systems being considered. These forces reside in the physical features, institutions, character, ideals, and economic resources of each country and people; and they can be understood only in the light of their history. A national school system is an instrument of the nation for the formation of the national will and the cultivation of the people's capacities to make that will effective. One key question asks how much freedom a particular nation allows individuals to control their own education and to use it for their own purposes. The last few years have seen a remarkable increase of interest in this subject among professors. The Comparative Education Society has been organized, and its official organ, the *Comparative Education Review,* appeared first in 1957.

9. EDUCATION FOR PEACE

Some would identify international education with comparative education; but if they are the same we need only one name. Others would include comparative education under international education as part of a larger whole, but this would be to subordinate a fairly well-defined subject with a method of its own to an area of studies that has neither limit nor system.

The study of the pedagogy of several countries is, as we have seen, sometimes taken as a phase of international education; but it is more appropriately considered as a part of the sections on teacher education in courses in comparative education. The same kind of reduction of lesser topics to parts of large subjects can be pressed much further. Most of the matters that have been included under international education can be assigned to some better established discipline. The history of education already includes a great many, as any book in this field will show. Geography and world history will absorb what remains after the usual professional subjects have enforced their claims. In that case, we should for international education substitute the education for international peace, not as another subject but as one of the great goals of all education. This goal is about as old as modern nationalism.

Education for peace has been promoted by leading educators since the time of Comenius. He proposed the establishment of a pansophic college where students from many nations were to gather universal knowledge to be applied to the harmonizing of international discord. Comenius was not the first but he was an earnest advocate of this idea (Chapter 8). He held that until a universal language could be perfected, a knowledge of languages, especially those of one's neighbors, would be useful. He would have favored the international exchange of teachers and students, the study of comparative education, and abolition of class privileges in education and other areas of life. He would have applauded Point Four, UNESCO, and other forms of international cooperation. He overemphasized the power of knowledge, but he desired much besides. He proposed to educate everyone in knowledge, virtue, and piety; he hoped to transform people.

To transform people by moderating the aggressive spirit of nationalism and chauvinism is the problem. This problem involves several tasks. To provide a fuller, rounded education of heart and soul as well as of intellect is necessary although difficult. The difficulty is increased by the fact that public schools do not stand outside the emotional currents which move a nation and are apt to carry a full load of nationalist prejudice. Even when educators favor a changed spirit, the public may be hostile as was demonstrated by the attacks in sections of the United States upon the United Nations and UNESCO and upon all efforts to teach pupils about these organizations.

There is also the condition that it needs only a single nation to start a war, rendering the best educational efforts of other nations ineffective. Any of the little wars ignited by the "peace-loving nations" may blaze up into a big war. On the other hand countries with popular governments are subject to emotional storms that may sweep across even old-line republics and create danger of a military explosion. For all these reasons international agencies and diplomacy must carry forward the peace-making and peace-keeping processes to which the schools must also contribute.

Something along educational lines was attempted even before World War I. Fannie Fern Andrews in America worked for the International Conference on Education at The Hague in 1914. Sixteen governments had prepared to send delegates, but the outbreak of war canceled the plan. At war's end there were unsuccessful efforts to commit the League of Nations to the promotion of international education. When these failed, the Committee of Intellectual Cooperation was formed by private efforts in 1921 and later associated with the League. Under the topic UNESCO, below, this is also briefly treated.

After World War I, German and French historians attempted to displace the biased and nationalistic history taught in their schools with objective national accounts. During the twenties they made great progress in developing more scientific history textbooks, but Hitler (1933) put a stop to this; and, quite in character with his policy, he published the "lies" which the French had admitted but suppressed the corresponding German "lies." The American historian Carleton J. H. Hayes published a survey of nationalism in a hundred French schoolbooks of the twenties in his *France, A Nation of Patriots* (New York, The Macmillan Company, 1930). The book is listed in Chapter 13.

The International Bureau of Education in Geneva was formed (1926) as a private venture but soon became an intergovernmental body. It served as an international clearing house of educational information. The World Federation of Educational Associations was founded at Oakland, California, in 1923. Governments—France, Great Britain, and the United States included—developed national programs of cultural relations with other countries. Under its Department of State, the United States started a policy of cultural cooperation with other nations in 1938. The preceding are only a few samples of the many international bodies which dispense educational and cultural services. In the following paragraphs we shall deal mainly with the exchange of persons for educational purposes. This is believed to be an effective form of international education.

International scholarships and teacher exchanges are part of a larger class of arrangements for foreign study and teaching. The Rhodes Scholarships at Oxford University were established by Cecil Rhodes, African diamond kind and empire founder, to make war "impossible" between the English-speaking and German peoples. They have, unfortunately, not accomplished this purpose, but according to Frank Aydelotte, American Secretary of the Rhodes Trust for many years, they have developed many hundreds of "world citizens," promoters of international friendship. Exchange of professors has been promoted by the Institute of International Education (1919), which for many years was directed by Stephen Duggan.

Student and teacher exchanges have developed in many countries since the beginning of the present century. A small-scale but interesting example along this line has been promoted by Peter Manniche, long head of a special kind of Danish folk high school, the International People's College of Elsinore. A newspaper item in the *Times Educational Supplement,* London, on its summer vacation project (1947) tells the story. It said: The College "has this month [August] entertained about ninety teachers from England and an equal number from eight European countries and British Guiana in South America."

In Europe there are international federations of teachers to promote the exchange of their members and of pupils also. An international federation of teachers' associations and an international federation of secondary school teachers held a joint meeting in Edinburgh in 1947. They made arrangements for the exchange of teachers and pupils, worked for the improved study of languages, and attempted to lay a better foundation for cooperation and understanding among the nations. A resolution was adopted asking UNESCO to develop plans and principles for the exchange of students and teachers. The second of the above associations (*Federation Internationale des Professeurs de l'Enseignement Secondaire Officiel,* or *F.I.P.E.S.O.*) has also undertaken the important task of creating a more democratic outlook in secondary education, a plan from which many European boys and girls could greatly profit.

In the United States, several thousand persons are exchanged annually with corresponding persons from as many as ninety countries to teach, study, lecture, or engage in research under the International Educational Exchange Program carried out by the Department of State, with the help of the Office of Education, and voluntary groups such as the National Association of Secondary School Principals. The exchanges were made possible by the Fulbright Act, Public Law 584, the 79th Congress, and the Smith-Mundt Act, Public Law 402, the 80th Congress. Private foundations, universities, and associations also make arrangements for the exchange of educators and students. The Guggenheim Fellowships have long been useful for this purpose.

The Fulbright Scholars are carefully chosen, and according to reports they compare not unfavorably with those sent out with the support of the Rockefeller, Guggenheim, and Ford foundations. The numbers also are not small. Since the beginning in 1947 a total of about twenty-eight thousand students, teachers, investigators, and technical specialists have received Fulbright aid. Senator J. William Fulbright has said that although the scheme has not yet remade the world, given time it may do so. The values like those of religion, he has said, are intangible. Senator Fulbright himself was a Rhodes Scholar. One of the values of the program results from the fact that many of the Fulbright and also of the Rhodes Scholars become teachers upon their return to America.

In the colleges and universities of the United States the number has been growing rapidly, and there are annually, at present, over forty thousand foreign students. They distribute themselves very unequally among possibly fourteen hundred institutions. This is a form of international education in reverse. They come to America, but they return home after completing their program; and their reports cannot but be an important factor in the international reputation of the United States. They should be met by active helpfulness and good will.

10. UNESCO

The United Nations formed in San Francisco in 1945 with its specialized agencies is an improved version of the League of Nations and its subsidiary bodies. Among the specialized agencies of the United Nations there are some that had been active under the League as well as new ones. Of the older ones we may particularly notice the International Labor Organization (ILO), the Food and Agriculture Organization (FAO), and the World Health Organization (WHO). These are named here because they often work with the new specialized agency, the United Nations Educational, Scientific, and Cultural Organization (UNESCO).

UNESCO was formed to apply the resources of education, science, and culture in attacking those problems of the world's peoples which might threaten international peace and security. There was an altruistic and humanitarian motive behind this action, and the thought was not wholly new. The League of Nations (1920) was aided by cooperating committees, one of which was the International Committee on Intellectual Cooperation (1924) with aims somewhat like those of UNESCO. Both were to promote education, the exchange of scholars between nations, the rights of intellectuals, and peace. One difference is plain. UNESCO tries to help the have-not persons, peoples, and nations as well as (if not rather than) intellectuals. It also receives better financial support.

The leaders of both bodies have been more distinguished than the leadership they were able to give. They were far greater in other fields than in administration. At the head of the International Committee on Intellectual Cooperation were Gilbert Murray, Chairman, and Albert Einstein, Henri Bergson, and Henri Bonnet. It would be difficult to find a more eminent quartet of intellectuals, but this was a case where administrative skill was needed. Yet the labors of the Committee were not without fruit. It investigated the teaching of history and history textbooks, and the teaching of art and music, two international languages, as they may be called. One result of its activities was the International Bureau of Education at Geneva, already mentioned. The Committee was liquidated after World War II, and UNESCO, with a broader mandate, took its place.

The United Nations Charter provides for an organization to promote peace and security by intellectual and moral means. A convention with delegates from forty-nine countries met in London in November, 1945, to form such a body. The resulting constitution of UNESCO argues in the memorable words of the Prime Minister of Great Britain, Clement Atlee, that "since wars begin in the minds of men it is in the minds of men that the defences of peace must be constructed." The criticism, sometimes heard, that the "mind" is not as important a cause of war as the Prime Minister supposed is flippant, for the constitution goes on to give due emphasis to economics and politics.

The tasks of UNESCO are, however, intellectual and moral. The Constitution would have it promote mutual understanding, equal educational opportunity, the diffusion of knowledge, extended library opportunities, exchange of teachers and students, and respect for justice, law, and fundamental freedoms. In applying these words from its primary law, UNESCO frequently uses education, science, and culture to fight poverty, hunger, dirt, and disease, and, on the mental level, racism and national greed and chauvinism. Certainly wars begin in the minds of men, and the absurd nationalism of the present can be moderated only by changing the minds of men. Incidentally, the word *racism* is found in the newer dictionaries only.

Membership in UNESCO is open to nations, and the present member-nations number eighty-two. Each member has one vote in the General Conference which is the legislative body, and which directs the work.

Delegates are chosen by national commissions formed in each state. Instead of the annual meetings of the early years, the General Conference now meets every two years. The first meeting at Paris was followed by other early convocations in Mexico City, Beirut, and Montevideo. An Executive Board and a Secretariat of some hundreds of international civil servants carry on the day-to-day business. The chief executive office is that of the Director-General. Early incumbents were Julian Huxley, British biologist, J. Torres Bodet of Mexico, and Luther Evans of the United States. The present Director-General is Dr. Vittorino Veronese of Italy. The interposition of national commissions between the member-nations and UNESCO was intended to reduce national pressures upon the international body; but in the Senator McCarthy period in the United States the device seemed ineffective.

In the beginning UNESCO had difficulty in settling upon a plan and program. So many projects were submitted to it by delegates and such diverse views were held of its proper functions that much of its energy was spent in program-making. The danger that UNESCO might become another scientific society or one dispensing social theory and propaganda was avoided. Fortunately, UNESCO has found ways of helping backward peoples through practical education to help themselves. This thought was developed by Bodet who, when he was Director-General, proposed three yardsticks for all projects, as follows: (1) Will the project promote the welfare of the masses and improve their living conditions? UNESCO is not "an assembly of mandarins." (2) Will it enlist the cooperation of intellectual leaders everywhere to work for humanity? If it can be done without educators, scientists, scholars, let it be done elsewhere. (3) Will it produce results quickly? UNESCO must succeed early if it is to survive.

Program, support, permanent membership, all were in doubt for some years. When the first General Conference met in 1946, the administration hoped for an $8,000,000 budget, but this estimate shrank by one-fourth. It has since been increased a great deal. There were only forty-three nations represented at the first General Conference. Some early members, being Russian satellites, soon withdrew or, we should say, were withdrawn. Russia remained away until 1954 when she joined as the seventieth member, and her satellites returned. At the time there were those who predicted that she was joining merely to make trouble. They were mistaken, but this is no proof that Russia is in full sympathy with the aims of UNESCO. In late 1958 the General Conference defeated Russia's efforts to gain a seat for Red China and her proposal to grant full accreditation to the delegates from satellite Hungary. The chief Russian delegate replied to these rebuffs by raising the question whether

Russia was getting from UNESCO the value of her contribution to it. The budget then (1958) was about $25,000,000 and Russia contributed thirteen per cent, the United States, over thirty-two per cent.

UNESCO spent much time in the early years making pronouncements and was criticized for talking instead of acting. Some statements, although not effective at once, were significant. The Universal Declaration of Human Rights was much criticized but significant. The Declaration's thirty substantive articles affirm (1) that all persons are born free and equal in dignity and rights; (2) that all are entitled to the essential human rights and freedoms without respect to race, color, sex, religion, or property; (3) that among these rights are life, liberty, security of person, freedom from slavery, torture, cruel or inhuman and degrading treatment and from attacks upon the honor and reputation of any person. It would seem that such statements are demanded because the promises of 1776 and 1789 have not in two centuries been fulfilled. The Declaration is not a legal but an educational instrument.

The spread of fundamental education is the primary means selected to aid peace and security. To remove illiteracy is an essential part of fundamental education. If the removal of illiteracy were easy, it would have been achieved long ago. Over one-half of the people of the world are unable to read and write in any useful degree. Many illiterates are found even in countries which take pride in their public school systems, such countries as the United States of America. For this there may be no sufficient excuse. But in parts of Asia and Africa where the rates of illiteracy are highest, tax yields are low, the birthrate high, and life expectancy short. The result is that there are few producers of economic goods and no margin of capital savings to pay for schools. UNESCO has made and published many studies of such conditions.

An opportunity to attack the problem in a Western nation occurred in 1947 when the General Conference met in Mexico. This is a country with a highly cultivated upper class in the capital and elsewhere but with many illiterates, low living standards, and poverty in rural areas, especially among the Indian population. When the Mexican government offered opportunity and facilities to institute a fundamental education scheme, UNESCO decided to make it one of a series of pilot experiments that might serve as models for other areas and countries.

The place chosen for the project is in the small state of Nayarit on the coast in west-central Mexico. The whole state is about as large as Vermont, but it has only half as many people; and the area chosen is a tropical plain drained by the Santiago River which winds its way from the sierras on the east to the Pacific Ocean. The district has a small city, about thirty villages, and a population of fifty thousand made up of businessmen, farmers, fishermen, laborers, Indian tribes, and their dependents. The experiment is an enlarged version of the cultural missions which have been carried on in many countries. Those also were intended as examples to the neighbors, examples of a method to develop socially and economically backward communities.

The fundamental education experiments directed by UNESCO are new only in the sense that they are large, well financed, and expertly administered. In the present case the promoters dealt with the occupations and economics of the people; they built a road across the sierras to provide access to markets and contacts with the socially advanced world outside; they showed how houses should be built; they attacked the causes of malaria and other tropical diseases; and with a well-drilling outfit they provided pure water. Schools were established in all villages, many with kindergartens. Personnel trained in the Mexican pilot project and a similar one in Egypt are working in five South American countries and in the Near East.

Parallel to the promotion of fundamental education is UNESCO's aid to the establishment of free and compulsory public school systems. Korea and Libya are among the countries aided in this matter. A third UNESCO activity is the provision, with the help of other specialized agencies of the United Nations, of technical assistance. Other agencies such as the United States Department of State, through the Point IV program, also work along this line. UNESCO's greatest success in recent years has been in giving technical assistance to education in less developed countries. "Education is the big push in UNESCO," said Luther Evans.

The library program is another activity that is likely to have helpful results. Few countries of the world, perhaps about ten, have modern library systems. UNESCO has led in establishing pilot libraries in New Delhi, India, and in Medellin, Colombia. The plans include not only modern processes in a central library but also branches and bookmobiles to take books to prospective readers. Not wholly unrelated to library development is UNESCO's work in promoting a universal copyright convention which went into operation in 1956. Other activities such as arid zone studies to make the once fruitful deserts bloom again, and the hope of conquering the Amazon Basin cannot be treated here. It was, no doubt, the former of these to which President Eisenhower referred in his speech to the Near East during the 1958 diplomatic and military crisis.

The great wars have done great harm to schools and children, but by revealing the weak spots in education they may have also helped to bring about some improvements. This would become true of France if her experiments were fully developed and if the results were applied everywhere. England has taken the great step of instituting a universal ladder system from the infant years through the secondary school. This plan also needs further expansion and refinement; and these may be expected to follow now that Britain is again entering upon a period of prosperity. Germany, though compelled to care for a large refugee population, has again instituted an effective school system upon somewhat more liberal lines than before. In these and other countries there is a continuing shortage of buildings and teachers and a new increase of pupils. Classes are over-large, and schools may be conducted in two or more shifts.

Nazi fanaticism and the war and, on the other hand, the resistance movement exerted the most evil influences upon many young lives. Schools and other mental and moral agencies have had a hard and not always successful task to bring them back to physical and mental health. Education should do what it can do to prevent war and so to make unnecessary the repair of its destruction, not to speak of its irreparable wastes and horrors. Education for peace should be carried on in schools; and UNESCO is a practical agency putting into effect what schools teach, by bringing the means of self-help to depressed countries, by helping to cure present ills, and by raising a vision and a hope. References are given below to magazines which carried the violent American criticisms of UNESCO and objections to American participation in it. Educational and general periodical guides provide further citations.

QUESTIONS ON CHAPTERS 21 AND 22

1.   By several means, planned and accidental, as told in Chapters 21 and 22, people obtained a new view of the condition of their schools. How could an adequate view of a nation's schools be presented to the people?

2.   How may we account for the differences between secondary education in France and the United States?

3.   Why does secondary education everywhere pose greater difficulties than elementary or higher education?

4.   What is the meaning of the phrase, "Slaves need no leaders?" Is the statement, as you interpret it, true?

5.   If a nation contributes to the support of church schools, should it not also aid the independent schools? And if it provides support, should it not also inspect and license them?

6.   After reading as widely as you can on Russian education, compare your conclusions with those of this textbook.

7.   Should special public schools be provided for talented young people, and can you recommend other ways of cultivating and directing their capacities?

8.   If international education and UNESCO are accepted and promoted, as it seems, mainly in the "democratic and peace-loving countries," how can they advance the cause of peace? Which are the "democratic and peace-loving countries"?

9.   Is the rising emphasis, in the United States, upon science and mathematics wise? How does this program differ, if it does differ, from the Russian?

10. Should language study aim at a speaking knowledge mainly, or a reading knowledge? Consider the several values of language study for people today.
11. By what tests can a school system be shown to be mature? Compare certain school systems with respect to their relative maturity. Include Prussia and Russia in your comparisons.
12. If television is extensively used what roles should be assigned to teachers?

FOR FURTHER READING AND STUDY
CHAPTERS 21 AND 22

The quarterly *International Review of Education*, The Hague, Holland, has been revived since its release from Nazi control. The founder, Friedrich Schneider, has returned to the publication. Professor Karl Bigelow from Teachers College, Columbia University, is on the editorial board. The *Comparative Education Review*, now in its second year, is published in New York. The London *Times Educational Supplement* and *School and Society* have been of great value in the preparation of this chapter and the following one.

The publications of UNESCO, including documents, reports, pronouncements, directories, studies, many of them pamphlets, are far too numerous to list. One of its publications is the quarterly *Fundamental and Adult Education*, which with others that are still in print may be obtained from UNESCO Publications Center, U.S.A., 801 Third Avenue, New York 22, New York. For some idea of the hostility aroused by UNESCO, see *Saturday Evening Post*, October 2, 1948; *American Mercury*, January, 1954, February, 1954, and August, 1956; and *Commonweal*, May 27, 1954. The article last cited deals critically with the outburst in Los Angeles.

The articles and references on "International Education" by W. W. Brickman (*Encyclopedia of Educational Research*, New York, The Macmillan Company, 1950) and on "Intergroup Education" by Lloyd Allen Cook, in the same volume, will carry the student of these topics a considerable distance.

The *Year Book of Education* was founded in 1932; and since 1953 it has been prepared under the joint editorial care of the Institute of Education, University of London, England, and Teachers College, Columbia University. It is published by Evans Brothers, Ltd., Russell Square, London, and the World Book Company, Yonkers-on-Hudson, New York.

CHAPTER 21

Ascher, Charles S., *Program-Making in Unesco 1946–1951*, Chicago, Public Administration Service, 1951, 84 pp., double-column.
Beach, Fred F., and Robert F. Will, *The State and Nonpublic Schools*, Washington, D. C., United States Government Printing Office, 1958, 152 pp.
Benjamin, Harold, *Under Their Own Command, Observations on the Nature of a People's Education for War and Peace*, New York, The Macmillan Company, 1947, 88 pp.
Brickman, W. W., "The World Challenge to Elementary and Secondary Education," *Educational Forum*, XVIII (May, 1956), 477–481.

Cramer, J. F., and G. S. Browne, *Contemporary Education, A Comparative Study of National School Systems*, New York, Harcourt, Brace and Company, 1956, 637 pp.

Kandel, I. L., *United States Activities in International Cultural Relations*, Washington, D. C., American Council on Education Studies, Volume IX, September, 1945; *The New Era in Education, A Comparative Study*, Boston, Houghton Mifflin Company, [1957], 388 pp. Professor Kandel, also edited the *Educational Yearbook of the International Institute of Teachers Colleges, Columbia University*, 1924–1944.

Laves, Walter H. C., and Charles A. Thomson, *UNESCO: Purpose, Progress, Prospects*, Bloomington, Indiana University Press, 1947, 469 pp.

Lindegren, Alina M., *Germany Revisited, Education in the Federal Republic*, Washington, D. C., United States Office of Education, Bulletin, 1957, No. 12, 107 pp. Bibliography, pp. 101–107.

Mallinson, Vernon, *An Introduction to the Study of Comparative Education*, London, William Heinemann, Ltd., [1957], 249 pp.

Pilgert, Henry P., *The West German Educational System*, Frankfurt-am-Main, Office of the United States High Commissioner for Germany, 1953, 136 pp.

Samuel, R. H., and R. Hinton Thomas, *Education and Society in Modern Germany*, London, Routledge and Kegan Paul, Ltd., [1949], 191 pp.

Schwarz, Leo W., *Refugees in Germany Today*, New York, Twayne Publishing Company, [1957], 168 pp. Bibliography.

Tandler, Fredrika, *Teaching About the United Nations . . .* , United States Office of Education, Bulletin, 1956, No. 8, 40 pp.

Teacher Exchange Opportunities, 1959–1960, Washington, D. C., United States Office of Education, 1958. Pamphlet issued annually.

UNESCO, *Fundamental Education*, New York, The Macmillan Company, 1947, 325 pp.

UNESCO, *Flight and Resettlement*, [Paris, 1955], 281 pp. Illustrated. First-hand stories and scientific studies by several contributors.

CHAPTER 22

Bestor, Arthur, *The Restoration of Learning, A Program for Redeeming the Unfulfilled Promise of American Education*, New York, Alfred A. Knopf, 1955, 459 pp.

Brickman, William W., "John Dewey's Foreign Reputation as an Educator," *School and Society*, LXX (October 22, 1949), 257–265, with bibliography.

Counts, George S., *The Challenge of Soviet Education*, New York, McGraw-Hill Book Company, 1957, 330 pp.

Counts, George S., and Nucia Lodge, *The Country of the Blind*, Boston, Houghton Mifflin Company, 1949, 378 pp.

Dale, Edgar, *Audio-Visual Methods in Teaching*, New York, Dryden Press, [1954], 534 pp.

Documentary and Reference Material on Education in the Soviet Union, Cambridge, Mass., The Massachusetts Institute of Technology, 1956, 2 vols.

Dunham, Franklin, and others, *Television in Education*, United States Office of Education, Bulletin, 1957, No. 21, 124 pp. Historical and descriptive; illustrated.

Education in the USSR, Washington, D. C., United States Office of Education, Bulletin, 1957, No. 14, 226 pp. With bibliography of English and Russian sources.

Essert, Paul L., *Creative Leadership of Adult Education*, New York, Prentice-Hall, Inc., 1951, 333 pp.

Furman, Bess, "Who Killed Federal Aid?" *Saturday Review*, September 8, 1956.

Hofstadter, Richard, and Walter P. Metzger, *The Development of Academic Freedom in the United States*, New York, Columbia University Press, 1955, 527 pp.

Kandel, I. L., *The Impact of the War Upon American Education*, Chapel Hill, University of North Carolina Press, 1948, 285 pp.; *American Education in the Twentieth Century*, Cambridge, Mass., Harvard University Press, 1957, 247 pp.

Kellogg, Flint, "Villard and the NAACP," *Nation*, February 14, 1959, pp. 137–140. An account of the origin of the National Association for the Advancement of Colored People.

Kempfer, Homer, and Grace S. Wright, *One Hundred Evening Schools*, Washington, D. C., United States Government Printing Office, 1949, 71 pp. (United States Office of Education Bulletin, 1949, No. 4).

Kline, George L. (Editor), *Soviet Education*, London, Routledge and Kegan Paul, Ltd., [1957], 192 pp. A collection of papers by Russian contributors, foreword by George S. Counts.

Korol, Alexander, *Soviet Education for Science and Technology*, New York, John Wiley and Sons, Inc., [1957], 513 pp.

London, Ivan D., "Evaluation of Some Current Literature about Soviet Education," in *Proceedings*, Fifth Annual Conference on Comparative Education, School of Education, New York University, April 25, 1958, bound with *School and Society*, November 8, 1958; also separately available.

Michels, Walter C., "The Teaching of Elementary Physics," *Scientific American*, April, 1958. This, and the Rosenbaum article below, are highly significant reports.

Richmond, Kenneth, *Education in the U.S.A., A Comparative Study*, London, Alvin Redman, Ltd., 1956, 227 pp.

Rosenbaum, E. P., "The Teaching of Elementary Mathematics," *Scientific American*, May, 1958.

Sawyer, W. W., *Mathematician's Delight*, Pelican Books, A 121, 1949, 238 pp. The author's view of the proper introduction to elementary mathematics differs from that described by E. P. Rosenbaum in the *Scientific American*.

Scott, C. Winfield, and Clyde M. Hill, *Public Education Under Criticism*, New York, Prentice-Hall, Inc., 1954, 414 pp.

Shalin, A. F., "Technical Education in the Union of Socialist Soviet Republics," Chapter 7, in *Year Book of Education*, 1956, Yonkers-on-Hudson, New York, World Book Company, 1956.

Siepmann, Charles A., *TV and Our School Crisis*, New York, Dodd, Mead and Company, 1958, 198 pp.

Stanley, Charles J., "Organized Interests and Federal Aid to Education," *School and Society*, January 6, 1951.

22 SOVIET AND AMERICAN EDUCATION

T
HE NATIONAL SCHOOL SYSTEMS OF WESTERN EUROPE AND THE Americas belong to a common family. They differ in many ways, but these ways are like those which distinguish the children of a common parentage; and it is not strange that all of their languages belong to the same far-ranging Indo-European speech. It is even less surprising that these school systems have a common foundation in the culture of the eastern and northern Mediterranean countries of Judea, Greece, and Rome. Much of the culture of those ancient lands was transmitted by the medieval Church and Empire.

On this road came the Judean-Christian religions and practical ethics, Greek philosophy, literature, mathematics, and science, and Roman law and government. Would that the destiny assigned to Rome by Vergil, to rule the nations and to maintain a lasting peace, had been attained; but Rome, though she did not establish perpetual peace, did well by the future otherwise. The civilizing elements brought to the West were molded into new forms by the Renaissance, the Reformation, the Enlightenment, and the democratic revolutions of the seventeenth and eighteenth centuries. These are the foundations and the forces of the school systems of France, Germany, England, and the United States. Local conditions and particular peoples have given the systems their special forms.

Twenty chapters of the present book have traced the evolution of formal education and its administration, first in private, then in church, and now in state schools; and some attention has been given to the present condition and operation of the four systems which we have named. To those four we now add a fifth, the system of the Union of the Socialist Soviet Republics. We shall in subsequent pages show how the historical foundations and present condition of the Soviet system differ from those of the other four. After a description of the main features of this system we shall deal briefly with its history and shall mention some of the contemplated changes. Later sections of the chapter will contain an account of recent changes and present conditions in the United States.

1. WHY WE WATCH SOVIET SCHOOLS

The Soviet educational system has aroused an extraordinary degree of interest in the West and especially in the United States. This interest has been increased by the observation of Russian technological progress. The effect might well be an overemphasis upon science and technology in American education. The question deserves the fullest consideration by those who guide pupils and frame curricula.

The technological success of the Soviet Union is of interest with respect to many and especially two fields, war and trade. The governments of the world pay attention to her fleets of planes and submarines, long-range weapons, and growing steel industry. And Russia is offering to supply India, Egypt, and other countries with agricultural, industrial, and military equipment, and to build the Aswan Dam on the Nile. She will continue her bid for a larger share of the world markets. These activities are neither new nor surprising, but her priority in putting into orbit two satellites, the Sputniks of 1957, was both. The United States was astounded by a result so contrary to her expectations, and American prestige abroad suffered an abrupt decline.

The West may have underestimated the Soviet educational achievement also. There is little doubt that the schools have had a share in the material advances of the Soviet Union. How great the share has been and how it has been accomplished are difficult questions. The freer access to that country in the last few years and the large number of Americans who are studying the system will produce more accurate answers. In the summer of 1958 some seventy American educators visited Russia under the auspices of the Comparative Education Society, and there were many others who took advantage of the opportunity. At the same time Russian students, athletes, farm leaders, and intelligentsia were visiting the United States. This is encouraging in more than one way, but one is the better understanding of Russian education that will be formed. Critical voices have recently begun to spread the opinion that there are flaws in the Russian system. The changes which are being introduced into it, such as the boarding schools and the manual labor period, also suggest a cautious attitude.

Changes in the Soviet school system are nothing new. The system passed through an experimental phase in the period following the Revolution. It did not emerge full-grown. In that early phase there was considerable fumbling, as one would expect; and the leaders were active in borrowing, trying out, and adapting the ideas and practices of other countries, particularly those of Germany and the United States. They were also fertile in educational invention and the end-result of their efforts is unlike any other system.

From the first they were interested mainly in methods and organization rather than in goals, which have always been those of the Communist Party of Russia. They found the liberal and progressive practices of the West unsuitable for their purposes. The system was changed after 1928 under Stalin and became fixed and rigid by 1938. Military training and the separate education of boys and girls were tried for brief periods and abandoned.

2. FORMATIVE IDEAS OF SOVIET EDUCATION

The school system was organized under Stalin who has been charged with the "betrayal of an ideal," the ideal of brotherhood in a classless and stateless society; but it is more probable that the monolithic state and the inflexible schools are the natural results of radical socialism. The school system has some strongly marked features, as will appear, but its efficiency does not come only from its structure, curriculum, and methods of teaching. Intangible forces have been effective. The pupils are the children of peasants or of parents removed from peasantry by a generation only, and they have seen a vision of a new world of ideas and opportunity for intelligent people. Their will to succeed, the whipped-up competition with the capitalist West, the worship of the state and its heroes, Lenin and Stalin, the honors, medals, and material prizes for scientists and engineers, all have had their effect. Evidence is appearing that these drives are now losing some of their potency, because many pupils have discovered that the prizes are beyond their reach.

One very great prize for workers in the abstract sciences and in their technical applications is the comparative safety of a career in mathematics, physics, chemistry, and engineering. Social scientists, psychologists, biologists, educators, composers, and writers have been sent to slave labor camps or purged when the Party line suddenly and unaccountably changed. It has been claimed, perhaps with considerable exaggeration, that every high official expects that his fall, even though delayed, is sure to come.

Another explanation for the industry shown by the youth of Russia may lie in the persistent political education which they receive in school, and in the youth organizations. In a little book, *I Want to Be Like Stalin*, we read: "Education for us is a vital public concern and is directed toward the strengthening of the Socialist State." That state which is the Soviet Union respects brains in those who will serve the regime. Even old Czarist Russia had a distinguished intelligentsia, novelists, historians, and scientists. The new Russia, as in so many other lines, carries forward old Russia's intellectual tradition also and, with greater resources and skill, tries to cultivate talent wherever it appears. But autocracies, old and new, although they reward genius and use it, are careful not to trust it too far.

The Soviet schools are organized, directed, and supported by the state, that is, by the Communist Party. Although a collective farm or a labor union may conduct a kindergarten or vocational school, these must be uniform with the state system in organization, curriculum, methods, and theory. There are no private schools in the Soviet Union; but the Russian Orthodox Church is allowed to maintain seminaries to train its priests, and Moslems and Jews have corresponding institutions.

In the schools for all pupils, the materialist-scientific philosophy of man and nature must be taught from kindergarten days on. The Party ideology provides a complete philosophy of life which is imposed upon everyone in school, in youth organizations, and in the system of political education for adults. How fully effective the teaching of atheism is, we cannot be certain. It is not wholly ineffective. A Moscow school principal is reported to have said: "After leaving my school any child is free to become a Christian, but, of course, this has never happened." Other sources report that many teachers go through the form of instilling the official doctrine but without conviction. Most teachers do not belong to the Party which numbers about 8,000,000 in a population of 200,000,000. The membership is growing.

The West, we know, does not accept the prevailing philosophy of Russia or her political system. Western philosophers are sufficiently sophisticated, but they sometimes lack commitment. Russian Party members not only know the required answers to the fundamental questions, but they are fully committed to the task of "building socialism." This greatly simplifies the educational problem. The social studies cease to be a controversial area. The answers to social questions become nearly as exact as those of physical science.

The West has been deeply moved by historical forces that hardly touched Russia. She was not affected by the revival of Greek and Latin learning and art, or the humanism and the new history and archaeology of the Renaissance. The devotional movements in the Roman Catholic Church did not reach her, nor did the Protestant Reformation with its powerful incentive to strive for the education of the common people. The Enlightenment and the democratic revolutions did not shake the autocracy, the orthodoxy, or the imperialism of the country of the Czars. Even now Russia has not changed as much as some observers imagine. The new autocracy is that of the Presidium and Premier; the new orthodoxy, that of materialism and Communism; and the new imperialism swallowed the Baltic nations and holds its neighbors in its powerful grip. One can see why the humanities are absent from the Soviet curriculum, why there is no freedom of discussion of controversial issues in Soviet schools, and why the people, though literate, are misinformed.

3. THE SOVIET TEN-YEAR SCHOOL

The educational task as thus simplified is carried out in a single-track school, uniform throughout the entire country. It has been a day school. The following schedule shows what is taught in it.

Table 1. Schedule of Soviet Ten-Year School

Subjects	Number of class-periods per week										Total
	Primary				Junior			Senior			
	1	2	3	4	5	6	7	8	9	10	
Ages:	7–8	8	9	10	11	12	13	14	16	16–17	
RUSSIAN LANGUAGE AND LITERATURE	13	13	13	9	9	8	6	5	4	4	84
MATHEMATICS	6	6	6	6	6	6	6	6	6	6	60
HISTORY	—	—	—	2	2	2	2	4	4	4	20
USSR CONSTITUTION	—	—	—	—	—	—	—	—	—	1	1
GEOGRAPHY	—	—	—	2	3	2	2	2	3	—	14
BIOLOGY	—	—	—	2	2	2	3	2	1	—	12
PHYSICS	—	—	—	—	—	2	3	3	4	4	16
ASTRONOMY	—	—	—	—	—	—	—	—	—	1	1
CHEMISTRY	—	—	—	—	—	—	2	2	3	4	11
PSYCHOLOGY	—	—	—	—	—	—	—	—	—	1	1
FOREIGN LANGUAGE	—	—	—	—	4	4	3	3	3	3	20
PHYSICAL EDUCATION	2	2	2	2	2	2	2	2	2	2	20
DRAWING	1	1	1	1	1	1	—	—	—	—	6
DRAFTING	—	—	—	—	—	—	1	1	1	1	4
SINGING	1	1	1	1	1	1	—	—	—	—	6
LABOR AND EXCURSIONS	1	1	1	1	2	2	2	3	2	2	17
Total	24	24	24	26	32	32	32	32	33	33	293
Number of subjects (carried by each pupil)	6	6	6	9	10	11	11	11	11	12	—

NOTE: The above schedule is a modified form of one in George S. Counts, *The Challenge of Soviet Education*, New York, McGraw-Hill Book Co., Inc. (1957), p. 77. By publisher's permission.

This schedule must be supplemented with further information if we are to grasp its meaning. Small towns may have only a seven-year, incomplete school and some rural sections only a four-year elementary school which may be compared with the German *Grundschule*. As in other parts of the world, there is a considerable gap between city and country school provisions. The Soviets hope to extend the ten-year school to all parts of the Union by 1960.

The complete ten-year school is an elementary and secondary school on a 4–3–3 plan. It is a comprehensive school covering all studies offered to children between the ages of seven and seventeen; it is coeducational; it is supposed to be classless, and it is intended to promote the abolition of social classes in the population. Bureaucracy, however, and education itself, tend to form new classes in Russia. This condition is the subject of strong complaints in the Communist Party press (*Times Educational Supplement*, London, January 1, 1954, p. 7).

The comprehensive elementary-secondary school of Russia forms a contrast with the parallel elementary school for the common people and secondary school for the elite in such countries as France and Germany. But in the latter countries there is a tendency toward the integration of the parallel systems, and in England this has been accomplished in theory by the Act of 1944. In Russia, on the contrary, there is appearing a new plan, the Khrushchev Reform, to be mentioned again (p. 584 f.), which may tend to develop a laboring proletariat on the one hand and a scientific-technological elite on the other.

A comparison with the American high school, which is different from the schools just mentioned, may prove instructive. The high school is comprehensive in its subject offerings, and it admits all qualified children of its district; but it separates pupils into different groups by assigning them to somewhat specialized curricula. In a large school a vast number of adjustments is possible so that some pupils may have an individual scheme. We sometimes call the high school a single-track school, but this term may be more correctly restricted to schools like the Russian or the German *Gymnasium* in which all pupils do the same work. But Germany also has alternate schools, as is shown in Chapter 14. Russia offers no choice, an appropriate scheme for an autocracy, and also a comparatively inexpensive plan.

The Soviet single-track is not without barriers or gates. The completion of the seventh year marks an important step in the child's progress. At that point there is a critical examination. Those who pass may proceed to the senior school and ultimate graduation, perhaps even to the university. At that point also, or even at the end of the junior division, special examinations may admit those who pass them to "technicums," a variety of practical schools, usually on the secondary level, which prepare pupils for skilled and semi-technical occupations.

The ten-year school is, therefore, a terminal school for some and a preparatory school for those who will continue in advanced institutions. Not all children are able to complete the course, but all must attend the school to the end of the compulsory period. Before 1949, attendance was compulsory only in urban districts; since 1949 education has been compulsory from age seven through the junior school at thirteen or fourteen; and by 1960 it is intended to extend the compulsory period everywhere to age seventeen. This and other predictions are to be taken as goals.

Below the elementary school there are nursery schools and kindergartens. These are directed not by the department of education but by the department of health. As in other countries preschool institutions are lacking in many rural parts. The technicums, as already mentioned, are mainly secondary institutions, drawing off students from the main system. Above the ten-year school there are many higher and technical institutions including thirty-seven universities, many technical and professional schools, research institutions, military and naval academies, and special schools for political enlightenment in Communist theory and doctrine. These latter prepare Party leaders and functionaries.

Barring the foreign languages where large schools can offer the pupils some choice between English, or German, or French, for example, all studies as listed in the above schedule are required and as far as possible are uniform in content and method throughout the Union. The Russian tongue is required either as the native tongue, as shown in the schedule, or in non-Russian-speaking republics, as an additional foreign language. Most of the world's leading languages are offered in different schools. The reading selections in Western languages are not usually taken from the literature of the country whose language is being studied; they are often synthetic pieces praising the great Soviet land and sounding its virtues; or they may be the writings of Communists from the country being studied. In contrast with some small countries like Holland or Luxembourg, which may require a pupil to study five or more foreign languages, the Soviet Union requires only one. Yet Russian educators claim that their aim is to give children an understanding of the cultures of foreign countries.

We should notice that most studies are pursued continuously for several years, not, as in many cases in the American high school, for a single semester or year. Russia follows the European habit of demanding continued application, not the American scheme of course credits which permits the pupil to "cash in" his work for graduation even though he may have forgotten what he had learned. In the European and Russian system the number of class exercises per week in a given subject is reduced and the subject is in most cases kept before the pupil until graduation day.

In the ten-year school, physics is studied for five years, biology for six, history for seven, and mathematics for ten.

Instruction in mathematics begins with primary arithmetic and includes algebra, geometry, trigonometry, and some references to non-Euclidean geometry, one of whose several inventors was a Russian, Lobatchevskii; and the teacher is required, by Party regulation, to make this fact clear to the pupils. Such an item should be left to the judgment of the teacher. The mathematics course includes a brief introduction to the history of elementary mathematics; but the mathematical content and methods are formal and conservative in comparison with advanced teaching practice in the West. The purpose is mainly practical, not the cultivation of independent thinking. With able pupils the scheme is effective in attaining the selected goal.

Recent information raises questions about the effectiveness of the methods with less able pupils. Soviet educators are said to be much disturbed by poor teaching and poor learning in mathematics and physics. In *Izvestia* (June 7, 1958) a soviet teacher reported that high school pupils are losing interest in schoolwork because they find that they will have to work in factories and on farms (*New York Times*, editorial, June 16, 1958). One teacher's report is not conclusive, but there is further evidence such as that of the following paragraph.

For some unexplained reasons, oral examinations prevail in Soviet education. The judgment of a former student upon this practice is as follows: "From personal observation the system of oral examinations seems one of the poorer aspects of the Russian educational system. Since there is a limit to the problems that one can solve orally, the examinations emphasize too much procedural knowledge (i.e., give the *rule* for multiplying fractions) and place a heavy premium upon memorization. The examinations when I took them were recitations, not discussions. It seems to me that this examination system contributes to 'formalism' as much as anything else" (*Documentary and Reference Material on Education in the Soviet Union*, Cambridge, Massachusetts Institute of Technology, 1956, p. 10, no name given).

Some Russians claim that the secondary schools are overloading the pupils. Thirty-three periods a week in the upper years, the heavy emphasis upon mathematics and science, and the excessive demand for memory work place great burdens upon young people, most of whom, as in other countries, will not be geniuses. The same kind of charge has been laid against the German and French schools, as we have shown. In both countries the same causes may have been at work, namely, high competition for scholarships and even for places in the higher institutions. The latter, at least, is a fact in the Soviet Union. The university system is expanding but not rapidly enough to absorb all or even a majority of the secondary school graduates. For at least two years, also, the government has warned that more engineers are being trained than the state industries can use. We return to the schedule. It shows that the child will be exposed to seventeen subjects. The exposure is brief in some cases: one hour a week for a year on the Soviet constitution, and the same for astronomy and psychology; but it is extended in other cases as the schedule indicates. The number of subjects carried at any one time by each pupil varies from six in the early years to eleven or twelve later. The number of class exercises also rises from twenty-four per week to thirty-three. Exclusive of examinations, the school-year extends to thirty-three weeks of class work and one week of excursions. The student can make the needed comparisons with American practice. As in some other European countries, the schools are in session six days a week.

The schedule reveals three main points of concentration in the curriculum. Native and foreign languages are given 104 week-hours, mathematics and science, 100, and history and the constitution, twenty-one. This leaves out geography which is partly a social study but is taught as a natural science. Languages will be hard for some, but we may assume that mathematics and science will be most difficult for many and that not all pupils complete the course. A large number of these are drawn off at the end of the seventh year, and others will fail in the senior school. Figures by Nicholas DeWitt show that only about one-third of the four to five million seven-year-olds who enter the system remain to graduate from the tenth grade (*Comparative Education Review*, June, 1958, p. 9). This is one measure of the success of the system; but we must recall that the ten-year school is not found everywhere.

Teachers for the elementary schools are prepared in training schools in a two-year course. The course for secondary teachers extends over four years and is offered in teachers' colleges. These are organized into faculties and departments. "Faculty" has the sense frequently given it in Europe and is approximately what Americans call a "school," as in School of Fine Arts. It is a major specialized division of a university. The faculties in teachers colleges are: physics and mathematics; natural sciences and geography; language and literature; foreign languages; and, in the larger colleges, a faculty of history. Not all teachers' colleges have a complete program, and they vary greatly in quality. All students must take the required courses in education and in the principles of Marxism, which are taught in special departments serving the whole college. It is to be noticed that there is no faculty, or even department, of philosophy.

Teachers' colleges are classified as higher institutions along with technical schools and universities, but those in the smaller cities do not always justify this ranking. The colleges are distributed over the Union, and large cities may have more than one. Leningrad has four and Moscow, three. Graduates who make the highest grades or who are members of the Party are assigned to ten-year, less able students to seven-year, schools. A former professor in a teachers' college has written: "Exceptions are made in the case of students who are Party members. Regardless of their academic accomplishments they are assigned to ten-year schools. Students who fail the state examinations are classified as 'course auditors' and assigned to teach in elementary schools. In all my experience, I have never known the State Examination Commission to fail a student who was a Party member" (from report by Ivan Rossianin in *Soviet Education*, edited by George L. Kline, London, 1957, p. 79). Similar reports are not infrequent, but Russian teachers deny their substance when Western visitors inquire.

Most officials, but not most teachers or students, are Party members. Higher institutions seem to have less autonomy now than they had under the Czar; and the surveillance of the universities and spying upon students were cultivated as an art and practiced as a vocation under the old regime.

4. HISTORICAL NOTE ON SOVIET EDUCATION

We shall not follow a chronological course. Because of the great interest at present in engineering education, we shall deal with it first; and after some attention to the literacy problem we shall trace the evolution of the schools from the Revolution. The Soviets have a variety of schools that run parallel to the ordinary elementary and secondary schools. Thus, there are opportunities to receive elementary and secondary instruction by correspondence. There are schools for the blind, the deaf, the dull, and those who are crippled or in poor health. We have already mentioned the technicums which prepare their pupils for practical work of various kinds. There are schools with curricula of two or three years for industrial and transport workers who have only an elementary education. Education is provided in children's homes; there are evening schools for rural youth; and until recently there was an apparatus for the removal of illiteracy. No group seems to be overlooked by the Soviets, but how widely these various facilities are available is not readily discovered.

Soviet higher education has grown out of the Czarist school system. The numbers of both institutions and students have increased rapidly. Women are admitted on an equal basis with men, and this was not done in old Russia. There is also a much greater degree of specialization in Soviet technical education than there was before the Revolution. The Soviets criticize the old Russian education as having been too general. They seem to have gone to the opposite extreme.

Under the Czars there were nine universities, attended almost exclusively by members of the upper classes. The present regime in 1957 opened its thirty-seventh university at Ufa near the Urals on the eastern edge of Europe. There are universities far east of the Ural Mountains, also. There are eight or nine hundred polytechnical, engineering, and special schools and institutes giving higher technical education. There are higher schools for workers in the food and fish industries, in oil geology, in electric power, in light industry of various kinds, and in many other specialties. A recent report claims that there are about 4,000 specialized secondary schools in the Union.

Specialists produced by these various institutions are said to be in great demand. Many are mainly technicians who work under the direction of engineers and scientists who understand the theoretical foundations of the techniques used. Russian institutions of higher and especially of technical and semi-technical education have had a decisive effect upon the rapid industrialization of the Soviet empire. It has been noticed that the technical schools have been moving eastward to aid the rapid growth of cities and industries in new regions. We have just noted also the eastern location of the newest university. The making of engineers out of peasants has been a great political achievement. In view of the fear frequently expressed that Russia is outpacing the United States in the preparation of engineers, a few figures are given here from a recent publication.

Table 2. Comparative Numbers of Graduates in Russia and the United States

	U.S.S.R.	U.S.
NUMBER OF HIGHER EDUCATION GRADUATES EMPLOYED IN THE NATIONAL ECONOMY	2,750,000	5,800,000
ESTIMATED NUMBER OF ABOVE TRAINED IN ENGINEERING AND THE SCIENCES	1,730,000	1,600,000
TOTAL NUMBER OF ENGINEERING GRADUATES	720,000	600,000
NUMBER OF ENGINEERING GRADUATES PER 1,000 POPULATION	3.6	3.6
PER CENT ENGINEERING GRADUATES ARE OF ALL HIGHER EDUCATION GRADUATES	26.0	10.4

NOTE: Information from Nicholas DeWitt, *Comparative Education Review*, June, 1958, p. 10; see also R. J. Havighurst, "Is Russia Really Out-producing Us in Scientists," *School and Society*, April 26, 1958.

Some considerations not included in the table or not apparent upon cursory view may be mentioned. The Soviet population numbers about 200 million and the American, 175 million. The numbers of engineering graduates are exactly proportional to the two populations, but the United States has twice as many college and university graduates as the Soviet Union. The broader sweep of higher education in America is one reason for this difference. Soviet education is largely practical and technical; it does not stress the humanities, the arts, social studies, philosophy, and other liberal and cultural disciplines to the extent that American education does. Even some engineering courses in the United States are partly liberal and are becoming more so.

The United States can prepare more engineers if more should be needed, but the present situation is confused. As in Russia, women could be induced to enter the technical fields, and many young men who do not go to college might make good engineers. Preparation for a technical profession requires time, and failure to act now might be costly. But one should not forget that the great numbers of engineers prepared after World War II found positions only because unforeseen conditions arose. It was the fighting in Korea, together with the rising industrial production, growing air transport, and missile and rocket research which have made many new jobs for technically educated men.

The present drive to increase the number of engineers almost without limit is contrary to the spirit of American education, which has never failed to emphasize, along with technical objectives, the ethical and humanistic components of life. The drive is not effective. College enrollments have increased annually since 1952, but engineering freshmen in 1958 were fewer than in 1957 by 7.6 per cent (*School and Society*, December 6, 1958, p. 427). We should also remember that the quality of engineering talent is far more important than numbers. If the American people wish to copy the technical education and materialist philosophy of Russia, they should do it with full knowledge. Even the Soviets admit that they have about reached the saturation point in engineering.

We have treated the growth of technical education first because of the present great interest in it, but, historically, fundamental education had the priority. Russia claims to have reversed the figures on illiteracy. From a population of whom four-fifths were illiterate she has raised the proportion of literate persons to four-fifths of the whole. This claim may be questioned if, as is asserted, the average numbers of years of school attendance in the Soviet Union as a whole is only about four years. This is hardly enough schooling to assure functional literacy. (For a critical view of this question see the essay by Nina Nar in *Soviet Education*, edited by George L. Kline and mentioned above.)

In the process of changing the people, the instrument used—that is, the educational system—was itself changed. Lenin had insisted that the infant can be molded easily, the child or youth less easily, and older persons hardly at all. From the first, therefore, the Soviets laid great importance upon the education of the smallest children. They established infant nurseries for children as young as six weeks, nursery schools for those between two and three years, and kindergartens for three- to seven-year-olds. Communist indoctrination begins soon after the child leaves the cradle.

There was another reason for these state institutions for the very young. Lenin wanted to free women from "petty household tasks and poverty" that crushed, stifled, and degraded them. Women were to be given the same privileges as men, including the privilege of helping to build socialism. Another and truer way of putting this is to say that by freeing mothers from housekeeping, the labor force was greatly increased. It has been estimated that a million women were thus enabled to join the working force in the early thirties when the industrialization drive began. These were found mainly in cities, for that is where nursery schools and kindergartens were established. Even today these institutions are available to only a small proportion of the appropriate age groups, and in this respect Russia does not differ from other Western countries.

Waifs, the homeless and fatherless children, made another problem. Such unfortunates by the thousands resulted from the famines of 1921 and 1933, from war, and from the early practice of easy divorce. Many boys and not a few girls roamed the streets, seeking food and shelter, stealing, and committing depredations. The Communist theory of the ultimate "withering away of the family" proved as mistaken as the parallel theory of the "withering away of the state." The former theory and the practice of "free love" produced a generation of children left by their unmarried or divorced mothers to be cared for in children's homes, if cared for at all. The situation was described in *The Waif* by "Nicholas Voinov."

In the pages which follow we shall trace some of the steps by which the fluid school system of the nineteen twenties became the hard, autocratic system of today. In the twenties, a three- or four-year elementary school was established, and this was expanded into a seven-year and then a nine-year school. Compulsory attendance regulations were announced in 1930 and extended in 1933. At first, school attendance began at the age of eight, but this left an awkward gap of one year since the kindergarten program ended at seven. The ten-year school, taking children at seven, closed the gap. Lenin had died in 1924, and the views of Stalin—the name means steel—began to affect the schools, at least, by 1928. In the middle thirties the present rigid and autocratic system became fully established although there have been some temporary changes. The separate education of the sexes, completely contrary to standard Communist theory, was one of these.

In Lenin's time school practices were comparatively free and easygoing.

Russian theorists, in the manner of John Dewey, declared that there could be no final system or universal philosophy of education. Each school was a sort of soviet with the pupils largely in control. The curriculum was often made up from day to day. This has been called the experimental period, and it continued in one phase or another until the thirties. Great emphasis was laid upon ideological and political indoctrination in socialism, sovietism, and Marxism-Leninism. This object is vigorously promoted not only in the "people's schools," but also in the special Party Schools and by every means of mass communication.

Polytechnical education, which Karl Marx had envisioned, was introduced. It involved the participation by the children in work processes, learning the uses of various tools, the qualities of materials, and the methods of constructing various simple objects. A related scheme introduced somewhat later has been called the activity program. It was, however, a Soviet creation and did not follow the ideas of John Dewey or Georg Kerschensteiner of Munich who developed a Western activity school. According to the Russian plan, children were to help in building socialism. They went out from school to harvest corn, kill potato bugs, carry lunches to workers, or to "liquidate illiteracy." The activity program, sometimes called the project method, was especially emphasized after the First Five Year Plan was undertaken (1928). According to the brigade method a group, rather than individual children, was held responsible for the completion of a task.

Parallel to such schemes there was also a foray into educational psychology or rather pedology, the study of child growth and development. An extensive program of testing and charting the qualities and growth of children was carried on. This was based upon the theory, soon to be repudiated by the Communists, that what a child becomes is determined not by environment and education but by native ability. The program came to a sudden, and for participants, an unhappy end. The Central Committee of the Party decreed in 1936 that the entire pedological experiment must be abandoned. The use of intelligence tests was forbidden, and some of the leaders in the testing program were purged.

Several years ago a London newspaper commented upon some of the "revolutions" in Soviet education: dropping intelligence tests and coeducation (since restored), projects, activity methods, and the reversion to lessons delivered by the teacher and discipline administered by him. The newspaper said: "The reason for this reversal of policy was strictly pragmatic. Russia badly needed an educated population, and the more advanced methods were simply not producing it. Sterner, more disciplined techniques were found to be necessary" (*Times Educational Supplement*, London, August 3, 1951, p. 613). In the following issue a correspondent replied that the new Soviet plan demonstrated simply "that if you wish every member of a population to think alike you dare not teach them to think for themselves."

Some who have come up through the Russian schools agree with this English teacher. The existence of these dissenters may be part of the reason for the recent decision to build boarding schools where the children can be confined to a socialist environment for twenty-four hours a day. Khrushchev in his speech to the Twentieth Congress of the Party (1956) gave no clear explanation of his demand for such schools. Did he want to appease the upper classes who had attained position under Stalin, or was he looking forward to the preparation of a new privileged group? He was not clear.

More than two hundred boarding schools were formed within a year, 1956–1957. These do not seem to cater for an upper class of parents nor to be preparing an elite group. Perhaps the first guess is the best, that the groups of children are to become partly self-governing collectives, small soviets, and that their work is to consist of a combination of mental and manual labor. The manual labor part was emphasized in a criticism of the whole system by Khrushchev in 1958. He declared that Soviet education was making pupils unwilling to work with their hands, and he called for a work and study program through which youth would earn its right to a chance in higher institutions.

A correspondent's account of Boarding School, No. 16, near Moscow hardly supports any of the above ideas. This English visitor found an old building, previously used for a day school, now housing 180 boys and girls, aged seven to twelve years. The wood and metal shops were moderately well equipped; the laboratories for biology, physics, and chemistry could not provide for much individual work. The library was well furnished with books, newspapers, and maps, and the reporter especially noticed translations from English works. There were tables for chess and other games. The rooms were comfortable, the food good and substantial. The director was a photography addict who lost no time in having his visitors pose for him. There were numerous pupil groups, an orchestra, a cinema club, sports organizations, and others. The teachers were young. They had "full control over the children." The curriculum was identical with that of every other elementary school in the Union. The director reacted with "shocked scorn" to the idea that Party members' children were given preferential treatment (*Times Educational Supplement*, London, November 22, 1957, p. 1491). The above is only what one man saw and saw fit to report, but it adds concrete detail to a subject that is often buried under generalizations.

After the launching of the first Sputnik, many Western observers seemed to consider the Soviet school system as nearly perfect. The introduction of the boarding schools should have given warning that Premier Khruschev thought it capable of further improvement. There has now been a further effort to perfect it. In September, 1958, Khrushchev proposed a new reorganization of the previously admired system. The new plan introduces manual work into the lower grades and upon completion of the seven-year school all children, except a small group of intellectuals, are to be put to work in field or factory. If they want to proceed with their schooling, they must attend night classes or take correspondence courses. Only the highly talented will be allowed the privilege of continued full-time schooling. Russia's need for a great labor force may be the reason for the change. Perhaps the boarding schools will, after all, be used to train an elite. The Khrushchev School Reform was approved by the Supreme Soviet at its meeting in December, 1958, to go into effect in the fall of 1959. It is meanwhile opposed by teachers and by many industrial managers, by the latter because they expect difficulty in using untrained youths in their farms and factories. We may be sure that the plan is not popular with the young people. Whether all this dissatisfaction will lead to modification remains to be seen (*Comparative Education Review*, February, 1959, article by Albert Boiter).

The remainder of this chapter will be used to trace American developments since World War II. The contrast with Russia will, with the introduction of the labor plan, be greater than ever.

5. POPULATION CHANGES AND AMERICAN SCHOOLS

To provide teachers and schools for the millions of new Americans is a problem everywhere in the country. The whole number of the people in the United States has grown by one-third in twenty years, and it reached the total of 175,000,000 during 1958. Twenty years ago no such result was expected; but just when the students of vital statistics had agreed that the population would become stationary at about 160 million, a great increase in the birth rate began; and this, without much help from immigration, has raised the population to the present level. Other countries are experiencing a similar expansion suggesting that the guess of Malthus may prove to have been correct. We shall deal only with the educational problem raised in the United States by this population increase.

Several millions of pupils were added to the elementary school enrollment after World War II, and the increase is continuing. At the same time university attendance was high because the veterans in great numbers accepted the educational offer of the government under the GI Bill. Meanwhile high school enrollment was low because of the low birth rate in the thirties. This accidental interlocking of high and low enrollments made possible some adjustments by shifting high school teachers to elementary schools and in some cases to universities. Such relief was temporary and partial and has come to an end. All levels of the educational system are full, and many institutions are hard pressed for teachers, buildings, books, and operating costs. The enrollment in all schools has increased more rapidly than the population, from 32,000,000 in 1948 to 43,000,000 in 1958.

The war caused a great exodus from the teaching profession. It was reported that 350,000 teachers left the schools after Pearl Harbor. If this number seems incredible, we should recall that many teachers leave the profession every year in normal times. After Pearl Harbor they left to enlist, to work in war industries, and to fill gaps which the war had caused in homes, business, and public life. Not many returned to teaching after the war. They had formed other connections, and teachers' salaries were lagging. There has been some improvement in salaries, but in many cases it was not sufficient to offset the increase in the cost of living. Teachers' college enrollments were low, and great numbers of emergency certificates were issued. Children were put on half-time schedules, or oversize classes were set up. When elementary classes have to be over thirty or even twenty-five, there is a teacher shortage.

A debate has been carried on in the press over the seriousness or even the existence of teacher and building shortages. By ignoring such facts as the above it is possible to argue that all is well. But the Ohio State Board of Education has reported that seventy thousand children in the state are attending school in buildings that are unfit for school use. If such conditions exist in Ohio it is probable, and reports affirm, that they exist elsewhere also. A law to lend federal funds for school construction was enacted by Congress, but it was unworkable. The White House Conference on Education (p. 593 f.) voted, two to one, for federal aid to provide school buildings but without result.

Besides the increase in the number of children to be housed and taught, there are other population changes that affect the schools. Immigration, especially from Puerto Rico into New York City, is one of these. Many people also are relocating within the United States, and when they move the receiving districts must provide school accommodations for them. There are four massive trends of this kind: the movement of Negroes from the South into the North and West; the general westward movement, especially into California which is now the second state in population; the movement from the country into the cities; and finally the growth of the suburbs which in some cases almost surround the cities and prevent their expansion. Everyone of these population changes creates great problems for the schools. One thinks first of the financial and school construction problems and the securing of qualified teachers. Wealthy suburbs often pay better salaries than some of the cities, and the two make it difficult for smaller towns and townships to maintain adequate staffs. The relocation also leads to the intermingling of different classes of people. The Pasadena crisis had several causes, but the influx of new people into that residential community is blamed for part of it.

Juvenile delinquency is another problem of the school and society today. It is not peculiar to the United States. England, France, Russia, and many other countries are likewise afflicted. We shall treat of American conditions only.

In the United States, according to the federal Children's Bureau, juvenile delinquency declined steadily, although slowly, from 1929 to 1939. It increased again in the war and since and seems to be at the highest rate in history. If the schools had the staffs to keep their playgrounds and gymnasiums open all day and every evening, if they could direct more club work, and if every school had a junior republic, some delinquency could no doubt be prevented. Waywardness has many causes including bad and broken homes, slums, the traffic in liquor and narcotics, the unrestricted sale of guns, and the failure of the schools to deal with early indications of future trouble. Considerable delinquency takes place in schools as the city papers make plain, and everyone from the board of education to the custodians has the obligation to prevent it as much as possible.

The study of the ways and means to moderate prejudice and group hostility and to promote cultural unity is called intergroup education or the study of human relations. There is an extensive literature but little scientific knowledge and no formulas for the achievement of the desired ends. Teachers seem to know little about intergroup or intercultural studies, and a course of reading in this field would be rewarding. They would at least learn what some of the causes and early manifestations of group conflict are. Although they might not gain any simple solutions, they would be forewarned; and the old proverb has a measure of truth.

6. FEDERAL AID FOR EDUCATION

Public schools in most countries derive their financial support from local, intermediate, and central governments or from two of these. In England school expenses are paid from the funds of local authorities and Parliamentary grants. In that country, as in most others, there are also miscellaneous funds derived from endowments, tuition, rents, and donations that meet a part, usually a small part, of the total costs. Although Parliament votes large grants for schools and universities, public and private, no one claims that the government does or attempts to influence what is to be taught. In France the communes, the departments, and the nation contribute, and the government does exercise control over the schools.

School costs in the United States are paid from local taxation, state appropriations, and federal appropriations for some special purposes such as vocational education, the operation of land-grant colleges, school lunches, and others. There are no regular federal appropriations for general education in the elementary and high schools. This is somewhat strange because the first Congressional action in favor of education was included in the so-called Survey Act of 1785 adopted by the Congress of the Confederation. It began the practice of granting lands for the support of schools and of a university in each state (p. 401). This beginning was also the end of federal support for general education in the states.

As the state systems developed it (1) became evident that the rich states are able to support a complete and excellent program with little effort while the poorer states can with the greatest effort offer only a less adequate program. Yet these are sister states in a nation boasting that it offers equal opportunity to all its people. This seems inconsistent and unwise because (2) the half-educated from any state move freely and at will to states with high educational standards. In the third place, the federal revenue system draws large sums from even the poorest states but will not return a single dollar to aid in teaching little children to read. Many people in both poor and rich states are opposed to federal aid because they think it will lead to federal control. This is not inevitable as England has shown; and also the difference between the state and national control may not be great.

Each of the three greatest wars of the United States has been followed by efforts to secure federal aid (pp. 436 f., 443, 490). Within the two years following the close of World War I, seventy bills and resolutions dealing with education were presented to Congress. One of these proposed a national Department of Education, "with power to shape national educational policy." These two ideas were not absent from the Smith-Towner Bill, introduced in 1919 and promoted by the National Education Association. This bill also included the matching principle whereby the states provide a sum equal to the amount received from the federal treasury, and it restricted aid to public schools only. The bill was not passed.

The struggle was repeated in World War II when a federal aid bill was reported out of committee and debated in the Senate (1943). It did not come to a vote. Senatorial opinion has usually been more favorable to federal aid than that of the House. The powerful Senator Robert A. Taft, long an opponent of federal aid, came out in favor of it. A second bill was actually passed by the Senate in 1948 by the decisive vote of 58 to 15. This bill called for a subsidy of $300,000,000 a year, three times the amount named in the Smith-Towner Bill; and from the bill of 1948 most federal controls had been removed. President Truman favored the bill, but the House, as in the case of the old Blair Bill, would not cooperate. Instead, the Congress appropriated about $90,000,000 for school lunches and vocational education.

To secure passage of special and limited appropriation bills is for obvious reasons far easier than to gain approval of a general law. The Congress also, to give another example, votes relief money to communities which are in difficulty from the erection of military, atomic, or other federal installations within their borders. Such establishments occupy property formerly subject to local taxation and may bring in families with children to be educated in the local schools. The government may provide financial help to local districts which have to carry this extra burden.

The Congress in 1958 was persuaded, by the cold war, the various hot wars, and the fears called out by the Sputniks, to enact a National Defense Education Act providing for a four-year program of federal aid to higher education. The title was doubtless intended to make the bill more palatable, and the act did not infringe upon the right of the states to protect their children from federal propaganda. The law did not grant money for the undergraduate scholarships for which the President had asked nor the much needed aid to school construction which the White House Conference (p. 594) had recommended.

The new law provides for student loans of as much as $1,000 annually for five years. One year after graduation these will begin to bear three per cent interest, and they are repayable in ten years. Special consideration will be given to elementary and secondary school teachers and to able students of mathematics, science, engineering, and foreign languages. The law is to aid the improvement of language-teaching methods and of the study of modern languages not now popular in American schools. The framers of the bill may have had Russian and other Slavic languages and perhaps Chinese, Japanese, and Arabic in mind. The Act provides funds, on the matching principle, for scientific and modern foreign language equipment; and funds to improve counseling, testing, the use of visual aids, and vocational education. It provides for the expenditure on the designated phases of higher education of about $900,000,000 over four years.

7. PROGRESSIVE EDUCATION IN RETREAT

This section reports the criticism directed against progressive education, and it is to serve as an introduction to the more violent assaults upon the schools which led to the organization of the National Citizens Commission to defend the schools. Some opponents of progressive education may not have understood the movement, and it is, in fact, complex and hard to define.

One way to define it is to say that progressive education is an application in schools of the principles of liberty, equality, and fraternity. Progressive education means freedom to grow naturally, freedom from arbitrary control, and free access to surroundings that will stimulate investigation and construction. It means equality of educational opportunity. And fraternity refers to the friendly society of children and adults. Friends, said Plato in the *Phaedrus*, can learn from each other with the finest results. This society is the school, a company of learners including teachers, for that is what teachers, as well as children, are—learners.

These are the principles of the Copernican revolution in education of which Rousseau was the proximate author, just as they were also the principles of the French Revolution which he is said to have inspired. And these are at least some of the essential principles of progressive education; but some think one necessary principle is lacking, namely, that the child must grow up in and for an existing society. We must live in our house, with whatever faults of construction it may have, while it is being rebuilt. John Dewey might not have agreed, and for some progressives and disciples of Dewey this concession spoils everything.

Dewey is given too much credit by some and too much blame by others for the rise of progressive education. We grant that he has been the great leader of the movement, but the conditions of the late nineteenth and early twentieth centuries made the movement inevitable. Some of these conditions were the interpretations of Rousseau by Pestalozzi and Froebel, the kindergarten, the rise of child psychology and scientific method, the stimulating thought of William James, G. Stanley Hall, and Francis W. Parker, the new elementary school with a broader curriculum and milder discipline, and the growing desires and influence of the common man. We admit that Dewey was the most active and ablest leader, but if he had not appeared there would have been others. There were indeed others, but they were overshadowed by Dewey.

Dewey believed that education should be a process of discovery, not one of instruction and drill. His opponents say children in progressive schools do not gain sufficient command of the fundamentals for further progress. Such schools they say are not really progressive. Dewey would have the school be a self-governing society, a democracy, that by actual practice prepares children for the practice of democracy in later life. We learn by doing. Opponents want discipline, control by the teacher. They say progressive schools are noisy, disorderly. Some of them claim that the United States is not a democracy; it is a republic. Dewey bases his program on the child's interests. Extreme progressives would let the child's interests direct the whole program of the school. Dewey and moderates generally would have the teacher guide, enlarge, and improve the child's interests, but his interests, not the adult interests of the teacher, are to be supreme. Education is life, not preparation for life; and its purpose is more life through scientific investigation. Only within this context do the humanities find a place in education.

American schools, not alone the progressive ones, have always been under fire from the Right and the Left alternately, or both together. There seems to be little prospect of a change, and informed and honest criticism is to be welcomed and carefully weighed. The Right had its innings after the break in the stock market in 1929. People were hard pressed to pay their taxes and resented the heavier burden caused by rising high school enrollments. One heard again the proposals of 1895 to abolish the free public high school or to make admission selective, or at least to discard the frills, even foreign languages, and to reduce the salaries of the teachers. Teachers had to wait for considerable periods in some cities for their wages.

Criticism of progressive education was another matter. It increased in the depression but much more after World War II. A group known as the Essentialists led by William C. Bagley charged that in progressive schools pupils did not learn the fundamental school arts well enough. Colleges had to set up remedial classes in composition and arithmetic. Investigators showed that these educational failures were not more numerous in progressive than in conventional schools. But the public demanded that the basic school arts be more thoroughly taught and that the emphasis upon drill be increased. Instruction and acquisition, not interest, became the slogan.

The high point of the attacks upon the schools was reached in the early fifties when it, indeed, became strident, irresponsible, and effective. Only the beginning of this hostile campaign could be seen in 1947 (p. 490). One effect, much later, was the dissolution in 1955 of the Progressive Education Association. Two years later the magazine *Progressive Education,* published since 1922, was also discontinued; and this announcement was greeted editorially in a daily paper as "a modest note of cheer in the news." Editors were not always so considerate. Several popular magazines opened their pages to slashing attacks on the progressives.

Teachers' colleges and university colleges of education have been frequent targets of the critics. Since most of these schools are favorable to at least a moderate progressivism, the attacks on them may be taken as, in part, criticisms of the progressive movement. Sometimes these schools are attacked also because they are unlike the liberal arts colleges, but this is a virtue. They have special functions with which liberal arts colleges have little concern unless they prepare teachers. Teachers' colleges are more justly accused of offering too many fragmented courses and that they often dwell on the obvious.

Charges of Communist teachers and teaching were frequently made, sometimes in vague general charges, sometimes by naming particular schools or persons. This was the Senator Joseph McCarthy era of unprincipled propaganda. Often school boards, as in Pasadena, California, were more easily intimidated than private institutions. In many cities, groups of the citizenry were organized in defense of the public schools, and there were also national associations formed for this purpose and for the broader aim to raise the effectiveness of public education. One of these was the National Citizens Commission for the Public Schools.

8. NATIONAL CITIZENS COMMISSION FOR THE PUBLIC SCHOOLS

A sinister campaign directed not against progressive practices but against public education itself followed the war. The opening for it may have been created by the attacks on the progressives; and the emotional disturbance of the war, the rise in prices, and the population shifts caused by the demand for workers in war industries roused the hostile elements to action. Some of the leaders talked like real Fascists and used the "big lie" and the underhanded methods of Fascism. Some of their organizations, for example, imitated the names of responsible teachers' associations. Only alert teachers were able to distinguish the National Council for American Education from the well-known American Council on Education and took the pains to inquire into the right of the new group to speak for the public schools.

Various "front" organizations issued pamphlets, published periodicals, and attempted to fan any smoldering dissatisfaction in local situations. They called public education socialistic and teachers communistic. One of their widely circulated publications was called, "How Red the Little Red Schoolhouse?" The little red schoolhouse was, of course, not red inside. The owner of a chain of newspapers that extends into several states called public education unconstitutional and contrary to the Ten Commandments. He seemed to be most concerned about school taxes. Textbooks in the social studies, some that were in wide use, were attacked and had to be withdrawn. As after World War I, several states passed teachers' oath laws.

There were, as indicated, economic and psychological causes for the dissatisfaction. To the rising costs, changes in the distribution of the population, the difficulties arising from the higher birth rate, and postwar shortages of teachers and buildings must be added the failure of the schools to keep the public informed about school conditions, needs, and plans. Especially unfortunate was the attempt to push new policies before the public was ready to endorse them. And wherever local dissatisfaction became known, the trouble-makers, who live and sometimes live well on trouble, moved in.

The National Citizens Commission for the Public Schools was formed in 1949 with Mr. Roy E. Larsen of *Time, Life,* and other magazines as chairman; but the suggestion for such a group was made by President James B. Conant of Harvard three years earlier. President Conant proposed that the leading citizens of the United States should spend at least one-tenth of the time and effort on the vital problems of public education that they spend on hospitals or the discussion of foreign policy.

The Commission proposed "to help Americans to realize how important our public schools are to our expanding democracy, and to arouse in each community the intelligence and will to improve our public schools." The Commission secured the cooperation of the Advertising Council in an effort to reach "every citizen in the United States." Press, radio, public meetings, and even posters in public conveyances were used to tell people about citizens committees in each community. Plans for raising money for school buildings, advice on the proper composition of school boards, and answers to unfounded charges against the schools were developed. The Commission reached millions of people and achieved great positive results. Other older organizations helped. These included the National Congress of Parents and Teachers, the General Federation of Women's Clubs, and many others.

How much influence the National Citizens Commission may have had upon the national administration in Washington may not be known; but President Eisenhower in his State of the Union Message in 1954 called for a White House Conference to report in November, 1955, on the condition of education in the country. Local and state meetings were held throughout the nation to study conditions and needs and to prepare plans for school improvement. Connecticut made one of the earliest state reports, and her problems were typical, were indeed the ones already mentioned several times: how to find and retain enough competent teachers, keep ahead of growing enrollments with buildings, and hold the interest and support of local constituencies. Not all of these could be bought with money, but school taxation and bond issues had high priority among school needs. The question: Would the people shoulder the necessary financial burden, revise the school tax laws, rationalize district boundaries, and provide for financial aid by the rich districts to the poorer ones and federal aid to the weaker states?

The White House Conference met in Washington in November, 1955.

The Chairman was Neil McElroy, a business executive and now Secretary of Defense. The delegates were chosen by state conferences and by a sub-committee of these which added others from labor, business, and welfare organizations from all parts of the country. They were a cross-section of middle-class America including housewives, farmers, doctors, executives, and a minority of educators.

The surprising decision of the Conference was a two-to-one vote in favor of federal aid for school construction. It was probably this unpalatable outcome that caused a conservative paper in mid-America to make the absurd charge that the conference had been "stacked." The total effect of the resolution turned out to be less important than had been hoped. The Congress passed a wholly unworkable law providing for loans to the states for school construction. The Conference also expressed its opinion on educational aims, school districts, school finance, teacher recruitment, and the maintenance of citizen interest in schools. The press covered the Conference (*Saturday Review*, December 21, 1955). The preparation for the Conference and the meeting itself performed an important service in providing a means of communication between the schools and the people in community, state, and nation.

Another effort to improve communication was made by the Kellogg Foundation which contributed $3,500,000, to be spent over a five-year period in the study of the general and professional education of school administrators and of means to protect the schools from those who were attempting to undermine public education. The subsidy was later increased, and the study was continued beyond the five-year period. In its report for the year 1955–1956, the Foundation said that the attacks upon public education were the reason that it was supporting the study. (The nature of the attacks can be seen in such books as the one by Scott and Hill, listed on p. 569, and other sources to which that book will serve as a guide.)

9. INTEGRATION AND STATES RIGHTS

By unanimous decision the Supreme Court in 1954 declared racial segregation in public schools to be unconstitutional. The decision was based upon the Fourteenth Amendment, adopted in 1868, which declares that "No State . . . [may] deny to any person within its jurisdiction the equal protection of the laws." The Amendment, therefore, in form and intent limits the powers of the states.

The judgment of the Court was directed particularly against the segregated schools for whites in the South, but it applies to all races and all public schools everywhere in the United States. Public schools from the kindergarten to the state universities must admit qualified persons without respect to race. This is merely another instance among many in which the high court has made new application of the Fourteenth Amendment. Nor is the segregation decision a unique instance in which the Court has acted to limit state control of schools. It is, therefore, idle for state officials to claim, as some do, that their states are sovereign political entities.

The Constitution as it is interpreted by the Supreme Court limits the powers and sovereignty of the states. It seems to be the fact that the federal government, from its first institution onward, has been extending its powers over the states. Now and then state legislatures and the Congress have acted to contain this process and have attempted to build a dike for this purpose. So today several states have enacted laws that, in order to prevent racial integration, would close all public schools. If the federal courts void these laws it will be another proof that the states are not as completely sovereign as some politicians claim. The answer to this question is beginning to appear, as we shall presently show.

A list of several Supreme Court decisions, which restrict each state in its function as public educator, will place the segregation decision in its proper class. In *Meyer* v. *Nebraska,* 262 U.S. 390, the Court in 1923 declared unconstitutional a state law which prohibited the teaching of foreign languages in the elementary grades, a teaching practice now much approved and in use. In the so-called Oregon Case, 268 U.S. 510, the Court denied the state the right to prohibit private schools. The Court has rendered several decisions on religion and matters of conscience in relation to public education. Two important ones were those in the McCollum Case, 330 U.S. 203 (1948), and *Zorach* v. *Clauson,* 343 U.S. 306 (1952). It was, perhaps, an unfriendly voice that called the Supreme Court our "national school board," but whether friendly or not the phrase implies the fact that states are not altogether sovereign in school affairs. The citizens whose education the states direct are citizens of the United States and of the state in which they live. On this point see, again, the Fourteenth Amendment. This dual citizenship should receive consideration from those who believe that each state is meeting its full responsibility in educating citizens, and from those who are against federal aid to education.

The education of Negroes was forbidden by law in many states of the South before the Civil War. During and after Reconstruction, there were some private and public efforts to provide schools for them. When all-white governments again came into control, compulsory segregation laws were enacted in seventeen states. It is these states, reaching from Delaware to Texas, which are principally affected by the school integration decision.

We shall trace the history further. The theory of Negro education was modified in 1896 by the doctrine that school facilities for the two races were to be "separate but equal." This was mainly theory and has remained theory. Negro schools are generally poorly built and equipped and their teachers poorly prepared and paid. Some excellent buildings for Negro children have been constructed in the South in an effort to head off integration, and there are other exceptions, but the difference exists at all levels. The land grant colleges for Negroes are not the equals of those for whites for reasons that are noted in Chapter 18.

The attitudes toward the Negro which were maintained at the South, after slavery, the Civil War, and Reconstruction, can be understood. The whites were only human, but their educational policy was doubtless a mistake in economics. Better education would have rendered the Negro population economically more productive and would have offered the South a market such as absentee owners, share croppers, and underpaid labor cannot provide. This was the argument of Booker Washington. The argument of the Supreme Court in its integration decision has been called sociological, but it is also inherently economic. At all events the Court did not interpret the Constitution in purely abstract terms as if it had no concern with social and economic fact.

The Court said: "Today, education is perhaps the most important function of state and local governments. . . . It is required in the performance of our most basic public responsibilities, even service in the armed forces. It is the very foundation of good citizenship." The Court concluded that "in the field of public education the doctrine of 'separate but equal' has no place. Separate educational facilities are inherently unequal."

In a later statement the Court directed the states and school districts to proceed "with all deliberate speed" in the integration of the schools. The belief has been expressed that, if the Court in 1954 had demanded immediate integration, compliance would have been more general. This is an opinion. It is a fact that in the interval the opponents organized the "white councils" to resist the order. Delay also gave opportunity for disorderly and lawless elements to concentrate in the areas where they could make trouble. There has been some violence in several places. Laws were enacted by Virginia and other states which required the closing of public schools where federal courts order integration. The Virginia laws were declared unconstitutional by the federal courts in February, 1959. This was a great defeat for the cause of segregation. Small-scale integration is proceeding in Virginia in Norfolk, Arlington, Alexandria, and elsewhere in the state, but Charlottesville has been granted a stay until the autumn school term of 1959. Resistance will be greatest in the southern and eastern counties which have a large Negro population. The National Association for the Advancement of Colored People may now move for further integration in North Carolina, where there is token integration now, and the segregated regions of the South will doubtless be whittled down; but some such areas may remain for some years.

Integration is complete in the District of Columbia and practically complete in the states of West Virginia, Missouri, and Oklahoma; it is proceeding in parts of Arkansas, Delaware, Kentucky, where Louisville gave an example of early and peaceful integration under the lead of a statesman-superintendent, Maryland, North Carolina, Tennessee, and Texas. It cannot be said that statesmanship could have gained early and peaceable integration everywhere, but it seems evident that selfish politicians have been the fomenters of trouble in some places. Separate schools for Negroes continue in South Carolina, Georgia, Florida, Alabama, Mississippi, and Louisiana. By their decisions, vacillating federal judges have given comfort to segregationists. In the Supreme Court all decisions and orders on the issue have been unanimous. Except in the Deep South, which is firmly opposed to integration, the present situation is unstable. The controversy can be followed in the newspapers and weekly news magazines. These are read abroad also, and the harm that has been done to the nation's prestige in Asia and Africa is considerable; the support given to lawlessness at home is another bad result of the struggle.

10. OPPORTUNITY FOR TALENT

The high school remained selective until the end of the nineteenth century, but then the rise of the junior high school, the lengthening of the compulsory attendance period, and the lack of jobs for youth in a country that was becoming industrialized brought more pupils into the upper schools. They did not all stay; but administrative wisdom as well as public demand led the schools to broaden their program and even dilute it with such subjects as grooming, dating, and table manners. It is not that these are unnecessary skills in civilized life, but only that they were formerly learned in the home, or in school were taught incidentally as needed.

Life-adjustment education is the name given to the type of instruction indicated above. It may include some more weighty subjects such as hygiene, family life, thrift, consumer education, citizenship, and further teaching of the common branches. Even with this kind of program for the unacademic youth, it is not fair to apply the derisive term "custodial institutions" to the high schools as if they merely kept the youth off the streets until they could go to work.

An exponent of vocational education, Charles Allen Prosser, in a resolution (1947) called upon the schools to provide for the education of "all American youth" to the age of eighteen. England has undertaken a corresponding program to age sixteen. The Prosser resolution started from the premise that 60 per cent of the young people are one- or two-talent persons who cannot master an academic curriculum, or are persons in such circumstances that, even if they acquired such knowledge, it would be of no use to them in the life which they would lead. The need, he thought, was for life-adjustment education for the 60 per cent. For comparison we may note that the English are finding about 60 or 70 per cent of their youth unable to cope with grammar school or technical school programs. These go to a modern school.

At this point our history tends to become a lesson in current events. Educators are dividing into several groups over the merits and demerits of the life-adjustment program. Publications of the National Education Association recommend it. Some private school leaders declare that such courses are a fraud foisted upon the public. Public high school teachers not infrequently oppose the lengthening of the compulsory attendance period to age eighteen and urge the repeal of the law where it is now in force. A half-dozen academic professors in leading universities are both the bitterest and the most vocal opponents and some of their books and addresses have called out protests and replies from educators. It is hard to know what the people think, but they pay the school tax and elect the school boards. They seem to favor schools for all the children whatever the number of their talents.

Children with many talents have generally been allowed to find or make their own way. Democracy favors equality and, DeTocqueville thought, mediocrity. What about equality of opportunity? The answer is that the kind of school which suits the one-talent child only irritates and bores the talented. Equal opportunity is not the same opportunity for all; it is simple arithmetic and narrative for some and quadratics and short-story writing for others. The talented are neglected in school because democracy is interpreted as equality of status; or because some schools are weak and many are overcrowded; or because teachers know far less chemistry, electronics, or whatever it may be than some of their bright pupils. The fault lies not in the teacher but in the failure to provide for the talented.

The National Science Foundation is carrying out plans to aid science teachers improve their understanding of science and science education. There is activity among mathematics teachers also. College professors, sometimes unjustly critical of education in the lower schools, need to become more familiar with the actual conditions and problems of high school teaching. One easy lesson would be that science is not the only field with which pupils should become somewhat familiar. Other fields to be considered would be the Russian language, English composition, American history, and good manners and morals.

School administrators and teachers sometimes suffer from a professional myopia. They see problems near at hand but need the corrections that laymen can provide. One such report was prepared in 1958 for the Rockefeller Brothers Fund. This study held, first, that we must not choose between a fair education for everyone and an excellent one for leaders. We must have both, and both must be better than they have been. Teachers must be given better academic and professional education. Salaries must be raised. The United States should not spend only $14,000,000,000 as is now done but should spend $30,000,000,000 on public education. A larger share of local taxes should be spent on education. The federal government already spends great sums for education but should bear a far larger proportion of the total cost. The report adds that the crisis in science education is real and is caused by the rapid increases in technology. This report does not tell how education is to be improved. More money by itself will not do it. It does not tell how the education of teachers is to be made better. There are several views on that subject, including the proposal to drop most or all of professional education for teachers which this report would, however, retain.

The Rockefeller Brothers Fund report seems to endorse the present emphasis upon the teaching of science and perhaps of technology. For a century technical education has served man's practical interests, guiding him toward the improvement not of industry only but also of agriculture, engineering, medicine, surgery, and, alas, warfare also. This so-called second industrial revolution began with the discovery of new sources of power, the dynamo which fascinated and shocked Henry Adams (1838–1918), and the gas engine which made plane and automobile feasible. Science has been the means of changing man's material conditions in the past few centuries more than in all previous time.

Schools now have the task of bringing science teaching up to the level demanded by the present age. Neither the schools nor the people are prepared for this difficult change. But there is a new seriousness and greater interest in academic work. A survey of the studies chosen in 1958 in the high schools of Maryland shows that the students with a high level of intelligence are choosing to take seven years of mathematics and science. This is a surprising change. If nearly all should continue and complete this program and if the change became general, it would constitute an academic revolution.

To raise the teaching of science and other subjects as well to the level demanded by present conditions should not be too difficult. College students are a little older, more mature, and less collegiate than they were. Some have completed their military service; many are married; a greater number are from working-class families; and a considerable proportion are earning part of their expenses. It is unfortunate that some cannot stay to complete their courses. This last condition existed fifty years ago, and many who dropped out for a time returned later and finished. All this proves their determination to achieve "success," if not scholarship.

The success of science teaching depends upon the intellectual and scientific understanding of the supporting public and upon the teacher, textbook, and equipment. The public is the controlling factor. Americans are eager for quick results of a practical kind such as roads, factories, markets, and jobs. They favor engineering at the expense of fundamental science. The teacher is not an independent agent and in his environment he is naturally prone to select the textbook and equipment which the public demands. The public has been satisfied in many cases with teachers who were themselves inadequately grounded in the principles of their sciences. It is in this context that the National Science Foundation chose to attempt to re-educate the science teacher as holding the key to the problem. School boards must either employ teachers with adequate preparation and pay them enough to keep them, or the teachers now in the schools must be re-educated. As one means of re-education, the Foundation uses the science teachers' institutes conducted in universities, either in six- or eight-week summer terms or, for teachers on leave, throughout the college year. Several million dollars are appropriated annually in support of the full-year program. This enrolls fewer teachers but produces results of a more fundamental kind.

The number of summer institutes is large enough to exert an influence upon the teaching of the whole country. For the summer of 1959, 350 institutes were scheduled. Almost every state had at least one and populous states had many. Others were held in Puerto Rico, Hawaii, and the city of Washington. Funds were available for the expenses of about 18,000 high school and college teachers. The institutes dealt with the teaching of most of the basic sciences and mathematics; in some the instruction was adapted to the needs of junior or senior high school teachers, and in others to those of college teachers.

The Foundation supports other programs also. It bears part of the expenses of the Physical Science Committee which is preparing a new high school textbook in physics and a set of simple laboratory apparatus as well as accessory manuals to aid pupils and teachers in the use of these new tools. The Foundation carries its campaign into the smaller colleges by sending university professors to give lectures and counsel to teachers and students in the science departments. The preparation of science films for use in school television is another current enterprise. The films have been made generally available to schools through Encyclopaedia Britannica Films. The science films of the future will be strictly scientific, avoiding the dramatic and distracting by-play of earlier attempts. Two examples are the high school films *Combustion* and *Chlorine* which are being distributed now.

There remains the further problem of gaining greater public interest and the financial support of foundations and professional associations for the improvement of education in the humanities, social studies, arts, and other knowledges and skills that do not bake bread. Not everyone should become a scientist or an engineer. Anyone who has observed the rise and sudden fall of many movements and fads in education knows that this is a real problem. Already it is reported that students have been enrolled in engineering who came to college with no intention of choosing that profession. It is not ten years since the profession was supposed to be saturated. Doubtless, at present more engineers and scientists are needed, and better ones. But science is not enough; knowledge is not enough. The spirit of man must be cultivated through religion, philosophy, literature, music, and all the great arts which interpret the inner life of man. Talents vary and education must be adapted to them, not they to it.

11. ADULT EDUCATION

All free nations have free institutions for the further education of those who are no longer full-time pupils or students. The exercise of freedom, mental health, changes in politics and in occupations make adult education necessary. Adult education in the United States has had a varied history. It may have begun in the evening schools of the eighteenth century. The lyceum, the Chautauqua Institution, and university extension began in the nineteenth century. One of the old forms is the public evening school which is prominent in larger towns. Since World War II, public school adult education has grown at a more rapid rate than the regular daytime schools; but its base to begin with was much smaller.

Training programs in banking and other kinds of business and industry are growing rapidly. The increasing number of high school graduates who do not go to college attend private business colleges or trade and technical schools in many cases. Students of this development are predicting great increases in such adult vocational schools.

Correspondence courses were offered in the United States in 1873 and have succeeded beyond any dreams of their early promoters. Private home-study courses are said to enroll more new students each year than the colleges. There are, probably, three hundred such schools in the United States, and they offer courses in almost every kind of subject. The schools are of every grade of competence and vary even in honesty. Only a minority are members of the National Home Study Council, which was organized in 1926 to protect students and reputable schools. The government offers correspondence courses to men in uniform through its United States Armed Forces Institute. The public forum and town meeting type of adult education grew rapidly in the nineteen forties. Town meetings are often broadcast by radio and television. The American Adult Education Association attempts to promote and coordinate activities in this field. It is a private voluntary body. The *Journal of Adult Education* is one of its publications.

University extension in the United States began about 1887. Like some other educational institutions for adults, it was borrowed from England; but it has developed in a less academic form in the United States than in the country of its origin. The most elaborate of the early forms of university extension was organized at the University of Chicago which was opened in 1892 under a president, William Rainey Harper, who was experienced in the teaching of adults, in and out of universities. His subject was the Hebrew language and literature, and he was so expert that at least one university professor of mathematics took his course to study Harper more than Hebrew. Under President Harper, the University of Chicago had not merely a department but a fully organized Division of University Extension. Off-campus classes, correspondence courses, a library department, a lecture-study department, and other services were announced, but only the correspondence department survived the general decline which came over university extension in its first period.

The second period opened at the University of Wisconsin. It was marked by a change from academic and liberal arts subjects to the idea of state-wide service on "the broadest basis." The University "Cannot escape," said President Charles R. Van Hise, "from taking on the function of carrying knowledge to the people." This he said is the definition of university extension. It means taking knowledge to the masses; and he might have included practical services, to dairymen, industrialists, labor unions, all who needed any help that the state university was able to give. The theory was that the state is the campus of the university.

As a result of this idea, and the federal legislation of 1914, the Smith-Lever Act, and of 1917, the Smith-Hughes Act, agricultural extension became by far the largest segment of university extension. It has four times as many enrollments as all other forms of university extension combined. Service to public education is another important form. And through institutes, forums, and conferences university extension aids service clubs, women's clubs, and other sections of the public. It deals also with matters of local and national policy and should probably treat controversial matters of opinion more than it does. Money and staff are other problems. There is a National University Extension Association to aid institutions in exchanging and pooling the knowledge that comes from experience in a field that needs better organization.

12. TELEVISION IN EDUCATION

Television in less than ten years has become a significant addition to the equipment of the school. Other recent additions include moving picture equipment, tape recorders, and the radio. History was made by the Federal Communications Commission in 1945 when it set aside the 88–92 megacycle band in FM radio for noncommercial use; and again in 1952 the Commission helped the school by setting aside about one in eight of the available television channels for use by educational institutions.

The earliest schools in the ancient world had no special equipment, not even desks; and if they used books, these were literary works. Ancient word lists that have been found were the early beginnings of the textbook which, in a multitude of forms and in all fields, is the most essential of all special aids to learning. Reference works such as the encyclopedia and the indispensable dictionary form the second attacking column in the battle against ignorance. In the fifteenth century the printing press came in to improve the form and reduce the cost of books and to make universal education feasible and also necessary. The list of helps to learning includes writing materials, maps, collections, and museums, laboratories, shops, kitchens, and gardens. From these artificial means the pupil goes out to nature and life, to the panorama of the sky, and land, and sea, and to the activities of man. Television is the most effective means of bringing that panorama and those activities indoors for study.

Television, in one way of looking at it, is only a more effective book, and more effective only in some fields and some ways of using it. The high school films *Combustion* and *Chlorine*, mentioned above in Section 11, do not include chemical formulae or the periodic table. These are handled in ordinary classwork with textbooks and charts, and drill. The educational world is in the experimental stage in its use of the new instrument. Yale University is reported to have been a pioneer in operating a closed-circuit TV station, heard only on the campus. Others are also using this plan for both entertainment and education. The results already obtained in New York City, Philadelphia, Pittsburgh, Oklahoma City, and many other places, coast to coast, have generated enormous enthusiasm. At the same time many are cautioning against overconfidence. Some fear that it might become an educational toy spreading entertainment rather than understanding. There is the danger that it may stress information too heavily. In the sciences, for example, the pupils will see experiments performed instead of themselves performing experiments. People have long complained that the modern laboratory with textbooks and manuals gives the student too much help. How can he become ingenious by merely following directions? Television and radio have the defects that when the performance ends the student has only a memory and memory is a weak faculty. The book can be read again, the experiment can be repeated, but the television performance when done is done.

The Fund for the Advancement of Education, a subsidiary of the Ford Foundation, is continuing its investigation of educational television which was carried on in 1957–1958 in the public schools of several large cities, including Detroit and Milwaukee. The investigation compared the results obtained by the ordinary method with those obtained from the use of television. The balance, according to a preliminary report, was in favor of the television classes. Other comparisons have been made in Maryland, North Carolina, and Oklahoma. In Oklahoma television was adapted to the capacities of gifted pupils in about fifty high schools. In New York State television lessons are supplied to two million pupils. One of its uses is in the teaching of English to the Spanish-speaking Puerto Ricans who are coming into the metropolis in large numbers. The Fund for the Advancement of Education is continuing its investigation during 1958–1959.

The thirty-fourth station for educational television began operation in Gainesville, Florida, in 1958. Permits have now been granted to eighty stations, and the expectation that fifty will be operating in 1959 is reported by the press. As with any new device there is the problem of finding the best use of it. Even a blackboard may be used unwisely. It was in such terms that the President of the Fund for the Advancement of Education, Alvin C. Eurich, evaluated the new instrument. He said: "Television is only an educational tool. It makes the best teachers available to more persons, as books make the best writers available. It won't do the whole job—but then books didn't either."

13. IN CONCLUSION

Customs, the arts, and the primary elements of civilization develop earlier than schools. The invention of writing, the appearance of religious books, and the need for business records make formal education necessary. This may be carried on by private instruction, but as the numbers of learners and teachers increase, the school becomes an economical instrument for the maintenance and improvement of education.

Schools teach counting, writing, and other so-called school skills, but they do more. They teach indirectly as well as explicitly. Children and youths in school learn from each other. A school is, or it should be, a society where children live and work in cooperation with each other and with the society outside the school. A New Jersey court once held that even the best and best-educated parents are not qualified to educate their children at home. Home education, the Court said, is necessarily inadequate because the children need to learn the social and democratic qualities and abilities which can be gained only in association with other children. This, although correct, is a somewhat sophisticated view of the matter. Early schools were for centuries largely knowledge and skill factories. Schools have developed far beyond those early conceptions. They have a history.

History is the record of human experience. Experience that is recorded can be examined at leisure at a later time and compared with new experience. Thus experience is amplified and criticized by later experience. Your experience can be compared with mine, that of America with that of England, and this process may bring wisdom.

The history of education performs a similar function in its proper field. Since formal education is usually carried on in schools, the history of schools is a part of the history of education. Schools were for many centuries carried on by private arrangements or, in Europe, by the Church. Today most schools are maintained by the state, and in the United States most schools are controlled by elected boards. The modern state finds it desirable to have all young people educated and aims to make schools accessible to all and adapted to the capacities of all. School buildings, the organization and administration of school systems, and many other topics become matters of school legislation. The history of education reports on the development of school systems, and comparative education studies these systems in relation to each other. School curricula, management, and teaching methods have all gone through progressive changes and are important topics in the history of education. Method depends upon many conditions, but equipment is an important factor. In 1947 German children were taught to read from lessons written on the blackboard because there were no acceptable books. Long ago there was no blackboard either. Today new equipment, such as the television set, is affecting teaching and may revolutionize some phases of it. The history of school equipment is a significant part of the history of education.

In the modern state the school is a national instrument, and public education varies with the nature of the state and its government. Governments have used the schools to select and train able and obedient public servants while providing only limited opportunities for the unselected masses. Governments have seized all means of popular knowledge and intercommunication and have used the schools to indoctrinate whole peoples with a philosophy of aggression and to inflame them with the desire for military conquest. We must not forget the lessons from the past and present dictatorships. The first lesson is that there is something radically wrong with a system that prevents the people from learning the economic and political conditions at home and abroad.

The history of education teaches that there is often a vast difference between theory and practice. It has been said that it is easier to teach twenty what should be done than to be one of the twenty to practice the teaching. The progressive education movement in the United States may serve as an example. Even to preserve the gains of the past may be difficult. And while inspiration may be gained from the great figures of history, from Pestalozzi or Horace Mann, they are not to be imitated. Their problems are not ours. We must seek new solutions of today's new issues. And yet, some old solutions have permanent value: to seek and to teach the truth, to respect the individual person, and to love our neighbor. These deserve to be specially mentioned because they are so often flouted today.

INDEX

AACHEN, 73; Council of, 75
Abbotsholme, 336, 360, 487, 554
Abelard, 88, 102, 117
Academies, French, 92, 170; German knightly, 92, 170; English, 170; American, 367, 403; Franklin's, 389; influence and defects of American, 390; becoming high schools, 501
Academy, Plato's, 32, 39
Academy of Sciences, French, 177
Accademia dei Lincei, 177
Accademia del Cimento, 177
Accrediting plans, high school, 510
Adams, John, president, 403
Adams, John Quincy, 427
Addison, Joseph, 347
Adelhard of Bath, 87, 88
Adler, Felix, 287, 473; and Ethical Culture Schools, 485
Adult education, 601–604, early forms, 601; correspondence schools, 601 f.; university and agricultural extension, 602 f.
Ælfric, 345
Aeneas Sylvius, 128
Aesop, 26, 71
Agassiz, Louis, 428, 465; summer school at Penikese, 488, 467; as teacher, 464
Agricola, Rudolph, 135, 149
Aims of education, Hebrew, 14; Greek, 15, 18; Spartan, 20 f.; Athenian, 23 f., 27 ff.; Plato's, 35; Alexandrian, 38 f.; early Roman, 44 f.; later Roman, 48; Quintilian's, 54 f.; early Christian, 62 f.; monastic, 72; chivalric, 91; in medieval cities, 99 ff.; of medieval universities, 106; in Italian Renaissance, 114, 119 f., 126, 131; Luther's, 155 ff.; Jesuit, 162; of Comenius, 192 ff.; philanthropinist, 202, 230 f.; Rousseau's, 208, 213; Condorcet's, 219 f.; of benevolent despots, 225; Pestalozzi's, 234, 244 f.; Herbart's, 256; Froebel's, 276, 278 ff.; Napoleon's, 297 f.; in France, 312 ff.; in German Republic, 332, 335; English, 347; American, 373, 398, 402 ff., 415, 417, 467 f.; Felix Adler's, 473 f., 485; F. W. Parker's, 477; Progressive, 485 ff., 491; high school, 519, 527; Soviet, 572 ff.
à Kempis, Thomas, 149

Akkad, 8; language of, 11
Akron (Ohio) law, 498
Alaric, 54
Alberti, Leon Battista, 117, 128, 133
Albert the Great, 89
Albigenses, 143
Alchemy, 87
Alcibiades, 30
Alcott, Amos Bronson, 484
Alcuin, 69, 74 f.
Aldhelm, 345
Aldus, printer, 125; his press, 145
Alexander the Great, 36
Alexandria, 37, 59 ff., 84, 92; catechetical school in, 63
Alfred the Great, 76, 345 f.
al-Khwarizmi, 85 ff.
Almagest, 88
al-Razes, 86
Alsted, J. H., 189
American Adult Education Association, 548 f.
American Education Fellowship, 490
American Institute of Instruction, 418
American Lyceum, 418 f.
Americanization of Pennsylvania Germans, 337, 382 f.
Andreae, John V., 170, 173; on education of small children, 269
Andrews, F. F., 559
Angell, James R., 486, 507
Antioch College, 407
Aporti, Ferrante, 272
Apperception, 254 ff.
Apprenticeship, 7 f., 96 ff., 157; indenture, 97; laws on, 161, 346; in American colonies, 369, 374–376
Aquinas, Thomas, 89, 115
Arabic language, 84, 86 ff.
Aramaic language, 13
Archaeology, 5, 7, 10; classical, 116
Archimedes, 37, 179
Aristarchus, 37
Aristotle, 22, 66, 71, 113, 120, 250, 253; educational theory, 36; his Lyceum, 39; his logical works, 88; recovery of his works, 88; intellectual crisis caused by, 89
Arithmetic, in Greek schools, 26 f.; Roman, 47; Hindu-Arabic notation, 87, 95; Pestalozzian mental and primary, 243 f., 463;

[607]

also mentioned, 58, 64, 97, 99, 145, 186, 373, 409
Arndt, Ernst Moritz, 321
Arnold, Matthew, 30, 309; as school inspector, 354
Ars dictaminis, 100
Ashurbanipal, 10 f., 14
Asceticism, 66 ff., 90
Association psychology, 173, 250 ff.; laws of, 251 f.; secondary laws of, 252 f.
Athens, 22 ff., 28 ff., 32 f., 37 f.
Athletics, 20 f., 28, 30, 36
Aufbauschule, 333, 336
Augustine, Saint, 59, 64, 120, 165, 253
Aurispa, 122
Averroes, 86 ff.
Avicenna, 86
Avignon, 119, 141
Aydelotte, Frank, 560

BACHE, ALEXANDER, 319, 322, 337; president Philadelphia Central High School, 501
Bacon, Francis, 170, 181, 418, 463; inductive method, 178
Badley, J. H., 360
Bagdad, 84 f.
Bagley, W. C., 591
Bailey, Ebenezer, 426, 500
Bailey, Liberty H., 469
Bain, Alexander, 253
Baldwin, Bird T., 476
Baldwin, Joseph, 447
Balliol College, 134
Bancroft, George, and the Round Hill School, 337
Bangor, Irish monastery, 68
Barnard, Henry, 246, 384, 422, 425, 505, 556; infant school promoter, 271; educational editor, 352, 418; on grading of schools, 497; organizer, normal institute, 448; on object-teaching, 464, 466 f.; kindergarten notice, 471; notice of Herbart, 483; chief Connecticut school officer, 471 f.; first United States Commissioner of Education, 444
Barnard, Frederick A. P., 513
Barzizza, G., 130
Basedow, J. B., 92, 197, 225 f., 227 ff.; 241, 320; general views, 227; early life, 227; his *Memorial*, 227 f.; his philanthropinum, 228 f.
Bates Case, 346
Bateus, William, 190
Batsch, A. J., and Froebel, 273
Battersea Training College, 246, 352
Bavaria, 60; reform of elementary schools, 322
Beccaria, Antonio, 134
Beck, Charles, 337
Bede, the Venerable, 68, 87, 345

Beecher, Catherine Esther, 446
Bell, Dr. Andrew, 384 ff., 355; religious character of his schools, 350
Bembo, 117
Benedictine Rule, 66 f.
Benedict, Saint, 66, 71
Benevolent despots, 225
Berea College, 407
Bergson, Henri, 562
Berlin, University, 230, 321, 545
Bessarion, 121, 124
Beza, Theodore, 159
Bible, 8, 139, 142 ff., 146 ff., 187, 348, 373; vernacular versions, 151; use in schools, 346
Birkbeck, George, 362, 548
Bismarck, 318, 326 f.; and the Kulturkampf, 327; and the socialists, 328
Blair Bill, 437
Blow, Susan, quoted, 280, 472
Board of Education, English national, 356
Bobbio, monastery, 68
Boccaccio, 120
Bodet, J. Torres, 563
Boelte, Maria, 471 f.
Boethius, 64, 76, 88
Boniface VIII, Pope, 140 f.
Boniface, Saint, 60
Bonnet, Henri, 562
Bonser, Frederick G., 508
Bookkeeping, development of, 95; subject, 99 ff., 226, 373; in American colonial schools, 389, 409
Borough Road Training College, opened by Lancaster, 351; government-aided, 354
Boston high school movement, 412, 499 f.
Boston Latin School, 381, 386, 409, 411, 497, 499
Boston schools, history of, 409–413; double-headed system, 409; in the Revolution, 410 f.; primary schools, 411; English Classical School, 412, 499, 514
Boyle, Robert, 180, 183
Bray, Thomas, 348
Breasted, James H., 6 f., 9 f., 338
Brethren of the Common Life, 135, 139, 147, 149
Briggs, Thomas H., 514; chairman, Committee on Orientation of Secondary Education, 522 f.
Brinsley, John, 188; use of monitors, 348
British and Foreign School Society, 351, 354
Brothers of the Christain Schools, 165, 297 f.; preparation of teachers by, 445
Brougham Committee, on condition of the poor of London, 349, 354
Brougham, Henry, 319; infant school promotion, 352; chairman investigating committee, 353 ff.; education bill, 354
Brown, Thomas, 252

Brown University, 391 f.
Bruni, Leonardo, 121, 128
Budé, William, 135
Bugenhagen, John, 157
Burk, Frederic, 481
Burschenschaft, association of students, 323
Burton, Warren, 464
Business Colleges, 408
Butler Education Act, *see* England
Butler, Nicholas Murray, 515
Butler, Richard A., 357, 539, 543
Byzantine Empire, 39, 54, 84, 95

CAESAR, 52 f., 133
Calendar, Egyptian, 7; Roman, 52
Calvin, John, 158; education, and educational activity, 159
Cambridge University, 105, 175 f., 340
Campanella, Thomas, 170; educational doctrines, 173
Campe, J. H., 229, 320
Capella, Martianus, 64, 87
Carnegie Foundation for the Advancement of Teaching, 513
Cassian, John, 66
Castellion, 159
Castiglione, Baldassare, 92, 133
Cassiodorus, 65 ff.
Catechetical Schools, 62 f.
Catechism, 230, 346 f., 376
Catechumenal schools, 62 f.
Cathedral schools, 59, 73, 92, 100 ff.
Cato's Distichs, 71, 150
Cato the Elder, 47
Cattell, J. McKeen, 340
Caxton, William, 70, 145
Cellini, Benvenuto, 117
Celtes, Conrad, 147
Centralized administration of schools, in France, 297, 306 f.; in Prussia, 319; proposed in United States, 404
Central schools, England, 359
Chalcondylas, D., 121
Character education, 12, 21, 27, 126, 130; Socratic, 33; Roman, 44 f.; monastic, 72 f.; chivalric, 91; in Locke, 185 f.; in Comenius, 192 f.; by the Jesuits, 161, 163; Rousseau on, 213, 217; Pestalozzi's efforts in, at Neuhof, 234, at Stanz, 237, at Yverdon, 243 f.; theory of Herbart on, 256 ff., 263 f.; in France, 313; in German youth-movement, 335; as high school ideal, 519, 522; as aim of National Honor Society, 522; and juvenile delinquency, 546 f.
Charity schools, 347, 376, 380
Charlemagne, 73, 80, 95, 292; his educational policy, 75 f.
Chaucer, 64, 92, 142, 152
Cheever, Ezekiel, 409
Chemistry, teaching laboratories, 339

Child labor, 353, 356, 416
Children's books, 229 f., 465
Childstudy, 283; in Europe, 475 f.; in United States, 475 f.
Chivalric education, 91
Chodowiecki, 228
Christianity, beliefs, 59 f.; and philosophy, 61 ff.; liberal tendencies, 147; and Platonism, 152; early practices, 153
Chrysoloras, Manuel, 121 f., 125, 130
Cicero, 37, 54 f., 120 f.; style and initiation in school, 115, 118, 133; outline for orations, 259
City schools, 100
City-states, Greek, 19; Italian, 112
Civilian Conservation Corps, 548
Civilization, early, 3 ff.
Classics, 120 ff.; recovery of, 112 ff., 120 ff.; basis of Renaissance humanism, 114; libraries of, 122 f.; printing of, 124 f.; chief authors used in schools, 128 f., 133 f.
Clement of Alexandria, 63
Clinton, DeWitt, 415
Cluny, 89
Colburn, Warren, 429
Colet, John, 139, 151, 345 f.
Collège de France, 135
Collège de Guyenne, 135
College Entrance Board, 513 ff.
Collège de Louis le Grand, 296
College of Philadelphia, 391
Collegiate School of the Dutch Reformed Church, 381
Colonial conditions in America, 367–372
Columba, Saint, 60
Columbanus, 68
Columbia University, 391 ff.; efforts to bring under state control, 440, Teachers College, 448; and manuel education, 474
Comenius, John Amos, 89, 170, 181, 187–197, 220, 250, 260, 268, 285, 323, 463; as author, 189 f.; textbooks, 190 ff.; theory of education, 192 ff.; quoted, 194; on school organization, 195; on education for peace, 192, 558
Commercial education, 99 ff.
Commission on Relation of School and College, 523 f.
Commission on Reorganization of Secondary Education, 518 ff.
Committee of Ten, 510 ff., 514
Committee on the Orientation of Secondary Educations, 522 f.
Compagnons de l'Université Nouvelle, Les, 308, 311, 535
Comparative Education, 557
Compulsory school attendance, 14, 405; urged by Luther, 157; in Denmark, 158; in German states, 227, 318; in England, 356 f. *and* age raised (1947), 504; in continuation schools, 358; Massachusetts

law, 405 f.; United States, 450 ff.; Germany, 547; in Russia, 582

Computus, 72, 75

Comstock, Anna B., 469 f.

Conant, J. B., 525

Conciliar party, 143 f.

Condillac, 203

Condorcet, 219–221, 295, 308, 404, 519

Conference for Education in the South, 438

Constitution of the German Republic, education in, 332 f.

Constitution of the United States, 398; lacking education clauses, 402, 419

Cooperative education, 407

Cooperative Study of Secondary School Standards, 526

Copernicus, Nicholas, 149, 177, 180; his method, 179, 259

Coram, Robert, 403

Cordier, Mathurin (Corderius), 135, 159; his *Colloquies*, 150

Correspondence schools, 548

Corvei, 70

Council of Arles, 344

Council of Constance, 143 f.

Counter-Reformation, 113, 172

Country Day Schools, 488 f.

Cousin, Victor, 246, 319, 337; Report on German schools and English translation, 299

Cowper-Temple Clause, 357

Cox Case, 346

Crates of Mallos, 46

Croyland, 70

Crusades, 89 f., 154, 294

Culture epochs, 210, 263, 285 f.; 484

Curriculum, 38, 58 f., 75, 99, 155, 164 f. 180, 353; in catechetical schools, 63; in Roman schools, 47; monastic, 70 f.; chivalric, 91; Renaissance, 126 ff., 132 ff.; elementary at Reformation, 157; Jesuit, 162 f.; Jansenist, 164 f.; realist, 171, 176 f.; Sulzer's, 202 f.; in *Emile*, 213 ff.; philanthropinist, 226, 228; Herbart's, 261 ff.; of secondary schools under Napoleon, 276; in France (1833), 299, (1938), 306, (1931), 310; in German Middle Schools, 330, and secondary schools, 331; English elementary, 358, secondary, 360 f.; and S. P. G. charity schools, 380; in American Latin Schools, 386 ff.; in American academies, 390; in high schools, 499 ff., 503–510, 520 f., *also*, 484, 497, 510 f., 515

Curry, J. L. M., 437

DANIEL OF MORLEY, 88

Dante, 113, 141

Dartmouth College, 340; case in Supreme Court, 440

Darwin, Charles, 37, 253, 283, 354

Davis, Jesse B., 517

Debatable issues, teaching of, 537 f.

DeGarmo, Charles, 265; publications, 483

Democracy, 19, 30; and nationalism, 295; early, in New England, 370; in American education, 363, 477 ff., 486, 492; an example of, 592 ff.

Demosthenes, 31, 48

Denman, J. S., organizer of teachers' institutes, 448

Denmark, 157 f.; folk high schools of, 548

Department of Science and Art, 361

Departments of education in universities, 448 f.

DeQuincey, Thomas, 113

Descartes, 170, 180, 308; on scientific method, 178; on distribution of ability, 181

Deutsche Oberschule, 333, 336

Deventer, 135, 148

Dewey, John, 259, 484, 490, 507; books by, 484, 486 f.; his University Elementary School, 485 f.; quoted, 486; theory of, 486 ff., 524, 583, 590

Dewitt, Nicholas, 578

Dexter, Edwin Grant, 511

Dickinson, John W., 464 f.

Dictamen, 71, 100

Dictata, 26

Diesterweg, F. A. W., supporter of Froebel, 283; teachers' seminary director, 323; writings banned, 325

Discipline, in Sparta, 20 f.; by Athenian pedagogue, 25; in monastic schools, 70; in medieval universities, 103 f., 105 f.; at the Renaissance, 131; view of Luther, 157; in Jesuit schools, 163; view of Rousseau, 213; Herbart's doctrine of, 256 f.; Lancasterian, 350; in district school, 424 f.

District system, 385, 388; defects of, 385 f., 423 f.

Doddridge, Philip, 176

Dominicans, 102, 152

Domitian, 55, 126

Donatus, Aelius, grammarian, 64

Douglas Commission, on vocational education, 508

Drawing, 36, 133, 177, 188, 205, 214 f., 226; in American schools, 505

Drobisch, Martin, 265

Duggan, Stephen, 560

Dupont de Nemours, Pierre, 403 f.

Dury, John, 174

EATON, AMOS, 407, 539

Ebers, Georg, 281

Eckart, 147

École des Roches, 487

Edgeworth, Maria, 246, 269

Educational magazines, 417 f.

Educational methods, 33, 63, 89, 130; Vittorino's, 131 f., 145; Jesuit, 163 f.; realist, 174 ff.; effect of science on, 180 f.; in language teaching, 187 f., 308 f.; Rousseau's, 212 ff.; Pestalozzian, 239–245, 352 f.; *also*, 334, 353

Educational theory, 32, 38, 54, 125–129, 133; *see* Comenius, Locke, Rousseau, Pestalozzi, Herbart, Froebel, Dewey

Education, definition of, 2

Edwards, Richard, 447

Eggleston, Edward, 425

Einstein, Albert, 562

Eliot, Charles William, 498, 511 f.; chairman Committee of Ten, 510

Elyot, Sir Thomas, 92

Emerson, George B., 426, 499

Emerson, R. W., 418

Encyclopedism, 38, 193

Encyclopedists, 201

Engels, Frederick, 324

Engineering, 42; French schools of, 297; early American schools of, 407

England, 60, 97, 100, 140 f.; Reformation in, 160 f.; infant schools of, 271; early schools of, 344 f.; Puritan educational program, 346; Society for the Propagation of the Gospel, 347; charity schools, 347 f.; monitorial systems, 348–351; influences from the Continent, 351 f.; state activity, 353–356; great educational commissions, 355 f.; Fisher Act., 357; Hadow reports, 357 f.; secondary schools, 359 ff.; Public Schools, 345, 360, 543; Butler Education Act, 358, 361, 539 ff.; tripartite plan, 541; selectiveness of schools, 542 f.

English academies, 175–177

English Poor and Apprenticeship Laws, 161

Erasistratus, 36

Erasmus, 64, 121, 139 f., 145 ff.

Eratosthenes, 38

Ernst, Otto, 329

Essentialists, 591

Ethical Culture Schools, 472, 485

Ethics, 12, 18, 32 f., 38 f.; Greek and Christian, 113, 129, 186

Eton College, 345

Etruscans, 42 f.

Euclid, 36 f., 87, 130

Eusebius, 63

Evacuation of children from cities, 534, 535

Evans, Luther, 563

Everett, Edward, 415, 427

Exchange of persons, 549, 560

Extracurricular activities, 520 f.

FACULTY PSYCHOLOGY, 253

Federal aid to education, 398; early land grants, 401; proposals after Civil War, 436 ff.; land-grant colleges, 439 ff.; for vocational education, 442 f., 508 f., 602; proposals after the World Wars, 443 f., 588 f.; National Defense Education Act, 589

Federigo, Duke of Urbino, 124

Felbiger, J. I. von, 319

Fellenberg, Emanuel, 226, 237 f., 246, 418; influence, 352; system in America, 406 f.

Fénelon, 165

Ferrara, 129, 149; Council of, 122

Ferry, Jules, 304, 309

Feudalism, 91

Fichte, J. G., 245, 320

Filelfo, 118, 122, 130

Fischer, Karl, youth leader, 335

Fisher Act (1918), 356 f.

Fithian, Philip Vickers, 377

Fleming Committee, 543

Fleury, Abbé Claude, 183, 308

Florence, 94 f., 112, 118, 124, 177

Flower, Enoch, 381

Folk High Schools, 361, 547, 560

Follen, Charles, 337

Ford Foundation, 561

Formal discipline, 31, 511 f.

Forster Act, 351, 356 f.

France, 18, 60, 90, 103, 135, 140 f., 292–315; teaching of nationalism in, 312 ff.; commissions on secondary education, 535; Langevin Plan, 535–537; secondary schooling extended, 536; reforms in curricula and method, 536 f.; over-pressure in school, 537; vocational education, 538

Francis of Assisi, Saint, 115

Franciscans, 102

Francke, August Hermann, 117, 347, 382

Franco-Prussian War, 303, 325

Frankenberg, Caroline, 471

Franklin, Benjamin, 184, 399, 362, 402; proposals for academy, 391

Frederick the Great, 318 f., 327

Free School Society of New York, 404 ff.

French Revolution, 207, 295; educational programs in, 296; influence, 321

Friends, religious society, 349; settlements in America, 371 ff.; educational activity, 380 f.; opposition to slavery, 414

Froben, J., printer, 125, 145, 151, 154

Froebel, F. A. W., 195, 245, 250, 268 f., 272–286, 556; education through creative work, 278; the kindergarten, 279 ff.; theory of organic development, 273 f.; play in education, 284 ff.; psychology of, 283 f.; influence upon infant school, 352; *also* 321, 323, 455, 462, 473

Froebel, Karl, 281

Frontier in America, influence upon education, 385, 399 f.; and travel, 399

Fulbright, Senator J. W., Fulbright Act, and Fulbright Scholars, 561

Fulda, monastery, 60, 68
Fund for the Advancement of Education, 604

GALEN, 85, 88
Galileo, 177, 179 f.
Gallaudet, Thomas Hopkins, 446
Gardiner Lyceum, 407
Garrison, William Lloyd, 414
Gaudig, Hugo, 336
Gaza, Theodore, 121, 149
Gedike, Frederick, 319
Geneva, 145, 158, 207; sumptuary laws of, 159; schools, 159 f.; birthplace of Rousseau, 205; location International Institute of Education, 559
Geographical discoveries, 113
Geography as school subject, 31 f., 177, 214 f.; Pestalozzian teaching of, 241 f.
George-Deen Act, 518
George Junior Republic, 487
George Peabody College for Teachers, 438
Gerard of Creniona, 88
Germany, and West Germany, 145 ff., 179, 318–341, 544–551; reforms in Napoleonic era, 320 f.; common schools in, 322 f., 546 ff.; political activity in, 322 f., 327, 544 f.; secondary schools, 330 f., 336, 542; Weimar Constitution, 332; current laws, 548 ff.; youth movement, 335; World War II and effects, 544–551; refugees in, 547, 551 f.; educational writings of Germans, 334; influence abroad, 337 f.; Potsdam Agreement, 546; new teaching methods and equipment, 549; National Socialism in, 336, 534, 538, 544 ff., 550.
Gesell, Arnold, 476
Giessen, University of, 339, 545
Gilbert, William, 178, 180
Gilds, 96 ff., 112, 173; their schools, 97
Girard, Gregoire, 226, 352
Girls, education of, 446; in Sparta, 21 f.; in Athens, 28; in the Renaissance, 128; in Emile, 218; by Moravians, 382; in private schools, 446; Boston High and Normal School, 500
Glasgow University, 176
Goethe, 191, 274, 320, 329
Gott, Samuel, 173, 269
Göttingen University, 251, 273, 275, 324
Gouge, Thomas, 347
Grading of schools, 429 f., 454 f., 497 f.
Graduate schools, American, 339
Grammar, developed by Sophists, 30 f.; in schools, 38, 71; medieval textbooks, 64
Grammar schools, 134; reformed, in England, 345; American, 386
Great Schism, 141 f., 144
Greaves, J. P., 238
Gregory I, Pope, 60, 76

Grimm, Hermann, and Jacob, 324
Griscom, John, 246, 411
Groos, Karl, 285
Groot, Gerhard, 147
Grundschule, 332, 336
Grundtvig, N. F. S., 548
Gruner, G. A., 274, 556
Guarino, Battista, 128 ff.
Guarino da Verona, 121 f., 129 ff.
Guggenheim Fellowships, 561
Guizot, F. P. G., 300, 450
Gutenberg, 145
Guyot, Arnold, 428
Gymnasium, as classical school, 134, 158; Prussian reformed, 322, 331, 333; imported into United States, 337

HADOW REPORTS, 357
Hailmann, William N., 472 f., 483
Hall, G. Stanley, 285, 340; promoter of child study, 475
Hall, S. R., 417; early school for teachers, 446; also, 462, 472, 590
Halle University, 228 f.
Hamburg, school dispute in, 99 ff., 545, 547
Hammurabi, Code of, 7, 9 f.
Handwork in elementary schools, 473 ff.
Handwriting, teaching of, 373
Hanseatic League, 95
Hanus, Paul H., 517
Harnisch, William, 322
Harper, William Rainey, 516, 602
Harrington, James, 173
Harris, William T., 429, 480
Harrower, John, 377
Harrow School, 345
Hartenstein, Gustav, 265
Hartley, David, 252
Hartlib, Samuel, 174
Harvard University, 340, 391 ff., 422
Harvey, William, 178 ff.
Haskins, Charles Homer, 111
Hawley, Gideon, 420, 427
Hawthorne, Nathaniel, 409
Hayes, C. J. H., 559
Hebrew studies, 139, 152 f.
Hecker, Julius, 177
Hegel, 251, 265, 274, 320
Hegius, Alexander, 135, 148
Heidelberg University, 148, 150, 189, 339, 545
Hellenistic Age, 36, 38 f., 52
Hellenizing, of Jews, 61; of Romans, 47; of Moslems, 82 ff.
Helots, 19
Helvetius, 203
Herbart, J. F., 241, 245, 250–265, 268, 336, 462; aim of education, 255 f.; apperception doctrine, 254 f., 258; curriculum theories, 261 ff.; doctrine of interest,

257 f., 261; formal steps, 258 ff.; methods, 259 f., 262 f.; influence, 264 f.
Herbartianism in the United States, 483 f., 512
Herder, J. G., 229
Herodotus, 22, 31, 262
Heusinger, J. G. H., 278
Hieronymians, 135, 139, 147, 149
Higher education, 32, 297, 391 ff., 403; land-grant colleges, 439–443; Dartmouth College Case, 440; state university origins, 440 f.; professional education of teachers, 448 f.
High school, American public, definitions of, 496 f.; relation to academy, 391; early high schools, 497–501; evolution from graded school, 497 f.; selective nature of, 500; opposition to, 502; accrediting of, 510; increasing attendance, 520; recent trends, 525 ff.
Hill, Thomas Wright, 360
Hindu numerals, 87, 95
Hinsdale, Burke A., 512
Hippocrates, 32, 180
History, 7, 31, 48; St. Augustine's theory of, 64; Rousseau on, 218; also, 114, 133, 171, 177, 186, 214, 226; nationalism in history-teaching, 294, 312 f., 559
History of education, 3, 329, 334, 350; lessons from, 570 ff.
Hitler, A., 294, 327, 336
Hitler Youth, 335
Hittites, 11
Hoar Bill, 436 f.
Hobbes, Thomas, 211
Holbrook, Josiah, 419
Holman, Henry, quoted, 350
Home and Colonial School Society, 446; organization of, 352; and Pestalozzi, 246; and infant schools, 271
Home economics, 509
Homer, and the Homeric poems, 20 f., 29, 32, 34, 37, 44, 120, 133
Hooker, Thomas, 370
Hoole, Charles, 188, 191
Hopkins Grammar School, 388
Hosea, 13
Huddlestone, Mr., 380
Humanism, classical, 113 f.; decline of, 132 f.; northern phase, 139 f., 149 ff.; at Geneva, 159
Humboldt, Alexander, 229
Humboldt, William, 229, 331; Minister of Education, 321 f.
Hume, David, 207
Humphrey, Duke, 134
Hunayn-ibn-Ishaq, 85
Huntington, Emily, 485
Huss, John, 143 f., 158, 372
Hutcheson, Francis, 176
Hutchinson, Ann, 370

Huxley, Julian, 563
Huyghens, Christian, 179
Hygiene, 90

IBN-RUSHD (Averroes), 86 f., 89
ibn-Sina (Avicenna), 86
Illiteracy, 12, 373, 416, 438, 564
Indiana University, 510
Individual instruction, 480 ff.
Individualism in education, of Hellenistic Age, 36 ff.; of chivalry, 91 f.; Abelard's method, 102; in the Renaissance, 117, 129; in theories of Locke, 184 f., and Rousseau, 204; of radical reformers in German Republic, 336; opposing public education, 353, 400; as mode of teaching, 481
Indulgences, 154
Industrial arts education, 216 f., 226; as developed by Heusinger and Froebel, 278; in American schools, 505 ff., 508; purposes of, 507
Industrial Revolution, 298
Infant school, 268–272, 357; Henry Barnard's interest in, 271, and criticism of, 271 f.; French, 300; British, 271, 351 f.; American, 271, 464
Inquisition, 143
Institute of International Education, 560
Intergroup education, 587
International Bureau of Education, 559
International Committee on Intellectual Cooperation, 561 f.
International education, 554–556
International Kindergarten Union, 282, 556
International People's College, 560
International Review of Education, 555, 557
Ireland, 60, 68
Ireland, Bishop John, 357
Irnerius, 102
Isidore of Seville, 65, 87
Ismar, F. A., 406
Isocrates, 31
Italy, 18, 31, 42 f., 60, 111 ff., 135, 149; in the Renaissance, 115 f.
Izvestia, 577

JACKMAN, WILBUR S., 469, 474
Jackson, Andrew, 400, 413
Jahn, F. L., 273, 276, 321 f., 324, 337
James of Venice, 88
James, Sir Eric, 543
James, William, 484, 486, 512, 590
Jefferson, Thomas, 19, 208, 413; education bill of 1779, 403
Jena, University of, 176, 251, 265, 273; and nationalist student movement, 323; war damage of, 545
Jerome of Prague, 143
Jerome, Saint, 59, 64, 120
Jesuit Society, 139, 159, 165, 170 f., 218,

327, 445; history of, 161–164; constitution and government, 161 f.; spread and success of schools, 162; use of monitors, 348

Johns Hopkins University, 339
Johnson, Andrew, 436
Johnson, Marietta, 448
Jones, Margaret E. M., 466
Josephus, 14
Joshua ben Gamala, 14
Judaism, 14
Julian, "The Apostate," 62
Jullien, Marc-Antoine, 557
Jundi-Shapur, 84 f.
Junior college, 515 f.
Junior high school, 514 f.
Justin Martyr, 61
Justinian, 32, 63, 84; Code of, 88
Juvenile delinquency, 534, 551–553, 582, 587

KALAMAZOO DECISION, 448, 501 f.
Kandel, Isaac L., 361, 557
Kant, Immanuel, 228, 251, 286, 322
Kay-Shuttleworth, James, 352, 354 f.
Keilhau, 276 f.
Kennet, Dr., White, 347
Kerschensteiner, Georg, 328f., 336, 538, 583
Khrushchev, Nikita, 584 ff.
Kindergarten, 268; promoters of, 281 ff.; American, 470–473; public, 472 f.; difficulties with, 472 f.; Dewey's definition of, 486
Knox, Samuel, 403 f.
Knox College, 406
Koran, 88
Kotschnig, W., 534
Kraus, Dr. John, 471 f.
Krause, K. C. F., 273 f.
Kriege, Matilda, and Alma, 471
Krüsi, Hermann, senior, 237, 245
Krüsi, Hermann, junior, 352 f., 468, 479
Kulturkampf, 327

LABOR UNIONS AND EDUCATION, 416 f.
La Chalotais, 305, 308
Lakanal, 296
Lancaster, Joseph, 348, 418, 445; early teaching, 349; ingenuity of, 349; writings, 350; American visit, 351
Land-grant colleges, 439–443, for Negroes, 442; problems of, 442 f.
Land grants for schools, 401 f.
Langethal, Henry, 276 ff., 279
Language studies, 37, 187–189, 194 f., 329, 387, 544; Rousseau's opposition to, 214; modern versus ancient languages, 309; in Russian schools, 576
Larsen, Roy E., 593
Larsson, Gustaf, 474
LaSalle, Jean Baptiste, 165
Lassalle, Ferdinand, 327

Latin language, at the Renaissance, 114 f.; authors read, 133; declining position in schools, 176; in the seventeenth century, 187 ff.; proposed reforms, 188, 189 ff.
Latin Grammar Schools, American, 369, 386, 388
Lazarus, Moritz, 285, 475
Leach, Arthur F., 97
League of Nations, 555, 561
Leeuwenhoek, Antonius van, 179
Lefèvre d'Etaples, Jacques, 151
Lehrfreiheit, in German universities, 324, 340
Leibnitz, W. von, 180, 253 f.
Leipzig University, 148, 227, 265, 339
Lenin, 582
Leo X, Pope, 153
Leo XIII, Pope, 327
Leonardo da Vinci, 117
Leonardo, Fibonacci, 87
Leontius Pilatus, 120
Lepeletier de Saint-Fargeau, 296
Lessing, G. E., 210
Libanius, 84
Liberal Education, 111, 113 f., 126 ff., 150; why limited in Soviet schools, 570, 573 f., 581
Libraries, 37, 53, 65; monastic, 69 ff.; classical, 122 ff.
Library of Congress, 444
Liebig, Justus, 339
Lietz, Hermann, 336
Life adjustment education, 597 f.
Lincoln, Abraham, 439
Lindisfarne, 60
Lindner, G. A., 265
Literacy, growth of, 90 f., 146, 154 ff., 564, 579
Litt, Theodore, 336
Livius Andronicus, 46
Locke, John, 22, 92, 170, 180, 181–187, 203 f., 211 f., 241, 250, 268, 295, 362, 370, 418, 463, 514; writings, 182 f.; and the Abbé Fleury, 183; his educational theory, 184 f.
Lollards, 142, 146, 345
London Infant School Society, 352
Lorain, P., 300
Louvain, 149, 187
Love, Samuel G., 474
Loyola, Saint Ignatius, 159, 161
Lübeck, 100
Lucretius, 51, 120
Luder, Peter, 149
Ludus, 45, 49
Lunacharskii, A. V., 553
Luther, Martin, 145, 149, 383; translator of Bible, 151; Ninety-five Theses, 154; on education, 156 f.
Lutheran movement, 153–158
Lutherans, 381 f.
Lyceum, of Aristotle, 39

MACHIAVELLI, 117 f.
Macmillan, Rachel, and Margaret, 287 f.
McMurry, Frank, 488
Madison, James, 19, 387, 403
Magna Charta, 294
Magyars, 81
Maimon, Moses ben, 89
Malaise of school-youth, 334 f.
Malpighi, Marcello, 180
Mandeville, B., 347
Mann, Horace, 246, 319, 337, 415, 424 ff., 463 ff., 505; characteristics, 427; on Germany, 325; work and achievement, 426 ff.; Secretary of Massachusetts Board of Education, 426
Mann, Mrs. Horace, 281
Manniche, Peter, 560
Mansbridge, Albert, 362
Mantua, 130 f.
Manual labor education, 406 f.
Manual training, 216 f., 226, 278, 505; in public schools, 506 ff.
Marcus Aurelius, 43
Marenholtz-Bülow, Bertha von, 281 f.
Martin, Saint, of Tours, 66, 74
Marwedel, Emma, 471
Marx, Karl, 327, 583
Massachusetts Institute of Technology, 500
Mathematics, 30, 32, 37, 48, 87; branches taught in colonial schools, 389
Mather, Sir William, 287
Maxwell, William N., 429
Mayo, Charles, 246, 352
Mayo, Elizabeth, 352
Medici, Lorenzo, 121; Cosimo de', 123, 124
Melanchthon, P., 158
Mennonites, 371, 382; opposition to slavery, 414
Merchant Taylors School, 97, 188
Meriam, Junius L., 488
Merrill, George A., 517
Methodists, 382
Middendorf, William, 276 ff.
Mill, James, 252 f.
Milton, John, 174 f.
Missionary colleges, American, 414
Mohammed, 83
Mohammedans, 80 f., 86, 294; sources of their learning, 82 f.; literary interests, 112
Monasticism, 66 ff.
Monastic schools, 68–73
Monitorial schools, 322, 348–351, 353, 417, 422; plan of, 349; controversy over, 350 f.; in the United States, 351, 404–406
Monophysites, 84
Montaigne, Michel, 22, 92, 206
Monte Cassino, 66, 68, 81
Montessori, Maria, 287, 540
Moravians, 372, 382
More, Sir Thomas, 146, 160, 173, 345

Morley, John, 218
Morrill Act, 407, 439, 441 f.
Morrison, J. C., 490
Morton, Charles, 176
Mozarabs, 86
Muhlenberg, Henry M., 381 f.
Müller, G. E., 265
Mulcaster, Richard, 170, 172, 188, 346
Murray, Gilbert, 562
Music in education, 9, 21, 27, 34, 36, 38, 48, 58, 71, 75, 133, 171, 186, 188, 214 f., 226; Boethius' schoolbook on, 64; in American schools, 504 f.
Mussolini, Benito, 294

NÄGELI, 244, 275
Napier, John, 180
Napoleon I, 237 f., 276, 296 f., 315, 319 f., 323, 402
Napoleon III, 301
National Association of Secondary School Principals, 521 f., 560
National Citizens Commission for the Public Schools, 592 f.
National Education Association, 418, 437, 479, 483, 514; on delinquency, 552
National Home Study Council, 548
National Honor Society, 522
Nationalism, 141, 292, 404; and school systems, 292; rise of, 293–295; extreme examples, 294; in history teaching, 559; and democracy, 295; in French schools, 312 ff.; in English education, 344, 353 ff.; and sectionalism, 400.
National school systems, 269
National Science Foundation, 598 ff.
National Socialism, 336, 534, 538, 544, 546, 550
National Society, of Dr. Bell's monitorial schools, 350, 354
National University Extension Association, 602
National Vocational Guidance Association, 517
National Youth Administration, 518
Nation-state, 19; and education according to Rousseau, 208 f., and La Chalotais, 218 f.
Natural punishment, 213
Nature study, Pestalozzian, 214 ff.; in American schools, 467–470; definition of, 467 f.; spread and influence, 469 f.
Nebuchadrezzar, 13
Neef, Joseph, 244, 246, 462
Negroes, separate schools for, 434 ff.; progress of Negro education, 438 f., 595
Neighborhood schools, 369, 378, 382, 388
Neo-Platonism, 61
Nestorians, 85
Netherlands, 95, 134, 139, 144, 147, 155; influence in United States, 160
Newcastle Commission, 355 f.

New England Association of Colleges and Preparatory Schools, 513
New Haven Gymnasium, 337
New Testament, 61, 146 ff.; Greek version of, 150 f.; vernacular translations, 151, 159
Newton, Isaac, 180
New York City, public school system established, 405
New York College for the Training of Teachers, 474
Niccoli, Niccolo, 120 f., 124
Nicholas V, Pope, 118, 121, 123 f.
Nicholas of Cusa, 149
"Nicholas Voinov," 553, 582
Nicolovius, G. H. L., 322
Niederer, John, 237
Nonconformists, English, 346 f.
Normal departments, in state universities, 448
Normal schools, 246; French system, 298; under the July monarchy, 300; attack upon, under Napoleon III, 301; expansion by Third Republic, 304; restriction of German teachers' seminaries, 325, and more generous regulations, 329 f.; English training colleges, 352; American, affected by German influence, 339; American development of, 445 ff.; objective methods in, 464 f.
North Central Association of Colleges and Secondary Schools, 513
Northwest Ordinance, 402
Norwich (Connecticut) Free Academy, 501
Norwood Committee, 542
Notre Dame, of Paris, 102
Novice, in monastery, 72 f.
Nursery school, 287 f.; influence upon by Dr. Montessori, 287; development, 287 f., 540

Oberlin, J. F., his infant schools, 269–272, 298; community leader, 270
Oberlin College, 270, 406
Oberrealschule, 177, 331, 333
Object-teaching, 352, 463; Oswego system, 465 ff.
Observation of teaching, 352
Oestreich, Paul, 336
Office of Education, United States, 444; publications of, 445
"Old field" schools, 369, 377
Old Testament, 61
Olympic Games, 30
Omar Khayyám, 86
Oratory of Divine Love, 164
Orbis Pictus, 191
Ordinance of 1785 and land grants for colleges, 401
Ordinance of 1787, 402
Origen, 63
Oswego Method, 363, 463 ff.

Owen, Robert, 270 f., 351; and New Harmony Community, 413
Oxford University, 102 f.; 124, 134, 142, 176, 181 f., 340, 560

Padua, University of, 130
Page, David P., 447, 463, 485
Paidonomos, 20
Palaestra, 25, 28
Palestine, 12 f., 43, 83
Papacy, 60, 90; attitude in school disputes, 99
Papal supremacy, 140, 143
Parent education, 195, 237, 278
Paris, 89, 93, 101 ff., 135, 145; University of, 101, 119, 187, 296
Parker, Francis Wayland, 449, 467, 474, 476–479, 482, 507; as author, 479; at Quincy, 476 ff.; and E. A. Sheldon, 476; democracy of, 477; in Chicago, 479; his relation to Progressive Education, 485, 590
Parsons, Frank H., 517
Pastorius, Francis Daniel, 371
Patrick, Saint, 60, 68
Patridge, Lelia, 477
Paulinus of Aquileia, 73
Paulsen, Friedrich, 336
Paul the Deacon, 71, 74
"Payment by results," 355 f.
Peabody, Elizabeth, 282, 471
Peabody, George, and the Peabody Fund, 437 f.
Pedagogue, 24 f.
Peirce, Cyrus, 447
Penn, William, educational views, 380 f.; and his Frame of Government, 381; also, 402
Pentathlon, 21, 28, 127
Pereira, Roderiquez, 203, 215
Pericles, 23, 28, 30 f., 113
Perioeci, 19, 20
Perkiomen School, 372
Persia, 11, 18, 84 ff.
Persian Wars, 23
Pestalozzi, J. H., 195, 202, 204, 225, 230 f., 231–247, 250, 268 f., 272, 283, 322, 418; analysis of subject-matter, 242 f.; his assistants, 237; language teaching, 242; methods, 239–245; at Burgdorf, 237; at Neuhof, 234 f.; at Stanz, 236 f.; at Yverdon, 238; influence, 352; his doctrines in America, 417, 428 f., 446, 455, 462 ff., 556
Pestalozzi Children's Village, 553 f.
Peter of Pisa, 73
Peter the Venerable, 88
Petrarch, 113, 115, 117–120, 123, 130
Petty, William, 174
Pfefferkorn, John, 153
Pfeiffer, Michael T., 244, 275
Philadelphia Central High School, 500 ff.
Philanthropinum, 183, 225
Philo, 61

Physical education, 20 f., 28, 36, 127, 131, 133, 202, 321; in the *Émile*, 211 f.; under Salzmann, 230, 243 f.; Jahn's contribution to, 275 f.; in schools under Spiess, 244, 279; in the United States, 337; *also*, 535, 584

Picket, Albert, 246, 415, 498; as educational journalist, 418

Pisa, 93, 118; Council of, 143

Place, Francis, 347

Plamann, John E., 273, 321 f.

Planta, Martin, 226 f.

Plato, 22, 29, 31–38, 43, 62, 113, 120, 251, 253, 414, 590

Platonic Academy, 121

Platonism, 414

Plato of Tivoli, 81

Platter, Thomas, 148

Play in education, in ancient Greece, 21; favored by Comenius, 195; later theory and practice, 284 ff.; in Froebel's system, 286

Plutarch, 46, 130, 133, 205

Poggio Bracciolini, 118, 120, 144

Population changes in the United States, 586

Porter, Noah, 384

Port Royalists, 165

Potsdam Agreement, 546

Potter, Bishop Alonzo, 415

Practical education, 45, 97, 107; Utopians' views on, 174; Locke on teaching a trade, 186; in French higher primary schools, 300; in German continuation and trade schools, 328 f.; in England, 358 f.; in the high school, 505–509

Prague, 103, 142 f.; University of, 148

Presbyterians, 372 f., 382, 387

Pre-school child, 195, 211 f., 287 f., 269

Priestley, Joseph, 176, 418

Primary schools, French, 296–300, 304–306, 312 ff.; American, 376–386, 411 f., 461–492

Princeton University, 391 f.

Printing, 124, 145 f., 148

Priscian, 64

Professional education of teachers in the United States, 445–450

Progressive Education, 484–492; under attack, 589 ff.

Progressive Education Association, 489, 523

Progress, theory of, 219

Propaganda-education, 555 f.

Propaganda for public education, 414–418

Prussia, 225, 227, 229, 238, 302, 322; kindergarten banned in, 281; school regulations of, 318; social reforms in, 321

Psychology, 183; educational, 251–254, 445; in preparation of teachers, 329; writers on, 334

Psychology of children, 202, 204 f., 268, 283

Ptolemy, C., 36, 38, 88

Public School Society, 404 ff.

Puritans, 176, 346; leavening influence of, 369 f.

Purmont, Philemon, 409

QUADRIVIUM, 58, 71

Quincy, Josiah, 500

Quincy Methods, 476–479

Quintilian, 45 f., 48 f., 53 ff., 120, 128 f., 144, 261

Quisling, 534

RACIAL SEGREGATION in public schools, 434 ff.; declared unconstitutional, 594 ff.; progress in desegregation, 596 f.

Raikes, Robert, 348

Ramsauer, John, 237, 244

Ramus, Peter, 188

Ratke, Wolfgang, 188, 196

Raumer, Karl von, 325

Realism, 170–197, 203

Realgymnasium, 331, 333

Realschule, 177, 331

Reddie, Cecil, 335, 360

Reformation, 113, 135, 139–166, 170, 172, 318, 346, 373, 383, 393

Reform Bill of 1832, English, 354

Regents, New York Board of, 402, 420, 427

Rehabilitation of veterans, 518

Reichenau, 68

Renaissance, 48, 55, 91, 94, 111–132, 171, 250, 393

Renan, Ernest, 87

Rensselaer Polytechnic Institute, 297, 407

Reuchlin, John, 152

Reyher, Andreas, 196

Rhetoric, development by Sophists, 33 ff.; in Greek encyclopedia, 38; in Roman education, 48; decay of Roman, 52 f.; one of Seven Liberal Arts, 71

Rhodes Scholarships, 560

Ribot Commission, 309 f.

Richards, Charles F., 508

Richter, Jean Paul, 285

Rickoff, Andrew Jackson, 465

Ritter, Karl, 230, 241

Robert of Chester, 88

Rochow, Eberhard von, 319

Rockefeller Brothers Fund report, 599

Roelantsen, Adam, 379

Rolland d'Erceville, Barthelémy, 308

Roman Britain, 344

Romans, The, 8, 9, 22, 26; traits of, 42 f.; spread of their culture, 42 f., 48; school organization of, 49 f.; their calendar, geography, science, 50 ff.; educational theory, 54 f.; *also*, 83, 113, 118, 141

Roman Catholic Church, 8, 42, 58; form of organization, 59; as preserver of learning, 60, 64 ff.; in opposition to secular learn-

ing, 65; wealth and income at Reformation, 140
Round Hill School, 337
Rousseau, 22, 197, 202 f., 204–218, 226, 250, 268, 283, 295, 308, 590; writings, 207 f.; plan of state education, 208 f.; analysis of *Émile*, 209 ff.; on child study, 475
Roxbury Latin School, 386
Royal Academy of Sciences, Berlin, 177
Royal Society of London, 177, 183
Royce, Josiah, 256
Rural schools, 318 f., 400 ff.; delay in development, 404
Rush, Benjamin, 165, 403
Russell, William, 246, 418
Russian educational system, 571–585; American interest in, 571; general character of, 572–574; lack of emphasis upon humanities, 573 f.; class-schedule examined, 574–579; comparisons, 576 f.; effectiveness, 577; teacher education, 578 f.; higher and polytechnical education, 579 ff.; past and prospective changes, 581–585; Russian interest in western education, 571 f.
Rutgers University, 391 f.
Ryerson, Egerton, 466

SADOLETO, JACOPO, 117 f.
St. Gall, 68, 144
St. Louis, U.S.A., 472
St. Paul, Apostle, 59, 61, 117, 146
St. Paul's School, 150, 188, 346
St. Peter's, in Rome, 81, 111, 121, 154
Salamanca, University of, 187
Salzmann, Christian G., 197, 229–231; advice to teachers, 230; books for children, 230
Sardanapalus, 10
Sáros-Patak, 191
Saxe-Gotha, 196 f., 227
Schiller, F. von, 285, 329
Schlatter, Michael, 382
Schmid, Joseph, 238
Schneider, Friedrich, 555
Scholasticus, 100
Schoolbooks, 26, 37, 44, 46, 68, 71; by Boethius, 64; by Bede, 68; in the Renaissance, 121; by Erasmus, 150; of the Port Royalists, 165; by Comenius, 189–192; in medieval England, 345; variety of, in early common schools, 425; need for, in West Germany, 546
Schoolhouses, and equipment, 452 ff.
School support, 383, 405; varied forms of, 383 f., 421 ff.; land grants for, 401 f., 422; state school funds, 422; of Negro schools, 438 f.
School tax, 354, 383, 421 ff.
Schurz, Mrs. Carl, 471, 552
Schwenkfeld, Casper, 372

Science in education, 170; proposals regarding, by the Utopians, 173 f.; scheme of Campanella, 173 f.; changes produced by, 180 f.; in elementary schools, 463 ff.
Science, development in modern times, 177–181
Science of education, 181; early American exponents of, 480
Scotch-Irish, the, 372 f.
Scotch-Irish schoolmasters, 387
Scotland, 60, 100, 141; and American education, 160
Search, Preston W., 480, 487 f., 506
Sears, Barnas, 437
Secondary education, 26, 47 ff., 97, 202, 336; French, 296 ff., 300 f.; French secondary school reforms, 308–312; German, 330 f.; English, 356 f., 359 f.; American colonial, 386–391; history of the high school, 496–528; Committee of Ten on, 510 ff.; accrediting plans, 510; standardizing associations, 513 f.; Russian, 574–579
Seguin, Edouard, 287
Seneca, Lucius Annaeus, 43, 51, 117, 119 f.
Semler, Christopher, 177
Septuagint, 61
Servetus, Michael, 159
Seven Liberal Arts, 38, 58, 64 f., 71
Shaw, Mrs. Pauline, supporter of kindergartens, 287, 471; of manual training, 474; of child study, 475; of vocational guidance, 517
Sheldon, Edward Austin, 465, 476
Sheriffhales, 175
Shrewsbury School, 345
Sloyd, 474
Smith, Goldwin, 561
Smith, Samuel H., 403 f.
Smith, Dr. William, 382, 391
Smith-Hughes Act, 518, 602
Smith-Mundt Act, 561
Smithsonian Institution, 444
Snedden, David, 508
Society for the Promotion of Christian Knowledge, 347, 351, 353
Society for the Propagation of the Gospel in Foreign Parts, 348, 362, 376, 379 f.
Socrates, 29 f., 32 ff.
Socratic Method, 33
Soldan, Louis, 483
Sophists, The, 30, 32, 34, 37
Sosigenes, 52
Spain, 18, 43, 54, 60, 81 ff.; Mohammedans in, 84; *also*, 141
Sparta, 20 ff., 36, 38, 185, 292
Spencer, Herbert, 213, 253, 285
Spencer, John Walton, 469
Spencerian handwriting, 408
Spens Report, 357
Speyer School, 488

Spiess, Adolph, 244, 279
Spiral plan of teaching, 89
Spranger, Eduard, 336
Stalin, 572, 582
Standardizing associations, of secondary schools, 513 f., 526
Stanz, 236 f., 553
State activity in education, Spartan, 19 ff.; Roman 53 f., 293; under Charlemagne, 75 f., 293; in the Reformation, 158, 166; in Saxe-Gotha, 196 f.; urged by La Chalotais, 218 f.; Basedow's plan for, 227; giving aid to private schools, 351, 354 ff.; in American states, 402
State and church cooperation in education, 293, 318
State school office, 420 f., 477
State school systems (U.S.A.), 419–421
State University of Iowa, 448
Stationers School, 97
Statute of Artificers, 345, 373
Stewart, Dugald, 252
Stoics, 43, 51, 117
Stow, David, 271, 352
Stowe, Calvin E., 246, 319, 322, 337
Straight, Henry H., 467 ff., 470, 485
Stubbs, Bishop William, 345
Student self-government, 521, 547
Sturm, John, 135, 139; organized classical gymnasium, 158, 331
Süvern, J. W., 322, 325, 332
Sulzer, John George, 202 f., 226, 319
Sumer, 8 f., 11, 14
Summer schools for teachers, 448
Sunday School, 348, 351, 411
Supervised study, 519
Symms-Eaton Academy, 387
Symonds, J. A., 111, 121

Tacitus, Cornelius, 45, 48, 53, 120
Talmudic school, 86
Tappan, Henry, 516
Tatian, 62
Tauler, J., 147
Taylor, J. Orville, 418
Teachers, 25; privileges of, at Rome, 53; early Christian, 63; their political views, 302, 324; professional isolation in Germany, 330; professional education of, 298 f., 304, 329, 334, 352, 449; orthodoxy of, 379; salaries (U.S.A.), 377, 379, 425, 428, 439; status and preparation, 541, 549 f., 578 ff., 586
Teachers College, Columbia University, 448
Teachers' colleges, 449
Teachers' institutes, 447 f.
Television in education, 603 f.
Tennent, Rev. William, 390 f.
Terence, 148, 151
Tertullian, 59, 61 ff.
Tetzel, J., 154

Textual scholarship, 151
Thayer, Gideon F., 426, 484
Thayer, Vivian T., 489
Theocritus, 44
Theodoric the Great, 54
Theodosius the Great, 54, 84
Thirty Schools Experiment, 523 ff.
Thorndike, Edward L., 480
Thorndike, Lynn, 4
Thucydides, 23, 31
Ticknor, Elisha, 411, 446
Ticknor, George, 340, 403
Tiedemann, F., 283
Tillinghast, Nicholas, 447
Tobler, J. G., 237
Trapezuntius, 121, 130
Trapp, E. C., 229
Traversari, 121
Trilingual colleges, 187
Troubled minds, 551 ff.
Turgot, R. J., 219
Turner, Ross, 505
Turnkunst, 337
Tuskegee Institute, 438
Tyndale, William, 146, 151

UNESCO, 553; education for peace, 558–565; tasks of, 562; General Conference of, 562 f.; support, 563; achievements, 564 f.
Unitarianism, 414
United Nations Agencies, 561
United States Armed Forces Institute, 548
United States Children's Bureau, 587
United States Military Academy, 297, 444
United States Naval Academy, 444
United States Office of Education, 444 f.
United States Supreme Court decisions on education, Dartmouth College decision, 440; segregation of races in public schools declared unconstitutional, 594–597; other decisions, 452, 595–597
Universal education proposed, 221, 348, 350; as aim, 381; spread of, 564
Universities, medieval, 101–106
University of Chicago Elementary School, 485 ff.
University of France, founded, 297; under Napoleon III, 304; in Third Republic, 306–308, 402
University of Michigan, 448, 510
University of Pennsylvania, 391 ff.; effort to bring under state control, 440
University of the State of New York, 297, 420
University of Virginia, 403
University practice school, 229
Urban II, Pope, 89 f., 154
Ursuline Sisters, 165
Utopias of the realists, 173 f.

Van Hise, Charles R., 602

Varro, M. T., 51, 53
Vaucluse, 119 f.
Vegio, Mafeo, 128
Venice, 93 f., 122, 145
Vergerius, 118, 125–128
Vergil, 43 f., 71, 119, 130
Vernacular schools, 100, 148, 156 ff., 171, 187 f., 196; in More's *Utopia*, 173; English, 188, 346
Veronese, V., 563
Vesalius, A., 177
Vespasian, Roman emperor, 53
Vespasiano da Bisticci, 122, 124
Vienna, University of, 149; city, 155
Vinet, Élie, 135, 139
Vittorino, 121, 126, 130–132, 194
Vivarium, monastery, 65, 68
Vives, Juan Luis, 172 f., 181, 194
Vocational education, 97, 170, 373; in America, 369, 406 f., 443, 508 f., 518, 549
Vocational guidance, 517 f., 547, 549
Volkmann, W. F., 264 f.
Vulgate Bible, 64, 117, 147

WABASH COLLEGE, 406
Wadsworth, James, 415
Waifs, 553, 582
Wake Forest College, 406
Waldenses, 142 f., 147 f.
Walther von der Vogelweide, 152
Wandering scholars, 148
War affecting youth, 533 ff., 551 f., 553
Warens, Madame de, 206
War-time education, 534
Washburne, Carleton, 482
Washington, Booker T., 438
Washington, George, 398; quoted, 415
Watson, John B., 476
Weaver, Eli W., 517
Webster, Daniel, 427
Webster, Noah, 428
Wehrli, J. J., 226, 352
Weld, Theodore, 406
Wellington, Duke of, 353
Wells, David A., 465
Wessel, John, 149
Western Literary Institute and College of Professional Teachers, 418

Western Reserve University, 406
Whitbread, Samuel, 353
Whitefield, George, 372
Whitehouse Conference on Education, 586, 593 f.
Whittier, J. G., 414, 461
Wickersham, James Pyle, 378, 437, 447
Wilderspin, Samuel, 271, 352
Willard, Emma, 446
William of Champeaux, 102
William and Mary College, 387, 393, 440
William Penn Charter School, 381, 386 f., 391
Williams, Roger, 370, 372
Winchester School, 345
Wirt, William J., 482
Witmer, Lightner, 476
Wittenberg University, Germany, 148, 153 f.
Wolff, Christian, 253
Wolke, C. H., 229
Woodbridge, W. C., 352, 406, 418
Woodhouse, John, 175 f.
Woodward, C. M., 479 f., 509 f.
World Federation of Educational Associations, 556, 559
World War II and education, 490, 492, 533–535, *et passim*
Worthington, Thomas, 415
Wrightstone, J. W., 440
Wundt, William, 340
Wycliffe, John, 142, 144, 147, 345 f.
Wyneken, Gustav, 335

XIMINES, CARDINAL, 151

YALE UNIVERSITY, 391 ff., 440
York, monastery of, 69, 74
Young, R. F., 357
Youth Congress, 335
Youth Movement, German, 335 f.
Yverdon, 231, 238, 244, 352, 556

ZAY, JEAN, 311
Zeller, Karl A., 322
Zeno, 31, 39
Zook, George F., 554
Zürich, 158, 553 f.
Zwingle, Ulrich, 158